HOUGHTON MIFFLIN HARCOURT

JOURNEYS

Grade 4

TEACHER'S EDITION

Program Authors

James F. Baumann · David J. Chard · Jamal Cooks
J. David Cooper · Russell Gersten · Marjorie Lipson
Lesley Mandel Morrow · John J. Pikulski · Héctor H. Rivera
Mabel Rivera · Shane Templeton · Sheila W. Valencia
Catherine Valentino · MaryEllen Vogt

Consulting Author

Irene Fountas

HOUGHTON MIFFLIN HARCOURT

Authors

Program Authors

James F. Baumann
Wyoming Excellence Chair of Literacy
Education
University of Wyoming
Laramie, Wyoming

RESEARCH CONTRIBUTIONS:
Reading teacher effectiveness, national
trends in elementary reading instruction

David J. Chard
Leon Simmons Endowed Chair
Southern Methodist University
Dallas, Texas

RESEARCH CONTRIBUTIONS:
Reading interventions, direct instruction
of comprehension, alphabetic principle on
the reading development of first graders

Jamal Cooks
Associate Professor
San Francisco State University
San Francisco, California

RESEARCH CONTRIBUTIONS:
Urban education; language, literacy, and
culture; popular culture in the classroom

J. David Cooper
Professor of Education, Retired
Ball State University
Muncie, Indiana

RESEARCH CONTRIBUTIONS:
Classroom instruction, classroom
management, development of programs
for Response to Intervention

Russell Gersten
Professor Emeritus, College of Education
University of Oregon
Eugene, Oregon

RESEARCH CONTRIBUTIONS:
English language learners, studies of
implementation, measurement of
classroom instruction, reading comprehension

Marjorie Lipson
Professor Emerita
Principal Investigator, Vermont Reads Institute
University of Vermont
Burlington, Vermont

RESEARCH CONTRIBUTIONS:
Struggling readers and reading
disabilities, reading comprehension,
school change and literacy improvement

Lesley Mandel Morrow
Professor of Literacy, Graduate School of
Education
Rutgers University, The State University of
New Jersey
New Brunswick, New Jersey

RESEARCH CONTRIBUTIONS:
Early literacy development, organization and
management of language arts programs

John J. Pikulski
Professor Emeritus, School of Education
University of Delaware
Newark, Delaware

RESEARCH CONTRIBUTIONS:
Early intervention to prevent reading
difficulties, teaching and developing
vocabulary

Héctor H. Rivera
Assistant Professor, School of Education
and Human Development
Southern Methodist University
Dallas, Texas

RESEARCH CONTRIBUTIONS:
Professional development for educators
who work with adolescent newcomers

Mabel Rivera
Research Assistant Professor at the Texas
Institute for Measurement, Evaluation, and
Statistics
University of Houston
Houston, Texas

RESEARCH CONTRIBUTIONS:
Education and prevention of reading
difficulties in English learners

Shane Templeton
Foundation Professor of Literacy Studies
The University of Nevada, Reno
Reno, Nevada

RESEARCH CONTRIBUTIONS:
Morphological knowledge in vocabulary
and spelling development; integrated
word study in the development of
phonics, spelling, and vocabulary

Sheila W. Valencia
Professor, Curriculum and Instruction
University of Washington
Seattle, Washington

RESEARCH CONTRIBUTIONS:
Literacy assessment, reading and writing
instruction, teacher development

Catherine Valentino
Author-in-Residence
Houghton Mifflin Harcourt
West Kingston, Rhode Island

RESEARCH CONTRIBUTIONS:
Inquiry-based learning in reading and
writing, motivating reluctant learners,
literacy through early childhood problem-
solving projects

MaryEllen Vogt
Distinguished Professor Emerita, College
of Education
California State University, Long Beach
Long Beach, California

RESEARCH CONTRIBUTIONS:
English language learners, Sheltered
Instruction Observation Protocol Model
for teaching English-language arts to
English language learners

Consulting Author

Irene Fountas
Professor of Education
Lesley University
Cambridge, Massachusetts

RESEARCH CONTRIBUTIONS:
Leveled texts, readers' and writers'
workshop, assessment, classroom
management and professional
development

TEACHER'S EDITION

HOUGHTON MIFFLIN HARCOURT

JOURNEYS

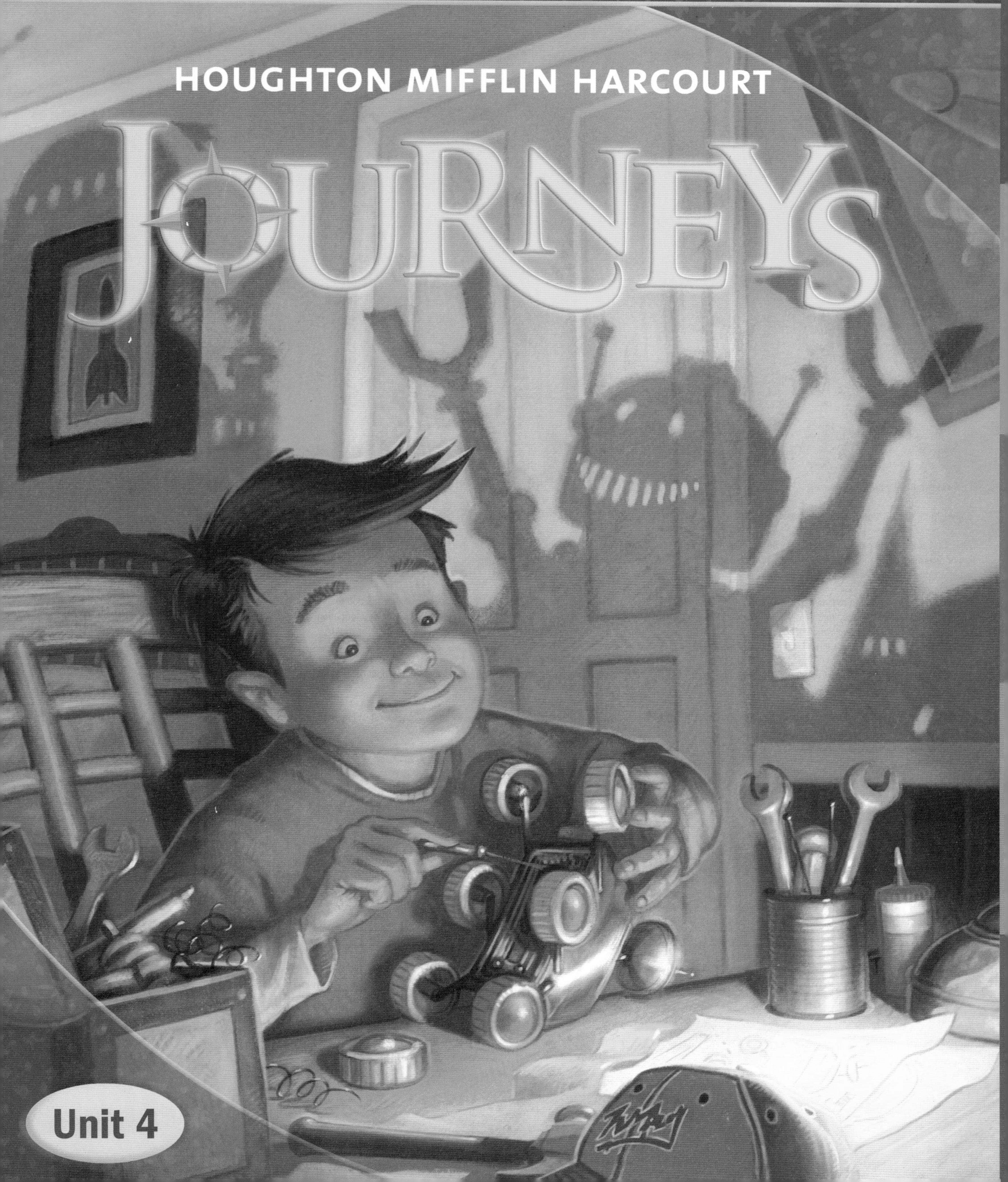

Unit 4

Printed in China

ISBN   978-0-547-61003-0

3 4 5 6 7 8 9 10   1548   20 19 18 17 16 15 14 13 12

4500351518   A B C D E F G

Reviewers

Reviewers

an Eckola
ake Geneva Schools
ake Geneva, WI

ue Fleming
racemor Elementary School
ansas City, MO

aura Heyboer
Woodside Elementary School
olland, MI

licole Lehr
iverview Elementary
Wautoma, WI

essica Martin
racemor Elementary
ansas City, MO

Valerie McCall
Elmwood Park Community Unit School District
Elmwood Park, IL

Edie Stearns
Bluff Creek Elementary
Chanhassen, MN

Connie Vang
Webster Elementary
Green Bay, WI

Steven Wernick
Washington County Public Schools
Hagerstown, MD

Contents

Lesson

16

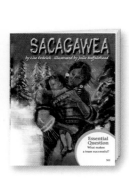

 **and Unit Wrap-Up** T349

Intervention

ELL English Language Learners

Resources

Implementing Interactive Instruction

http://www.hmhschool.com

Whole Group & Small Group Instruction

Transforming teacher-led instruction

- Teach critical reading skills using interactive lessons and *Projectables*
- Project eBook selections and target skills
- Provide guided practice for target skills
- Teach vocabulary words

Digital Centers

Application and Practice

- Interactive centers reinforce weekly skills
- *Leveled Readers, Student eBooks,* practice activities
- Full audio support for all *Leveled Readers*

Family Support @ Home

Extend learning opportunities

- Interactive activities for homework
- Keep parents involved with school-home connections in English and Spanish

Additional Digital Support
Teacher Resources
Lesson Planning
Professional Development

- Teacher One-Stop Lesson Planning
- Comprehension Expedition CD-ROM
- WriteSmart CD-ROM
- Picture Card Bank for ELL Support
- Student Book Audiotext CD

Focus Wall

Easy Navigation for Teachers

to Suggested Weekly Plan

Student Book
- Student eBook
- Online Audio
- Online Teacher's Edition

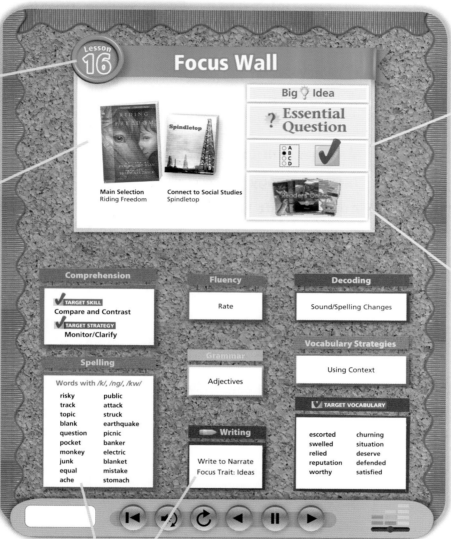

Focus Wall

Big Idea

? Essential Question

○ A
● B
○ C
○ D   ✔

Main Selection
Riding Freedom

Connect to Social Studies
Spindletop

Readers Online

Comprehension
✔ TARGET SKILL
Compare and Contrast
✔ TARGET STRATEGY
Monitor/Clarify

Fluency
Rate

Decoding
Sound/Spelling Changes

Spelling
Words with /k/, /ng/, /kw/

risky	public
track	attack
topic	struck
blank	earthquake
question	picnic
pocket	banker
monkey	electric
junk	blanket
equal	mistake
ache	stomach

Grammar
Adjectives

Vocabulary Strategies
Using Context

TARGET VOCABULARY

escorted	churning
swelled	situation
relied	deserve
reputation	defended
worthy	satisfied

Writing
Write to Narrate
Focus Trait: Ideas

Online Assessment System
- Link to this lesson's Weekly Test
- Unit and Benchmark Tests available

Online Leveled Readers
- Link to this lesson's Readers
- Full audio support

Instruction and Resources on Demand
- Links to *Student Book* and *Teacher's Edition* pages for this lesson
- Game-like practice, powered by *Destination Reading*
- *Projectables, BLMs*, and other lesson resources
- Differentiated Instruction

Single Log In

Unit 4 Planning and Pacing

Big Idea
There is more than one secret to success.

	Essential Question	**Lesson 16** *What traits do successful people have in common?*	**Lesson 17** *What steps can you take toward success?*
Whole Group	**Vocabulary** **Vocabulary Strategies**	☑ Target Vocabulary ☑ Using Context	☑ Target Vocabulary ☑ Suffixes *-ion, -ation, -ition*
	Comprehension **Reading**	☑ **Target Skill** Compare and Contrast **Target Strategy** Monitor/Clarify **Author's Craft** Personification **Main Selection** "Riding Freedom" **Paired Selection** "Spindletop"	☑ **Target Skill** Sequence of Events **Target Strategy** Summarize **Author's Craft** Word Choice **Main Selection** "The Right Dog for the Job" **Paired Selection** "The Sticky Coyote"
	Fluency **Decoding**	☑ **Fluency** Rate ☑ **Decoding** Sound/Spelling Changes	☑ **Fluency** Intonation ☑ **Decoding** More Sound/Spelling Changes
Whole Group	**Research Skill/ Media Literacy** **Listening/Speaking**	Skimming/Scanning Texts and Sources Evaluate Media Sources	Taking Notes/Identifying Sources Evaluate and Adapt Spoken Language
Language Arts	**Grammar** **Spelling** **Writing**	☑ **Grammar** Adjectives ☑ **Spelling** Words with /k/, /ng/, and /kw/ ▱ **Writing** Descriptive Paragraph Focus Trait: Ideas	☑ **Grammar** Adverbs ☑ **Spelling** Words with Final /j/ and /s/ ▱ **Writing** Friendly Letter Focus Trait: Voice
SMALL GROUP Options	**Vocabulary Reader**	Differentiate *Stagecoach Travel*	Differentiate *Animals Helping People*
	Leveled Readers	● *Elizabeth's Stormy Ride* ▲ *Perilous Passage* ■ *Come to Nicodemus* ◆ *A Dangerous Trip*	● *Animal Doctors* ▲ *A Rural Veterinarian* ■ *Helping Wild Animals* ◆ *Taking Care of Animals*
	Differentiate Instruction	Differentiate Comprehension and Vocabulary Strategies	Differentiate Comprehension and Vocabulary Strategies

Key ● Struggling Readers   ▲ On-Level Readers   ■ Advanced Readers   ◆ English Language Learners   ☑ Tested skills

Unit Project

You've Earned It!
Students will determine the criteria for and create an award to be presented to a book character.

Checkpoints
☐ Discuss characters from previously read books, noting the character's qualities and reaction to events.
☐ Decide on the award and draw, design, or create the award.
☐ Make a poster and write a speech for the award presentation.
☐ Present the award.

Lesson 18

How can people share their successes?

☑ Target Vocabulary
☑ Homphones, Homonyms, and Homographs

☑ **Target Skill** Understanding Characters
Target Strategy Question
Author's Craft Point of View
Main Selection "Moon Runner"
Paired Selection "A Day for the Moon"

☑ **Fluency** Accuracy and Self-Correction
☑ **Decoding** Recognizing Prefixes

Online Searches: Reliable Sources

Prepare for Oral Summaries

☑ **Grammar** Prepositions and Prepositional Phrases
☑ **Spelling** Prefixes *re-, un-, dis-*
✏ **Writing** Narrative Composition
☑ Focus Trait: Word Choice

Differentiate *The First Lady of Track*

● *Tammy's Goal*
▲ *Baseball Boys*
■ *The Friendship Garden*
◆ *Baseball Friends*

Differentiate Comprehension and Vocabulary Strategies

Lesson 19

Why might a leader use persuasion?

☑ Target Vocabulary
☑ Use a Dictionary

☑ **Target Skill** Persuasion
Target Strategy Infer/Predict
Author's Craft Idioms
Main Selection "Harvesting Hope: The Story of Cesar Chavez"
Paired Selection "The Edible Schoolyard"

☑ **Fluency** Stress
☑ **Decoding** More Common Suffixes

Using Keywords in Online Searches

Deliver a Summary

☑ **Grammar** Transitions
☑ **Spelling** Suffixes *-ful, -less, -ness, -ment*
✏ **Writing** Prewrite: Personal Narrative
☑ Focus Trait: Organization

Differentiate *Tough Times*

● *Songs for the People*
▲ *The People's President*
■ *The Story of Dorothea Lange*
◆ *A President for the People*

Differentiate Comprehension and Vocabulary Strategies

Lesson 20
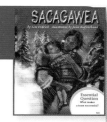

What makes a team successful?

☑ Target Vocabulary
☑ Compound Words

☑ **Target Skill** Main Ideas and Details
Target Strategy Visualize
Author's Craft Onomatopoeia
Main Selection "Sacagawea"
Paired Selection "Native American Nature Poetry"

☑ **Fluency** Phrasing: Punctuation
☑ **Decoding** VCCV Pattern and Word Parts

Taking Notes/Sorting Evidence/Citing Online Sources
Interpret Poetry

☑ **Grammar** Abbreviations
☑ **Spelling** Words with VCCV Pattern
✏ **Writing** Draft, Revise, Edit, Publish: Personal Narrative
Focus Trait: Ideas

Differentiate *Lewis and Clark's Packing List*

● *John Wesley Powell*
▲ *Writer from the Prairie*
■ *Chief Washakie*
◆ *Laura Ingalls Wilder*

Differentiate Comprehension and Vocabulary Strategies

Test Preparation and Assessment

5 Steps for Success

1

Where Do I Start?

Comprehensive Screening Assessment

- Group-administered tests
- Initial screening of previous year's skills: Language Arts, Decoding, and Writing, plus passages for Comprehension and Vocabulary
- Includes an optional group Spelling test

Diagnostic Assessment

- Individually administered tests
- Diagnosis of basic reading skills, plus passages for reading in context

2

Every **Day**

In Your Teacher's Edition

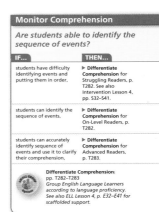

Monitor Progress features in the Teacher's Edition

- Monitor progress
- Differentiate instruction successfully

Corrective Feedback in the Teacher's Edition

- Provide immediate and helpful feedback

Online Assessment System

- Weekly Tests
- Benchmark and Unit Tests

 Common Core Assessment

- All Journeys assessments are correlated to the Common Core State Standards.

3 Every **Week**

Group-administered assessment of
- Target Vocabulary
- Comprehension
- Decoding
- Vocabulary Strategies
- Language Arts

4 Every **Unit**

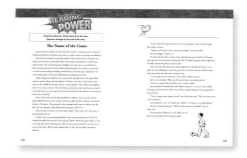

Reading Power in the Student Book

Benchmark and Unit Tests

- Group-administered, criterion-referenced
- Measure the unit's reading and writing skills

5 Twice a **Year**

Units 3 and 5 Benchmark Tests

- Comprehensive, cumulative midyear and yearly assessments
- Group-administered, criterion-referenced

Diagnostic Assessment

- Can be re-administered to document progress of struggling readers

Discuss the Unit: Never Give Up!

- Have students turn to the Unit 4 Opener photograph. Have a volunteer read the unit title.

- Ask students to describe how the photograph of the surfer on the page connects to the title.

  1 Ask students to describe an experience they have had in which they faced a challenge or needed to complete a difficult task.

  2 Have them tell about a time when they thought about giving up but decided not to. What made them keep going?

  3 Encourage students to tell about a book they have read in which a character faces a challenge and doesn't give up. How does this character keep going?

Connect to the Big Idea

There is more than one secret to success.

- Have students turn the page to the photograph of the skier. Ask them to tell how this photograph relates to the unit title, *Never Give Up!*

- Have a volunteer read the Big Idea. Discuss how never giving up connects to the idea of success.

- Briefly discuss what makes a task successful. Is success only measured by the outcome? Can success depend on other "secrets," such as confidence, hard work, and teamwork?

- Encourage students to give examples of a successful task or project and explain why it turned out so well.

Student Book

**Essential
Question**
There is more
than one secret
to success.

401

Student Book

Preview the Literature

- Ask students to scan the contents of the Table of Contents on **Student Book p. 401**, noting titles and topics of interest to them.

- Have students make predictions about how the selections expand upon concepts related to the Big Idea, based on selection titles and covers. Prompt discussion by asking how success and never giving up might be involved in a woman relearning how to drive a stagecoach after a bad accident; a dog being trained for a specific job; two girls competing in a race; Cesar Chavez working for farm workers' rights; and Sacagawea guiding Lewis and Clark's expedition through the wilderness.

You've Earned It!

Students will determine the criteria for an award to be presented to a book character. They will create a poster to explain the award and describe the winner. Students will then create the award and deliver a presentation.

SHARE OBJECTIVES

- Summarize plot events and demonstrate understanding of characters.
- Work productively with others in teams.
- Deliver an informative and persuasive presentation.

DEVELOP BACKGROUND

- Have students discuss characters in books they've previously read who overcame obstacles.
- Tell students that they will give a presentation about a character who they believe should earn an award for the way he or she overcame obstacles.

Materials

- pens, pencils, markers
- poster and construction paper
- scissors
- Classroom Library books for reference

Step 1

Plan and Gather Tell students they will be giving an award to a character who overcame a great obstacle.

a Students discuss characters from previously-read books.

b Students take notes on the character's qualities and how he or she is affected by plot events.

c Students decide on an award they would give their character and draw, design, or otherwise create the award.

Step 2

Organize Tell students they will be making a poster that they will use during an award presentation for their character. Explain that in their speech, they should focus on character qualities and use persuasive language.

a Students design and create a poster that organizes the information in their notes.

b Students use their notes, the poster, and the award to develop a draft of their speech.

Step 3

Complete and Present Remind students that they will use their notes, the award and the poster in their oral presentation of the award.

a Students revise their drafts for persuasive language, spelling, grammar, and mechanics.

b Students rehearse their presentations, exchanging feedback on communicating effectively.

c Students present the award and poster to the class.

ELL ENGLISH LANGUAGE LEARNERS

Scaffold

Beginning Using gestures, illustrations, and simplified language, teach words used to describe characters' qualities.	**Advanced** Have pairs choose characters and discuss qualities that helped those characters overcome obstacles.
Intermediate Guide students to complete sentence frames about characters' qualities, such as ____ *is brave because* ____.	**Advanced High** Have students write a paragraph about a character who overcame an obstacle. Have them explain how that character's qualities helped solve the problem.

Study Skills

For instruction in the following applicable study skills, see the lessons in the **Resources** section, pp. R2–R7.

Unit 4 Study Skills

p. R2	• Brainstorm • Solve Problems
p. R3	• Make a Hypothesis • Support a Proposition
p. R4	• Follow Multi-step Directions • Collect Information from Surveys
p. R5	• Prepare Oral Reports • Make Oral Presentations
p. R6	• Use Text Structure to Outline • Analyze Incorrect Inferences • Follow Oral Directions
p. R7	• Review Internet Strategy: Steps 1 and 2

How Do Children Learn to Decode Print?

Phonics and Beyond

How do children learn to decode print? Decoding is getting from the printed letters to the right sounds. In an alphabetic language, the most reliable way to decode a word is to use phonics—to know the sounds that the various letters stand for and to blend those sounds together to form words. The *Report of the National Reading Panel* (2000) concludes that children who are taught phonics early, systematically, and explicitly do better in beginning reading; they also maintain their skills when decoding instruction is followed by the language, content-area, and comprehension instruction needed for high-level and long-term reading achievement.

What do children need in order to be successful in developing and applying phonics skills? Since phonics is the knowledge of how letters relate to sounds, beginning readers need familiarity with both letters and sounds. Of the two, letters are easier to learn; they are concrete, we can point to them, and they have names. Phonemic awareness is more abstract. While young children are usually familiar with the sounds of oral language, they are not often consciously aware that speech is composed of a limited number of identifiable sounds. This conscious awareness of the sounds in spoken language is called phonemic awareness. A substantial number of children find phonemic awareness very difficult; nonetheless, it is essential for them to develop this awareness.

John J. Pikulski

Is phonics all there is to decoding? Not by a long shot. In addition, children also need to learn to recognize larger "chunks" of words, such as phonograms, syllables, prefixes, and suffixes. Children must also learn to use context when phonics gets them close to—but not exactly at—the correct pronunciation, or to determine which of two or more pronunciations is correct (for example, *bow* as in "a tied ribbon" or *bow* as in "to lean forward").

In addition, in English, even some short words cannot be decoded easily with phonics alone. For example, the word *said,* using the most common letter–sound associations, would rhyme with *raid*; instead, it rhymes with *red*! These potentially confusing spellings are fairly common among words that we use frequently; therefore, they are called high-frequency words and receive special attention.

Another key skill is fluency. With high-quality decoding instruction and lots of opportunities to apply decoding skills in meaningful text, children learn to read accurately, rapidly, and automatically, gaining meaning as they decode. When children can decode automatically and read fluently, they can then focus their efforts on understanding what they read. Fluency allows children to access meaning in a wide variety of interesting and informative texts and, ultimately, become life-long readers.

Understanding the Common Core State Standards

Writing Standards

The Common Core State Standards provide rigorous and increasingly complex student expectations in crucial areas of learning. In the Writing strand, emphasis is placed on real-world writing forms and applications. As students progress across grade levels, they are asked to write longer and more sophisticated pieces.

A main objective of the Common Core writing standards is to develop students' competencies in integrating and using digital tools and technology to produce and publish their writing as well to collaborate with others. Beyond their school years, students will continue to build on those competencies as they move toward success.

Research

One of the most challenging aspects of the Common Core writing standards is the emphasis they place on research. The standards require students to participate in research and demonstrate a deep understanding of a topic. The goal is to empower students to be thoughtful, focused writers who can gather evidence, analyze their findings, and produce logical, well-supported arguments.

Textual Evidence

When working with students on research, you might find them unsure how to incorporate textual evidence into their writing. Explain to students that when they take notes, they should either paraphrase the information or quote exact words. As students write, they can use their notes to incorporate the paraphrases or direct quotations in their writing.

Additional Support

It is important to establish a learning environment in which students feel comfortable collaborating with peers and exchanging constructive feedback about writing projects. Offer encouragement in the form of positive feedback at every opportunity. Use Routines to support struggling students and Options for Reteaching to support students' mastery of skills. *HMH Journeys* provides teachers with the texts and comprehensive instruction they need to help students meet the Common Core State Standards and reach educational goals appropriate to each grade level.

Extending the Common Core State Standards: A Preview

Unit 4: Never Give Up!

Extend the Common Core State Standards with these lessons.

- Introduce the Story: "Hercules' Quest,"
- Introduce the Folktale: "Zomo's Friends"
- Comprehension: Compare and Contrast Themes
- Comprehension: Compare and Contrast Patterns of Events
- Vocabulary Strategies: Words from Mythology
- Vocabulary Strategies: Adages and Proverbs
- Grammar: Ordering Adjectives
- Writing: Conclusions in Narrative Writing

Reading Standards for Literature K–5

Key Ideas and Details

RL.4.1 Refer to details and examples in a text when explaining what the text says explicitly and when drawing inferences from the text.

RL.4.2 Determine a theme of a story, drama, or poem from details in the text; summarize the text.

RL.4.3 Describe in depth a character, setting, or event in a story or drama, drawing on specific details in the text (e.g., a character's thoughts, words, or actions).

Craft and Structure

RL.4.4 Determine the meaning of words and phrases as they are used in a text, including those that allude to significant characters found in mythology (e.g., Herculean).

Range of Reading and Level of Text Complexity

RL.4.10 By the end of the year, read and comprehend literature, including stories, dramas, and poetry, in the grades 4–5 text complexity band proficiently, with scaffolding as needed at the high end of the range.

Reading Standards: Foundational Skills K–5

Phonics and Word Recognition

RF.4.3a Use combined knowledge of all letter-sound correspondences, syllabication patterns, and morphology (e.g. roots and affixes) to read accurately unfamiliar multisyllabic words in context and out of context.

Fluency

RF.4.4b Read grade-level prose and poetry orally with accuracy, appropriate rate, and expression.

RF.4.4c Use context to confirm or self-correct word recognition and understanding, rereading as necessary.

Writing Standards K–5

Text Types and Purposes

W.4.3b Use dialogue and description to develop experiences and events or show the responses of characters to situations.

W.4.3d Use concrete words and phrases and sensory details to convey experiences and events precisely.

W.4.3e Provide a conclusion that follows from the narrated experiences or events.

Production and Distribution of Writing

W.4.4 Produce clear and coherent writing in which the development and organization are appropriate to task, purpose, and audience. (Grade-specific expectations for writing types are defined in standards 1–3 above.)

W.4.5 With guidance and support from peers and adults, develop and strengthen writing as needed by planning, revising, and editing. (Editing for conventions should demonstrate command of Language standards 1–3 up to and including grade 4 on pages 28 and 29.)

Range of Writing

W.4.10 Write routinely over extended time frames (time for research, reflection, and revision) and shorter time frames (a single sitting or a day or two) for a range of discipline-specific tasks, purposes, and audiences.

Speaking & Listening Standards K–5

Comprehension and Collaboration

SL.4.1a Come to discussions prepared, having read or studied required material; explicitly draw on that preparation and other information known about the topic to explore ideas under discussion.

Presentation of Knowledge and Ideas

SL.4.4 Report on a topic or text, tell a story, or recount an experience in an organized manner, using appropriate facts and relevant, descriptive details to support main ideas or themes; speak clearly at an understandable pace.

Language Standards K–5

Conventions of Standard English

L.4.2d Spell grade-appropriate words correctly, consulting references as needed.

Vocabulary Acquisition and Use

L.4.4a Use context (e.g., definitions, examples, or restatements in text) as a clue to the meaning of a word or phrase.

SUGGESTIONS FOR BALANCED LITERACY

Use *Journeys* materials to support a Readers' Workshop approach. See the Lesson 16 resources on pages 24, 70–71.

Lesson 16

Focus Wall

Main Selection
Riding Freedom

Connect to Social Studies
Spindletop

Big Idea
There is more than one secret to success.

? Essential Question
What traits do successful people have in common?

Comprehension

✔ **TARGET SKILL**

Compare and Contrast

✔ **TARGET STRATEGY**

Monitor/Clarify

Spelling

Words with /k/, /ng/, /kw/

risky	public
track	attack
topic	struck
blank	earthquake
question	picnic
pocket	banker
monkey	electric
junk	blanket
equal	mistake
ache	stomach

Fluency

Rate

Grammar

Adjectives

Writing

Write to Narrate
Focus Trait: Ideas

Decoding

Sound/Spelling Changes

Vocabulary Strategies

Using Context

✔ TARGET VOCABULARY

escorted	churning
swelled	situation
relied	deserve
reputation	defended
worthy	satisfied

Week at a Glance

Key Skills This Week

Target Skill:
Compare and Contrast

Target Strategy:
Monitor/Clarify

Vocabulary Strategies:
Using Context

Fluency:
Rate

Decoding:
Sound/Spelling Changes

Research Skill:
Skimming and Scanning Texts and Sources

Grammar:
Adjectives

Spelling:
Words with /k/, /ng/, /kw/

Writing:
Descriptive Paragraph

✔ Assess/Monitor

☑ **Vocabulary,** p. T54

☑ **Comprehension,** p. T54

☑ **Decoding,** p. T55

☑ **Language Arts,** p. T55

☑ **Fluency,** p. T55

Whole Group

READING

Paired Selections

Riding Freedom
Historical Fiction
Student Book, pp. 406–417

Spindletop
SOCIAL STUDIES / Informational Text
Student Book, pp. 418–421

Accelerated Reader®
Practice Quizzes for the Selection

Vocabulary

Student Book, pp. 402–403

Background and Comprehension

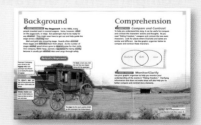

Student Book, pp. 404–405

LANGUAGE ARTS

Grammar
Student Book, pp. 422–423

Writing
Student Book, pp. 424–425

Small Group

See pages T58–T59 for Suggested Small Group Plan.

TEACHER-LED

Leveled Readers

● **Struggling Readers**

▲ **On Level**

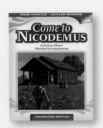

■ **Advanced**

◆ **English Language Learners**

Vocabulary Reader

WHAT MY OTHER STUDENTS ARE DOING

Ready-Made Work Stations

Word Study

Think and Write

Comprehension and Fluency

Digital Center

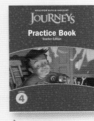

▲ **On Level**

● **Struggling Readers**

■ **Advanced**

◆ **English Language Learners**

Lesson 16 Blackline Masters
- Target Vocabulary 16.1
- Selection Summary 16.2
- Graphic Organizers 16.3–16.6 ●▲■◆
- Critical Thinking 16.7–16.10 ●▲■◆
- Running Records 16.11–16.14 ●▲■◆
- Weekly Tests 16.1–16.9

Graphic Organizer Transparency 14

Additional Resources
- Genre: Fiction, p. 4
- Reading Log, p. 12
- Vocabulary Log, p. 13
- Listening Log, p. 14
- Proofreading Checklist, p. 15
- Proofreading Marks, p. 16
- Writing Conference Form, p. 17
- Writing Rubric, p. 18
- Instructional Routines, pp. 19–26
- Graphic Organizer 14: Venn Diagram, p. 40

JOURNEYS DIGITAL Powered by DESTINATION Reading

For Students
- Student eBook
- Comprehension Expedition CD-ROM
- Leveled Readers Online
- WriteSmart CD-ROM

For Teachers
- Online TE and Focus Wall
- Online Assessment System
- Teacher One-Stop
- Destination Reading Instruction

Week at a Glance

Intervention

STRATEGIC INTERVENTION: TIER II

Use these materials to provide additional targeted instruction for students who need Tier II strategic intervention.

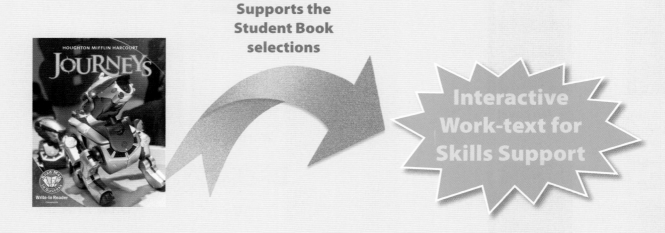

Supports the Student Book selections

Interactive Work-text for Skills Support

Write-In Reader:

The Fastest Rider in the West

• Engaging selection connects to main topic.
• Reinforces this week's target vocabulary and comprehension skill and strategy.
• Opportunities for student interaction on each page.

Assessment

Progress monitoring every two weeks.

For this week's Strategic Intervention lessons, see Teacher's Edition pages S2–S11.

INTENSIVE INTERVENTION: TIER III

• The materials in the Literacy Tool Kit help you provide a different approach for students who need Tier III intensive intervention.
• Interactive lessons provide focused instruction in key reading skills, targeted at students' specific needs.
• Lesson cards are convenient for small-group or individual instruction.
• Blackline masters provide additional practice.
• A leveled book accompanies each lesson to give students opportunities for additional reading and skill application.
• Assessments for each lesson help you evaluate the effectiveness of the intervention.

Lessons provide support for

• Phonics and Word Study Skills
• Vocabulary
• Comprehension Skills and Literary Genres
• Fluency

ELL English Language Learners

SCAFFOLDED SUPPORT

Use these materials to ensure that students acquire social and academic language proficiency.

JOURNEYS DIGITAL **Powered by DESTINATIONReading**
- Leveled Readers Online
- Picture Card Bank Online

Language Support Card

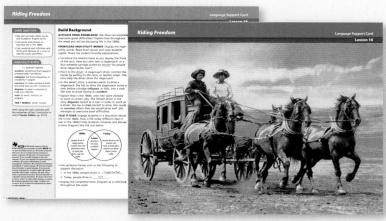

- Builds background for the main topic and promotes oral language.
- Develops high-utility vocabulary and academic language.

Leveled Reader

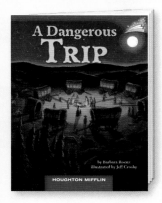

- Sheltered text connects to the main selection's topic, vocabulary, skill, and strategy.

Scaffolded Support

ELL ENGLISH LANGUAGE LEARNERS

Scaffold

Beginning Help students list familiar modes of transportation. Point out common features, such as wheels, windows, and seats.

Intermediate Pre-teach unfamiliar vocabulary from the diagram on p. 404 using gestures, visuals, or simplified language.

Advanced Discuss with students the difficulties a stagecoach driver might have had while guiding horses over unfamiliar territory.

Advanced High Point out the last sentence of the first paragraph of **p. 404**. Ask students how it might feel in such a situation. Have them work with a partner to write a short paragraph about it using Vocabulary words.

See ELL Lesson 16, pp. E2–E11 for scaffolded support.

- Notes throughout the Teacher's Edition scaffold instruction to each language proficiency level.

Vocabulary in Context Cards 151–160

escorted
Guides who knew the western trails well often escorted, or led, travelers.

swelled
The number of wagons heading west swelled, or grew, in the 1850s.

relied
This family built a house of sod. They relied, or depended, on materials they found.

- Provide visual support and additional practice for Target Vocabulary words.

For this week's English Language Learners lessons, see Teacher's Edition pages E2–E11.

Weekly Plan

		Day 1	**Day 2**
Whole Group	**Oral Language** Listening Comprehension	**Read Aloud** "Getting the Story," T12–T13 ☑ Introduce Vocabulary, T13	**Turn and Talk,** T19
	Vocabulary Comprehension Skills and Strategies **Reading**	☑ **Comprehension** Preview the Target Skill, T13 ☑ **Introduce Vocabulary** Vocabulary in Context, T14–T15 **Develop Background** ☑ Target Vocabulary, T16–T17	**Introduce Comprehension** ☑ Compare and Contrast, T18–T19 Monitor/Clarify, T18–T19 **Read "Riding Freedom,"** T20–T31 Focus on Genre, T20 Stop and Think, T27, T29, T30
	Cross-Curricular Connections Fluency Decoding	☑ **Fluency** Model Rate, T12	☑ **Fluency** Teach Rate, T38
Whole Group Language Arts	**Spelling Grammar Writing**	☑ **Spelling** Words with /k/, /ng/, /kw/: Pretest, T44 ☑ **Grammar** Daily Proofreading Practice, T46 Teach Adjectives, T46 ☑ **Write to Narrate: Descriptive Paragraph** Analyze the Model, T50	☑ **Spelling** Words with /k/, /ng/, /kw/: Word Sort, T44 ☑ **Grammar** Daily Proofreading Practice, T47 Teach Adjectives after *be*, T47 ☑ **Write to Narrate: Descriptive Paragraph** Focus Trait: Ideas, T51
	Writing Prompt	*Compare and contrast transportation in the 1800s and today.*	*Describe a time you set a goal and the steps you took to achieve it.*

COMMON CORE
Correlations

Read Aloud RF.4.4b **Fluency** RF.4.4b **Spelling** L.4.2d **Write to Narrate** W.4.3b, W.4.3d, W.4.4, W.4.5, W.4.10	**Read** RL.4.1, RL.4.2, RL.4.3, RL.4.4, RL.4.10, RF.4.4b, SL.4.1a **Fluency** RF.4.4b **Spelling** L.4.2d **Write to Narrate** W.4.3b, W.4.3d, W.4.4, W.4.5, W.4.10

Suggestions for Small Groups (See pp. T57–T71.)
Suggestions for Intervention (See pp. S2–S11.)
Suggestions for English Language Learners (See pp. E2–E11.)

JOURNEYS DIGITAL   **Powered by**
DESTINATIONReading®
Teacher One-Stop: Lesson Planning

Day 3

Turn and Talk, T31
Oral Language, T31

Read "Riding Freedom," T20–T31
Develop Comprehension, T22, T24, T26, T28
☑ **Target Vocabulary**
"Riding Freedom," T22, T24
Your Turn, T31
Deepen Comprehension
☑ Compare and Contrast
Story Details, T36–T37

Cross-Curricular Connections
Social Studies, T23
☑ **Fluency**
Practice Rate, T23
Decoding
☑ Sound/Spelling Changes, T39

☑ **Spelling**
Words with /k/, /ng/, /kw/: Word Families, T45
☑ **Grammar**
Daily Proofreading Practice, T47
Teach Articles, T47

☑ **Write to Narrate: Descriptive Paragraph**
Prewrite, T51

Explain why you think Charlotte's behavior was wise or unwise.

Turn and Talk SL.4.1a
Oral Language SL.4.1a
Read RL.4.1, RL.4.2, RL.4.3, RL.4.4, RL.4.10, RF.4.4b, SL.4.1a
Target Vocabulary RL.4.4
Fluency RF.4.4b
Decoding RF.4.3a
Spelling L.4.2d
Write to Narrate W.4.3b, W.4.3d, W.4.4, W.4.5, W.4.10

Day 4

Text to World, T35

Read "Spindletop," T32–T35
Connect to Social Studies, T32
Target Vocabulary Review, T33
Develop Comprehension, T34
Weekly Internet Challenge, T34
Making Connections, T35
☑ **Vocabulary Strategies**
Using Context, T40–T41

☑ **Fluency**
Practice Rate, T33

☑ **Spelling**
Words with /k/, /ng/, /kw/: Connect to Writing, T45
☑ **Grammar**
Daily Proofreading Practice, T48
Review Adjectives, T48

☑ **Write to Narrate: Descriptive Paragraph**
Draft, T52

Write a journal entry as if you were a gold seeker traveling to California.

Read RF.4.4b
Vocabulary Strategies RL.4.4, RF.4.4c, L.4.4a
Fluency RF.4.4b
Spelling L.4.2d
Write to Narrate W.4.3b, W.4.3d, W.4.3e, W.4.4, W.4.5, W.4.10

Day 5

Listening and Speaking, T43

Connect and Extend
Read to Connect, T42
Independent Reading, T42
Extend Through Research, T43

☑ **Fluency**
Progress Monitoring, T55

☑ **Spelling**
Words with /k/, /ng/, /kw/: Assess, T45
☑ **Grammar**
Daily Proofreading Practice, T48
Connect Grammar to Writing, T48–T49

☑ **Write to Narrate: Descriptive Paragraph**
Revise for Ideas, T52

Tell about the important lessons you can learn by reading this week's literature.

Listening and Speaking SL.4.4
Connect and Extend SL.4.1a, SL.4.4
Fluency RF.4.4b
Spelling L.4.2d
Write to Narrate W.4.3b, W.4.3d, W.4.3e, W.4.4, W.4.5, W.4.10

Your Skills for the Week

☑ **Vocabulary**
Target Vocabulary Strategies: Using Context

☑ **Comprehension**
Compare and Contrast
Monitor/Clarify

☑ **Decoding**
Sound/Spelling Changes

☑ **Fluency**
Rate

☑ **Language Arts**
Spelling
Grammar
Writing

Weekly Leveled Readers

Differentiated Support for This Week's Targets

 **TARGET SKILL**

Compare and Contrast

 **TARGET STRATEGY**

Monitor/Clarify

TARGET VOCABULARY	
escorted	churning
swelled	situation
relied	deserve
reputation	defended
worthy	satisfied

Additional Tools

Vocabulary in Context Cards

Comprehension Tool: Graphic Organizer Transparency 14

? Essential Question

What traits do successful people have in common?

Vocabulary Reader

Level Q

Build Target Vocabulary

- Introduce the Target Vocabulary in context and build comprehension using the Target Strategy.

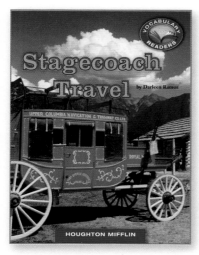

Vocabulary Reader

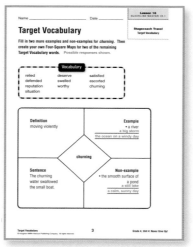

Blackline Master 16.1

Intervention

Scaffolded Support

- Provide extra support in applying the Target Vocabulary, Target Skill, and Target Strategy in context.

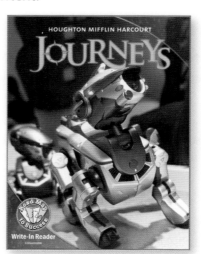

Write-In Reader

For Vocabulary Reader Lesson Plans, see Small Group pages T60–T61.

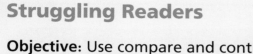
Leveled Readers

Level N

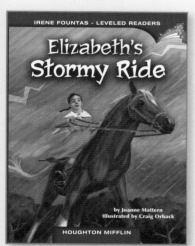

Struggling Readers

Objective: Use compare and contrast and the monitor/clarify strategy to read *Elizabeth's Stormy Ride.*

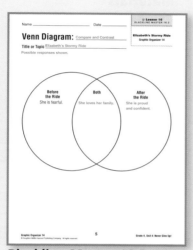

Blackline Master 16.3

Level S

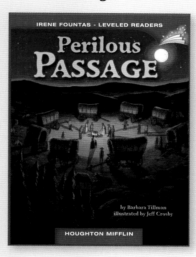

On Level

Objective: Use compare and contrast and the monitor/clarify strategy to read *Perilous Passage.*

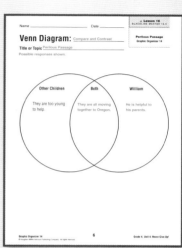

Blackline Master 16.4

Level S

Advanced

Objective: Use compare and contrast and the monitor/clarify strategy to read *Come to Nicodemus.*

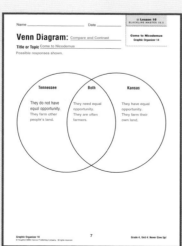

Blackline Master 16.5

Level S

English Language Learners

Objective: Use compare and contrast and the monitor/clarify strategy to read *A Dangerous Trip.*

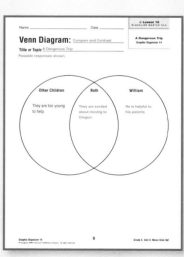

Blackline Master 16.6

For Leveled Reader Lesson Plans, see Small Group pages T64–T67.

Ready-Made Work Stations

Manage Independent Activities

Use the Ready-Made Work Stations to establish a consistent routine for students working independently. Each station contains three activities. Students who experience success with the *Get Started!* activity move on to the *Reach Higher!* and *Challenge Yourself!* activities, as time permits.

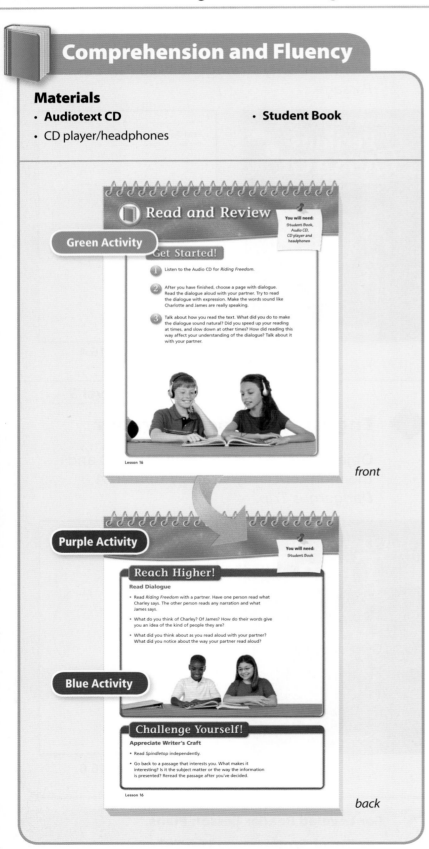

Comprehension and Fluency

Materials
- **Audiotext CD**
- CD player/headphones
- **Student Book**

Read and Review

You will need:
Student Book, Audio CD, CD player and headphones

Green Activity

Get Started!

1. Listen to the Audio CD for *Riding Freedom*.

2. After you have finished, choose a page with dialogue. Read the dialogue aloud with your partner. Try to read the dialogue with expression. Make the words sound like Charlotte and James are really speaking.

3. Talk about how you read the text. What did you do to make the dialogue sound natural? Did you speed up your reading at times, and slow down at other times? How did reading this way affect your understanding of the dialogue? Talk about it with your partner.

Lesson 16

front

Purple Activity

You will need:
Student Book

Reach Higher!

Read Dialogue

- Read *Riding Freedom* with a partner. Have one person read what Charley says. The other person reads any narration and what James says.

- What do you think of Charley? Of James? How do their words give you an idea of the kind of people they are?

- What did you think about as you read aloud with your partner? What did you notice about the way your partner read aloud?

Blue Activity

Challenge Yourself!

Appreciate Writer's Craft

- Read *Spindletop* independently.

- Go back to a passage that interests you. What makes it interesting? Is it the subject matter or the way the information is presented? Reread the passage after you've decided.

Lesson 16

back

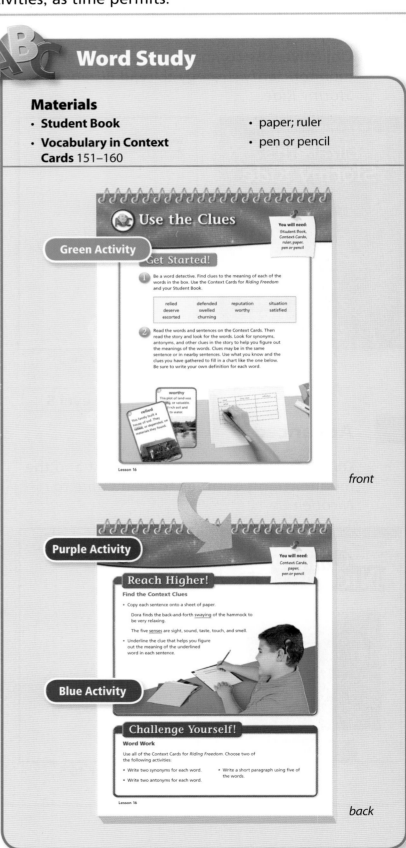

Word Study

Materials
- **Student Book**
- **Vocabulary in Context Cards** 151–160
- paper; ruler
- pen or pencil

Use the Clues

You will need:
Student Book, Context Cards, ruler, paper, pen or pencil

Green Activity

Get Started!

1. Be a word detective. Find clues to the meaning of each of the words in the box. Use the Context Cards for *Riding Freedom* and your Student Book.

relied	defended	reputation	situation
deserve	swelled	worthy	satisfied
escorted	churning		

2. Read the words and sentences on the Context Cards. Then read the story and look for the words. Look for synonyms, antonyms, and other clues in the story to help you figure out the meanings of the words. Clues may be in the same sentence or in nearby sentences. Use what you know and the clues you have gathered to fill in a chart like the one below. Be sure to write your own definition for each word.

Lesson 16

front

Purple Activity

You will need:
Context Cards, paper, pen or pencil

Reach Higher!

Find the Context Clues

- Copy each sentence onto a sheet of paper.

  Dora finds the back-and-forth swaying of the hammock to be very relaxing.

  The five senses are sight, sound, taste, touch, and smell.

- Underline the clue that helps you figure out the meaning of the underlined word in each sentence.

Blue Activity

Challenge Yourself!

Word Work

Use all of the Context Cards for *Riding Freedom*. Choose two of the following activities:

- Write two synonyms for each word.
- Write two antonyms for each word.
- Write a short paragraph using five of the words.

Lesson 16

back

Think and Write

Materials
- **Student Book**
- paper
- pen or pencil

front

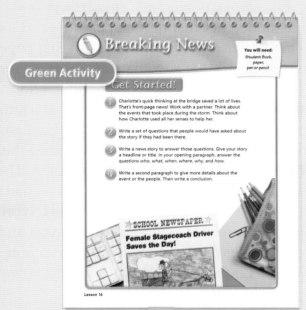

back

Independent Activities

Have students complete these activities at a computer center or a center with an audio CD player.

LAUNCH **Comprehension and Grammar Activities**

- Practice and apply this week's skills.

LAUNCH **Student eBook**

- Read and listen to this week's selections and skill lessons.

LAUNCH **WriteSmart CD-ROM**

- Review student versions of this week's writing model.

LAUNCH  **Audiotext CD**

- Listen to books or selections on CD.

Single Log In

Teacher Read Aloud

Model Fluency

Rate Explain that when good readers read aloud, their rate should be appropriate for the text—that is, not too fast or too slow.

- Display **Projectable 16.1**. As you read each sentence, model how to read at a rate that is appropriate for the text.

- Point out that reading for different purposes affects the rate at which you read.

- Reread the sentences together with students at a rate that is appropriate for the text.

Getting the Story

In 1887, a young reporter for a New York City newspaper received a daring first assignment: go undercover and expose the conditions at a well-known mental institution. "Could I pass a week in the insane ward at Blackwell's Island?" the reporter later wrote. "I said I could and I would. And I did."

The reporter's name was Nellie Bly. At a time when there were few women journalists, Bly was determined to prove herself **worthy** of the job. Going into a mental hospital must have set her stomach **churning** nervously, but it wasn't the first challenging **situation** she'd plunged into, and it wouldn't be the last. **1**

Bly was born Elizabeth Cochran in a small town in Pennsylvania. She landed her first newspaper job—and took her pen name—at the *Pittsburgh Dispatch*. When that paper's popular columnist declared that a woman who worked for a living was a "monstrosity," Bly **swelled** with indignation. Women didn't **deserve** such an insult! She fired off a letter to the paper. Impressed, the editors hired her. For her first story, Bly interviewed working women, then described their lives and **defended** their abilities, in an article called "The Girl Puzzle." Nellie Bly cared about people's lives and had a knack for getting them to talk to her. She wasn't **satisfied** when the *Dispatch* assigned her to write about fashion and flowers, so she packed her bags and left her editors a note: "I'm off for New York. Look out for me. Bly."

Projectable 16.1

Projectable 16.1

Riding Freedom | Fluency | Rate

Read Aloud: Model Oral Fluency

Getting the Story

In 1887, a young reporter for a New York City newspaper received a daring first assignment: go undercover and expose the conditions at a well-known mental institution. "Could I pass a week in the insane ward at Blackwell's Island?" the reporter later wrote. "I said I could and I would. And I did."

The reporter's name was Nellie Bly. At a time when there were few women journalists, Bly was determined to prove herself **worthy** of the job. Going into a mental hospital must have set her stomach **churning** nervously, but it wasn't the first challenging **situation** she'd plunged into, and it wouldn't be the last.

Fluency
© Houghton Mifflin Harcourt Publishing Company. All rights reserved.

Grade 4, Unit 4: Never Give Up!

The editors didn't have to look out for long. Nellie Bly's name soon began to appear in the *New York World*, the paper that sent her undercover to the mental asylum. Because of what she wrote about the cruel treatment there, horrified officials began to make changes. For another story, she got herself arrested, then wrote about the harsh treatment of prisoners. She exposed a health clinic that used unqualified doctors. **2**

Nellie Bly was a pioneer in investigative reporting. Readers **relied** on her to dig for the facts and get "the story behind the story." She developed a strong **reputation** for her work. But another kind of story made her an international celebrity. Her newspaper wanted to send a reporter around the world to try to beat the record of a character in the novel, *Around the World In 80 Days*. Naturally, Bly wanted the assignment. When she threatened to go to another newspaper if they sent a man instead, her paper gave in. Refusing to be **escorted** by a chaperone, Bly circled the world by steamship, train, handcart, and burro—sending stories back to her eager readers. She arrived home in 72 days, 6 hours, and 11 minutes, breaking the fictional record. Nellie Bly said she could do it, and she did. **3** **4**

Listening Comprehension

Preview the Target Skill

Read aloud the passage at an appropriate rate. Then ask the following questions.

1 Draw Conclusions *Why was Nellie Bly determined to prove herself worthy of the job? She wanted to prove that a woman could be a good journalist.*

2 Compare and Contrast *How did Nellie's assignments differ at the two newspapers? In Pittsburgh, she was assigned to write about fashion and flowers; in New York, she wrote about the treatment of mental patients and prisoners.*

3 Character Traits *Why is Nellie Bly considered a pioneer in investigative reporting? She would dig for the facts and get "the story behind the story."*

4 Cause and Effect *What would have happened if Nellie had not gotten the assignment to go around the world? She would have gone to work at another paper.*

✔ Target Vocabulary

Reread "Getting the Story" aloud.

As you read, pause briefly to explain each highlighted vocabulary word.

- Discuss the meaning of each word as it is used in the Read Aloud.

worthy good enough for something

churning vigorously mixing or stirring

situation a set of circumstances

swelled got larger

deserve earn something

defended speak or write in support of something

satisfied accepting

relied depended on

reputation people's opinions about someone or something

escorted guided or accompanied by someone

✓ Introduce Vocabulary

SHARE OBJECTIVE

- Understand and use the Target Vocabulary words.

Teach

Display the **Vocabulary in Context Cards**, using the routine below. Direct students to **Student Book pp. 402–403**. See also **Instructional Routine 9**.

1 **Read and pronounce the word.** Read the word once alone, then together with students.

2 **Explain the word.** Read aloud the explanation under *What Does It Mean?*

3 **Discuss vocabulary in context.** Together, read aloud the sentence on the front of the card. Help students explain and use the word in new sentences.

4 **Engage with the word.** Ask and discuss the *Think About It* question with students.

Apply

Give partners or small groups one or two **Vocabulary in Context Cards**.

- Help students start the *Talk It Over* activity on the back of their card.

- Have students complete activities for all the cards during the week.

Lesson 16

Vocabulary in Context

✓ **TARGET VOCABULARY**

escorted

swelled

relied

reputation

worthy

churning

situation

deserve

defended

satisfied

Vocabulary Reader

Context Cards

402

1 escorted
Guides who knew the western trails well often escorted, or led, travelers.

2 swelled
The number of wagons heading west swelled, or grew, in the 1850s.

3 relied
This family built a house of sod. They relied, or depended, on materials they found.

4 reputation
When customers were happy about a shop, its owner earned a good reputation.

ELL ENGLISH LANGUAGE LEARNERS

Scaffold

Beginning Use actions to demonstrate the meaning of *escort, swell,* and *churn.* Then have students perform the action as you say each word.

Advanced Ask students questions to confirm their understanding. For example: *I escorted Maria to her new classroom. Why might I have done this?*

Intermediate Have students complete sentence frames for each Vocabulary word. For example,
If you work hard all day, you _____ a rest. (deserve)

Advanced High Have partners ask and answer questions about each Vocabulary Word. For example, *How might you feel if your stomach were churning?*

See ELL Lesson 16, pp. E2–E11, for scaffolded support.

- Study each **Context Card**.
- Break the longer words into syllables. Use a dictionary to confirm.

5 worthy

This plot of land was worthy, or valuable. It had rich soil and access to water.

6 churning

Dark clouds and churning winds over the plains could signal a tornado.

7 situation

Mail carriers were prepared for any situation, or event, as they rode alone.

8 deserve

Kids who worked hard on the farm would deserve an occasional treat.

9 defended

Westward travelers defended themselves from harm by circling their wagons.

10 satisfied

Despite the hard work and danger, some settlers were satisfied with life in the West.

403

Monitor Vocabulary

Are students able to understand and use Target Vocabulary words?

IF...	THEN...
students have difficulty understanding and using most of the Target Vocabulary words,	▶ use **Vocabulary in Context Cards** and differentiate the **Vocabulary Reader**, *Stagecoach Travel*, for Struggling Readers, p. T60. *See also Intervention Lesson 16, pp. S2–S11.*
students can understand and use most of the Target Vocabulary words,	▶ use **Vocabulary in Context Cards** and differentiate the **Vocabulary Reader**, *Stagecoach Travel*, for On-Level Readers, p. T60.
students can understand and use all of the Target Vocabulary words,	▶ differentiate the **Vocabulary Reader**, *Stagecoach Travel*, for Advanced Readers, p. T61.

Vocabulary Reader, *pp. T60–T61*
Group English Language Learners according to language proficiency.

VOCABULARY IN CONTEXT CARDS 151–160

1 escorted

Guides who knew the western trails well often escorted, or led, travelers.

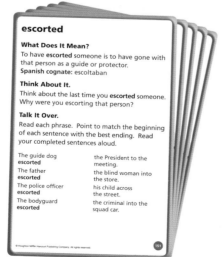

escorted

What Does It Mean?
To have escorted someone is to have gone with that person as a guide or protector.
Spanish cognate: escoltaban

Think About It.
Think about the last time you escorted someone. Why were you escorting that person?

Talk It Over.
Read each phrase. Point to match the beginning of each sentence with the best ending. Read your completed sentences aloud.

The guide dog escorted	the President to the meeting.
The father escorted	the blind woman into the store.
The police officer escorted	his child across the street.
The bodyguard escorted	the criminal into the squad car.

front   back

Develop Background

SHARE OBJECTIVES

- Learn about important ideas in "Riding Freedom."
- Build background using the Target Vocabulary words.

 ENGLISH LANGUAGE LEARNERS

Scaffold

Beginning Help students list familiar modes of transportation. Point out common features, such as wheels, windows, and seats.

Intermediate Use the diagram on p. 404 to have students discuss the stagecoach.

Advanced Discuss with students the difficulties a stagecoach driver might have had while guiding horses over unfamiliar territory.

Advanced High Point out the last sentence of the first paragraph on p. 404. Ask students how it might feel in such a situation. Have them work with a partner to write a short paragraph about it, using Vocabulary words.

See ELL Lesson 16, pp. E2–E11 for scaffolded support.

 Target Vocabulary

1 Teach/Model

- Use the diagram of the stagecoach on **Student Book p. 404** t explain that "Riding Freedom" is about a stagecoach driver v faces a dangerous situation.

- Use **Vocabulary in Context Cards** to review the student-frien explanations of each Target Vocabulary word.

- Have students silently read **Student Book p. 404**. Then read t passage aloud.

2 Guided Practice

Ask students the first item below and discuss their responses. Continue this way until students have answered a question ab each Target Vocabulary word.

1. Tell about a time when you **relied** on a friend to help you a task.

2. Describe a **situation** that made you smile.

3. What are the dangers of trying to swim across a **churning** river?

4. Why is it a good idea to be **escorted** across a busy street b crossing guard?

5. Tell about a character from a story who **defended** himself herself when faced with a conflict.

6. What could happen to a boat on a lake if the waves sudde **swelled** to three times their normal size?

7. List three reasons why you feel you **deserve** good grades.

8. Describe some ways you might build a **reputation** for bein honest.

9. What characteristics would make someone **worthy** of trus

10. What might you do after a large meal to show you feel **satisfied**?

Background

✓ TARGET VOCABULARY **The Stagecoach** In the 1800s, many people traveled west in covered wagons. Some, however, relied on the stagecoach, or stage. But passengers had to be ready for any situation. They might even have to get out and help guide the stage across a churning river!

Mail and gold also moved by stage. Guards often escorted these stages and defended them from attack. As the number of stages swelled, good drivers grew to deserve praise for their skills. One company, Wells Fargo, earned a reputation for being worthy because it usually got satisfied riders and cargo through safely.

Parts of a Stagecoach

gers' belongings
arried on the
ge rack. Each
ger was allowed
wenty-five pounds
age.

river's seat was
f the ground so that
ver could easily see

w shades were
f oiled leather to
ut dust as well as
d snow.

The **boot**, or back area, held the mail that was shipped along with the passengers.

The **steps** into the coach could be folded up after passengers had climbed aboard.

3 Apply

- Have partners take turns reading a paragraph on **Student Book p. 404** to one another.

- Tell partners to pause at and explain each highlighted vocabulary word as they read.

Introduce Comprehension

SHARE OBJECTIVES

• Understand compare and contrast.
• Identify similarities and differences in text.
• Use the Monitor/Clarify strategy to check understanding of similarities and differences.

SKILL TRACE

Compare and Contrast	
▶ Introduce	**T18–19**, T36–T37
Differentiate	T62–T63
Reteach	T70
Review	Lesson 24
Test	Weekly Tests, Lesson 16

ELL ENGLISH LANGUAGE LEARNERS

Scaffold

Beginning Write the following sentence frames on the board: *A _____ and a _____ are alike. One difference between them is _____.* Work with students to complete them orally using classroom objects.

Intermediate Ask these questions, and encourage answers with complete sentences: *How is a stagecoach like a car? What are the differences between them?*

Advanced Draw a Venn diagram on the board, and guide students to complete it using the answers to the questions above.

Advanced High Have partners write two or more sentences that use *both* and *but* in this pattern: *A _____ and a _____ both have _____, but _____.*

See ELL Lesson 16, pp. E2–E11, for scaffolded support.

✔ ## Compare and Contrast; Monitor/Clarify

1 Teach/Model

 Academic Language

compare to find ways that two or more things are similar

contrast to find ways that two or more things are different

• Tell students that when readers **compare**, they think about similarities. When readers **contrast**, they think about differences.

• Read and discuss **Student Book p. 405**. Have students use the Academic Language in the discussion.

• Display **Projectable 16.2**. Have students read "New Home."

COMPARE AND CONTRAST Point out that signal words, such as *different*, *but*, *though*, and *same* help readers to find similarities and differences.

• Explain that a Venn diagram helps organize text details, to compare and contrast story elements such as setting.

> Think Aloud *The land back in Silas's home had busy streets, but the land in his new home is empty. I'll write those details in the Venn diagram.*

MONITOR/CLARIFY Tell students that they can monitor their understanding of a text and then reread to clarify their understanding.

> Think Aloud *As I read, I can pay attention to how well I understand the text. Silas compares and contrasts the setting of his old and new homes. I'm not sure how he feels about the new place, though. I'll reread to try to figure that out.*

Projectable 16.2

Projectable 16.2

Riding Freedom Introduce Comprehension Compare and Contrast; Monitor/Clarify

Compare and Contrast; Monitor/Clarify

New Home
Mama napped while Silas looked out the window of the stagecoach. This land seemed so much emptier and quieter than the land back home. Silas was used to busy streets, but there were no streets here. Instead, there was just a dusty trail. Silas saw nothing but tall grasses and the occasional tree off in the distance. He pictured the thick, friendly trees that formed a canopy over Main Street back home. This land seemed so different from home, but when he and Mama joined Papa on the new farm, they would be the same happy family again.

Compare and Contrast Use a Venn diagram to show similarities and differences in the text.

Old Place
busy streets
big friendly trees

Both
home
happy family

New Place
empty, quiet
land
dusty trail
tall grass
few trees

Monitor/Clarify Use a Venn diagram to clarify your understanding of similarities and differences.

Introduce Comprehension
© Houghton Mifflin Harcourt Publishing Company. All rights reserved.
Grade 4, Unit 4: Never Give Up!

Comprehension

✓ TARGET SKILL Compare and Contrast

To help you understand the story, it can be useful to compare and contrast the characters' actions and thoughts. As you read "Riding Freedom," compare and contrast the two main characters. Look for places where Charlotte and James are similar and different. Use the graphic organizer below to compare and contrast these characters.

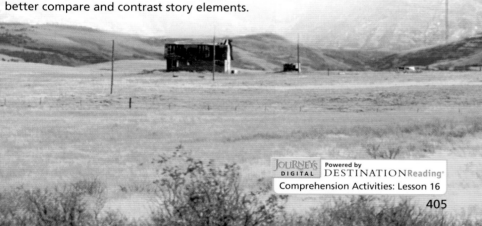

Charlotte   Both   James

✓ TARGET STRATEGY Monitor/Clarify

Use your graphic organizer to help you monitor your understanding of the events in "Riding Freedom." Clarifying information that does not make sense will also help you to better compare and contrast story elements.

2 Guided Practice

Guide students to copy and complete Venn diagrams for "New Home." Then review the diagrams together.

3 Apply

Turn and Talk Have partners use their Venn diagrams to discuss similarities and differences in the text.

Have students use a Venn diagram to compare and contrast another fictional text. Have them identify similarities and differences in characters' actions and thoughts.

Monitor Comprehension

Are students able to compare and contrast story details?

IF...	THEN...
students have difficulty comparing and contrasting information,	▶ **Differentiate Comprehension** for Struggling Readers, p. T62. *See also Intervention Lesson 16, pp. S2–S11.*
students can compare and contrast information,	▶ **Differentiate Comprehension** for On-Level Readers, p. T62.
students can accurately monitor to clarify comparisons and contrasts,	▶ **Differentiate Comprehension** for Advanced Readers, p. T63.

Differentiate Comprehension pp. T62–T63. *Group English Language Learners according to language proficiency. See also ELL Lesson 16, pp. E2–E11, for scaffolded support.*

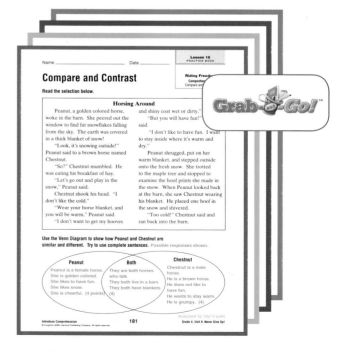

Practice Book p. 181
See Grab-and-Go™ Resources for additional leveled practice.

Introduce the Main Selection

TARGET SKILL

COMPARE AND CONTRAST Explain that as they read, students will use **Graphic Organizer 14: Venn Diagram** to compare and contrast these characters and story events:

- Charlotte's accident and her ability to drive a stagecoach
- how the characters react to the situation on the bridge

TARGET STRATEGY

MONITOR/CLARIFY Students will use a Venn diagram to **monitor** events in the story and **clarify** comparisons.

GENRE: Historical Fiction

- Read the genre information on **Student Book p. 406** with students.
- Share and discuss **Genre Blackline Master: Fiction.**
- Preview the selection and model identifying the characteristics of the genre.

Think Aloud *The illustrations of people seem to show realistic characters. The drawings of stagecoaches and horses tell me this story takes place in the past. The characters' clothing reminds me of the Old West.*

- As you preview the story, have students identify other features of historical fiction.

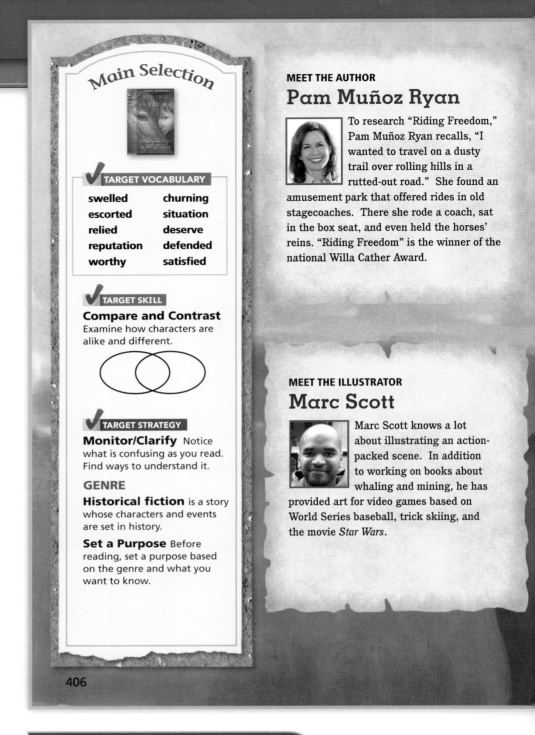

Main Selection

TARGET VOCABULARY

swelled	churning
escorted	situation
relied	deserve
reputation	defended
worthy	satisfied

TARGET SKILL

Compare and Contrast Examine how characters are alike and different.

TARGET STRATEGY

Monitor/Clarify Notice what is confusing as you read. Find ways to understand it.

GENRE

Historical fiction is a story whose characters and events are set in history.

Set a Purpose Before reading, set a purpose based on the genre and what you want to know.

406

MEET THE AUTHOR
Pam Muñoz Ryan

To research "Riding Freedom," Pam Muñoz Ryan recalls, "I wanted to travel on a dusty trail over rolling hills in a rutted-out road." She found an amusement park that offered rides in old stagecoaches. There she rode a coach, sat in the box seat, and even held the horses' reins. "Riding Freedom" is the winner of the national Willa Cather Award.

MEET THE ILLUSTRATOR
Marc Scott

Marc Scott knows a lot about illustrating an action-packed scene. In addition to working on books about whaling and mining, he has provided art for video games based on World Series baseball, trick skiing, and the movie *Star Wars*.

Reading the Selection

	Pre-reading	Reading
Supported	**SELECTION SUMMARY** Use **Blackline Master 16.2** to give students an overview before they read. **AUDIOTEXT CD** Have students listen to the selection as they follow along in their books.	**AUTHOR'S MESSAGE** After reading the selection, discuss with students the author's message about determination and overcoming difficulties.
Independent	**PREVIEW** Have students look at the title and illustrations and discuss predictions and clues. Some students may read the story independently first.	**TEXT EVIDENCE** Pause after pp. **409, 411, 414,** and **416.** Have students write a question and answer and the page number where evidence for the answer is found. Discuss students' responses.

Riding Freedom

by Pam Muñoz Ryan
selection illustrated by Marc Scott

Essential Question

What traits do successful people have in common?

407

? Essential Question

- Read aloud the **Essential Question** on **Student Book p. 407**. *What traits do successful people have in common?*

- Tell students to think about this question as they read "Riding Freedom."

Set Purpose

- Explain that good readers set a purpose for reading, based on their preview of the selection and what they know about the genre.

Think Aloud *Historical fiction tells about events that could have happened in the past. The illustrations show a stagecoach driver and horses. One purpose might be to understand why this story is called "Riding Freedom."*

- Have students share and record in their journals their reading purposes.

JOURNEYS DIGITAL
Powered by
DESTINATIONReading®
Student eBook: Read and Listen

Name _____ Date _____

Riding Freedom

Pages 408–409
During the 1800s, Charlotte disguises herself as a boy to work with horses. After moving to California to drive stagecoaches an accident leaves her partly blind. Charlotte is determined to learn how to drive again. She takes out a larger team each day, retrains her other senses, memorizes the route, and sets a goal for herself of ten roundtrips.

Pages 410–411
Charlotte tells her partner James that she wants to drive the stage across the river on its regular route. James worries she can't handle the job but agrees to give her a chance. There is a bad storm on the day of the test. James is nervous, but Charlotte knows she can handle the coach.

Pages 412–413
The coach reaches a bridge over a river with high water. Charlotte checks the safety of the bridge. Then she escorts the passengers and James across because the weakened bridge cannot support the stage and their weight. When everyone is safely across, Charlotte goes back for the stagecoach.

Pages 414–415
Charlotte moves the nervous horses slowly forward. When the wooden bridge starts to splinter, she cracks her whip and makes the horses run across the bridge. Just as the coach reaches the far bank, the bridge falls into the river.

Page 416
Charlotte jumps off the coach and calms the horses. The relieved passengers thank her for helping them. Charlotte knows James won't try to stop her from driving ever again.

Blackline Master 16.2

Develop Comprehension

Pause at the stopping points to ask students the following questions.

1 Identify Story Structure

What is the main problem Charlotte faces? She became partially blind and now must relearn to drive a coach.

2 ✔ **TARGET VOCABULARY**

Which of Charlotte's senses do you think she relied on most after her accident? Charlotte relied on touch, smell, and sound. She also had a "sixth sense" for dealing with horses.

3 Draw Conclusions

What do Charlotte's disguise and desire to drive a coach again tell about her character? Sample answer: She is very determined and will do whatever it takes to do what she loves— working with horses.

4 Understanding Characters

What does Charlotte's goal tell about her? Sample answer: She is determined and persistent. Being a good driver is important to her.

In the mid-1800s, when most girls are not allowed to have paid jobs, Charlotte Parkhurst disguises herself as a boy in order to work with horses. She goes by the name of "Charley" and keeps her true identity a secret. Years later, "Charley" moves from Rhode Island to an area near Sacramento, California. There, she and her friends, James and Frank, drive horse-drawn stagecoaches for a living. Suddenly, a bad accident leaves Charlotte partially blind. Now with only one good eye left, Charlotte must relearn how to drive a coach.

The next day, she overturned the coach completely but was able to jump free. What was she doing wrong? She knew how to drive a team. She didn't need training with the horses or the ribbons. She knew those things by heart. It was her eye she didn't know. She needed to train her one good eye. She needed to learn how to use it all over again.

408

ELL ENGLISH LANGUAGE LEARNERS

Scaffold

Beginning Using the illustrations, preview the selection with students. Have them repeat the names of the people and objects in the illustrations.

Advanced After reading pages 408–409, have students restate the ideas and ask clarifying questions.

Intermediate While reading the introduction aloud, pause to explain these words using gestures, visuals, or simplified language: *disguises, identity, secret, accident,* and *partially.*

Advanced High After reading pages 408–409, have students write one or two sentences, summarizing what they have learned so far.

See ELL Lesson 16, pp. E2–E11, for scaffolded support.

She started taking a smaller team out every day. First a two-horse team. Then a four. Finally, with six-in-the-hand. Charlotte had been proving herself her whole life and she wasn't about to stop now. She didn't even care if Frank and James caught on to what she was doing. They might as well see me trying, she thought.

She learned the different sounds the horses' hooves made on different types of roads. If the road was hard, the hooves made a hollow, clopping sound. If the road was soft, the hooves made a dull, thudding sound. She relied on her one good eye to take over for the other. She trusted her senses. And the sixth sense she had for handling horses. **2**

Charlotte drove back and forth over her route and memorized every rock and tree. She set a goal for herself. If she made ten clean, round-trip runs, she'd know she was as good as the next driver. After that, she'd just have Frank and James to convince. **3** **4**

409

Practice Fluency

Rate Read aloud the second paragraph on **Student Book p. 408** while students follow along. As you read the paragraph, model reading more slowly, at a rate that would be more appropriate for complicated informational text.

Discuss with students why reading the text at a faster pace might sound more appropriate for fiction.

- Tell students that Charlotte's story is to be read for enjoyment. Good readers read narrative text at a faster rate than when reading for information.

- Have students echo-read each sentence after you read it.

See **p. T38** for a complete fluency lesson on reading rate.

CROSS-CURRICULAR CONNECTION

Social Studies

Have students turn to the diagram of the stagecoach shown on **Student Book p. 404**. Explain that Wells Fargo provided regular mail service by stage between St. Louis and San Francisco. The six-horse stagecoach shown here carried mail, passengers, and luggage over the vast plains. By 1866, Wells Fargo ran most of the stagecoach traffic in the West. Explain that with the completion of the Transcontinental Railroad in 1869, the importance of the stagecoach started to decline. Have students discuss why the new technology of the railroad helped lead to the end of stagecoach travel.

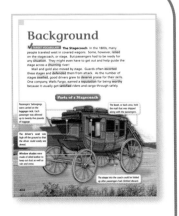

Develop Comprehension

5 ✔ **TARGET VOCABULARY**

*What is the **situation** in which Charlotte finds herself?* Sample answer: She wants to prove she can still drive a coach.

6 **Draw Conclusions**

Why is James worried that Charlotte might have trouble driving the stagecoach? Charlotte wears an eye patch, and James is worried about her because of her vision.

7 **Predict Characters' Actions**

How could Charlotte's earlier training help her during the storm? Sample answer: Charlotte could use her retrained senses to find landmarks along the road.

8 **Analyze Supporting Details**

How does the author use details to describe the storm? The author shows the storm's wildness with phrases like "came down in washtubs" and "flying in every direction."

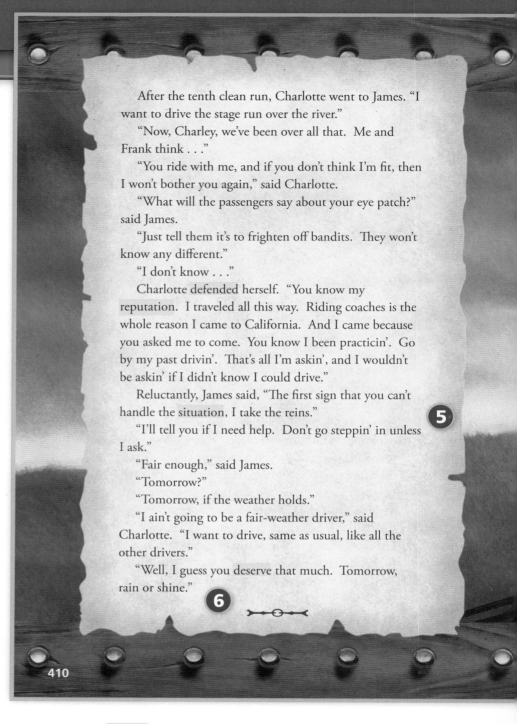

After the tenth clean run, Charlotte went to James. "I want to drive the stage run over the river."

"Now, Charley, we've been over all that. Me and Frank think . . ."

"You ride with me, and if you don't think I'm fit, then I won't bother you again," said Charlotte.

"What will the passengers say about your eye patch?" said James.

"Just tell them it's to frighten off bandits. They won't know any different."

"I don't know . . ."

Charlotte defended herself. "You know my reputation. I traveled all this way. Riding coaches is the whole reason I came to California. And I came because you asked me to come. You know I been practicin'. Go by my past drivin'. That's all I'm askin', and I wouldn't be askin' if I didn't know I could drive."

Reluctantly, James said, "The first sign that you can't handle the situation, I take the reins."

"I'll tell you if I need help. Don't go steppin' in unless I ask."

"Fair enough," said James.

"Tomorrow?"

"Tomorrow, if the weather holds."

"I ain't going to be a fair-weather driver," said Charlotte. "I want to drive, same as usual, like all the other drivers."

"Well, I guess you deserve that much. Tomorrow, rain or shine."

410

ELL ENGLISH LANGUAGE LEARNERS

Scaffold

Beginning For each question, accept one-word responses and expand student responses into sentences. For example, if a student's response to question 6 is "her eye," expand the answer by saying, *Yes, James is worried about Charlotte's eye.* Have students repeat the expanded response and confirm their understanding.

Advanced Have students respond to the questions in complete sentences. Provide corrective feedback as needed.

Intermediate Provide part of the response for each question and have students complete it. Then have students repeat the complete response. Confirm their understanding.

Advanced High Have students tell how they know the answer to each question based on details from the story.

See ELL Lesson 16, pp. E2–E11, for scaffolded support.

It was one of those storms where the rain came down in washtubs, but the stage was scheduled to go. The coach was chock-full of passengers, baggage, and mail pouches that had to get through. Charlotte was soaked clear through by the time the baggage was secured. James rode shotgun next to her.

The wind wouldn't let up, and the rain came flying in every which direction. James seemed nervous.

"Charley, I can't even see the road!" he yelled.

"Then it's a good thing I'm drivin', 'cause I can smell it, and I can hear it!" yelled Charlotte.

James sat back as the coach headed into the storm. **7**
The mud was so thick it reached the hubs, but Charlotte still found the road. **8**

411

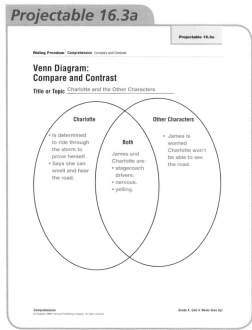

Projectable 16.3a

Riding Freedom | **Comprehension** Compare and Contrast

Venn Diagram:
Compare and Contrast

Title or Topic Charlotte and the Other Characters

Charlotte
- Is determined to ride through the storm to prove herself.
- Says she can smell and hear the road.

Both
James and Charlotte are:
- stagecoach drivers.
- nervous.
- yelling.

Other Characters
- James is worried Charlotte won't be able to see the road.

Comprehension
© Houghton Mifflin Harcourt Publishing Company. All rights reserved.

Grade 4, Unit 4: Never Give Up!

✓ **TARGET STRATEGY**

Monitor/Clarify

MODEL THE STRATEGY

- Remind students that when they read something that doesn't make sense, they need to stop and figure out what they don't understand and how to clarify their understanding. Point out that comparing and contrasting characters and story details can help them monitor their understanding.

- Display **Projectable 16.3a**. Point out that students can use a completed Venn diagram to help them monitor and clarify their understanding of the story.

- Model how to use the Monitor/Clarify strategy as you begin recording details from **Student Book p. 411** in the Venn Diagram.

Think Aloud *The first time I read this page, I don't see much difference between James and Charlotte. They both seem nervous. I can write that in the middle of the diagram. I reread to clarify my understanding. When I do this, I see that while James is just nervous, Charlotte is nervous but also determined to do the job. I can write that detail on one side of the diagram.*

- Have students use **Graphic Organizer 14** to begin their own Venn diagram as they read. Students should compare and contrast characters and story details. Have students practice using the Monitor/Clarify strategy to clarify their understanding.

Develop Comprehension

9 Summarize

What is the third paragraph on page 412 mainly about? Sample answer: Charlotte checks the bridge to make sure it will withstand the weight of the stagecoach.

10 Compare and Contrast

Contrast James's and Charlotte's actions at the bridge. James stays with the passengers, but Charlotte goes to check on how safe the bridge is to cross.

11 Analyze Character Traits

How do Charlotte's actions on pp. 412–413 show she can handle the problems caused by the storm? Sample answer: She escorts the passengers to safety and returns for the horses and coach.

12 Understanding Details

Why does the author use so many details to describe how Charlotte checks the bridge? Sample answer: The author wants to show how careful Charlotte is about safety and why she thinks the bridge won't support any extra weight.

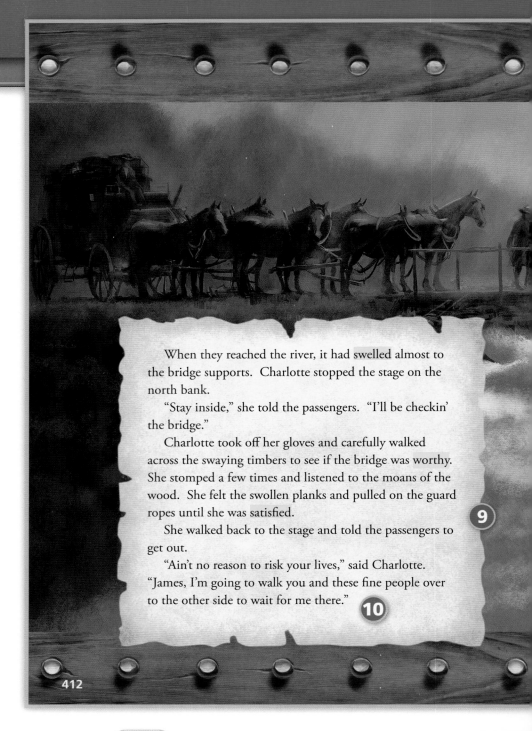

When they reached the river, it had swelled almost to the bridge supports. Charlotte stopped the stage on the north bank.

"Stay inside," she told the passengers. "I'll be checkin' the bridge."

Charlotte took off her gloves and carefully walked across the swaying timbers to see if the bridge was worthy. She stomped a few times and listened to the moans of the wood. She felt the swollen planks and pulled on the guard ropes until she was satisfied.

She walked back to the stage and told the passengers to get out.

"Ain't no reason to risk your lives," said Charlotte. "James, I'm going to walk you and these fine people over to the other side to wait for me there."

412

ELL — ENGLISH LANGUAGE LEARNERS

Scaffold

Beginning Use gestures and the illustration on pp. 412–413 to explain the steps Charlotte took to escort the passengers safely across the bridge.

Advanced Say: *How would you describe Charlotte on these pages?* Make a word web of words that students say to describe the character.

Intermediate Work with students to describe the steps Charlotte took to escort the passengers to safety.

Advanced High Have students work in pairs to discuss what Charlotte is like. Ask partners to write sentences that describe Charlotte based on her actions.

See ELL Lesson 16, pp. E2–E11, for scaffolded support.

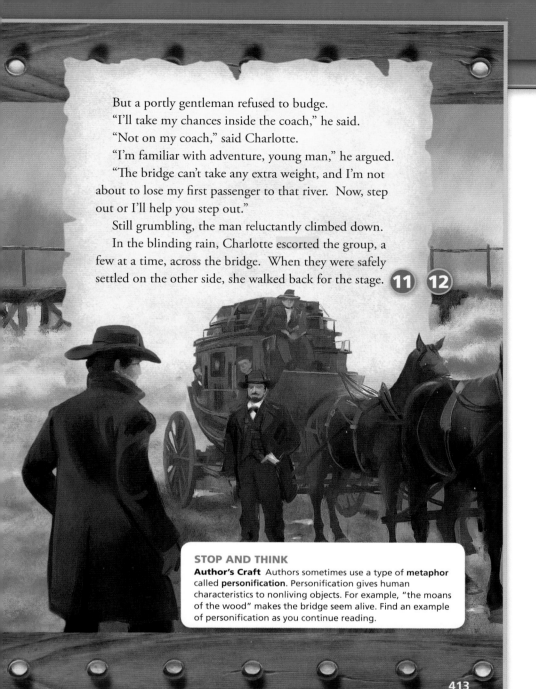

But a portly gentleman refused to budge.

"I'll take my chances inside the coach," he said.

"Not on my coach," said Charlotte.

"I'm familiar with adventure, young man," he argued.

"The bridge can't take any extra weight, and I'm not about to lose my first passenger to that river. Now, step out or I'll help you step out."

Still grumbling, the man reluctantly climbed down.

In the blinding rain, Charlotte escorted the group, a few at a time, across the bridge. When they were safely settled on the other side, she walked back for the stage. **11** **12**

> **STOP AND THINK**
> **Author's Craft** Authors sometimes use a type of **metaphor** called **personification**. Personification gives human characteristics to nonliving objects. For example, "the moans of the wood" makes the bridge seem alive. Find an example of personification as you continue reading.

413

STOP AND THINK
Author's Craft: Personification

- Explain to students that **personification** is a literary device an author uses to describe nonhuman objects or ideas as if they had human characteristics.

- Write the following sentence on the board: *The rain tap danced on the roof.* Point out that this is an example of personification, since rain obviously cannot tap dance—only people can do that. Explain that this use of personification is a more vivid and interesting way to describe the rain.

- Point out that authors use personification to make their writing more lively and interesting for readers.

- Use the **Stop and Think** feature on **Student Book p. 413** to model the thinking.

> **Think Aloud** *An example of personification might be "the moans of the wood." Wood cannot moan. Only humans can moan, usually when they aren't feeling good. This gives the idea that the wood in the bridge is strained and in bad condition. It is also a sensory detail, describing how the bridge sounds.*

- Have students answer the **Stop and Think** question about personification on **Student Book p. 413**.

Develop Comprehension

13 **Author's Craft**
How does the author use language in this scene to create a feeling in the reader? Sample answer: The author uses words and details such as "thunder growled," "groaned," "raced," "huddled," and "anxiously" to create a feeling of danger in the reader.

14 **Draw Conclusions**
Why are the passengers huddled together and watching anxiously from the other side? Sample answer: The passengers see that the river is a few feet below the wheels of the coach. They are worried that Charlotte, the horses, and the coach may not make it across the racing river.

15 **Analyze Story Structure**
How does driving through the storm help Charlotte resolve her main problem? Sample answer: It shows she can handle the horses and coach during a crisis. If the weather had been good, her skills would not have been tested as much.

16 **Identify Sequence of Events**
Summarize the events on pp. 414–415. As thunder and lightning strike, Charlotte drives onto the bridge. The bridge rocks and splinters, so Charlotte cracks the whip, causing the horses to run. As the coach reaches the far bank, the bridge collapses.

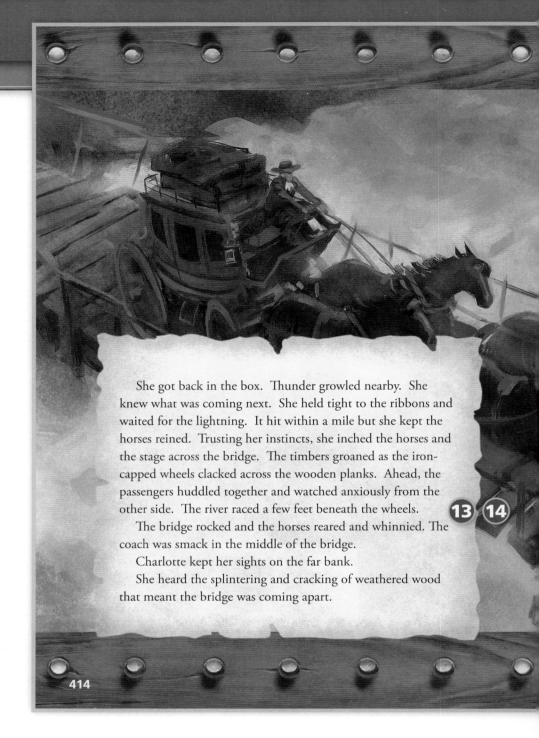

She got back in the box. Thunder growled nearby. She knew what was coming next. She held tight to the ribbons and waited for the lightning. It hit within a mile but she kept the horses reined. Trusting her instincts, she inched the horses and the stage across the bridge. The timbers groaned as the iron-capped wheels clacked across the wooden planks. Ahead, the passengers huddled together and watched anxiously from the other side. The river raced a few feet beneath the wheels.

The bridge rocked and the horses reared and whinnied. The coach was smack in the middle of the bridge.

Charlotte kept her sights on the far bank.

She heard the splintering and cracking of weathered wood that meant the bridge was coming apart.

414

She stood up in the box. "Keep them straight on the bridge, Charlotte." Dashing the water from her good eye and gathering the reins in a firm grip, she cracked her whip and yelled, "Away!"

She was thrown back into the box. The horses jibbed, side to side, but she held tight to the ribbons. They flew across like scared jackrabbits. The back wheels barely turned on solid ground when the bridge collapsed and dropped into the churning river.

"Whoa, my beauties! Whoa!" yelled Charlotte. **15 16**

> ✔ **STOP AND THINK**
> **Compare and Contrast** Compare and contrast the thoughts and emotions of Charlotte to those of the passengers as she guides the stagecoach across the bridge.

415

STOP AND THINK

✔ **TARGET SKILL**

COMPARE AND CONTRAST

- Remind students that comparing and contrasting story details as they read will help deepen their understanding of the characters and events.

- Have students complete the Stop and Think activity on **Student Book p. 415.**

- If students have difficulty comparing and contrasting story details, see **Comprehension Intervention** below for extra support.

- Have students continue their graphic organizers. Display **Projectable 16.3b** and work with students to add to the Venn diagram.

❓ Essential Question

Discuss what Charlotte's actions in this story tell about her courage, bravery, and determination. Have students compare her traits with those of successful people they know about.

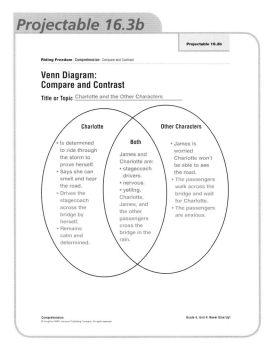

Projectable 16.3b

COMPREHENSION INTERVENTION

✔ **TARGET SKILL** **Compare and Contrast**

SKILL SUPPORT Remind students that they can compare and contrast story characters to help better understand why things happen in a story. Model finding the similarities and differences between Charlotte and the other characters:

Charlotte got soaked in the rain, but the passengers stayed dry, so they are different. James stood shivering in the rain, too, so they are similar. However, when Charlotte makes the passengers exit the coach, they all are soaked. When the similarities and differences between the characters change, I know that something important is happening in the story.

Read aloud **Student Book p. 414.** Have students describe what the passengers do in this scene. They huddle together anxiously. Have them describe what Charlotte does. She bravely guides the horses across the bridge.

Have students continue filling in their graphic organizers.

STOP AND THINK

 **TARGET STRATEGY**

Monitor/Clarify

- Remind students that monitoring, or checking their comprehension as they read, will help them better understand what they read. When they find an idea that seems puzzling, they should stop to clarify what they have read before continuing.

- Have students answer the Stop and Think question on **p. 416**. If necessary, have students reread to find the answer.

- Have students use their completed graphic organizers to discuss how successful Charlotte was in achieving the goal she set for herself at the beginning of the story.

- If students have difficulty using the Monitor/Clarify strategy, see **Comprehension Intervention** below for extra support.

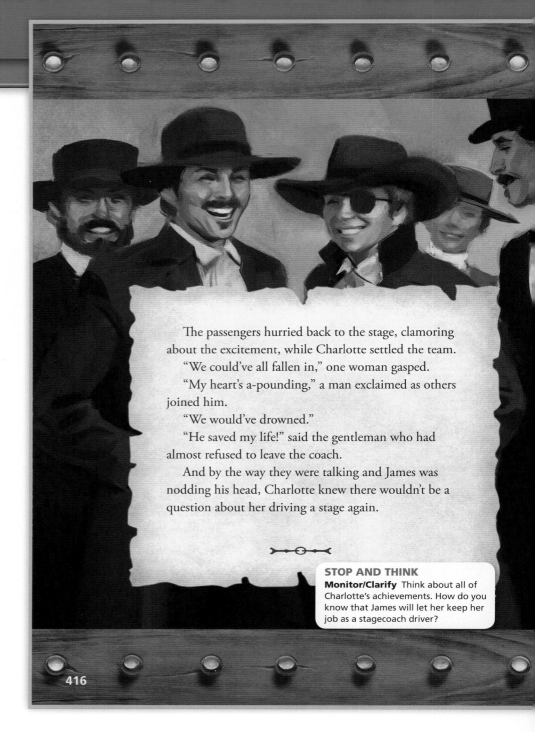

The passengers hurried back to the stage, clamoring about the excitement, while Charlotte settled the team.

"We could've all fallen in," one woman gasped.

"My heart's a-pounding," a man exclaimed as others joined him.

"We would've drowned."

"He saved my life!" said the gentleman who had almost refused to leave the coach.

And by the way they were talking and James was nodding his head, Charlotte knew there wouldn't be a question about her driving a stage again.

STOP AND THINK
Monitor/Clarify Think about all of Charlotte's achievements. How do you know that James will let her keep her job as a stagecoach driver?

416

COMPREHENSION INTERVENTION

 **TARGET STRATEGY**   Monitor/Clarify

STRATEGY SUPPORT Remind students that when they monitor their understanding, they check or confirm their understanding as they read. When they come to text that doesn't make sense, they should pause to clarify their understanding. Model the monitor/clarify strategy by reviewing what Charlotte achieved on the bridge.

If I do not understand why James smiled and nodded at Charlotte, I should stop to clarify what I have just read. I see that Charlotte just successfully drove the stagecoach across the bridge, and now all the passengers are congratulating Charlotte. A nod usually means agreement, so James might be impressed with what Charlotte accomplished.

Have students continue to complete their graphic organizers, and remind them to stop to clarify anything they do not understand.

Your Turn

What an Attitude!

Short Response Charlotte must keep her true identity as a woman a secret in order to drive a stagecoach. What does this tell you about attitudes toward women in the mid-1800s? Write a paragraph comparing attitudes toward women in Charlotte's day to attitudes toward women today.
SOCIAL STUDIES

Steal the Scene

Draw a Picture Charlotte had some challenging and exciting experiences. Work with a small group to choose a scene from the story. Choose roles. Use details from the story to make your scene realistic and exciting. Rehearse the scene and then perform it for classmates.
SMALL GROUP

Do You Trust Me?

Turn and Talk Think about the point in the story where Charlotte tries to convince James that she can drive the stage again. With a partner, discuss the problem each character faces as they try to come to a decision. How are their problems similar and different? How do each character's traits affect the way the problem is solved?
COMPARE AND CONTRAST

417

Retelling Rubric

4	**Excellent**	Students provide detailed descriptions and opinions supported by several relevant details from the text and illustrations.
3	**Good**	Students provide descriptions and opinions supported by one or two details from the text and illustrations.
2	**Fair**	Students do not respond to the entire prompt and/or do not support their opinions.
1	**Unsatisfactory**	Students provide inaccurate, unsupported descriptions and/or opinions.

Your Turn

Have students complete the activities on page 417.

What an Attitude! Tell students that an *attitude* toward something is an overall feeling about it. For example, if somebody gets excited about playing with puppies or going to the zoo, this person has a positive attitude toward animals. Provide students with a Venn diagram to help them organize their paragraphs about attitudes toward women in both time periods.
(SOCIAL STUDIES)

Steal the Scene Tell students that a scene in a play focuses on just one or two events. Have students skim the text, choose their scenes, and brainstorm for possible sound effects. As students rehearse their scenes, circulate around the room and provide acting and speaking tips. (SMALL GROUP)

Do You Trust Me? Before students work in partners, post a T-chart with the columns Charlotte and James. Complete the chart as you discuss the two characters' problems. Then have partners answer the questions in the Student Book. Finally, ask: *How would you feel if you were in Charlotte's shoes? In James's shoes?* (COMPARE AND CONTRAST)

Oral Language Have partners describe Charlotte's character traits. Students should use details from the story and illustrations to give examples of how Charlotte's actions reveal her traits. Use the Retelling Rubric at the left to evaluate students' responses.

Connect to Social Studies

PREVIEW THE INFORMATIONAL TEXT

- Tell students that this selection is an online encylopedia entry giving factual information about the beginning of the oil industry in Texas. Have students read the title and subtitles, preview the photographs and note the email message on page 420. Then have students read the informational text independently.

DISCUSS DIGITAL MEDIA CONVENTIONS

- Discuss with students the different kinds of information that students have found using **digital media**, such as CD-ROMs and websites.

- Point out that different types of print and digital media have their own **conventions**, or rules, for how to write and communicate. Explain that articles in an online magazine or encyclopedia have similar writing conventions to books. Others, such as weblogs and emails, are often written less formally and more personally.

digital media	print, video, and audio content usually accessed by computer or electronic device
email	mail-type messages sent from one computer or electronic device to another

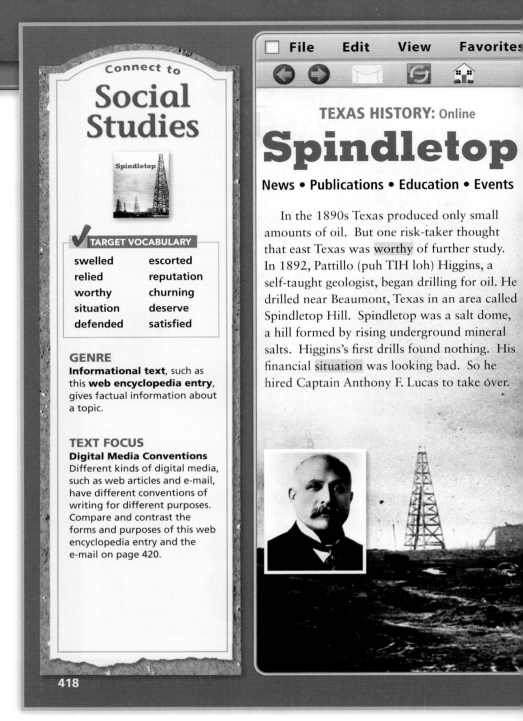

Connect to Social Studies

Spindletop

✓ TARGET VOCABULARY

swelled	escorted
relied	reputation
worthy	churning
situation	deserve
defended	satisfied

GENRE
Informational text, such as this **web encyclopedia entry**, gives factual information about a topic.

TEXT FOCUS
Digital Media Conventions Different kinds of digital media, such as web articles and e-mail, have different conventions of writing for different purposes. Compare and contrast the forms and purposes of this web encyclopedia entry and the e-mail on page 420.

418

File   Edit   View   Favorites

TEXAS HISTORY: Online
Spindletop
News • Publications • Education • Events

In the 1890s Texas produced only small amounts of oil. But one risk-taker thought that east Texas was worthy of further study. In 1892, Pattillo (puh TIH loh) Higgins, a self-taught geologist, began drilling for oil. He drilled near Beaumont, Texas in an area called Spindletop Hill. Spindletop was a salt dome, a hill formed by rising underground mineral salts. Higgins's first drills found nothing. His financial situation was looking bad. So he hired Captain Anthony F. Lucas to take over.

 ENGLISH LANGUAGE LEARNERS

Scaffold

Beginning Use simplified language and the images to help students understand that *oil* is the liquid fuel from the ground used to power cars.

Advanced Have partners answer the following question using evidence from the text: *Why was getting oil out of the ground in Texas difficult to do?*

Intermediate Pose simple questions about oil and where it comes from to develop students' understanding. Discuss with students their responses and clarify understanding as needed.

Advanced High Have students give oral sentences summarizing the information they read on pages 418–419

See ELL Lesson 16, pp. E2–E11, for scaffolded support.

OIL: Spindletop

The Lucas Geyser

Lucas was a leading geologist with a reputation as an expert on salt domes. He began drilling at Spindletop in 1899. At first, he, too, had no luck. The money he relied on was running out. Lucas escorted businessmen to Beaumont, hoping that they would invest in the well. Most of them felt that he did not deserve their help. But Lucas defended his ideas about salt domes and oil. Finally, his investors were satisfied that his project was worthwhile, and the funds came in.

On the morning of January 10, 1901, Lucas's team drilled down 1,139 feet—and found oil. "The Lucas Geyser," as it came to be called, blew oil more than 150 feet in the air. In time, it would produce 100,000 barrels per day. Until then, few oil fields in Texas had produced more than 25 barrels per day! **1**

The Spindletop Gusher, 1901

419

Practice Fluency

Rate Have students listen as you read aloud the paragraph on **Student Book p. 418**.

- Remind students that good readers use different rates of reading for different purposes. This page contains information about dates and places. To read informational text, the reader may need to slow down for complete understanding.

- Have students partner read each sentence. Remind them to read at a rate that helps them understand the text.

JOURNEYS DIGITAL
Powered by
DESTINATIONReading®
Student eBook: Read and Listen

TARGET VOCABULARY REVIEW

✓ **TARGET VOCABULARY** Vocabulary in Context Cards – Word Sort

Have students work in groups to review the Vocabulary in Context Cards. Then have them sort the Target Vocabulary words into categories. For example, students might sort the words by parts of speech or by other things the words have in common. Then have each student select at least one word from each category and write a sentence for that word. After students complete the activity, ask volunteers to share their sentences.

Develop Comprehension

Pause at the stopping points to ask the following questions.

1 Compare and Contrast

How were Pattillo Higgins and Captain Anthony Lucas alike? How were they different? Alike: Both wanted to find oil in Texas; Different: Higgins was not successful, but Lucas was successful.

2 ✓ TARGET VOCABULARY

What do you mean if you say "The number of students at school has **swelled***.?" The population of students has grown very quickly.*

Interpret Digital Media Conventions

• Tell students that the online encyclopedia article "Spindletop" is one example of digital media, and the email on **p. 420** is another. Explain that the article is written with standard writing conventions. Point out that the email is less formal, written as if the writer is leaving a note with a quick message.

• Model comparing and contrasting.

Think Aloud Spindletop has headings, dates, facts, and paragraphs with main ideas. This is more like a magazine or book. The email writer, though, used a less formal style, like a message to someone he knows.

• Have students look for other similiarities and differences between the article and the email.

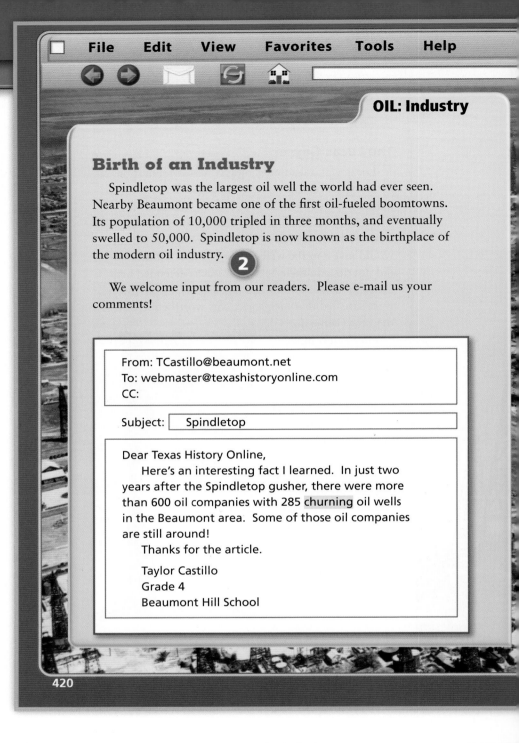

OIL: Industry

Birth of an Industry

Spindletop was the largest oil well the world had ever seen. Nearby Beaumont became one of the first oil-fueled boomtowns. Its population of 10,000 tripled in three months, and eventually swelled to 50,000. Spindletop is now known as the birthplace of the modern oil industry. **2**

We welcome input from our readers. Please e-mail us your comments!

From: TCastillo@beaumont.net
To: webmaster@texashistoryonline.com
CC:

Subject: Spindletop

Dear Texas History Online,
   Here's an interesting fact I learned. In just two years after the Spindletop gusher, there were more than 600 oil companies with 285 churning oil wells in the Beaumont area. Some of those oil companies are still around!
   Thanks for the article.

   Taylor Castillo
   Grade 4
   Beaumont Hill School

420

Weekly Internet Challenge

Using Keywords; adjust keywords as needed

• Review Internet Strategy, Step 1: Plan a Search.

• Remind students that the purpose of a search engine is to perform research on the Internet.

• Explain that good researchers can choose keywords effectively to find useful information and data.

INTERNET STRATEGY

1. **Plan a Search** by identifying what you are looking for and how to find it.

2. **Search and Predict** which sites will be worth exploring.

3. **Navigate** a site to see how to get around it and what it contains.

4. **Analyze and Evaluate** the quality and reliability of the information.

5. **Synthesize** the information from multiple sites.

Making Connections

Text to Self

Write a Letter Imagine that you have traveled back in time to the mid-1800s. What differences do you notice between your neighborhood now and in the past? Write a letter to a friend in which you compare and contrast the two settings.

Text to Text

Compare and Contrast How are the challenges faced by Charlotte Parkhurst similar to those faced by Pattillo Higgins (right) and Anthony Lucas in Texas? How are they different? Show evidence from the text.

Text to World

Connect to Social Studies In "Riding Freedom," Charlotte Parkhurst overcomes a physical challenge in order to continue doing what she loves. Work in a group to identify a famous person you have heard or read about who has done something similar, and discuss his or her experiences.

421

Making Connections

Text to Self

Students may need help imagining their neighborhoods during the mid-1800s. If possible, guide them to print resources and Internet sites where they can learn about their communities in the past and find ideas for features to focus on in their letters.

Text to Text

To help students identify similarities and differences between Charlotte Parkhurst and the Texas oil pioneers, have them create a Venn diagram to compare and contrast the challenges these characters faced. Remind them to use evidence from both texts.

Text to World

Remind students that in a good discussion, all participants are polite to each other, speak in turn, and listen attentively while others speak. Suggest that they create a list of questions before they start to guide their discussion.

"Spindletop" Challenge

• Ask students to brainstorm keywords for an Internet search about how the city of Beaumont, Texas, grew rapidly because of oil. If students need additional help, suggest using such keywords as *Texas oil industry, Beaumont Texas,* and *oil boom.*

• Have students start with the first term, check their results, then add additional search terms and evaluate the results.

• Discuss how the other information from the selection such as the dates involved in the town's growth, people who became rich because of Texas oil, and the importance of oil in Texas, could help them to choose additional effective keywords to use.

Deepen Comprehension

SKILL TRACE

Compare and Contrast	
Introduce	T18–T19, **T36–T37**
Differentiate	T62–T63
Reteach	T70
Review	Lesson 24
Test	Weekly Tests, Lesson 16

ELL ENGLISH LANGUAGE LEARNERS

Scaffold

Beginning Compare and contrast the illustrations in *Riding Freedom*. Use sentence frames like these: *In this picture, _____, but in this picture, _____. In both pictures, _____.*

Intermediate Guide students to compare and contrast story details: *How is Charlotte different from the passengers? How is this storm different from most rainstorms?*

Advanced Have partners come up with oral sentences to tell how this story is similar to and different from most adventure stories.

Advanced High Have students explain how women's work in Charlotte's time was different from a woman's career choices today.

See ELL Lesson 16, p. E2–E11, for scaffolded support.

✔ Compare and Contrast Story Details

1 Teach/Model

AL *Academic Language*

compare, **contrast**, **similarity**

- Remind students that readers look for comparisons and contrasts that the author points out. Readers also **compare** and **contrast** story characters, settings, and other details from different parts of the story on their own.

- Explain that readers deepen their understanding of a story when they think about how characters and other parts of the story are similar and different.

- Display **Projectable 16.4** and discuss **Deepen Comprehension Question 1**.

- Review the three sections of the Venn diagram. Model thinking about contrasts to answer the question.

Think Aloud *The most important difference is that Charlotte can't see as well as she did before her accident. After the accident, she must relearn how to drive a stagecoach using one eye and her other senses.*

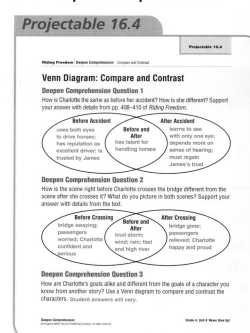

Projectable 16.4

Projectable 16.4

Riding Freedom Deepen Comprehension Compare and Contrast

Venn Diagram: Compare and Contrast

Deepen Comprehension Question 1

How is Charlotte the same as before her accident? How is she different? Support your answer with details from pp. 408–410 of *Riding Freedom*.

Before Accident: uses both eyes to drive horses; has reputation as excellent driver; is trusted by James

Before and After: has talent for handling horses

After Accident: learns to see with only one eye; depends more on sense of hearing; must regain James's trust

Deepen Comprehension Question 2

How is the scene right before Charlotte crosses the bridge different from the scene after she crosses it? What do you picture in both scenes? Support your answer with details from the text.

Before Crossing: bridge swaying; passengers worried; Charlotte confident and serious

Before and After: loud storm; wind; rain; fast and high river

After Crossing: bridge gone; passengers relieved; Charlotte happy and proud

Deepen Comprehension Question 3

How are Charlotte's goals alike and different from the goals of a character you know from another story? Use a Venn diagram to compare and contrast the characters. Student answers will vary.

Deepen Comprehension
© Houghton Mifflin Harcourt Publishing Company. All rights reserved.

Grade 4, Unit 4: Never Give Up!

2 | Guided Practice

- Reread with students p. 411 through the end of "Riding Freedom" as they answer **Deepen Comprehension Question 2** on **Projectable 16.4**. Use these prompts to guide them:

- *On p. 411, James yells that he can't even see the road. Charlotte yells back, "Then it's a good thing I'm drivin'." Why are they both yelling? What do Charlotte's words reveal about her?* The wind and rain are loud. Charlotte feels confident and brave.

- *Reread p. 412 to find details about the river and the bridge. How is the scene different on p. 415?* The bridge is shaky but whole above the swollen river before Charlotte drives the stagecoach across. Just after she crosses, the bridge collapses into the churning water.

- Guide students to complete the Venn diagram on their own for **Question 2**.

GUIDED DISCUSSION Use the prompt below to discuss Charlotte's goals, preparing students for **Deepen Comprehension Question 3**.

- *What are Charlotte's goals?* She wants to be able to drive stagecoaches again. She wants to prove that she can be just as good as when she had the use of both eyes.

3 | Apply

Turn and Talk Have partners list Charlotte's goals. Ask them to name other story characters before choosing one with goals similar to Charlotte's. Have them use a Venn diagram to answer **Deepen Comprehension Question 3** on **Projectable 16.4**.

WRITE ABOUT READING Have partners use the ideas in their Venn diagram for **Deepen Comprehension Question 3** to write two paragraphs that compare and contrast the story characters.

Monitor Comprehension

Are students able to compare and contrast story details and ideas?

IF...	THEN...
students have difficulty comparing and contrasting story details and ideas,	▶ use the Leveled Reader for **Struggling Readers**, *Elizabeth's Stormy Ride*, p. T64.
students have a basic understanding of comparing and contrasting story details and ideas,	▶ use the Leveled Reader for **On-Level Readers**, *Perilous Passage*, p. T65.
students can accurately compare and contrast story details and ideas,	▶ use the Leveled Reader for **Advanced Readers**, *Come to Nicodemus*, p. T66.

 Leveled Readers: pp. T64–T67. Use the Leveled Reader for **English Language Learners**, *A Dangerous Trip*, p. T67. *Group English Language Learners according to language proficiency level.*

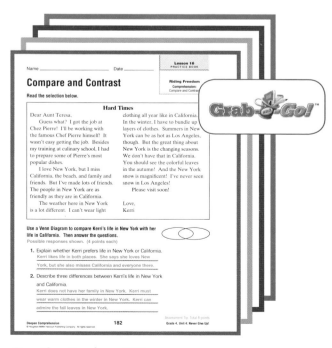

Practice Book p. 182
See Grab-and-Go™ Resources for additional leveled practice.

Deepen Comprehension • **T37**

Fluency

☑ Rate

1 | Teach/Model

- Tell students that reading rate is the speed at which a reader can correctly read a text.

- Have students follow along as you read aloud **Student Book p. 411**. Ask them to listen for the pronunciations of difficult words or phrases.

- Note for them where you use punctuation to direct your pauses and breathing.

- Explain that an appropriate reading rate is not necessarily a fast rate. Discuss how to adjust reading rate in order to better understand the details in the passage.

2 | Guided Practice

- Together, read aloud **Student Book p. 412**.

- Guide students to adjust their reading rate as needed to understand the passage.

- If students have difficulty with the concept of rate, guide them to pause after each phrase and at the end of each sentence.

- See also **Instructional Routine Card 7**.

3 | Apply

- Tell students that with practice, they can improve their reading rate.

- Have partners take turns reading the pages aloud to each other at a rate appropriate for understanding.

- Allow each student to read the section three or four times.

Decoding

 ## Sound/Spelling Changes

1 Teach/Model

ANALYZE RELATED WORDS Write the word *electric* on the board and read it aloud. Break the word into syllables and read each one aloud with students: e/lec/tric.

- Point out that the letter *c* at the end of *electric* stands for the /k/ sound.

- Write the related words *electricity* and *electrician* on the board and read them aloud. Break each word into syllables:

  e/lec/tric/i/ty   e/lec/tri/cian

- Underline the suffixes *-ity* and *-ian* in these words. Point out to students that when these suffixes are added, the /k/ sound at the end of *electric* becomes the /s/ sound in *electricity* and the /sh/ sound in *electrician*.

- Tell students that if they are unsure how to pronounce a word with sound/spelling changes like these, they should try each sound until the word sounds like one they know.

2 Practice/Apply

DECODE WORD PAIRS Write on the board the following pairs of words with sound/spelling changes. Have students break the words into syllables and read them aloud. Tell students to identify the sound for the letter *c* in each word.

public / publicity
pub/lic, /k/; pub/lic/i/ty, /s/

toxic / toxicity
tox/ic, /k/; tox/ic/i/ty, /s/

optical / optician
op/ti/cal, /k/; op/ti/cian, /sh/

elastic / elasticity
e/las/tic, /k/; e/las/tic/i/ty, /s/

Corrective Feedback

If students have trouble decoding words with sound/spelling changes, use the model below.

Correct the error. *Remember that the sound of the letter c in related words may be pronounced /k/, /s/, or /sh/.*

Model how to decode the words. Write the words *optical* and *optician* for students. *In the word* optical, *the c has the /k/ sound. This word (point to* optician*) looks like* optical. *But when I pronounce the c with a /k/ sound, it doesn't make sense. I'll try again with the /sh/ sound. This time I read the word* optician. *This is a word I know.*

Guide students to try different sounds for the second *c* in the words *electric, electricity,* and *electrician. What are the sounds for c in these words? (/k/, /s/, /sh/)*

Check students' understanding. *Read these three words. (electric, electricity, electrician)*

Reinforce Have students repeat the process with the words *elastic* and *elasticity*.

Vocabulary Strategies

SHARE OBJECTIVE

- Use context to determine the meaning of unfamiliar and multiple-meaning words.

SKILL TRACE

Using Context	
Introduce	T184–T185, Unit 1
Differentiate	T68–T69
Reteach	T70
▶ Review	**T40–T41**
Test	Weekly Tests, Lesson 16

ELL ENGLISH LANGUAGE LEARNERS

Scaffold

Beginning Pair unfamiliar words with familiar words. For example: *My friend walked with me. He escorted me home.*

Intermediate Help students use prior knowledge to determine word meanings: *Charlotte escorted the man across the bridge. She went with him. Where might you have escorted a friend?*

Advanced Have partners work together to find context clues for words in the selection.

Advanced High Have students work independently to list new words and context clues from the selection.

See ELL Lesson 16, pp. E2–E11, for scaffolded support.

✔ Using Context

1 Teach/Model

AL *Academic Language*

context the words and sentences around a word that give readers clues to its meaning

- Explain that **context** refers to the words and sentences around an unfamiliar word. Context can give clues to a word's meaning.

- Point out that there are several types of context clues. Discuss with students how to use the following types of context clues:

Context Clues

Definition/Example	Look for a definition or for words and ideas that are examples.
Synonym/Antonym	Look for a word or phrase with the same meaning or an opposite meaning.
General	Look at the situation or events in the text. Then use prior knowledge and experience to determine meaning.

- Model looking around the word to understand the meaning of *escorted* on **p. 413** of "Riding Freedom."

Think Aloud *I'm not sure what* escorted *means. I notice the author doesn't give an example or a definition of the word. When I reread the sentences before the word, I see that the passengers got out of the stagecoach. Charlotte made them get out. When I read ahead, I learn that she walked them across the bridge. So I think* escorted *means "walked with" or "led."*

2 Guided Practice

- Display the top half of **Projectable 16.5** and read "Ridin' the Pony Express" aloud.

- Display the graphic organizer on the bottom of **Projectable 16.5**.

- Read aloud the two words in the chart. Guide students to identify context clues that can help them determine each word's meaning.

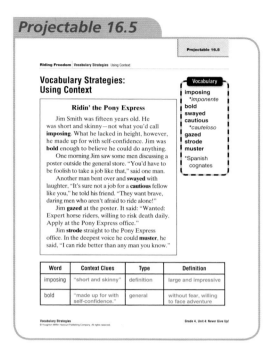

Projectable 16.5

Riding Freedom Vocabulary Strategies Using Context

Vocabulary Strategies: Using Context

Ridin' the Pony Express

Jim Smith was fifteen years old. He was short and skinny—not what you'd call **imposing**. What he lacked in height, however, he made up for with self-confidence. Jim was **bold** enough to believe he could do anything.

One morning Jim saw some men discussing a poster outside the general store. "You'd have to be foolish to take a job like that," said one man.

Another man bent over and **swayed** with laughter, "It's sure not a job for a **cautious** fellow like you," he told his friend. "They want brave, daring men who aren't afraid to ride alone!"

Jim **gazed** at the poster. It said: "Wanted: Expert horse riders, willing to risk death daily. Apply at the Pony Express office."

Jim **strode** straight to the Pony Express office. In the deepest voice he could **muster**, he said, "I can ride better than any man you know."

Vocabulary
imposing
*imponente
bold
swayed
cautious
*cauteloso
gazed
strode
muster
*Spanish cognates

Word	Context Clues	Type	Definition
imposing	"short and skinny"	definition	large and impressive
bold	"made up for with self-confidence."	general	without fear, willing to face adventure

3 Apply

- Have partners make a graphic organizer like the one in **Projectable 16.5**. Tell them to use context clues and types to determine the meanings of the rest of the boldfaced words in the passage on **Projectable 16.5**. Then have students discuss the context clues and types and explain how they clarify the meaning of each word.

- Have students look in a dictionary or glossary for definitions of any words that are still unfamiliar.

Monitor Vocabulary Strategies

Are students able to use context clues to determine word meaning?

IF...	THEN...
students have difficulty identifying and using context clues,	▶ **Differentiate Vocabulary Strategies** for Struggling Readers, p. T68. *See also Intervention Lesson 16, pp. S2–S11.*
students can identify and use context clues most of the time,	▶ **Differentiate Vocabulary Strategies** for On-Level Readers, p. T68.
students can consistently identify and use context clues,	▶ **Differentiate Vocabulary Strategies** for Advanced Readers, p. T69.

Differentiate Vocabulary Strategies: pp. T68-T69.
Group English Language Learners according to language proficiency.

Using Context

Read each sentence or pair of sentences. Then circle the answer that best explains the meaning of the underlined word. (2 points each)

1. Don't shove so hard on the wagon. Just give it a <u>nudge</u>.
   a. kick   **b. gentle push**   c. flower

2. There were no factories or businesses on the street—only the <u>dwellings</u> of people who lived there.
   a. houses   b. cars   c. barns

3. After several mechanics failed to fix the car, we found a person who was <u>capable</u> of making the repair.
   a. has the ability to   b. does not understand   c. wants to

4. They did a <u>thorough</u> job picking up the bedroom. Not one thing remained on the floor.
   a. fast   b. sloppy   **c. complete**

5. The class didn't shout in protest when they got the big assignment, but several students <u>grumbled</u> about how hard it was.
   a. muttered   b. hummed   c. yelled

6. Bill thought he was safe at first, but the umpire thought he was out. Bill was angry about the call and started to <u>quarrel</u> with the umpire.
   a. discuss quietly   **b. argue**   c. dance

7. The trees <u>sway</u> in heavy winds, but they don't fall over.
   a. swing back and forth   b. march   c. circle

Practice Book p. 183
See Grab-and-Go™ Resources for additional leveled practice.

Connect and Extend

Riding Freedom   **Spindletop**

Vocabulary Reader

Struggling Readers   **On-Level Readers**

Advanced Readers   **English Language Learners**

Read to Connect

SHARE AND COMPARE TEXTS Have students compare and contrast this week's reading selections. Use the following questions to guide the discussion:

- What difficulties did characters face? How are their difficulties similar? How are they different?

- Using evidence from the books you've read this week, explain how the setting in each story affected the characters. How did the setting contribute to the difficulties they faced?

CONNECT TEXT TO WORLD Use these prompts to help deepen student thinking and discussion. Accept students' opinions, but encourage them to support their ideas with text details and other information from their reading.

- How can one person's courage and determination affect others?

- What situations in this week's readings remind you of situations happening in the world today?

Independent Reading

BOOK TALK Have student pairs discuss their independent reading for the week. Tell them to refer to their Reading Log or journal and paraphrase what the reading was about. To focus the students' further discussions, have them discuss the following:

- how the cultural or historical context of the text supports their understanding

- the selections' messages or main ideas

- the authors' styles

Reading Log

Extend Through Research

SKIMMING AND SCANNING TEXTS AND SOURCES Explain to students that they do not have to read an entire piece of writing to get information from it. Sometimes they can simply skim or scan a piece to gain an overview of the information contained in the piece. **Skimming** is quickly reviewing text to get an overall sense of it. **Scanning** is looking for specific words and phrases in which you are interested.

- Discuss how to skim text: **read** the title and the headings; **look** at the illustrations, photographs, and captions; **look** at boxed lists, tables, and charts; and **read** the first and last paragraphs.

- Explain that in scanning students should **read** quickly to find key words, then **read** more carefully when they find the information they are interested in.

- Have students choose a textbook chapter, magazine article, or other informational text that includes chapters and headings. Have student partners work together to write a set of questions about information they would like to find. Then have partners skim and scan the text and text features to gain an overview of the text and find the answers. Have them take notes on their findings.

Listening and Speaking

EVALUATE MEDIA SOURCES Tell students that they will give oral presentations on how to evaluate media sources. Have them create lists of sequenced instructions on how to view a media source. Provide students with the following questions to help them in their planning:

- **Author, Artist, or Presenter:** Is the person giving the information qualified?

- **Date:** How old is the information? Is it up to date?

- **Content:** Is the information accurate? Are there errors? Is there enough information to let you form an opinion?

- **Bias:** Is the information trying to persuade readers in a certain way?

As students give their presentations, have the audience use the Listening Log to record what they learned. Give students the opportunity to respond by asking questions, restating the instructions in sequence, and following the oral instructions to evaluate a media source.

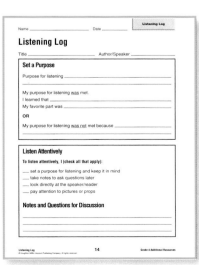

Listening Log

Spelling Words with /k/, /ng/, and /kw/

SHARE OBJECTIVE

- Spell words with the /k/, /ng/, and /kw/ sounds.

Spelling Words

Basic

risky	junk	picnic
track	equal	banker
topic	ache	electric
blank	public	blanket
✪ question	attack	mistake
pocket	struck	stomach
monkey	earthquake	

Review

quick, squeeze, shark, second, circus

Challenge

request, skeleton, peculiar, attic, reckless

✪ Forms of these words appear in "Riding Freedom."

ELL ENGLISH LANGUAGE LEARNERS

Preteach

Spanish Cognates

Write and discuss these Spanish cognates for Spanish-speaking students.

electric • *eléctrico(a)*

stomach • *estómago*

Day 1

❶ TEACH THE PRINCIPLE

- Administer the **Pretest**. Use the Day 5 sentences.

- Write *risky, track*, and *public* on the board. Guide students to identify the letters in each word that make the /k/ sound. *(k, ck, c)* Repeat with the sounds /ng/ and /kw/, using the chart below.

/k/	**k** *as in* ris**k**y **ck** *as in* tra**ck** **c** *as in* publi**c**
/ng/	**n** *as in* ju**n**k
/kw/	**qu** *as in* **qu**estion

❷ PRACTICE/APPLY

Guide students to identify the sounds and spellings of the remaining Spelling Words.

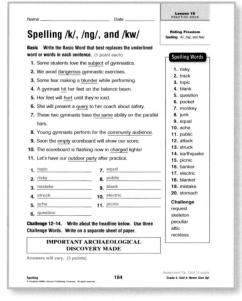

Practice Book p. 184

Day 2

❶ TEACH WORD SORT

- Set up three rows as shown below. Model adding a Spelling Word to each row.

- Have students copy the chart. Guide students to write each Spelling Word in the correct row.

/k/	electric
/ng/	monkey
/kw/	equal

❷ PRACTICE/APPLY

Have students find /k/, /ng/, and /kw/ words in "Riding Freedom" and add them to their charts.

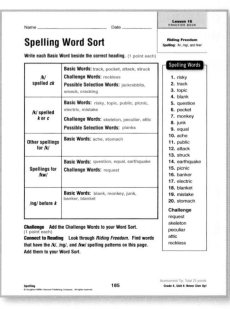

Practice Book p.185

Day 3

1 TEACH WORD FAMILIES

- **WRITE** *equal* on the board. Define it: "having the same amount or number."

- **WRITE** *equality* on the board. Define it: "having the same rights."

- **ASK:** *What is the connection between these words? Both contain the letters e-q-u-a-l; both mean two things are the same in some way.*

- With students, list and discuss more words related to *equal*. Samples: *unequal, equally, equation, equaling, equate*

2 PRACTICE/APPLY

- **WRITE** *question* on the board. Define it: "a sentence worded in a way to find out something."

- **WRITE** *questionable, questioner, questionnaire.* Have students look these words up in a dictionary or electronic resource.

- **ASK:** *What is the connection among the words* question, questionable, questioner, *and* questionnaire?

➤ Have students write their answers.

Day 4

1 CONNECT TO WRITING

- Read and discuss the prompt below.

> **Write to Describe**
>
> Write a paragraph describing what it might be like to ride in a stagecoach. Use details from your Vocabulary or Leveled Reader.

2 PRACTICE/APPLY

- Guide students as they plan and write their descriptive paragraphs (see p. T52).

- Remind students to proofread their writing for errors in spelling words with /k/, /ng/, and /kw/.

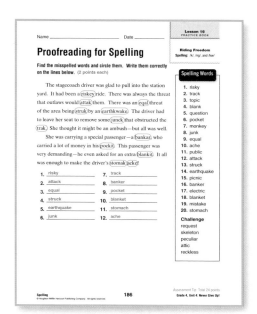

Practice Book p. 186

Day 5

ASSESS SPELLING

- Say each boldfaced word below, read the sentence, and then repeat the word.

- Have students write the bold-faced word.

Basic

1. It is **risky** to hike too far alone.
2. Alexa runs on the **track** team.
3. The speaker knew her **topic** well.
4. She filled in the **blank** spaces.
5. I asked a **question** about math.
6. My **pocket** is full of coins.
7. The **monkey** is very loud.
8. Please recycle the **junk** mail.
9. Rosa Parks wanted **equal** rights.
10. I **ache** when I have the flu.
11. Juan loves **public** speaking.
12. Lions **attack** to save a cub.
13. Sara **struck** the ball hard.
14. The **earthquake** did no harm.
15. Did ants spoil the **picnic**?
16. A **banker** can make loans.
17. Plug in the **electric** stove.
18. My wool **blanket** is so warm.
19. I made a **mistake** on the test.
20. My **stomach** is empty.

Grammar ☑ Adjectives

SHARE OBJECTIVES

- Identify adjectives and the nouns they describe.
- Use adjectives and articles in writing and speaking.

ELL ENGLISH LANGUAGE LEARNERS

Scaffold

Beginning Use the following sentence frames to demonstrate how to use adjectives to describe a noun.

> The river is _____. *long*
> Charlotte is _____. *brave*

Intermediate Use the following sentence frames to demonstrate how to combine sentences with adjectives.

> The river is _____. *big*
> The river flows _____. *south*
> The _____ river flows _____. *big, south*

Advanced Have students describe objects around the room using adjectives. Provide them with sentence frames, such as the following:

> My desk is _____.
> The walls are _____.

Advanced High Have student pairs take turns using adjectives in oral descriptions of objects from around the room.

See ELL Lesson 16, pp. E2–E11, for scaffolded support.

JOURNEYS DIGITAL **Powered by DESTINATIONReading®**
Grammar Activities: Lesson 16
Grammar Songs CD: Track 7

Day 1 TEACH

DAILY PROOFREADING PRACTICE
was Charlotte brave to drive the coach. *Was; ?*

❶ TEACH ADJECTIVES

- Display **Projectable 16.6**. Explain that an **adjective** describes a noun or pronoun. Point out that adjectives tell *what kind*, *how many* or *which one*. Tell students that an adjective typically comes before the noun that it describes.

  Projectable **16.6**

- Model identifying what noun the adjectives describe in the example sentence: *The stagecoach carried four tired travelers*.

> **Think Aloud** *I ask this Thinking Question:* **What words describe a noun?** *Four and* tired *describe* travelers. *So* four *and* tired *must be adjectives that tell about the noun* travelers.

❷ PRACTICE/APPLY

- Work with students to complete items 1–6 on **Projectable 16.6**.

- Work with students to identify adjectives to describe the following nouns.

  night   lightning
  horse   stagecoach

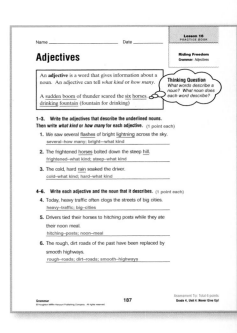

Day 2 TEACH

DAILY PROOFREADING PRACTICE

The whether was rainy, stormy. *weather; rainy and*

① TEACH ADJECTIVES AFTER *BE*

Projectable **16.7**

- Display **Projectable 16.7**. Point out to students that adjectives do not always occur near the noun or pronoun they describe. Tell them the adjective can come after a form of the verb *be* in a sentence.

- Remind students that the verb *be* has special forms, such as *am/was, are/were, is/was.*

- Model identifying the adjective and the noun it describes in this sentence: *The journey was long.*

> **Think Aloud** *I see a form of the verb* be *in this sentence:* was. *The word after* was *is an adjective because it tells "what kind", so it must describe the subject of the sentence,* journey.

② PRACTICE/APPLY

- Work with students to complete items 1–8 on **Projectable 16.7**.

- Write the following sentence frames on the board. Have students orally add adjectives to describe the nouns.

The sky was _____.
Sample answers: bright, dark, stormy

They are _____ all day.
Sample answers: noisy, playing, busy

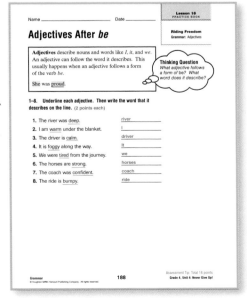

Day 3 TEACH

DAILY PROOFREADING PRACTICE

The wet passengers hudled togethr. *huddled; together*

① TEACH ARTICLES

Projectable **16.8**

- Display **Projectable 16.8**. Explain that an article is a type of adjective. Use the example sentences to explain when to use the **articles** *a (when the following word begins with a consonant)* and *an (when the following word begins with a vowel)*. Then explain when to use the article *the.*

- Display the following sentences:

  I saw a parade.
  I saw an exciting parade.
  I saw the Labor Day Parade.

Explain that the article *a* describes any parade, the article *an* describes a specific kind of parade, and the article *the* describes a specific parade.

② PRACTICE/APPLY

- Work with students to complete items 1–10 on **Projectable 16.8**.

- Call out several nouns. Have students respond by using *a, an* or *the* with the noun, as appropriate. Discuss students' responses.

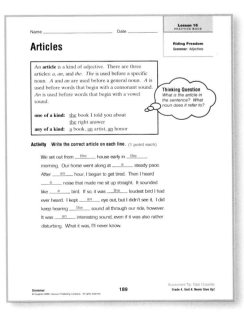

Day 4 REVIEW

DAILY PROOFREADING PRACTICE

Charlotte drives an stagecoche. *a; stagecoach*

❶ REVIEW ADJECTIVES

- Remind students that an **adjective** is a word that describes a noun, and an **article** is a type of adjective that refers to either a general or a specific noun.

- Have students turn to **Student Book p. 422**. Read aloud the paragraph and review the example sentences. Then have students complete the **Turn and Talk** activity with a partner.

❷ SPIRAL REVIEW

Writing Proper Nouns Review with students that **proper nouns** are capitalized. Explain that proper nouns can include the names of specific people, places, and things. Point out that book titles are also capitalized. Work with students to identify the proper nouns in the following sentences.

Be careful on that bridge, Brenda! *Brenda*
"Riding Freedom" is an interesting story. *"Riding Freedom"*
We are going to Omaha. *Omaha*
My mother is in the United States Senate. *United States Senate*

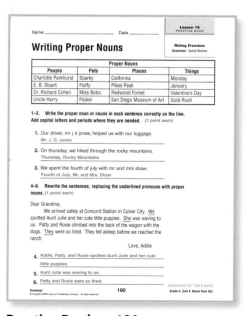

Practice Book p. 190

Day 5 CONNECT TO WRITING

DAILY PROOFREADING PRACTICE

An river was churnin under the bridge. *A; churning*

❶ CONNECT TO WRITING

- Tell students that it is important to make writing flow smoothly to keep the reader focused and interested.

- Point out that an important part of revising is combining sentences using adjectives so writing does not sound choppy.

- Display the following sentences. Guide students to combine them using adjectives.

  The students returned from the field trip.
  They were tired.
  The tired students returned from the field trip.

❷ PRACTICE/APPLY

- Display these sentence pairs. Have students combine each pair.

  The driver climbed onto the stagecoach.
  The stagecoach was old.
  The driver climbed onto the old stagecoach.
  The sun was bright.
  Maria shielded her eyes from the sun.
  Maria shielded her eyes from the bright sun.

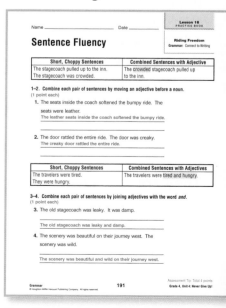

Practice Book p. 191

Grammar

What Is an Adjective? An **adjective** is a word that gives information about a noun. Some adjectives tell *what kind*. Others tell *how many*. They often appear right before the nouns they describe. Sometimes adjectives appear after a form of the verb *be*. They give information about the noun in front of the verb.

Academic Language

adjective

adjective of purpose

What Kind	How Many
Charlotte used her good eye.	She made ten runs successfully.

An **adjective of purpose** is a special type of adjective. It tells what a noun is used for.

The campers slept in sleeping bags.   (bags for sleeping)

They cooked bacon in a frying pan.   (a pan for frying)

Turn and Talk With a partner, find the adjectives that tell about the underlined nouns. Which adjectives tell *what kind*? Which tell *how many*? Which are adjectives of purpose?

1. The brave <u>driver</u> looked at the muddy <u>road</u>.
2. She tied one <u>horse</u> to a hitching <u>post</u>.
3. She left three <u>horses</u> with her young <u>partner</u>.
4. She stepped into a waiting <u>room</u>.
5. She wanted the doctor to look at her bad <u>eye</u>.

422

Sentence Fluency To make your writing flow smoothly, you can move adjectives to combine sentences. If two choppy sentences tell about the same noun, try moving an adjective from one sentence to another. You can place an adjective before a noun to combine sentences.

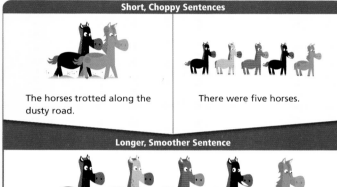

Short, Choppy Sentences

The horses trotted along the dusty road.

There were five horses.

Longer, Smoother Sentence

The five horses trotted along the dusty road.

Connect Grammar to Writing

As you revise your writing, look for short, choppy sentences that may repeat a noun. Try combining these sentences by moving an adjective.

423

Turn and Talk

1. *brave, what kind; muddy, what kind*
2. *one, how many; hitching, adjective of purpose*
3. *three, how many; young, what kind*
4. *waiting, adjective of purpose*
5. *bad, what kind*

CONNECT GRAMMAR TO WRITING

- Have students turn to **Student Book p. 423** and read the page with them.

- Discuss how the short, choppy sentences in the examples were combined to form a smoother sentence. Point out how the adjective *five* was added to the first short sentence to form the longer sentence.

- Tell students that as they revise their descriptive paragraphs, they should look for opportunities to use adjectives to combine choppy sentences.

- Review the Common Errors at right with students.

COMMON ERRORS

Error: That is **a** insect.

Correct: That is **an** insect.

Error: I know **them** boys.

Correct: I know **those** boys.

Error: She bought a boat **huge**!

Correct: She bought a **huge** boat!

Error: He picked **a** prettiest flower.

Correct: He picked **the** prettiest flower.

Write to Narrate Focus Trait: Ideas

SHARE OBJECTIVES

- Understand the features of a descriptive paragraph.
- Demonstrate focused ideas in writing.
- Write a descriptive paragraph about a personal experience.

Academic Language

describe to tell what someone or something is like or about

vivid detail a detail that helps readers clearly picture what is being described

topic sentence a sentence that introduces the topic of a paragraph; it comes at the beginning of the paragraph

ELL ENGLISH LANGUAGE LEARNERS

Scaffold

Beginning Work with students to brainstorm words associated with their topics. Then demonstrate how to use the following sentence frames.

They are _____ in the _____.
The _____ is near the _____.

Intermediate Guide students to use the sentence frames as they draft their descriptive paragraphs.

Advanced Have partners take turns describing their paragraph topics orally as they prewrite.

Advanced High As students prewrite, have them use a thesaurus to find more descriptive words.

See ELL Lesson 16, pp. E2–E11, for scaffolded support.

JOURNEYS DIGITAL **Powered by**
DESTINATIONReading®
WriteSmart CD-ROM

Day 1 ANALYZE THE MODEL

❶ INTRODUCE THE MODEL

- Tell students that they will be writing a descriptive paragraph in this lesson.
- Display **Projectable 16.9** and read aloud the Writing Model. Discuss the following:

What Is a Descriptive Paragraph?

- It **describes**, or tells about, a person, place, thing, or event.
- It begins with a **topic sentence** that explains what the paragraph is about.
- It includes **vivid details**–words that describe the person, place, thing, or event clearly.
- Vivid details keep readers interested by helping them to form pictures in their minds.

- Use the Projectable to point out that a descriptive paragraph begins with a topic sentence and contains details that describe the topic.

❷ PRACTICE/APPLY

- Have students identify the topic sentence, vivid details, and exact words in the second paragraph.

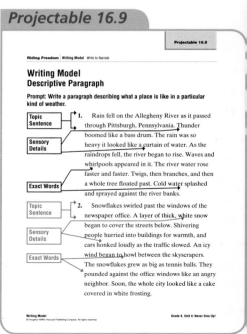

Projectable 16.9

LESSON	FORM	TRAIT
16	**Descriptive Paragraph**	**Ideas**
17	Friendly Letter	Voice
18	Narrative Composition	Word Choice
19	Prewrite: Personal Narrative	Organization
20	Draft, Revise, Edit, Publish: Personal Narrative	Ideas

Day 2 TEACH THE FOCUS TRAIT

1 INTRODUCE THE FOCUS TRAIT: IDEAS

- Explain that writers use vivid details in a descriptive paragraph to help the reader picture what is being described. Vivid details can also show how writers feel about a subject.

Connect to "Riding Freedom"	
Instead of this...	**...the author wrote this.**
She knew the bridge was coming apart.	"She heard the splintering and cracking of the weathered wood that meant the bridge was coming apart." (p. 414)

- Point out that this vivid description helps the reader imagine the scene and conveys its tension.

2 PRACTICE/APPLY

- Write: *The storm was loud*. Work with students to revise this sentence by adding vivid details.

- Write: *The forest was as quiet as _____*. Tell students to complete the simile to create a vivid image.

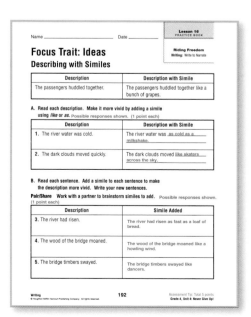

Practice Book p. 192

Day 3 PREWRITE

1 TEACH PLANNING A PARAGRAPH

- Display **Projectable 16.10** and read aloud the prompt. Ask students to think about a special place with which they are familiar.

- Explain that a graphic organizer can help them plan their writing.

2 PRACTICE/APPLY

- Point out the topic in the center of the web on **Projectable 16.10**. Explain to students that the topic should be mentioned in the first sentence of their paragraph.

- Tell students that each detail in the outer circles should relate to the topic. Tell them that these details will make up the body of the paragraph.

- Work with students to complete the web.

- Have students choose a topic for their descriptive paragraphs. Distribute **Graphic Organizer 15**. Guide students to complete the web.

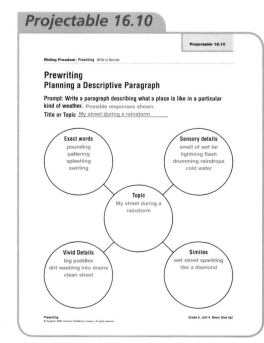

Projectable 16.10

Day 4 DRAFT

① BEGIN A DRAFT

- Have students begin their drafts using their prewriting webs. Discuss with them the following:

> **1. Introduce** the place you will be describing in the first sentence.

> **2. Organize** your ideas so the descriptions make sense to the reader.

> **3. Include** vivid details that help readers picture the place in their minds. Use adjectives and strong, exact descriptions to draw in the reader.

> **4. Conclude** by noting why this place is special or important to you.

② PRACTICE/APPLY

- Have students draft their descriptive paragraphs. Remind them to use the graphic organizers they completed for prewriting.

Day 5 REVISE FOR IDEAS

① INTRODUCE THE STUDENT MODEL

- Remind students that good writers use vivid details to communicate their ideas clearly.

- Read aloud the top of **Student Book p. 424**. Discuss the revisions made by the student writer. Point out that the revision in the first sentence helps readers imagine the sound of the thunder.

② PRACTICE/APPLY

- Display **Projectable 16.11**. Work together to revise the rest of the paragraph. Point out where vivid details could better communicate Claire's ideas.

- Work with students to answer the *Reading as a Writer* questions on **Student Book p. 425**. Discuss their responses.

- **Revising** Have students revise their paragraphs using the Writing Traits Checklist on **Student Book p. 424**.

- **Proofreading** For proofreading support, have students use the **Proofreading Checklist Blackline Master**.

Projectable 16.11

Write to Narrate

☑ Ideas In "Riding Freedom," the author creates a colorful simile—a comparison using *like* or *as*—when she says that the horses ran "like scared jackrabbits." When you revise a **description** for a personal narrative, add similes to paint vivid word pictures.

Claire drafted a descriptive paragraph about a bus ride during a rainstorm. Then she reread her draft and added some similes.

Writing Traits Checklist

☑ Ideas
Did I use similes to paint vivid pictures?

☑ Organization
Are all my details about one main idea?

☑ Word Choice
Do my words say just what I mean?

☑ Voice
Did I show how it feels to be in the place I describe?

☑ Sentence Fluency
Did I combine short, choppy sentences so they read smoothly?

☑ Conventions
Did I use correct spelling, grammar, and mechanics?

424

Revised Draft

sounded like dynamite exploding

Bang! The thunder ~~was really loud!~~

Everyone on the bus shrieked, and

then the older kids started laughing.

Some kindergartners burst out crying.

~~They were (scared)~~ All of a sudden,

rain began hammering on the roof.

like a drum roll

It grew louder and louder.

Final Copy

A Ride to Remember
by Claire Amaral

Bang! The thunder sounded like dynamite exploding. Everyone on the bus shrieked, and then the older kids started laughing. Some scared kindergartners burst out crying. All of a sudden, rain began hammering on the roof. It grew louder and louder like a drum roll. My window fogged up, and down in front, the windshield wipers were jerking back and forth like a conductor keeping time to some super-fast music. When the bus stopped and the door opened, the water in the street was up to the curb. The kids who got off had to leap to the sidewalk. For once, I was glad my stop was last!

In my final paper, I added some similes. I also combined two short sentences by moving an adjective.

Reading as a Writer

What do Claire's similes help you see or hear? Where can you add similes in your own description?

425

Writing Traits Scoring Rubric

	Focus/Ideas	☑ Organization	Voice	☑ Word Choice	☑ Sentence Fluency	Conventions
4	Adheres to the topic, is interesting, has a sense of completeness. Ideas are well developed.	Ideas and details are clearly presented and well organized.	Connects with reader in a unique, personal way.	Includes vivid verbs, strong adjectives, specific nouns.	Includes a variety of complete sentences that flow smoothly, naturally.	Shows a strong command of grammar, spelling, capitalization, punctuation.
3	Mostly adheres to the topic, is somewhat interesting, has a sense of completeness. Ideas are adequately developed.	Ideas and details are mostly clear and generally organized.	Generally connects with reader in a way that is personal and sometimes unique.	Includes some vivid verbs, strong adjectives, specific nouns.	Includes some variety of mostly complete sentences. Some parts flow smoothly, naturally.	Shows a good command of grammar, spelling, capitalization, punctuation.
2	Does not always adhere to the topic, has some sense of completeness. Ideas are superficially developed.	Ideas and details are not always clear or organized. There is some wordiness or repetition.	Connects somewhat with reader. Sounds somewhat personal, but not unique.	Includes mostly simple nouns and verbs, and may have a few adjectives.	Includes mostly simple sentences, some of which are incomplete.	Some errors in grammar, spelling, capitalization, punctuation.
1	Does not adhere to the topic, has no sense of completeness. Ideas are vague.	Ideas and details are not organized. Wordiness or repetition hinders meaning.	Does not connect with reader. Does not sound personal or unique.	Includes only simple nouns and verbs, some inaccurate. Writing is not descriptive.	Sentences do not vary. Incomplete sentences hinder meaning.	Frequent errors in grammar, spelling, capitalization, punctuation.

See also **Writing Rubric Blackline Master** and Teacher's Edition pp. R18–R21.

Progress Monitoring

Assess

- Weekly Tests
- Fluency Tests
- Periodic Assessments

✔ Vocabulary
Target Vocabulary
Strategies: Using Context

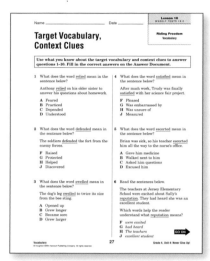

Weekly Tests 16.2–16.3

✔ Comprehension
Compare and Contrast

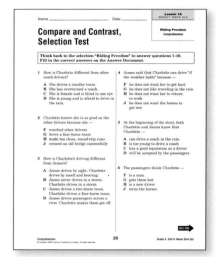

Weekly Tests 16.4–16.5

Respond to Assessment

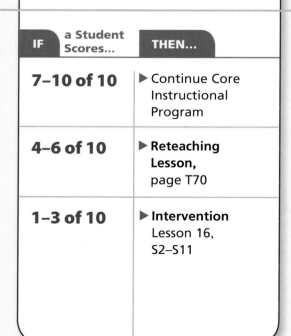

IF a Student Scores...	THEN...
7–10 of 10	▶ Continue Core Instructional Program
4–6 of 10	▶ **Reteaching Lesson,** page T70
1–3 of 10	▶ **Intervention** Lesson 16, S2–S11

IF a Student Scores...	THEN...
7–10 of 10	▶ Continue Core Instructional Program
4–6 of 10	▶ **Reteaching Lesson,** page T70
1–3 of 10	▶ **Intervention** Lesson 16, S2–S11

Powered by DESTINATIONReading®

- **Weekly Tests**
- **Online Asessment System**

Decoding
Sound/Spelling Changes

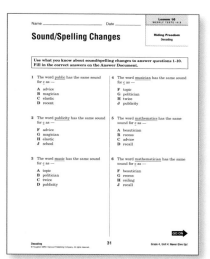

Weekly Tests 16.6–16.7

IF	a Student Scores...	THEN...
	7–10 of 10	▶ Continue Core Instructional Program
	4–6 of 10	▶ Reteaching Lesson, page T71
	1–3 of 10	▶ Intervention Lesson 16, S2–S11

☑ Language Arts
Grammar: Adjectives

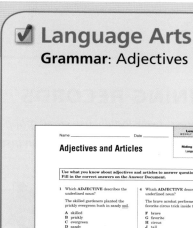

Weekly Tests 16.8–16.9

Writing Traits Rubrics
See *TE pp. R18–R21.*

IF	a Student Scores...	THEN...
	7–10 of 10	▶ Continue Core Instructional Program
	4–6 of 10	▶ Reteaching Lesson, page T71
	1–3 of 10	▶ Intervention Lesson 16, S2–S11

☑ Fluency

Fluency Plan
Assess one group per week.
Use the suggested plan below.

	Struggling Readers	Weeks 1, 3, 5
▲	On Level	Week 2
■	Advanced	Week 4

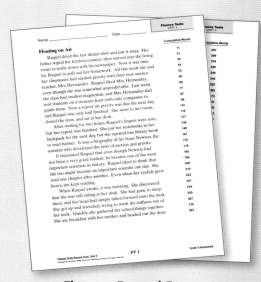

Fluency Record Form

Fluency Scoring Rubrics
See *Grab-and-Go™ Resources Assessment* for help in measuring progress.

Progress Monitoring

Small Group

RUNNING RECORDS

To assess individual progress, occasionally use small group time to take a reading record for each student. Use the results to plan instruction.

 **Struggling Readers**

 On Level

 Advanced

 **English Language Learners**

For running records, see
Grab-and-Go™ Resources: Lesson 16, pp. 13–16.

Behaviors and Understandings to Notice

- Self-corrects errors that detract from meaning.
- Self-corrects intonation when it does not reflect the meaning.
- Rereads to solve words and resumes normal rate of reading.
- Demonstrates phrased and fluent oral reading.
- Reads dialogue with expression.

- Demonstrates awareness of punctuation.
- Automatically solves most words in the text to read fluently.
- Demonstrates appropriate stress on words, pausing and phrasing, intonation, and use of punctuation.
- Reads orally at an appropriate rate.

Weekly
Small Group Instruction

Day 1

Vocabulary Reader
- *Stagecoach Travel*, T60–T61

Vocabulary Reader

Day 2

Differentiate Comprehension
- Target Skill: Compare and Contrast, T62–T63
- Target Strategy: Monitor/Clarify, T62–T63

Day 3

Leveled Readers
- ● *Elizabeth's Stormy Ride*, T64
- ▲ *Perilous Passage*, T65
- ■ *Come to Nicodemus*, T66
- ◆ *A Dangerous Trip*, T67

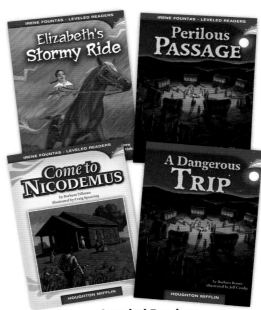

Day 4

Differentiate Vocabulary Strategies
- Using Context, T68–T69

Day 5

Options for Reteaching
- Vocabulary Strategies: Using Context, T70
- Comprehension Skill: Compare and Contrast, T70
- Language Arts: Adjectives/Write to Narrate, T71
- Decoding: Sound/Spelling Changes, T71

Leveled Readers

Ready-Made Work Stations

Independent Practice
- Comprehension and Fluency, T10
- Word Study, T10
- Think and Write, T11
- Digital Center, T11

Comprehension and Fluency **Word Study** **Think and Write** **Digital Center**

Suggested Small Group Plan

Teacher-Led

	Day 1	Day 2	Day 3
Struggling Readers	**Vocabulary Reader** *Stagecoach Travel*, Differentiated Instruction, p. T60	**Differentiate Comprehension:** Compare and Contrast; Monitor/Clarify, p. T62	**Leveled Reader** *Elizabeth's Stormy Ride*, p. T64
On Level	**Vocabulary Reader** *Stagecoach Travel*, Differentiated Instruction, p. T60	**Differentiate Comprehension:** Compare and Contrast; Monitor/Clarify, p. T62	**Leveled Reader** *Perilous Passage*, p. T65
Advanced	**Vocabulary Reader** *Stagecoach Travel*, Differentiated Instruction, p. T61	**Differentiate Comprehension:** Compare and Contrast; Monitor/Clarify, p. T63	**Leveled Reader** *Come to Nicodemus*, p. T66
English Language Learners	**Vocabulary Reader** *Stagecoach Travel*, Differentiated Instruction, p. T61	**Differentiate Comprehension:** Compare and Contrast; Monitor/Clarify, p. T63	**Leveled Reader** *A Dangerous Trip*, p. T67

What are my other students doing?

	Day 1	Day 2	Day 3
Struggling Readers	• **Reread** *Stagecoach Travel*	• **Vocabulary in Context Cards** 151–160; *Talk It Over* Activities • **Complete** Leveled Practice SR16.1	• **Listen** to Audiotext CD of "Riding Freedom"; Retell and discuss • **Complete** Leveled Practice SR16.2
On Level	• **Reread** *Stagecoach Travel*	• **Reread** "Riding Freedom" with a partner • **Complete** Practice Book p. 181	• **Reread** for Fluency: *Perilous Passage* • **Complete** Practice Book p. 182
Advanced	• **Vocabulary in Context Cards** 151–160 *Talk It Over* Activities	• **Reread and Retell** "Riding Freedom" • **Complete** Leveled Practice A16.1	• **Reread** for Fluency: *Come to Nicodemus* • **Complete** Leveled Practice A16.2
English Language Learners	• **Reread** *Stagecoach Travel*	• **Listen** to Audiotext CD of "Riding Freedom"; Retell and discuss • **Complete** Leveled Practice ELL16.1	• **Vocabulary in Context Cards** 151–160 *Talk It Over* Activities • **Complete** Leveled Practice ELL16.2

Ready-Made Work Stations

Assign these activities across the week to reinforce and extend learning.

Comprehension and Fluency
Read and Review

Word Study
Use the Clues

Day 4

Differentiate Vocabulary Strategies:
Using Context, p. T68

Differentiate Vocabulary Strategies:
Using Context, p. T68

Differentiate Vocabulary Strategies:
Using Context, p. T69

Differentiate Vocabulary Strategies:
Using Context, p. T69

Day 5

Options for Reteaching, pp. T70–T71

Options for Reteaching, pp. T70–T71

Options for Reteaching, pp. T70–T71

Options for Reteaching, pp. T70–T71

Day 4

• **Partners: Reread**
Elizabeth's Stormy Ride
• **Complete** Leveled
Practice SR16.3

• **Vocabulary in Context Cards**
151–160
Talk It Over Activities
• **Complete** Practice Book p. 183

• **Reread** for Fluency: "Riding
Freedom"
• **Complete** Leveled Practice A16.3

• **Partners: Reread** for Fluency:
A Dangerous Trip
• **Complete** Leveled
Practice ELL16.3

Day 5

• **Reread** for Fluency: "Riding
Freedom"
• **Complete** Work Station activities
• **Independent Reading**

• **Complete** Work Station activities
• **Independent Reading**

• **Complete** Work Station activities
• **Independent Reading**

• **Reread** *Stagecoach Travel* or "Riding
Freedom"
• **Complete** Work Station activities

Think and Write
Breaking News

JOURNEYS DIGITAL
Powered by
DESTINATIONReading

Digital Center

Weekly To-Do List

This Weekly To-Do List helps students
see their own progress and move on
to additional activities independently.

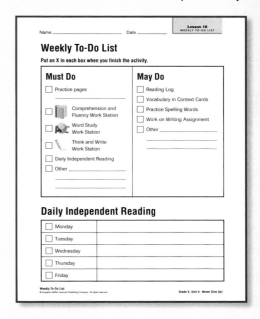

Reading Log

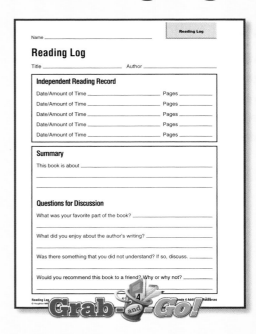

Vocabulary Reader
Stagecoach Travel

Summary

Traveling by stagecoach in the Old West took a long time and could be uncomfortable and sometimes even dangerous.

✓ TARGET VOCABULARY	
relied	swelled
defended	worthy
reputation	satisfied
situation	escorted
deserve	churning

Struggling Readers

• Explain that people who traveled west by stagecoach in the 1800s had a very long trip. Tell students also that the romantic view of stagecoach travel as sometimes seen in movies is not really accurate. Things were much tougher than that—the real stagecoach travels had very long hours, cramped seating, and even stagecoach robbers.

• Guide students to preview the **Vocabulary Reader**. Read aloud the headings. Ask students to describe the images, using Target Vocabulary when possible.

• Have students alternate reading pages of the selection aloud. Guide them to use context to determine the meanings of unfamiliar words. As necessary, use the **Vocabulary in Context Cards** to review the meanings of vocabulary words.

• Assign the **Responding Page** and **Blackline Master 16.1**. Have partners work together to complete the pages.

On Level

• Tell students that people who traveled west by stagecoach in the nineteenth century could expect a difficult journey. Explain that stagecoach travel was not necessarily an exciting adventure, as sometimes seen in movies, and that the difficulties included long hours, cramped seating, and even stagecoach robbers. Guide students to preview the **Vocabulary Reader**.

• Remind students that context clues can help them determine the meaning of an unknown word. Tell students to use context clues to confirm their understanding of Target Vocabulary and to learn the meanings of new words.

• Assign the **Responding Page** and **Blackline Master 16.1**. Have students discuss their responses with a partner.

JOURNEYS
DIGITAL | Powered by
DESTINATIONReading®
Leveled Readers Online

Advanced

- Have students preview the selection and make predictions about what they will read, using information from the preview and prior knowledge.

- Tell students to read the selection with a partner. Ask them to stop and discuss the meanings of unknown words as necessary.

- Assign the **Responding Page** and **Blackline Master 16.1**. For the Write About It activity, remind students to use facts and details to support their ideas. Tell them to give a clear description of another way to travel.

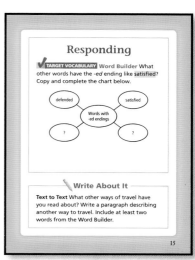

Stagecoach Travel, p. 15

ELL English Language Learners

Group English Language Learners according to language proficiency.

Beginning

Conduct a picture walk with students. Then read the Vocabulary Reader aloud with them, pausing to explain the Target Vocabulary words, as necessary.

Advanced

Read aloud p. 11. Have students write one or two sentences to tell what *churning* means. Have them complete the sentence frame: *My stomach was churning because* _____.

Intermediate

Use the photographs to preteach the following selection vocabulary: *worthy, defended,* and *reputation.* Using these words, have students choose a photograph to describe.

Advanced High

Have students read p. 8. Ask them what the author wants readers to understand. Have them include the word *reputation* as they discuss the author's purpose.

Blackline Master 16.1

Differentiate Comprehension
☑ Compare and Contrast; Monitor/Clarify

Struggling Readers

I DO IT

- Explain that comparing shows how things are alike, while contrasting shows differences.

- Read aloud p. 413. Model how to infer details that compare and contrast.

  Think Aloud *Charlotte wants the portly gentleman to go over the bridge. The man wants to ride in the coach, but Charlotte insists that they all walk. So, that is a difference between them.*

WE DO IT

- Use p. 416 to guide students to compare and contrast the passengers and Charlotte after they cross the bridge.

- Create a Venn diagram together. Write *Both are safe across the bridge* in the center. Use these prompts to guide students to complete the diagram. Ask: *How do the passengers act? excited How does Charlotte act? She seems calm, trying to settle the horses.*

YOU DO IT

- Have partners reread p. 415 together and complete a Venn diagram to compare Charlotte and the passengers.

- Have partners use the diagram to answer this question: *What problem do they both want to solve? They both want to cross the bridge safely.*

On Level

I DO IT

- Read p. 411 of the selection.

- Explain that readers use characters' actions and words to compare and contrast them.

- Model with a Think Aloud.

  Think Aloud *James and Charlotte are both yelling. But James is worried that he can't see the road. Charlotte yells back to tell him not to worry, since she can hear and smell the road.*

WE DO IT

- Read p. 413 together.

- Help students compare and contrast Charlotte's words and actions with that of the portly gentleman's. Explain that a character's words and actions are important clues.

- Work with students to complete a Venn diagram on the board.

YOU DO IT

- Have pairs of students complete a Venn diagram comparing and contrasting Charlotte's words and actions in a dangerous situation in "Riding Freedom" and another character's words and actions in another adventure story they have previously read.

- Have students use the Venn diagram to help them write a paragraph comparing and contrasting the characters.

Advanced

I DO IT	**WE DO IT**	**YOU DO IT**

I DO IT

- Explain that students can compare and contrast a character's behavior in different parts of a story to see how the character changes.

- Use Charlotte's words and actions to discuss what she is like at the beginning and at the end of "Riding Freedom."

- Use a Venn diagram to model comparing and contrasting.

WE DO IT

- Have students read pp. 413 and 416. Work with them to compare and contrast Charlotte's and the portly gentleman's words and actions before and after crossing the bridge. Have them record details in a Venn Diagram.

- Ask: *What does the portly man think about crossing the bridge at first? He thinks he knows best, and he should stay in the stagecoach. How does he feel at the end? He's happy he listened to Charlotte, saying that she saved his life.*

YOU DO IT

- Have students reread pp. 411–416. Tell them to write a paragraph comparing and contrasting what James thought about Charlotte before and after she drove the stagecoach across the bridge.

- Encourage students to make a Venn diagram before they write.

ELL English Language Learners

Group English Language Learners according to language proficiency.

Write the following sentence frames on the board. *A cat and a dog are both _____. A cat is _____, but a dog is _____.* Complete some of these frames to review compare and contrast. Write the answers in a Venn diagram on the board. Then use the following scaffolded activities based on students' language proficiency.

Beginning

Have students look at the illustration on p. 411 of "Riding Freedom." Ask: *Do Charlotte and James both have a hat? yes Does Charlotte have a moustache? no Does James have an eye patch? no*

Intermediate

Have students look at the illustration on p. 411 of "Riding Freedom." Say: *How is Charlotte different from James? Charlotte has an eye patch. James has a moustache. How are they alike? Both wear hats.*

Advanced

Have students read p. 413 and tell two ways in which the man and Charlotte are the same. *Both are in the rain; both want to cross the bridge. What is one difference? Charlotte insists that the man let her escort him across the bridge.*

Advanced High

Have partners complete a Venn diagram telling how James and Charlotte are alike and different. Ask partners to take turns using their completed diagrams to describe Charlotte and James.

Targets for Lesson 16

TARGET SKILL

Compare and Contrast

TARGET STRATEGY

Monitor/Clarify

✓ **TARGET VOCABULARY**

relied	swelled
defended	worthy
reputation	satisfied
situation	escorted
deserve	churning

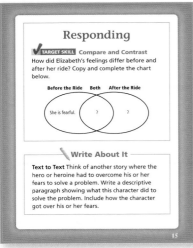

Elizabeth's Stormy Ride, p. 15

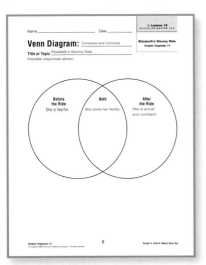

Blackline Master 16.3

Leveled Readers

Struggling Readers

 Elizabeth's Stormy Ride

GENRE: HISTORICAL FICTION

SUMMARY Elizabeth rides her horse in a storm to seek help for her mother, who is in labor. Elizabeth braves the storm to get to the midwife, who safely delivers the baby.

Introducing the Text

- Discuss key vocabulary from the story. Explain that people sometimes have to overcome obstacles to get what they need.

- Remind students that using a Venn diagram can help them organize information to compare and contrast in a story.

Supporting the Reading

- As you listen to students read, pause to discuss these questions.

COMPARE AND CONTRAST p. 13 *Compare Mama's facial expression with Mrs. Baldwin's at the end. How are they different? Mama's face is "white with pain." Mrs. Baldwin has a "big smile."*

MONITOR/CLARIFY p. 8 *Why was Elizabeth worried that it was getting dark? She would not be able to find her way through the woods using her mother's directions if she could not see well.*

Discussing and Revisiting the Text

CRITICAL THINKING After discussing *Elizabeth's Stormy Ride* together, have students read the instructions on the top half of **Responding** p. 15. Use these teaching points to guide them as they revisit the text.

- Have volunteers read aloud the story details listed in their Venn diagrams.

- Have them compare and contrast other story events on **Blackline Master 16.3**.

- Distribute **Blackline Master 16.7** to further develop students' critical thinking skills.

FLUENCY: RATE Model reading at a rate that allows students to understand the text and make it enjoyable. Then have partners echo-read p. 8, focusing on rate.

JOURNEYS DIGITAL | Powered by DESTINATIONReading®
Leveled Readers Online

On Level

▲ *Perilous Passage*

GENRE: HISTORICAL FICTION

Summary The Ambrose family begins a difficult 2,000-mile trip to Oregon to start a new life. William, the eldest son, braves challenges during the dangerous trip.

Introducing the Text

- Discuss key vocabulary from the story. Explain that people sometimes move to a different place in order to find a better life. Before there were cars, people traveled by wagon and by foot.

- Remind students that authors do not always draw attention to comparisons in the text. Good readers pay attention to details as they read to identify comparisons.

Supporting the Reading

- As you listen to students read, pause to discuss these questions.

COMPARE AND CONTRAST p. 5 *What is the difference between the Ambrose family's wagon and a Prairie Schooner? The family wagon had no storage space; the schooner had hidden storage space, and it could float on water.*

MONITOR/CLARIFY p. 4 *Who is William referring to when he asks about Meg and Nan? Meg and Nan were the horses that were sold.*

Discussing and Revisiting the Text

CRITICAL THINKING After discussing *Perilous Passage* together, have students read the instructions on the top half of **Responding** p. 15. Use these teaching points to guide them as they revisit the text.

- Have partners identify similarities and differences among characters in the story.

- Have them compare and contrast other story events on **Blackline Master 16.4**.

- Distribute **Blackline Master 16.8** to further develop students' critical thinking skills.

FLUENCY: RATE Have partners read and reread their favorite parts of *Perilous Passage* to improve rate and fluency.

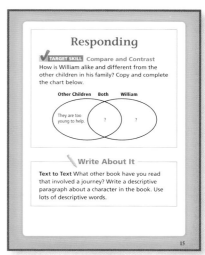

Perilous Passage, p. 15

Blackline Master 16.4

Targets for Lesson 16

TARGET SKILL

Compare and Contrast

TARGET STRATEGY

Monitor/Clarify

TARGET VOCABULARY

relied	swelled
defended	worthy
reputation	satisfied
situation	escorted
deserve	churning

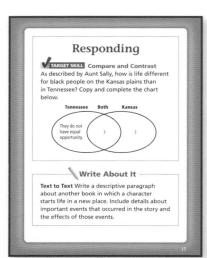

Come to Nicodemus, p. 15

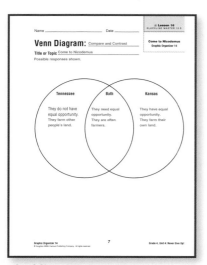

Blackline Master 16.5

Leveled Readers

Advanced

 Come to Nicodemus

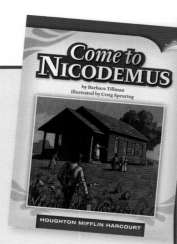

GENRE: HISTORICAL FICTION

Summary In a series of letters to her nephew Benjamin, Aunt Sally describes her new life in an all-black settlement in Nicodemus, Kansas. Sally encourages Benjamin's family to come.

Introducing the Text

- Tell students that sometimes families have to move away from their homes for better opportunities.

- Remind students that sometimes authors use comparisons as a basis for their writing or parts of the stories they tell. Active readers keep track of these comparisons to make meaning as they read.

Supporting the Reading

- As you listen to students read, pause to discuss these questions.

COMPARE AND CONTRAST p. 4 *How do the living conditions differ from the first settlements to when Aunt Sally writes her August 9 letter? At first people lived in dugouts and life was hard. Later, things were better—they had hotels and shops.*

MONITOR/CLARIFY p. 11 *Based on the illustration on p. 11, what do you think "Ho for Kansas!" means? Sample answer: It encourages people to join a group moving to Kansas in search of a better life.*

Discussing and Revisiting the Text

CRITICAL THINKING After discussing *Come to Nicodemus* together, have students read the instructions on the top half of **Responding** p. 15. Use these teaching points to guide them as they revisit the text.

- Have volunteers read aloud the comparisons listed in their Venn diagrams.

- Have them compare and contrast other story events on **Blackline Master 16.5**.

- Distribute **Blackline Master 16.9** to further develop students' critical thinking skills.

FLUENCY: RATE Have volunteers read parts of *Come to Nicodemus* aloud, adjusting their rate for accuracy and understanding.

JOURNEYS DIGITAL Powered by **DESTINATIONReading** Leveled Readers Online

ELL **English Language Learners**

◆ A Dangerous Trip

GENRE: HISTORICAL FICTION

Summary The Ambrose family begins a difficult journey to Oregon to start a new life. William, the eldest son, faces challenges that show his bravery.

Introducing the Text

- Explain that people move to different places in order to find a better life. Sometimes, people must endure great hardships when they move to a new location.

- Remind students that good readers compare and contrast text clues to help them understand characters in a story.

Supporting the Reading

- As you listen to students read, pause to discuss these questions.

COMPARE AND CONTRAST p. 14 *What is the difference between the Ambrose family's wagon and a Prairie Schooner? The family wagon had no storage space; the schooner had hidden storage space, and it could float across rivers.*

MONITOR/CLARIFY p. 6 *How do the oxen and the wagon get across the river? The oxen pull the empty wagon, which floats.*

Discussing and Revisiting the Text

CRITICAL THINKING After discussing *A Dangerous Trip* together, have students read the instructions on the top half of **Responding** p. 15. Use these teaching points to guide them as they revisit the text.

- Have volunteers read aloud the comparisons listed in their Venn diagrams.

- Have them compare and contrast other story events on **Blackline Master 16.6**.

- Distribute **Blackline Master 16.10** to further develop students' critical thinking skills.

FLUENCY: RATE Have pairs of students practice reading their favorite parts of *A Dangerous Crossing* at a rate that makes the text understandable and enjoyable.

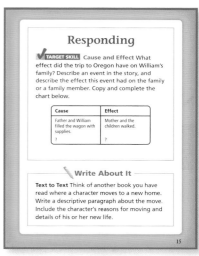

A Dangerous Trip, p. 15

Blackline Master 16.6

Differentiate Vocabulary Strategies ☑ Using Context

Struggling Readers

I DO IT

- Display the **Vocabulary in Context Card** for *escorted*.

- Remind students that good readers use context to find clues to the meaning of unfamiliar words.

- Explain that looking around an unfamiliar word helps readers use context clues.

WE DO IT

- Read aloud the context sentence on the front of the card.

- Have students look in the sentence to figure out the meaning of *escorted*. Guide them as they discuss clues to the meaning.

> Guides who knew the trails well often escorted, or led, travelers.

- Point out that the author used a synonym for *escorted*.

YOU DO IT

- Have students restate the context sentence for *escorted* and the meaning "to have accompanied someone."

- Have pairs brainstorm other situations using *escorted*. For example, *The teacher escorted students to the library*.

- Have students write a short sentence using the word *escorted* and then illustrate it.

On Level

I DO IT

- Remind students that looking around a word helps readers figure out an unfamiliar word's meaning.

- Review the five types of context clues: *definition, example, synonym, antonym, general*.

- Point out that definition context clues define the word within the same sentence. General context clues may be spread over several sentences.

WE DO IT

- On the board, list unfamiliar words students have identified in the selection.

- Guide students to use context clues to find the meaning of the words on the list. Reread passages containing the words. Identify context clues that help determine each word's meaning. Have students indicate the type of each context clue.

YOU DO IT

- Have students write sentences to show their understanding of the unfamiliar words.

- Have partners read each other's sentences and use the context around each word to confirm its meaning.

- Tell partners to indicate the type of context clues they identify.

Advanced

I DO IT

- Write these sentences on the board:
  She trusted her senses to guide her as she drove.
  My dog growls when she senses a stranger is nearby.

- Explain that many words have more than one meaning. Using context clues is a good way to know which meaning is correct.

- Review the five types of context clues: *definition, example, synonym, antonym,* and *general.*

WE DO IT

- Help students use context to predict the meaning of the word *senses* in each sentence on the board.

- Guide students as they use a dictionary to confirm their predictions of the meaning of *senses* in each sentence.

YOU DO IT

- Have pairs identify the type of context clue used in each sentence on the board.

- Have students write additional sentences using the word *senses* and its different meanings.

ELL English Language Learners

Group English Language Learners according to language proficiency.

Write *worthy, churning, situation, swelled, deserve, defended, satisfied, relied, reputation,* and *escorted* on the board. Have students repeat after you as you pronounce each word.

Beginning

Display the **Vocabulary in Context Card** for *escorted.* Have students listen for the word as you read the sentence. Point out and discuss the picture. Then have students demonstrate the word's meaning.

Intermediate

Have students listen as you explain each word's meaning. Use the words in questions based on the selection. Have students provide answers based on their understanding of the story. Example: *Did Charlotte deserve to keep driving the coach?* *Yes, she proved that she could drive it safely.*

Advanced

Have students write each word on one side of an index card. Have them use a dictionary to confirm the word's meaning. Ask them to write it and a sentence using the word on the reverse side of the card. Have partners work together to brainstorm new sentences using the word.

Advanced High

Have students generate an example and a non-example for each word. For example, *anxious*: *example: worried* *non-example: a book*

 Options for Reteaching

Vocabulary Strategies

Using Context

I DO IT

- Remind students that context refers to the words and sentences around a word.
- Explain that readers use context to figure out the meaning of unfamiliar words.
- Review the five types of context clues: *example*, *definition*, *synonym*, *antonym*, and *general*.

WE DO IT

- Have a volunteer read aloud the first two sentences on **Student Book p. 408.**
- Model how to use context to figure out the meaning of *disguises*.

  Think Aloud *I can use the words around* disguises *to help me figure out what it means. The sentence before says that girls were not allowed to have jobs, but Charlotte had one and she was a girl. The sentence after says that she kept her true identity a secret. I think* disguises *means she is "hiding her identity by changing her appearance."*

- Have a volunteer look up *disguises* (the verb) in a dictionary and read the definition aloud. Discuss how using context can lead to the correct definition.

YOU DO IT

- Have partners reread sections of "Riding Freedom" and identify unfamiliar words.
- Have them use context to determine the meaning of each unfamiliar word.
- Have them use dictionaries to verify their decisions.
- Provide corrective feedback if students need additional support.

Comprehension Skill

Compare and Contrast

I DO IT

- Remind students that they can compare and contrast to find ways in which stories are alike and ways in which they are different.
- Remind students that they can look for signal words such as *but*, *instead*, *however*, *different*, and *same* to help them find comparisons in the text.

WE DO IT

- Have students read the **Student Book p. 409** aloud and help them identify signal words that show a comparison of the sounds Charlotte could hear the horses' hooves make on different roads.
- Model how to compare and contrast.

  Think Aloud *I see the signal word* different. *That tells me to look for story details that are not alike. I see that Charlotte can hear different sounds the horses' hooves make. On a hard road, the hooves make a hollow, clopping sound. On a soft road, they make a dull, thudding sound. I can write this in a Venn diagram to keep track of the difference. In the Both section, I can put that the horses hooves make sounds on both kinds of roads.*

- Help students compare and contrast how Charlotte's experiences would be if she had the use of both her eyes.

YOU DO IT

- Distribute **Graphic Organizer 14.**
- Have students compare and contrast James and Charlotte on **Student Book pp. 410-411.** *James is not sure about Charlotte's being ready, but she is sure. James is nervous about riding in the storm, but Charlotte is confident and determined.*
- Have partners complete the graphic organizer.

Language Arts

 # Adjectives/Write to Narrate

I DO IT

- Remind students that adjectives are words that describe nouns. Adjectives tell *what kind* or *how many*.
- Tell students that some adjectives appear before a noun, while others appear after a form of the verb *be*.
- Remind students that adjectives can be used to combine sentences to make writing flow smoothly.

WE DO IT

- Remind students that narrative writing often includes descriptive, vivid adjectives and other details.
- Have students turn to **Student Book p. 409.** Read aloud with them the second paragraph.
- Model analyzing the narrative paragraph for descriptive details.

  Think Aloud *This paragraph describes the different sounds that the horses' hooves make depending on the type of road they use. The sound is described as hollow and clopping when the road is hard, and dull and thudding when the road is soft. These descriptions help me "see" and "hear" what is happening in the text.*

- Work with students to find and discuss other examples of descriptive detail in the selection.

YOU DO IT

- Encourage students to use vivid details as they write their narrative paragraphs.
- Have partners take turns reading their narrative paragraphs to each other.
- Have partners discuss what they were able to "see" or "hear" through the descriptive details.

Decoding

 # Sound/Spelling Changes

I DO IT

- Remind students that some related words, such as *public* and *publicity*, have sound/spelling changes.
- Provide this example: The *c* in *public* has a /k/ sound; the *c* in *publicity* has a /s/ sound.
- Tell students that if they are unsure of how to prononce a word with sound/spelling changes, they should try pronouncing it with each sound until it sounds like a word they know.

WE DO IT

- Write on the board the related words *muscle* and *muscular*. Tell students that when the suffix *-ar* is added to the noun *muscle*, the adjective *muscular* is formed.
- Use this model to point out the sound/spelling changes in these related words.

  Think Aloud *The letter* c *in* muscle *stands for the /s/ sound. In the word* muscular, *though, the letter c stands for the /k/ sound. When I pronounce the* c *in this word with the /s/ sound, it doesn't sound like a word I know. When I pronounce the* c *with the /k/ sound, I read the word* muscular, *which is a word I know.*

- Work with students to identify sound/spelling changes in the related words *optical* and *optician*.

YOU DO IT

- Have partners identify the sound/spelling changes in the related words *toxic/toxicity* and *elastic/elasticity*.
- Have students find other related words with sound/spelling changes and share their findings with the class.

Teacher Notes

Preteaching for Success!

Comprehension:
Sequence of Events

Help students understand the importance of the sequence of events for readers and writers.

- Be sure students know that by understanding the sequence of events, they are better able to answer questions about the plot.
- Tell students that signal words such as *soon, afterwards,* and *finally* can help them find the order of events in a story.
- Have students work to fill out a sequence of events chart like the one on Student Book p. 430 to explain the events of their day.

Challenge Yourself!

Write an Advertisement

After reading the selection "The Right Dog for the Job," have students write advertisements for a school that trains guide dogs.

- Have each student write a magazine or radio advertisement for a school that trains guide dogs. The advertisement should include how the dogs will improve the lives of the people they are trained to help.
- Students can provide drawings, or write parts for actors who will read the scripts.
- Ask students to perform their advertisements in front of the class, or display their artwork in the classroom.

Short Response

W.4.3d Use concrete words and phrases and sensory details to convey experiences and events precisely.

Write a paragraph to explain what the lives of seeing-impaired people would be like if they did not have guide dogs to help them. Provide details from the text.

Scoring Guidelines	
Excellent	Student has written a paragraph to explain what the lives of seeing-impaired people would be like without guide dogs and has provided details from the text.
Good	Student has written a paragraph to explain what the lives of seeing-impaired people would be like without guide dogs but has not provided details from the text.
Fair	Student has written a paragraph but has not addressed the writing prompt.
Unsatisfactory	Student has not written a paragraph.

Writing Minilesson

Skill: Write to Narrate—Friendly Letter

Teach: Explain to students that when they write friendly letters, they should try to show feelings.

Thinking Beyond the Text

Writing Prompt: Write a friendly letter to thank someone for a gift.

1. Have students brainstorm people and gifts that mean a lot to them.
2. Remind students to use adverbs to help them describe verbs in their letters. Be sure students know that adverbs tell *how, when,* or *where,* and often end in -*ly.*
3. Encourage students to revise their letters to make sure they are showing feelings and that they sound like themselves.

Group Share: Have volunteers read their letters to small groups. If possible, let students deliver their letters to the addressees.

Cross-Curricular Activity: Social Studies

Active Citizens

This selection tells about a woman and a dog that work together to help seeing-impaired people. Discuss some of the skills the trainer and dog practice. How do these skills help seeing-impaired people? As a class, learn about local organizations that train guide dogs.

Common Core State Standards
for English Language Arts

Reading Standards for Literature K–5
Integration of Knowledge and Ideas
RL.4.9 Compare and contrast the treatment of similar themes and topics (e.g., opposition of good and evil) and patterns of events (e.g., the quest) in stories, myths, and traditional literature from different cultures.

Reading Standards for Informational Text K–5
Key Ideas and Details
RI.4.1 Refer to details and examples in a text when explaining what the text says explicitly and when drawing inferences from the text.

RI.4.2 Determine the main idea of a text and explain how it is supported by key details; summarize the text.

Craft and Structure
RI.4.4 Determine the meaning of general academic and domain-specific words or phrases in a text relevant to a *grade 4 topic or subject area*.

RI.4.5 Describe the overall structure (e.g., chronology, comparison, cause/effect, problem/solution) of events, ideas, concepts, or information in a text or part of a text.

Range of Reading and Level of Text Complexity
RI.4.10 By the end of year, read and comprehend informational texts, including history/social studies, science, and technical texts, in the grades 4–5 text complexity band proficiently, with scaffolding as needed at the high end of the range.

Reading Standards: Foundational Skills K–5
Phonics and Word Recognition
RF.4.3a Use combined knowledge of all letter-sound correspondences, syllabication patterns, and morphology (e.g. roots and affixes) to read accurately unfamiliar multisyllabic words in context and out of context.

Fluency
RF.4.4b Read grade-level prose and poetry orally with accuracy, appropriate rate, and expression.

Writing Standards K–5
Production and Distribution of Writing
W.4.5 With guidance and support from peers and adults, develop and strengthen writing as needed by planning, revising, and editing. (Editing for conventions should demonstrate command of Language standards 1–3 up to and including grade 4 on pages 28 and 29.)

Research to Build and Present Knowledge
W.4.7 Conduct short research projects that build knowledge through investigation of different aspects of a topic.

W.4.8 Recall relevant information from experiences or gather relevant information from print and digital sources; take notes and categorize information, and provide a list of sources.

Range of Writing
W.4.10 Write routinely over extended time frames (time for research, reflection, and revision) and shorter time frames (a single sitting or a day or two) for a range of discipline-specific tasks, purposes, and audiences.

Speaking & Listening Standards K–5
Comprehension and Collaboration
SL.4.1a Come to discussions prepared, having read or studied required material; explicitly draw on that preparation and other information known about the topic to explore ideas under discussion.

Presentation of Knowledge and Ideas
SL.4.4 Report on a topic or text, tell a story, or recount an experience in an organized manner, using appropriate facts and relevant, descriptive details to support main ideas or themes; speak clearly at an understandable pace.

SL.4.6 Differentiate between contexts that call for formal English (e.g., presenting ideas) and situations where informal discourse is appropriate (e.g., small-group discussion); use formal English when appropriate to task and situation. (See grade 4 Language standards 1 on pages 28 and 29 for specific expectations.)

Language Standards K–5
Conventions of Standard English
L.4.2d Spell grade-appropriate words correctly, consulting references as needed.

Knowledge of Language
L.4.3c Differentiate between contexts that call for formal English (e.g., presenting ideas) and situations where informal discourse is appropriate (e.g., small-group discussion).

Vocabulary Acquisition and Use
L.4.5b Recognize and explain the meaning of common idioms, adages, and proverbs.

SUGGESTIONS FOR BALANCED LITERACY

Use *Journeys* materials to support a Readers' Workshop approach. See the Lesson 17 resources on pages 25, 72–73.

Focus Wall

Main Selection
The Right Dog
for the Job

**Connect to
Traditional Tale**
The Sticky Coyote

Big Idea
There is more than one secret to success.

? Essential Question
What steps can you take toward success?

Comprehension

 **TARGET SKILL**
Sequence of Events

 **TARGET STRATEGY**
Summarize

Spelling

Spelling Final /j/ and /s/

glance	baggage
judge	office
damage	message
package	bridge
twice	chance
stage	notice
carriage	ridge
since	manage
practice	palace
marriage	bandage

Fluency

Intonation

Grammar

Adverbs

Writing

Write to Narrate

Focus Trait:
Voice

Decoding

More Sound/Spelling Changes

Vocabulary Strategies

Suffixes -ion, -ation, -ition

✔ TARGET VOCABULARY

reward	confidence
graduate	patiently
symbol	confesses
foster	ceremony
disobey	performs

Week at a Glance

Key Skills This Week

Target Skill:
Sequence of Events

Target Strategy:
Summarize

Vocabulary Strategies:
Suffixes -ion, -ation, -ition

Fluency:
Intonation

Decoding:
More Sound/Spelling Changes

Research Skill:
Taking Notes/Identifying Sources

Grammar:
Adverbs

Spelling:
Words with Final /j/ and /s/

 Writing:
Friendly Letter

✔ Assess/Monitor

✔ **Vocabulary,** p. T126

✔ **Comprehension,** p. T126

✔ **Decoding,** p. T127

✔ **Fluency,** p. T127

✔ **Language Arts,** p. T127

Whole Group

READING

Paired Selections

The Right Dog for the Job
Narrative Fiction
Student Book, pp. 430–440

Accelerated Reader

Practice Quizzes for the Selection

The Sticky Coyote
TRADITIONAL TALE
Readers' Theater/Trickster Tale
Student Book, pp. 442–445

Vocabulary

Student Book, pp. 426–427

Background and Comprehensio

Student Book, pp. 428–429

LANGUAGE ARTS

Grammar
Student Book, pp. 446–447

 **Writing**
Student Book, pp. 448–449

Small Group

See pages T130–T131 for Suggested Small Group Plan.

TEACHER-LED

Leveled Readers

 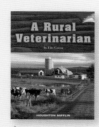

● **Struggling Readers** ▲ **On Level**

 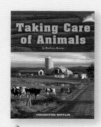

■ **Advanced** ◆ **English Language Learners**

Vocabulary Reader

WHAT MY OTHER STUDENTS ARE DOING

Ready-Made Work Stations

Word Study **Think and Write**

Comprehension and Fluency **Digital Center**

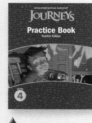 

● **Struggling Readers** ■ **Advanced** ◆ **English Language Learners**

▲ **On Level**

Grab-and-Go!

Lesson 17 Blackline Master
- Target Vocabulary, 17.1
- Selection Summary, 17.2
- Graphic Organizer 17.3–17.6 ●▲■◆
- Critical Thinking 17.7–17.10 ●▲■◆
- Running Records 17.11–17.14 ●▲■◆
- Weekly Tests 17.1–17.9

Graphic Organizer Transparency 4

Additional Resources
- Genre: Nonfiction, p. 5
- Reading Log, p. 12
- Vocabulary Log, p. 13
- Listening Log, p.14
- Proofreading Checklist, p.15
- Proofreading Marks, p.16
- Writing Conference Form, p.17
- Writing Rubric, p.18
- Instructional Routines, pp.19–26
- Graphic Organizer 4: Flow Chart, p. 3.

JOURNEYS DIGITAL

For Students
- Student eBook
- Comprehension Expedition CD-ROM
- Leveled Readers Online
- WriteSmart CD-ROM

For Teachers
- Online TE and Focus Wall
- Online Assessment System
- Teacher One-Stop
- Destination Reading Instruction

Week at a Glance

Intervention

STRATEGIC INTERVENTION: TIER II

Use these materials to provide additional targeted instruction for students who need Tier II strategic intervention.

Supports the Student Book selections

Interactive Work-text for Skills Support

Write-In Reader:

Monkey Business

- Engaging selection connects to main topic.
- Reinforces this week's target vocabulary and comprehension skill and strategy.
- Opportunities for student interaction on each page.

Assessment

Progress monitoring every two weeks.

For this week's Strategic Intervention lessons, see Teacher Edition pages S12–S21.

INTENSIVE INTERVENTION: TIER III

- The materials in the Literacy Tool Kit help you provide a different approach for students who need Tier III intensive intervention.
- Interactive lessons provide focused instruction in key reading skills, targeted at students' specific needs.
- Lesson cards are convenient for small-group or individual instruction.
- Blackline masters provide additional practice.
- A leveled book accompanies each lesson to give students opportunities for additional reading and skill application.
- Assessments for each lesson help you evaluate the effectiveness of the intervention.

Lessons provide support for

- Phonics and Word Study Skills
- Vocabulary
- Comprehension Skills and Literacy Genres
- Fluency

ELL English Language Learners

Powered by JOURNEYS DIGITAL / DESTINATIONReading
- Leveled Readers Online
- Picture Card Bank Online

SCAFFOLDED SUPPORT

Use these materials to ensure that students acquire social and academic language proficiency.

Language Support Card

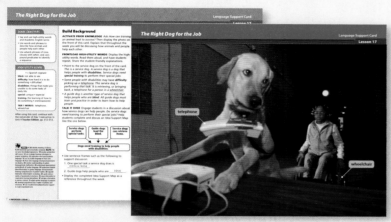

- Builds background for the main topic and promotes oral language.
- Develops high-utility vocabulary and academic language.

Leveled Reader

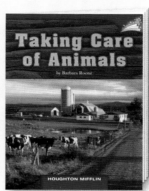

- Sheltered text connects to the main selection's topic, vocabulary, skill, and strategy.

Scaffolded Support

ELL ENGLISH LANGUAGE LEARNERS

Scaffold

Beginning Help students list common working animals. Guide students to identify horses, cattle, sheep, dogs, and other animals.

Intermediate Pre-teach unfamiliar vocabulary in *The Right Dog for the Job* using gestures, visuals, or simplified language.

Advanced Discuss with students the difficulties a service animal might have while training to assist a person with disabilities.

Advanced High Ask students to discuss what it feels like to receive a reward for something. Have them work with a partner to write a short paragraph about a reward they would like to receive, using Target Vocabulary.

See ELL Lesson 17, p. E12-E21, for scaffolded support.

- Notes throughout the Teacher's Edition scaffold instruction to each language proficiency level.

Vocabulary in Context Cards 161–170

- Provide visual support and additional practice for Target Vocabulary words.

For this week's English Language Learners lessons, see Teacher's Edition, pages E12–E21.

? Essential Question What steps can you take toward success?

	Day 1	Day 2
Oral Language Listening Comprehension	**Teacher Read Aloud** "Let Me Be Brave," T84–T85 ☑ Target Vocabulary, T85	**Turn and Talk,** T91
Vocabulary **Comprehension** Skills and Strategies **Reading**	☑ **Comprehension** Preview the Target Skill, T85 ☑ **Introduce Vocabulary** Vocabulary in Context, T86–T87 **Develop Background** ☑ Target Vocabulary, T88–T89	**Introduce Comprehension** ☑ Sequence of Events, T90–T91 Summarize, T90–T91 **Read "The Right Dog for the Job,"** T92–T102 Focus on Genre, T92 Stop and Think, T95, T99, T101
Cross-Curricular **Connections** **Fluency** **Decoding**	☑ **Fluency** Model Intonation, T84	☑ **Fluency** Teach Intonation, T110
Spelling **Grammar** **Writing**	☑ **Spelling** Words with Final /j/ and /s/: Pretest, T116 ☑ **Grammar** Daily Proofreading Practice, T118 Teach Adverbs, T118 ☑ **Write to Narrate: Friendly Letter** Analyze the Model, T122	☑ **Spelling** Words with Final /j/ and /s/: Word Sort, T116 ☑ **Grammar** Daily Proofreading Practice, T119 Extend Adverbs, T119 ☑ **Write to Narrate: Friendly Letter** Focus Trait: Voice, T123
Writing Prompt	*List traits that a successful service animal must have.*	*Write a "Help Wanted" advertisement that describes the perfect service animal.*

Whole Group

Whole Group Language Arts

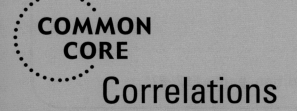

Teacher Read Aloud RF.4.4b
Comprehension RF.4.4b
Introduce Vocabulary RI.4.4
Develop Background RI.4.4
Fluency RF.4.4b
Spelling L.4.2d
Write to Narrate W.4.5

Turn and Talk RI.4.5
Introduce Comprehension RI.4.1, RI.4.2, RI.4.5
Read RI.4.1, RI.4.2, RI.4.4, RI.4.5, RI.4.10, RF.4.4b, L.4.5b
Fluency RF.4.4b
Spelling L.4.2d
Write to Narrate W.4.5

Suggestions for Small Groups (See pp. T130–T131.)
Suggestions for Intervention (See pp. S12–S21.)
Suggestions for English Language Learners (See pp. E12–E21.)

JOURNEYS DIGITAL Powered by DESTINATIONReading
Teacher One-Stop: Lesson Planning

Day 3

Turn and Talk, T103
Oral Language, T103

Read "The Right Dog for the Job", T92–T102
Develop Comprehension, T94, T96, T98, T100
☑ **Target Vocabulary**
"The Right Dog for the Job," T94, T96, T98, T100, T102
Your Turn, T103
Deepen Comprehension
☑ Infer Sequence of Events, T108–T109

Cross-Curricular Connection
Science, T97
☑ **Fluency**
Practice Intonation, T97
☑ **Decoding**
More Sound/Spelling Changes, T111

☑ **Spelling**
Words with Final /j/ and /s/:
    Multiple Meaning Words, T117
☑ **Grammar**
Daily Proofreading Practice, T119
Teach Adverbs, T119

☑ **Write to Narrate: Friendly Letter**
Prewrite, T123

Describe the steps that a guide dog must go through before graduation.

Turn and Talk SL.4.1a
Oral Language SL.4.1a
Read RI.4.1, RI.4.2, RI.4.4, RI.4.5, RI.4.10, RF.4.4b, L.4.5b
Target Vocabulary L.4.5b
Deepen Comprehension RI.4.5
Fluency RF.4.4b
Decoding RF.4.3a
Spelling L.4.2d
Write to Narrate W.4.5, L.4.3c

Day 4

Text to World, T107

Read "The Sticky Coyote," T104–T106
Connect to Traditional Tales, T104
Target Vocabulary Review, T105
Develop Comprehension, T106
Weekly Internet Challenge, T106
Making Connections, T107
☑ **Vocabulary Strategies**
Suffixes *-ion, -ation, -ition,* T112–T113

☑ **Fluency**
Practice Intonation, T105

☑ **Spelling**
Words with Final /j/ and /s/:
    Connect to Writing, T117
☑ **Grammar**
Daily Proofreading Practice, T120
Review Adverbs, T120

☑ **Write to Narrate: Friendly Letter**
Draft, T124

Write a short scene that shows how Coyote scares the animals.

Text to World W.4.7, W.4.8, W.4.10, SL.4.4
Read RL.4.9, RF.4.4b
Making Connections W.4.7, W.4.8, W.4.10, SL.4.4
Vocabulary Strategies RF.4.3a
Fluency RF.4.4b
Spelling W.4.10, L.4.2d
Write to Narrate W.4.5

Day 5

Listening and Speaking, T115

Connect and Extend
Read to Connect, T114
Independent Reading, T114
Extend Through Research, T115

☑ **Fluency**
Progress Monitoring, T127

☑ **Spelling**
Words with Final /j/ and /s/:
    Assess, T117
☑ **Grammar**
Daily Proofreading Practice, T120
Connect Grammar to Writing, T120–T121

☑ **Write to Narrate: Friendly Letter**
Revise for Voice, T124

Explain why Coyote would not make a good service animal.

Listening and Speaking SL.4.6
Connect and Extend W.4.8, SL.4.1a, SL.4.6, L.4.3c
Fluency RF.4.4b
Spelling L.4.2d
Write to Narrate W.4.5, L.4.3c

Your Skills for the Week

☑ **Vocabulary**
Target Vocabulary Strategies: Suffixes *-ion, -ation, -ition*

☑ **Comprehension**
Sequence of Events
Summarize

☑ **Decoding**
More Sound/Spelling Changes

☑ **Fluency**
Intonation

☑ **Language Arts**
Spelling
Grammar
Writing

Weekly Leveled Readers

Differentiated Support for This Week's Targets

✓ **TARGET SKILL**

Sequence of Events

✓ **TARGET STRATEGY**

Summarize

✓ **TARGET VOCABULARY**

reward	confidence
graduate	patiently
symbol	confesses
foster	ceremony
disobey	performs

Additional Tools

Vocabulary in Context Cards

Comprehension Tool: Graphic Organizer Transparency 4

? Essential Question

What steps can you take toward success?

Vocabulary Reader

Level N

Build Target Vocabulary

• Introduce the Target Vocabulary in context and build comprehension using the Target Strategy.

Vocabulary Reader

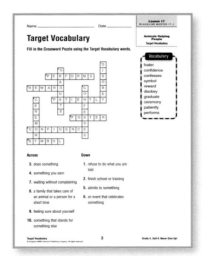

Blackline Master 17.1

Intervention

Scaffolded Support

• Provide extra support in applying the Target Vocabulary, Target Skill, and Target Strategy in context.

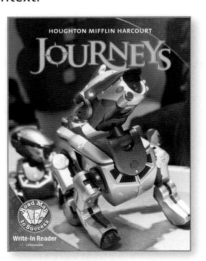

Write-In Reader

 For Vocabulary Reader Lesson Plans, see Small Group pages T132–T133.

JOURNEYS DIGITAL · **Powered by** DESTINATIONReading®
Leveled Readers Online

Leveled Readers

Struggling Readers

Level N

Objective: Use sequence of events and the summarize strategy to read *Animal Doctors*.

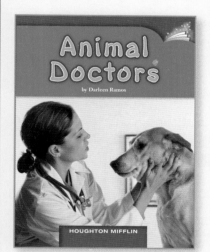

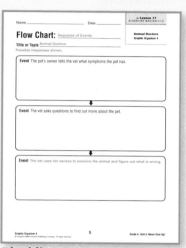

Blackline Master 17.3

On Level

Level R

Objective: Use sequence of events and the summarize strategy to read *A Rural Veterinarian*.

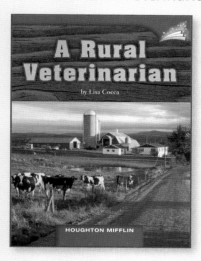

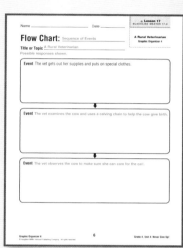

Blackline Master 17.4

Advanced

Level T

Objective: Use sequence of events and the summarize strategy to read *Helping Wild Animals*.

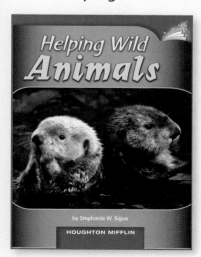

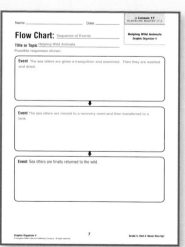

Blackline Master 17.5

English Language Learners

Level R

Objective: Use sequence of events and the summarize strategy to read *Taking Care of Animals*.

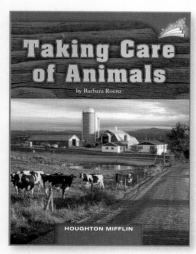

Blackline Master 17.6

 For Leveled Reader Lesson Plans, see Small Group pages T136–T139.

Weekly Leveled Readers • **T81**

Ready-Made Work Stations

Manage Independent Activities

Use the Ready-Made Work Stations to establish a consistent routine for students working independently. Each station contains three activities. Students who experience success with the *Get Started!* activity move on to the *Reach Higher!* and *Challenge Yourself!* activities, as time permits.

Comprehension and Fluency

Materials
- **Audiotext CD**
- CD Player/headphones
- **Student Book**
- **Reading Log**
- pencil or pen

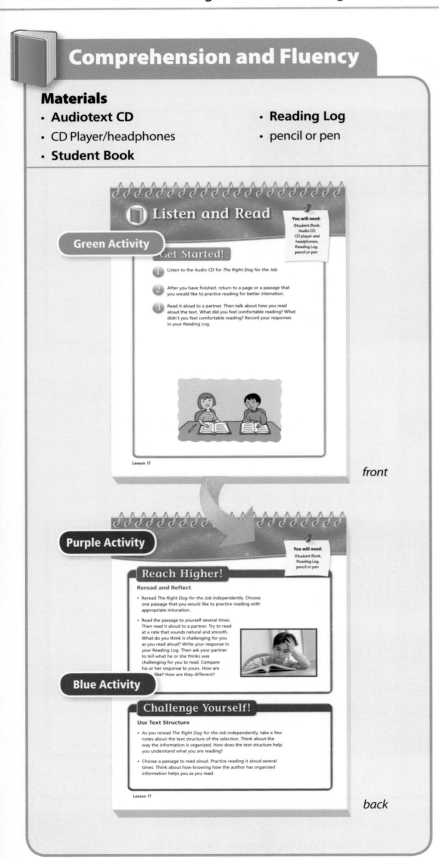

Green Activity

Listen and Read

You will need: Student Book, Audio CD, CD player and headphones, Reading Log, pencil or pen

Get Started!

1. Listen to the Audio CD for *The Right Dog for the Job*.

2. After you have finished, return to a page or a passage that you would like to practice reading for better intonation.

3. Read it aloud to a partner. Then talk about how you read aloud the text. What did you feel comfortable reading? What didn't you feel comfortable reading? Record your responses in your Reading Log.

Lesson 17 — *front*

Purple Activity

Reach Higher!

Reread and Reflect

- Reread *The Right Dog for the Job* independently. Choose one passage that you would like to practice reading with appropriate intonation.

- Read the passage to yourself several times. Then read it aloud to a partner. Try to read at a rate that sounds natural and smooth. What do you think is challenging for you as you read aloud? Write your response in your Reading Log. Then ask your partner to tell what he or she thinks was challenging for you to read. Compare his or her response to yours. How are they alike? How are they different?

You will need: Student Book, Reading Log, pencil or pen

Blue Activity

Challenge Yourself!

Use Text Structure

- As you reread *The Right Dog for the Job* independently, take a few notes about the text structure of the selection. Think about the way the information is organized. How does the text structure help you understand what you are reading?

- Choose a passage to read aloud. Practice reading it aloud several times. Think about how knowing how the author has organized information helps you as you read.

Lesson 17 — *back*

Word Study

Materials
- ruler
- paper
- pencil or pen

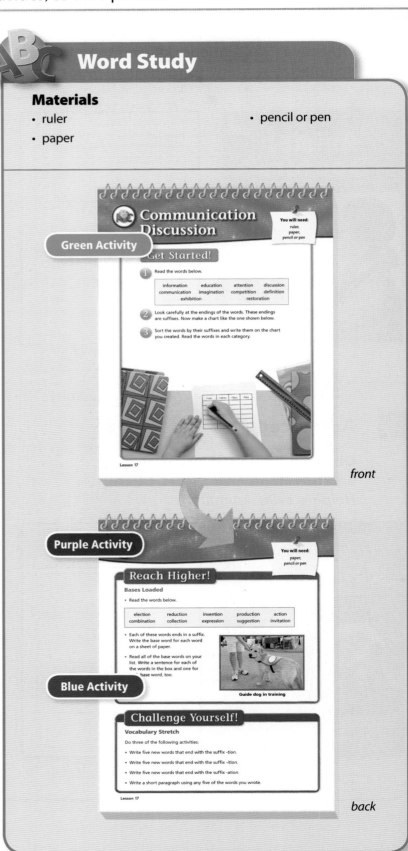

Green Activity

Communication Discussion

You will need: ruler, paper, pencil or pen

Get Started!

1. Read the words below.

information	education	attention	discussion
communication	imagination	competition	definition
	exhibition	restoration	

2. Look carefully at the endings of the words. These endings are suffixes. Now make a chart like the one shown below.

3. Sort the words by their suffixes and write them on the chart you created. Read the words in each category.

Lesson 17 — *front*

Purple Activity

Reach Higher!

Bases Loaded

- Read the words below.

| election | reduction | invention | production | action |
| combination | collection | expression | suggestion | invitation |

- Each of these words ends in a suffix. Write the base word for each word on a sheet of paper.

- Read all of the base words on your list. Write a sentence for each of the words in the box and one for base word, too.

Guide dog in training

Blue Activity

Challenge Yourself!

Vocabulary Stretch

Do three of the following activities:

- Write five new words that end with the suffix -tion.
- Write five new words that end with the suffix -ition.
- Write five new words that end with the suffix -ation.
- Write a short paragraph using any five of the words you wrote.

Lesson 17 — *back*

Think and Write

Materials

- computer with Internet access
- books, magazines
- index cards
- encyclopedia
- paper, pencil/pen
- colored pencils or markers

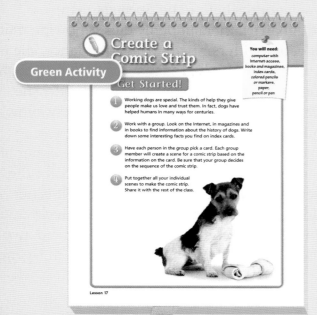

Green Activity

Create a Comic Strip

You will need:
computer with Internet access, books and magazines, index cards, colored pencils or markers, paper, pencil or pen

Get Started!

1. Working dogs are special. The kinds of help they give people make us love and trust them. In fact, dogs have helped humans in many ways for centuries.

2. Work with a group. Look on the Internet, in magazines and in books to find information about the history of dogs. Write down some interesting facts you find on index cards.

3. Have each person in the group pick a card. Each group member will create a scene for a comic strip based on the information on the card. Be sure that your group decides on the sequence of the comic strip.

4. Put together all your individual scenes to make the comic strip. Share it with the rest of the class.

Lesson 17

front

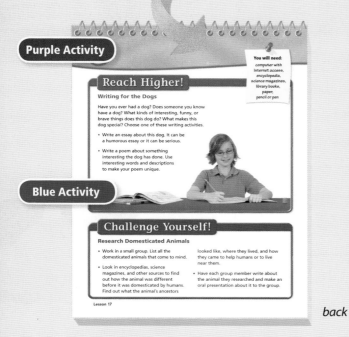

Purple Activity

You will need:
computer with Internet access, encyclopedia, science magazines, library books, paper, pencil or pen

Reach Higher!

Writing for the Dogs

Have you ever had a dog? Does someone you know have a dog? What kinds of interesting, funny, or brave things does this dog do? What makes this dog special? Choose one of these writing activities.

- Write an essay about this dog. It can be a humorous essay or it can be serious.

- Write a poem about something interesting the dog has done. Use interesting words and descriptions to make your poem unique.

Blue Activity

Challenge Yourself!

Research Domesticated Animals

- Work in a small group. List all the domesticated animals that come to mind.

- Look in encyclopedias, science magazines, and other sources to find out how the animal was different before it was domesticated by humans. Find out what the animal's ancestors

looked like, where they lived, and how they came to help humans or to live near them.

- Have each group member write about the animal they researched and make an oral presentation about it to the group.

Lesson 17

back

Independent Activities

Have students complete these activities at a computer center or a center with an audio CD player.

 LAUNCH ▶

Comprehension and Grammar Activities

- Practice and apply this week's skills.

 LAUNCH ▶

Student eBook

- Read and listen to this week's selections and skill lessons.

LAUNCH ▶

WriteSmart CD-ROM

- Review student versions of this week's writing model.

 LAUNCH ▶

Audiotext CD

- Listen to books or selections on CD.

Single Log In

Teacher Read Aloud

Model Fluency

Intonation Explain that when good readers read aloud, they vary their intonation, or pitch.

- Display **Projectable 17.1.** As you read each sentence, model how to read while varying your intonation.

- Point out that varying intonation can help make the meaning of a text clearer.

- Reread the sentences together with students, varying your intonation in order to make the meaning of the text clear.

Let Me Be Brave

Many people witnessed Liinah Bukenya win the 50-meter backstroke in the 2003 Special Olympics in Dublin, but they did not see all of the difficulties she had to overcome just to be there.

Even though Liinah was born with a mental disability, she always wanted to swim. Her coach started her with armband floats, but as she gained **confidence**, Liinah was able to **graduate** to swimming without help. At first, she could barely make it across the pool. The more she practiced, the better she got. Soon Liinah sped through the water like a fish. **1**

Then, just two months before the Special Olympics, tragedy strikes. Liinah's father suddenly dies. Knowing that she **performs** better with her parents in attendance, she is faced with a problem. If she **confesses** this to her coach, he may cut her from the team. If she doesn't tell anyone, she will have to face her fears alone. Liinah decides to swallow her sadness and keep practicing.

Before she knows it, the day of the biggest race of her life is upon her. Liinah's stomach is jumpy as she waits for the race to start. Her eager eyes scan the large crowd. It is her first trip away from her home in Uganda, and she feels completely alone. Even though her family can't attend, two Irish social workers working with **foster** children in Uganda

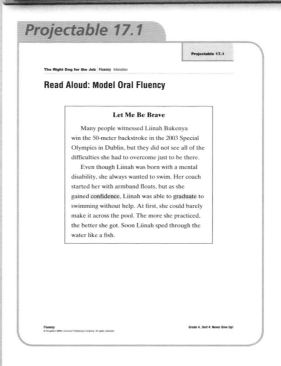

Projectable 17.1

have met Liinah in her country. Liinah looks into the crowd and catches their smiling faces. She smiles back, takes a deep breath, and **patiently** waits for the start of the race. **2**

Suddenly, the buzzer sounds, and Liinah springs into action. Using every muscle, she glides swiftly through the water. She is in the lead, but she knows other racers are close behind and working to catch her. Liinah's muscles scream for her to slow down, but she will **disobey** the urge until she reaches the edge of the pool. Suddenly, the crowd cheers, and Liinah knows she has won! **3**

Later, in a grand **ceremony**, Queen Sylvia Nagginda of Uganda presents Liinah with a shiny gold medal to **reward** her hard work. The medal is a sparkling **symbol** of Liinah's great effort. She smiles as the Queen gives her a big hug. **4**

Listening Comprehension

Preview the Target Skill

Read aloud the passage using appropriate intonation. Then ask students the following questions.

1 Sequence of Events
What events led to Liinah participating in the Special Olympics swim competition? Sample answer: Liinah always wanted to swim; she worked with a coach; she learned how to swim without help; she practiced.

2 Summarize
Summarize how Liinah handled the tragedy in her life with great courage. Liinah kept practicing so her coach would not cut her from the team. She kept her sadness to herself.

3 Sequence of Events
What occurred in Liinah's life just before she won the race? When the buzzer sounded she swam fast and took the lead; her muscles were screaming to stop, but she kept on going.

4 Monitor/Clarify
What happened to Liinah after the race? The crowd cheered for her. In an awards ceremony, the Queen of Uganda presented Liinah with a gold medal to reward her efforts and gave her a big hug.

Target Vocabulary

Reread "Let Me Be Brave" aloud.

As you read, pause briefly to explain each highlighted vocabulary word.

Discuss the meaning of each word as it is used in the Read Aloud.

confidence feeling sure about abilities

graduate to finish school or training

performs acts

confesses admits something is true

foster cared for by an adult for a period of time

patiently waiting calmly, without getting annoyed

disobey not do what you are told

ceremony a special event celebrating something

reward to give a person something they have earned

symbol an object that stands for something else

☑ Introduce Vocabulary

SHARE OBJECTIVE

• Understand and use the Target Vocabulary words.

Teach

Display and discuss the **Vocabulary in Context Cards,** using the routine below. Direct students to **Student Book pp. 426–427.** See also **Instructional Routine 9.**

1 **Read and pronounce the word.** Read the word once alone, then together with students.

2 **Explain the word.** Read aloud the explanation under *What Does It Mean?*

3 **Discuss vocabulary in context.** Together, read aloud the sentence on the front of the card. Help students explain and use the word in new sentences.

4 **Engage with the word.** Ask and discuss the *Think About It* question with students.

Apply

Give partners or small groups one or two **Vocabulary in Context Cards.**

• Help students start the *Talk It Over* activity on the back of the card.

• Have students complete activities for all the cards during the week.

Lesson 17

Vocabulary in Context

☑ **TARGET VOCABULARY**

reward
graduate
symbol
foster
disobey
confidence
patiently
confesses
ceremony
performs

Vocabulary Reader   Context Cards

426

1 **reward**
Many dogs reward the hard work of their caretakers with affection.

2 **graduate**
Some dogs graduate to show they have completed obedience school.

3 **symbol**
For some dogs, a leash is a symbol, or sign, of outdoor fun.

4 **foster**
Some service dogs live with foster caretakers for a short time.

ELL **ENGLISH LANGUAGE LEARNERS**

Scaffold

Beginning Use actions to demonstrate the meaning of *reward, performs,* and *patiently.* Then have students perform the actions as you say each word.

Advanced Ask students questions to confirm their understanding, such as, *Would you walk with confidence after winning the state science fair? Why?*

Intermediate Have students complete sentence frames for each Vocabulary word. For example, *If you _____ people, you give them something they have earned. (reward)*

Advanced High Have partners ask and answer questions about each Vocabulary word. For example, *Why are students so happy when they graduate?*

See ELL Lesson 17, pp. E12–E21, for scaffolded support.

- Study each **Context Card**.
- Use context clues to determine the meanings of these words.

disobey

Well-trained dogs don't disobey, or ignore, their owners' commands.

confidence

Praising a dog helps it gain confidence that it is learning well.

patiently

Show dogs must remain calm and wait patiently for long periods.

confesses

This girl confesses, or admits, that daily care of a dog is hard work.

ceremony

Dogs who win awards may be honored in a special event known as a ceremony.

performs

This working dog performs its job by herding sheep.

427

VOCABULARY IN CONTEXT CARDS 161–170

reward

Many dogs reward the hard work of their caretakers with affection.

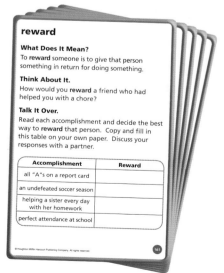

reward

What Does It Mean?
To **reward** someone is to give that person something in return for doing something.

Think About It.
How would you **reward** a friend who had helped you with a chore?

Talk It Over.
Read each accomplishment and decide the best way to **reward** that person. Copy and fill in this table on your own paper. Discuss your responses with a partner.

Accomplishment	Reward
all "A"s on a report card	
an undefeated soccer season	
helping a sister every day with her homework	
perfect attendance at school	

front   back

Monitor Vocabulary

Are students able to understand and use Target Vocabulary words?

IF...	THEN...
students have difficulty understanding and using most of the Target Vocabulary words,	▶ use **Vocabulary in Context Cards** and differentiate the **Vocabulary Reader**, *Animals Helping People*, for Struggling Readers, p. T132. *See also Intervention Lesson 17, pp. S12–S21.*
students can understand and use most of the Target Vocabulary words,	▶ use **Vocabulary in Context Cards** and differentiate the **Vocabulary Reader**, *Animals Helping People*, for On-Level Readers, p. T132.
students can understand and use all of the Target Vocabulary words,	▶ use **Vocabulary in Context Cards** and differentiate the **Vocabulary Reader**, *Animals Helping People*, for Advanced Readers, p. T133.

SMALL GROUP Options

Vocabulary Reader, pp. T132–T133
Group English Language Learners according to language proficiency.

Develop Background

- Learn about important ideas in "The Right Dog for the Job."
- Build background using the Target Vocabulary words.

ELL **ENGLISH LANGUAGE LEARNERS**

Scaffold

Beginning Help students list common working animals. Guide students to identify horses, cattle, sheep, dogs, and other animals.

Intermediate Demonstrate the meaning of the Vocabulary Words in *The Right Dog for the Job* using simplified language.

Advanced Have students complete the following sentence frame: *Service animals are trained to _____ people*. Then have partners discuss how animals can help people.

Advanced High Have partners discuss what it feels like to receive a reward for something. Have them work with a partner to write short sentences about a reward they would like to receive, using Target Vocabulary.

See ELL Lesson 17, p. E12–E21, for scaffolded support.

☑ Target Vocabulary

1 | Teach/Model

- Use the chart of Service Dog Tasks on **Student Book p. 428** to explain that "The Right Dog for the Job" is about a dog who **performs** tasks that help people in amazing ways.
- Use **Vocabulary In Context Cards** to review the student-friendly explanations of each Target Vocabulary word.
- Have students silently read **Student Book p. 428**. Then read the passage aloud.

2 | Guided Practice

Ask students the first item below and discuss their responses. Continue in this way until students have answered a question about each Target Vocabulary word.

1. Describe an activity that gives you **confidence** in yourself.
2. Why might it be bad if drivers **disobey** traffic signs?
3. Tell about a time when you had to wait **patiently** for something.
4. Explain how the flag is an important **symbol** in the United States.
5. When people take in **foster** animals, they care for them. How does this benefit the community?
6. It is fun to watch when an animal **performs**. What tricks have you seen?
7. If someone **confesses** to not knowing an answer, what should he or she do?
8. What could you do to **reward** an animal for good behavior?
9. Describe a **ceremony** that you have attended or witnessed.
10. What would you like to do after you **graduate** from school?

Background

☑ TARGET VOCABULARY **Service Animals** Do you know dogs that show confidence, don't disobey, and behave patiently? Some dogs with these traits go into training to become service animals. Service animals help people with disabilities. They are a symbol of the cooperation between humans and animals. Not all service animals are canine, however. Cats, monkeys, and birds can be trained too!

A service animal trainer is part foster parent and part coach. The trainer must make sure the animal performs its tasks very well. If the animal doesn't succeed, the trainer confesses that it won't be a good service animal after all. But if all goes well, the trainer is glad to reward the animal with a ceremony so that it may graduate and get to work.

Using this chart, name some specific ways that a service dog might help someone.

Service Dog Tasks

	For a person with difficulty seeing:	▸ Find a clear path for the person. ▸ Help the person avoid obstacles such as low-hanging branches and large objects.
	For a person with difficulty hearing:	▸ Alert the person to doorbells and smoke alarms. ▸ Alert the person when someone is approaching from behind or from the side.
	For a person with difficulty moving:	▸ Pull the person in wheelchair. ▸ Help the person get up after a fall.

3 | Apply

- Have partners take turns reading aloud a paragraph on **Student Book p. 428** to one another.

- Tell partners to pause at and explain each highlighted vocabulary word as they read.

- Have each partner use one vocabulary word in a new sentence.

Introduce Comprehension

SHARE OBJECTIVES

- Identify the sequence of events in text.
- Describe the relationship of ideas organized in sequence.
- Use the sequence of events to summarize text.

SKILL TRACE

Sequence of Events

Introduce	T90–T91
Differentiate	T134–T135
Reteach	T142
Review	T108–T109
Test	Weekly Tests, Lesson 17

ELL ENGLISH LANGUAGE LEARNERS

Scaffold

Beginning Write these sentences on the board, and read them aloud: *First, I eat breakfast. Then I brush my teeth.* Have students act out the activities in order.

Intermediate Have students use the following sentence frames to describe what they did before school: *First, I _____. Then I _____. Finally, I _____.* Point out the signal words.

Advanced Using the third event on **Projectable 17.2,** draw a flow chart. Work with students to complete it.

Advanced High Have partners say three events in order, using signal words such as *first, then,* and *finally.*

See also ELL Lesson 17, pp. E12–E21, for scaffolded support.

 Sequence of Events; Summarize

1 Teach/Model

AL *Academic Language*

infer to figure out something that is not directly stated

sequence of events the order in which events take place in time

- Tell students that the order of events in a text is called the **sequence of events.** Point out that signal words such as *first, before,* and *after* can help readers **infer,** or figure out, where events belong in the sequence.

- Read and discuss with students **Student Book p. 429.** Have them use the Academic Language.

- Display **Projectable 17.2.** Have students read "Hearing Dogs."

SEQUENCE OF EVENTS Explain that signal words can help readers understand event order.

- Tell students that you will use the Flow Chart to record the passage's sequence of events.

Projectable 17.2

Projectable 17.2

The Right Dog for the Job | Introduce Comprehension Sequence of Events; Summarize

Sequence of Events; Summarize

Hearing Dogs

International Hearing Dog, Inc. (IHDI) trains dogs for people who are deaf or hard-of-hearing. First, they rescue dogs from animal shelters and make sure they are healthy. Then they train the dogs for four to eight months. The dogs learn to respond to normal sounds you would hear in a house: the doorbell, telephone, smoke alarm, or alarm clock. They learn basic commands such as "sit," "stay," and "down."

After the dog completes training, IHDI places the hearing dog in its new home. The trainer works with the dog and its new master for a week. After 90 days, the dog becomes certified as a hearing dog!

Sequence of Events Use a Flow Chart to put the sequence of events in order.

Event: IHDI rescues dogs from animal shelters.

Event: IHDI trains the dogs for four to eight months.

Event: A dog is placed with its new owner and goes through a week of training. After 90 days, the dog is certified as a hearing dog.

Summarize Use the Flow Chart to summarize important parts of the text.

Introduce Comprehension
© Houghton Mifflin Harcourt Publishing Company. All rights reserved.   Grade 4, Unit 4: Never Give Up!

Think Aloud *IHDI rescues dogs and trains them for service. The signal word* after *tells me that a dog being placed with its new owner comes after the dog is trained, but before it is certified.*

SUMMARIZE Explain that readers can use sequence of events to summarize, or retell, the main events of a text.

Think Aloud *I understand the main events involved in choosing and training a hearing dog after reading the text.*

Comprehension

✔ **TARGET SKILL** **Sequence of Events**

As you read "The Right Dog for the Job," notice the sequence, or order, in which events take place. Some events may happen at the same time, but others follow one another. Look for dates and clue words, such as *next, then,* and *now,* to help you. Use a graphic organizer like this one to help you identify the sequence of events in the story.

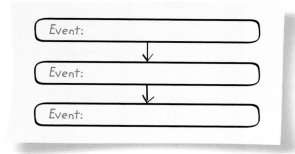

✔ **TARGET STRATEGY** **Summarize**

As you read, use the sequence of events and your graphic organizer to help you summarize, or briefly restate, the most important events of the selection. You should use your own words in your summary to help make sure you understand the selection. Summarizing also helps to show how the author organizes events.

JOURNEYS **DIGITAL** **Powered by** DESTINATION Reading®
Comprehension Activities: Lesson 17

429

Monitor Comprehension

Are students able to identify sequence of events?

IF...	THEN...
students have difficulty identifying the sequence of events,	▶ **Differentiate Comprehension** for Struggling Readers, p. T134. *See also Intervention Lesson 17, pp. S12–S21.*
students can identify the sequence of events,	▶ **Differentiate Comprehension** for On-Level Readers, p. T134.
students can accurately use sequence of events to summarize text,	▶ **Differentiate Comprehension** for Advanced Readers, p. T135.

 Differentiate Comprehension: pp.T134-T135. *Group English Language Learners according to language proficiency. See also ELL Lesson 17, pp. E12–E21, for scaffolded support.*

2 Guided Practice

Have students work with a partner to copy and complete their own Flow Charts for "Hearing Dogs." Then have them review their Flow Charts together.

3 Apply

Turn and Talk Have partners use their Flow Charts to discuss the sequence of events in the text.

Have students determine the sequence of events in another text they have read recently. Have them record the sequence of events in a Flow Chart and share with a partner.

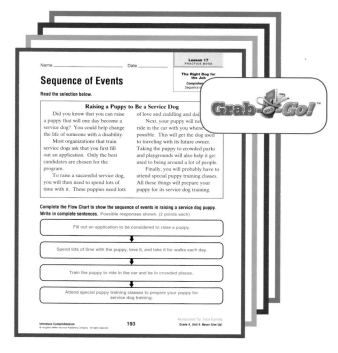

Practice Book, p. 193
See Grab-and-Go™ Resources for additional leveled practice.

Introduce Comprehension (SB p. 429) • **T91**

Introduce the Main Selection

TARGET SKILL

SEQUENCE OF EVENTS Explain that as they read, students will use **Graphic Organizer 4: Flow Chart** to record two sequences:

• events before Ira began training

• things that Ira learns during his service-dog training

TARGET STRATEGY

SUMMARIZE Students will use **Graphic Organizer 4** to summarize events in both sequences.

GENRE: Narrative Nonfiction

• Read the genre information on **Student Book p. 430** with students.

• Share and discuss **Genre Blackline Master: Nonfiction**.

• Preview the selection, and model identifying characteristics of the genre.

 *Think Aloud*

The title and photographs tell me this selection is about a dog that works. The photos make me think about a real dog with a job. These are clues that this text is nonfiction.

• As you preview, ask students to identify other features of narrative nonfiction.

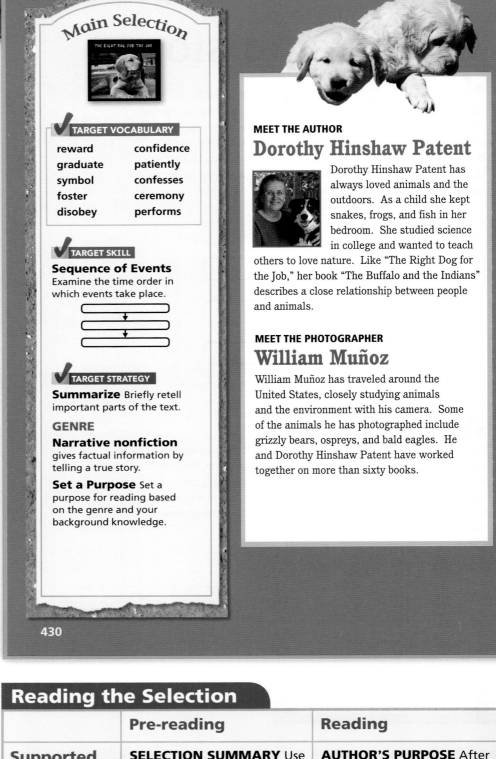

Main Selection

THE RIGHT DOG FOR THE JOB

✓ TARGET VOCABULARY

reward	confidence
graduate	patiently
symbol	confesses
foster	ceremony
disobey	performs

✓ TARGET SKILL

Sequence of Events
Examine the time order in which events take place.

✓ TARGET STRATEGY

Summarize Briefly retell important parts of the text.

GENRE

Narrative nonfiction gives factual information by telling a true story.

Set a Purpose Set a purpose for reading based on the genre and your background knowledge.

MEET THE AUTHOR

Dorothy Hinshaw Patent

Dorothy Hinshaw Patent has always loved animals and the outdoors. As a child she kept snakes, frogs, and fish in her bedroom. She studied science in college and wanted to teach others to love nature. Like "The Right Dog for the Job," her book "The Buffalo and the Indians" describes a close relationship between people and animals.

MEET THE PHOTOGRAPHER

William Muñoz

William Muñoz has traveled around the United States, closely studying animals and the environment with his camera. Some of the animals he has photographed include grizzly bears, ospreys, and bald eagles. He and Dorothy Hinshaw Patent have worked together on more than sixty books.

430

Reading the Selection

	Pre-reading	Reading
Supported	**SELECTION SUMMARY** Use Blackline Master 17.2 to give students an overview before they read. **AUDIOTEXT CD** Have students listen to the selection as they follow along in their books.	**AUTHOR'S PURPOSE** After reading the selection, discuss with students the author's purpose in explaining the steps Ira's trainer took so that Ira would be successful.
Independent	**PREVIEW** Have students look at the title and the photos and discuss what they think the selection will be about. Some students may read the story independently.	**TEXT EVIDENCE** Pause after pp. 433, 435, and 439. Have students write a question, answer, and page number where the evidence for the answer can be found. After reading, discuss students' responses.

THE RIGHT DOG FOR THE JOB

Ira's Path from Service Dog to Guide Dog

by Dorothy Hinshaw Patent
photographs by William Muñoz

Essential Question

What steps can you take toward success?

431

? Essential Question

- Read aloud the **Essential Question** on **Student Book p. 431.** *What steps can you take toward success?*

- Tell students to think about this question as they read "The Right Dog for the Job."

Set Purpose

- Explain that good readers set a purpose for reading based on their preview of the selection and what they know about the genre, as well as what they want to learn by reading.

- Model setting a reading purpose.

Think Aloud
I've seen guide dogs before, and I've always wondered how they are trained to do things like stop at red lights. I'll read to find out how guide dogs are trained.

- Have students share and record their reading purposes in journals.

JOURNEYS DIGITAL **Powered by** DESTINATIONReading®
Student eBook: Read and Listen

Blackline Master 17.2

Develop Comprehension

Pause at the stopping points to ask students the following questions.

1 ✔ **TARGET VOCABULARY**

Why might a **foster** *puppy coordinator need someone with patience, kindness, and experience raising dogs? Sample answer: Because a person like this will help to raise puppies who can later become service dogs.*

2 ✔ **TARGET SKILL**

Sequence of Events

Describe how the puppies changed and grew during their first six weeks of life. When they were born, their eyes and ears were closed. They grew, and their eyes and ears opened. Soon they began playing. At four weeks, they began to eat puppy food. At six weeks, they did not need their mother's milk.

3 **Main Idea and Details**

Why do you think Sandy might be a good choice to raise Ira? Sample answer: She knows how to handle golden retrievers because she already has one.

4 **Draw Conclusions**

What important task does Ira learn to perform very early? Why is this an important task for a service dog? Sample answer: He learns to retrieve things. It is important because he may have to retrieve things for the person with disabilities he is placed with.

Ira was born on Shy Bear Farm in Montana, along with his sister, Ivy, and his brother, Ike. Like all newborn puppies, the three young golden retrievers have closed eyes, velvety ears, and very soft fur. But unlike most puppies, these three were born for a special purpose. By the time they are two years old, each is expected to have become a service dog, helping a person who has difficulty moving around on his or her own to lead a fuller life. Ira, Ivy, and Ike are part of PawsAbilities, Canine Partners for People with Disabilities.

Brea, the puppies' mother, and Kathleen Decker, PawsAbilities' foster puppy coordinator, take good care of the puppies. They grow bigger and stronger. Their eyes and ears open so they can take in the world around them. Soon they are romping and playing together, getting bolder each day. Kathleen begins to feed them puppy food when they are four weeks old. By the age of six weeks, they no longer need their mother's milk. Soon it will be time to leave home.

Before they can help people with disabilities, service dogs need to learn to deal confidently with the world and whatever it might present to them—loud noises, smelly buses, crowds of people.

1

2

432

ELL **ENGLISH LANGUAGE LEARNERS**

Scaffold

Beginning Using the photos, preview the selection with students. Help them name objects they recognize, especially any of the Target Vocabulary pictured.

Advanced After reading pp. 432–433, have students describe the things that have happened to Ira so far.

Intermediate Explain that Ira is a kind of dog called a retriever that was originally bred for hunting. Help students understand the meaning of *retrieve.*

Advanced High After reading pp. 432–433, have students write three things summarizing what they have learned so far.

See ELL Lesson 17, pp. E12–E21, for scaffolded support.

Each puppy goes to live with a special person called a foster puppy raiser. The puppy becomes a member of the family, where it gets plenty of love, attention, and praise as the puppy raiser introduces it to the world.

When they are about eight weeks old, Ira, Ivy, and Ike meet their puppy raisers. Ira goes home with Sandy Welch, a sixth-grade teacher in Lolo, Montana. Sandy already has her own beautiful golden retriever, Laddy Griz. Laddy and Ira quickly become friends. Kathleen visits Ira and Sandy a month later. She wants to see how Ira is doing and check on his service-dog skills. **3**

One of the most important tasks a service dog performs is retrieving things such as dropped keys. Sandy has already been working on this skill with Ira, so Kathleen throws her keys and tells Ira to fetch them. He runs over, picks them up in his mouth, and brings them back to Kathleen. Good news—Ira is already on his way to becoming a service dog! **4**

✔ **STOP AND THINK**
Sequence of Events Explain, in chronological order, the events that happen to Ira on page 433.

Ira retrieves Kathleen's keys.

433

STOP AND THINK

✔ **TARGET SKILL**
Sequence of Events

- Remind students that charting the sequence of events as they read narrative nonfiction is a good way to keep track of important information.

- Display **Projectable 17.3a**.

- Model how to fill in the first event in Ira's life on the Flow Chart. Then fill in the third event.

- Prompt students to identify the event that happens after Ira goes to live with Sandy, but before Kathleen visits Ira. *Ira becomes friends with Sandy's dog, Laddy Griz.*

- Have students use **Graphic Organizer 4** to complete the **Stop and Think** activity on p. 433.

- If students have difficulty identifying the sequence of events, see **Comprehension Intervention** below.

- Have students continue to fill in their graphic organizers as they read.

COMPREHENSION INTERVENTION

✔ **TARGET SKILL**   Sequence of Events

SKILL SUPPORT Remind students that events in a text are often told in chronological, or time, order. Signal words such as *first, meanwhile,* and *later* can help readers determine the sequence of events. Guide students to find the signal words and phrases in these sentences:

• *After school, Mary went to the library and borrowed two books.* after

• *She returned the books three weeks later.* three weeks later

Read aloud the second paragraph on page 433. Have students find and name the events that happened to Ira on page 433. Ira goes to live with Sandy, a puppy trainer, where he will begin training as a service dog.

Guide students to add text events to their graphic organizers.

Projectable 17.3a

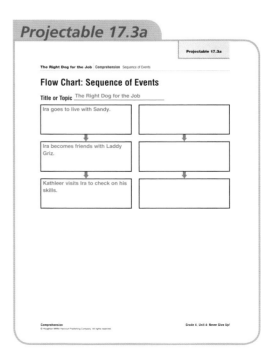

Develop Comprehension

5 ✔ TARGET VOCABULARY

*Why might a **symbol** be more useful than words to identify wheelchair-access areas? Sample answers: The symbol can help people who might not be able to read or who don't know the language used on the sign.*

6 **Analyze Supporting Details**

What text clues on these pages support the idea that all puppies need training in order to become service dogs? Sample answers: The puppies have to learn how to walk at heel on a leash; they learn to lie quietly under a table.

7 **Compare and Contrast**

Explain how Ira's experiences with Kathleen are different from those with Sandy, the puppy raiser. Kathleen teaches Ira specific tasks, such as retrieving keys and opening doors; Sandy helps Ira get used to different places and situations.

All along, the puppy raisers meet as a group to learn how to teach the young dogs what they need to know. The puppies have to learn how to come or to sit on command and how to walk at heel on a leash.

Kathleen also shows them how to teach the puppies to press a wheelchair-access sign with their paw. The symbol appears on buttons that open doors automatically when pressed. Kathleen uses a plastic lid attached to a stick with a strip of cloth. On the lid is the wheelchair-access sign. She puts a dog treat on the deck and covers it with the lid. One by one, the puppies sniff and push the lid with their noses, trying to get at the treat. But only when they scratch at it with a foot does Kathleen lift the stick so the puppy is rewarded. **5**

Ivy tries to figure out how to get at the treat under the plastic lid.

434

ELL ENGLISH LANGUAGE LEARNERS

Scaffold

Beginning Use simplified language, visuals, and gestures to explain *walk at heel* and *farmer's market*.	**Advanced** Have students respond to the questions in complete sentences. Provide corrective feedback as needed.
Intermediate For each question, accept one-word responses and expand them into sentences. For example, if a student's response to question 6 is "walk on a leash," expand by saying, "Yes, Ira learns to walk on a leash, but he learns to walk in a certain way—at heel." Have students repeat the expanded response and confirm their understanding.	**Advanced High** Have students tell how they know the answer to each question based on details from the story.

See ELL Lesson 17, pp. E12–E21, for scaffolded support.

Ira gets off the bus.

Next, the group goes to the bus station. The bus company loans PawsAbilities a bus and driver. The puppies practice getting on and off over and over again. They ride around town and learn to stay calm on the bus as it stops and starts. By the end of the day, riding the bus has become as natural as a trip in the car.

The puppy raisers take the dogs wherever they can, such as to sporting events and the farmers' market. Every two weeks, the group meets at a different place somewhere in town. At the mall, the puppies learn not to be distracted at the pet store or by the crowds of people walking by. They also practice pushing the button with the wheelchair sign to open the door. At the university, they learn how to pull open a door using a tug made of rope tied to the knob. At the library, they learn to lie quietly under the table while the puppy raisers look through books. They also learn how to enter the elevator correctly, walking right beside the puppy raiser instead of going in front or behind. It would be dangerous if the elevator door closed on the leash. **7**

6

435

CROSS-CURRICULAR CONNECTION

Science

Have students turn to **Student Book p. 428.** Tell students that many of the tasks on the chart are also performed by trained capuchin monkeys. Like service dogs, capuchins are trained from an early age. They are used mainly to help people who are paralyzed as a result of spinal cord injuries.

Why might a trained monkey be more helpful than a dog for someone with a spinal cord injury? Monkeys are able to do things like turn knobs and open cabinets, so they could be helpful to those who have restricted movement.

Student Book, p. 428

✔ TARGET STRATEGY
Summarize

- Explain that summarizing helps readers organize information by including only the main points or most important events. Help students identify the important events on **pp. 434–435.**

  > **Think Aloud** *Not all of the words on these pages are part of the main idea. For example, knowing that dogs are trained to become service animals by doing things over and over again is important, but knowing what each of those things are is not.*

- Ask volunteers to summarize Ira's experiences on **p. 435.** *Sample answer: Ira learns how to remain calm in everyday situations, such as riding on buses and going to the library.*

Practice Fluency

Intonation Read aloud the first paragraph on **Student Book p. 435** as students follow along.

- Tell students that good readers change the pitch in their voices when reading a sentence that starts with a time-order word such as "First," or "Next."

- Have students choral read the paragraph, taking care to change intonation for time-order words.

See **p. T110** for a complete fluency lesson on reading with intonation.

Develop Comprehension

✔ **8 | TARGET SKILL**

Sequence of Events

What is the next important part of Ira's training? Sandy begins to bring Ira to her classroom two days a week so he can learn other skills.

9 Draw Conclusions

Why does Sandy tell students not to pet a service dog in training? Sample answer: It might distract the dog from a task.

10 Use Text and Graphic Features

How does the photograph on page 436 make the information given in the selection clearer? Sample answer: It provides both a visual and text reference for the last paragraph on the page, where children take turns calling Ira's name.

✔ **11 | TARGET VOCABULARY**

When Ira performs a task correctly, he usually receives food as a **reward**. *What are some other kinds of rewards he could receive? Sample answers: a pat on the head, a chew toy*

Sandy brings Ira to her classroom two days a week. She explains to her students the importance of training Ira correctly.

"Ira needs to learn to lie down by himself and stay there, even **8** if he gets bored," she says. "You have to leave him alone, even if he wants to be petted, so he doesn't get distracted from his job. You can also help teach the other children not to pet a service dog in training." **9**

Ira has his own corner of the room, where he must lie quietly on his rug. If he gets up and wanders around, Sandy says in a firm voice, "Rug!" Then she tells Ira to sit, lie down, or stay. He must also learn to always stay close to the person he is helping.

When Sandy and the students work with Ira, they form a circle and bring Ira into the center. Then one of the children calls him. He knows he'll get a treat if he lays his head in the child's lap. The children take turns calling him, helping him learn to come reliably every time he is called. Then they help teach him to use his nose to push a light switch, another important job for a service dog to learn.

Ira learns to come when he is called.

10

436

It takes lots of practice for Ira to learn to flip a
light switch with his nose instead of his mouth.

Ira goes all over the school, so he gets used to noisy places
like the cafeteria and the gym during pep rallies. Sandy also
takes him to other classrooms and tells the other students about
service dogs.

As summer approaches, Sandy's students must say good-bye
to Ira. Each child gets a chance to say what having Ira in the
classroom meant to her or him.

"I feel special because I got to help train Ira," says one.

"I never liked dogs before Ira came, but now I like having
him around," confesses another.

"Having Ira in the classroom has made me feel beyond
wonderful," says a third.

To reward the children for their help, Sandy arranges a field
trip to Shy Bear Farm. The students take turns making dog toys,
working on scrapbooks for Ira's new companion, touring the
farm, and playing with the six-week-old puppies. They also get
to say one last good-bye to Ira.

(11)

✔ **STOP AND THINK**
Summarize Using your own
words, summarize the skills Ira
learns at Sandy's school.

437

STOP AND THINK

✔ **TARGET STRATEGY**
Summarize

- Remind students that a summary
  includes only the main ideas or the
  most important points of a selection.
  Summaries should also follow the
  order of the text events.

- Have students complete the **Stop and
  Think** activity on **Student Book p. 437**.

- If students have difficulty summarizing
  what Ira learned at Sandy's school, see
  Comprehension Intervention below for
  extra support.

- Have students continue adding text
  events to their graphic organizers.
  Display **Projectable 17.3b** and work
  with students to add to the Flow Chart.

Projectable 17.3b

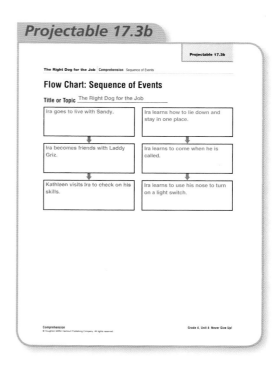

COMPREHENSION INTERVENTION

✔ **TARGET STRATEGY** **Summarize**

STRATEGY SUPPORT Remind students that they can use the sequence of
events and their flow charts to help summarize, or briefly restate, the main events in
the text. Model summarizing what they have learned so far about Ira: *Ira learned to
fetch keys and to ride a bus. Then he learned to open doors with a
wheelchair-access sign and to enter an elevator beside his handler.*

Read aloud **p. 436**. Point out that the story has shifted to a new setting. *What is
the setting on p. 436?* Sandy's classroom *What new things does Ira learn?*
to lie quietly on his rug, to do what he is told, to stay close to the person he's helping,
to come when called, to push a light switch with his nose

Guide students to add text events to their graphic organizers.

Develop Comprehension

12 **Make Inferences**

Why might Ira be able to learn a new career? Sample answer: He's smart, patient, and easily trained.

13 ✔ **TARGET VOCABULARY**

I wonder why it is important for a guide dog to have **confidence.** *I know that confidence is being sure of yourself. Maybe it takes confidence for a dog to learn new skills. What might be another reason that* **confidence** *is important for a service dog? Sample answer: Confidence helps a service dog know when to disobey for its owner's safety.*

14 **Understand Idioms**

What does the expression "running a red light" mean? It means going through a red light without stopping.

15 **Compare and Contrast**

Explain how service dogs and guide dogs are similar and how they are different. Similar—obedient, smart, confident, calm, loving; Different—a service dog always obeys and does things like picking up dropped keys; a guide dog wears a special harness, can disobey its owner for safety reasons, and guides its owner through traffic

---

As summer starts it's time for Ira to leave Sandy and go for more detailed service-dog training. But his assigned training facility isn't ready yet. Glenn Martyn, director of PawsAbilities, can't find another service-dog group that can use Ira. Everyone worries. What will happen? Can Ira learn a new career?

Though they rarely take dogs raised and trained elsewhere, Guide Dogs for the Blind in San Rafael, California, steps in. "Ira has lots of confidence, which is very important in a guide dog, so we'll give Ira a chance," says their coordinator. "But we'll have to change his name. Each dog we train has a different name, and we already have one called Ira. We'll just change the spelling to 'Irah' so he won't have to learn a new name." **12**

Now Irah needs to learn a whole new set of skills, which takes four to five months. He has to get used to wearing a guide-dog harness. Trainer Stacy Burrow helps him learn many things, such as stopping at street corners and crossing only when the way is clear.

The most important thing a guide dog must learn is intelligent disobedience. Knowing when to disobey can enable a guide dog to save its owner's life. For example, if the blind person tells the dog to go forward when a car is running a red light, the dog must refuse to obey. Irah is smart. He passes the program with flying colors. **14**

13

Stacy works with Irah on the Guide Dogs for the Blind campus.

15

STOP AND THINK

Author's Craft The author's **word choice** often includes signal words such as *next* and *all along* to explain the sequence of events. Find a signal word or phrase on page 439.

438

ELL **ENGLISH LANGUAGE LEARNERS**

Scaffold

Beginning Have students study the photo on p. 438. Explain that Irah will learn to be a guide dog for the blind. Point out the harness.

Advanced After students read p. 438, have them tell you what Irah needs to learn how to do.

Intermediate Have students complete the following sentence frames: *Irah must learn how to _____. He also must learn how to _____.*

Advanced High Have students work with a partner to give an oral summary of what Irah learns in his training as a guide dog.

See ELL Lesson 17, pp. E12–E21, for scaffolded support.

After training, Irah is paired with Don Simmonson, a piano tuner who had already retired two guide dogs after they got too old to work. Irah and Don work together for three weeks in San Rafael, learning to be a team. Then it's time to graduate.

Sandy comes from Montana for the graduation. She gets to see Irah and meet Don before the ceremony. Irah and Sandy are delighted to be together again, but Irah clearly knows his place is now with Don.

During the graduation ceremony, Don's name is announced when his turn comes. Sandy hands Irah over to Don. Irah is Don's dog now, and the two will be loving, giving partners. Sandy will miss Irah, but she is happy that he has found a home with someone like Don.

At home in Kennewick, Washington, Don and Irah continue to learn to work together. Grayson, Don's retired guide dog, also lives with them. Grayson and Irah become fast friends, playing together just like Irah and Laddy did.

Stacy, Sandy, and Irah stand by as Don speaks at the graduation.

439

STOP AND THINK
Author's Craft: Word Choice

- Writers use signal words to help readers understand the sequence of events.

- Signal words often are found at points where things change in a story. Some examples of signal words are *before, after, next, all along, first,* and *later,* and time words like *two months.*

- Model answering the **Stop and Think** question on **p. 438**.

Think Aloud *Irah goes through a lot of changes, so I will look for signal words to show each change. The first word on the page is a signal word—after. Irah and Don worked together for three weeks, so three weeks helps me understand that time has passed.*

Turn and Talk

? Essential Question

Have partners discuss the kinds of things service and guide dogs such as Irah are trained to do. What steps are taken to make sure that Irah is a successful guide dog?

Develop Comprehension

16 ✔ TARGET VOCABULARY

Describe a time when Irah might have learned to wait **patiently***.*
Sample answer: Sandy made Irah lie on his rug for long periods of time. He may have wanted to get up, but he was not allowed to.

17 Analyze Characters' Feelings

Explain how their experiences working with Irah might make Sandy's students feel now. Sample answer: They're proud of their roles in Irah's training, which may make them more confident about their own abilities.

18 ✔ TARGET SKILL

Sequence of Events

What do Don and Irah get to do at the end of the selection? Sandy invites them to the eighth-grade graduation of the students who helped train Irah when he was a puppy.

When Don goes to work, Irah guides him. Once they enter the room with the piano, Don says, "Irah, find the piano," and Irah leads him to it. Then Don gets to work and Irah lies down nearby, waiting patiently, as he learned to do in Sandy's classroom. He is there for Don whenever he is needed. **16**

"I'm so glad Irah and I found each other," Don says. "He's just the right dog for me."

Sandy and Don become friends, and, as a surprise, Sandy invites Don to the eighth-grade graduation of the children who helped train Irah.

Don's wife, Robbie, drives their motor home to Montana for the graduation. After Sandy talks to the audience about Irah and Don, she shows a movie of their graduation from Guide Dogs for the Blind. Then she announces that Don and Irah are in the auditorium, and Joey, Irah's favorite student, escorts them to the stage. The surprised students are delighted to see the results of their hard work and the hard work of so many others. Their own canine student, Irah, is now a working guide dog! **17** **18**

Joey escorts Don and Irah to the stage for their big moment.

440

Your Turn

Best Friends

Short Response Dogs and humans have been helping each other for thousands of years. Humans feed and shelter dogs. Dogs help herd animals and protect their owners. Write a paragraph about other ways dogs and humans help each other.
SOCIAL STUDIES

Train a Puppy

Make a Flyer With a partner, make a flyer inviting people to become foster puppy raisers. Briefly summarize what puppy raisers need to do. Be sure to include drawings of puppies.
PARTNERS

The Writer's Reasons

Turn and Talk With a partner, make a list of the steps it took to turn Ira into a guide dog. Discuss what you think is the most important thing a dog raiser can do to train a successful guide dog.
SEQUENCE OF EVENTS

441

Have students complete the activities on page 441.

Best Friends Students may have little prior knowledge about how dogs and humans can help each other. Provide resources such as nonfiction books and online articles about the relationships between people and dogs.
SOCIAL STUDIES

Train a Puppy Show students examples of flyers that they might find on a public bulletin board. Point out text features such as fonts of different styles and sizes, boldface or italic text, and graphics. Have students refer to the selection as they write tips and draw pictures of puppies. PARTNERS

The Writer's Reasons Give students a timeline template to use as they list the steps of training Ira. Have students look for repetition of certain words or phrases in the steps. This will help them select the most important thing to do when training a successful guide dog. SEQUENCE OF EVENTS

Oral Language Have partners give each other oral instructions on how to teach a dog to do one of the tasks described in the selection. Have partners restate each other's instructions and then follow them by pretending to do the steps. Use the Retelling Rubric at the left to evaluate students' responses.

Retelling Rubric

4	Excellent	Students provide clear, logical, sequential instructions that are very easy for their partners to follow.
3	Good	Students provide accurate, sequential instructions that are relatively easy for their partners to follow.
2	Fair	Students provide basic instructions that are a bit challenging for their partners to follow.
1	Unsatisfactory	Students provide unclear, nonsequential instructions that are difficult or impossible for their partners to follow.

Connect to Traditional Tales

PREVIEW THE TRICKSTER TALE

- Tell students that this selection is a kind of traditional story known as a **trickster tale**. Ask students to read the definition of a trickster tale and preview the selection by reading the title and cast of characters.

DISCUSS TRICKSTERS

- Tell students that a *trickster* is a clever character, usually an animal, who plays tricks on other characters. Often the trickster is greedy or boastful. Sometimes another character fools the trickster.

- Tell students that the trickster tries to outsmart another character. He may succeed, or he may be outsmarted himself.

- Define key terms. A trickster can be a clever, greedy, and boastful character. However, not every trickster has these qualities. Sometimes a trickster can show qualities, such as regret and humility, that make the character more likeable.

- As students read, have them compare and contrast the actions of Coyote with the actions of trickster characters from other tales.

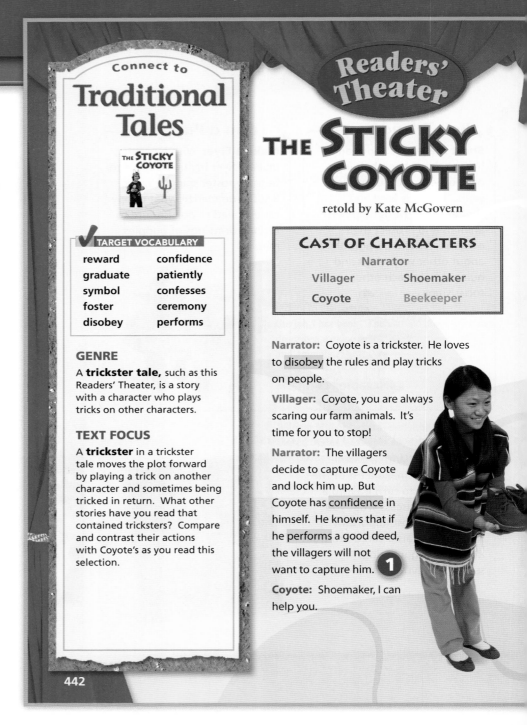

Connect to

Traditional Tales

THE STICKY COYOTE

✓ **TARGET VOCABULARY**

reward	confidence
graduate	patiently
symbol	confesses
foster	ceremony
disobey	performs

GENRE

A **trickster tale,** such as this Readers' Theater, is a story with a character who plays tricks on other characters.

TEXT FOCUS

A **trickster** in a trickster tale moves the plot forward by playing a trick on another character and sometimes being tricked in return. What other stories have you read that contained tricksters? Compare and contrast their actions with Coyote's as you read this selection.

442

Readers' Theater

THE STICKY COYOTE

retold by Kate McGovern

CAST OF CHARACTERS

Narrator

Villager	Shoemaker
Coyote	Beekeeper

Narrator: Coyote is a trickster. He loves to disobey the rules and play tricks on people.

Villager: Coyote, you are always scaring our farm animals. It's time for you to stop!

Narrator: The villagers decide to capture Coyote and lock him up. But Coyote has confidence in himself. He knows that if he performs a good deed, the villagers will not want to capture him.

Coyote: Shoemaker, I can help you.

ELL **ENGLISH LANGUAGE LEARNERS**

Scaffold

Beginning Read the cast of characters with students, and help them identify the characters in the photographs. Be sure students understand the play format.

Advanced Have students practice reading the characters' lines orally, using appropriate expression. Model expression as necessary.

Intermediate Have students complete the following sentence frames:

_____ likes to play tricks.

_____ is carrying _____ in the pot.

Coyote made the _____ laugh.

Advanced High Have partners take turns asking and answering questions about the characters in the story.

See ELL Lesson 17, pp. E12–E21, for scaffolded support.

Shoemaker: How?

Coyote: I see you have made some special shoes for Beekeeper's daughter.

Shoemaker: That's right. She will wear them for a ceremony at school. She is going to graduate this year.

Coyote: I will deliver the shoes to Beekeeper for you.

Narrator: So Coyote takes the shoes and heads to Beekeeper's house. He hopes the villagers will want to reward him for his kindness. Suddenly, Coyote sees Beekeeper coming down the path carrying a big pot. On the front is a picture of a bee.

Coyote: That bee is a symbol. There must be honey in that pot. Yum!

Narrator: Coyote waits patiently for Beekeeper. Then Coyote drops the shoes to distract Beekeeper.

Beekeeper: Why are these shoes on the ground?

Narrator: When Beekeeper puts down her pot of honey, Coyote quickly grabs it and eats some honey.

Coyote: Mmm. Sticky and delicious. Wait, what's this? A fly is stuck on my snout!

Narrator: Coyote rolls on the ground to get the fly off, but his sticky fur gets covered with twigs and leaves. Some villagers see Coyote and think he is a monster. They run away.

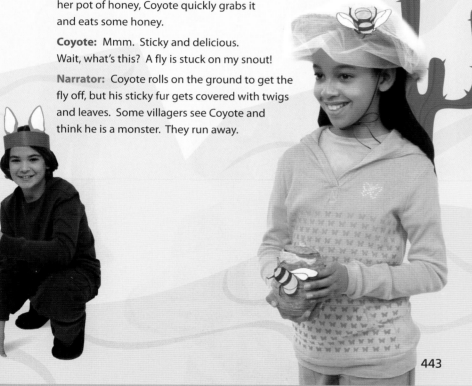

443

Practice Fluency

Intonation Have students listen as you read aloud relevant dialogue on **Student Book pp. 442–444.**

- Remind students that good readers change intonation for different types of sentences. Question marks and exclamation marks tell readers to change pitch, or the levels of sound in their voices.

- Have students partner read this selection. Remind them to change intonation appropriately as they read questions and exclamations.

TARGET VOCABULARY REVIEW

✓ **TARGET VOCABULARY** **Vocabulary in Context Cards – Find the Word**

Have students work with a partner. One partner chooses a word and then says, "I am thinking of a word that means (definition)." The other student must find the correct card, read the word, and repeat the definition. Partners then switch roles until all the words are used.

Develop Comprehension

1 Cause and Effect

What makes the villagers want to capture Coyote and lock him up? Coyote was scaring the farm animals.

2 ✔ **TARGET VOCABULARY**

*Why do you think Coyote **confesses** to what he has done, instead of hiding or playing more tricks? He wants to be honest because he wants the villagers to like him and let him stay.*

3 Main Idea and Details

How does Coyote get the villagers to let him stay? He plays a trick on them and makes them laugh.

INTERPRET A TRICKSTER TALE

• Review the features of a trickster tale, and model how to explain what happens after Coyote outsmarts one of the villagers.

Think Aloud *Coyote drops the shoes in order to trick the beekeeper. He gets the honey he wants, but he also ends up scaring the villagers. Instead of lying about it, Coyote confesses to what he has done. This shows he is not really a bad person. In fact, the villagers laughed, so clever Coyote got what he wanted after all.*

• For additional practice with character types, have students complete the activity on **Student Book p. 691.**

Coyote: I am a mess! I will go into the river to clean myself off.

Narrator: Coyote washes the leaves off his fur.

Villager: There was a monster covered in leaves and sticks. Where did it go?

Coyote: That was no monster. It was I, Sticky Coyote. I was covered with honey and dirt and leaves.

Narrator: When Coyote confesses what he has done, the villagers laugh. **2**

Villager: What would we do without you, Coyote? You make us laugh. Of course you can stay in our village.

Coyote: Thank you, friends. I am happy to stay. I will try not to cause so much trouble.

Narrator: Since then, Coyote often helps the villagers. He even protects them sometimes, like a foster parent. Every now and then, however, he still loves to play a good trick. **3**

444

Weekly Internet Challenge

Narrowing a Search

• Review Internet Strategy, Step 2: Search and Predict.

• Explain that using quotation marks to search for "trickster tale" will yield far fewer results than a search without quotation marks.

• Describe how adding a plus sign or a minus sign can further narrow the search results; for example, "trickster tale" + coyote.

INTERNET STRATEGY

1. **Plan a Search** by identifying what you are looking for and how to find it.

2. **Search and Predict** which sites will be worth exploring.

3. **Navigate** a site to see how to get around it and what it contains.

4. **Analyze and Evaluate** the quality and reliability of the information.

5. **Synthesize** the information from multiple sites.

Making Connections

 Text to Self

Working with Animals Have you ever cared for an animal or trained a pet? Write a paragraph about a lesson you have learned from working with an animal or watching other people work with animals.

 Text to Text

Compare and Contrast Think about what you have read in "The Right Dog for the Job" and "The Sticky Coyote." Then research golden retrievers and coyotes to find out how they are similar and different. Make a poster that compares the two animals. Include a picture of each animal on your poster.

golden retriever

coyote

 Text to World

Connect to Social Studies Ira was first trained as a service dog and then as a guide dog. What other jobs and services can dogs be trained to do? Work with a group to research other ways dogs are trained to help humans. Present your findings to the class.

445

"The Sticky Coyote" Challenge

- Have students brainstorm a list of keywords to perform an Internet search about other trickster tales involving a coyote.

- Enter *"trickster tale"* + *coyote* as keywords, and perform an Internet search.

- Look at the number of results returned. Monitor students as they add another keyword by using a plus or minus sign and perform another Internet search.

- Explain to students that the addition of other keywords, with plus or minus signs, can narrow their search results even further.

- Have students share their findings with the class.

Making Connections

 Text to Self

Suggest that students begin by making a list of things they have done to care for a pet or what they have observed by watching someone else care for an animal. Then have them write a paragraph explaining three or four things done to meet the pet's needs.

 Text to Text

Have students use a Venn diagram to help them identify similarities and differences between golden retrievers and coyotes. Then have them list the similarities and differences side by side before creating their posters.

 Text to World

Explain to students that dozens of different dog breeds have been trained to do specific jobs. Suggest that they research the various breeds of dogs to find out what some of these special jobs are. Have them find photographs of the breeds in books or on the Internet to share with the class.

Deepen Comprehension

SKILL TRACE

Sequence of Events	
Introduce	T90–T91
Differentiate	T134–T135
Reteach	T142
Review	**T108–T109**
Test	Weekly Tests, Lesson 17

ELL ENGLISH LANGUAGE LEARNERS

Scaffold

Beginning Use the selection photos to review the steps in Ira's training as a service dog. Work with students as you list on the board what happened as Ira grew older and was trained.

Intermediate Provide sentence frames using signal words such as *first, then, after,* and *later.* Have students use the frames to state events from pp. 432–440.

Advanced Have students take turns naming events in Ira's life using signal words, such as *First Ira was a little puppy. Then he _____.*

Advanced High Have partners orally summarize the sequence of events that took place when Ira started his guide-dog training.

See ELL Lesson 17, pp. E12–E21, for scaffolded support.

☑ Infer Sequence of Events

1 Teach/Model

AL *Academic Language*

infer, sequence of events

• Explain that some events in a selection occur in a certain order. This time-order is known as the **sequence of events**. Readers should notice the sequence of events to better understand the selection.

• Authors do not always tell every event. Readers may need to use clues from the text and their own knowledge to **infer**, or figure out, events that the author has left out of the sequence.

• Signal words such as *first, next, then, finally, yesterday, tomorrow, now, before, after, later, ago, afterward, meanwhile, eventually,* and *immediately* provide clues to the sequence of events.

• Point out that sometimes authors interrupt the sequence by giving events that happened earlier or later in time.

• Remind students that they can monitor their comprehension of a text by using a Flow Chart to summarize the events in order.

• Display **Projectable 17.4.** Model using sequence of events to answer **Deepen Comprehension Question 1** and complete the first Flow Chart.

Think Aloud *The author writes about Ira's training process by describing each step as it happens. Ira is raised by a trainer from the time he is eight weeks old. He learns skills such as retrieving things such as lost keys. Then he learns to obey commands. Finally, he practices going out in public.*

Projectable 17.4

Projectable 17.4

The Right Dog for the Job | Deepen Comprehension Summarize Sequence of Events

Flow Chart: Summarize Sequence of Events

Deepen Comprehension Question 1
How does Ira get trained? Think about the order in which Ira learns what he needs to know to become a service dog. Support your answer with details from pp. 433–437.

| He learns to retrieve things, such as lost keys. |
| He learns to obey simple commands. |
| He practices his skills in public. |

Deepen Comprehension Question 2
How does Ira get ready to go out into public as a service dog? Support your answer with details from pp. 433–437.

| A trainer uses treats to teach puppies to press wheelchair access signs. |
| Puppy raisers take the dogs on buses and to public events. |
| Trainers teach puppies to handle doors and elevators. |

Deepen Comprehension Question 3
How does Ira find a placement after his original facility cannot take him?

Deepen Comprehension
© Houghton Mifflin Harcourt Publishing Company. All rights reserved.

Grade 4, Unit 4: Never Give Up!

Monitor Comprehension

Are students able to infer the sequence of events in a selection?

IF...	THEN...
students have difficulty determining events in a sequence,	▶ use the Leveled Reader for **Struggling Readers,** *Animal Doctors,* p. T136.
students have a basic understanding of sequence of events,	▶ use the Leveled Reader for **On-Level Readers,** *A Rural Veterinarian,* p. T137.
students can accurately infer events to complete a sequence,	▶ use the Leveled Reader for **Advanced Readers,** *Helping Wild Animals,* p. T138.

Use the Leveled Reader for **English Language Learners,** *Taking Care of Animals,* p. T139.

2 Guided Practice

- Reread **pp. 433–434** of "The Right Dog for the Job" with students.

- Explain that authors sometimes depart from sequential order by mentioning events that have already happened, repeating an event from another viewpoint, or skipping ahead to build suspense. Have students find an example where the author told an event out of sequence.

- Read and discuss **Deepen Comprehension Question 2** on **Projectable 17.4**. Use these prompts to guide students:

- *How does a trainer teach a puppy to press wheelchair-access signs?* The trainer uses treats and a plastic lid with the weelchair sign on it.

- *How does a puppy raiser get the puppy used to being out in public?* The puppy raiser takes the dog on buses and to public events.

- *What special skills do the dogs learn in public?* They learn how to handle doors and elevators.

- Have students complete the flow chart for **Question 2.**

GUIDED DISCUSSION Ask students to identify words that help them infer the sequence of events in this selection. Tell them to use the words they found to help them summarize the selection.

3 Apply

Turn and Talk Have students reread **p. 438** of "The Right Dog for the Job." Then have partners make a Flow Chart showing the sequence of events on the page. Have students work together to discuss and complete **Deepen Comprehension Question 3** on **Projectable 17.4**.

WRITE ABOUT READING Have students write their responses to **Deepen Comprehension Question 3**. Ask volunteers to share their responses.

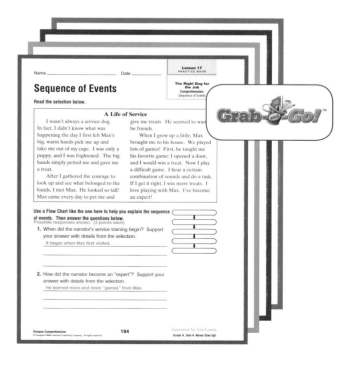

Practice Book p. 194
See Grab-and-Go™ Resources for additional leveled practice.

Fluency

- Read aloud with grade-appropriate fluency.
- Read fluently by adjusting intonation.

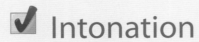

Intonation

1 Teach/Model

- Tell students that good readers change their intonation, or the tone and pitch in their voices, as they read to help communicate information accurately. For example, a rise in pitch at the end of a sentence indicates that a question is being asked.

- Have students turn to "The Right Dog for the Job," on **Student Book p. 433**. Point out the last paragraph ("One of the most important…").

- Read the paragraph in a monotone voice. Then reread the paragraph, modeling how to change your intonation to demonstrate the meaning of the words.

- Discuss how you changed your voice to show the ideas in the paragraph.

2 Guided Practice

Echo-read with students the last paragraph on **Student Book p. 440,** using punctuation to guide intonation.

- Guide students to change their intonation as they come to punctuation such as exclamation points. See **Routine Card 6.**

- Have partners take turns reading the paragraph aloud with changes in their voice. Listen in to monitor intonation.

3 Apply

- Tell students that with practice, they can improve their intonation.

- Have partners take turns reading **Student Book p. 440** aloud, using intonation appropriate to the text. Listen in to monitor fluency and self-correction.

- Allow each student to read the page three or four times.

Decoding

 More Sound/Spelling Changes

- Recognize words with sound/spelling changes.
- Decode words with sound/spelling changes.

1 Teach/Model

CONNECT TO SPELLING Point out the sound and spelling changes that occur in *marriage*, *baggage*, and other spelling words for the week. Write the words *marry* and *marriage* on the board. Have students repeat the words. Explain to students that the *y* in *marry* changes to *i* when adding the suffix *-age* to form *marriage*.

- Model how to decode *marriage*. Break the words into syllables and read each one aloud with students: *mar | ry*, *marri | age*. Point out that while *marry* and *marriage* have different pronunciations, their meanings are related. By recognizing the suffix *-age*, students can find a base word with which they are already familiar.

- Write *pack* on the board. Point out that adding the suffix *-age* forms the derived word *package*.

- Remind students that words derived from other words sometimes have a sound or spelling change.

2 Practice/Apply

DECODE WORDS WITH MORE SOUND/SPELLING CHANGES Write on the board the words below. Have students model how to decode the first word step by step. Have partners work to decode the other words and note the spelling changes, if any. Use **Projectable S1** to guide instruction with the decoding strategy.

band | bandage
band; band | age; no change

slip | slippage
slip; slip | page; add a second *p*

carry | carriage
car | ry; car | riage; *y* becomes *i*

- Call on volunteers to read the words and note familiar base words, such as *slip* in *slippage*.

- Have partners list examples of words with sound/spelling changes. Have them decode the words, noting the sound/spelling change.

- Use the **Corrective Feedback** if students need additional help.

Corrective Feedback

If students have trouble decoding words with sound/spelling changes, use the model below.

Correct the error. *Remember that the /j/ sound may be spelled with the suffix -age.*

Model how to decode the words. *In the word* passage *I recognize the suffix* -age. *I don't recognize the word* passage, *but I do know the base word* pass. *The suffix* -age *has the /j/ sound, and I already know how to pronounce* pass. *Therefore, this word must be pronounced* passage.

Guide students to try different examples to decode and recognize other words with the -age ending. *The words* package *and* carriage *both have the* -age *ending. What are the base words?* (pack, carry)

Check students' understanding. *Name two more words with the suffix* -age. (sample responses: shortage, baggage)

Reinforce Have partners reread the main selection looking for more words with *-age*.

Vocabulary Strategies

SHARE OBJECTIVE

• Learn and use words with suffixes -*ion*, -*ation*, and -*ition*.

SKILL TRACE

Suffixes	
Introduce	T42–T43, Unit 2
Differentiate	T140–T141
Reteach	T142
▶ **Review**	T42–T43, T260–T261, Unit 3; **T112–T113**; T262–T263, Unit 5; T212–T213, Unit 6
Test	Weekly Tests, Lesson 17

ELL ENGLISH LANGUAGE LEARNERS

Scaffold

Beginning Write *confess* and *confession* on the board. Say each word as you point to it. Circle the -*ion* ending in *confession* as you explain that the ending -*ion* is a suffix.

Intermediate Write the word *graduation* on the board. Circle the -*ion* ending. Help partners identify three more words with suffixes in "The Right Dog for the Job."

Advanced Have student partners find five words with suffixes in "The Right Dog for the Job." Students should identify the base word, using a dictionary as needed.

Advanced High Have students write three sentences using suffixed words and their base words. For example, *I can't wait to celebrate your birthday! It's a perfect time for a celebration.* (*celebrate, celebration*)

See ELL Lesson 17, pp. E12–E21, for scaffolded support.

✔ Suffixes -*ion*, -*ation*, -*ition*

1 Teach/Model

AL *Academic Language*

suffix an affix attached at the end of a base word or root that changes the meaning of the word

---

• Remind students that when a **suffix** is added to the end of a base word or root, the meaning of the word changes.

• Explain that the suffixes -*ion*, -*ation*, and -*ition* come at the end of the word and changes a verb to a noun. Words with these suffixes usually tell about a process, action, or result.

• Write the following sentence on the board: *We went to the graduation ceremony.* Read it aloud with students.

• Model looking at word parts and context to understand the meaning of *graduation*.

> **Think Aloud** *I'm trying to figure out the meaning of* graduation *in this sentence. I recognize the word,* graduate. *I know* graduate *means "to get a degree or diploma." I'm not sure what the* -ion *means. The context tells me there is a ceremony.* Graduation *must be the time and place you graduate.*

• Ask: *What else can we do to figure out a word, if looking at the word parts and looking around the word doesn't help?* (*look in a dictionary*)

• Repeat the process with the word *satisfaction*.

2 Guided Practice

- Display the top of **Projectable 17.5** and read aloud "Surfing Dogs."

- Display the Web on the bottom half of **Projectable 17.5.**

- Have students identify the words with suffixes -*ion*, -*ation*, and -*ition* from the passage. Circle or highlight the words and use them to complete the Web.

3 Apply

- Have partners use context and knowledge of base words and suffixes to figure out the meaning of the unknown words in the Web.

- Tell them to look in a dictionary to confirm the meaning of each word.

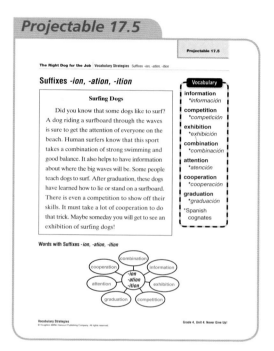

Projectable 17.5

Monitor Vocabulary Strategies

Are students able to identify and use these suffixes?

IF...	THEN...
students have difficulty identifying and using these suffixes,	▶ **Differentiate Vocabulary Strategies** for Struggling Readers, p. T140. *See also Intervention Lesson 17, pp. S12–S21.*
students can identify and use some words with these suffixes,	▶ **Differentiate Vocabulary Strategies** for On-Level Readers, p. T140.
students can identify and use words with these suffixes,	▶ **Differentiate Vocabulary Strategies** for Advanced Readers, p. T141.

 Differentiate Vocabulary Strategies: pp. T140–T141 *Group English Language Learners according to language proficiency.*

Practice Book p. 195
See Grab-and-Go™ Resources for additional leveled practice.

Connect and Extend

- Make connections across texts.
- Read independently for a sustained period of time.
- Take notes and identify sources correctly.
- Discuss and apply tips for evaluating and adapting spoken language.

The Right Dog for the Job   **The Sticky Coyote**

Vocabulary Reader

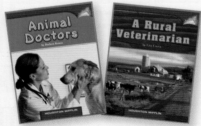

Struggling Readers   *On-Level Readers*

Advanced Readers   *English Language Learners*

Read to Connect

SHARE AND COMPARE TEXTS Have students compare and contrast this week's selections to make connections. Use the following questions:

- Compare and contrast how the people and animals in this week's selections achieved success. What qualities did they need to succeed?

- Using evidence from this week's selections, explain how the information about animals helping people added to what you already knew about animals.

CONNECT TEXT TO SELF Use these prompts to help deepen student thinking and discussion. Accept students' opinions, but encourage them to support their ideas with text details and other information from their reading.

- What is a career you are thinking about for your future? What will it take to successfully achieve that goal?

- In what ways do you or someone you know rely on animals for care, companionship, or some type of service?

Independent Reading

BOOK TALK Have student pairs discuss their independent reading for the week. Tell them to refer to their Reading Log or journal and paraphrase what the reading was about. To focus students' discussions, tell them to talk about one or more of the following:

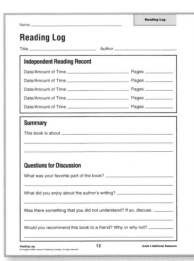

- different ways that animals help people,

- careers that involve working with animals.

Reading Log

Extend Through Research

TAKING NOTES/IDENTIFYING SOURCES Tell students that when they are doing research for a report, they will need to take notes. Remind them that they should paraphrase and not copy the information word for word.

- Using **Student Book p. 435,** model taking notes on how puppies are trained. Write the notes on the board.

    puppies taken to bus station

    practice getting on and off buses

    learn to stay calm

- Point out that notes may not be complete sentences.

- Explain that a report should include a list of sources including books and websites that the writer used to research the topic of the report. For books, students should include the book's title, author, and page number. For a website, they should list the website's address, or URL.

Listening and Speaking

EVALUATE AND ADAPT SPOKEN LANGUAGE Explain to students that many languages have specific words that are used when speaking formally. For example, people may use a different sort of language when speaking to their friends than they do when speaking to people in authority or to strangers.

- Have students reread **Student Book p. 436** and identify the command word used to train Ira.

- Have partners brainstorm a list of command words that could be used for the tasks described on the page.

- Tell students to select two commands and adapt them to use in a formal setting. Have them practice saying the commands using complete sentences. Then have partners share the command sentences with the class. While students are reciting their sentences, have audience members use the **Listening Log** to record how well each pair adapted informal commands into formal sentences.

Listening Log

Spelling ☑ Words with Final /j/ and /s/

Spelling Words

Basic

glance	since	✪ chance
judge	✪ practice	notice
damage	marriage	ridge
package	baggage	manage
twice	office	palace
✪ stage	message	bandage
carriage	bridge	

Review ✪ once, dance, ✪ change, ✪ age, bounce

Challenge
fringe, average, fleece, fragrance, excellence

✪ Forms of these words appear in "The Right Dog for the Job."

ELL ENGLISH LANGUAGE LEARNERS

Preteach

Spanish Cognates

Write and discuss these Spanish cognates for Spanish-speaking students.

office • *oficina*

package • *paquete*

Day 1

❶ TEACH THE PRINCIPLE

• Administer the Pretest. Use the Day 5 sentences.

• Write *judge* and *package* on the board. Guide students to identify the letters in each word that make the final /j/ sound. *(ge)* Repeat with the final /s/ sound using the chart.

Connect to Phonics	
These sounds...	**can be spelled...**
/j/	**ge** *as in* jud**ge**
	ge *as in* packa**ge**
/s/	**ce** *as in* glan**ce**
	ce *as in* practi**ce**

❷ PRACTICE/APPLY

Guide students to identify words with final /j/ and /s/ in the remaining Spelling Words.

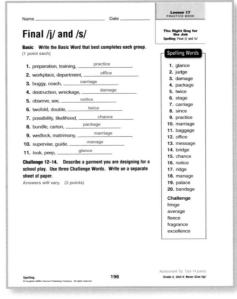

Practice Book p. 196

Day 2

❶ TEACH WORD SORT

• Set up two rows as shown. Model adding a Spelling Word to each row.

• Have students copy the chart. Guide students to write each Spelling Word on the row where it belongs.

/j/	baggage
/s/	palace

❷ PRACTICE/APPLY

Have students add words from "The Right Dog for the Job" to the sort.

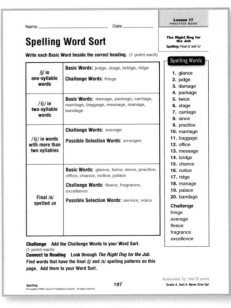

Practice Book p. 197

Day 3

❶ TEACH MULTIPLE-MEANING WORDS

- **WRITE** *My teacher will judge the science contest.* Define *judge*: "decide the winner."

- **WRITE** *The judge talked to the jury.*

- **ASK** What is the meaning of *judge* in this sentence? *an official who hears cases in a court of law*

- With students, list and discuss more meanings of *judge*. *Sample answers: person who knows enough to give a useful opinion; make decisions in a court of law; form an opinion on*

❷ PRACTICE/APPLY

- **WRITE** *stage, bridge, chance*

- **ASK** *How are these words like* judge? *They have more than one meaning.*

- Have partners look up each word in a dictionary or in an electronic resource to find two definitions for each word. Then, ask them to think of a sentence for each definition.

✏️ Have students write their answers.

Day 4

❶ CONNECT TO WRITING

- Read and discuss the prompt below.

✏️ **WRITE TO NARRATE**
Write a letter to a friend telling why you might like to train a service or guide dog. Use details from what you read this week.

❷ PRACTICE/APPLY

- Guide students as they plan and write their friendly letters (see p. T124).

- Remind students to proofread their writing.

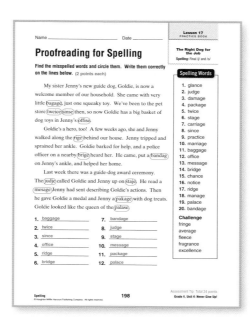

Practice Book p. 198

Day 5

ASSESS SPELLING

- Say each boldfaced word, read the sentence, and then repeat the word.

- Have students write the boldfaced word.

Basic

1. She gave the picture a **glance**.
2. Who will **judge** the show?
3. An early frost will **damage** the crops.
4. I got a **package** in the mail.
5. You are **twice** as old as I am.
6. Frogs are in a tadpole **stage** early in life.
7. A baby **carriage** is expensive.
8. The sun has been up **since** six.
9. I **practice** singing every day.
10. We wished the couple a happy **marriage**.
11. Check your **baggage** here.
12. The doctor's **office** is closed.
13. The **message** was in a bottle.
14. The **bridge** was built in 1910.
15. This is your last **chance**.
16. Did you **notice** my haircut?
17. The sun rose over the **ridge**.
18. I can **manage** the children.
19. The king lives in a grand **palace**.
20. The nurse put a **bandage** on the wound.

Grammar ☑ Adverbs

SHARE OBJECTIVES

- Identify adverbs and the verbs they describe.
- Use adverbs in writing and speaking.

ELL ENGLISH LANGUAGE LEARNERS

Scaffold

Beginning

Use the following sentence frames to demonstrate how to use adverbs to describe verbs.

The girl speaks _____ to the teacher. *often*

Sarah _____ walks down the hall. *slowly*

Intermediate

Use the sentence frames above to demonstrate how to use precise adverbs.

The girl speaks *quietly* to the teacher.

Sara *sluggishly* walks down the hall.

Advanced

Have students use adverbs to describe actions they do. Provide them with sentence frames such as the following:

I _____ eat my lunch. *quickly*

I play _____ at recess. *happily*

Advanced High

Have student pairs take turns orally describing their actions using adverbs.

See ELL Lesson 17, pp. E12–E21, for scaffolded support

Day 1 TEACH

DAILY PROOFREADING PRACTICE
An girl walked to the crouded bus stop.
A; crowded

① TEACH ADVERBS

- Display **Projectable 17.6**. Explain that an **adverb** tells something about a verb. Point out that some adverbs tell *how*. Tell students that an adverb that tells how usually ends in *–ly*.

  > Projectable **17.6**

- Model identifying the adverb and the verb it tells about in this sentence: *Poppi sits quietly by Anna's desk.*

Think Aloud *To identify the adverb and the verb it tells about, I ask these Thinking Questions:* **What is the verb?** *sits* **What word tells how about the verb?** Quietly *tells how Poppi sits.* Quietly *is the adverb.*

② PRACTICE/APPLY

- Complete **Projectable 17.6** with students.

- Write the following sentence on the board. Work with students to identify the verb and an adverb that tells *how* about the verb.

Pedro ran happily to meet his friend.
verb: ran; adverb: happily

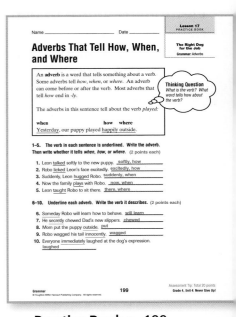

Practice Book p. 199

AL **Academic Language**

adverb a word that describes a verb

adverb of frequency tells how often an action happens

adverb of intensity tells how much or to what degree an action happens

Day 2 TEACH

DAILY PROOFREADING PRACTICE

The child waited patiently for the buss, bus.

1 EXTEND ADVERBS

Projectable 17.7

- Display **Projectable 17.7**. Point out that an **adverb of frequency** can tell *how often* an action happens. An **adverb of intensity** can tell *how much* or *to what degree* an action happens.

- Model identifying the verb and then the adverb that tells *how often* in this sentence: *Maria rarely wears sandals to school.*

> **Think Aloud** *To identify the adverb and the verb it tells about, I ask these Thinking Questions:* **Which word is the verb?** *wears* **Which word tells** how often *or* how much? *rarely*

2 PRACTICE/APPLY

- Complete **Projectable 17.7** with students.

- List the following verbs on the board. Have students use each verb in an oral sentence. Then have them use an adverb that tells *how often* or *how much* for each verb.

go	write
hold	talk

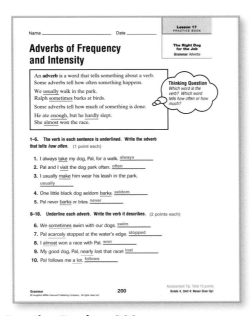

Practice Book p. 200

Day 3 TEACH

DAILY PROOFREADING PRACTICE

The bus stops alot to pik up children. *a lot; pick*

1 TEACH ADVERBS

Projectable 17.8

- Display **Projectable 17.8**. Explain that an adverb can be used at the beginning, middle, or end of a sentence.

- Model identifying the adverb in the example sentences: *Sometimes the guide dog needs a break. She eats a snack quickly and returns to work. I walk with her proudly.*

> **Think Aloud** *To identify the adverb and where in the sentence is used, I ask these Thinking Questions:* **Where is the adverb that tells about the verb?** *Sometimes, quickly, proudly* **In what part of the sentence is the adverb?** *beginning, middle, end*

2 PRACTICE/APPLY

- Complete the other examples on **Projectable 17.8** with students.

- Have students give oral sentences that place adverbs at the beginning, middle, and end of the sentences.

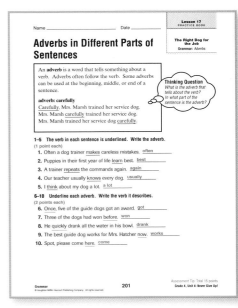

Practice Book p. 201

Day 4 REVIEW

DAILY PROOFREADING PRACTICE

The children walks to the store quick. *walk/walked, quickly*

① REVIEW ADVERBS

Remind students that an **adverb** tells something about a verb. Adverbs that tell *how* usually end in -*ly*. **Adverbs of frequency** tell how often an action happens. **Adverbs of intensity** describe how much an action happens.

② SPIRAL REVIEW

Possessive Nouns Review with students that a singular possessive noun shows ownership by one person or thing. Remind students that a plural possessive noun shows ownership by more than one person or thing.

• Write the following sentences on the board. Have students identify the type of possessive noun in each sentence.

The boys' jackets were in the car. *plural possessive noun*

The women's dresses are on sale. *plural possessive noun*

The child's toy is big. *singular possessive noun*

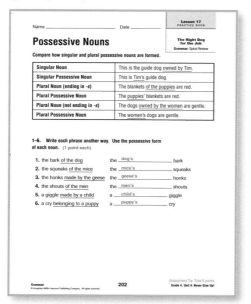

Practice Book p. 202

Day 5 CONNECT TO WRITING

DAILY PROOFREADING PRACTICE

They wait patient for a drinking of water. *patiently, drink*

① CONNECT TO WRITING

• Explain that precise adverbs tell readers how, when, and where things happen.

• Point out that adverbs make writing more interesting and easier to understand.

② PRACTICE/APPLY

• Display the following sentences. Have students identify the adverbs and decide if they tell *how* or *how often* something happens.

The children enter the room quietly. *quietly; how*

The teacher always says hello to them. *always; how often*

Lately, the students read their own books. *Lately; how often*

• Have students turn to **Student Book p. 446**. Read aloud the paragraph to review how to use **adverbs**. Discuss the example sentences. Then have students complete the **Try This!** activity.

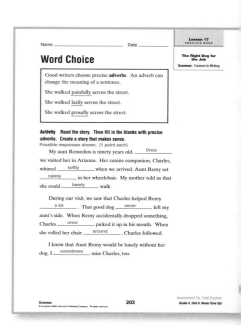

Practice Book p. 203

Grammar

What Is an Adverb? An **adverb** is a word that describes a verb. Adverbs give us more information about an action verb or a form of the verb *be*. They tell *how, when,* or *where*. Most adverbs telling *how* end with *-ly*.

Academic Language

adverb

adverb of frequency

adverb of intensity

Adverbs

How: The puppy happily chased its tail.

When: Later she barked at a noisy bird.

Where: Her mother was nearby.

An **adverb of frequency** tells how often something happens. **Adverbs of intensity** tell to what degree or how much something happens.

Adverb of Frequency: Puppies usually love walks.

Adverb of Intensity: Our puppy almost caught a squirrel.

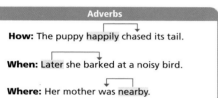 **Write the following sentences on a piece of paper and identify the adverbs. Note whether they tell about intensity or frequency.**

1. A cat visits our yard often.
2. Our dog barks loudly.
3. She nearly jumps through the window.

446

Word Choice When you write, use precise adverbs to create clear pictures of how, when, and where things happen for your readers. Precise adverbs also help to make your writing more interesting and easier to understand.

Less Precise Adverb	More Precise Adverb
A well-trained dog often follows orders.	A well-trained dog reliably follows orders.

Less Precise Adverb	More Precise Adverb
A service dog does not get distracted.	A service dog rarely gets distracted.
My dog doesn't leave my side.	My dog never leaves my side!

Connect Grammar to Writing

As you revise your friendly letter, look for opportunities to use precise adverbs. Use descriptive language to help readers create clear pictures in their minds.

447

Try This!

1. *often, frequency*
2. *loudly, intensity*
3. *nearly, intensity*

CONNECT GRAMMAR TO WRITING

- Have students turn to **Student Book p. 447** and read the page with them.

- Discuss with students how using adverbs can describe the intensity of frequency of an action and make the sentences easier to understand.

- Tell students that as they revise their friendly letters, they should look for opportunities to use adverbs.

- Review the Common Errors at right with students.

COMMON ERRORS

Error: Don **careful** picks up the puppy.

Correct: Don **carefully** picks up the puppy.

Error: The students did **good** on the test.

Correct: The students did **well** on the test.

Error: Ira runs **quicklier**.

Correct: Ira runs **quickly**.

Write to Narrate Focus Trait: Voice

- Write a friendly letter that includes thoughts and feelings.
- Identify the parts of a friendly letter.

Academic Language

greeting the opening address to a person in a letter

closing the closing address at the end of the letter

ELL ENGLISH LANGUAGE LEARNERS

Scaffold

Beginning Place categories of Formal and Friendly on the board. Fill in the formal side with expressions that are formal, like *Good Afternoon, Very good,* and *I appreciate that.* Then write matching friendly expressions. *(Hey!/What's up?; Cool!; Thanks)*

Intermediate Provide examples of formal sentences. Have students come up with friendly sentences that mean the same thing. Example: *My dog is so playful. My dog is so fun.*

Advanced Have partners brainstorm friendly greetings they use each day with friends. Then guide them to come up with formal phrases they use with teachers.

Advanced High Have partners take turns sharing formal expressions and choosing friendly expressions to substitute.

See ELL Lesson 17, pp. E12–E21, for scaffolded support.

JOURNEYS DIGITAL Powered by **DESTINATIONReading®** WriteSmart CD-ROM

Day 1 ANALYZE THE MODEL

❶ INTRODUCE THE MODEL

- Tell students that they will be writing a friendly letter in this lesson. Point out that they will be writing a longer type of narrative at the end of the unit.
- Discuss the following:

What is a Friendly Letter?

- It is a letter to someone the writer knows well, written in a friendly way.
- It begins with a **greeting** to the person receiving the letter, such as "Dear Martha."
- It ends with a friendly **closing** and signature, such as, "Love, Trudy."

- Display **Projectable 17.9**. Read aloud the Writing Model and identify the parts of the letter.

❷ PRACTICE/APPLY

- Work with students to label the conventions of a friendly letter in Writing Model 2.
- Work with students to find what happened first, next, and last in Writing Model 2.

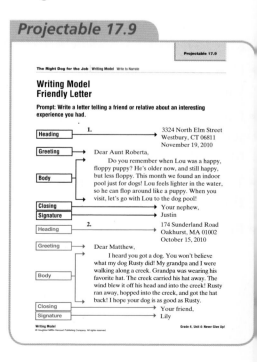

Projectable 17.9

LESSON	FORM	TRAIT
16	Descriptive Paragraph	Ideas
17	**Friendly Letter**	**Voice**
18	Narrative Composition	Word Choice
19	Prewrite: Personal Narrative	Organization
20	Draft, Revise, Edit, Publish: Personal Narrative	Ideas

Day 2 TEACH THE FOCUS TRAIT

1 INTRODUCE THE FOCUS TRAIT: VOICE

• Explain that writers convey their feelings by using words that they would use in normal speech. It helps the reader connect to the writer's text.

Connect to "The Right Dog for the Job"	
Instead of this...	**...the author wrote this.**
Ira has learned the right thing to do.	"Good news—Ira is already on his way to becoming a service dog!" (p. 433)

• Point out how the author can use words and expressions to maintain a friendly tone.

2 PRACTICE/APPLY

• Work with students to rewrite the following sentence in a friendly tone: *The students learned.* *Sample answer: The students really understood what they were taught.*

• Have students use a more friendly voice to rewrite the sentence: *Dogs help people. Sample answer: Dogs are the best! They are so caring and helpful. They often become best friends with people.*

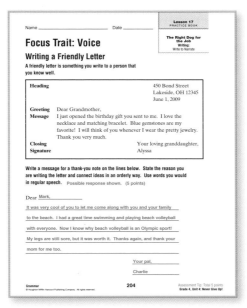

Practice Book p. 204

Day 3 PREWRITE

1 TEACH PLANNING A FRIENDLY LETTER

• Display **Projectable 17.10** and read aloud the prompt. Ask students to think about a friend or relative to whom they would like to write.

• Remind students that a Flow Chart can help them organize the events they want to write about in the order in which they happened.

2 PRACTICE/APPLY

• Point out the topic at the top of **Projectable 17.10**. Help students list interesting things that might happen at a dog show. Remind them that the ideas should all come from the topic. Help them complete the Flow Chart.

• Remind students that they should begin with a topic sentence. All the following sentences should be details that support the opening sentence.

• Work with students to complete the Flow Chart.

• Have students choose topics for their own friendly letters. Guide students to complete a Flow Chart for their own letters.

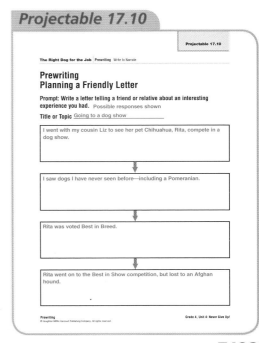

Day 4 DRAFT

① BEGIN A DRAFT

- Have students use their Flow Charts to draft their letters. Discuss with them the following:

> 1. **Begin** by addressing the person receiving the letter. Start out with a topic sentence that states what you will be describing in your letter.

> 2. **Organize** the events in order. Use an informal, friendly voice.

> 3. **Include** details about the event or experience. Use expressions that really sound like you. Use colorful, friendly words to help the reader understand your experience and feelings.

> 4. **Conclude** by noting why this experience was something you wanted to share. End the letter with a closing and your signature.

② PRACTICE/APPLY

- Have students draft their friendly letters. Remind them to use the graphic organizers they completed for prewriting.

- Remind students to use a friendly, informal voice.

Day 5 REVISE FOR VOICE

① INTRODUCE THE STUDENT MODEL

- Remind students that good writers show their voice in their friendly letters by choosing words and phrases that show their feelings and personalities.

- Read the top of **Student Book p. 448** with the class. Discuss with students the revisions made by the student writer, Anthony. Ask: *How does each version show Anthony's personality?*

② PRACTICE/APPLY

- Display **Projectable 17.11**. Work with students to add the other revisions Anthony made before creating his final copy. Ask students how each change improved his letter and whether there are any other changes they would make.

- Work with students to answer the *Reading as a Writer* questions on **Student Book p. 449**. Discuss students' responses.

- **Revising** Have students revise their letters using the Writing Traits Checklist on **Student Book p. 448**.

- **Proofreading** For proofreading support, have students use the **Proofreading Checklist Blackline Master.**

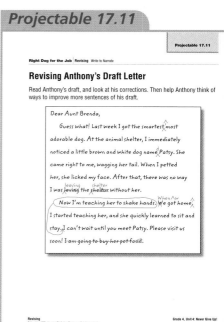

Projectable 17.11

Projectable 17.11

Right Dog for the Job | Revising Write to Narrate

Revising Anthony's Draft Letter

Read Anthony's draft, and look at his corrections. Then help Anthony think of ways to improve more sentences of his draft.

Dear Aunt Brenda,

   Guess what! Last week I got the smartest, most adorable dog. At the animal shelter, I immediately noticed a little brown and white dog named Patsy. She came right to me, wagging her tail. When I petted her, she licked my face. After that, there was no way I was leaving the shelter without her.

   Now I'm teaching her to shake hands. When we got home, I started teaching her, and she quickly learned to sit and stay. I can't wait until you meet Patsy. Please visit us soon! I am going to buy her pet food.

Revising

Grade 4, Unit 4: Never Give Up!

Write to Narrate

☑ Voice In "The Right Dog for the Job," Don lets his feelings come through when he says, "I'm so glad Irah and I found each other." When you revise your **friendly letter**, don't just tell what happened. Let your words show how you really feel. Use the Writing Traits Checklist as you revise your writing.

Anthony drafted a letter to his aunt about getting a dog. Then he revised some parts to let his feelings come through more clearly.

Writing Traits Checklist

☑ **Ideas**
Does my ending wrap up my main idea?

☑ **Organization**
Did I tell the events in chronological order?

☑ **Sentence Fluency**
Did I combine short, choppy sentences so they read smoothly?

☑ **Word Choice**
Did I choose vivid, interesting words?

☑ **Voice**
Did I sound like myself and show my feelings?

☑ **Conventions**
Did I use correct spelling, grammar, and mechanics?

Revised Draft

Dear Aunt Brenda,
Guess what! Last week I got the
∧ ~~Last week I got a dog. She is~~ smartest, most adorable dog.
~~a very good dog.~~ At the animal
shelter, I noticed a little brown and
white dog named Patsy. ~~I noticed~~
~~her immediately.~~ She came right
to me, wagging her tail. When I
petted her, she licked my face. ∧ ~~So~~ I can't
wait until you meet Patsy.
~~I decided that I wanted her.~~

448

Final Copy

14 West Orchard Street
Nashville, Tennessee 37215
June 30, 2008

Dear Aunt Brenda,

Guess what! Last week I got the smartest, most adorable dog. At the animal shelter, I immediately noticed a little brown and white dog named Patsy. She came right to me, wagging her tail. When I petted her, she licked my face. After that, there was no way I was leaving the shelter without her. When we got home, I started teaching her, and she quickly learned to sit and stay. Now I'm teaching her to shake hands. I can't wait until you meet Patsy. Please visit us soon!

Love,

Anthony

In my final letter, I made changes to better show my feelings. I also combined two short sentences by moving an adverb.

Reading as a Writer

Which parts show how Anthony feels about his dog Patsy? Where can you show more feeling in your letter?

449

Writing Traits Scoring Rubric

	Focus/Ideas	☑ Organization	Voice	☑ Word Choice	☑ Sentence Fluency	Conventions
4	Adheres to the topic, is interesting, has a sense of completeness. Ideas are well developed.	Ideas and details are clearly presented and well organized.	Connects with reader in a unique, personal way.	Includes vivid verbs, strong adjectives, specific nouns.	Includes a variety of complete sentences that flow smoothly, naturally.	Shows a strong command of grammar, spelling, capitalization, punctuation.
3	Mostly adheres to the topic, is somewhat interesting, has a sense of completeness. Ideas are adequately developed.	Ideas and details are mostly clear and generally organized.	Generally connects with reader in a way that is personal and sometimes unique.	Includes some vivid verbs, strong adjectives, specific nouns.	Includes some variety of mostly complete sentences. Some parts flow smoothly, naturally.	Shows a good command of grammar, spelling, capitalization, punctuation.
2	Does not always adhere to the topic, has some sense of completeness. Ideas are superficially developed.	Ideas and details are not always clear or organized. There is some wordiness or repetition.	Connects somewhat with reader. Sounds somewhat personal, but not unique.	Includes mostly simple nouns and verbs, and may have a few adjectives.	Includes mostly simple sentences, some of which are incomplete.	Some errors in grammar, spelling, capitalization, punctuation.
1	Does not adhere to the topic, has no sense of completeness. Ideas are vague.	Ideas and details are not organized. Wordiness or repetition hinders meaning.	Does not connect with reader. Does not sound personal or unique.	Includes only simple nouns and verbs, some inaccurate. Writing is not descriptive.	Sentences do not vary. Incomplete sentences hinder meaning.	Frequent errors in grammar, spelling, capitalization, punctuation.

See also ***Writing Rubric Blackline Master*** and Teacher's Edition pp. R18–R21.

Progress Monitoring

Assess

- **Weekly Tests**
- **Periodic Assessments**
- **Fluency Tests**

✓ Vocabulary

Target Vocabulary
Strategies: Suffixes *-ion, -ation, -ition*

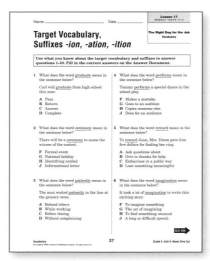

Weekly Tests 17.2–17.3

✓ Comprehension

Sequence of Events

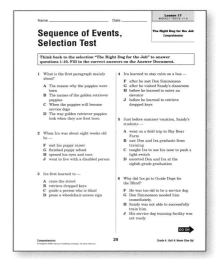

Weekly Tests 17.4–17.5

Respond to Assessment

IF a Student Scores...	THEN...
7–10 of 10	▶ Continue Core Instructional Program.
4–6 of 10	▶ **Reteaching Lesson 17,** page T142
1–3 of 10	▶ **Intervention** Lesson 17, pages S12–S21

IF a Student Scores...	THEN...
7–10 of 10	▶ Continue Core Instructional Program.
4–6 of 10	▶ **Reteaching Lesson 17,** page T142
1–3 of 10	▶ **Intervention** Lesson 17, pages S12–S21

 **Powered by**
DESTINATIONReading®

- **Weekly Tests**
- **Online Assessment System**

☑ Decoding
More Sound/Spelling Changes

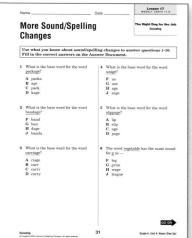

Weekly Tests 17.6–17.7

☑ Language Arts
Grammar: Adverbs

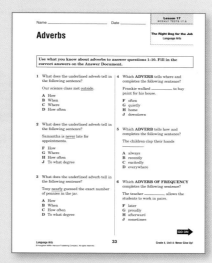

Weekly Tests 17.8–17.9

Writing Traits Rubrics
See TE pp. R18–R21.

☑ Fluency

Fluency Plan
Assess one group per week.
Use the suggested plan below.

● Struggling Readers	Weeks 1, 3, 5
▲ On Level	Week 2
■ Advanced	Week 4

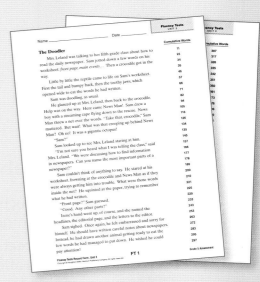

Fluency Record Form

Fluency Scoring Rubrics
See Grab-and-Go™ Resources *Assessment* for help in measuring progress.

IF a Student Scores...	THEN...
7–10 of 10	▶ Continue Core Instructional Program.
4–6 of 10	▶ **Reteaching Lesson 17,** page T143
1–3 of 10	▶ **Intervention** Lesson 17, pages S12–S21

IF a Student Scores...	THEN...
7–10 of 10	▶ Continue Core Instructional Program.
4–6 of 10	▶ **Reteaching Lesson 17,** page T143
1–3 of 10	▶ **Intervention** Lesson 17, pages S12–S21

Progress Monitoring

Small Group

RUNNING RECORDS

To assess individual progress, occasionally use small group time to take a reading record for each student. Use the results to plan instruction.

 Struggling Readers

 On Level

Grab-and-Go™ Resources Lesson 17, pp. 13–16

 Advanced

 English Language Learners

Behaviors and Understandings to Notice

- Self-corrects errors that detract from meaning.
- Self-corrects intonation when it does not reflect the meaning.
- Rereads to solve words and resumes normal rate of reading.
- Demonstrates phrased and fluent oral reading.
- Reads dialogue with expression.

- Demonstrates awareness of punctuation.
- Automatically solves most words in the text to read fluently.
- Demonstrates appropriate stress on words, pausing and phrasing, intonation, and use of punctuation.
- Reads orally at an appropriate rate.

Vocabulary Reader
- *Animals Helping People*, T132–T133

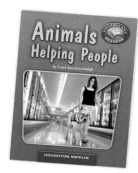

Vocabulary Reader

Differentiate Comprehension
- Target Skill: Sequence of Events, T134–T135
- Target Strategy: Summarize, T134–T135

Leveled Readers
- ● *Animal Doctors*, T136
- ▲ *A Rural Veterinarian*, T137
- ■ *Helping Wild Animals*, T138
- ◆ *Taking Care of Animals*, T139

Differentiate Vocabulary Strategies
- Using Suffixes *-ion, -ation, -ition*, T140–T141

Options for Reteaching
- Vocabulary Strategies: Using Suffixes *-ion, -ation, -ition*, T142
- Comprehension Skill: Sequence of Events, T142
- Language Arts: Adverbs/Write to Narrate, T143
- Decoding: More Sound/Spelling Changes, T143

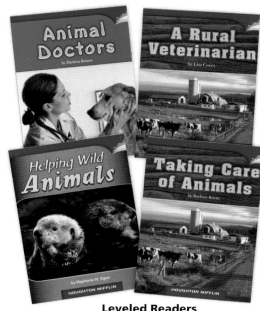

Leveled Readers

Ready-Made Work Stations

Independent Practice
- Comprehension and Fluency, T82
- Word Study, T82
- Think and Write, T83
- Digital Center, T83

Comprehension and Fluency

Word Study

Think and Write

Digital Center

Suggested Small Group Plan

	Day 1	Day 2	Day 3
Teacher-Led			
Struggling Readers	**Vocabulary Reader** *Animals Helping People*, Differentiated Instruction, p. T132	**Differentiate Comprehension:** Sequence of Events; Summarize, p. T134	**Leveled Reader** *Animal Doctors*, p. T136
On Level	**Vocabulary Reader** *Animals Helping People*, Differentiated Instruction, p. T132	**Differentiate Comprehension:** Sequence of Events; Summarize, p. T134	**Leveled Reader** *A Rural Veterinarian*, p. T137
Advanced	**Vocabulary Reader** *Animals Helping People*, Differentiated Instruction, p. T133	**Differentiate Comprehension:** Sequence of Events; Summarize, p. T135	**Leveled Reader** *Helping Wild Animals*, p. T138
English Language Learners	**Vocabulary Reader** *Animals Helping People*, Differentiated Instruction, p. T133	**Differentiate Comprehension:** Sequence of Events; Summarize, p. T135	**Leveled Reader** *Taking Care of Animals*, p. T139

	Day 1	Day 2	Day 3
What are my other students doing?			
Struggling Readers	• **Reread** *Animals Helping People*	• **Vocabulary in Context Cards** 161–170 *Talk It Over* Activities • **Complete** Leveled Practice SR17.1	• **Listen** to Audiotext CD of "The Right Dog for the Job"; Retell and discuss • **Complete** Leveled Reader SR17.2
On Level	• **Reread** *Animals Helping People*	• **Reread** "The Right Dog for the Job" with a partner • **Complete** Practice Book p. 193	• **Reread** for Fluency: *A Rural Veterinarian* • **Complete** Practice Book p. 194
Advanced	• **Vocabulary in Context Cards** 161–170 *Talk It Over* Activities	• **Reread and Retell** "The Right Dog for the Job" • **Complete** Leveled Practice A17.1	• **Reread** for Fluency: *Helping Wild Animals* • **Complete** Leveled Practice A17.2
English Language Learners	• **Reread** *Animals Helping People*	• **Listen** to Audiotext CD of "The Right Dog for the Job"; Retell and discuss • **Complete** Leveled Practice ELL17.1	• **Vocabulary in Context Cards** 161–170 *Talk It Over* Activities • **Complete** Leveled Practice ELL17.2

Ready-Made Work Stations

Assign these activities across the week to reinforce and extend learning.

Comprehension and Fluency
Listen and Read

Word Study
Communication Discussion

Weekly To-Do List

This Weekly To-Do List helps students see their own progress and move on to additional activities independently.

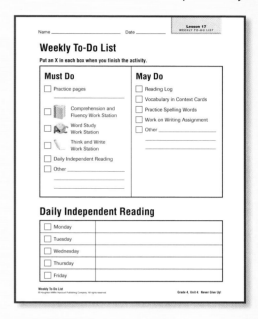

Day 4	Day 5
Differentiate Vocabulary Strategies: Using Suffixes *-ion, -ation, -ition,* p. T140	**Options for Reteaching,** pp. T142–T143
Differentiate Vocabulary Strategies: Using Suffixes *-ion, -ation, -ition,* p. T140	**Options for Reteaching,** pp. T142–T143
Differentiate Vocabulary Strategies: Using Suffixes *-ion, -ation, -ition,* p. T141	**Options for Reteaching,** pp. T142–T143
Differentiate Vocabulary Strategies: Using Suffixes *-ion, -ation, -ition,* p. T141	**Options for Reteaching,** pp. T142–T143

- **Partners: Reread** *Animal Doctors*
- **Complete** Leveled Practice SR17.3

- **Reread** for Fluency: "The Right Dog for the Job"
- **Complete** Work Station activities
- **Independent Reading**

- **Vocabulary in Context Cards** 161–170 *Talk It Over* Activities
- **Complete** Practice Book p. 195

- **Complete** Work Station activities
- **Independent Reading**

- **Reread** for Fluency: "The Right Dog for the Job"
- **Complete** Leveled Practice A17.3

- **Complete** Work Station activities
- **Independent Reading**

- **Partners: Reread** for Fluency: "Taking Care of Animals"
- **Complete** Leveled Practice ELL17.3

- **Reread** *Animals Helping People* or "The Right Dog for the Job"
- **Complete** Work Station activities

Think and Write
Create a Comic Strip

JOURNEYS DIGITAL Powered by **DESTINATION** Reading**

Digital Center

Reading Log

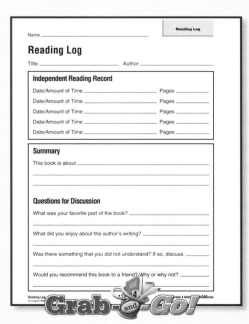

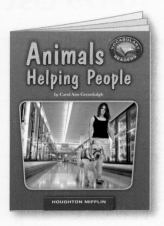

Vocabulary Reader
Animals Helping People

Summary

There are many animals both in the wild and in homes that have helped humans. These animals help, not because they have to, but because they are guided by instinct or training.

✔ TARGET VOCABULARY

reward	confidence
graduate	patiently
symbol	confesses
foster	ceremony
disobey	performs

Struggling Readers

- Explain to students that service animals are trained to help people. These animals can help people with disabilities perform certain activities, such as crossing busy streets.

- Guide students to preview the selection. Read aloud the headings. Ask students to describe the images, using Target Vocabulary when possible. Ask why would it be important that a service animal have *confidence*?

- Have students alternate reading pages of the selection aloud. Guide them to use context clues to determine the meanings of unfamiliar words. As necessary, use the **Vocabulary in Context Cards** to review the meanings of Vocabulary words.

- Assign the **Responding Page** and **Blackline Master 17.1**. Have partners work together to complete the pages.

On Level

- Explain to students that people with disabilities may need help with seeing, hearing, and other activities, and that dogs and other animals can be trained to assist them. Guide students to preview the selection.

- Remind students that context clues can help them determine the meaning of an unknown word. Tell students to use context clues to confirm their understanding of Target Vocabulary and to learn the meanings of new words.

- Have students alternate reading pages of the selection aloud. Tell them to use context clues to determine the meanings of unfamiliar words.

- Assign the **Responding Page** and **Blackline Master 17.1**. Have students discuss their responses with a partner.

Advanced

- Have students preview the selection and make predictions about what they will read, using information from the preview and prior knowledge.

- Remind students to use context clues to help them determine the meanings of unfamiliar words.

- Tell students to read the selection with a partner. Ask them to stop and discuss the meanings of unfamiliar words as necessary.

- Assign the **Responding Page** and **Blackline Master 17.1**. For the Write About It activity, remind students to use facts and details to support their ideas. Ask: *What are some jobs that a service monkey performs for people?*

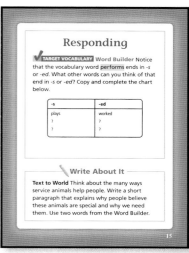

Animals Helping People, p. 15

Blackline Master 17.1

ELL English Language Learners

Group English Language Learners according to language proficiency.

Beginning

Have students look through *Animals Helping People*. Have them identify the animals they recognize. Then read *Animals Helping People*, stopping at the Target Vocabulary and explaining the words, as necessary.

Advanced

Have students reread *Animals Helping People*. Check students' understanding of the Target Vocabulary words by having partners use the words in oral sentences.

Intermediate

Have partners work together to perform panto-mimes demonstrating the meanings of the following selection Vocabulary: *reward, ceremony, confidence,* and *patiently*.

Advanced High

Have students reread *Animals Helping People*. Guide them to tell the sequence of events in the selection using Target Vocabulary words.

 **SMALL GROUP Options**

Differentiate Comprehension
 ☑ Sequence of Events; Summarize

Struggling Readers

I DO IT

- Explain to students that summarizing means using their own words to briefly retell the events in a story.

- Read aloud the last paragraph on p. 433 of "The Right Dog for the Job" and summarize the events in order. As you model, use transition words.

  Think Aloud *To train Ira, Kathleen throws her keys. Then she tells Ira, "Fetch!" Ira runs to the keys and picks them up. Then he brings them to Kathleen.*

WE DO IT

- Have students read the last paragraph on p. 436.

- Help students identify the main events in this passage.

- Record on the board the main events as students name them. Then work with students to number the events in chronological order.

- Fill in a Flow Chart on the board with the sequence of events for the paragraph.

YOU DO IT

- Have students read p. 440 of "The Right Dog for the Job."

- Have them complete a Flow Chart for the section.

- Ask a volunteer to read aloud the sequential sentences in their chart.

- Point out that the sentences form a summary of the selection.

On Level

I DO IT

- Read aloud p. 432 through the start of paragraph two on p. 433 of "The Right Dog for the Job."

- Explain that a strong summary often lists ideas or events in sequence.

- Model listing events in a Flow Chart to create a summary of the puppies' first weeks of life.

WE DO IT

- Have students read pp. 434–435 of "The Right Dog for the Job."

- Point out that this passage covers an extended period of time.

- Work with students to identify signal words in the passage. Then help them determine the sequence of events.

- On the board, fill in a Flow Chart with students' responses. Have volunteers use the sequence of events to summarize the passage.

YOU DO IT

- Have students read p. 439 of "The Right Dog for the Job" and complete a Flow Chart for the passage.

- Tell partners to cut out the boxes of their charts. Have students shuffle the boxes and then arrange them in chronological order.

- Have partners use their event boxes to write a summary of p. 439.

- Have volunteers share their summaries.

Advanced

I DO IT

- Read aloud p. 433 of "The Right Dog for the Job."

- Explain that authors sometimes interrupt the sequence of events by stating events that happen earlier or later in time.

Think Aloud *Ira goes home with Sandy Welsh at eight weeks of age. The author mentions Kathleen's visit in the same paragraph. Sandy must have worked with Ira on his skills first.*

WE DO IT

- Have students read p. 436 independently.

- Remind students that authors sometimes provide additional information about events that happen at the same time.

- *How does bringing Ira to school help with his training? He learns to lie quietly and gets used to noisy places. How do Sandy's students help with Ira's training? They do not distract him. They teach him to come when called and teach him to push a light switch with his nose.*

YOU DO IT

- Have students finish reading "The Right Dog for the Job" and complete a Flow Chart for the selection.

- Have students use their completed Flow Charts to write a paragraph summarizing the selection.

- Invite students to model how they used the Summarize strategy to complete their Flow Charts.

ELL English Language Learners

Group English Language Learners according to language proficiency.

Draw a sequence-of-events Flow Chart on the board. Then choose one of the following activities for additional support, as appropriate.

Beginning

Write *one, two, three* on the board. Next to each word, write their ordinals: *first, second, third.* Tell students to use ordinal numbers when they tell the order of what they do after they wake up in the morning.

Intermediate

Remind students to use ordinal numbers to talk about sequence of events. Read page 432 of "The Right Dog for the Job." Ask: *What happens first? Ira and his siblings are born.* Help students fill in the chart on the board with what happens next.

Advanced

Have students pick a page from the selection and copy the sequence of events chart from the board. Help students fill in the chart with the events from the page they chose. Have them tell what happened first, second, and third.

Advanced High

Have students work in pairs to discuss the sequence of events from the selection. Have students add as many events as they need. Then have them give an oral summary of the selection.

Targets for Lesson 17

 **TARGET SKILL**

Sequence of Events

 **TARGET STRATEGY**

Summarize

 **TARGET VOCABULARY**

foster	disobey
confidence	graduate
confesses	ceremony
symbol	patiently
reward	performs

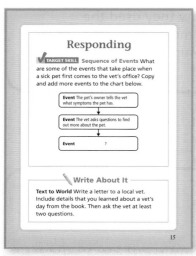

Animal Doctors, p. 15

Blackline Master 17.3

Leveled Readers

Struggling Readers

● *Animal Doctors*

GENRE: INFORMATIONAL TEXT

Summary Veterinarians must be good listeners and observers. From routine annual checkups to emergency care and operations, vets tend to a wide range of animals.

Introducing the Text

- Explain that the word *vet* is short for *veterinarian*. Veterinarians are doctors who care for animals.

- Remind students that using a Flow Chart can help them organize information into the correct sequence, or order, of events

Supporting the Reading

- As you listen to students read, pause to discuss these questions.

SEQUENCE OF EVENTS p. 9 *What might a pet owner do after a pet has had surgery and recovered? Pick the pet up at the clinic; ask the doctor for any post-operation instructions.*

SUMMARIZE p. 11 *How do the heading and photos on this page help you to summarize the paragraph? They indicate that the main idea is pet emergencies, such as a dog eating food that it should have avoided.*

Discussing and Revisiting the Text

CRITICAL THINKING After discussing *Animal Doctors*, have students read the instructions on **Responding** p. 15. Use these points to guide students as they revisit the text.

- Have partners identify the sequence of events on pp. 6–7 of *Animal Doctors* and list events 1 and 2 in **Blackline Master 17.3**. Have students list the final event in box 3.

- Distribute **Blackline Master 17.7** to develop students' critical thinking skills.

FLUENCY: INTONATION Model using tone and pitch as you read aloud. Have partners echo-read p. 3 to practice reading with appropriate intonation.

Small Group

Day 3

JOURNEYS
DIGITAL | Powered by
DESTINATIONReading®
Leveled Readers Online

On Level

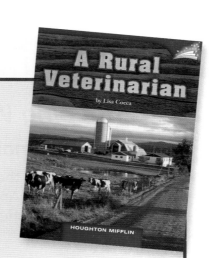

▲ *A Rural Veterinarian*

GENRE: INFORMATIONAL TEXT

Summary The work of a rural veterinarian is unique, and work days are long. Rural vets must travel from farm to farm in a single day to see all the patients that need their care.

Introducing the Text

• Explain that rural vets work with farm animals like cows and chickens. Tell students that rural areas are areas that are far away from towns and cities.

• Remind students that the sequence of events is the order in which events take place over time. Sometimes signal words such as *first, next,* and *finally* indicate sequence of events.

Supporting the Reading

• As you listen to students read, pause to discuss these questions.

SEQUENCE OF EVENTS p. 2 *What can you infer from how early a farm veterinarian's day begins?* A farm veterinarian can be called at odd hours of the day.

SUMMARIZE p. 12 *What is being described in the section under the heading "The Road to Becoming a Vet"?* the steps it takes to become a veterinarian

Discussing and Revisiting the Text

CRITICAL THINKING After discussing *A Rural Veterinarian*, have students read the instructions on **Responding** p. 15. Use these points as they revisit the text.

• Have students identify the sequence of events at the vet's first stop and list the events in order on **Blackline Master 17.4.** Then have students summarize the vet's first stop using their flow charts.

• Distribute **Blackline Master 17.8** to further develop students' critical thinking skills.

FLUENCY: INTONATION Have students practice reading their favorite parts of *A Rural Veterinarian* using appropriate tone and pitch.

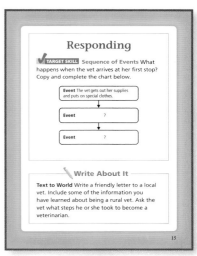

A Rural Veterinarian, p. 15

Blackline Master 17.4

Targets for Lesson 17

Sequence of Events

 TARGET STRATEGY

Summarize

 **TARGET VOCABULARY**

foster	disobey
confidence	graduate
confesses	ceremony
symbol	patiently
reward	performs

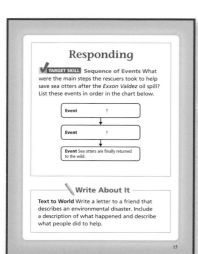

Helping Wild Animals, p. 15

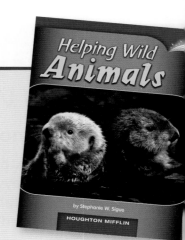

Blackline Master 17.5

Leveled Readers

Advanced

▢ *Helping Wild Animals*

GENRE: INFORMATIONAL TEXT

Summary In 1989, the *Exxon Valdez* spilled oil off the coast of Alaska. Animals were in danger. In cases like this and others, wildlife rehabilitators step in to help.

Introducing the Text

- Explain that natural disasters or accidents, such as ocean oil spills, can endanger the health of wild animals.

- Remind students that a sequence of events refers to the order events happened.

Supporting the Reading

- As you listen to students read, pause to discuss these questions.

SEQUENCE OF EVENTS p. 2 *What must have happened before the Exxon Valdez spilled oil into the sea? There must have been an accident or mistake that caused the oil spill.*

SUMMARIZE pp. 10–11 *Summarize the action you should take if you see an injured wild animal. Don't touch the animal. Call wildlife rehabilitation or a vet.*

Discussing and Revisiting the Text

CRITICAL THINKING Have students discuss *Helping Wild Animals* and read the instructions on **Responding** p. 15. Use these points to guide students as they revisit the text.

- Have partners identify the sequence of events described on pp. 5–6. Point out that students must identify the main events that took place before the sea otters were returned to the wild. Then have students list the events on **Blackline Master 17.5.**

- Distribute **Blackline Master 17.9** to develop students' critical thinking skills.

FLUENCY: INTONATION Have students read with appropriate intonation.

JOURNEYS DIGITAL Powered by DESTINATIONReading®
Leveled Readers Online

ELL English Language Learners

◆ *Taking Care of Animals*

GENRE: INFORMATIONAL TEXT

Summary Farm veterinarians travel from farm to farm, treating animals, performing surgery, and helping animals give birth.

Introducing the Text

• Explain that veterinarians are doctors who take care of animals rather than people. Point out that the word *vet* is short for *veterinarian*.

• Remind students that events are usually presented in order, or sequence, to the reader. Tell students to pay attention to the order of events as they read. A flow chart can help them to keep track of the order of events.

Supporting the Reading

• As you listen to students read, pause to discuss these questions.

SEQUENCE OF EVENTS p. 4 *What will happen after the vet leaves the cow with her new calf? The cow will feed and care for the calf.*

SUMMARIZE pp. 7–8 *What are two ways the vet determines what is wrong with the horse? She examines the horse with her hands and takes an X-ray.*

Discussing and Revisiting the Text

CRITICAL THINKING Have students discuss *Taking Care of Animals* and read the instructions on **Responding** p. 15. Use these points as they revisit the text.

• Have students work with a partner to identify two more events on p. 4 of *Taking Care of Animals* and list the events in the appropriate boxes of **Blackline Master 17.6**. Then have them read the three events aloud to check their understanding of sequence of events.

• Distribute **Blackline Master 17.10** to develop students' critical thinking skills.

FLUENCY: INTONATION Model reading aloud the first paragraph on p.12. Have students echo-read the paragraph, reading with appropriate intonation.

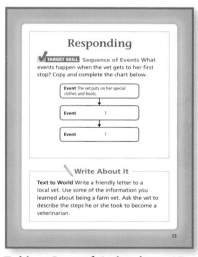

Taking Care of Animals, p. 15

Blackline Master 17.6

Differentiate Vocabulary Strategies ☑ Suffixes *-ion, -ation, -ition*

Struggling Readers

I DO IT

- Display **Vocabulary in Context Card 162:** *graduate*

- Explain that a suffix comes at the end of a base word and changes the word's meaning. On the board, show students that the suffix *-ion* can be added to *graduate* to form the word *graduation*.

- Explain that the suffixes *-ion, -ation,* and *-ition* make words into nouns that tell about a process, action, or result.

WE DO IT

- Read aloud the sample dictionary entry for *graduate* below:

> *graduate* **1.** Someone who has completed the last year in a school and has received a diploma **2.** To finish a course of study in a school and receive a diploma

- Discuss how adding the suffix *-ion* to *graduate* forms the word *graduation,* which means "the completion of a course of academic study."

- Read the card's context sentence.

YOU DO IT

- Tell students to restate the context sentence using the Vocabulary word *graduate* and the meaning "to finish a course of study and receive a diploma." *Possible response: The guide dog is at his (or her) graduation.*

- Have students write a sentence for the word *graduation.*

On Level

I DO IT

- Remind students that a suffix is an affix attached at the end of a base word that changes the word's meaning.

- Remind students that the suffix *-ion* turns verbs into nouns that tell about a process, action, or result. When added to base words, the final syllables change to *-ation* or *-ition.*

WE DO IT

- On the board, list student suggestions of words that contain the suffixes *-ion, -ation,* and *-ition,* such as *election, implementation,* and *definition.*

- Read the list with students and identify the base words and how the suffix changed the base words' meaning.

YOU DO IT

- Have students select three words with the suffixes *-ion, -ation,* or *-ition* and write sentences to demonstrate students' understanding.

- Have students read **Student Book p. 439.** Tell them to find one of the Target Vocabulary Words for Lesson 17. Then have them find the same word with a suffix.

Advanced

I DO IT

- Write on the board the suffixes *-ion, -ation,* and *-ition,* and the following word sets:

    inform, information
    imagine, imagination
    adopt, adoption
    compete, competition

- Remind students that the suffix *-ion* tells about a process, action, or result.

WE DO IT

- Note the parts of speech of the paired words.

- Read the list with students and identify the base words. Discuss how the base words were changed by adding the suffix *-ion, -ation,* or *-ition.*

YOU DO IT

- Have students list and define additional words with the suffixes *-ion, -ation,* and *-ition.*

- Ask students to work with a partner to underline the base words in each word.

- Have partners share their words with the class.

imagination : imagine

ELL English Language Learners

Group English Language Learners according to language proficiency.

Write *reward, graduate,* and *confess* on the board. Have students repeat after you as you pronounce each word.

Beginning

Write *graduate* and *graduation* on the board. Circle the *-ion* in *graduation.* Explain to students how the addition of the suffix changes the meaning of the word. Use both words in an example sentence.

Intermediate

Write *confess* and *confession* on the board. Ask: *What is the difference between the two words?* Explain how the addition of the suffix changes the word's meaning. Ask students to name another *-ion* word.

Advanced

Explain to students how the suffix *-ion* changes the meaning of a word. Have students use a dictionary to identify the base word in the following words: *imagination, adoption, competition.*

Advanced High

Have students use the words *graduate, graduation; compete, competition* in oral sentences.

Differentiate Vocabulary Strategies • **T141**

✔ Options for Reteaching

Vocabulary Strategies

✔ Suffixes *-ion, -ation, -ition*

I DO IT

- Remind students that a suffix is an affix added to the end of a word that changes the meaning of the word.

- Explain that the suffix *-ion* is a suffix that makes words into nouns that tell about a process, action, or result.

WE DO IT

- Display **Projectable 17.5.** Help students identify words containing the suffixes *-ion*, *-ation*, and *-ition*.

- Model how to apply the Vocabulary Strategy to determine the meaning of the word *cooperation*.

Think Aloud *I know the base word of* cooperation *is* cooperate. *To cooperate is to work in a friendly way with others. The suffix* -ion *tells about cooperating and turns the word into a noun. So it makes* cooperating *into a thing rather than an action.* Cooperation *must be a form of friendliness and helpfulness among people who are doing something together.*

- Have a volunteer look up *cooperation* in a dictionary and read the definition aloud.

Noun	Verb
information	inform
competition	compete
exhibition	exhibit
combination	combine
attention	attend

YOU DO IT

- Have partners apply the Vocabulary Strategy to determine the meanings of *information, competition, exhibition, combination,* and *attention.*

- Have students make a chart listing the noun form and verb form of each word.

- Provide corrective feedback if students need additional support.

Comprehension Skill

✔ Sequence of Events

I DO IT

- Remind students that a sequence of events is the order in which events take place in time. Point out that authors do not always supply every event. Readers may need to infer or figure out events that the author has left out.

- Explain that at certain points in a text, the author may depart from the sequence by giving events that happened earlier or later in time. Tell students to use clue words *(before, next),* or times or dates to retell events.

WE DO IT

- Have students read aloud the second and third paragraphs on **Student Book p. 433** and identify the sequence of events that begins when puppies meet their puppy raisers.

- Model how to identify each event in the sequence.

Think Aloud *Ira goes home with Sandy, and Kathleen visits Ira a month later. The next paragraph describes an important service dog task— Ira must learn how to retrieve things. The purpose of Kathleen's visit is to check on Ira's service dog skills. During the visit, Ira shows Kathleen what Sandy has taught him earlier by picking up her keys.*

- Have volunteers name each step in the sequence.

YOU DO IT

- Distribute **Graphic Organizer 4.**

- Have students list the events described on p. 436, in order. *Sandy's students help train Ira. Students form a circle with Ira in the center. Then they take turns calling him. Ira gets treats for laying his head in their laps. They teach him to push a light switch.*

- Have partners complete the Flow Chart.

- Review the completed graphic organizers as a class.

Language Arts

 Adverbs/Write to Narrate

I DO IT

- Remind students that an adverb is a word that describes a verb. Adverbs answer the questions *how, when,* or *where* an action takes place.

- List the following verbs on the board: *walked, read, sings.* Model answering questions to assign an adverb to each verb.

Think Aloud *To describe* walked, *I ask how did the person or animal walk? One answer is* quickly: walked quickly. *To describe* read, *I ask when did the person read? I can answer* yesterday: read yesterday. *To describe* sings, *I ask where did the person sing? I can answer with* everywhere: Tami sings everywhere.

WE DO IT

- Work together to describe an action students are familiar with.

- Guide students to use adverbs to describe the action. Have them use an adverb that tells how, when, and where for the action they chose.

- Ask students to help you write sentences that contain adverbs. Write the sentences on the board. Ask volunteers to come to the board and circle the adverbs.
Example: *The butterfly sailed smoothly over the flower. It gracefully landed on a petal and soon fluttered its wings. Then it flew away.* smoothly, gracefully, soon, away

YOU DO IT

- Have pairs of students write three or four sentences with adverbs in them.

- Have students tell what question is answered by each adverb they used.

Decoding

 More Sound/Spelling Changes

I DO IT

- Remind students that they can find base words in words that have added a prefix or suffix. Model how to decode *package*.

Think Aloud *The base word is* pack, *which is a verb. If I add the suffix -age, the word becomes a noun,* package, *meaning a thing or group of things packed or wrapped up.*

WE DO IT

- Write *marriage* and *baggage* on the board.
- Write the headings *Base Word* and *Derived Word* on the board. Ask students for examples of words to put under each heading.

Base Word	Derived Word
pack	package
marry	marriage
bag	baggage

YOU DO IT

- Have partners work together to identify the base words of *bandage* and *carriage*.

- Have students read the words and note common letter patterns.

- Use the **Corrective Feedback** on page T111 if students need additional help.

Teacher Notes

Moon Runner

Preteaching for Success!

Comprehension:

Understanding Characters

Remind students that they can understand a story better if they understand the characters and their actions.

- Have students name some of their favorite stories and then name several characters from each of them.
- Tell students that understanding characters means knowing why they do and say things.
- Have students choose a story they know and use a graphic organizer like the one on Student Book p. 454 to help them understand one of the characters.

Challenge Yourself!

An Athlete's Poem

After reading the selection "Moon Runner," have each student write a poem about the kind of professional athlete he or she would like to be.

- Have students brainstorm about the types of sports they like best.
- Ask each student to write a poem to describe himself or herself doing that sport and succeeding. Explain that the poem can be true or imaginary.
- Remind students that their poems do not have to rhyme, but they should have a rhythm, a good pace, and vivid language.

✓ Short Response

W.4.3d Use concrete words and phrases and sensory details to convey experiences and events precisely.

Write a paragraph about a time when you competed in a sport. Compare your experience with the events of the story.

Scoring Guidelines

Excellent	Student has written a paragraph to explain a time when he or she competed in a sport and has compared the experience with events in the story.
Good	Student has written a paragraph to explain a time when he or she competed in a sport but has not compared the experience with events in the story.
Fair	Student has written a paragraph but has not addressed the writing prompt.
Unsatisfactory	Student has not written a paragraph.

Writing Minilesson

Skill: Write to Narrate—Descriptive Paragraph

Teach: Remind students that description is an important part of narrative writing.

Thinking Beyond the Text

Writing Prompt: Write a paragraph describing a person who likes to compete in sports.

1. Have students include words, actions, and thoughts of the characters.
2. Tell students that including prepositions and prepositional phrases will help to give details and tell about time and location.
3. Encourage students to use synonyms to help them avoid repeating the same words.

Group Share: Have volunteers read their paragraphs aloud. Post them in a display titled "Competition."

Cross-Curricular Activity: Science

The Cycle of the Moon

In the selection, Mina wishes that it were time for the Chinese Moon Festival. Explain that during this festival families and friends gather to watch the full moon. As a class, research when the next full moon will take place. Mark the date on the class calendar. That day, remind students to step outside and enjoy it!

Common Core State Standards
for English Language Arts

Reading Standards for Literature K–5
Key Ideas and Details
RL.4.1 Refer to details and examples in a text when explaining what the text says explicitly and when drawing inferences from the text.

RL.4.3 Describe in depth a character, setting, or event in a story or drama, drawing on specific details in the text (e.g., a character's thoughts, words, or actions).

Craft and Structure
RL.4.4 Determine the meaning of words and phrases as they are used in a text, including those that allude to significant characters found in mythology (e.g., Herculean).

RL.4.6 Compare and contrast the point of view from which different stories are narrated, including the difference between first- and third-person narrations.

Range of Reading and Level of Text Complexity
RL.4.10 By the end of the year, read and comprehend literature, including stories, dramas, and poetry, in the grades 4–5 text complexity band proficiently, with scaffolding as needed at the high end of the range.

Reading Standards for Informational Text K–5
Key Ideas and Details
RI.4.2 Determine the main idea of a text and explain how it is supported by key details; summarize the text.

Range of Reading and Level of Text Complexity
RI.4.10 By the end of year, read and comprehend informational texts, including history/social studies, science, and technical texts, in the grades 4–5 text complexity band proficiently, with scaffolding as needed at the high end of the range.

Reading Standards: Foundational Skills K–5
Phonics and Word Recognition
RF.4.3a Use combined knowledge of all letter-sound correspondences, syllabication patterns, and morphology (e.g. roots and affixes) to read accurately unfamiliar multisyllabic words in context and out of context.

Fluency
RF.4.4c Use context to confirm or self-correct word recognition and understanding, rereading as necessary.

Writing Standards K–5
Text Types and Purposes
W.4.3a Orient the reader by establishing a situation and introducing a narrator and/or characters; organize an event sequence that unfolds naturally.

W.4.3d Use concrete words and phrases and sensory details to convey experiences and events precisely.

W.4.3e Provide a conclusion that follows from the narrated experiences or events.

Production and Distribution of Writing
W.4.5 With guidance and support from peers and adults, develop and strengthen writing as needed by planning, revising, and editing. (Editing for conventions should demonstrate command of Language standards 1–3 up to and including grade 4 on pages 28 and 29.)

Research to Build and Present Knowledge
W.4.7 Conduct short research projects that build knowledge through investigation of different aspects of a topic.

W.4.8 Recall relevant information from experiences or gather relevant information from print and digital sources; take notes and categorize information, and provide a list of sources.

Range of Writing
W.4.10 Write routinely over extended time frames (time for research, reflection, and revision) and shorter time frames (a single sitting or a day or two) for a range of discipline-specific tasks, purposes, and audiences.

Speaking & Listening Standards K–5
Comprehension and Collaboration
SL.4.1a Come to discussions prepared, having read or studied required material; explicitly draw on that preparation and other information known about the topic to explore ideas under discussion.

SL.4.1b Follow agreed-upon rules for discussions and carry out assigned roles.

SL.4.1c Pose and respond to specific questions to clarify or follow up on information, and make comments that contribute to the discussion and link to the remarks of others.

SL.4.1d Review the key ideas expressed and explain their own ideas and understanding in light of the discussion.

Presentation of Knowledge and Ideas
SL.4.4 Report on a topic or text, tell a story, or recount an experience in an organized manner, using appropriate facts and relevant, descriptive details to support main ideas or themes; speak clearly at an understandable pace.

Language Standards K–5
Conventions of Standard English
L.4.1e Form and use prepositional phrases.

L.4.1g Correctly use frequently confused words (e.g., *to, too, two; there, their*).

L.4.2d Spell grade-appropriate words correctly, consulting references as needed.

Knowledge of Language
L.4.3a Choose words and phrases to convey ideas precisely.

Vocabulary Acquisition and Use
L.4.4c Consult reference materials (e.g., dictionaries, glossaries, thesauruses), both print and digital, to find the pronunciation and determine or clarify the precise meaning of key words and phrases.

L.4.5c Demonstrate understanding of words by relating them to their opposites (antonyms) and to words with similar but not identical meanings (synonyms).

SUGGESTIONS FOR BALANCED LITERACY

Use *Journeys* materials to support a Readers' Workshop approach.
See the Lesson 18 resources on pages 26, 74–75.

Focus Wall

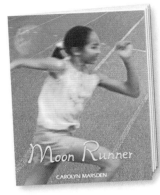

Main Selection
Moon Runner

Connect to Social Studies
A Day for the Moon

Big Idea
There is more than one secret to success.

Essential Question
How can people share their successes?

Comprehension

✔ **TARGET SKILL**

Understanding Characters

✔ **TARGET STRATEGY**

Question

Fluency

Accuracy and Self-Correction

Decoding

Recognizing Prefixes
re-, un-, dis-

Vocabulary Strategies

Homophones, Homonyms, and Homographs

Grammar

Prepositions and Prepositional Phrases

Spelling

Prefixes *re-, un-, dis-*

unused	untrue
refresh	unload
dislike	recall
replace	displease
unpaid	uneven
redo	rebuild
disorder	restart
unplanned	uncover
distrust	untidy
rewind	discolor

Writing

Write to Narrate

Focus Trait:
Word Choice

TARGET VOCABULARY

gigantic	deliberately
miniature	jealous
especially	haze
lapped	lure
vanished	crisp

Key Skills This Week

Target Skill:
Understanding Characters

Target Strategy:
Question

Vocabulary Strategies:
Homophones, Homonyms, and Homographs

Fluency:
Accuracy and Self-Correction

Decoding:
Recognizing Prefixes
re-, un-, dis-

Research Skill:
Onine Searches: Reliable Sources

Grammar:
Prepositions and Prepositional Phrases

Spelling:
Prefixes *re-, un-, dis-*

 Writing:
Narrative Composition

 Assess/Monitor

☑ **Vocabulary,** p. T198

☑ **Comprehension,** p. T198

☑ **Decoding,** p. T199

☑ **Language Arts,** p. T199

☑ **Fluency,** p. T199

Whole Group

READING

Paired Selections

Moon Runner
Realistic Fiction
Student Book, pp. 454–465

A Day for the Moon
SOCIAL STUDIES / Informational Text
Student Book, pp. 466–469

Practice Quizzes for the Selection

Vocabulary

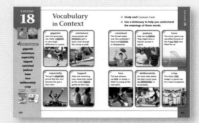

Student Book, pp. 450–451

Background and Comprehensio

Student Book, pp. 452–453

LANGUAGE ARTS

Grammar
Student Book, pp. 470–471

Writing
Student Book, pp. 472–473

Small Group

See pages T202–T203 for Suggested Small Group Plan.

TEACHER-LED

Leveled Readers

 **Struggling Readers**

On Level

 **Advanced**

English Language Learners

Vocabulary Reader

WHAT MY OTHER STUDENTS ARE DOING

Word Study

Think and Write

Comprehension and Fluency

Digital Center

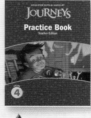

On Level

Struggling Readers

Advanced

English Language Learners

Lesson 18 Blackline Master
- Target Vocabulary 18.1
- Selection Summary 18.2
- Graphic Organizer 18.3–18.6
- Critical Thinking 18.7–18.10
- Running Records 18.11–18.14
- Weekly Tests 18.2–18.14

Graphic Organizer Transparency 1

Additional Resources
- Genre: Fiction, p. 4
- Reading Log, p. 12
- Vocabulary Log, p. 13
- Listening Log, p. 14
- Proofreading Checklist, p. 15
- Proofreading Marks, p. 16
- Writing Conference Form, p. 17
- Writing Rubric, p. 18
- Instructional Routines, pp. 19–26
- Graphic Organizer 1: Column Chart, p. 27

For Students
- Student eBook
- Comprehension Expedition CD-ROM
- Leveled Readers Online
- WriteSmart CD-ROM

For Teachers
- Online TE and Focus Wall
- Online Assessment System
- Teacher One-Stop
- Destination Reading Instruction

Week at a Glance

Intervention

STRATEGIC INTERVENTION: TIER II

Use these materials to provide additional targeted instruction for students who need Tier II strategic intervention.

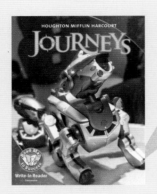

Supports the Student Book selections

Interactive Work-text for Skills Support

Write-In Reader:
Right on Track

- Engaging selection connects to main topic.
- Reinforces this week's target vocabulary and comprehension skill and strategy.
- Opportunities for student interaction on each page.

Support

Progress monitoring every two weeks.

For this week's Strategic Intervention lessons, see Teacher's Edition pages S22–S31.

INTENSIVE INTERVENTION: TIER III

- The materials in the Literacy Tool Kit help you provide a different approach for students who need Tier III intensive intervention.
- Interactive lessons provide focused instruction in key reading skills, targeted at students' specific needs.
- Lesson cards are convenient for small-group or individual instruction.
- Blackline masters provide additional practice.
- A leveled book accompanies each lesson to give students opportunities for additional reading and skill application.
- Assessments for each lesson help you evaluate the effectiveness of the intervention.

Lessons provide support for:

- Phonics and Word Study Skills
- Vocabulary
- Comprehension Skills and Literary Genres
- Fluency

ELL English Language Learners

SCAFFOLDED SUPPORT

Use these materials to ensure that students acquire social and academic language proficiency.

Language Support Card

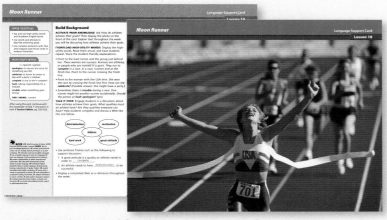

- Builds background for the main topic and promotes oral language.
- Develops high-utility vocabulary and academic language.

Leveled Reader

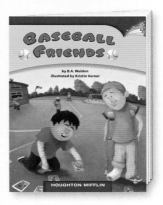

- Sheltered text connects to the main selection's topic, vocabulary, skill, and strategy.

Scaffolded Support

ELL ENGLISH LANGUAGE LEARNERS

Scaffold

Beginning Help students list familiar sports activities. Point out common favorites like running, basketball, football, soccer, baseball, and swimming. Use photographs of each sport and point to them as you say the activity name aloud.

Intermediate Have students name their favorite sports. Ask students if they are *jealous* of any famous athletes.

Advanced Discuss with students what it feels like to be jealous of someone. Why do people sometimes feel *jealous* of one another?

Advanced High Have student partners work together to write a short paragraph explaining something they are *especially* good at doing.

See ELL Lesson 18, p. E22–E31, for scaffolded support.

- Notes throughout the Teacher's Edition scaffold instruction to each language proficiency level.

Vocabulary in Context Cards 171–180

- Provide visual support and additional practice for Target Vocabulary words.

For this week's English Language Learners lessons, see Teacher's Edition, pages E22–E31.

? Essential Question How can people share their successes?

	Day 1	Day 2
Oral Language Listening Comprehension	**Read Aloud** "Darnell Tries Harder," T156–T157 ☑ Target Vocabulary, T157	**Turn and Talk, T163**
Vocabulary **Comprehension** Skills and Strategies **Reading** 	☑ **Comprehension** Preview the Target Skill, T157 ☑ **Introduce Vocabulary** Vocabulary in Context, T158–T159 **Develop Background** ☑ Target Vocabulary, T160–T161 	**Introduce Comprehension** ☑ Understanding Characters, T162–T163 Question, T162–T163 **Read "Moon Runner,"** T164–T174 Focus on Genre, T164 Stop and Think, T167, T169, T174
Cross-Curricular **Connections** **Fluency** **Decoding**	☑ **Fluency** Model Accuracy and Self-Correction, T156	☑ **Fluency** Teach Accuracy and Self-Correction, T182
Spelling **Grammar** **Writing**	☑ **Spelling** Prefixes *re-, un-, dis-*: Pretest, T188 ☑ **Grammar** Daily Proofreading Practice, T190 Teach Prepositions, T190 ☑ **Write to Narrate: Narrative** **Composition** Analyze the Model, T194	☑ **Spelling** Prefixes *re-, un-, dis-*: Word Sort, T188 ☑ **Grammar** Daily Proofreading Practice, T191 Teach Prepositional Phrases, T191 ☑ **Write to Narrate: Narrative** **Composition** Focus Trait: Word Choice, T195
Writing Prompt	*Describe your favorite outdoor game*	*Explain why you think Mina was right or wrong to lose the tryout race.*

Whole Group

Whole Group Language Arts

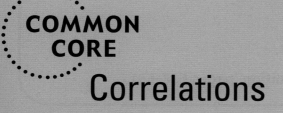

COMMON CORE
Correlations

Day 1	Day 2
Comprehension RF.4.4c **Fluency** RF.4.4c **Spelling** L.4.2d **Grammar** L.4.1e **Write to Narrate** W.4.3a, W.4.3d, W.4.5	**Turn and Talk** RL.4.1 **Introduce Comprehension** RL.4.1, RL.4.3 **Read** RL.4.1, RL.4.3, RL.4.4, RL.4.6, RL.4.10, RF.4.4c **Fluency** RF.4.4c **Spelling** L.4.2d **Grammar** L.4.1e **Write to Narrate** W.4.3a, W.4.3d, W.4.5, L.4.3a

Suggestions for Small Groups (See pp. T201–T215.)
Suggestions for Intervention (See pp. S22–S31.)
Suggestions for English Language Learners (See pp. E22–E31.)

JOURNEYS DIGITAL Powered by DESTINATIONReading·
Teacher One-Stop: Lesson Planning

Day 3

Turn and Talk, T175
Oral Language, T175

Read "Moon Runner," T164–T174
Develop Comprehension, T166, T168, T170, T172
☑ **Target Vocabulary**
"Moon Runner," T166, T168, T172
Your Turn, T175
Deepen Comprehension
☑ Understanding Characters, T180–T181

Cross-Curricular Connection
Science, T173
☑ **Fluency**
Practice Accuracy and Self-Correction, T173
☑ **Decoding**
Recognizing Prefixes *re-, un-, dis-,* T183

☑ **Spelling**
Prefixes *re-, un-, dis-:* **Analogies,** T189
☑ **Grammar**
Daily Proofreading Practice, T191
Extend Prepositional Phrases, T191
☑ **Write to Narrate:**
Narrative Composition
Prewrite, T195

Write about a time you had to make a sacrifice to save a friendship.

Turn and Talk SL.4.1a, SL.4.1b, SL.4.1c, SL.4.1d
Read RL.4.1, RL.4.3, RL.4.4, RL.4.6, RL.4.10, RF.4.4c
Deepen Comprehension RL.4.1, RL.4.3
Fluency RF.4.4c
Decoding RF.4.3a
Spelling L.4.2d
Grammar L.4.1e
Write to Narrate W.4.3a, W.4.3d, W.4.5

Day 4

Text to World, T179

Read "A Day for the Moon," T176–T178
Connect to Social Studies, T176
Target Vocabulary Review, T177
Develop Comprehension, T178
Weekly Internet Challenge, T178
Making Connections, T179
☑ **Vocabulary Strategies**
Homophones, Homonyms, and Homographs, T184–T185

☑ **Fluency**
Practice Accuracy and Self-Correction, T177

☑ **Spelling**
Prefixes *re-, un-, dis-:* **Connect to Writing,** T189
☑ **Grammar**
Daily Proofreading Practice, T192
Review Prepositional Phrases, T192
☑ **Write to Narrate:**
Narrative Composition
Draft, T196

Write an email that invites people to join your friends for an activity.

Text to World W.4.7, W.4.8, SL.4.4
Read RI.4.2, RI.4.10, RF.4.4c
Making Connections RI.4.10, W.4.7, W.4.8, W.4.10, SL.4.4
Vocabulary Strategies L.4.1g, L.4.4c
Fluency RF.4.4c
Spelling L.4.2d
Grammar L.4.1e
Write to Narrate W.4.3a, W.4.3d, W.4.3e, W.4.5, L.4.5c

Day 5

Listening and Speaking, T187

Connect and Extend
Read to Connect, T186
Independent Reading, T186
Extend Through Research, T187

☑ **Fluency**
Progress Monitoring, T199

☑ **Spelling**
Prefixes *re-, un-, dis-:* **Assess,** T189
☑ **Grammar**
Daily Proofreading Practice, T192
Connect Grammar to Writing, T192–T193
☑ **Write to Narrate:**
Narrative Composition
Revise for Word Choice, T196

Describe how you define a successful friendship.

Connect and Extend SL.4.1a
Fluency RF.4.4c
Spelling L.4.2d
Grammar L.4.1e
Write to Narrate W.4.3a, W.4.3d, W.4.3e, W.4.5, L.4.5c

Your Skills for the Week

☑ **Vocabulary**
Target Vocabulary Strategies:
Homophones, Homonyms, and Homographs

☑ **Comprehension**
Understanding Characters
Question

☑ **Decoding**
Recognizing Prefixes *re-, un-, dis-*

☑ **Fluency**
Accuracy and Self-Correction

☑ **Language Arts**
Spelling
Grammar
Writing

Weekly Leveled Readers

Differentiated Support for This Week's Targets

✓ **TARGET SKILL**

Understanding Characters

✓ **TARGET STRATEGY**

Question

✓ **TARGET VOCABULARY**

gigantic	jealous
miniature	haze
especially	lure
lapped	deliberately
vanished	crisp

Additional Tools

Vocabulary in Context Cards

Comprehension Tool: Graphic Organizer Transparency 1

❓ Essential Question

How can people share their successes?

Vocabulary Reader

Level O

Build Target Vocabulary

• Introduce the Target Vocabulary in context and build comprehension using the Target Strategy.

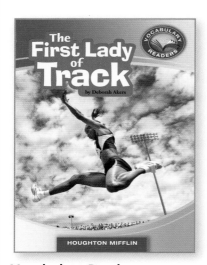

Vocabulary Reader

Blackline Master 18.1

Intervention

Scaffolded Support

• Provide extra support in applying the Target Vocabulary, Target Skill, and Target Strategy in context.

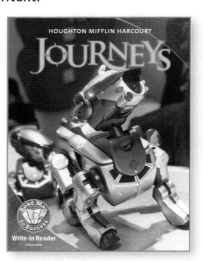

Write-In Reader

For Vocabulary Reader Lesson Plans, see Small Group pages T204–T205.

Leveled Readers

Struggling Readers
Level N

Objective: Use understanding characters and the question strategy to read *Tammy's Goal*.

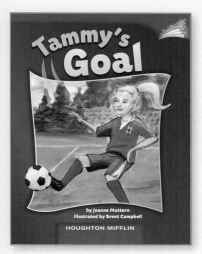

Blackline Master 18.3

On Level
Level P

Objective: Use understanding characters and the question strategy to read *Baseball Boys*.

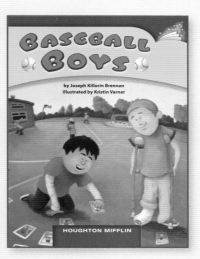

Blackline Master 18.4

Advanced
Level S

Objective: Use understanding characters and the question strategy to read *The Friendship Garden*.

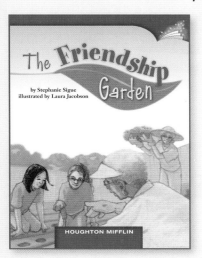

Blackline Master 18.5

English Language Learners
Level P

Objective: Use understanding characters and the question strategy to read *Baseball Friends*.

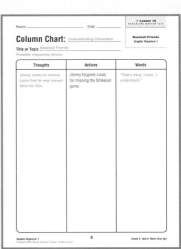

Blackline Master 18.6

**For Leveled Reader Lesson Plans,
see Small Group pages T208–T211.**

Ready-Made Work Stations

Manage Independent Activities

Use the Ready-Made Work Stations to establish a consistent routine for students working independently. Each station contains three activities. Students who experience success with the *Get Started!* activity move on to the *Reach Higher!* and *Challenge Yourself!* activities, as time permits.

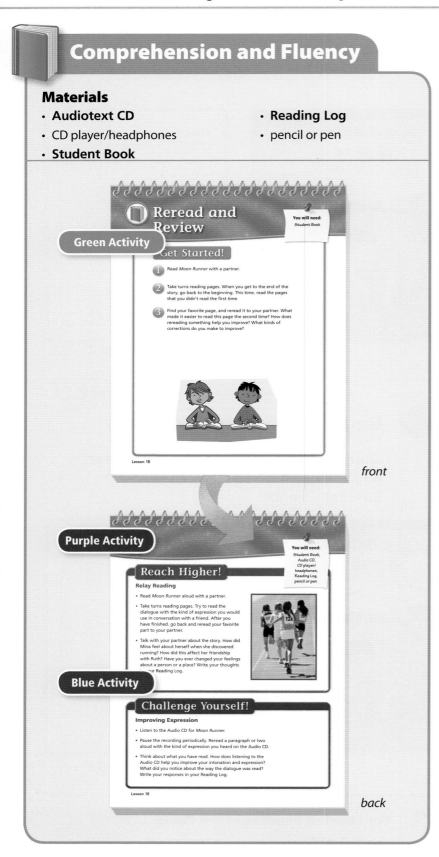

Comprehension and Fluency

Materials
- **Audiotext CD**
- CD player/headphones
- **Student Book**
- **Reading Log**
- pencil or pen

Green Activity

Reread and Review

You will need: Student Book

Get Started!

1. Read *Moon Runner* with a partner.

2. Take turns reading pages. When you get to the end of the story, go back to the beginning. This time, read the pages that you didn't read the first time.

3. Find your favorite page, and reread it to your partner. What made it easier to read this page the second time? How does rereading something help you improve? What kinds of corrections do you make to improve?

Lesson 18

front

Purple Activity

Reach Higher!

You will need: Student Book, Audio CD, CD player/headphones, Reading Log, pencil or pen

Relay Reading

- Read *Moon Runner* aloud with a partner.

- Take turns reading pages. Try to read the dialogue with the kind of expression you would use in conversation with a friend. After you have finished, go back and reread your favorite part to your partner.

- Talk with your partner about the story. How did Mina feel about herself when she discovered running? How did this affect her friendship with Ruth? Have you ever changed your feelings about a person or a place? Write your thoughts your Reading Log.

Blue Activity

Challenge Yourself!

Improving Expression

- Listen to the Audio CD for *Moon Runner*.

- Pause the recording periodically. Reread a paragraph or two aloud with the kind of expression you heard on the Audio CD.

- Think about what you have read. How does listening to the Audio CD help you improve your intonation and expression? What did you notice about the way the dialogue was read? Write your responses in your Reading Log.

Lesson 18

back

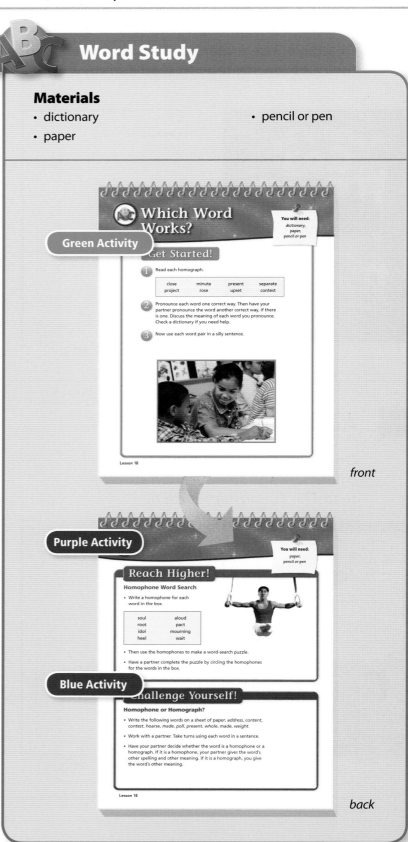

Word Study

Materials
- dictionary
- paper
- pencil or pen

Green Activity

Which Word Works?

You will need: dictionary, paper, pencil or pen

Get Started!

1. Read each homograph.

close	minute	present	separate
project	rose	upset	contest

2. Pronounce each word one correct way. Then have your partner pronounce the word another correct way, if there is one. Discuss the meaning of each word you pronounce. Check a dictionary if you need help.

3. Now use each word pair in a silly sentence.

Lesson 18

front

Purple Activity

Reach Higher!

You will need: paper, pencil or pen

Homophone Word Search

- Write a homophone for each word in the box.

soul	aloud
root	pact
idol	mourning
heel	wait

- Then use the homophones to make a word-search puzzle.

- Have a partner complete the puzzle by circling the homophones for the words in the box.

Blue Activity

Challenge Yourself!

Homophone or Homograph?

- Write the following words on a sheet of paper: *address, content, contest, hoarse, made, poll, present, whole, made, weight.*

- Work with a partner. Take turns using each word in a sentence.

- Have your partner decide whether the word is a homophone or a homograph. If it is a homophone, your partner gives the word's other spelling and other meaning. If it is a homograph, you give the word's other meaning.

Lesson 18

back

Think and Write

Materials
- library books, magazines/newspapers
- colored pencils or markers
- paper
- pencil or pen

Go for Your Goals!

Green Activity

Get Started!

You will need: library books, magazines/newspapers, paper, pencil or pen

1. Do some research about Wilma Rudolph. Find out the challenges she faced and how she overcame them. Learn about Rudolph's athletic achievements. Look for information about what she did after she was no longer a track star.

2. Next, research Wilma Rudolph Day. When is it, and why do you think that day was chosen?

3. Use the information you find to write a brief biography of Wilma Rudolph.

Lesson 18

front

Purple Activity

Reach Higher!

Run for Fun

You will need: library books, colored pencils or markers, magazines/newspapers, paper, pencil or pen

- Running is one of the best forms of exercise. What can you find out about this exercise? Use library books, as well as magazine and newspaper articles, to do your research.

- Check out rules that beginning runners should follow. How do runners warm up before running and cool down afterwards? What equipment do they need? Is there a best time to run? How do they stay safe from injury?

- Make a pamphlet or handout to help others get started running safely. Use pictures to make your points.

Blue Activity

Challenge Yourself!

Fitness Fuel

- What healthful foods make up the best diet for an athlete? Research sports magazines, or interview someone who might know about such things. Use questions such as these: How much protein, carbohydrates, fruits, and vegetables do you need? What vitamins and minerals should you have? What's the right amount of fluids or water? How much time each day should an athlete spend practicing?

- Write the results of your research or interview, and share it with classmates you know who are interested in sports.

Lesson 18

back

JOURNEYS DIGITAL — Powered by DESTINATIONReading®

Independent Activities

Have students complete these activities at a computer center or a center with an audio CD player.

LAUNCH > **Comprehension and Grammar Activities**
- Practice and apply this week's skills.

LAUNCH > **Student eBook**
- Read and listen to this week's selections and skill lessons.

LAUNCH > **WriteSmart CD-ROM**
- Review student versions of this week's writing model.

LAUNCH > **Audiotext CD**
- Listen to books or selections on CD.

Single Log In

Teacher Read Aloud

Model Fluency

Accuracy and Self-Correction Explain that when good readers read aloud, they work to increase automatic and successful word recognition. They also monitor their reading and correct words when necessary.

- Display **Projectable 18.1**. As you read each sentence, model how to read with automatic word recognition and self-correction.

- Point out that automatic word recognition and self-correction help make better sense of the text.

- Reread the sentences together with students, demonstrating automatic word recognition and self-correction.

Darnell Tries Harder

Darnell rolled out of bed on a **crisp** fall morning. He looked out his window and smiled as his dog Skeeter trotted towards the bike path that ran through the backyard. Their neighbor pushed her new baby in a stroller along the path towards the park. From the window they looked like the **miniature** characters in his sister's model train set. He looked up the path and saw a light **haze** on "The Hill." He didn't know if the towering giant had another name. In the neighborhood, it was always just called "The Hill."

Climbing the **gigantic** hill on your bike unofficially separated big kids from little kids in the neighborhood. Darnell had never made it all the way to the top of that hill, although most of his friends had by now. His smile **vanished** as he saw his older sister Lannie zip out of the garage on her shiny red bike. She pedaled slowly and **deliberately** across the grass, but took off once she hit the smooth pavement. Watching her climb "The Hill" made **①** Darnell **jealous**. He and his sister competed at everything, **especially** sports. Lannie had only climbed it for the first time last month, but she seemed to do it every day now.

Projectable 18.1

After breakfast, Darnell waited until the **lure** of her newest book on soccer had called Lannie to her room. Now was his chance to try without her watchful eyes! He walked his bike through the backyard and stared at the hill. 'I'm just going to do it,' he thought. He hopped on and pushed down hard on the pedals. He picked up speed, and the breeze **lapped** at his face.

"What are *you* up to?" came Lannie's singsong voice from behind. She caught up to him just as they reached the hill. "See you at the top!" she yelled. Lannie pulled slightly ahead as they reached the halfway point. This was the steepest part, the part he had never passed. Darnell bit down, stood on his pedals, and pushed even harder. He passed the midway **2** mark and pulled slightly ahead of Lannie; he was going to make it!

In a flurry, they both reached the top, completely out of breath. Darnell couldn't decide if his heart was pounding more from the ride or the excitement. Lannie looked over and grinned at him. "Nice ride, but I think it was a tie. Race you to the bottom!" **3**

Listening Comprehension

Preview the Target Skill

Read aloud the passage with accuracy and self-correction. Then ask the following questions.

1 Understanding Characters
How does Darnell feels about his sister at the beginning of the story? His smile vanishes when he sees her on her bike; he is jealous as she climbs the hill.

2 Understanding Characters
How does Darnell's respond to Lannie's taunting? When Lannie taunts him, Darnell becomes even more determined; at the halfway point he bites down, pulls ahead of his sister, and reaches the top.

3 Cause and Effect
Why might Lannie have said, "Race you to the bottom!"? Sample answer: Darnell and Lannie often competed, expecially in sports. Lannie thought their race to the top ended in a tie, so she extended it to include riding down.

✔ Target Vocabulary

- Reread "Darnell Tries Harder" aloud.
- As you read, pause briefly to explain each highlighted vocabulary word.
- Discuss the meaning of each word as it is used in the article.

crisp dry and cool

miniature very small; tiny

haze a mist in the air

gigantic huge; enormous

vanished disappeared

deliberately done on purpose

jealous want what someone else has

especially mainly; particularly

lure attraction

lapped moved gently against

✓ Introduce Vocabulary

Teach

Display and discuss the **Vocabulary in Context Cards,** using the routine below. Direct students to **Student Book pp. 450–451.** See also **Instructional Routine 9.**

1 **Read and pronounce the word.** Read the word once alone, then together with students.

2 **Explain the word.** Read aloud the explanation under *What Does It Mean?*

3 **Discuss vocabulary in context.** Together, read aloud the sentence on the front of the card. Help students explain and use the word in new sentences.

4 **Engage with the word.** Ask and discuss the *Think About It* question with students.

Apply

Give partners or small groups one or two **Vocabulary in Context Cards.**

• Help students start the *Talk It Over* activity on the back of their card.

• Have students complete activities for all the cards during the week.

Lesson 18

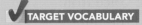
✓ **TARGET VOCABULARY**

gigantic
miniature
especially
lapped
vanished
jealous
haze
lure
deliberately
crisp

Vocabulary Reader   Context Cards

450

Vocabulary in Context

1 gigantic
Just one good play can make a gigantic, or very large, difference in a game.

2 miniature
Some people call miniature golf a sport, even though the course is small.

3 especially
This girl is especially proud that she won because she got a slow start.

4 lapped
After the swimming race, these kids rested as the water lapped gently at their legs.

ELL **ENGLISH LANGUAGE LEARNERS**

Scaffold

Beginning Use actions to demonstrate the meaning of *miniature, gigantic,* and *lapped.* Then have students demonstrate the meaning as you say each word aloud.

Advanced Ask students questions to confirm their understanding. *Do you think it's safe for people to drive in a haze of clouds? Why or why not?*

Intermediate Have students use sentence frames for each Vocabulary word. For example, *Don't be _____ of your friend's accomplishments. jealous* Have them repeat the sentences.

Advanced High Have partners ask and answer questions about each vocabulary word. For example, *Would you be concerned if your lunch vanished?*

See ELL Lesson 18, pp. E22–E31, for scaffolded support

- Study each Context Card.
- Use a dictionary to help you understand the meanings of these words.

5 vanished

The fly ball sailed over this outfielder's head and vanished, or disappeared.

6 jealous

Kids can be jealous. They might envy a friend's success in sports.

7 haze

The soccer game was cancelled because of this foggy haze that filled the air.

8 lure

The best pitchers can lure, or tempt, a hitter to swing at the next pitch.

9 deliberately

On most relay teams, the best runner goes last deliberately, or on purpose.

10 crisp

This sharp, crisp image is a good one for a team scrapbook.

451

VOCABULARY IN CONTEXT CARDS 171–180

gigantic

Just one good play can make a gigantic, or very large, difference in a game.

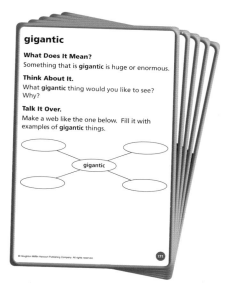

gigantic

What Does It Mean?
Something that is gigantic is huge or enormous.

Think About It.
What gigantic thing would you like to see? Why?

Talk It Over.
Make a web like the one below. Fill it with examples of gigantic things.

gigantic

171

front   back

Monitor Vocabulary

Are students able to understand and use Target Vocabulary words?

IF...	THEN...
students have difficulty understanding and using most of the Target Vocabulary words,	▶ use **Vocabulary in Context Cards** and differentiate the **Vocabulary Reader,** *The First Lady of Track,* for Struggling Readers, p. T204. *See also Intervention Lesson 18, pp. S22–S31.*
students can understand and use most of the Target Vocabulary words,	▶ use **Vocabulary in Context Cards** and differentiate the **Vocabulary Reader,** *The First Lady of Track,* for On-Level Readers, p. T204.
students can understand and use all of the Target Vocabulary words,	▶ differentiate the **Vocabulary Reader,** *The First Lady of Track,* for Advanced Readers, p. T205.

SMALL GROUP Options

Vocabulary Reader, pp. T204–T205.
Group English Language Learners according to language proficiency.

Develop Background

 ENGLISH LANGUAGE LEARNERS

Scaffold

Beginning Show students photographs of well-known sports such as running, basketball, football, soccer, baseball, and swimming. Have students repeat after you as you point to each photograph and say the activity name aloud.

Intermediate Have students use the photographs above to name their favorite sports. Ask students if they are *jealous* of any famous athletes.

Advanced Discuss with students what it feels like to be *jealous*. Ask: *Why do people sometimes feel jealous of one another?*

Advanced High Have student partners work together to write a short paragraph explaining something they are *especially* good at doing.

See ELL Lesson 18, p. E22–E31, for scaffolded support.

 Target Vocabulary

1 | Teach/Model

- Use the photograph of sportsmanship on **Student Book p. 452** to explain that "Moon Runner" is about a girl whose talent for running makes her friend **jealous.**

- Use **Vocabulary in Context Cards** to review the student-friendly explanations of each Target Vocabulary word.

- Have students silently read **Student Book p. 452**. Then read the passage aloud.

2 | Guided Practice

Ask students the first item below and discuss their responses. Continue in this way until students have answered a question about each Target Vocabulary word.

1. Describe a fun, outdoor activity that will always **lure** you out of your house.

2. What is your favorite thing to do on a **crisp** fall day? Explain.

3. If the sky is filled with **haze,** how might it affect drivers?

4. If water **lapped** against you, would you expect it to hurt? Explain.

5. Would you be surprised if someone **deliberately** tried to win a game or a race? Explain.

6. In which subject at school are you **especially** good?

7. What did you do the last time one of your belongings **vanished**?

8. If a friend feels **jealous**, how can he or she best handle the situation?

9. Using specific details, describe something **miniature** in your house.

10. If I told you that the rhinoceros at the zoo was big, but the elephant was **gigantic**, which animal was larger?

Background

✔ TARGET VOCABULARY **Being a Good Sport** Does a game of baseball or soccer ever lure you and your friends outside? Many kids love outdoor sports, whether the sky is crisp and clear or filled with a rainy haze. Some people even have happy memories of playing in cold weather while the wind lapped against their faces.

Games give everyone a chance to compete and have fun, but what happens when you face a good friend in a contest? Do you deliberately keep from doing your best, or do you try especially hard to win? Many friendships have vanished because of jealous feelings. A contest can be miniature or gigantic in its importance. How would you try to be a good sport?

...se to be a ...port whether ...in a baseball ...a track meet, ...elling bee.

3 Apply

• Have partners take turns reading a paragraph of the passage on **Student Book p. 452** to one another.

• Tell partners to pause at and explain each highlighted vocabulary word as they read. Have partners use a dictionary to look up any words they do not understand.

• Have each partner use one vocabulary word in a new sentence.

Introduce Comprehension

SHARE OBJECTIVES

- Infer characters' feelings and motives based on their behavior.
- Ask questions to understand characters and their relationships.

SKILL TRACE

Understanding Characters

Introduce	**T162–T163**, T180–T181
Differentiate	T206–T207
Reteach	T214
Review	Lesson 29
Test	Weekly Tests, Lesson 18

ELL ENGLISH LANGUAGE LEARNERS

Scaffold

Beginning Using Student Book pp. 455–464, teach the word *characters*. Point out the characters in the story. Discuss how the characters might be feeling in the illustrations.

Intermediate Display these sentence frames: *If I am angry, I might _____. When I feel jealous, I _____.* Guide students to complete the sentences. Then have them explain how they might act when they feel so.

Advanced Ask students to explain orally how they might tell how someone is feeling. Discuss things that a person might say or do that reveals how they feel?

Advanced High Have students write two or three sentences that show through words or actions how a person is feeling. Have a partner read the sentence and explain what the character is feeling.

See ELL Lesson 18, pp. E22–E31, for scaffolded support.

✔ Understanding Characters; Question

1 Teach/Model

AL *Academic Language*

character a person or animal in a story

infer to figure out something that is not stated directly

- Explain that authors create story **characters** that seem like real people. They feel, act, and talk in a believable way.

- Read and discuss with students **Student Book p. 453**. Have them use the Academic Language in the discussion.

- Display **Projectable 18.2**. Have students students read "A Friend in Need."

UNDERSTANDING CHARACTERS Students can compare what they know about how real people think and act with the behavior of the characters in a story to **infer** the characters' feelings and motives.

- Explain that you will use the Column Chart to record the characters' thoughts, actions, and words.

Projectable 18.2

Think Aloud *I read that Brady has failed another math test. He worries what his parents will say. I'll begin by recording what Brady thinks and says in the chart.*

QUESTION Explain that asking questions about what a character does and why can help students fully understand the story.

Think Aloud *The author begins with an important action: "Brady hung his head." Right away I want to know, "Why did he do that?" I'll look for the answer to this question as I continue. As I read on, Brady's action helps me understand that he feels upset.*

Comprehension

✓ TARGET SKILL Understanding Characters

As you read "Moon Runner," try to figure out the characters' feelings and motives, or reasons for their behavior. Think about the ways they think and interact with each other. How would you or someone you know behave in similar situations? Make a graphic organizer like the one below. It will help you keep track of the characters' thoughts, actions, and words.

Thoughts	Actions	Words

✓ TARGET STRATEGY Question

Use your graphic organizer to help you ask important questions about a character's behavior and personality. For example, you might ask *why* a character acts a certain way or says certain things. It is useful to ask yourself questions before, during, and after reading a text.

JOURNEYS DIGITAL Powered by DESTINATIONReading®
Comprehension Activities: Lesson 18

453

Monitor Comprehension

Are students able to understand characters' motives and feelings?

IF...	THEN...
students have difficulty understanding characters,	▶ **Differentiate Comprehension** for Struggling Readers, p. T206. *See also Intervention Lesson 18, pp. S22–S31.*
students can understand characters,	▶ **Differentiate Comprehension** for On-Level Readers, p. T206.
students can accurately question the text to understand characters,	▶ **Differentiate Comprehension** for Advanced Readers, p. 207.

SMALL GROUP Options **Differentiate Comprehension:** pp. T206–T207. *Group English Language Learners according to language proficiency. See also ELL Lesson 18, pp. E22–E31, for scaffolded support.*

2 Guided Practice

Guide partners to copy and complete their own column charts for "A Friend in Need." Then review their charts as a class, discussing what questions students asked to arrive at their inferences.

3 Apply

Turn and Talk Have partners use their Column Charts to question and discuss the characters' motives and feelings.

Ask students to think about characters in another text. Have them record the characters' thoughts, actions, and words in a Column Chart and use their completed charts to infer characters' feelings and motives.

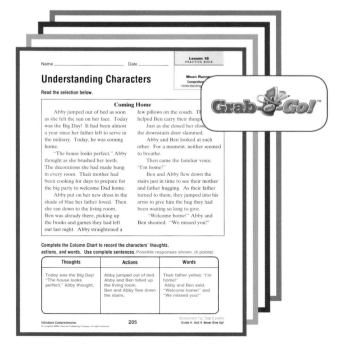

Practice Book p. 205
See Grab-and-Go™ Resources for additional leveled practice.

Introduce the
Main
Selection

TARGET SKILL

UNDERSTANDING CHARACTERS

Explain that as they read, students will use **Graphic Organizer 1: Column Chart** to record details about the main characters, including:

• Mina and Ruth's thoughts, actions, and words

TARGET STRATEGY

QUESTION Students will use a Column Chart to ask questions about why characters think, talk, and act as they do in order to tell more about characters and their realtionships.

GENRE: Realistic Fiction

• Read the genre information on **Student Book p. 454** with students.

• Share and discuss **Genre Blackline Master: Fiction**

• Preview the selection and model identifying the characteristics of the genre.

Think Aloud *The illustrations make the yard and park look like places I've seen. The people seem realistic and the story seems to have a present-day setting.*

• As you preview, ask students to identify other features of realistic fiction.

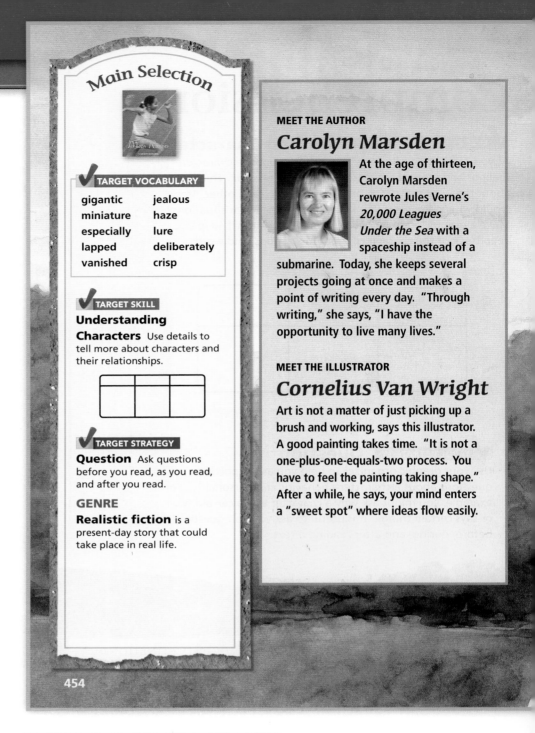

Main Selection

✓ TARGET VOCABULARY

gigantic	jealous
miniature	haze
especially	lure
lapped	deliberately
vanished	crisp

✓ TARGET SKILL

Understanding Characters Use details to tell more about characters and their relationships.

✓ TARGET STRATEGY

Question Ask questions before you read, as you read, and after you read.

GENRE

Realistic fiction is a present-day story that could take place in real life.

454

MEET THE AUTHOR

Carolyn Marsden

At the age of thirteen, Carolyn Marsden rewrote Jules Verne's *20,000 Leagues Under the Sea* with a spaceship instead of a submarine. Today, she keeps several projects going at once and makes a point of writing every day. "Through writing," she says, "I have the opportunity to live many lives."

MEET THE ILLUSTRATOR

Cornelius Van Wright

Art is not a matter of just picking up a brush and working, says this illustrator. A good painting takes time. "It is not a one-plus-one-equals-two process. You have to feel the painting taking shape." After a while, he says, your mind enters a "sweet spot" where ideas flow easily.

Reading the Selection

	Pre-reading	Reading
Supported	**SELECTION SUMMARY** Use **Blackline Master 18.2** to give students an overview before they read. **AUDIOTEXT CD** Have students listen to the selection as they follow along in their books.	**AUTHOR'S MESSAGE** After reading the selection, discuss students' inferences about characters' feelings and motives.
Independent	**PREVIEW** Have students use the title, introduction, and illustrations to discuss predictions and clues. Some students may read the story independently.	**TEXT EVIDENCE** Pause after pp. 457, 461, and 464 and have students write questions that can be answered using text evidence in the story. After reading, discuss students' questions and answers.

Moon Runner

by **Carolyn Marsden**

selection illustrated by
Cornelius Van Wright

Essential Question

How can people share their successes?

455

❓ Essential Question

- Read aloud the **Essential Question** on **Student Book p. 455**. *How can people share their successes?*

- Tell students to think about this question as they read "Moon Runner."

Set Purpose

- Explain that good readers set a purpose for reading, based on their preview of the selection and what they know about the genre, as well as what they want to learn by reading.

- Model setting a reading purpose.

Think Aloud   *There's a crescent moon in some pictures, and the selection title includes the word "moon." I wonder what the connection is between the moon and running. If I read the story, maybe I will find out.*

- Have students share and record in their journals their reading purposes.

JOURNEYS DIGITAL Powered by **DESTINATIONReading**
Student eBook: Read and Listen

Name _____ Date _____

Lesson 18
BLACKLINE MASTER 18.2

Moon Runner

Moon Runner
Selection Summary

Pages 456–457
Mina joins a new school and makes friends with Ruth. When track tryouts start, Mina finds she can run faster than Ruth. Mina loses a race on purpose. This causes tension between the girls. Mina worries that Ruth is jealous and won't want to be friends anymore.

Pages 458–459
Mina tries to say she's sorry for letting Ruth win the race. Ruth says she knew Mina let her win and that has upset her. She wants to know who is really the fastest runner. Ruth decides they should go to the park right then and race each other.

Pages 460–461
Mina agrees to race. Ruth gives her the Fellow Friends Handshake. Mina thinks of the Chinese Moon Festival, and she wishes she could celebrate with Ruth. When they get to the park, they stretch and warm up. Ruth asks some young boys passing by to help them judge the race.

Pages 462–463
When the race starts, Mina finds herself holding back at first. But she doesn't like the way it feels to fall behind. She decides she will not hold back. She will run as hard as she can. Ruth is running beside her. Mina feels they are running like antelopes across a plain.

Page 464
Mina wins the race, and Ruth smiles. The girls lay in a field of small flowers and look up at the sky. Mina sees the crescent of the new moon in the sky. She feels that she is growing round and whole just like the moon. Then she thanks Ruth for helping her try her best.

Selection Summary   4   Grade 4, Unit 4: Never Give Up!
© Houghton Mifflin Harcourt Publishing Company. All rights reserved.

Blackline Master 18.2

Develop Comprehension

Pause at the stopping points to ask students the following questions.

1 ✓ **TARGET VOCABULARY**

*Why might Mina **deliberately** talk to Ruth when Mina really wanted to hide? Sample answer: Mina wanted to see how Ruth felt about what had happened between them.*

2 Draw Conclusions

How might Ruth feel if she knew that Mina had let her win the race? Sample answers: Ruth might think it was dishonest or bad sportsmanship; it might hurt her pride.

3 Cause and Effect

On p. 457, Mina talks about changes in the Fellow Friends group. What effect does Mina identify? Sample answer: Most of the time the four friends do not play together anymore. Ruth and Sammy play together; Mina and Alana play together.

When Mina joins a new school, she quickly becomes "Fellow Friends" with Ruth, Alana, and Sammy. But things begin to change once track tryouts start. Mina suddenly discovers that she is a fast runner. Everyone is surprised, especially Ruth. Ruth has always been one of the best athletes at school, but during a tryout race, she and Mina tie for first place. Secretly, Mina knows that she is a faster runner than Ruth. Rather than hurt Ruth's feelings, Mina loses another tryout race deliberately. Now the girls know their friendship is in trouble. They sit outside of Ruth's house eating chips and drinking lemonade.

As Mina sat down in the lawn chair, she wished it was still the day the Fellow Friends had welcomed her into the group.

Little brown birds hopped along the branches of the walnut tree. Did they ever get jealous or scared?

She wanted to hide from Ruth, covering her face with the glass of lemonade. Instead, she said, "Ruth, do you think . . ." She paused, not knowing how to put it. "Do you think the Fellow Friends group is falling apart?"

> **STOP AND THINK**
> **Author's Craft** Authors tell stories from different **points of view**. Sometimes they are actually in the story and sometimes they are outside the story, speaking as a narrator. From what point of view is this story told? How do you know?

456

ELL **ENGLISH LANGUAGE LEARNERS**

Scaffold

Beginning Using the illustrations, preview the selection with students. Help them name and identify characters' feelings.	**Advanced** After reading pp. 456–457, have students summarize the problem, how Mina is feeling, and why she feels that way.
Intermediate Read pp. 456–457 with students. Then guide them to complete sentence frames about the text, such as: *Mina wanted to _____ from Ruth. She felt _____.*	**Advanced High** After reading pages 456–457, have students write two sentences that show something Mina did that revealed how she was feeling.

See ELL Lesson 18, pp. E22–E31, for scaffolded support.

Ruth looked up from her glass. "Why do you ask that?"

Mina shrugged and forced herself to go on. "Well, you and Sammy play alone a lot now. And Alana and I do, too."

"Yeah. I noticed." Ruth flicked a leaf off her forearm.

3 "This started when track started."

Ruth stared into her empty glass, as though studying the flecks of lemon pulp that clung to the sides.

457

STOP AND THINK
Author's Craft: Point of View

- Remind students that **point of view** is the narrator's view of events. It is how a narrator sees and interprets what is happening.

- Explain that sometimes a story is told by a character in the story. This narrator uses the pronouns *I*, *me*, and *we* and tells the story from the **first-person point of view**.

- Point out that at other times, the narrator is outside the story. The narrator is not a character in the story, but observes the events and characters using the pronouns *he*, *she*, and *they* to describe what happens. Explain that this kind of narration is called **third-person point of view**. Remind students that in a story with third-person point of view, the narrator knows what characters think, feel, say, and do.

- Have students complete the **Stop and Think** activity on **Student Book p. 456.**

Develop Comprehension

④ Identify Author's Purpose
Why do you think the author includes a description of the birds and their actions? Sample answers: To show how friends can help each other; to make a connection between friendship and teamwork; even though only one of the birds "wins" the chip, all three birds share the prize.

⑤ ✔ TARGET VOCABULARY
What foods might **lure** *you to the dinner table? Why? Responses will vary.*

⑥ Cause and Effect
Why does the author say that Mina's legs "felt as though they needed braces"? Sample answer: Mina is nervous at the thought of racing her friend and her legs feel weak.

Would she keep on staring into the glass, or set it down and leave? The conversation might end and never start up again. Mina had to keep talking. "I've never run before, at least not in races, or with anyone timing me," she said. "I didn't mean to tie you in the race. I didn't know I could."

"It wasn't your fault," Ruth said.

"But it still made you mad."

"Yeah. Sometimes."

Mina put down her glass and then picked it up again, needing something to hold on to. "But I didn't mean to tie you."

"Don't apologize."

A bird landed on the other side of the table. It cocked its head, first to one side and then the other, eyeing the bag of chips. *Just one, please? Just a nibble?*

④ Ruth reached into the bag and tossed a chip toward the bird. It began to tug at it, trying to break off a bite. Two more flew down to help.

> ✔ **STOP AND THINK**
> **Question** Why is it hard for Mina to talk to Ruth?

458

ELL **ENGLISH LANGUAGE LEARNERS**

Scaffold

Beginning For each question, accept one-word answers and expand student responses into sentences. For example, if a student's response to question 5 is "pizza," expand the answer by saying, "Yes, pizza might lure me to the dinner table because I like cheese and tomatoes."

Advanced Have students respond to the questions in complete sentences. Provide corrective feedback as needed.

Intermediate Provide part of a response for each question, and have students complete it. Then have students repeat the complete response to confirm their understanding.

Advanced High Have students tell how they know the answer to each question based on details from the story.

See ELL Lesson 18, pp. E22–E31, for scaffolded support.

"You came out of nowhere and ran as fast as me," Ruth said. "I've worked all my life to be good at sports. I practice soccer three times a week. And here you come . . . But it's okay. Really, it's okay."

Mina felt like one of the tiny birds—out on the end of a branch, but with no wings. Yet she had to continue. "In the tryouts I tried to run slower."

"I know you did. And that was even worse. You know, Mina, when athletes compete, it isn't fair if someone doesn't try their hardest. You made me feel like I didn't really win. Or like at any time you could surprise me and beat me and I won't know what hit me."

"I didn't know what else to do."

"Yeah, I knew you lost on purpose because we're friends. A real athlete wouldn't have done that."

"But I'm not a real athlete," said Mina. "I'm a girlie girl."

Ruth laughed so loudly that the birds flew off. "You're one fast girlie girl."

Ruth's laughter made Mina laugh, too. Then she interlocked her fingers and looked down into the tight ball her hands made. She sighed and looked up. "I just want to be a Fellow Friend."

5 Ruth threw another chip to lure the birds back before turning to Mina. She squinted and screwed up her face against the bright sun. "It's too late. You're already more than a friend."

"What do you mean?"

"A friend is a friend. I've got lots. But there's not a lot of people I can race against." She paused. "I got an idea. I want to know something. Let's go over to the park right now and race."

6 Mina's legs suddenly felt as though they needed braces. She wondered if Wilma Rudolph had ever felt this weak. And yet there was no escaping this race.

"If you don't race, we'll never know if you can beat me. I'll never be able to think of myself as the fastest."

459

STOP AND THINK

✔ **TARGET STRATEGY** **Question**

- Remind students that readers check their understanding of text by asking questions. Point out that questioning characters' behavior can help readers understand their feelings and motives.

- Have students answer the **Stop and Think** question on **p. 458**.

- If students have difficulty with understanding Mina and Ruth's relationship, see **Comprehension Intervention** below for extra support.

- Display **Projectable 18.3a**. Remind students that a Column Chart can help keep track of character traits. Guide students fill out the Column Chart using the Question strategy:

  Have you ever felt nervous talking to a friend? Why? answers will vary *Why might Ruth be jealous of Mina?* Sample answer: she thinks Mina is a better runner

- Have students use **Graphic Organizer 1** to begin their own column charts as they read.

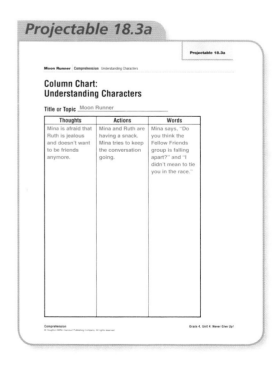

Projectable 18.3a

COMPREHENSION INTERVENTION

✔ **TARGET STRATEGY** Question

STRATEGY SUPPORT Remind students that asking questions before, during, and after reading will help them better understand the story. Model the strategy by asking a question, having the students answer, and explaining how that helps them understand the reading:

Why is Ruth moody and quiet? She is upset. *Why is Ruth upset with Mina?* She is jealous and also upset that Mina didn't try her hardest. *What does this tell you?* Ruth values good sportsmanship and honesty.

Tell students to continue asking themselves questions about the story as they read. Guide students to add story details to their graphic organizers as they answer questions they generate about the text.

Develop Comprehension

7 Draw Conclusions

Why do you think Ruth wants to do the Fellow Friends Handshake?
Sample answer: She still wants to be friends with Mina.

8 Understanding Characters

Why does Mina wish she could celebrate the Chinese Moon Festival now? She says so because the festival celebrates friendship; she wishes she could just share a moon cake with Ruth and make everything better.

9 Analyze Story Structure

Based on what you have read, predict what you think will happen at the race. Sample answer: Mina might win the race because she might not lose on purpose this time.

"Okay," Mina said slowly. "I'll race you."

7 Ruth held out her hands, the fingertips salty and greasy from the chips, ready for the Fellow Friends Handshake.

The park was just down the street from Ruth's house. As they walked, Mina thought of how the Chinese Moon Festival was a special time to celebrate friendship. If only it were fall instead of spring. If only she could just offer Ruth a simple moon cake. . . .

When they reached the spread of green grass, Ruth headed for an olive tree with a patch of bare dirt underneath. "Let's run from that pine tree over there to here." She marked a line with her toe. "That's about fifty meters." **8**

Mina nodded. Would it really be okay to win? She followed Ruth to the pine, where she marked a second line.

460

Ruth leaned into the tree trunk and stretched one leg behind her, bouncing into the heel.

Not wanting to copy Ruth, Mina bent over to touch her toes.

"Hey, guys," Ruth called to two small boys crossing the grass. She cupped her hands around her mouth: "Can you help us with our race?"

The boys came closer, one in a striped T-shirt, the other wearing a purple baseball cap turned backward.

Ruth beckoned to the one with the cap. "You stand here." She pointed to the start line she'd drawn. "You'll count down for us." She pointed to the line by the olive tree. "You're over there," she told the other boy. "Watch who puts their foot across the line first. Watch closely because the race could be close." **9**

461

Question
Model the Strategy

- Remind students that readers ask questions about what they read before, during, and after reading to check and improve their understanding of the text.

- Tell students that stopping to question what they read can help them understand details that tell more about characters and their relationships. Point out the question Mina asks herself at the bottom of **p. 460,** "Would it really be okay to win?"

- Model using questions to understand how looking at Mina's behavior can tell more about Mina's and Ruth's relationship.

Think Aloud *I already know from Mina's own thoughts, actions, and words that she cares about her relationship with Ruth. When I read Mina's question to herself on page 460, I think about how I'd feel if I were Mina. I think Mina asks herself this question because she's worried that if she tries hard to win the race, Ruth will be upset again.*

- Have students continue their graphic organizers. Tell them to use their Column Charts to discuss what they know about Mina's and Ruth's relationship so far.

Develop Comprehension

10 ✔ **TARGET VOCABULARY**

Explain the most likely reason Mina's thoughts of holding back **vanished**. *Sample answer: She didn't want to feel the way she felt when she lost a race on purpose.*

11 Figurative Language

Why do you think the author uses a simile that compares the girls to African antelopes? Sample answer: It helps readers visualize the way the girls looked as they ran.

12 Analyze Author's Purpose

Why do you think the author uses such vivid, sensory details to describe Mina's experience? Sample answer: It shows how much she enjoys running.

Mina suddenly wished Ruth would offer another Fellow Friends Handshake, but Ruth was busy wiping her palms on her shorts.

The boy counted—"Three, two, one"—and then shouted: "Go!"

Mina plunged forward, shoving hard against the dirt with her toes. All her holding back vanished. She was off!

But the next moment, as though a whisper of wind had crossed her path, she found herself slowing—like in the tryouts when she had fallen behind on purpose. Way behind. That had felt awful.

462

She'd won once. It was time to win again.

At that moment, the world fell silent. The air filled with the smell of orange blossoms, a thick haze of sweetness. The sunshine cascaded, lovely and soft, around her head and shoulders. The tiniest breeze lapped at her as she ran. There was all the time in the world to complete the short distance between here and the tree.

She didn't turn her head to look, but Mina knew that Ruth was running beside her. They ran like the African antelopes she'd seen in a movie—loping over a yellow plain, **11** beneath trees with flat, horizontal branches.

12

463

Practice Fluency

Accuracy and Self-Correction Read aloud the last paragraph on **Student Book p. 462** as students follow along.

Ask: *What would happen if I said, "That had felt awesome," instead of "awful"? The meaning changes, and it wouldn't make sense. Awesome means something totally different from* awful.

- Tell students that good readers monitor their reading and correct themselves so that the text makes sense.

- Have students echo-read the paragraph, taking care to correct words as they read.

See **p. T182** for a complete fluency lesson on reading with accuracy and self-correction.

Turn and Talk

? Essential Question

Have partners imagine a situation in which they must compete for a prize that only one of them can win. Have them use details from the text to brainstorm ways friends can compete and still remain friends.

CROSS-CURRICULAR CONNECTION

Connect to Science

Have students turn to the illustration on p. 455. *What shape does the moon have here?* a crescent Explain that the moon seems to change shape over time. This is because the moon receives its light from the sun, and the amount of the moon that we see lighted depends on where the moon is in the sky relative to Earth. Explain that as the moon moves around Earth, it seems to grow or shrink from a crescent to a full moon and back again. You may wish to use a ball and a flashlight to demonstrate this. Tell students that a full moon occurs about every twenty-eight days.

Student Book, p. 455

STOP AND THINK

 **TARGET SKILL**

Understanding Characters

- Remind students that the ways characters think and interact with one another tell readers about the characters' feelings and motives.

- Have them answer the **Stop and Think** question on **Student Book p. 464.**

- If students have difficulty using the characters' thoughts, words, and inter-actions to understand characters, see **Comprehension Intervention** below for extra support.

- Have students use their completed Column Charts to discuss how Mina's and Ruth's feelings have changed throughout the story.

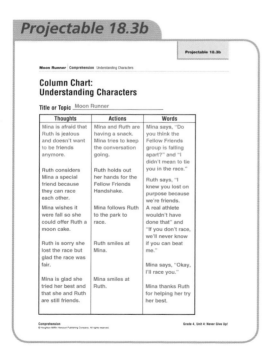

Projectable 18.3b

One gigantic leap took Mina sailing high and forward, over the line. The leap carried her past the boy in the striped shirt.

The silence broke. "You won!" shouted the boy, pointing at Mina.

She glanced down at herself. Then, even though her breath was coming in great heaving gulps, she looked at Ruth.

Ruth was leaning over, her hands on her knees, breathing hard. Finally, she lifted her face and managed to smile.

The boys wandered off, and Mina and Ruth lay down on the grass, cradled in a large nest of miniature white flowers. Their breathing calmed into the same rhythm.

The sun was still up, but Mina noticed a crisp crescent in the sky. For the next two weeks it would grow until it reached its night of complete fullness. Mina closed her eyes. She was glad she'd run against Ruth. Like the moon, she was beginning to feel round and whole herself.

"Thanks," said Mina after the shadow of the olive tree had edged across their faces.

"For what?"

"For helping me try my best."

> ✔ **STOP AND THINK**
> **Understanding Characters** Think about what Ruth said to Mina earlier in the story. What does Ruth's smile here tell you about her reaction to their race in the park?

464

COMPREHENSION INTERVENTION

✔ **TARGET SKILL**   **Understanding Characters**

SKILL SUPPORT Readers can analyze how characters think and behave to infer their feelings and motives. Model using Ruth's and Mina's thoughts, actions, and words to understand more about their relationship.

> **Think Aloud** *Earlier, on p. 459, Ruth told Mina that "when athletes compete, it isn't fair if someone doesn't try their hardest." After the last race, Ruth doesn't win, but she smiles at Mina. Ruth's words and actions help me understand how she feels. I think she is happy that she and Mina both tried hard to win. Ruth loves to race, and she knows she can race her friend another day and maybe win that time.*

Guide students to identify how Ruth's and Mina's friendship has changed throughout the story.

Your Turn

In Their Shoes

Write About Friendship
Mina wished she could honor her friendship with Ruth by giving her a moon cake at the Moon Festival. Think about how you show your friends that you care about them. Write a paragraph that describes some of the caring things that you do for your friends.
PERSONAL RESPONSE

Everyone Wins

Make an Award Ruth doesn't win the race with Mina at the end of the story, but she shows she is a good sport. In a small group, design and make an award for Ruth. Include her name and three or four words that describe her good qualities. SMALL GROUP

Do Your Best

Turn and Talk With a partner, discuss why Ruth smiled at Mina after their race in the park. What do you think caused Mina to try to win the race instead of deliberately losing? Make a list of the character traits that drive both Ruth and Mina's actions in the story. Discuss with your partner how these traits influenced the story.
UNDERSTANDING CHARACTERS

465

Retelling Rubric

4	Excellent	Students accurately identify the problem, describe the steps toward Mina's and Ruth's solution, and show excellent listening skills.
3	Good	Students accurately identify the problem, describe most steps toward Mina's and Ruth's solution, and show good listening skills.
2	Fair	Students show a basic knowledge of the problem and solution, and their listening skills are fair.
1	Unsatisfactory	Students neither address the prompt nor show any awareness of strong listening skills.

Your Turn

Have students complete the activities on page 465.

In Their Shoes Help students brainstorm ways of being caring toward friends. Remind students that giving a gift is only one way to show we care. We can also do something, say something, or write something to show how much we care about a friend. Tell students to provide several supporting details in their paragraphs. PERSONAL RESPONSE

Everyone Wins Show students examples of awards, such as certificates, ribbons, and trophies. If possible, give students sample certificate and ribbon templates. Help students as they brainstorm for adjectives describing Ruth—for example, *fast, determined,* and *strong.* SMALL GROUP

Do Your Best Remind students that a character trait is a quality that every person has. We use adjectives to describe character traits. For example, Ruth is a brave character, and Mina is an honest character. Ask: *What do you think would happen in the story if Ruth and Mina had different character traits? Explain.*

UNDERSTANDING CHARACTERS

Oral Language Have small groups discuss how Mina and Ruth resolve their problem. Tell students to listen carefully and build upon the ideas of others. Use the Retelling Rubric at the left to evaluate students' responses.

Connect to Social Studies

PREVIEW THE INFORMATIONAL TEXT

- Tell students that this selection is an online article that gives information about Moon Festivals. Have students read the title, subtitles, and the advertisement on page 468. Then have them read the online article independently.

DISCUSS DIGITAL MEDIA CONVENTIONS

- Tell students that there are different types of **digital media**, such as online articles, e-mails, forums, and online announcements. Point out that each type of digital media has certain **conventions**, or rules and features, that separate it from other types.

- Explain that conventions include the types of words and sentences used, the tone of the language, and other features, such as headings and dates.

- Discuss with students how different conventions of digital media can help readers understand the type of information presented and the author's purpose for writing.

- Guide students to compare and contrast the different conventions of this online article and Internet press release.

chart	used to explain information graphically
schedule	a plan that tells what things will happen, in a specific order, at a certain time and place
blog	somebody's personal account of what happened

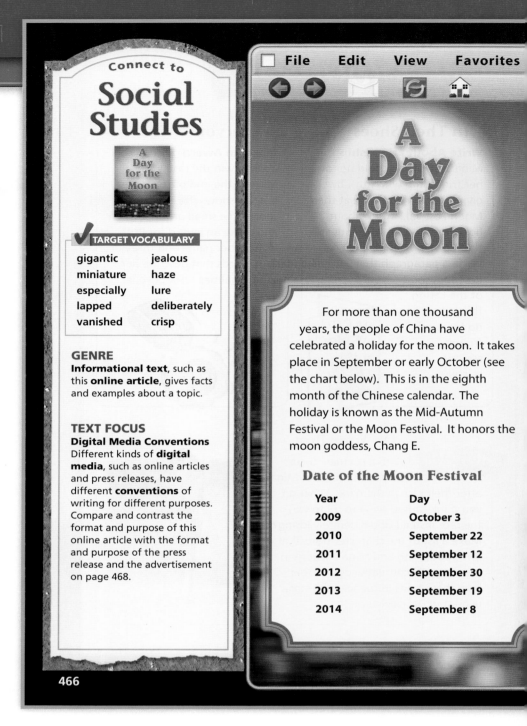

Connect to Social Studies

A Day for the Moon

✓ TARGET VOCABULARY

gigantic	jealous
miniature	haze
especially	lure
lapped	deliberately
vanished	crisp

GENRE
Informational text, such as this **online article**, gives facts and examples about a topic.

TEXT FOCUS
Digital Media Conventions Different kinds of **digital media**, such as online articles and press releases, have different **conventions** of writing for different purposes. Compare and contrast the format and purpose of this online article with the format and purpose of the press release and the advertisement on page 468.

466

File   Edit   View   Favorites

A Day for the Moon

For more than one thousand years, the people of China have celebrated a holiday for the moon. It takes place in September or early October (see the chart below). This is in the eighth month of the Chinese calendar. The holiday is known as the Mid-Autumn Festival or the Moon Festival. It honors the moon goddess, Chang E.

Date of the Moon Festival

Year	Day
2009	October 3
2010	September 22
2011	September 12
2012	September 30
2013	September 19
2014	September 8

 ENGLISH LANGUAGE LEARNERS

Scaffold

Beginning Use illustrations and simplified language to define the words *festival* and *legend*. Have students relate the words to any festivals their home culture may celebrate.

Advanced Have partners take turns reading aloud p. 467. Pose simple questions to clarify students' understanding.

Intermediate Read aloud pp. 466–467. Guide students to complete sentence frames such as, *Chang E drank the _____. She floated up to the _____.*

Advanced High Have students use the text to write an answer to this question: *What are moon cakes and why do people like them?*

See ELL Lesson 18, pp. E22–E31, for scaffolded support.

The Legend of Chang E

The skill of Hou Yi (HOO YEE) with a bow and arrow made other archers jealous. Yet they cheered when his arrows erased nine gigantic suns that had been burning up the Earth. The emperor rewarded Hou Yi with a potion. If he drank half of it, he would live forever. But Hou Yi's wife, Chang E, found the potion first and drank it all. She floated up, up, up to the moon. You can still see Chang E whenever the haze clears around the full mid-autumn moon. **1**

Lanterns and Moon Cakes

The Moon Festival is filled with customs. People still light candles in lanterns and deliberately float them in rivers. They look like miniature moons, gently lapped by the water. For many, the biggest treat of the holiday is the moon cake. It **2** will lure you with its crisp coating and sweet filling. The moon cake is an especially favorite part of the holiday. Anyone wanting one by day's end usually finds that it has vanished. **3**

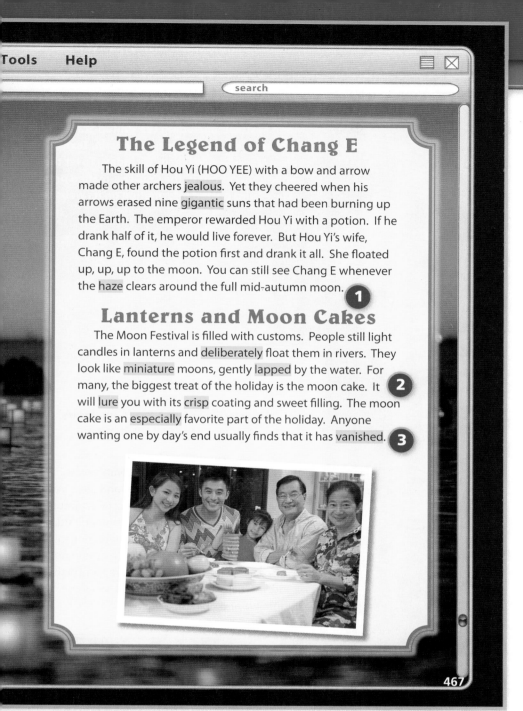

467

Practice Fluency

Accuracy and Self-Correction Have students listen as you read aloud the paragraph on **Student Book p. 466.**

- Remind students that good readers monitor their reading and correct words so that the text makes sense.

- Have students use the repeated-reading routine as they practice reading the paragraph. Remind them to monitor their reading and correct when necessary to connect words with meaning.

JOURNEYS DIGITAL Powered by DESTINATIONReading®
Student eBook: Read and Listen

TARGET VOCABULARY REVIEW

✓ **TARGET VOCABULARY** **Vocabulary in Context Cards**

Have students work in pairs to review the Vocabulary in Context Cards. Then have partners write a short paragraph that describes a topic or event, using five or six of the words. Tell them that topic or event should contain details to help readers fully picture what is being described. After students complete the activity, have volunteers share their paragraphs.

Develop Comprehension

1 **Main Idea and Details**
What fact of nature do you think this legend is attempting to explain?
It explains why some people believe they can see the face of a man or woman "in the moon."

2 ✓ **TARGET VOCABULARY**
How might the Moon Festival in Austin, Texas **lure** *you to attend?*
Sample answers: seeing the acrobats; moon cakes; learning about Asian culture

3 **Main Idea and Details**
What details support that author's statement that moon cakes are a favorite holiday treat? Sample answer: crisp outside, stuffed with sweet filling

Interpret Conventions

- Tell students that the online article and press release have different conventions because they give different kinds of information. Use this model:

> **Think Aloud** *The online article tells me about Moon Festivals in general, not a specific one. There is a history of how they started and a description of what people often do at Moon Festivals.*

- Guide students to identify the conventions of the press release on **Student Book p. 468**. Then have them compare and contrast the conventions of the two texts.

File   Edit   View   Favorites   Tools   Help

Many cities around the world celebrate Moon Festivals, including the United States. In 2007, the Chinatown Center in Austin, Texas held a Moon Festival on its birthday. To let the public know about it, the Center e-mailed press releases and posted information on its website.

Chinatown Center
中國城
1-Year Anniversary & Moon Festival Celebration
中秋佳節 TẾT TRUNG THU 請來參加我們的週年慶 KỶ NIỆM 1 NĂM
SEPTEMBER 22-23, 2007
WWW.CHINATOWNAUSTIN.COM

FOR IMMEDIATE RELEASE:
Over 5,000 Attend Chinatown Center's 1-Year Anniversary & Moon Festival Celebration

Austin, TX, September 27, 2007 — Central Texas's largest Moon Festival celebration was held at Austin's Chinatown Center on their 1-year Anniversary. The two-day event occurred Saturday, September 22nd and Sunday, September 23rd, 2007. This was the largest Asian celebration in Central Texas with over 5,000 people attending. The free event included singers from around the world, martial artists, Asian dancers, Japanese drumming, and Chinese guitar.

A Moon festival parade

468

Weekly Internet Challenge

Navigating the Site

- Review Internet Strategy, Step 3: Navigate.
- Have students navigate to a site about the Moon Festival.
- Review the use of site buttons to navigate the site and have students practice using them.
- Explain that researchers may use the "Find" feature to explore whether the site contains the information they need.

INTERNET STRATEGY

1. **Plan a Search** by identifying what you are looking for and how to find it.
2. **Search and Predict** which sites will be worth exploring.
3. **Navigate** a site to see how to get around it and what it contains.
4. **Analyze and Evaluate** the quality and reliability of the information.
5. **Synthesize** the information from multiple sites.

Making Connections

Making Connections

 Text to Self

Write About Friendship

Think of a time when you competed against a friend. Write a paragraph that describes what happened. What did you learn from the experience?

 Text to Text

Ways to Succeed
Does success always involve winning? Think about "Riding Freedom," "The Right Dog for the Job," and "Moon Runner." Tell what success means in each of these selections.

 Text to World

Connect to Social Studies
People celebrate the Moon Festival with moon cakes. Research another food that is used by a culture to celebrate a holiday. Find out how it is made and when it is eaten. Gather information from at least two different sources. Share what you learn with a partner. Then have your partner summarize the information for sense. Revise as necessary and present your findings to the class.

469

"A Day for the Moon" Challenge

• Have students look at the picture on **Student Book p. 467.** Ask: *How could you find out how to make your own moon cakes?* by locating a recipe on the Internet or in a cookbook

• Have students brainstorm keywords for an Internet search, and examine URLs from search results.

• Have students open websites most likely to have a recipe they can use. Then have them use navigation buttons to explore the sites to find a recipe.

• Have students tell what features of the sites help make it easier to find the recipe and use it.

 Text to Self

To help students prewrite, have them make a list of words that describe how they felt before, during, and after the competition. Then have them write their paragraphs. Have volunteers share their finished paragraphs.

 Text to Text

Have students use a Column Chart to jot down notes about what success meant in each of the three stories they have read in this unit. Then have them summarize what success meant to each main character.

 Text to World

Encourage students to use one Internet source and one book or encyclopedia to do their research. Remind them of the Internet search strategies they have learned, and have them write the URLs or book titles of the sources they used. Have partners exchange feedback on what they learned from each other about the ways different cultures celebrate holidays with certain foods, and how their sources helped them understand the background of the celebrations.

Deepen Comprehension

SKILL TRACE

Understanding Characters

Introduce	T162–163, **T180–T181**
Differentiate	T206–T207
Reteach	T214
Review	Lesson 29
Test	Weekly Tests, Lesson 18

ELL ENGLISH LANGUAGE LEARNERS

Scaffold

Beginning Use story illustrations to help students think about Mina and Ruth. Work with them to complete sentence frames such as, *Mina feels_____. Ruth wants _____.*

Intermediate Provide the sentence frames above, and have students complete them orally using information on pp. 457–458.

Advanced Point out that much of what we know about Mina is from her thoughts. Have students find these passages on pp. 457–458 and read them aloud and explain what they learn about Mina.

Advanced High Have students write cartoon speech balloons to show what they think each girl is thinking on pp. 457–458.

See ELL Lesson 18, pp. E22–E31, for scaffolded support.

✓ Understanding Characters

1 Teach/Model

AL *Academic Language*

character, **infer**, **traits**

- Explain that authors make choices about what their **characters** are like, how they behave, and what their motives are.

- Explain that authors can create a plot conflict by creating characters with contrasting **traits** and motives. Point out that the plot advances as characters and their relationships change.

- Tell students that everything a character says and does reveals his or her feelings and desires. Point out that as they read, they should pay attention to how those feelings and desires changes as the plot develops.

- Have students reread **pp. 456–459** of "Moon Runner."

- Display **Projectable 18.4.** Discuss **Deepen Comprehension Question 1.**

- Remind students that a Column Chart organizes the characters' thoughts, actions, and words. Analyzing this information helps readers understand characters' behavior and motives.

- Model analyzing Mina's and Ruth's comments to complete the Column Chart and answer the question.

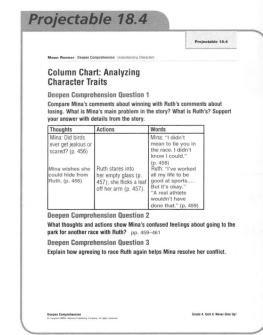

Projectable 18.4

Moon Runner | Deepen Comprehension Understanding Characters

Column Chart: Analyzing Character Traits

Deepen Comprehension Question 1
Compare Mina's comments about winning with Ruth's comments about losing. What is Mina's main problem in the story? What is Ruth's? Support your answer with details from the story.

Thoughts	Actions	Words
Mina: Did birds ever get jealous or scared? (p. 456)		Mina: "I didn't mean to tie you in the race. I didn't know I could." (p. 458)
Mina wishes she could hide from Ruth. (p. 456)	Ruth stares into her empty glass (p. 457); she flicks a leaf off her arm (p. 457).	Ruth: "I've worked all my life to be good at sports.... But it's okay." "A real athlete wouldn't have done that." (p. 459)

Deepen Comprehension Question 2
What thoughts and actions show Mina's confused feelings about going to the park for another race with Ruth? pp. 459–461

Deepen Comprehension Question 3
Explain how agreeing to race Ruth again helps Mina resolve her conflict.

Deepen Comprehension
© Houghton Mifflin Harcourt Publishing Company. All rights reserved.

Grade 4, Unit 4: Never Give Up!

Think Aloud *Analyzing a character's thoughts, actions, and words helps me understand why they act the way they do. When Mina talks, she keeps trying to apologize for winning. She seems really worried about what Ruth thinks. I think Mina cares about their friendship.*

Monitor Comprehension

Are students able to analyze characters' traits?

IF...	THEN...
students have trouble analyzing characters' traits,	▶ use the Leveled Reader for **Struggling Readers**, *Tammy's Goal*, p. T208.
students can analyze character traits most of the time,	▶ use the Leveled Reader for **On-Level Readers**, *Baseball Boys*, p. T209.
students can accurately analyze characters' traits,	▶ use the Leveled Reader for **Advanced Readers**, *The Friendship Garden*, p. T210.

Leveled Readers, pp. T208–T211
Use the Leveled Reader for **English Language Learners**, *Baseball Friends*, p. T211. *Group English Language Learners according to language proficiency.*

2 | Guided Practice

- Reread p. 459–462 of "Moon Runner" with students. Clarify unfamiliar words: *especially* means "to a great degree."

- Read and discuss **Deepen Comprehension Question 2** on **Projectable 18.4.** Use these prompts to guide students:

  - *How does Mina react to Ruth's suggestion about racing again? When Mina agrees to race, she answers slowly.*

  - *Why does Mina think about the Moon Festival as the girls walk to the park? Mina is more concerned about her friendship than running, and the Moon Festival is a celebration of friendship.*

  - *What words tell you that Mina is ready to stand on her own and do her best? She wonders if it would really be okay to win.*

- Complete the Column Chart for **Deepen Comprehension Question 2.**

GUIDED DISCUSSION Guide students as they identify moments when the changes in the characters determine the way the story's plot unfolds. Work with them to consider ways that Ruth or Mina might have acted differently if they had different character traits. *Suggested pages: pp. 456, 459, 462.*

3 | Apply

Turn and Talk Have partners each take a role—Mina or Ruth—and reread the dialogue in "Moon Runner." Then have them make a Column Chart and work together to discuss and complete **Deepen Comprehension Question 3** on **Projectable 18.4.**

▶ Write About Reading Have students write their responses to **Deepen Comprehension Question 3.**

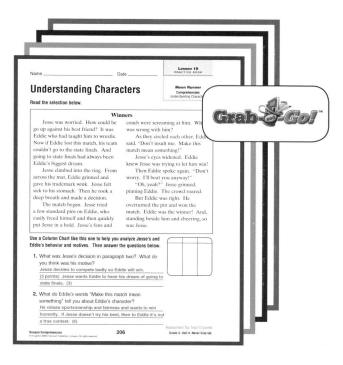

Practice Book p. 206
See Grab-and-Go™ Resources for additional leveled practice.

Deepen Comprehension • **T181**

Fluency

SHARE OBJECTIVES

- Read aloud with grade-appropriate fluency.
- Read with accuracy and self-correct as necessary for comprehension.

Accuracy and Self-Correction

1 Teach/Model

- Tell students that good readers work to increase accuracy. They also monitor their reading and correct mistakes so that the text makes sense.

- Have students turn to "Moon Runner," **Student Book p. 457.** Help students find the last sentence ("Ruth stared into…").

- Read the sentence slowly, in a choppy manner, as if you are having trouble recognizing some of the words. Then reread the sentence in a more fluent manner, modeling accuracy. Make a mistake in reading and pause to correct it.

2 Guided Practice

- Together, read aloud the first paragraph on **Student Book p. 458.**

- Listen as students read to monitor their fluency, as they practice accuracy and self-correct as necessary.

- If students are struggling, have them reread the last paragraph of **Student Book p. 458** and guide them as they practice.

- Discuss how you monitored your comprehension while reading. See also **Instructional Routine 7.**

3 Apply

- Tell students that with practice, they can improve their accuracy and learn to self-correct as they read.

- Have small groups take turns reading a paragraph of the selection aloud while practicing automatic word recognition and self-correction.

- See also **Instructional Routine Card 8: Partner Reading** for additional practice.

Decoding

 Recognizing Prefixes *re-, un-, dis-*

1 Teach/Model

PREVIEW PREFIXES Review with students that a prefix is added to the beginning of a base word to change its meaning. Remind students that recognizing prefixes can help them decode unfamiliar words.

- Model how to find the prefix and base word in *disorder*. Write the word on the board, and circle the prefix, *dis-*. Tell students that *dis-* is a prefix that was added to the base word, *order*. Say the word aloud with students: dis | order.

- See also **Instructional Routines 5** and **6**.

2 Practice/Apply

DECODE WORDS WITH PREFIXES Write the words from the chart below on the board: *disavows, review, unopened, misunderstand, nonfiction, incapable, impossible*. Guide students as they decode the first three words step by step.

For decoding with prefixes...	...break the word after the prefix and before the base word.
dis	dis | a | vow
re	re | view
un	un | opened
mis	mis | understand
non	non | fiction
in	in | capable
im	im | possible

- Have students work together to note the prefixes and base words in the other words in the chart, to decode and pronounce them.

- The have students read aloud each word in the chart.

Use the **Corrective Feedback** if students need additional help.

Corrective Feedback

If students have trouble decoding words with prefixes , use the model below.

Correct the error. Point out the prefix and the base word in review. *re/view*

Model how to decode the word. *This word has a prefix and a base word. I can say the prefix, re-, and the base word, view. When I say them together in a sequence, the word is review. That sounds like a word I know.*

Guide students to find the prefix and base word in rebuild. *re/build*

Check students' understanding. *Read these three words:* restart, reuse, recall.

Reinforce Have students repeat the process with the word *discolor*.

Vocabulary Strategies

SHARE OBJECTIVE

• Learn to recognize and use homonyms, homophones, and homographs.

SKILL TRACE

Homophones, Homonyms, Homographs	
Introduce	T184–T185
Differentiate	T212–T213
Reteach	T214
Test	Weekly Tests, Lesson 18

ELL ENGLISH LANGUAGE LEARNERS

Scaffold

Beginning Write *hair* and *hare* on the board and say each word aloud with students. Point to *hair* and show students a picture of human or animal hair. Repeat the process for the word *hare*. Explain that *hair* and *hare* sound the same but have different spellings and meanings, and that words like these are called homophones.

Intermediate Use procedure above to explain these words: *right/write, see/sea,* and *too/two.*

Advanced Write: *Alice went to the boat sale to buy a new sail.* Have students underline the homophones. *(sale/sail)* Have students write their own sentences with homophones and share with a partner to continue the exercise.

Advanced High Have students identify a pair of homophones, homographs, and homonyms and share them with the class. Students should provide a definition for each word.

See ELL Lesson 18, pp. E22–E31, for scaffolded support.

☑ Homophones, Homonyms, and Homographs

1 Teach/Model

AL *Academic Language*

homonyms words that sound the same and are spelled the same, but have different meanings (wooden *shed* vs. *shed* snakeskin)

homophones words that sound the same and may be spelled differently, but have different meanings (*bear* cub vs. *bare* feet)

homographs words that are spelled alike but may have different pronunciations and different meanings. Some are pronounced the same (*bear* cub vs. *bear* a burden), while others have different pronunciations (tie a *bow* vs. take a *bow*)

• Explain that a **homonym** and a **homophone** are words that sound the same. For example, *steel* and *steal* are homophones and *well* and *well* are homonyms. Use each word in a sentence.

• Point out that **homographs** are words that are spelled alike but have different meanings and are sometimes pronounced differently. For example, *bass* the fish and *bass* the musical instrument. Note that homographs are usually found in the dictionary listed as completely separate entry words.

• Write on the board: *The water lapped at his feet as he stood close to the water's edge.*

• Model using context clues to identify the meaning of the homograph *lap*.

Think Aloud *I can see the small word or word part,* lap *in the longer word* lapped. *I know my* lap *is the place I put my napkin. I also know that* lap *is a verb that means "to move in little waves." I look at the words around* lapped *and see that this meaning makes sense. The water is gently moving over his feet as he stands near the water's edge.*

Monitor Vocabulary Strategies

Are students able to identify and use homonyms, homographs, and homophones?

IF...	THEN...
students have difficulty identifying and using homonyms, homographs, and homophones,	▶ **Differentiate Vocabulary Strategies** for Struggling Readers, p. T212. *See also Intervention Lesson 18, pp. S22–S31.*
students can identify and use homonyms, homographs, and homophones most of the time,	▶ **Differentiate Vocabulary Strategies** for On-Level Readers, p. T212.
students can consistently identify and use homonyms, homographs, and homophones,	▶ **Differentiate Vocabulary Strategies** for Advanced Readers, p. T213.

Differentiate Vocabulary Strategies pp. T212–T213. *Group English Language Learners according to language proficiency.*

---

2 Guided Practice

- Display the passage at the top of **Projectable 18.5** and point out the boldfaced words. Then read "Training for Your First Marathon" aloud.

- Help students use context to figure out the meaning of *project*. Provide the following sentence and guide students to use context to determine an alternate meaning for *project*: *The bookcases project from the wall*.

- Discuss with students the two pronunciations and two different meanings for the word *project*. Work with students as they use the lesson criteria to determine whether *project* is a homonym, homophone, or homograph. *homograph*

- Display the Web at the bottom of **Projectable 18.5** and write project in an outer circle. Write the remaining boldfaced words in the Web as students brainstorm homonyms, homophones, or homographs for each one. *morning/mourning, pact/packed; route; sole/soul; heel/heal; lapped*

Projectable 18.5

Projectable 18.5

Moon Runner Vocabulary Strategies Homophones, Homonyms, and Homographs

Homophones, Homonyms, Homographs

Vocabulary
project
  *proyecto
sole
route
  *ruta
heel
pact
  *pacto
morning
lapped
*Spanish cognates

Training for Your First Marathon

Training before a first marathon can be a big **project.** Many athletes like to do their running in the **morning.** Sometimes it's good to make a **pact** with a running buddy to get up and run your **route** together each training day. It's important to wear the right shoes. Go to a shoe store where they will make sure the **sole** and the **heel** of the shoe are right for you. You'll be glad you're wearing good shoes once you've **lapped** other runners on the track.

[Web diagram with center "Homophones, Homonyms, Homographs" and outer circles: morning, project, lapped, route, heel, pact, sole]

Vocabulary Strategies
© Houghton Mifflin Harcourt Publishing Company. All rights reserved.

Grade 4, Unit 4: Never Give Up!

3 Apply

- Have partners use passage context to determine the meanings of the remaining boldfaced words. Have students use the homonyms, homophones, or homographs in sentences that convey the meaning of each word, and confirm the definitions in a dictionary.

- Have students look in a dictionary for the definitions of any words that are still unfamiliar.

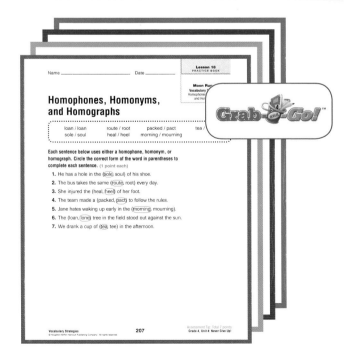

Practice Book p. 207
See Grab-and-Go™ Resources for additional leveled practice.

Connect and Extend

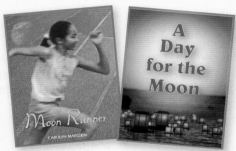

Moon Runner   **A Day for the Moon**

Vocabulary Reader

Struggling Readers   *On-Level Readers*

Advanced Readers   English Language Learners

Read to Connect

SHARE AND COMPARE TEXTS Have students compare and contrast this week's reading selections. Use the following discussion points:

- Using evidence from the selections you read this week, explain the reasons behind the characters' actions.

- Choose two selections from this week's readings. Explain how they might help someone who is in competition with a friend.

CONNECT TEXT TO WORLD Use these prompts to help deepen student thinking and discussion. Accept students' opinions, but encourage them to support their ideas with text details and other information from their reading.

- Imagine a world with no competition. Would people be better off? Why or why not? Defend your answer using evidence from this week's readings.

- How can competition be viewed in a positive way?

Independent Reading

BOOK TALK Have student pairs discuss their independent reading for the week. Tell them to refer to their Reading Log or journal and paraphrase what the reading was about. Have students discuss the following:

- what motivated the characters in their stories

- how the author revealed the characters' feelings and motives

- how the characters differed from one another

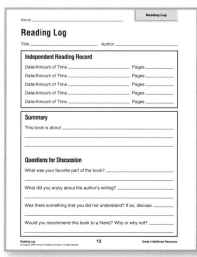

Reading Log

Extend Through Research

ONLINE SEARCHES: RELIABLE SOURCES Tell students that when they use the Internet to find information, they must be careful about where they find their information and which sites to trust as sources. Explain that not all websites contain accurate information. For instance, certain encyclopedia sites are not considered reliable resources, because anyone can add or subtract information from them. The reader does not know who wrote the material or whether the information is true.

- Discuss the various extensions at the end of a website URL, such as *.com, .org, .edu,* and *.gov.* Explain what each stands for (commerce, organization, educational institutions, government agencies). Discuss with students which would be more likely to have information they could trust.

- Ask students to tell which website would be more likely to have accurate information about pandas— a website created by the science department of a college or a website written by a third-grader for a school report? Have them explain their thoughts.

Listening and Speaking

PREPARE FOR ORAL SUMMARIES Have students select an article from a magazine. Tell them to prepare a two-minute summary of their article. Remind students that a good summary includes the main ideas and details.

- To get ready, have students list the main ideas of the article. Under each main idea they should list two or three details.

- Have students deliver their oral summaries to a partner. Students should be able to identify the main idea and details from their partner's summary. Have them record these in their Listening Logs.

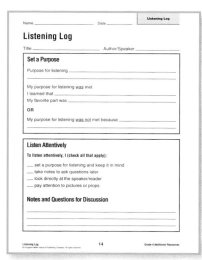

Listening Log

Spelling ☑ Prefixes *re-*, *un-*, *dis-*

- Spell words with the prefixes *re-*, *un-*, and *dis-*.

Spelling Words

Basic

unused	unplanned	uneven
refresh	distrust	rebuild
dislike	rewind	✪ restart
replace	untrue	✪ uncover
unpaid	unload	untidy
✪ redo	recall	discolor
disorder	displease	

Review

reuse, unfair, rewrite, unclear, untie

Challenge

disband, rearrange, ✪ discontinue, refund, unusual

✪ Forms of these words appear in "Moon Runner."

ELL ENGLISH LANGUAGE LEARNERS

Preteach

Spanish Cognates

Write and discuss these Spanish cognates for Spanish-speaking students.

discolor • *descolorar*

Day 1

❶ TEACH THE PRINCIPLE

- Administer the **Pretest**. Use the Day 5 sentences.

- Write *refresh* and *recall* on the board. Guide students to identify the prefix in each word. *re-* Repeat with the prefixes *un-* and *dis-*, using the chart below.

re- [again]	re- as in **re**fresh
re- [back]	re- as in **re**call
un- [not]	un- as in **un**paid
un- [reverse of]	un- as in **un**cover
dis- [opposite of]	dis- as in **dis**trust
dis- [to remove]	dis- as in **dis**color

❷ PRACTICE/APPLY

Guide students to identify words with the prefixes *re-*, *un-*, and *dis-* in the remaining Spelling Words.

Practice Book p. 208

Day 2

❶ TEACH WORD SORT

- Set up three rows as shown. Model adding a Spelling Word to each row.

- Have students copy the chart. Guide students to write each Spelling Word where it belongs.

re-	redo
un-	uneven
dis-	dislike

❷ PRACTICE/APPLY

Have students add words from "Moon Runner."

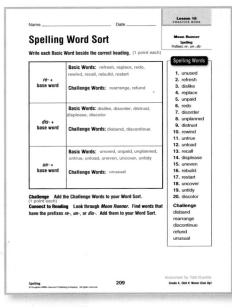

Practice Book p. 209

Day 3

❶ TEACH ANALOGIES

- **WRITE** this analogy: *Smile is to grin as hate is to* _____. Explain that a word analogy is an equation in which the first pair of words has the same relationship as the second pair of words.

- **ASK** *How are* smile *and* grin *related?* *same meaning; synonyms*

- **ASK** Which Spelling Word has almost the same meaning as *hate?* *(dislike)* Write *dislike* on the line.

- Follow the steps above with this analogy: *Calm is to tense as neat is to* _____. Help students discover that the word pairs are opposites, or antonyms, and have them find the missing spelling word. *(untidy)*

❷ PRACTICE/APPLY

- **WRITE** these analogies: *happy is to joyful as false is to* _____; *rude is to polite as believe is to* _____; *kind is to caring as remember is to* _____.

- **ASK** *Which Spelling Word belongs on each blank?* *untrue, distrust, recall*

➡ Have students write their answers.

Day 4

❶ CONNECT TO WRITING

- Read and discuss the prompt below.

> ✏ **WRITE TO NARRATE**
> Write a story about someone who is good at sports. Use details from your Vocabulary or Leveled Reader.

❷ PRACTICE/APPLY

- Guide students as they plan and write their narratives (see p. T196).

- Remind students to proofread their writing for errors in spelling words with the prefix *re-, un-,* and *dis-*.

Proofreading for Spelling

Find the misspelled words and circle them. Write them correctly on the lines below. (2 points each)

Everyone in town thought Max had won the race, but Ginny knew that was untru. She was one of the unpayed volunteers at the finish line handing out water and towels to the athletes. As she gathered the unussed towels, Ginny said that the track coach would uncovr who should replaise Max as the winner.

Even though I knew I'd won, I was sure that changing the outcome would be difficult. They'd have to redue the race results in the paper, too.

The next day, the coach said, "I dislik and destrust rumors. Rumors discoler the reputation of this race. Since I don't recal seeing who won, I want to rifresh my memory. I am going to rewinde and restaart the race tape." When he realized that I'd won instead of Max, I was relieved.

Spelling Words
1. unused
2. refresh
3. dislike
4. replace
5. unpaid
6. redo
7. disorder
8. unplanned
9. distrust
10. rewind
11. untrue
12. unload
13. recall
14. displease
15. uneven
16. rebuild
17. restart
18. uncover
19. untidy
20. discolor

Challenge
disband
rearrange
discontinue
refund
unusual

1. untrue
2. unpaid
3. unused
4. uncover
5. replace
6. redo
7. dislike
8. distrust
9. discolor
10. recall
11. refresh
12. rewind
13. restart

Practice Book p. 210

Day 5

ASSESS SPELLING

- Say each boldfaced word, read the sentence, and then repeat the word.

- Have students write the boldfaced word.

Basic

1. We have an **unused** room.
2. I take a bath to **refresh** myself.
3. We **dislike** spicy food.
4. I will **replace** the plate.
5. The loan will help him settle his **unpaid** bills.
6. I had to **redo** my report.
7. The room was in **disorder** after the party.
8. We took an **unplanned** trip.
9. Why do you **distrust** me?
10. Please **rewind** the tape.
11. The story was **untrue**.
12. The movers will **unload** this.
13. Do you **recall** her name?
14. Your actions **displease** me.
15. The car bounced on the **uneven** road.
16. They will **rebuild** their house.
17. Please **restart** the movie.
18. He will **uncover** the scheme.
19. You have an **untidy** room.
20. Bleach will **discolor** your clothes.

Grammar Prepositions and Prepositional Phrases

- Identify prepositions and prepositional phrases.
- Use prepositions and prepositional phrases in writing and speaking.

ELL ENGLISH LANGUAGE LEARNERS

Scaffold

Beginning Complete the following sentence frames with various prepositions to demonstrate how different prepositions change the meaning of the phrase.

The dog walks _____ his owner.

My bird loves to sit _____ his swing.

Intermediate Use the following sentence frames to demonstrate how to use prepositions.

The dog walks _____ the park. *to*

My bird loves to sit _____ his cage. *in*

Advanced Have students use prepositional phrases to describe a room. Provide them with sentence frames, such as the following:

My bed is _____. *in the corner*

I read books _____. *at my desk*

Advanced High Have student pairs take turns orally describing a room using prepositional phrases.

See ELL Lesson 18, pp. E22–E31, for scaffolded support.

JOURNEYS DIGITAL Powered by **DESTINATIONReading®**
Grammar Activities: Lesson 18
Grammar Songs CD: Track 8

Day 1 TEACH

DAILY PROOFREADING PRACTICE
The dog awften sleeps on the couch *often; couch.*

1 TEACH PREPOSITIONS

- Display **Projectable 18.6**. Explain that a preposition is a word that shows a connection between other words in a sentence. Point out that some prepositions describe time, while others describe place.

Projectable
18.6

- Model identifying the preposition in the example sentence: *The dog walks along the sidewalk.*

Think Aloud *To identify the preposition, I ask this Thinking Question:* **What word shows a connection between other words in the sentence?** *The word* along *connects other words in the sentence. Therefore,* along *is the preposition in this sentence.*

2 PRACTICE/APPLY

- Complete items 1–10 on **Projectable 18.6** with students.

- Write the following sentences on the board. Have students use the Thinking Question to identify the preposition in each sentence.

The dog in the blue collar is my pet. *in*

We take our dog on a walk every day. *on*

Name _____ Date _____

Lesson 18
PRACTICE BOOK

Prepositions

Moon Runner
Grammar: Prepositions and Prepositional Phrases

A **preposition** shows the connection between words in a sentence. Some prepositions describe time, such as *before, after,* or *during.* Others describe place, such as *over, in, on, above,* or *below.*

Thinking Question
What word shows a connection between other words in the sentence?

preposition
The runners raced on the track.

1–10. Find the preposition in each underlined phrase. Write the preposition on the line. (1 point each)

1. The track team will practice inside the gym. — inside
2. We use the outdoor track during warm weather. — during
3. Jack and Liam arrange the hurdles on the track. — on
4. Pedro easily leaps over every hurdle. — over
5. Then I bang my knee into the third hurdle. — Into
6. I stumble a bit before I fall. — before
7. Then I tumble to the ground. — to
8. The coach kneels beside me. — beside
9. She wraps a bandage around my knee. — around
10. After a long, hard practice, everyone is tired. — After

Grammar
© Houghton Mifflin Harcourt Publishing Company. All rights reserved.
211
Assessment Tip: Total 10 points
Grade 4, Unit 4: Never Give Up!

Practice Book p. 211

preposition a word that shows a connection between other words in a sentence
prepositional phrase begins with a preposition and ends with a noun or pronoun

Day 2 TEACH

DAILY PROOFREADING PRACTICE

is the cat with the long tail your cat. *Is; ?*

1 TEACH PREPOSITIONAL PHRASES

Projectable 18.7

• Display **Projectable 18.7**. Explain that a **prepositional phrase** begins with a preposition and ends with a noun or a pronoun. Point out that all the words in between are part of the prepositional phrase.

• Model identifying the prepositional phrase in this sentence: *There is a new running track behind our school.*

Think Aloud *I see a prepositional phrase in this sentence. I know that* behind *is a preposition and the noun that ends the phrase is* school. *So the prepositional phrase is* behind our school.

2 PRACTICE/APPLY

• Complete items 1–6 on **Projectable 18.7** with students.

• Write the following sentences on the board. Have students complete each sentence using a prepositional phrase.

The cat sits _____.
Sample answer: in the tree

The girl _____ holds the cat.
Sample answer: on the bench

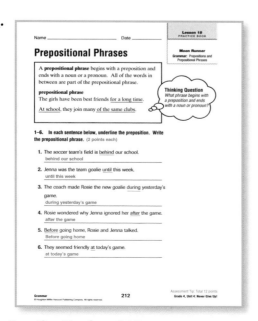

Practice Book p. 212

Day 3 TEACH

DAILY PROOFREADING PRACTICE

my pet fish live in there aquarium. *My; their*

1 EXTEND PREPOSITIONAL PHRASES

Projectable 18.8

• Display **Projectable 18.8**. Explain that a prepositional phrase can give more detail in a sentence. Tell students that a prepositional phrase can provide details such as *where, when, or how.*

• Model identifying the prepositional phrase in this example sentence: *The fish swam around the pond.*

Think Aloud *I know that* around *is a preposition and the noun that ends the phrase is* pond. *So the prepositional phrase is* around the pond. *The preposition* around *tells where the fish swam.*

2 PRACTICE/APPLY

• Complete items 1–10 on **Projectable 18.8** with students.

• Have students use prepositional phrases to describe classroom objects. Remind students that they can use prepositions and prepositional phrases to show *where, when,* or *how.*

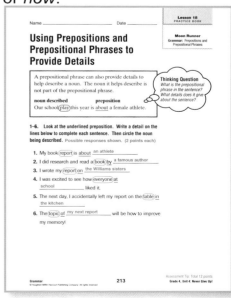

Practice Book p. 213
Prepositions and Prepositional Phrases • **T191**

Day 4 REVIEW

DAILY PROOFREADING PRACTICE

The bird land on the bransh. *lands; branch*

① REVIEW PREPOSITIONAL PHRASES

Have students turn to **Student Book p. 470**. Read aloud the paragraph to review **prepositions** and **prepositional phrases**. Discuss the example sentences. Then have students complete the **Turn and Talk** activity with a partner.

② SPIRAL REVIEW

Verbs in the Present Review with students that a *verb in the present* shows action that is happening now.

Write the following sentences on the board. Have students identify the verb in the present in each sentence.

Birds flip their wings rapidly. *flip*

This bird always eats at the feeder. *eats*

The birdhouse rarely has birds in it. *has*

Day 5 CONNECT TO WRITING

DAILY PROOFREADING PRACTICE

My father bot me a pet four my birthday. *bought; for*

① CONNECT TO WRITING

• Explain to students that they can add interesting and helpful information to their writing by using prepositional phrases.

• Point out that an important part of revising is looking for sentences that can be made more descriptive by adding prepositional phrases.

② PRACTICE/APPLY

• Display the following sentences. Guide students to identify the prepositional phrases.

My new kitten sleeps in my lap. *in my lap*

The kitten with the stripes is mine. *with the stripes*

• Write these sentence frames on the board. Have students orally give a prepositional phrase to complete each sentence. *Sample answers are shown.*

The cat walks _____. *into the house*

The bird perches _____. *on its nest*

The fish _____ swims quickly. *in the bowl*

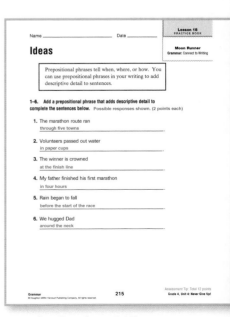

Practice Book p. 214

Practice Book p. 215

Grammar

What Is a Preposition? What Is a Prepositional Phrase? A **preposition** is a word that shows a connection between other words in a sentence. A **prepositional phrase** begins with a preposition and ends with a noun or pronoun. Prepositions are used to convey location, time, or to provide details.

Academic Language

preposition
prepositional phrase

Prepositions and Prepositional Phrases	
Convey location:	*prepositional phrase* *preposition* *noun* Birds hopped along the branches.
Convey time:	*prepositional phrase* *preposition* *noun* We watched them for an hour.
Provide details:	*prepositional phrase* *preposition* *noun* The topic of the discussion was friendship.

Turn and Talk With a partner, find the prepositions in the underlined prepositional phrases. Tell whether each prepositional phrase conveys location, time, or provides other details.

1. Both <u>of the girls</u> will race.

2. The park is <u>down the street</u>.

3. The race will begin <u>in ten minutes</u>.

4. The boy <u>with a purple baseball cap</u> will help.

470

Ideas In your writing, you can use prepositional phrases to add helpful and interesting information to your sentences. Elaborating your sentences helps the reader visualize what you are describing in your narrative.

Less Descriptive Sentence	More Descriptive Sentence
The girls raced each other.	The girls raced each other to the big tree.

Connect Grammar to Writing

As you revise your narrative composition, look for sentences that you can make more descriptive by adding prepositional phrases.

471

Turn and Talk

1. *of; provides details*
2. *down; conveys location*
3. *in; conveys time*
4. *with; provides details*

CONNECT GRAMMAR TO WRITING

• Have students turn to **Student Book p. 471**. Read the Ideas paragraph with students.

• Read the short sentence in the table aloud. Point out to the students that the sentence gives no description. Then read the long sentence in the table. Explain that the prepositional phrase adds description to the sentence.

• Tell students that as they revise their narrative compositions, they should look for opportunities to use prepositional phrases.

• Review the Common Errors at right with students.

COMMON ERRORS

Error: The party should start **about** three o'clock.

Correct: The party should start **at** three o'clock.

Error: This gift is different **than** that gift.

Correct: This gift is different **from** that gift.

Write to Narrate ☑ Focus Trait: Word Choice

ELL ENGLISH LANGUAGE LEARNERS

Scaffold

Beginning Work with students to think of a list of words that describe their topics. Guide them to use a thesaurus to find synonyms.

Intermediate Guide students to use sentence frames such as the following as they begin drafting their narratives:

I met my friend _____ .

My friend likes to _____ .

We had fun together when we _____ .

Advanced Have students take turns describing their compositions to a partner. Have the partners suggest alternative synonyms for key language.

Advanced High As students prewrite, have them use resources such as a thesaurus to find more descriptive words.

See ELL Lesson 18, pp. E22–E31, for scaffolded support.

JOURNEYS DIGITAL **Powered by** DESTINATIONReading®
WriteSmart CD-ROM

Day 1 ANALYZE THE MODEL

❶ INTRODUCE THE MODEL

- Tell students they will be writing a narrative composition.
- Display **Projectable 18.9** and read aloud the Writing Model. Discuss the following:

What Is a Narrative Composition?

- It describes an event or story.
- An interesting opening catches readers' attention of the reader in the beginning.
- The writer uses **synonyms** to add a variety of words that keep readers engaged.

❷ PRACTICE/APPLY

- Use **Projectable 18.9** to identify the opening, vivid details, and endings of the first passage.
- Work with students to identify the opening, vivid details, and ending in Writing Model 2.

Projectable 18.9

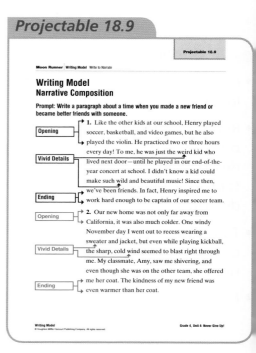

LESSON	FORM	TRAIT
16	Descriptive Paragraph	Ideas
17	Friendly Letter	Voice
18	**Narrative Composition**	**Word Choice**
19	Prewrite: Personal Narrative	Organization
20	Draft, Revise, Edit, Publish: Personal Narrative	Ideas

Language Arts

Writing

Day 2 TEACH THE FOCUS TRAIT

☑ INTRODUCE THE FOCUS TRAIT: WORD CHOICE

- Explain that authors vary their descriptive words to keep the text interesting.

- Tell students that authors use synonyms to avoid reusing the same words and to help create vivid details.

Connect to "Moon Runner"	
Instead of this...	**...the author wrote this.**
Ruth held out her dirty hands to shake.	"Ruth held out her hands, the fingertips salty and greasy from the chips, ready for the Fellow Friends Handshake." (p. 460)

- Discuss how the author's vivid description helps readers visualize Ruth's hands. Ask students to identify a synonym for *dirty* that the author uses.
greasy

② PRACTICE/APPLY

- Write: *Amy was happy she had won.* Work with students to revise this sentence by finding a synonym for *happy* that might be more interesting or exact.

- Write: *The rain fell.* Then write: *The rain poured down.* Discuss the difference between the two sentences. Have students revise the first sentence.

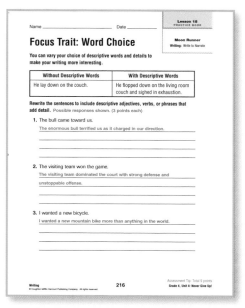

Practice Book p. 216

Day 3 PREWRITE

① TEACH PLANNING A NARRATIVE COMPOSITION

- Display **Projectable 18.10** and read the prompt aloud. Ask students to think about a special experience they have had with making a friend.

- Explain that the Flow Chart will help them plan their narrative compositions.

② PRACTICE/APPLY

- Point out the labels *Event* and *Detail* in **Projectable 18.10**. Tell students that the Flow Chart organizes events in the beginning, middle, and end of the narrative composition. The details tell more about each event.

- Tell students they will use a Flow Chart to plan their own narrative compositions. Point out that the event and details in the first box will become the opening. Work with students to complete the Flow Chart.

- Have students choose topics for their narrative compositions. Guide students to complete their own Flow Charts to plan their compositions.

Projectable 18.10

Projectable 18.10

Moon Runner Prewriting Write to Narrate

Prewriting
Planning a Narrative Paragraph

Prompt: Write a paragraph about a time when you made a new friend or became better friends with someone. Possible responses shown.

Title or Topic ____ Running for Class President

Event
My best friend and I both ran for class president.

Detail
nearly ended our friendship

↓

Event
I won the election.

Detail
her posters better—class loved my speech, though

↓

Event
In the end, we made up.

Detail
Competing with each other pushed us to do our best.

Prewriting
© Houghton Mifflin Harcourt Publishing Company. All rights reserved.   Grade 4, Unit 4: Never Give Up!

Day 4 DRAFT

① BEGIN A DRAFT

- Have students use their flow charts to begin their first draft. Discuss with them the following.

> 1. **Introduce** your friend and the experience you will be describing in the first sentence.

↓

> 2. **Organize** the events in the correct order.

↓

> 3. **Include** vivid details about the events to help readers visualize what happens. Use exact synonyms instead of repeated words.

↓

> 4. **Conclude** your narrative by noting what you learned from the experience.

② PRACTICE/APPLY

- Have students draft their narrative composition using the Flow Charts they completed for prewriting.

Day 5 REVISE FOR WORD CHOICE

① INTRODUCE THE STUDENT MODEL

- Remind students that good writers vary their descriptive words to avoid repetition.

- Read the draft on **Student Book p. 472**. Discuss the revisions the author made. Point out that the words *terrific* and *smacked* are colorful synonyms for *great* and *hit*.

② PRACTICE/APPLY

- Display **Projectable 18.11**. Work with students to revise the rest of the draft. Point out where better synonyms could make Tina's writing more colorful.

- Work with students to answer the *Reading as a Writer* questions on **Student Book p. 473**. Discuss students' responses.

- **Revising** Have students revise their paragraphs using the Writing Traits Checklist on **Student Book p. 472**.

- **Proofreading** For proofreading support, have students use the **Proofreading Checklist Blackline Master**.

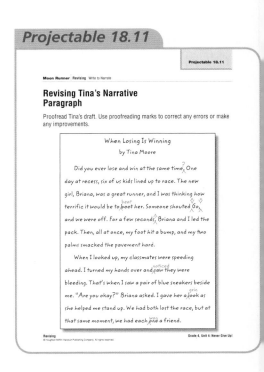

Projectable 18.11

Write to Narrate

☑ **Word Choice** In "Moon Runner," the author uses synonyms to avoid repeating words. For example, instead of repeating *looked*, she uses *stared* or *glanced*. When you revise your **narrative composition**, replace repeated words with more exact synonyms. As you revise, use the Writing Traits Checklist.

Tina drafted a paragraph about how she made a new friend. Later, she replaced some words with synonyms.

Writing Traits Checklist

☑ **Ideas**
Did I include vivid details?

☑ **Organization**
Did I write an interesting opening?

☑ **Word Choice**
Did I use synonyms to avoid repeating words?

☑ **Voice**
Did I tell what I was thinking and feeling?

☑ **Sentence Fluency**
Did I vary the way my sentences begin?

☑ **Conventions**
Did I use correct spelling, grammar, and mechanics?

Revised Draft

Did you ever lose and win at the same time? One day at recess, six of us kids lined up to race. The new girl, Briana, was a great runner, and I was thinking how ~~great~~ it would be to beat her. Someone shouted "Go," and we were off. ~~Briana and I led the pack~~ for a few seconds. Then, all at once, my foot hit a bump, and my two palms ~~hit~~ the pavement hard.

terrific (inserted above "great")

smacked (inserted above "hit")

Final Copy

When Losing Is Winning
by Tina Moore

Did you ever lose and win at the same time? One day at recess, six of us kids lined up to race. The new girl, Briana, was a great runner, and I was thinking how terrific it would be to beat her. Someone shouted "Go," and we were off. For a few seconds, Briana and I led the pack. Then, all at once, my foot hit a bump, and my two palms smacked the pavement hard. When I looked up, my classmates were speeding ahead. I turned my hands over and saw they were bleeding. That's when I noticed a pair of blue sneakers beside me. "Are you okay?" Briana asked. I gave her a grin as she helped me stand up. We had both lost the race, but at that same moment, we had each won a friend.

In my final paper, I replaced some repeated words with synonyms. I also varied a sentence by moving a phrase to the beginning.

Reading as a Writer

What synonyms did Tina use to avoid reusing the same words? What repeated words in your paper can you replace with synonyms?

472

473

Writing Traits Scoring Rubric

	Focus/Ideas	☑ Organization	Voice	☑ Word Choice	☑ Sentence Fluency	Conventions
4	Adheres to the topic, is interesting, has a sense of completeness. Ideas are well developed.	Ideas and details are clearly presented and well organized.	Connects with reader in a unique, personal way.	Includes vivid verbs, strong adjectives, specific nouns.	Includes a variety of complete sentences that flow smoothly, naturally.	Shows a strong command of grammar, spelling, capitalization, punctuation.
	Mostly adheres to the topic, is somewhat interesting, has a sense of completeness. Ideas are adequately developed.	Ideas and details are mostly clear and generally organized.	Generally connects with reader in a way that is personal and sometimes unique.	Includes some vivid verbs, strong adjectives, specific nouns.	Includes some variety of mostly complete sentences. Some parts flow smoothly, naturally.	Shows a good command of grammar, spelling, capitalization, punctuation.
2	Does not always adhere to the topic, has some sense of completeness. Ideas are superficially developed.	Ideas and details are not always clear or organized. There is some wordiness or repetition.	Connects somewhat with reader. Sounds somewhat personal, but not unique.	Includes mostly simple nouns and verbs, and may have a few adjectives.	Includes mostly simple sentences, some of which are incomplete.	Some errors in grammar, spelling, capitalization, punctuation.
1	Does not adhere to the topic, has no sense of completeness. Ideas are vague.	Ideas and details are not organized. Wordiness or repetition hinders meaning.	Does not connect with reader. Does not sound personal or unique.	Includes only simple nouns and verbs, some inaccurate. Writing is not descriptive.	Sentences do not vary. Incomplete sentences hinder meaning.	Frequent errors in grammar, spelling, capitalization, punctuation.

See also **Writing Rubric Blackline Master** and Teacher's Edition pp. R18–R21.

Progress Monitoring

Assess

- Weekly Tests
- Periodic Assessments
- Fluency Tests

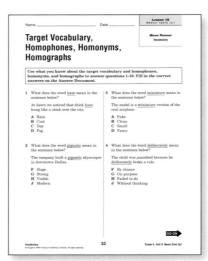

☑ Vocabulary

Strategies: Homophones, Homonyms, Homographs

Weekly Tests 18.7–18.8

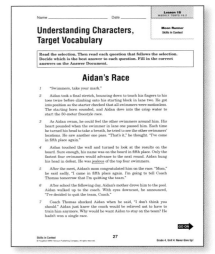

☑ Skills in Context

Understanding Characters
Target Vocabulary

Weekly Tests 18.2–18.6

Respond to Assessment

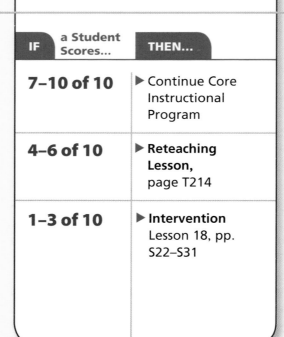

IF a Student Scores...	THEN...
7–10 of 10	▶ Continue Core Instructional Program
4–6 of 10	▶ Reteaching Lesson, page T214
1–3 of 10	▶ Intervention Lesson 18, pp. S22–S31

IF a Student Scores...	THEN...
7–10 of 10	▶ Continue Core Instructional Program
4–6 of 10	▶ Reteaching Lesson, page T214
1–3 of 10	▶ Intervention Lesson 18, pp. S22–S31

Journeys DIGITAL Powered by **DESTINATIONReading®**
- **Weekly Tests**
- **Online Assessment System**

 # Decoding

Recognizing Prefixes
re-, un-, dis-

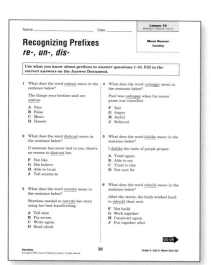

Weekly Tests 18.11–18.12

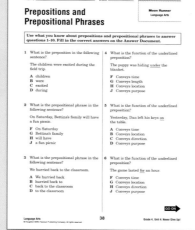 # Language Arts

Grammar: Prepositions and Prepositional Phrases

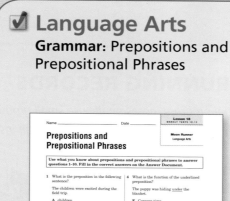

Weekly Tests 18.13–18.14

Writing Traits Rubrics
See *TE pp. R18–R21.*

Fluency

Fluency Plan
Assess one group per week.
Use the suggested plan below.

● Struggling Readers	**Weeks 1,3,5**
▲ On Level	**Week 2**
■ Advanced	**Week 3**

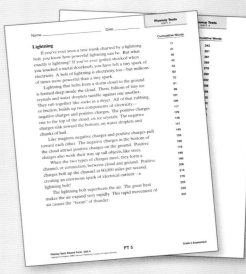

Fluency Record Forms

Fluency Scoring Rubrics
See *Grab-and-Go™ Resources Assessment* for help in measuring progress.

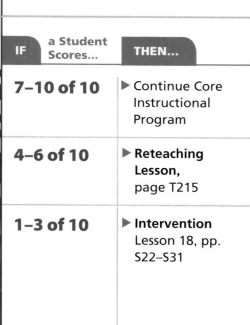

IF a Student Scores...	THEN...
7–10 of 10	▶ Continue Core Instructional Program
4–6 of 10	▶ Reteaching Lesson, page T215
1–3 of 10	▶ Intervention Lesson 18, pp. S22–S31

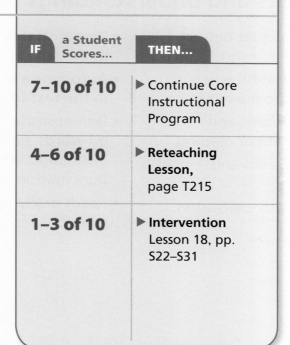

IF a Student Scores...	THEN...
7–10 of 10	▶ Continue Core Instructional Program
4–6 of 10	▶ Reteaching Lesson, page T215
1–3 of 10	▶ Intervention Lesson 18, pp. S22–S31

Progress Monitoring

 **Small Group**

RUNNING RECORDS

To assess individual progress, occasionally use small group time to take a reading record for each student. Use the results to plan instruction.

● **Struggling Readers**

▲ **On Level**

■ **Advanced**

◆ **English Language Learners**

Grab-and-Go™ Resources: Lesson 18, pp. 13–16.

Behaviors and Understandings to Notice

- Self-corrects errors that detract from meaning.
- Self-corrects intonation when it does not reflect the meaning.
- Rereads to solve words and resumes normal rate of reading.
- Demonstrates phrased and fluent oral reading.
- Reads dialogue with expression.

- Demonstrates awareness of punctuation.
- Automatically solves most words in the text to read fluently.
- Demonstrates appropriate stress on words, pausing and phrasing, intonation, and use of punctuation.
- Reads orally at an appropriate rate.

Weekly
Small Group Instruction

Day 1

Vocabulary Reader
• *The First Lady of Track*, T204–T205

Vocabulary Reader

Day 2

Differentiate Comprehension
• Target Skill: Understanding Characters, T206–T207
• Target Strategy: Question, T206–T207

Day 3

Leveled Readers
● *Tammy's Goal*, T208
▲ *Baseball Boys*, T209
■ *The Friendship Garden*, T210
◆ *Baseball Friends*, T211

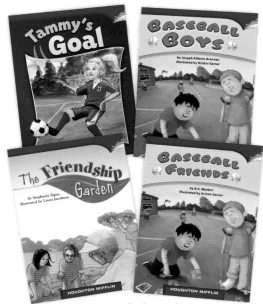

Day 4

Differentiate Vocabulary Strategies
• Homophones, Homonyms, Homographs, T212–T213

Leveled Readers

Day 5

Options for Reteaching
• Vocabulary Strategies: Homophones, Homonyms, and Homographs, T214
• Comprehension Skill: Understanding Characters, T214
• Language Arts: Prepositions and Prepositional Phrases/Write to Narrate, T215
• Decoding: Recognizing Prefixes *re-, un-, dis-*, T215

Ready-Made Work Stations

Independent Practice
• Comprehension and Fluency, p. T154
• Word Study, p. T154
• Think and Write, p. T155
• Digital Center, p. T155

Comprehension and Fluency　　**Word Study**　　**Think and Write**　　**Digital Center**

Teacher-Led

	Day 1	Day 2	Day 3
Struggling Readers	**Vocabulary Reader** *The First Lady of Track*, Differentiated Instruction, p. T204	**Differentiate Comprehension:** Understanding Characters; Question, p. T206	**Leveled Reader** *Tammy's Goal*, p. T208
On Level	**Vocabulary Reader** *The First Lady of Track*, Differentiated Instruction, p. T204	**Differentiate Comprehension:** Understanding Characters; Question, p. T206	**Leveled Reader** *Baseball Boys*, p. T209
Advanced	**Vocabulary Reader** *The First Lady of Track*, Differentiated Instruction, p. T205	**Differentiate Comprehension:** Understanding Characters; Question, p. T207	**Leveled Reader** *The Friendship Garden*, p. T210
English Language Learners	**Vocabulary Reader** *The First Lady of Track*, Differentiated Instruction, p. T205	**Differentiate Comprehension:** Understanding Characters; Question, p. T207	**Leveled Reader** *Baseball Friends*, p. T211

What are my other students doing?

	Day 1	Day 2	Day 3
Struggling Readers	• **Reread** *The First Lady of Track*	**Vocabulary in Context Cards** 171–180 *Talk It Over* Activities • **Complete** Leveled Practice SR18.1	• **Listen** to Audiotext CD of "Moon Runner"; Retell and discuss • **Complete** Leveled Reader, SR18.2
On Level	• **Reread** *The First Lady of Track*	**Reread** "Moon Runner" with a partner • **Complete** Practice Book p. 205	• **Reread** for Fluency: *Baseball Boys* • **Complete** Practice Book, p. 206
Advanced	• **Vocabulary in Context Cards** 171–180 *Talk It Over* Activities	**Reread and Retell** "Moon Runner" • **Complete** Leveled Practice A18.1	• **Reread** for Fluency: *The Friendship Garden* • **Complete** Leveled Practice, A18.2
English Language Learners	• **Reread** *The First Lady of Track*	**Listen** to Audiotext CD of "Moon Runner"; Retell and discuss • **Complete** Leveled Practice ELL18.1	• **Vocabulary in Context Cards** 171–180 *Talk It Over* Activities • **Complete** Leveled Practice ELL18.2

Ready Made-Work Stations

Assign these activities across the week to reinforce and extend learning.

Comprehension and Fluency
Reread and Review

Word Study
Which Word Works?

Day 4

Differentiate Vocabulary Strategies:
Homophones, Homonyms, and
Homographs, p. T212

Differentiate Vocabulary Strategies:
Homophones, Homonyms, and
Homographs, p. T212

Differentiate Vocabulary Strategies:
Homophones, Homonyms, and
Homographs, p. T213

Differentiate Vocabulary Strategies:
Homophones, Homonyms, and
Homographs, p. T213

Day 5

Options for Reteaching,
pp. T214–T215

Options for Reteaching,
pp. T214–T215

Options for Reteaching,
pp. T214–T215

Options for Reteaching,
pp. T214–T215

- **Partners: Reread**
Tammy's Goal
- **Complete** Leveled
Practice, SR18.3

- **Vocabulary in Context Cards**
171–180 *Talk It Over* Activities
- **Complete** Practice Book p. 207

- **Reread** for Fluency: "Moon Runner"
- **Complete** Leveled Practice A18.3

- **Partners: Reread** for Fluency:
Baseball Friends
- **Complete** Leveled Practice ELL18.3

- **Reread** for Fluency: "Moon Runner"
- **Complete** Work Station activities
- **Independent Reading**

- **Complete** Work Station activities
- **Independent Reading**

- **Complete** Work Station activities
- **Independent Reading**

- **Reread** *The First Lady of Track* or
"Moon Runner"
- **Complete** Work Station activities

Think and Write
Go For Your Goals!

JOURNEYS DIGITAL Powered by **DESTINATION**Reading®

Digital Center

Weekly To-Do List

This Weekly To-Do List helps students
see their own progress and move on
to additional activities independently.

Name _____	Date _____	Lesson 18 WEEKLY TO-DO LIST

Weekly To-Do List
Put an X in each box when you finish the activity.

Must Do	May Do
☐ Practice pages	☐ Reading Log
☐ Comprehension and Fluency Work Station	☐ Vocabulary in Context Cards
☐ Word Study Work Station	☐ Practice Spelling Words
☐ Think and Write Work Station	☐ Work on Writing Assignment
☐ Daily Independent Reading	☐ Other _____
☐ Other _____	

Daily Independent Reading

☐ Monday	
☐ Tuesday	
☐ Wednesday	
☐ Thursday	
☐ Friday	

Weekly To-Do List
© Houghton Mifflin Harcourt Publishing Company. All rights reserved.

Grade 4, Unit 4: Never Give Up!

Reading Log

Name _____		Reading Log

Reading Log
Title _____ Author _____

Independent Reading Record

Date/Amount of Time _____	Pages _____
Date/Amount of Time _____	Pages _____
Date/Amount of Time _____	Pages _____
Date/Amount of Time _____	Pages _____
Date/Amount of Time _____	Pages _____

Summary
This book is about _____

Questions for Discussion
What was your favorite part of the book? _____

What did you enjoy about the author's writing? _____

Was there something that you did not understand? If so, discuss. _____

Would you recommend this book to a friend? Why or why not? _____

Grab-and-Go!

Vocabulary Reader

The First Lady of Track

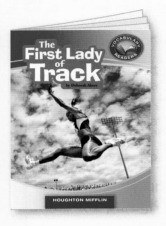

Summary

For many years, women were excluded from competitive sports. Jackie Joyner-Kersee was one of the first great female athletes. Joyner-Kersee went on to win two gold medals in the 1988 Olympics.

✓ TARGET VOCABULARY

jealous	miniature
vanished	crisp
haze	lure
lapped	especially
gigantic	deliberately

Struggling Readers

- Explain to students that women have not always had the same opportunities that men have had in competitive sports. Have students name famous female athletes with whom they are familiar.

- Guide students to preview the Vocabulary Reader. Read aloud the headings. Ask students to describe the images, using Target Vocabulary words when possible.

- Have students alternate reading pages of the Vocabulary Reader aloud. Guide them to use context clues to determine the meanings of unfamiliar words. As necessary, use the **Vocabulary in Context Cards** to review the meanings of vocabulary words.

- Assign the **Responding Page** and **Blackline Master 18.1**. Have partners work together to complete the pages.

On Level

- Explain to students that Jackie Joyner-Kersee was an exceptional athlete who won two gold medals in the 1988 Summer Olympics. Guide students to preview the selection.

- Remind students that context clues can help them determine the meaning of an unknown word. Tell students to use context clues to confirm their understanding of Target Vocabulary words and to learn the meanings of new words.

- Have students alternate reading pages of the Vocabulary Reader aloud. Tell them to use context clues to determine the meanings of unknown words.

- Assign the **Responding Page** and **Blackline Master 18.1**. Have students discuss their responses with a partner.

Advanced

- Have students preview the **Vocabulary Reader** and make predictions about what they will read, using information from their preview and their prior knowledge.

- Tell students to read the text with a partner. Ask them to stop and discuss the meanings of unknown words as necessary.

- Assign the **Responding Page** and **Blackline Master 18.1**. For the Write About It activity, ask students to describe why Jackie Joyner-Kersee was especially interested in helping children from disadvantaged backgrounds.

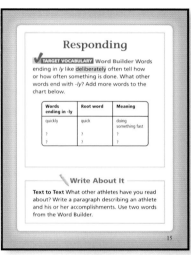

The First Lady of Track, p. 15

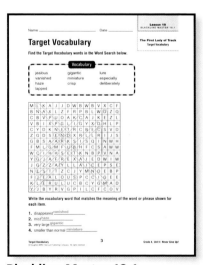

Blackline Master 18.1

ELL English Language Learners

Group English Language Learners according to language proficiency.

Beginning

Write the words *gigantic* and *miniature* on the board. Use actions to show students that these words are opposites. Have students name or use actions to demonstrate things that are gigantic and miniature.

Advanced

Have students choose two characters from *The First Lady of Track* and write a sentence about each character using one of the vocabulary words.

Intermediate

Use visuals, simplified language, and gestures to preteach the following Target Vocabulary words: *especially, vanished, lure,* and *crisp.* Then have students complete sentence frames such as, *I like ice cream, especially_____.*

Advanced High

Have students reread *The First Lady of Track* to find sentences that use the Target Vocabulary. Tell them to rewrite each sentence, replacing the Target Vocabulary word with a synonym.

Differentiate Comprehension
☑ Understanding Characters; Question

Struggling Readers

I DO IT

- Remind students that understanding why characters act the way they do can help them understand the story.
- Have students ask themselves questions about what characters think (thoughts), do (actions), and say (words). Tell them that these are unique traits.
- Read aloud p. 456 of "Moon Runner" and model questions.

  Think Aloud *Why does Mina wonder if birds get jealous or scared? Is she afraid of losing her friend?*

WE DO IT

- Have students read p. 458.
- Help students identify text details that help them better understand the character of Mina. Ask the following questions and discuss students' thoughts: *Why does Mina keep talking? Why does she say she didn't mean to tie Ruth?*

YOU DO IT

- Have students reread pp. 457–458, this time focusing on the character of Ruth.
- Have students use a Column Chart to track text details about Ruth. Encourage them to ask themselves questions about what Ruth thinks, says, and does, to better understand her.
- Have volunteers describe their understanding of Ruth.

On Level

I DO IT

- Read p. 458 of "Moon Runner."
- Explain that readers' understanding of characters can change. Tell students they can ask questions to learn more about the characters.
- On the board, create a Column Chart with the columns labeled *Thoughts, Actions,* and *Words.* Then use this model:

  Think Aloud *For "Title or Topic," I write "Mina." For "Thoughts," I write, "She must keep the conversation going."*

WE DO IT

- Have students read the first half of p. 459.
- Guide students to identify text details about Ruth by posing these questions: *How do the things she thinks, says, and does help you understand her character?* Add students' responses about Ruth's thoughts, words, and actions in row 2 of the Column Chart on the board.
- Ask students to describe Ruth based on the information they have so far.

YOU DO IT

- Have students read the rest of "Moon Runner" and ask themselves questions about Mina and Ruth.
- Have students copy the Column Chart and add more text details about Mina and Ruth.
- Discuss how their understanding of Mina and Ruth's characters may have changed from the beginning of the story to the end.

Advanced

I DO IT

- Read aloud pp. 456–457 of "Moon Runner."

- Explain that an author may provide information about characters by describing their actions. Use this model:

  Think Aloud *The author describes how Mina and Ruth both handle their lemonade glasses. What does this tell me about their characters? These actions tell that they are both nervous about the conversation they are having.*

WE DO IT

- Have students read pp. 460–461 independently.

- Ask: *What do Ruth's thoughts, words, and actions tell you about Ruth as a competitive athlete? Thoughts—She probably wants Mina to know that they are friends even though they are racing against each other. Words—She asks boys to judge the race. Actions—She marks the start and finish line; she stretches before the race.*

YOU DO IT

- Ask students to read pp. 462–464.

- Have them use a completed Column Chart to write a paragraph explaining how the characters of Mina and Ruth are similar. Have them support their ideas with text details.

- Invite students to share how they used the Question Strategy to complete their Column Charts.

ELL English Language Learners

Group English Language Learners according to language proficiency.

Review with students a completed Column Chart for "Moon Runner." Help student use academic language to describe the main characters' thoughts, feelings, and actions, and how their relationship changed in the story.

Beginning	Intermediate	Advanced	Advanced High
Guide students to use the completed Column Chart to complete these sentence frames: *At the beginning, Mina felt ____. When they raced again, Mina felt ____. At the end, Mina's and Ruth's friendship ____.*	Remind students that to understand character, we keep track of a character's thoughts, words, and actions. Have students copy the sentence frames at left from the board. Have them fill in the frames with Mina's thoughts, words, and actions. Allow students time to share their work.	Have partners make a Column Chart using a page from the story. Guide students as they fill in the chart to show the thoughts, actions, and words for the character(s) from the page they chose. Have students use their charts to figure out the characters' feelings and motives.	Have partners make a Column Chart and analyze one of the boys. Explain that students will need to infer traits based on the characters' thoughts, actions, and words. Have students share their ideas with the class.

Targets for Lesson 18

✓ **TARGET SKILL**

Understanding Characters

✓ **TARGET STRATEGY**

Question

✓ **TARGET VOCABULARY**

jealous	miniature
vanished	crisp
haze	lure
lapped	especially
gigantic	deliberately

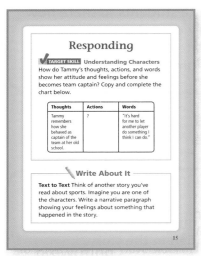

Tammy's Goal, p. 15

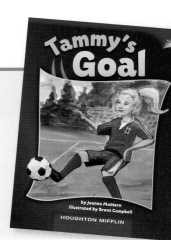

Leveled Readers

Struggling Readers

● *Tammy's Goal*

GENRE: REALISTIC FICTION

SUMMARY Tammy makes the soccer team at her school. Her election as team captain and her friendship with Orlando help her learn about teamwork.

Introducing the Text

• Explain that the word *goal* has multiple meanings.

• Remind students that a Column Chart can help them understand a character by organizing his or her thoughts, actions, and words.

Supporting the Reading

• As you listen to students read, pause to discuss these questions.

UNDERSTANDING CHARACTERS p. 6 *What does Tammy's memory of playing soccer at her old school tell you about Tammy? That she does not know how to share the ball; that she does not understand the idea of teamwork.*

QUESTION *Tammy asks Orlando about his shoelaces. What other questions might you ask Orlando? Sample answer: Why do you love playing soccer?*

Discussing and Revisiting the Text

CRITICAL THINKING After discussing *Tammy's Goal*, have students read the instructions on **Responding** p. 15. Use these points to guide students as they revisit the text.

• Have partners identify the actions on p. 11 that show what Tammy was like before becoming team captain and list them in the columns on **Blackline Master 18.3**.

• Distribute **Blackline Master 18.7** to further develop students' critical thinking skills.

FLUENCY: ACCURACY AND SELF-CORRECTION Model reading accurately and self-correcting when mispronouncing a word. Then have students echo-read p. 4 and focus on reading with accuracy.

Blackline Master 18.3

JOURNEYS
DIGITAL **Powered by**
DESTINATIONReading®
Leveled Readers Online

On Level

▲ **Baseball Boys**

GENRE: REALISTIC FICTION

Summary Louis shares a love of baseball cards with the new boy, Noah. Louis's friend Jimmy gets jealous. In the end, all three boys become friends.

Introducing the Text

- Explain that baseball fans often choose to collect baseball cards.

- Remind students that paying close attention to a character's thoughts, actions, and words helps readers to better understand a character.

Supporting the Reading

- As you listen to students read, pause to discuss these questions.

UNDERSTANDING CHARACTERS p. 13 *What does Jimmy's choice to not tell Louis and Noah that he is upset tell you about him?* *that Jimmy is understanding and values friendship*

QUESTION p. 2 *What can you ask if you don't know how Noah feels as a new student?* *Sample answer: What was it like to go somewhere where I didn't know anyone?*

Discussing and Revisiting the Text

CRITICAL THINKING After discussing *Baseball Boys*, have students read the instructions on **Responding** p. 15. Use these points to guide students as they revisit the text.

- Have partners identify the actions and words that show how Jimmy feels about his friendship with Louis in the columns on **Blackline Master 18.4**. In the third column, have them infer what Jimmy's actions and words say about his character.

- Distribute **Blackline Master 18.8** to further develop students' critical thinking skills.

FLUENCY: ACCURACY AND SELF-CORRECTION Have students practice reading their favorite parts of *Baseball Boys* with accuracy. Encourage students to self-correct as necessary.

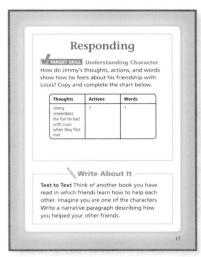

Baseball Boys, p. 15

Blackline Master 18.4

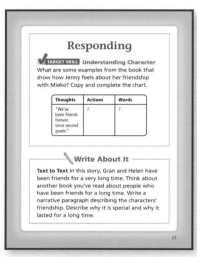

The Friendship Garden, p. 15

Blackline Master 18.5

Leveled Readers

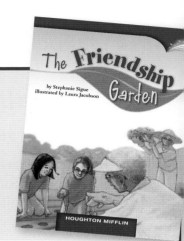

Advanced

▇ *The Friendship Garden*

GENRE: REALISTIC FICTION

Summary Jenny and Mieko are sad that Mieko is moving. Jenny's grandma and her friend Helen show the girls that long-distance friendships work.

Introducing the Text

• Explain that the characters in this story take a special interest in gardening.

• Remind students that part of understanding characters is paying close attention to a character's thoughts, actions, and words throughout a story. Good readers infer what a character is like based on the character's behavior.

Supporting the Reading

• As you listen to students read, pause to discuss these questions.

UNDERSTANDING CHARACTERS pp. 10–11 *How does Gran's and Helen's friendship change how the girls feel about Mieko's move? They are hopeful that their friendship can last, too.*

QUESTION p. 14 *What question could you ask about Jenny's and Mieko's future plans? Sample answer: Will they plan to send each other seeds from their gardens? Why?*

Discussing and Revisiting the Text

CRITICAL THINKING After discussing *The Friendship Garden*, have students read the instructions on **Responding** p. 15. Use these points to guide students as they revisit the text.

• Have partners list the actions and words that show how Jenny feels about Mieko on **Blackline Master 18.5**. Have students infer how they reflect Jenny's ideas about friendship.

• Distribute **Blackline Master 18.9** to further develop' critical thinking skills.

FLUENCY: ACCURACY AND SELF-CORRECTION Have students practice reading with accuracy using their favorite parts of *The Friendship Garden*.

English Language Learners

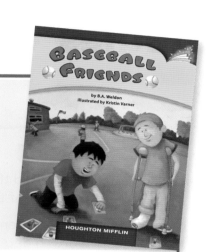

◆ Baseball Friends

GENRE: REALISTIC FICTION

Summary Louis and Jimmy love baseball. When Louis becomes friends with new boy Noah, Jimmy is jealous. By the end, all the boys are friends.

Introducing the Text

- Explain that friends often have similar interests, like baseball.

- Remind students that you can learn about characters by paying attention to what the characters say, think, and do.

Supporting the Reading

- As you listen to students read, pause to discuss these questions.

UNDERSTANDING CHARACTERS pp. 5–6 *What does it say about Louis that he is able to make new friends so easily? Louis is confident and friendly.*

QUESTION p. 10 *Why is Jimmy jealous when Louis becomes friends with Noah? He misses spending time with Louis and feels left out.*

Discussing and Revisiting the Text

CRITICAL THINKING After discussing *Baseball Friends*, have students read the instructions on **Responding** p. 15. Use these points to guide students as they revisit the text.

- Have students list the thoughts, actions, and words that show how Jimmy feels about Louis on **Blackline Master 18.6**.

- Distribute **Blackline Master 18.10** to further develop students' critical thinking skills.

FLUENCY: ACCURACY AND SELF-CORRECTION Model reading accurately and self-correcting when mispronouncing a word. Have students read several sentences aloud and ask them to repeat any words they find difficult.

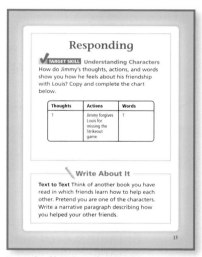

Baseball Friends, p. 15

Blackline Master 18.6

Differentiate Vocabulary Strategies ✓ Homophones, Homonyms, Homograph

Struggling Readers

■ I DO IT

- Display **Vocabulary in Context Card 4**: *lapped*.

- Explain that *lapped* is an example of a homograph. Explain that homographs are words that are spelled the same but have different meanings. *Lapped* can mean "the action of waves on a shore" or "to complete a circuit around something."

- Remind students that looking at the text around a word and using a dictionary are ways to learn a word's meaning.

WE DO IT

- Read aloud the context sentence on the front of the card.

- Guide students to look around the word to determine the definition of *lapped* in the context of the sentence. Then work with them to confirm the meaning using a dictionary.

> *lapped* **1.** moved in little waves against something. **2.** went one time around something, like a racecourse.

YOU DO IT

- Have students restate the context sentence using the vocabulary word *lapped* with the meaning "moved in little waves."

- Have partners write a new sentence for each of the meanings of the word *lapped*.

The waves quietly lapped against the lakeshore. She lapped the racetrack four times to run a mile.

On Level

■ I DO IT

- Explain that *homophones* are two or more words that sound alike but have different spellings and meanings, such as *to*, *too*, and *two*; *homographs* are words that are spelled the same but have different meanings and sometimes different pronunciations, such as a *bow* of a ship or a *bow* in a child's hair.

WE DO IT

- Work with students to identify homophones and homographs from the selection, such as: *egg*, *heel*, *lapped*, and *close*. List these words on the board.

- Have students reread the passages containing the words. Guide them to use context clues to determine the meaning of each word.

YOU DO IT

- Have students write sentences to demonstrate their understanding of each word.

- Have students read each other's sentences using the context around each word to confirm its meaning.

Advanced

I DO IT

- Explain that *homophones* are words that sound alike but have different spellings and meanings; *homographs* are words that are spelled the same but have different meanings or pronunciations; *homonyms* are words that are spelled and pronounced alike but have different meanings.

WE DO IT

- Write the following on the board: *mourning/morning, aloud/allowed sore/soar, bear/bare, duck, rose, minute, present,* and *separate.*

- Draw a Column Chart and label the columns *homophone, homograph,* and *homonym.*

- Work with students to put each word in the appropriate column. Point out that some words may be in multiple columns like *bear* and *bare.*

YOU DO IT

- Have students use another familiar text to select, list, and define one word each from the homophone, homonym, and homograph sets.

ELL English Language Learners

Group English Language Learners according to language proficiency.

Write *gigantic, miniature, especially, lapped, vanished, jealous, haze, lure, deliberately,* and *crisp* on the board. Have students repeat after you as you pronounce each word.

Beginning

Display **Vocabulary in Context Card 7** and say *haze*. Have students repeat the word after you. Have them read the sentence on the card and tell you when *haze* has ever made their outdoor plans change. Ask students if they can think of a homonym for *haze*.

Intermediate

Randomly distribute the **Vocabulary in Context Cards** to students. Guide them to read the card and then draw a picture of what the card says. If they are able, they can illustrate their own sentence to show they know the definition of the word.

Advanced

Display all the **Vocabulary in Context Cards** from Lesson 18. Have students choose a card and pantomime the sentence on the card. Have the rest of the class try to figure out which Target Vocabulary word is being pantomimed.

Advanced High

Write the Target Vocabulary words on index cards. Have each student or group of students choose a word. Then have students look in a dictionary or thesaurus to find any homonyms, homophones, or homographs for the Target Vocabulary words.

☑ Options for Reteaching

Vocabulary Strategies

☑ Homophones, Homonyms, and Homographs

I DO IT

- Review *homophones, homonyms,* and *homographs.*
- Remind students that *homonyms* sound the same, are spelled the same, but have different meanings. *Homophones* sound the same but are spelled differently or have different meanings.
- *Homographs* are words that are spelled alike but have different word meanings. Some homographs have different pronunciations.

WE DO IT

- Display **Projectable 18.5.** Read aloud the passage.
- Help students identify *homonyms, homophones,* and *homographs.*
- Model how to apply the vocabulary strategy to figure out whether words are homonyms, homophones or homographs.

Think Aloud *The word* pact *sounds like the word for what we did before we took a vacation last summer.* Packed *and* pact *must be homophones. They have the same sound, but they are spelled differently and have different meanings.*

- Work with students to use context to figure out the meanings of *pact* and *packed.* Guide them to use a dictionary to confirm the meanings.

Word	Homophone/Homonym	Homograph
project		project
lapped		lapped
sole	soul	
route	root	
morning	mourning	

YOU DO IT

- Have partners work together to identify *homonyms, homophones,* and *homographs* for the following words in the passage on **Projectable 18.5:** *project, lapped, sole, route, heel,* and *morning.*
- Have them use dictionaries to confirm meanings.

Comprehension Skill

☑ Understanding Characters

I DO IT

- Remind students that to *analyze* is to look at or study something carefully. Character traits are the ways of speaking or behaving that show what a character is like.
- Point out that authors create characters with differing traits and motives. This creates conflict and makes the plot and theme clearer.

WE DO IT

- Read aloud with students the fourth paragraph on **Student Book p. 456.** Work with them to identify the thoughts and words that tell more about Mina.
- Model how to identify Mina's character traits.

Think Aloud *The author writes that Mina wanted to hide from Ruth. That shows that Mina does not like to confront people. But Mina speaks anyway. That shows she is brave. Even when she doesn't know how to say something, she goes ahead and tries. She seems determined to try to resolve the problem that has come between them.*

- Guide students to identify actions that suggest character traits for Ruth on **Student Book p. 456.**

YOU DO IT

- Distribute **Graphic Organizer 4.**
- Have students identify how Mina's reaction to Ruth's challenge on **Student Book p. 461** helps the two characters resolve their conflict. *Though Mina agrees to race Ruth again, she is really more interested in friendship than the results of any race, but she is willing to try her best. As a result, Mina is also being true to herself.*
- Have students work with partners to complete the graphic organizer.
- Review the completed graphic organizers.

Language Arts

 # Prepositions and Prepositional Phrases/Write to Narrate

I DO IT

- Remind students that a preposition is a link between words in sentences. Prepositions can show time, place, and direction. Prepositional phrases start with a preposition and end with a noun or pronoun.
- List the following prepositions on the board: *after, above, across.*

  Think Aloud *I can write a sentence using* after *to show time: We went to the park* after lunch. *I know* after *is the preposition, and* after lunch *is the prepositional phrase. After tells when I went to the park. I can write sentences using* above *and* across, *too, to show place and direction.*

WE DO IT

- Work together to generate a sentence using a prepositional phrase that shows place.
- Guide students to identify the preposition and the prepositional phrase in the sentence.
- Have partners work together to write sentences with prepositional phrases. Guide them to identify whether the preposition shows time, place, or direction.

YOU DO IT

- Have pairs of students write three to four additional sentences using prepositional phrases.
- Then have partners identify whether the preposition shows time, place, or direction.

Decoding

 # Recognizing Prefixes *re-, un-, dis-*

I DO IT

- Remind students that a prefix is an affix that comes before a word and changes its meaning.
- Explain that the prefix *re-* means "again." The prefix *un-* means "not" or "the opposite of." The prefix *dis-* means "not" or "undo."
- Model how to decode *disorder* step by step.

  Think Aloud *I know that some words are made up of a prefix added to a base word. This word has the prefix* dis- *at the beginning The base word is* order. *The meaning is "not in order" or "not in sequence."*

WE DO IT

- Write *refresh, unopened,* and *dislike* on the board.
- Help students use the prefix and base word to decode each word. Discuss with students how the prefixes change the meaning of each word.

YOU DO IT

- Have partners work together to decode *replace, unpaid,* and *distrust.*
- Have students read the words aloud.
- Use **Corrective Feedback** on **p. T183** if students need additional help.

Teacher Notes

Preteaching for Success!

Comprehension:

Persuasion

Remind students to watch for what the author is trying to persuade them to think or do.

- Be sure students know what it means to persuade someone to do something. Say: *When you persuade someone, you convince that person to agree with your way of thinking.*
- Explain to students that finding the author's reasons and supporting details will help them understand the author's goals.
- Have students choose something they would like to persuade a classmate to do. Have them use a graphic organizer like the one on Student Book p. 478 to list reasons and supporting details.

Challenge Yourself!

Stand Up for Your Rights

After reading the selection "Harvesting Hope: The Story of Cesar Chavez," have students make posters that persuade people to stand up for causes.

- Have students think about things they feel strongly about and would like to stand up for.
- Ask students to make posters that try to persuade people to stand up for their causes. Each poster should give some factual information and suggestions about what should be done.
- Ask students to hang their posters in the classroom.

✓ Short Response

W.4.2b Develop the topic with facts, definitions, concrete details, quotations, or other information and examples related to the topic.

Write a paragraph to explain why Cesar's teacher hung a sign on him that said "I am a clown." Explain how that made Cesar feel.

Scoring Guidelines	
Excellent	Student has written a paragraph to explain why the teacher hung the sign and has written about how that made Cesar feel.
Good	Student has written a paragraph to explain why the teacher hung the sign but has not written about how that made Cesar feel.
Fair	Student has written a paragraph but has not addressed the writing prompt.
Unsatisfactory	Student has not written a paragraph.

Writing Minilesson

Skill: Write to Narrate—Personal Narrative Paragraph

Teach: Tell students that when they write to narrate, it can be in a long or short form.

Thinking Beyond the Text

Writing Prompt: Write a paragraph about a person who helped to make a change in your life.

1. Help students think about people who would make good subjects.
2. Remind students to use transition words to help them indicate time order or to indicate a conclusion.
3. Encourage students to make events charts to help them organize their ideas.

Group Share: Have students share their paragraphs in small groups.

Cross-Curricular Activity: Social Studies

Participate in Government

This selection tells how Cesar Chavez led a march to Sacramento, the capital of California, to ask government leaders to work for better treatment of farm workers. Discuss with students where people from their state can go to talk to government leaders. (the state capital) Explain that all citizens have the right to tell the government that they think certain laws are unfair. Ask students if there are any laws they think should be changed.

Reading Standards for Informational Text K–5

Key Ideas and Details

RI.4.1 Refer to details and examples in a text when explaining what the text says explicitly and when drawing inferences from the text.

RI.4.2 Determine the main idea of a text and explain how it is supported by key details; summarize the text.

RI.4.3 Explain events, procedures, ideas, or concepts in a historical, scientific, or technical text, including what happened and why, based on specific information in the text.

Craft and Structure

RI.4.4 Determine the meaning of general academic and domain-specific words or phrases in a text relevant to a *grade 4 topic or subject area*.

RI.4.5 Describe the overall structure (e.g., chronology, comparison, cause/effect, problem/solution) of events, ideas, concepts, or information in a text or part of a text.

Integration of Knowledge and Ideas

RI.4.7 Interpret information presented visually, orally, or quantitatively (e.g., in charts, graphs, diagrams, time lines, animations, or interactive elements on Web pages) and explain how the information contributes to an understanding of the text in which it appears.

RI.4.8 Explain how an author uses reasons and evidence to support particular points in a text.

RI.4.9 Integrate information from two texts on the same topic in order to write or speak about the subject knowledgeably.

Range of Reading and Level of Text Complexity

RI.4.10 By the end of year, read and comprehend informational texts, including history/social studies, science, and technical texts, in the grades 4–5 text complexity band proficiently, with scaffolding as needed at the high end of the range.

Reading Standards: Foundational Skills K–5

Phonics and Word Recognition

RF.4.3a Use combined knowledge of all letter-sound correspondences, syllabication patterns, and morphology (e.g. roots and affixes) to read accurately unfamiliar multisyllabic words in context and out of context.

Fluency

RF.4.4b Read grade-level prose and poetry orally with accuracy, appropriate rate, and expression.

Writing Standards K–5

Text Types and Purposes

W.4.3a Orient the reader by establishing a situation and introducing a narrator and/or characters; organize an event sequence that unfolds naturally.

W.4.3b Use dialogue and description to develop experiences and events or show the responses of characters to situations.

W.4.3c Use a variety of transitional words and phrases to manage the sequence of events.

Production and Distribution of Writing

W.4.4 Produce clear and coherent writing in which the development and organization are appropriate to task, purpose, and audience. (Grade-specific expectations for writing types are defined in standards 1–3 above.)

W.4.5 With guidance and support from peers and adults, develop and strengthen writing as needed by planning, revising, and editing. (Editing for conventions should demonstrate command of Language standards 1–3 up to and including grade 4 on pages 28 and 29.)

Research to Build and Present Knowledge

W.4.8 Recall relevant information from experiences or gather relevant information from print and digital sources; take notes and categorize information, and provide a list of sources.

Range of Writing

W.4.10 Write routinely over extended time frames (time for research, reflection, and revision) and shorter time frames (a single sitting or a day or two) for a range of discipline-specific tasks, purposes, and audiences.

Speaking & Listening Standards K–5

Comprehension and Collaboration

SL.4.1a Come to discussions prepared, having read or studied required material; explicitly draw on that preparation and other information known about the topic to explore ideas under discussion.

Presentation of Knowledge and Ideas

SL.4.6 Differentiate between contexts that call for formal English (e.g., presenting ideas) and situations where informal discourse is appropriate (e.g., small-group discussion); use formal English when appropriate to task and situation. (See grade 4 Language standards 1 on pages 28 and 29 for specific expectations.)

Language Standards K–5

Conventions of Standard English

L.4.2d Spell grade-appropriate words correctly, consulting references as needed.

Vocabulary Acquisition and Use

L.4.4c Consult reference materials (e.g., dictionaries, glossaries, thesauruses), both print and digital, to find the pronunciation and determine or clarify the precise meaning of key words and phrases.

L.4.5b Recognize and explain the meaning of common idioms, adages, and proverbs.

L.4.5c Demonstrate understanding of words by relating them to their opposites (antonyms) and to words with similar but not identical meanings (synonyms).

SUGGESTIONS FOR BALANCED LITERACY

Use *Journeys* materials to support a Readers' Workshop approach. See the Lesson 19 resources on pages 27, 76–77.

Lesson 19

Focus Wall

Main Selection
Harvesting Hope: The
Story of Cesar Chavez

Connect to Science
The Edible Schoolyard

Big Idea
There is more than
one secret to success.

? Essential Question
Why might a leader use
persuasion?

Comprehension

 **TARGET SKILL**
Persuasion

 **TARGET STRATEGY**
Infer/Predict

Spelling

Suffixes *-ful, -less,*
-ness, -ment

colorful	clumsiness
weakness	pavement
movement	peaceful
endless	fondness
truthful	neatness
illness	speechless
cheerful	statement
useless	wasteful
beautiful	penniless
restless	treatment

Fluency

Stress

Grammar

Transitions

Writing

Write to Narrate

Focus Trait:
Organization

Decoding

More Common Suffixes

Vocabulary Strategies

Use a Dictionary

TARGET VOCABULARY

overcome	publicity
association	violence
capitol	conflicts
drought	horizon
dedicate	brillant

Key Skills This Week

Target Skill:
Persuasion

Target Strategy:
Infer/Predict

Vocabulary Strategies:
Use a Dictionary

Fluency:
Stress

Decoding:
More Common Suffixes

Research Skill:
Online Searches: Keywords

Grammar:
Transitions

Spelling:
Suffixes *-ful, -less, -ness, -ment*

✏️ Writing:
Prewrite: Personal Narrative

✔ Assess/Monitor

☑ **Vocabulary,** p. T270

☑ **Comprehension,** p. T270

☑ **Decoding,** p. T271

☑ **Fluency,** p. T271

☑ **Language Arts,** p. T271

Whole Group

READING

Paired Selections

Harvesting Hope: The Story of Cesar Chavez
Biography
Student Book, pp. 478–489

Accelerated Reader
Practice Quizzes for the Selection

The Edible Schoolyard
SCIENCE/Informational Text
Student Book, pp. 490–493

Vocabulary

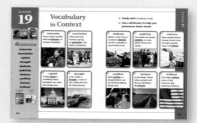

Student Book, pp. 474–475

Background and Comprehensi

Student Book, pp. 476–477

LANGUAGE ARTS

Grammar
Student Book, pp. 494–495

✏️ Writing
Student Book, pp. 496–497

Small Group

See pages T274–T275 for Suggested Small Group Plan.

TEACHER-LED

Leveled Readers

● Struggling Readers

▲ On Level

■ Advanced

◆ English Language Learners

Vocabulary Reader

WHAT MY OTHER STUDENTS ARE DOING

Ready-Made Work Stations

Word Study

Think and Write

Comprehension and Fluency

Digital Center

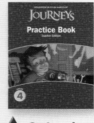
▲ On Level

● Struggling Readers

■ Advanced

◆ English Language Learners

Grab-and-Go!

Lesson 19 Blackline Master
- Target Vocabulary 19.1
- Selection Summary 19.2
- Graphic Organizer 19.3–19.6 ●▲■◆
- Critical Thinking 19.7–19.10 ●▲■◆
- Running Records 19.11–19.14 ●▲■◆
- Weekly Tests 19.2–19.9

Graphic Organizer Transparency 7

Additional Resources
- Genre: Biography, p. 8
- Reading Log, p. 12
- Vocabulary Log, p. 13
- Listening Log, p. 14
- Proofreading Checklist, p. 15
- Proofreading Marks, p. 16
- Writing Conference Form, p. 17
- Writing Rubric, p. 18
- Instructional Routines, pp. 19–26
- Graphic Organizer 7: Idea-Support Map, p. 33

Journeys Digital Powered by Destination Reading

For Students
- Student eBook
- Comprehension Expedition CD-ROM
- Leveled Online Readers
- WriteSmart CD-ROM

For Teachers
- Online TE and Focus Wall
- Online Assessment System
- Teacher One-Stop
- Destination Reading Instruction

Week at a Glance

Intervention

STRATEGIC INTERVENTION: TIER II

Use these materials to provide additional targeted instruction for students who need Tier II strategic intervention.

Supports the Student Book selections

Interactive Work-text for Skills Support

Write-In Reader:

Harriet Tubman, American Hero

- Engaging selection connects to main topic.
- Reinforces this week's target vocabulary and comprehension skill and strategy.
- Opportunities for student interaction on each page.

Assessment

Progress monitoring every two weeks.

For this week's Strategic Intervention lessons, see Teacher's Edition pages S32–S41.

INTENSIVE INTERVENTION: TIER III

- The materials in the Literacy Tool Kit help you provide a different approach for students who need Tier III intensive intervention.
- Interactive lessons provide focused instruction in key reading skills, targeted at students' specific needs.
- Lesson cards are convenient for small-group or individual instruction.
- Blackline masters provide additional practice.
- A leveled book accompanies each lesson to give students opportunities for additional reading and skill application.
- Assessments for each lesson help you evaluate the effectiveness of the intervention.

Lessons provide support for

- Phonics and Word Study Skills
- Vocabulary
- Comprehension Skills and Literacy Genres
- Fluency

ELL English Language Learners

SCAFFOLDED SUPPORT

Use these materials to ensure that students acquire social and academic language proficiency.

JOURNEYS DIGITAL Powered by DESTINATIONReading®
- Leveled Readers Online
- Picture Card Bank Online

Language Support Card

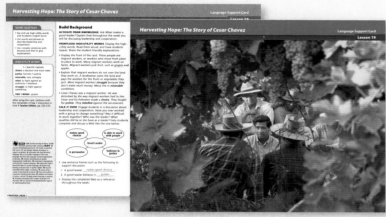

- Builds background for the main topic and promotes oral language.
- Develops high-utility vocabulary and academic language.

Leveled Reader

- Sheltered text connects to the main selection's topic, vocabulary, skill, and strategy.

Scaffolded Support

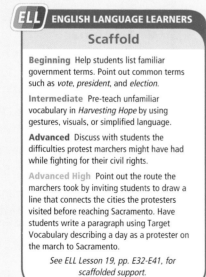

ELL ENGLISH LANGUAGE LEARNERS

Scaffold

Beginning Help students list familiar government terms. Point out common terms such as *vote*, *president*, and *election*.

Intermediate Pre-teach unfamiliar vocabulary in *Harvesting Hope* by using gestures, visuals, or simplified language.

Advanced Discuss with students the difficulties protest marchers might have had while fighting for their civil rights.

Advanced High Point out the route the marchers took by inviting students to draw a line that connects the cities the protesters visited before reaching Sacramento. Have students write a paragraph using Target Vocabulary describing a day as a protester on the march to Sacramento.

See ELL Lesson 19, pp. E32–E41, for scaffolded support.

- Notes throughout the Teacher's Edition scaffold instruction to each language proficiency level.

Vocabulary in Context Cards 181–190

- Provide visual support and additional practice for Target Vocabulary words.

For this week's English Language Learners lessons, see Teacher's Edition, pages E32–E41.

Essential Question Why might a leader use persuasion?

		Day 1	Day 2
Whole Group	**Oral Language** Listening Comprehension	**Teacher Read Aloud** "The Father of India," T228–T229 ☑ Target Vocabulary, T229	**Turn and Talk**, T235
	Vocabulary **Comprehension** Skills and Strategies **Reading**	☑ **Comprehension** Preview the Target Skill, T229 ☑ **Introduce Vocabulary** Vocabulary in Context, T230–T231 **Develop Background** ☑ Target Vocabulary, T232–T233	**Introduce Comprehension** ☑ Persuasion, T234–T235 Infer/Predict, T234–T235 **Read "Harvesting Hope,"** T236–T246 Focus on Genre, T236 Stop and Think, T239, T243, T245
	Cross-Curricular **Connections** **Fluency** **Decoding**	☑ **Fluency** Model Stress, T228	☑ **Fluency** Teach Stress, T254
Whole Group Language Arts	**Spelling** **Grammar** **Writing**	☑ **Spelling** Suffixes: -ful, -less, -ness, -ment: **Pretest**, T260 ☑ **Grammar** Daily Proofreading Practice, T262 Teach Transition Words, T262 ☑ **Write to Narrate: Plan a Personal Narrative** Analyze the Model, T266	☑ **Spelling** Suffixes: -ful, -less, -ness, -ment: Word Sort, T260 ☑ **Grammar** Daily Proofreading Practice, T263 Teach Transition Words, T263 ☑ **Write to Narrate: Plan a Personal Narrative** Focus Trait: Organization, T267
	Writing Prompt	*Write a list of what you would like and dislike about traveling all the time.*	*Imagine you are a migrant worker. Write a story about how you live.*
COMMON CORE Correlations		**Teacher Read Aloud** RF.4.4b **Introduce Vocabulary** RI.4.4 **Develop Background** RI.4.4 **Fluency** RF.4.4b **Spelling** L.4.2d **Grammar** W.4.3c **Write to Narrate** W.4.3a, W.4.3b, W.4.4, W.4.5	**Turn and Talk** RI.4.8 **Introduce Comprehension** RI.4.8 **Read** RI.4.1, RI.4.3, RI.4.4, RI.4.5, RI.4.8, RI.4.10, RF.4.4b, L.4.5b **Fluency** RF.4.4b **Spelling** L.4.2d **Grammar** W.4.3c **Write to Narrate** W.4.3a, W.4.3b, W.4.4, W.4.5

Suggestions for Small Groups (See pp. T274–T275.)
Suggestions for Intervention (See pp. S32–S41.)
Suggestions for English Language Learners (See pp. E32–E41.)

JOURNEYS DIGITAL Powered by DESTINATIONReading®
Teacher One-Stop: Lesson Planning

Day 3

Turn and Talk, T247
Oral Language, T247

Read "Harvesting Hope,"
T236–T246
Develop Comprehension, T238,
T240, T242, T244, T246
☑ **Target Vocabulary**
"Harvesting Hope: The Story of
Cesar Chavez," T238, T240,
T242, T244, T246
Your Turn, T247
Deepen Comprehension
☑ Persuasion, T252–T253

Cross-Curricular Connection
Social Studies, T241
☑ **Fluency**
Practice Stress, T241
☑ **Decoding**
More Common Suffixes, T255

☑ **Spelling**
Suffixes *-ful, -less, -ness, -ment*:
Word Families, T261
☑ **Grammar**
Daily Proofreading Practice, T263
Teach Transition Words, T263

☑ **Write to Narrate: Plan a
Personal Narrative**
Prewrite, T267

*Describe what it takes to be a
leader who fights for change.*

Turn and Talk SL.4.1a
Oral Language SL.4.1a
Read RI.4.1, RI.4.3, RI.4.4, RI.4.5, RI.4.8,
RI.4.10, RF.4.4b, L.5.b
Deepen Comprehension RI.4.8
Fluency RF.4.4b
Spelling L.4.2d, L.4.5c
Grammar W.4.3c
Write to Narrate W.4.3a, W.4.3b,
W.4.4, W.4.5

Day 4

Text to World, T251

**Read "The Edible
Schoolyard,"** T248–T251
Connect to Science, T248
Target Vocabulary Review, T249
Develop Comprehension, T250
Weekly Internet Challenge, T250
Making Connections, T251
☑ **Vocabulary Strategies**
Use a Dictionary, T256–T257

☑ **Fluency**
Practice Stress, T254

☑ **Spelling**
Suffixes *-ful, -less, -ness, -ment*:
Word Families, T261
☑ **Grammar**
Daily Proofreading Practice, T264
Review Transition Words, T264

☑ **Write to Narrate: Plan a
Personal Narrative**
Prewrite, T268

*Write an advertisement that
persuades people to help in
your community.*

Text to World W.4.8
Read RI.4.1, RI.4.2, RI.4.7, RI.4.9, RI.4.10,
RF.4.4b, W.4.8
Making Connections RI.4.9, RI.4.10,
W.4.8
Vocabulary Strategies L.4.4c
Fluency RF.4.4b
Spelling L.4.2d
Grammar W.4.3c
Write to Narrate W.4.3a, W.4.3b,
W.4.4, W.4.5

Day 5

Listening and Speaking, T259

Connect and Extend
Read to Connect, T258
Independent Reading, T258
Extend Through Research, T259

☑ **Fluency**
Progress Monitoring, T271

☑ **Spelling**
Suffixes *-ful, -less, -ness, -ment*:
Assess, T261
☑ **Grammar**
Daily Proofreading Practice, T264
Connect Grammar to Writing,
T264–T265

☑ **Write to Narrate: Plan a
Personal Narrative**
Prewrite, T268

*Write a speech to persuade
people that there should be a
Cesar Chavez Day.*

Listening and Speaking SL.4.6
Connect and Extend RI.4.9, W.4.8,
SL.4.1a, SL.4.6
Fluency RF.4.4b
Spelling L.4.2d
Grammar W.4.3c
Write to Narrate W.4.3a, W.4.3b,
W.4.4, W.4.5

Your Skills for the Week

☑ **Vocabulary**
Target Vocabulary
Strategies: Use a
Dictionary

☑ **Comprehension**
Persuasion
Infer/Predict

☑ **Decoding**
More Common
Suffixes *-ful, -less,
-ness, -ment*

☑ **Fluency**
Stress

☑ **Language Arts**
Spelling
Grammar
Writing

Weekly Leveled Readers

Differentiated Support for This Week's Targets

 **TARGET SKILL**

Persuasion

 **TARGET STRATEGY**

Infer/Predict

TARGET VOCABULARY

overcome	publicity
association	violence
capitol	conflicts
drought	horizon
dedicate	brilliant

Additional Tools

Vocabulary in Context Cards

Comprehension Tool: Graphic Organizer Transparency 7

? Essential Question

Why might a leader use persuasion?

Vocabulary Reader

Level S

Build Target Vocabulary

• Introduce the Target Vocabulary in context and build comprehension using the Target Strategy.

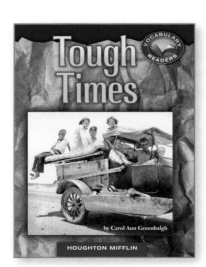

Vocabulary Reader

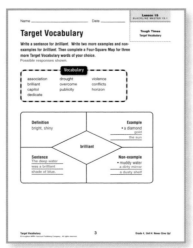

Blackline Master 19.1

Intervention

Scaffolded Support

• Provide extra support in applying the Target Vocabulary, Target Skill, and Target Strategy in context.

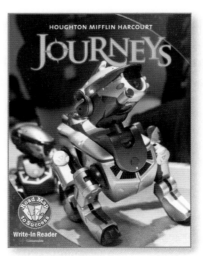

Write-In Reader

 For Vocabulary Reader Lesson Plans, see Small Group pages T276–T277.

Leveled Readers

Struggling Readers
Level P

Objective: Use persuasion and the infer/predict strategy to read *Songs for the People.*

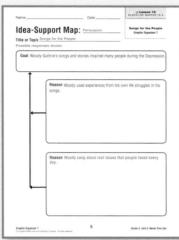

Blackline Master 19.3

On Level
Level R

Objective: Use persuasion and the infer/predict strategy to read *The People's President.*

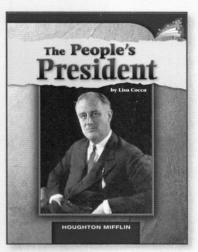

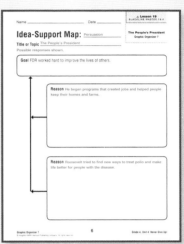

Blackline Master 19.4

Advanced
Level U

Objective: Use persuasion and the infer/predict strategy to read *The Story of Dorothea Lange.*

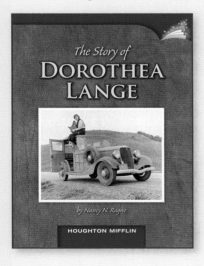

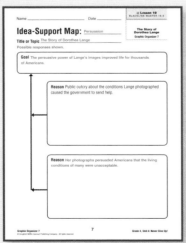

Blackline Master 19.5

English Language Learners
Level R

Objective: Use persuasion and the infer/predict strategy to read *A President for the People.*

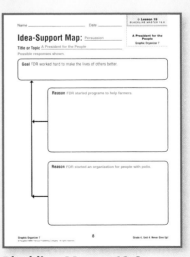

Blackline Master 19.6

 For Leveled Reader Lesson Plans, see Small Group pages T280–T283.

Ready-Made Work Stations

Manage Independent Activities

Use the Ready-Made Work Stations to establish a consistent routine for students working independently. Each station contains three activities. Students who experience success with the *Get Started!* activity move on to the *Reach Higher!* and *Challenge Yourself!* activities, as time permits.

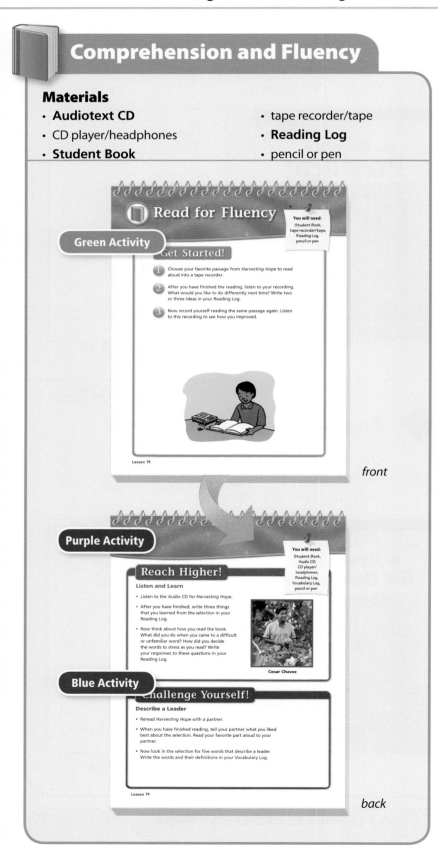

Comprehension and Fluency

Materials
- **Audiotext CD**
- CD player/headphones
- **Student Book**
- tape recorder/tape
- **Reading Log**
- pencil or pen

Read for Fluency

You will need: Student Book, tape recorder/tape, Reading Log, pencil or pen

Green Activity

Get Started!

1. Choose your favorite passage from *Harvesting Hope* to read aloud into a tape recorder.
2. After you have finished the reading, listen to your recording. What would you like to do differently next time? Write two or three ideas in your Reading Log.
3. Now record yourself reading the same passage again. Listen to this recording to see how you improved.

front

Purple Activity

You will need: Student Book, Audio CD, CD player/ headphones, Reading Log, Vocabulary Log, pencil or pen

Reach Higher!

Listen and Learn

- Listen to the Audio CD for *Harvesting Hope*.
- After you have finished, write three things that you learned from the selection in your Reading Log.
- Now think about how you read the book. What did you do when you came to a difficult or unfamiliar word? How did you decide the words to stress as you read? Write your responses to these questions in your Reading Log.

Cesar Chavez

Blue Activity

Challenge Yourself!

Describe a Leader

- Reread *Harvesting Hope* with a partner.
- When you have finished reading, tell your partner what you liked best about the selection. Read your favorite part aloud to your partner.
- Now look in the selection for five words that describe a leader. Write the words and their definitions in your Vocabulary Log.

Lesson 19

back

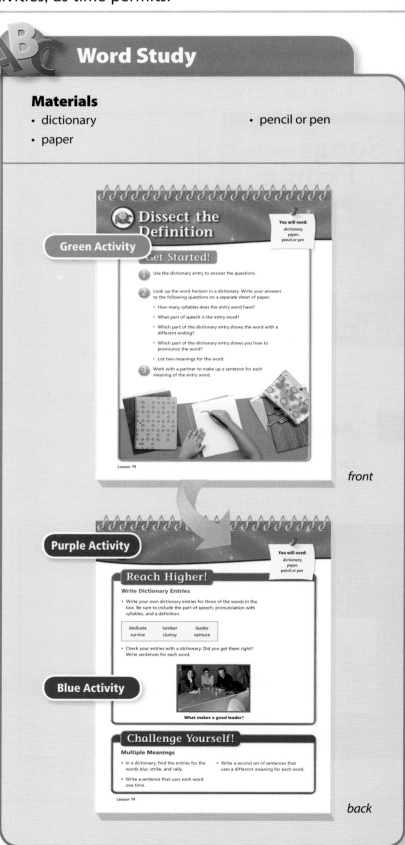

Word Study

Materials
- dictionary
- paper
- pencil or pen

Dissect the Definition

You will need: dictionary, paper, pencil or pen

Green Activity

Get Started!

1. Use the dictionary entry to answer the questions.
2. Look up the word *horizon* in a dictionary. Write your answers to the following questions on a separate sheet of paper.
   - How many syllables does the entry word have?
   - What part of speech is the entry word?
   - Which part of the dictionary entry shows the word with a different ending?
   - Which part of the dictionary entry shows you how to pronounce the word?
   - List two meanings for the word.
3. Work with a partner to make up a sentence for each meaning of the entry word.

front

Purple Activity

You will need: dictionary, paper, pencil or pen

Reach Higher!

Write Dictionary Entries

- Write your own dictionary entries for three of the words in the box. Be sure to include the part of speech, pronunciation with syllables, and a definition.

| dedicate | lumber | leader |
| survive | clumsy | venture |

- Check your entries with a dictionary. Did you get them right? Write sentences for each word.

Blue Activity

What makes a good leader?

Challenge Yourself!

Multiple Meanings

- In a dictionary, find the entries for the words *blur*, *strike*, and *rally*.
- Write a sentence that uses each word one time.
- Write a second set of sentences that uses a different meaning for each word.

Lesson 19

back

T226 • Unit 4 Lesson 19

Think and Write

Materials
- **Student Book**
- computer with Internet access
- library books, magazines/ newspapers
- pencil or pen; paper
- colored pencils

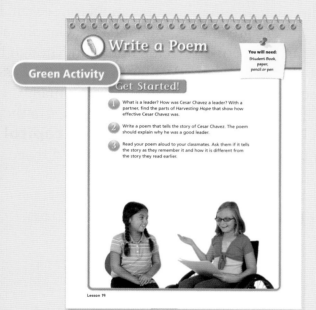

Write a Poem

Green Activity

You will need: Student Book, paper, pencil or pen

Get Started!

1. What is a leader? How was Cesar Chavez a leader? With a partner, find the parts of *Harvesting Hope* that show how effective Cesar Chavez was.

2. Write a poem that tells the story of Cesar Chavez. The poem should explain why he was a good leader.

3. Read your poem aloud to your classmates. Ask them if it tells the story as they remember it and how it is different from the story they read earlier.

Lesson 19

front

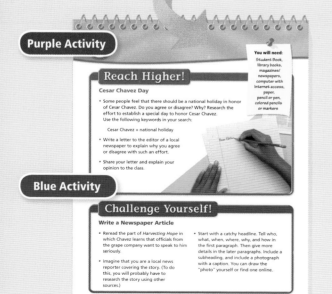

Purple Activity

Reach Higher!

Cesar Chavez Day

You will need: Student Book, library books, magazines/ newspapers, computer with Internet access, paper, pencil or pen, colored pencils or markers

- Some people feel that there should be a national holiday in honor of Cesar Chavez. Do you agree or disagree? Why? Research the effort to establish a special day to honor Cesar Chavez. Use the following keywords in your search:

  Cesar Chavez + national holiday

- Write a letter to the editor of a local newspaper to explain why you agree or disagree with such an effort.

- Share your letter and explain your opinion to the class.

Blue Activity

Challenge Yourself!

Write a Newspaper Article

- Reread the part of *Harvesting Hope* in which Chavez learns that officials from the grape company want to speak to him seriously.

- Imagine that you are a local news reporter covering the story. (To do this, you will probably have to research the story using other sources.)

- Start with a catchy headline. Tell who, what, when, where, why, and how in the first paragraph. Then give more details in the later paragraphs. Include a subheading, and include a photograph with a caption. You can draw the "photo" yourself or find one online.

Lesson 19

back

Independent Activities

Have students complete these activities at a computer center or a center with an audio CD player.

LAUNCH ➤ **Comprehension and Grammar Activities**

- Practice and apply this week's skills.

LAUNCH ➤ **Student eBook**

- Read and listen to this week's selections and skill lessons.

LAUNCH ➤ **WriteSmart CD-ROM**

- Review student versions of this week's writing model.

LAUNCH ➤ **Audiotext CD**

- Listen to books or selections on CD.

Single Log In

Teacher Read Aloud

Model Fluency

Stress Explain that when good readers read aloud they stress, or emphasize, certain words.

- Display **Projectable 19.1.** As you read each sentence, model how to stress important words to make the meaning of the text clearer.

- Point out that stressing different words can change the meaning of a sentence.

- Reread the sentences together with students, stressing important words.

The Father of India

Imagine living in a place where those in charge were from another country. Even though your ancestors had lived on the land for thousands of years, another government took over and decided who could own land, how much tax your family had to pay on simple things like salt, whether you could go to school, and what you could do when you grew up. India, a land of both **drought** and heavy rains, had been ruled by the British for a hundred years. But one day, one man would **dedicate** his life to persuading the British to give India its freedom.

Many Indians wanted to be free of the British, but they didn't agree with each other on how to win their freedom. In the midst of all the disagreements, Mohandas K. Gandhi, a small, frail-looking man, got everyone's attention. Though he adopted simple clothes and a modest lifestyle, Gandhi was an engaging speaker. In his work to **overcome** unfair British laws, Gandhi gave many persuasive speeches in the British Empire. Heads of government in London's **capitol** building took notice. In his speeches, Gandhi stated that only by acting together in protest, could Indians free themselves. Gandhi won over many Indians and became a leader of a new **association** called the Congress party.

Projectable 19.1

Projectable 19.1

Harvesting Hope | Fluency | Stress

Read Aloud: Model Oral Fluency

The Father of India

Imagine living in a place where those in charge were from another country. Even though your ancestors had lived in the land for thousands of years, another government took over and decided who could own land, how much tax your family had to pay on simple things like salt, whether you could go to school, and what you could do when you grew up. India, a land of both drought and heavy rains had been ruled by the British for a hundred years. But one day, one man would dedicate his life to persuading the British to give India its freedom.

Gandhi reasoned that the best way to resist unfair rules was to protest without **violence**. Peaceful action was persuasive action, even when British police were hitting, yelling, or arresting protesters. When Indians used non-violence in **conflicts** with British police, there was a lot of **publicity** that embarrassed the British. This caused people around the world to support India's struggles.

One of the most famous things Gandhi did was to lead people on a march that protested unfair salt laws. The British believed all of the salt belonged to them and they could tax Indians whatever they wanted for it. Gandhi, and thousands of people who marched with him, walked for 23 days to the city of Dandi. Perhaps the **brilliant** sea, sparkling in the sun, offered the weary protesters hope. Turning toward the **horizon**, Gandhi reached down to pick up a lump of salt. This action sent a message to the British that the people of India would no longer obey their unfair salt laws.

It took many years of practicing non-violence before Gandhi and his supporters could persuade the British to give India its independence. Then, in 1947, Gandhi and his supporters saw the birth of a free India. Indians honored him by calling him the "father of the nation."

Listening Comprehension

Preview the Target Skill

Read aloud the passage, using an appropriate rate. Then ask the following questions.

1 Persuasion

What groups do you think Gandhi was trying to convince? He was trying to convince the British to give India its freedom and the Indian people to act together in protest.

2 Persuasion

What did Gandhi do to try to convince others? Why was it so effective? Gandhi chose peaceful protests. It was effective because the publicity embarrassed the British.

3 Character's Traits

What do you understand about Gandhi's character from the way his group tried to fight the salt tax? He was a very strong, effective leader.

 Target Vocabulary

- Reread "The Father of India" aloud.
- As you read, pause briefly to explain each highlighted vocabulary word.
- Discuss the meaning of each word as it is used in the article.

drought a time with little or no rain

dedicate set aside for a special purpose

overcome defeat

capitol a building where government meets

association a club or organization

violence use of physical force

conflicts disagreements or fights

publicity information given to the public to get attention

brilliant bright and shining

horizon where the earth meets the sky

☑ Introduce Vocabulary

SHARE OBJECTIVE

• Understand and use the Target Vocabulary words.

Teach

Display and discuss the **Vocabulary in Context Cards**, using the routine below. Direct students to **Student Book pp. 474–475.** See also **Instructional Routine 9.**

1 **Read and pronounce the word.** Read the word once alone, then together with students.

2 **Explain the word.** Read aloud the explanation under *What does it mean?*

3 **Discuss vocabulary in context.** Together, read aloud the sentence on the front of the card. Help students explain and use the word in new sentences.

4 **Engage with the word.** Ask and discuss the *Think About It* question with students.

Apply

Give partners or small groups one or two **Vocabulary in Context Cards.**

• Help students start the *Talk It Over* activity on the back of the card.

• Have students complete activities for all the cards during the week.

Lesson 19

Vocabulary in Context

☑ TARGET VOCABULARY

overcome
association
capitol
drought
dedicate
publicity
violence
conflicts
horizon
brilliant

Vocabulary Reader

Context Cards

1 overcome
Cesar Chavez worked hard to overcome, or conquer, hardships.

2 association
These kids have formed a group, or association, that cleans up beaches.

3 capitol
A state capitol is a building where lawmakers can make and change laws.

4 drought
In the 1930s, a drought, or lack of rain, made life hard for many farmers.

474

ELL ENGLISH LANGUAGE LEARNERS

Scaffold

Beginning Use actions and facial expressions to demonstrate the meaning of *overcome*. Then have students perform the action as you say the word.

Advanced Ask questions to confirm students' understanding. For example, *The UN works to resolve international conflicts. Why is this an important job?*

Intermediate Have students complete sentence frames for each Vocabulary word. For example, **Elliot sees the _____ on the *horizon*.**

Advanced High Have partners ask each other questions about each Vocabulary word. For example, *How do you think farmers feel when there is a drought?*

See ELL Lesson 19, pp. E32–E41, for scaffolded support.

- Study each **Context Card**.
- Use a dictionary to help you pronounce these words.

dedicate

Martin Luther King Jr. wanted to dedicate his life to equality. It was his life's work.

publicity

The media can spread publicity, or news, about events and causes.

violence

Many people believe change should come through peaceful ways, not violence.

conflicts

Most conflicts, or disagreements, can be solved by talking things over.

horizon

In the fields, Chavez often worked until the sun fell below the horizon.

brilliant

The bright, brilliant colors of the American flag symbolize freedom.

475

Monitor Vocabulary

Are students able to understand and use Target Vocabulary words?

IF...	THEN...
students have difficulty understanding and using most of the Target Vocabulary words,	▶ use **Vocabulary in Context Cards** and differentiate the **Vocabulary Reader**, *Tough Times*, for Struggling Readers, p. T276. *See also Intervention Lesson 19, pp. S32–S41.*
students can understand and use most of the Target Vocabulary words,	▶ use **Vocabulary in Context Cards** and differentiate the **Vocabulary Reader**, *Tough Times*, for On-Level Readers, p. T276.
students can understand and use all of the Target Vocabulary words,	▶ differentiate the **Vocabulary Reader**, *Tough Times*, for Advanced Readers, p. T277.

Vocabulary Reader, pp. T276–T277 *Group English Language Learners according to language proficiency.*

VOCABULARY IN CONTEXT CARDS 181–190

overcome

Cesar Chavez worked hard to overcome, or conquer, hardships.

overcome

What Does It Mean?
To **overcome** a difficulty is to solve it or conquer it.

Think About It.
What character traits help to **overcome** difficulties?

Talk It Over.
Read each situation. Based on the information provided, decide whether the person was able to **overcome** the problem.

Situation	Did the person *overcome* the problem?
The firefighter rescued the kitten from the tree.	
I lost my homework, and I still cannot find it.	
My mother missed her plane and won't get to her meeting on time.	
The battery in my toy died, so I replaced it with a new one.	

front   back

Develop Background

 ENGLISH LANGUAGE LEARNERS

Scaffold

Beginning Use simplified language to explain the concepts on Student Book p. 476.

Intermediate Have students complete this sentence frame. *Migrant workers needed help because _____.*

Advanced Have partners use Target Vocabulary words to discuss why migrant workers needed help.

Advanced High Point out the route the marchers took by inviting students to draw a line that connects the cities the protesters visited before reaching Sacramento. Have students work together to describe a day as a protester on the march to Sacramento.

See ELL Lesson 19, pp. E32–E41, for scaffolded support.

☑ Target Vocabulary

1 Teach/Model

- Use the photograph of Cesar Chavez on **Student Book p. 476** to explain that "Harvesting Hope" is about a man who marches to the **capitol** to fight for the rights of farm workers.
- Use **Vocabulary in Context Cards** to review student-friendly explanations of each Target Vocabulary word.
- Have students silently read **Student Book p. 476.** Then read the passage aloud.

2 Guided Practice

Ask students the first item below and discuss their responses. Continue in this way until students have answered a question about each Target Vocabulary word.

1. Tell about a time when you watched the sun set beyond the **horizon**.
2. What steps must a student take to **overcome** a problem in school?
3. Firefighters **dedicate** themselves to their work. What other jobs require a lot of hard work?
4. What is something you have seen that is a **brilliant** shade of red?
5. People handle **conflicts** differently. Explain a good way to deal with a problem.
6. Describe a world that has no **violence**.
7. Name an **association** or club you belong to or would like to join.
8. Where is the **capitol** of the United States located?
9. How can positive **publicity** help a politician get elected?
10. Explain what happens to plant and animal life during a **drought**.

Background

✓ **TARGET VOCABULARY** **Migrant Farm Workers** American farmers have grown fruits and vegetables for centuries. Some crops grow in huge fields that stretch to the horizon. Often these plants must be tended and harvested by hand, a time-consuming process. To overcome this problem, farmers began hiring migrants, or traveling workers.

For many years, migrants were poorly treated but were expected to dedicate themselves to their work. They worked under the hot, brilliant sun for low wages. Conflicts arose between migrants and farm owners. To strike, or refuse to work, could lead to violence. For a long time, migrants had no association to help them and no contact with officials in the state capitol. There was no publicity to tell people about their situation. Then a young man named Cesar Chavez came along.

As the result of a drought in the 1930s, many people from the Great Plains moved to California and became migrant farm laborers. Cesar Chavez was one of them.

3 | Apply

- Have partners take turns reading a paragraph on **Student Book p. 476** to one another.

- Tell partners to pause at and explain each highlighted vocabulary word as they read.

- Have each partner use one vocabulary word in a new sentence.

Introduce Comprehension

SHARE OBJECTIVES

- Recognize an author's use of language to influence readers.
- Make inferences/use textual evidence.

SKILL TRACE

Persuasion	
Introduce	T234–T235
Differentiate	T278–T279
Reteach	T286
Review	T252–T253
Test	Weekly Tests, Lesson 19

ELL ENGLISH LANGUAGE LEARNERS

Scaffold

Beginning Discuss the meaning of *persuade*. Give examples of things someone might try to *persuade* someone to do (*not smoke, eat healthy food, go to a certain movie*).

Intermediate Display these sentence frames: *You should _____. It is _____.* Discuss possible ways to complete them using persuasive language.

Advanced Have student partners act out how they would persuade a friend to play a new game with them.

Advanced High Have students role-play an interview for a job. Have them use persuasive language.

See ELL Lesson 19, pp. E32–E41, for support.

✓ Persuasion; Infer/Predict

1 Teach/Model

AL *Academic Language*

persuade to convince someone to think or act in a certain way

author's goal what an author wants readers to think or do

- Explain that sometimes authors write to **persuade** readers to think or act a certain way. This kind of text is called *persuasive text*. Advertisements are one kind of persuasive text.

- Read and discuss with students **Student Book p. 477**. Have them use the Academic Language in the discussion.

- Display **Projectable 19.2**. Have students read "Helping the Forgotten Poor."

PERSUASION Tell students that as they read, they should ask: What is the **author's goal**? What does the author want me to think? What details does the author give to persuade me?

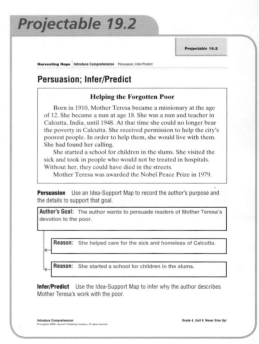

Projectable 19.2

Think Aloud *The passage tells about Mother Teresa's work with the poor in Calcutta. It says she started a school. She also took care of sick people so they did not die in the streets. I think the author wants to persuade me that Mother Teresa was devoted to helping the poor.*

INFER/PREDICT Use the chart to infer what the author wants you to think about Mother Teresa and her work.

Think Aloud *When I read these things, I infer that Mother Teresa did many things to help the poor. I think she must have been a special person.*

Comprehension

✓ TARGET SKILL **Persuasion**

As you read "Harvesting Hope," think about whether the author is trying to persuade, or convince, you to think or act in a certain way. Ask yourself, *What is the author trying to persuade me to do? How does the author use language to persuade me?* Use a graphic organizer like the one below to help you identify the author's goal and reasons.

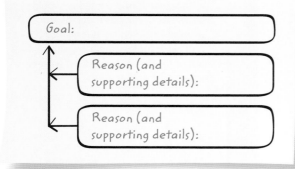

Goal:

Reason (and supporting details):

Reason (and supporting details):

✓ TARGET STRATEGY **Infer/Predict**

Sometimes the author's reasons are not stated directly in the text. Use your graphic organizer to infer those reasons by using details and evidence from the text. Inferring unstated details can help you decide if you agree with the author.

JOURNEYS DIGITAL | Powered by DESTINATIONReading®
Comprehension Activities: Lesson 19

477

2 Guided Practice

Have partners complete their own Idea-Support Map for "Helping the Forgotten Poor." Then have them review their charts together.

3 Apply

Turn and Talk Have partners use their Idea-Support Maps to discuss whether they agree with the author.

As students read the main selection, have them use an Idea-Support Map to understand what drove Cesar Chavez to do the things he did.

Monitor Comprehension

Are students able to recognize persuasion?

IF...	THEN...
students have difficulty recognizing persuasion,	▶ **Differentiate Comprehension** for Struggling Readers, p. T278. *See also Intervention Lesson 19, p. S32–S41.*
students can recognize persuasion,	▶ **Differentiate Comprehension** for On-Level Readers, p.T278.
students can accurately recognize persuasion and make appropriate inferences and predictions,	▶ **Differentiate Comprehension** for Advanced Readers p. T279.

SMALL GROUP Options

Differentiate Comprehension pp. T278–T279. *Group English Language Learners according to academic ability and language proficiency. See also ELL Lesson 19, pp. E32–E41, for scaffolded support.*

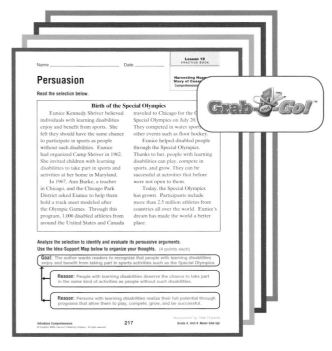

Practice Book p. 217
See Grab-and-Go™ Resource for additional leveled practice.

Introduce the
Main
Selection

TARGET SKILL

PERSUASION Explain that as they read, students will use **Graphic Organizer 3: Idea-Support Map** to record these points about the author's purpose:

- the author's goal; that is, what the author wants to convince readers to do or think

- the reasons and details (facts/examples) that support this goal

Use **Projectable 19.2** to model filling in the Idea-Support Map.

TARGET STRATEGY

INFER/PREDICT Students will use the **Idea-Support Map** to make **inferences** about the use of persuasion.

GENRE: Biography

- Review the genre information on **Student Book p. 478** with students.

- Share and discuss the **Genre Blackline Master: Biography**.

- Preview the selection and model identifying characteristics of the genre.

Think Aloud
The title gives the name of a real person—Cesar Chavez. It is told from a different person's point of view. I think this selection is a biography.

- As you preview, ask students to identify other features of biography.

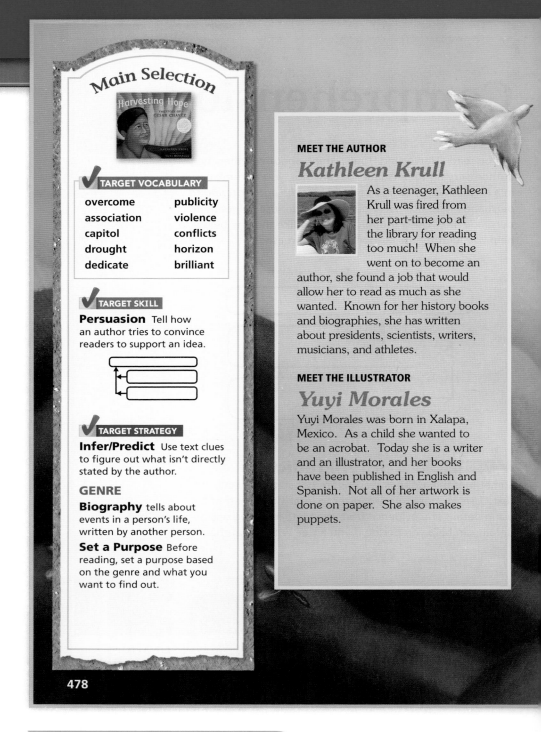

Main Selection

Harvesting Hope

✓ TARGET VOCABULARY

overcome	publicity
association	violence
capitol	conflicts
drought	horizon
dedicate	brilliant

✓ TARGET SKILL

Persuasion Tell how an author tries to convince readers to support an idea.

✓ TARGET STRATEGY

Infer/Predict Use text clues to figure out what isn't directly stated by the author.

GENRE

Biography tells about events in a person's life, written by another person.

Set a Purpose Before reading, set a purpose based on the genre and what you want to find out.

478

MEET THE AUTHOR
Kathleen Krull

As a teenager, Kathleen Krull was fired from her part-time job at the library for reading too much! When she went on to become an author, she found a job that would allow her to read as much as she wanted. Known for her history books and biographies, she has written about presidents, scientists, writers, musicians, and athletes.

MEET THE ILLUSTRATOR
Yuyi Morales

Yuyi Morales was born in Xalapa, Mexico. As a child she wanted to be an acrobat. Today she is a writer and an illustrator, and her books have been published in English and Spanish. Not all of her artwork is done on paper. She also makes puppets.

Reading the Selection

	Pre-reading	Reading
Supported	**SELECTION SUMMARY** Use **Blackline Master 19.2** to help students identify main ideas and details. **AUDIOTEXT CD** Have students listen to the selection as they follow along in their books.	**AUTHOR'S MESSAGE** Have students find places in the text where the author shows that Cesar Chavez tried to persuade people.
Independent	**PREVIEW** Have students look at the title and illustrations on the first few pages and discuss predictions and clues. Some students may read the story independently first.	**TEXT EVIDENCE** Pause at the bottom of pp. 483 and 485. Have students predict what might occur next in the text. Pause later to confirm or revise students' predictions.

Harvesting Hope

THE STORY OF CESAR CHAVEZ

by Kathleen Krull   *illustrated by Yuyi Morales*

Essential Question

Why might a leader use persuasion?

479

? Essential Question

- Read aloud the Essential Question on **p. 479**. *Why might a leader use persuasion?*

- Tell students to think about this question as they read "Harvesting Hope: The Story of Cesar Chavez."

Set Purpose

- Explain that good readers set a purpose for reading, based on their preview of the selection and what they know about the genre, as well as what they want to learn by reading.

- Model setting a reading purpose.

Think Aloud *I know a little about Cesar Chavez, but I'd like to know more. I don't know much about how he got to be a leader. Maybe this selection will tell me.*

- Have students share their reading purposes and record them in their journals.

JOURNEYS DIGITAL **Powered by DESTINATIONReading®**
Student eBook: Read and Listen

Name _____ Date _____

Harvesting Hope: The Story of Cesar Chavez

Pages 480–481
We meet Cesar Chavez and learn about his early life. Cesar's life is turned upside down by hard times due to a terrible drought. The Chavez family loses their ranch and is forced to move west. Their first home in California is a battered shack with a dirt floor.

Pages 482–483
Cesar and his family work in the fields harvesting fruits and vegetables as migrant farmworkers. It is a hard life. Workers who complain are treated poorly. The treatment of the farmworkers upsets Cesar. He remembers his old life and believes farmwork should not be so harsh.

Pages 484–485
Cesar dedicates his life to fighting for justice. He helps start the National Farm Workers Association. In 1965, Delano vineyard owners cut the farmworkers' pay. The farmworkers strike against the grape company.

Pages 486–487
The grape company fights the strike. Cesar refuses to use violence as a weapon. Instead, he organizes a march. The Delano police try to stop the march, but Cesar forces them to back down. Word spreads of the marchers' cause.

Page 488
Cesar receives a surprise message. The grape company is ready to recognize the National Farm Workers Association. They promise Cesar a contract and better working conditions. Cesar returns and announces the historic contract. He has achieved his goal.

Selection Summary   4   Grade 4, Unit 4: Never Give Up!

Lesson 19
BLACKLINE MASTER 19.2

Harvesting Hope

Selection Summary

Blackline Master 19.2

Develop Comprehension

Pause at the stopping points to ask students the following questions.

1 Identify Story Structure

Why does the selection begin with an introduction about Cesar's life in Arizona? The introduction tells the reader about Cesar's life before the period covered in the selection.

2 ✓ TARGET VOCABULARY

*How might a **drought** affect the foods you eat? Sample answer: If a drought reduced the amount of corn available, I might have to eat more wheat or rice instead.*

3 Author's Use of Language

Why do you think the author uses such terms as battered *and* filthy *to describe the place where Cesar's family lived in California? to help the reader make a strong emotional connection to the family's surroundings*

1 As a boy, Cesar Chavez (SEH sahr CHAH vehz) lived on his family's big ranch in Arizona. His family had a big house and all the food they could want. Cesar loved to play with his cousins and his brother Richard. He liked to listen to his relatives' tales of life back in Mexico.

~ ❀ ~

2 Then, in 1937, the summer Cesar was ten, the trees around the ranch began to wilt. The sun baked the farm soil rock hard. A drought (drowt) was choking the life out of Arizona. Without water for the crops, the Chavez family couldn't make money to pay its bills.

480

ELL ENGLISH LANGUAGE LEARNERS

Scaffold

Beginning Using the illustrations, preview the selection with students. Help students discuss what is happening in each scene.

Advanced Have students tell in their own words what it was like for Cesar to work as a field worker.

Intermediate Explain the following words using gestures, visuals, or simplified language: *possessions, spasms, torment, wilt.*

Advanced High After reading pp. 480-483, have students write a short summary of what they have learned so far.

See ELL Lesson 19, pp. E32–E41, for scaffolded support.

There came a day when Cesar's mother couldn't stop crying. In a daze, Cesar watched his father strap their possessions onto the roof of their old car. After a long struggle, the family no longer owned the ranch. They had no choice but to join the hundreds of thousands of people fleeing to the green valleys of California to look for work.

Cesar's old life had vanished. Now he and his family were migrants—working on other people's farms, crisscrossing California, picking whatever fruits and vegetables were in season.

When the Chavez family arrived at the first of their new homes in California, they found a battered old shed. Its doors were missing and garbage covered the dirt floor. Cold, damp air seeped into their bedding and clothes. They shared water and outdoor toilets with a dozen other families, and overcrowding made everything filthy. The neighbors were constantly fighting, and the noise upset Cesar. He had no place to play games with Richard. Meals were sometimes made of dandelion greens gathered along the road.

③

> **STOP AND THINK**
> **Infer/Predict** Why does the Chavez family tolerate the poor living conditions? What evidence from the text tells you this?

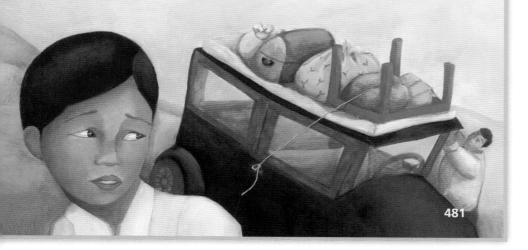

481

STOP AND THINK

✓ **TARGET STRATEGY** Infer/Predict

MODEL THE STRATEGY

- Explain that authors do not always state every idea directly. Readers sometimes must infer, or read "between the lines," to determine meaning.

- Have students complete the **Stop and Think** activity on p. 481. Use the following model to assist them:

  Think Aloud *Thousands of other migrants were seeking work. This was the only way for the Chavez family to make money. I can infer that the family did not have much choice but to accept the terrible conditions.*

- If students have difficulty making inferences, see **Comprehension Intervention** below for extra support.

- Tell students that when he grew up, Chavez worked to change things for farmworkers. Have students use **Projectable 19.3a** to keep track of evidence in the text that helps them infer what led Chavez want to make changes.

Projectable 19.3a

> Projectable 19.3a
>
> Harvesting Hope Comprehension Persuasion
>
> **Idea-Support Map: Persuasion**
> Title or Topic Harvesting Hope: The Story of Cesar Chavez
>
> Cesar wants people to work hard to improve conditions for farm workers.
>
> He saw that farm workers were treated like farm tools. Workers who complained were beaten up or fired.
>
> Comprehension
> Grade 4, Unit 4: Never Give Up!

COMPREHENSION INTERVENTION

✓ **TARGET STRATEGY** Infer/Predict

STRATEGY SUPPORT Remind students that *inferring* means figuring out ideas not directly stated in the text. Model identifying the key events that have happened so far:

A drought caused the Chavez family to lose their ranch in Arizona. Then they joined the many thousands of migrants looking for seasonal work.

Read aloud the description of the family's struggle on p. 481. Ask students to identify details that show what life was like in California. *Sample answer: living in a shed; damp bedding; filthy conditions; fighting neighbors.* Encourage students to connect what they know about the world and their own experiences to make inferences about what it is like for the family to tolerate such conditions. Then guide them to add more text details to their graphic organizers.

Develop Comprehension

4 **Identify Fact and Opinion**
Is the statement that "lettuce had to be the worst" a fact or an opinion?
an opinion *How do you know?*
because it states how someone feels about something

5 **Identify Cause and Effect**
What causes Cesar to not feel safe at school? Cesar is punished when he forgets to speak in English.

6 ✔ **TARGET VOCABULARY**
What is another word for **conflicts**?
disagreements, fights

7 **Draw Conclusions** *Using text details, what can you conclude about how the migrant workers' treatment affected them?* They were always afraid of what would happen to them if they complained.

Cesar swallowed his bitter homesickness and worked alongside his family. He was small and not very strong, but still a fierce worker. Nearly every crop caused torment. Yanking out beets broke the skin between his thumb and index finger. Grapevines sprayed with bug-killing chemicals made his eyes sting and his lungs wheeze. Lettuce had to be the worst. Thinning lettuce all day with a short-handled hoe would make hot spasms shoot through his back. Farm chores on someone else's farm instead of on his own felt like a form of slavery.

The Chavez family talked constantly of saving enough money to buy back their ranch. But by each sundown, the whole family had earned as little as thirty cents for the day's work. As the years blurred together, they spoke of the ranch less and less.

The towns weren't much better than the fields. WHITE TRADE ONLY signs were displayed in many stores and restaurants. None of the thirty-five schools Cesar attended over the years seemed like a safe place, either. Once, after Cesar broke the rule about speaking English at all times, a teacher hung a sign on him that read, I AM A CLOWN. I SPEAK SPANISH. He came to hate school because of the conflicts, though he liked to learn. Even he considered his eighth-grade graduation a miracle. After eighth grade he dropped out to work in the fields full-time.

482

ELL **ENGLISH LANGUAGE LEARNERS**

Scaffold

Beginning For each question, accept one-word responses, expanding student responses into complete sentences. For example, if a student's response to question 5 is "punished," expand the answer by saying, "Yes, Cesar was punished when he forgot to speak English." Have students repeat the expanded response.

Advanced Have students respond to the questions in complete sentences. Provide corrective feedback as needed.

Intermediate Provide part of a response for each question and have students complete it. Then have students repeat the complete response and confirm their understanding.

Advanced High Have students tell how they know the answer to each question based on details from the story.

See ELL Lesson 19, pp. E32–E41, for scaffolded support.

His lack of schooling embarrassed Cesar for the rest of his life, but as a teenager he just wanted to put food on his family's table. As he worked, it disturbed him that landowners treated their workers more like farm tools than human beings. They provided no clean drinking water, rest periods, or access to bathrooms. Anyone who complained was fired, beaten up, or sometimes even murdered.

7

So, like other migrant workers, Cesar was afraid and suspicious whenever outsiders showed up to try to help. How could they know about feeling so powerless? Who could battle such odds?

Yet Cesar had never forgotten his old life in Arizona and the jolt he'd felt when it was turned upside down. Farmwork did not have to be this miserable.

483

Practice Fluency

Stress Read aloud the last paragraph on **Student Book p. 483** as students follow along. As you read, model how to stress important points.

- Tell students that good readers can stress important words to make them stand out from the text. Words can be set apart from the remainder of the text by the author, and a good reader can recognize why this is done.

- Have students choral-read the paragraph, taking care to stress the words *not* and *miserable*.

See p. T254 for a complete fluency lesson on stressing words while reading aloud.

CROSS-CURRICULAR CONNECTION

Social Studies

Display a photo of dust bowl migrants, such as the ones taken by Dorothea Lange during the 1930s. Explain that when drought struck the Midwest and other states in the 1930s, many farmers lost their farms. Thousands traveled to California, where they hoped to find work picking crops. It was the largest migration of people in U.S. history. *What can you tell about the people in this photo?* Their lives are hard; they are poor. *How do you think they feel?* tired, discouraged, helpless *Why do you think the photographer took this picture?* to show how the farmers lived and what they went through Have students do research to find out why the drought area became known as the "dust bowl."

Develop Comprehension

8 **Make Inferences** *What do you think Cesar Chavez probably wanted to do when he felt embarrassed?* stop talking and end the meeting *Why do you think he forced himself to keep talking?* Sample answer: He believed in what he was doing and was determined to succeed.

9 ✔ **TARGET VOCABULARY**

Which of these would help workers **overcome** *feeling powerless: being given free food, fighting for their rights, lack of education, a living wage, safer working conditions?* fighting for their rights, a living wage, safer working conditions

10 **Infer Author's Viewpoint** *How does the author want readers to feel about La Causa? Use evidence from the selection.* Sample answer: She wants readers to sympathize with the workers' cause; she calls them "poorly paid" and "hunched over."

Reluctantly, he started paying attention to the outsiders. He began to think that maybe there was hope. And in his early twenties, he decided to dedicate the rest of his life to fighting for change.

Again he crisscrossed California, this time to talk people into joining his fight. At first, out of every hundred workers he talked to, perhaps one would agree with him. One by one—this was how he started.

At the first meeting Cesar organized, a dozen women gathered. He sat quietly in a corner. After twenty minutes, everyone started wondering when the organizer would show up. Cesar thought he might die of embarrassment.

"Well, I'm the organizer," he said—and forced himself to keep talking, hoping to inspire respect with his new suit and the mustache he was trying to grow. The women listened politely, and he was sure they did so out of pity. **8**

484

But despite his shyness, Cesar showed a knack for solving problems. People trusted him. With workers he was endlessly patient and compassionate. With landowners he was stubborn, demanding, and single-minded. He was learning to be a fighter.

In a fight for justice, he told everyone, truth was a better weapon than violence. "Nonviolence," he said, "takes more guts." It meant using imagination to find ways to overcome powerlessness.

More and more people listened.

One night, 150 people poured into an old abandoned theater in Fresno. At this first meeting of the National Farm Workers Association, Cesar unveiled its flag—a bold black eagle, the sacred bird of the Aztec Indians.

La Causa (lah KOW sah)—The Cause—was born.

It was time to rebel, and the place was Delano. Here, in the heart of the lush San Joaquin (hwah KEEN) Valley, brilliant green vineyards reached toward every horizon. Poorly paid workers hunched over grapevines for most of each year. Then, in 1965, the vineyard owners cut their pay even further.

Cesar chose to fight just one of the forty landowners, hopeful that others would get the message. As plump grapes drooped, thousands of workers walked off that company's fields in a strike, or *huelga* (WEHL gah).

Grapes, when ripe, do not last long.

> **STOP AND THINK**
> **Author's Craft** Authors sometimes use **idioms**, or phrases that mean something different than the meaning of the individual words put together. An idiom used on this page is "Nonviolence takes more than guts." As you continue reading, look for other idioms. What do they mean?

485

STOP AND THINK
Author's Craft: Idioms

* Idioms are phrases that mean something different than the individual words put together.

* There are many idioms in English, and people use them in their everyday speech. Writers often use idioms in their writing to make the story more interesting.

* Have students complete the **Stop and Think** question about idioms. Use the following model to assist them:

> **Think Aloud** *I read that Chavez said "nonviolence takes more guts." I know that to have guts means to have courage. Saying that something "takes guts" is an idiom. I think what he meant was that it took more courage to be nonviolent than to fight.*

* Guide students to find the idiom "get the message" in the next to last paragraph, and to identify and discuss its meaning.

Develop Comprehension

11 **Identify Author's Message**
Why does the author repeat here that Cesar Chavez refused to respond to the company's attacks with violence? Sample answer: to remind readers that Chavez believed in using nonviolence. He believed the truth was the most powerful weapon.

12 ✔ **TARGET VOCABULARY**
How might a peaceful march provide **publicity** *for the farmworkers' cause? Sample answer: Newspaper and TV coverage of the event creates public interest in how farmworkers live, and in the actions of the grape company and local police force.*

13 **Compare and Contrast** *How does the marchers' treatment at the beginning of the march compare with their welcome at the end? Sample answer: At first the police try to stop the march, and the workers must sleep outside. But, as word spreads, people offer them food and drink, more people join the march, and they are greeted with feasts, flowers, and music.*

？Essential Question

Have partners discuss reasons a leader might need to persuade people. Have them discuss reasons Chavez had, and the different groups he had to persuade.

The company fought back with everything from punches to bullets. Cesar refused to respond with violence. Violence would only hurt *La Causa*.

Instead, he organized a march—a march of more than three hundred miles. He and his supporters would walk from Delano to the state capitol in Sacramento to ask for the government's help.

Cesar and sixty-seven others started out one morning. Their first obstacle was the Delano police force, thirty of whose members locked arms to prevent the group from crossing the street. After three hours of arguing—in public— the chief of police backed down. Joyous marchers headed north under the sizzling sun. Their rallying cry was *Sí Se Puede* (see seh PWEH deh), or "Yes, It Can Be Done."

11

486

The first night, they reached Ducor. The marchers slept outside the tiny cabin of the only person who would welcome them.

Single file they continued, covering an average of fifteen miles a day. They inched their way through the San Joaquin Valley, while the unharvested grapes in Delano turned white with mold. Cesar developed painful blisters right away. He and many others had blood seeping out of their shoes.

The word spread. Along the way, farmworkers offered food and drink as the marchers passed by. When the sun set, marchers lit candles and kept going.

Shelter was no longer a problem. Supporters began welcoming them each night with feasts. Every night was a rally. "Our pilgrimage is the match," one speaker shouted, "that will light our cause for all farmworkers to see what is happening here."

Eager supporters would keep the marchers up half the night talking about change. Every morning, the line of marchers swelled, Cesar always in the lead.

On the ninth day, hundreds marched through Fresno.

The long, peaceful march was a shock to people unaware of how California farmworkers had to live. Now students, public officials, religious leaders, and citizens from everywhere offered help. For the grape company, the publicity was becoming unbearable. **(12)**

And on the vines, the grapes continued to rot.

In Modesto, on the fifteenth day, an exhilarated (ihg ZIHL uh ray tehd) crowd celebrated Cesar's thirty-eighth birthday. Two days later, five thousand people met the marchers in Stockton with flowers, guitars, and accordions. **(13)**

> ✔ **STOP AND THINK**
> **Persuasion** What are some words and phrases that the author uses on this page to persuade the reader that the march is starting to affect people?

487

STOP AND THINK

✔ **TARGET SKILL Persuasion**

- Remind students that authors sometimes use word choice or reasons and examples to persuade readers.

- Have students answer the **Stop and Think** question. Use **Comprehension Intervention** below, if needed.

- Explain to students that sometimes authors write about characters who try to persuade others.

- Display **Projectable 19.3b** and model the thinking:

> **Think Aloud** *I read how Cesar persuaded people to join his cause. I can infer that his goal is to persuade the growers to improve conditions for the workers.*

- Guide students to complete their maps. Discuss how the author succeeds in persuading readers of the importance of Cesar Chavez.

Projectable 19.3b

Harvesting Hope Comprehension Persuasion

Idea-Support Map: Persuasion
Title or Topic _____ Harvesting Hope: The Story of Cesar Chavez

Cesar wants people to work hard to improve conditions for farm workers.

He saw that farm workers were treated like farm tools. Workers who complained were beaten up or fired.

Chavez organized a march. People became upset when they learned how the workers were treated.

COMPREHENSION INTERVENTION

✔ **TARGET SKILL**   Persuasion

SKILL SUPPORT Remind students that authors use persuasion to convince readers of something. This may be through word choice or arguments. Recall what has happened in Delano:

- *The growers cut the workers' pay, so the workers walked off the job.*
- *The grape company fought back violently. Cesar organized a march.*

Read aloud the last paragraph on p. 486. *What words and phrases might influence readers to feel sympathy towards the marchers?* police locking arms; joyous marchers; sizzling sun; painful blisters; long, peaceful march

Tell students that as they read, the should watch for words and phrases intended to influence them.

Develop Comprehension

14 **Analyze Story Structure**
What events helped resolve the farmworkers' problem? The march helped resolve the problem; the owners didn't want attention and gave the workers a contract and better conditions.

15 ✓ **TARGET VOCABULARY**
*Why did Cesar Chavez make the contract announcement from the **capitol** building steps? The capitol is the seat of the state government, and he wanted to show a connection between the law and farmworkers' rights.*

That evening, Cesar received a message that he was sure was a prank. But in case it was true, he left the march and had someone drive him all through the night to a mansion in wealthy Beverly Hills. Officials from the grape company were waiting for him. They were ready to recognize the authority of the National Farm Workers Association, promising a contract with a pay raise and better conditions.

Cesar rushed back to join the march.

On Easter Sunday, when the marchers arrived in Sacramento, the parade was ten-thousand-people strong.

From the steps of the state capitol building, the joyous announcement was made to the public: Cesar Chavez had just signed the first contract for farmworkers in American history.

488

ELL **ENGLISH LANGUAGE LEARNERS**

Scaffold

Beginning Call attention to the picture. Ask: *Is Cesar Chavez happy or sad?* (happy) *Why?* (He had won his fight. The workers had a contract with better pay and conditions.)

Intermediate Discuss *prank*. Have students give an example of a prank. Discuss *mansion* and *wealthy*. Ask: *Who lives in a mansion?* (rich, or wealthy, people)

Advanced Have students summarize how Chavez was able to persuade the grape company owners to recognize the NFWA.

Advanced High Have students write a short paragraph telling why Cesar Chavez is considered an important leader.

See ELL Lesson 19, pp. E32–E41, for scaffolded support.

Your Turn

Leading the Way

Write about History Cesar Chavez worked hard to gain rights for farm workers. Think about another leader who championed the rights of others. Write a paragraph describing what the person belived in and what he or she did to bring about change.
SOCIAL STUDIES

Lift Every Voice

Write a Song People often sing during marches. With a partner, write words for a song the farm workers could sing during the march to Sacramento. Use the tune of a familiar song as your melody. In the song, say why they are marching and what they hope to gain. PARTNERS

Don't Fight—March!

Turn and Talk With a partner, discuss the result of the march to Sacramento. Why do you think Cesar Chavez used persuasion instead of violence to get what he and the farm workers wanted? What finally persuaded the grape growers to give in to his demands? PERSUASION

489

Retelling Rubric

4	Excellent	Students form insightful opinions, support their opinions with several details from the selection, and express their opinions fluidly.
3	Good	Students form reasonable opinions, support their opinions with one or two details from the selection, and express their opinions clearly.
2	Fair	Students form legitimate opinions but provide little to no support from the selection.
1	Unsatisfactory	Students neither express a clear opinion nor support their responses.

Your Turn

Have students complete the activities on page 489.

Leading the Way Help students generate topics by asking them about other human rights heroes they have studied. If students need additional support, provide reference sources such as a biographic encyclopedia. Make sure students address both parts of the prompt when they write their paragraphs. SOCIAL STUDIES

Lift Every Voice Have students skim the selection and identify the workers' purposes and goals. Then provide songbooks or lists of songs that are familiar to students. Encourage students to use rhyme in their song lyrics. PARTNERS

Don't Fight—March! Remind students that the *result* of something is its outcome—what happens in the end. *Persuasion* means getting someone to do or believe something by showing that it is a good idea. Ask: *What do you think would have happened if Chavez had used violence instead of persuasion?* PERSUASION

Oral Language Have students form opinions about Cesar Chavez and how he led the fight for change. Then have students share their opinions with a partner or the class. Students should use examples from the selection to support their opinions. Use the Retelling Rubric at the left to evaluate students' responses.

Connect to Science

PREVIEW THE INFORMATIONAL TEXT

• Explain to students that the selection is a magazine article. It gives information about a garden kept by 6th graders at a school in California. Ask students to read the title, subtitles, and preview the photographs and the graph on p. 492. Then have students read the informational text independently.

DISCUSS GRAPHS

• Tell students that informational text may include a graph. A graph is a diagram that shows how different facts and numbers relate to each other.

• Remind students that a graph often uses symbols. To understand the information in the graph, it is important to understand what each symbol means.

• A graph usually has a key that explains the symbols.

• Tell students to look for and explain the following features of a diagram as they read "The Edible Schoolyard."

symbol	a mark used to visually represent something
key	a list of symbols and their meanings
title	a word or phrase that tells what the chart is about

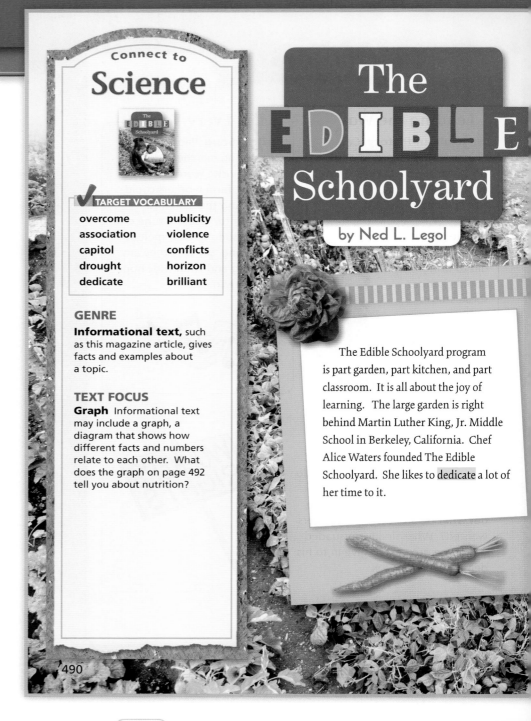

Connect to Science

The Edible Schoolyard

✓ **TARGET VOCABULARY**

overcome	publicity
association	violence
capitol	conflicts
drought	horizon
dedicate	brilliant

GENRE

Informational text, such as this magazine article, gives facts and examples about a topic.

TEXT FOCUS

Graph Informational text may include a graph, a diagram that shows how different facts and numbers relate to each other. What does the graph on page 492 tell you about nutrition?

490

The EDIBLE Schoolyard

by Ned L. Legol

The Edible Schoolyard program is part garden, part kitchen, and part classroom. It is all about the joy of learning. The large garden is right behind Martin Luther King, Jr. Middle School in Berkeley, California. Chef Alice Waters founded The Edible Schoolyard. She likes to dedicate a lot of her time to it.

ELL ENGLISH LANGUAGE LEARNERS

Scaffold

Beginning Go through the article with students, pointing to and naming the vegetables and plants shown. Have students repeat the words.

Advanced Have students give oral sentences summarizing the information they read on page 490.

Intermediate Create sentence frames such as the following and have students complete them. ***The children grow _____ and _____ in the _____.***

Advanced High Have students write a short summary of the article. Have them include what they think the 6th graders have learned from working in the garden.

See ELL Lesson 19, pp. E32–E41, for scaffolded support.

FROM THE PAGES OF
WEEKLY READER

WR

Inside the Edible Schoolyard

Every year, the school's sixth-grade students plant, tend, and harvest the crops from the garden. They learn about the effects that changing climate and weather have on the plants. During a drought, for example, they must water the garden more often. This keeps everything alive and healthy.

The students grow many types of fruits, vegetables, and herbs. Brilliant colors surround the kids as they work in the garden that stretches toward the horizon.

Time to Get Cooking

The students also learn how to cook healthy meals with the food they grow. The school houses many different students and cultures. So, the meals vary from Indian curries to Mediterranean grape leaves. Some of the kids learn to overcome their fear of unknown foods.

If there are conflicts in the kitchen or the garden, students must work to solve them. The program fits with Martin Luther King, Jr.'s vision of inclusion, equality, and peaceful growth without violence.

The Edible Schoolyard has inspired similar programs around the country. These Florida students are part of the Plant a Thousand Gardens program.

491

Practice Fluency

Stress Have students listen as you read aloud the first paragraph on **Student Book p. 491.**

- Tell students that an author may use certain words to help clarify the meaning of a passage. Explain that words such as *every*, *everything*, and *more* are important for clarifying meaning.

- Have students partner-read the paragraph. Remind them to stress words that help to clarify meaning.

JOURNEYS DIGITAL **Powered by**
DESTINATIONReading
Student eBook: Read and Listen

TARGET VOCABULARY REVIEW

✓ **TARGET VOCABULARY** **Vocabulary in Context Cards**

Have student pairs use the Vocabulary in Context Cards to review the selection vocabulary. Have them take turns choosing a card, reading the word, and then finding that word in "The Edible Schoolyard." Have them read the sentence containing the word aloud. Then have the partner supply a new sentence using the same word.

Develop Comprehension

Pause at the stopping points to ask students the following questions.

① ✓ TARGET VOCABULARY
*How might a **drought** affect the students' garden? It would mean they would have to water the garden more often, or else the plants would die.*

② Main Idea and Details
What do students do with the food they grow? They learn to cook healthy meals.

③ Author's Purpose *Why do you think the author wrote this article? to explain about a student garden project in California and what the students have learned*

INTERPRET A GRAPH

• Have students study the graph. Explain that the size of the colored boxes with the names of the groups are an important clue.

• Model the thinking:

> **Think Aloud** *Each part of the graph is a different color and size, and shows a different food group. The size of the box and the numbers below it tell how much of that group I should eat daily.*

• Ask: *Which groups should I eat the most of? grains, vegetables, and milk The least? oils How much should I eat from the vegetable group each day? 2.5 (two and a half) cups*

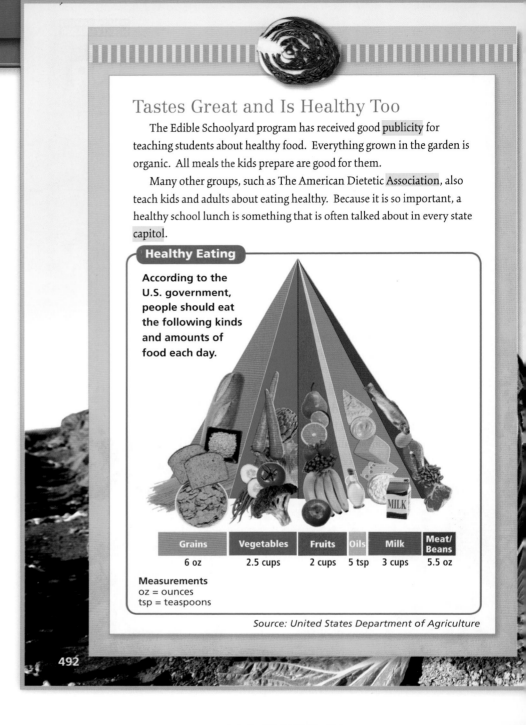

Tastes Great and Is Healthy Too

The Edible Schoolyard program has received good publicity for teaching students about healthy food. Everything grown in the garden is organic. All meals the kids prepare are good for them.

Many other groups, such as The American Dietetic Association, also teach kids and adults about eating healthy. Because it is so important, a healthy school lunch is something that is often talked about in every state capitol.

Healthy Eating

According to the U.S. government, people should eat the following kinds and amounts of food each day.

Grains	Vegetables	Fruits	Oils	Milk	Meat/Beans
6 oz	2.5 cups	2 cups	5 tsp	3 cups	5.5 oz

Measurements
oz = ounces
tsp = teaspoons

Source: United States Department of Agriculture

492

Weekly Internet Challenge

Choosing Useful Websites

• Review the Internet Strategy, Step 4: Analyze and Evaluate.

• Explain that websites can be quickly evaluated by reading the website's description and paying attention to the extension, such as .gov or .edu.

• Point out that not all Internet sites are equally reliable.

INTERNET STRATEGY

1. **Plan a Search** by identifying what you are looking for and how to find it.

2. **Search and Predict** which sites will be worth exploring.

3. **Navigate** a site to see how to get around it and what it contains.

4. **Analyze and Evaluate** the quality and reliability of the information.

5. **Synthesize** the information from multiple sites.

Making Connections

 Text to Self

Write a Paragraph Think of a time when you had to be persistent to solve a problem. Describe that occasion. Explain the problem that you had to solve and how being persistent helped you solve the problem.

 Text to Text

Compare and Contrast Think about some of the experiences had by Cesar Chavez in "Harvesting Hope" and Mina in "Moon Runner." How are they similar? How are they different? Record your thoughts in a Venn diagram.

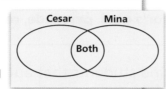

 Text to World

Connect to Social Studies Farming is an important industry in many communities. Work with a partner to list the different agricultural products that are grown in or near your community. Share your findings with the class.

493

"The Edible Schoolyard" Challenge

- Have partners look at **Student Book p. 492.** Ask them to list five fruits and five vegetables from the page. Have them do a Web search on the vitamin content of the foods on their lists.

- Tell students they will get hundreds of results, so they must determine which sites might be useful. Point out that they can evaluate a site's usefulness by reading the brief description (usually on the first page). They can also check the extension for sites they think will be most reliable.

- Have students open a site they think will be useful and reliable and explain why they would trust the information on the site.

Making Connections

 Text to Self

Have students prewrite by making a list of problems they have solved in the past month or so. Have them choose one that was particularly difficult to solve. Have them list the steps they took to solve the problem, and then write their paragraphs.

Text to Text

Supply copies of **Graphic Organizer 14: Venn Diagram.** Remind students how to fill in the diagram to compare and contrast characters and events from a fictional work with those in a biography.

 Text to World

Have students use Internet resources, an encyclopedia, or library or text books to find the information. Students might also make connections between the climate of your community and the type of products raised.

Deepen Comprehension

SKILL TRACE

Persuasion	
Introduce	T234–T235
Differentiate	T278–T279
Reteach	T286
Review	**T252–T253**
Test	Weekly Tests, Lesson 19

ELL **ENGLISH LANGUAGE LEARNERS**

Scaffold

Beginning Ask yes/no questions to review the effect of the author's persuasive text details. *Does the author say that Cesar eats poor food? Do we feel sad for Cesar?*

Intermediate Give students sentence frames that focus on persuasive text details, such as *To persuade the reader, the author _____.*

Advanced Have students tell in their own words how Cesar persuades farm workers to join his movement.

Advanced High Have students write sentences that summarize the author's goals in "Harvesting Hope."

See ELL Lesson 19, pp. E32–E41, for scaffolded support.

✔ Persuasion

1 Teach/Model

AL *Academic Language*

author's goal, **persuade**, **reasons**, **evaluate**

• Remind students that authors sometimes try to **persuade** others to think or act in a certain way.

• A character may also have a **goal** to try to persuade others. The author of a text may state the character's goal and give reasons to explain why that goal is important to the character.

• Explain to students that an Idea-Support Map can help them **evaluate** how well the author or the character uses **reasons** to achieve his or her goals.

• Have students reread **pp. 480–481** of "Harvesting Hope."

• Display **Projectable 19.4** and discuss **Deepen Comprehension Question 1.**

• Remind students that an Idea-Support Map will help them see how the author presents information to persuade readers.

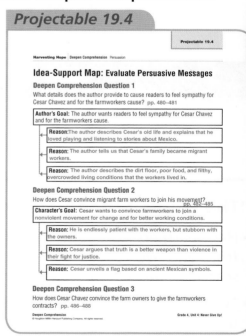

Projectable 19.4

Think Aloud *The author's goal here is to have readers feel sympathy for Cesar and the migrant workers. The author first describes Cesar's early life playing on the ranch and listening to stories about Mexico. Readers will probably think: "My life is much like Cesar's early childhood." But then the author tells us that one day this old life vanished. Like other people, they lost their home. They became migrant workers. Then the author describes the filthy, battered shed with the dirt floor that was their new home. The author describes the overcrowded conditions, the poor food they had to eat in California, and the poor treatment the workers received at the hands of the farm owners.*

Monitor Comprehension

Are students able to evaluate the author's or character's use of persuasive language?

IF...	THEN...
students have difficulty evaluating persuasive language,	▶ use the Leveled Reader for **Struggling Readers,** *Songs for the People*, p. T280.
students have a basic understanding of evaluating persuasive language,	▶ use the Leveled Reader for **On-Level Readers,** *The People's President*, p. T281.
students can accurately evaluate persuasive messages,	▶ use the Leveled Reader for **Advanced Readers,** *The Story of Dorothea Lange*, p. T282.

Use the Leveled Reader for **English Language Learners**, *A President for the People*, p. T283. *Group English Language Learners according to language proficiency level.*

2 | Guided Practice

- Reread pp. 482–485 of "Harvesting Hope" with students. Discuss **Deepen Comprehension Question 2** on **Projectable 19.4.** Use these prompts to guide students:

- *How was life dangerous for migrant workers? The chemicals were probably bad for their lungs. People who complained about conditions were beaten or murdered.*

- *How did Cesar plan to fight the injustice and work for change? He wanted to start a nonviolent movement that would use truth as a weapon.*

- *Why might it be hard to get the workers to join a movement for change? They were afraid they'd be fired or hurt. They might also feel it was useless or hopeless.*

- Have students complete the Idea-Support Map for Question 2.

GUIDED DISCUSSION Have students identify persuasive words that the author uses to get us to sympathize with Chavez and the workers. Tell them to explain why these words influence the reader. *Sample answers: pp. 482: torment, sting, wheeze, hot spasms; 483: fired, murdered; 485: patient, compassionate; workers hunched*

3 | Apply

Turn and Talk Have students reread pp. 486-487 of "Harvesting Hope." Tell partners to make an Idea-Support Map for the selection and work together to answer **Deepen Comprehension Question 3** on **Projectable 19.4.** Invite volunteers to share their responses.

WRITE ABOUT READING Have students write their responses to **Deepen Comprehension Question 3.** Ask volunteers to share their responses.

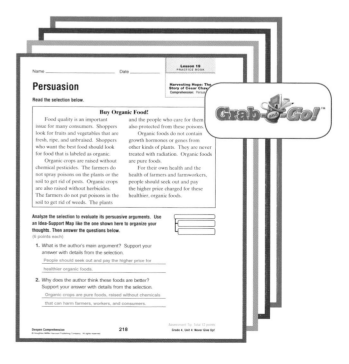

Practice Book p. 218
See Grab-and-Go™ Resources for additional leveled practice.

Fluency

Stress

1 | Teach/Model

- Tell students that good readers stress, or emphasize, certain words as they read. Stressing different words can change the meaning of a sentence.

- Have students turn to "Harvesting Hope," **Student Book p. 482**. Help students find the second-to-last sentence ("Even he considered…").

- Read the sentence in a monotone voice. Reread the sentence and stress the word *he,* modeling how emphasizing a word can change meaning. Discuss how you stressed your voice on the word *he.*

2 | Guided Practice

Together, read aloud the last two paragraphs on **Student Book p. 483,** stressing words as necessary.

- If students are struggling with the concept of stress, have them reread the last two paragraphs of **Student Book p. 483** and guide students as they stress certain words.

- Have partners take turns reading the paragraphs aloud while stressing certain words. Listen to monitor their fluency.

- See also **Instructional Routine 7.**

3 | Apply

- Tell students that with practice, they will learn to stress the correct words in a sentence as they read.

- Allow each student to read the section three or four times.

Decoding

 ## More Common Suffixes

- Recognize common suffixes.
- Decode words with common suffixes.

1 Teach/Model

RECOGNIZE COMMON SUFFIXES Remind students that suffixes are affixes added to the end of base words. Students can increase their ability to decode words by recognizing common suffixes. Model how to find the suffix in *homesickness*.

- Write the word *homesickness* on the board and say it aloud with students. Underline the suffix, -*ness*. Then break the base word, *homesick*, into syllables with students: home | sick.

2 Practice/Apply

DECODE COMMON SUFFIXES Write on the board the words below. Have students model how to decode the first two words step by step.

colorful	weakness
col | or | ful	weak | ness
movement	speechless
move | ment	speech | less
illness	endless
ill | ness	end | less
beautiful	statement
beau | ti | ful	state | ment

- Have partners work to decode the remaining words. Call on students to read the words and note the common suffixes, such as -*less* in *endless*.

- Have partners categorize spelling words with the suffixes -*ful*, -*less*, -*ness*, and -*ment*. Students should identify the suffix and read the words aloud to their partner.

- Use the **Corrective Feedback** if students need additional help.

Corrective Feedback

If students have trouble decoding words with common suffixes, use the model below.

Correct the error. *Remember that identifying suffixes will help you read new words.*

Model how to decode the word. *In the word plentiful I see the suffix -ful. I know that a syllable break comes before a suffix. Plenti looks like plenty, a base word I know. I see that the y changed to i when -ful was added. Knowing the suffix helps me to decode the word.*

Guide students to try different examples to decode and recognize other words with the suffix -*ful*. *What are other words you know that end with -ful?* (Example: *bountiful, healthful, helpful*)

Check students' understanding. *Decode these words into the suffix and base word.* (play, -*ful*; hope, -*ful*; peace, -*ful*)

Vocabulary Strategies

SHARE OBJECTIVES

- Use a dictionary to determine meaning, syllabication, and pronunciation of unfamiliar words.
- Understand dictionary organization.

SKILL TRACE

Use a Dictionary

Introduce	T332–T333, Unit 1
Differentiate	T284–T285
Reteach	T286
Review	**T256–T257**; T114–T115, Unit 5
Test	Weekly Tests, Lesson 19

ELL ENGLISH LANGUAGE LEARNERS

Scaffold

Beginning Guide students to use a dictionary to find the entry for *brilliant*. Say the word with students and point out the parts of a dictionary entry, such as pronunciation, part of speech, and definition.

Intermediate Have small groups use a dictionary to find the entry for *dedicate*. Guide students to find the part of speech, definition, and pronunciation.

Advanced Have partners use a dictionary to find two meanings for the word *drought*. Have students explain how they know which meaning of the word was used in *Harvesting Hope*.

Advanced High Have students identify two words in "Harvesting Hope" they are unfamiliar with and use a dictionary to look up the words. Have students share their results with a partner.

See ELL Lesson 19, pp. E32–E41, for scaffolded support.

✔ Use a Dictionary

1 Teach/Model

AL *Academic Language*

dictionary entry a word listed in the dictionary along with its meaning, pronunciation, and other information

pronunciation how a word is pronounced and divided into syllables

pronunciation key an explanation of the symbols used in pronunciations

- Explain to students that a dictionary can help them determine the meaning and **pronunciation** of unknown words.

- Point out that each **dictionary entry** lists all the meanings of the word and shows how to pronounce it.

- Explain that the pronunciation uses special symbols to show how to pronounce and break a word into syllables. A **pronunciation key** explains what these symbols mean. Pronunciation keys often appear at the bottom of each page of a dictionary.

- Write the following sentence on the board: *We saw the brilliant blue sky through the window*.

- Display **Projectable 19.5.** Model using context to understand the meaning of *brilliant*.

Think Aloud *I'm not sure how to pronounce* brilliant *or what it means. The context tells me* brilliant *must have something to do with describing the color of the sky. Brilliant must mean something that is very bright.*

- **Ask:** *What else can we do to figure out a word if looking in and around the word doesn't help? What can we do if we don't know how to pronounce a word? (Look in a dictionary.)*

2 Guided Practice

- Display the top of **Projectable 19.5** and read aloud "Cesar Chavez Day."

- Display the Web on the bottom of **Projectable 19.5**.

- Have students identify the Vocabulary words from the passage. Circle or highlight the words and use them to complete the Web.

- Remind students that they can use a dictionary to help them with pronunciation, parts of speech, word endings, and syllabication.

Projectable 19.5

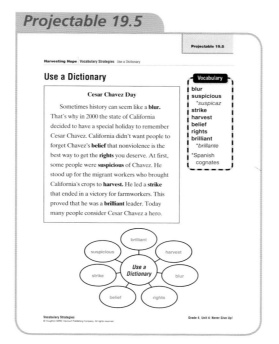

Projectable 19.5

Harvesting Hope: Vocabulary Strategies Use a Dictionary

Use a Dictionary

Cesar Chavez Day

Sometimes history can seem like a **blur.** That's why in 2000 the state of California decided to have a special holiday to remember Cesar Chavez. California didn't want people to forget Chavez's **belief** that nonviolence is the best way to get the **rights** you deserve. At first, some people were **suspicious** of Chavez. He stood up for the migrant workers who brought California's crops to **harvest.** He led a **strike** that ended in a victory for farmworkers. This proved that he was a **brilliant** leader. Today many people consider Cesar Chavez a hero.

Vocabulary
- blur
- suspicious
  - *suspicaz
- strike
- harvest
- belief
- rights
- brilliant
  - *brillante

*Spanish cognates

Web: brilliant, harvest, suspicious, Use a Dictionary, strike, blur, belief, rights

Vocabulary Strategies
© Houghton Mifflin Harcourt Publishing Company. All rights reserved.
Grade 4, Unit 4: Never Give Up!

Monitor Vocabulary Strategies

Are students able to use a dictionary and to identify dictionary parts?

IF...	THEN...
students have difficulty using a dictionary,	▶ **Differentiate Vocabulary Strategies** for Struggling Readers, p. T284. *See also Intervention Lesson 19, pp. S32–S41.*
students can use and identify dictionary parts most of the time,	▶ **Differentiate Vocabulary Strategies** for On-Level Readers, p. T284.
students can consistently use and identify dictionary parts,	▶ **Differentiate Vocabulary Strategies** for Advanced Readers, p. T285.

Differentiate Vocabulary Strategies: pp. T284–T285. *Group English Language Learners according to language proficiency.*

3 Apply

- Display **Projectable S8** for students. Have partners apply Steps 1 and 2 to determine the meaning of each word.

- Then have students look in a dictionary for the definition of the words to see if they were correct.

- Finally, have students write sentences using each word. Tell them to use the dictionary to help them determine correct pronunciation, parts of speech, word endings, and syllabication.

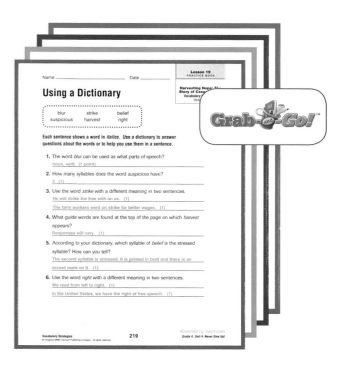

Name _____ Date _____

Lesson 19
PRACTICE BOOK

Using a Dictionary

Harvesting Hope: The Story of Cesar...
Vocabulary...
Dict...

| blur | strike | belief |
| suspicious | harvest | right |

Each sentence shows a word in *italics*. Use a dictionary to answer questions about the words or to help you use them in a sentence.

1. The word *blur* can be used as what parts of speech?
   noun, verb (1 point)

2. How many syllables does the word *suspicious* have?
   3 (1)

3. Use the word *strike* with a different meaning in two sentences.
   He will strike the tree with an ax. (1)
   The farm workers went on strike for better wages. (1)

4. What guide words are found at the top of the page on which *harvest* appears?
   Responses will vary. (1)

5. According to your dictionary, which syllable of *belief* is the stressed syllable? How can you tell?
   The second syllable is stressed. It is printed in bold and there is an accent mark on it. (1)

6. Use the word *right* with a different meaning in two sentences.
   We read from left to right. (1)
   In the United States, we have the right of free speech. (1)

Assessment Tip: Total 8 points

Vocabulary Strategies
© Houghton Mifflin Harcourt Publishing Company. All rights reserved.
219
Grade 4, Unit 4: Never Give Up!

Practice Book p. 219
See Grab-and-Go™ Resources for additional leveled practice.

Connect and Extend

Harvesting Hope   **The Edible Schoolyard**

Vocabulary Reader

Struggling Readers   *On-Level Readers*

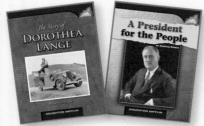

Advanced Readers   *English Language Learners*

Read to Connect

SHARE AND COMPARE TEXTS Have students compare and contrast this week's reading selections. Use the following questions to guide the discussion.

- Compare and contrast the leaders you read about this week. What is similar about their ways of creating change? What is different?

- How do the people in this week's selections work together to overcome hard times?

CONNECT TEXT TO WORLD Use these prompts to help deepen student thinking and discussion. Accept students' opinions, but encourage them to support their ideas with text details and other information from their reading.

- How did the work of Cesar Chavez, Dolores Huerta, and President Roosevelt change the lives of farmers and farm workers?

- What are some of the ways the people you read about overcame injustice in the world? How did they use nonviolent solutions?

Independent Reading

BOOK TALK Have student pairs discuss their independent reading for the week. Tell them to refer to their Reading Log or journal and paraphrase what the reading was about. To focus students' discussions, tell them to talk about one or more of the following:

- how the leaders overcame problems

- how the leaders used persuasion

- how the work of these leaders made a difference in peoples' lives

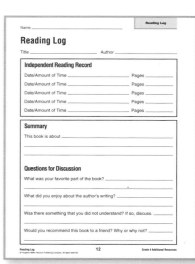

Reading Log

Extend Through Research

USING KEYWORDS IN ONLINE SEARCHES Remind students that they should gather data from at least three sources of information when they are writing a research report. They can then read through their notes to sort information and evidence into categories, eliminate unnecessary details, and narrow the information down to find the answer to their research question. Tell students that using keywords to narrow their online searches will make their research easier and more focused.

- Have students decide on a research topic related to this week's reading.

- Have small groups brainstorm a list of questions about the topic that they would like to have answered through their research.

- Tell group members to develop a list of keywords for their questions that will help narrow their search results. Remind students that keywords can be single words or words joined by the + sign, such as *Cesar Chavez + march*.

- Have students use their keywords to perform an online search to find the answers to their research questions.

- As a class, discuss whether students' keywords led them to the correct information, and which keywords worked best.

Listening and Speaking

DELIVER A SUMMARY Tell students to choose a favorite poem. Have them read the poem to determine what message the poet is trying to convey, and then deliver a short oral summary of the poem that tells the poem's message.

Allow students to prepare their summaries. Tell them to focus on:

- making eye contact with the audience.

- pronouncing each word clearly.

Tell students that they should be prepared to answer questions about the poem and their interpretation. Explain that they should be able to adapt information from their oral summaries to be explained more informally to their classmates.

While students give their oral summaries, have audience members write in their Listening Logs. They should record questions and comments, such as what they have learned about the poem and whether they agree with the speaker's interpretation. Have students ask questions and share their comments with the speaker.

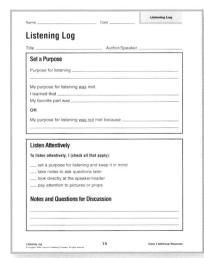

Listening Log

Spelling ✓ Suffixes -ful, -less, -ness, -ment

SHARE OBJECTIVE

- Spell words with the suffixes -ful, -less, -ness, and -ment.

Spelling Words

Basic

colorful	useless	✪ neatness
weakness	beautiful	speechless
movement	restless	statement
✪ endless	clumsiness	wasteful
✪ truthful	pavement	penniless
illness	peaceful	✪ treatment
cheerful	fondness	

Review

kindness, careful, sickness, helpless, fearful

Challenge

numbness, ailment, resourceful, ✪ cleanliness, appointment

✪ Forms of these words appear in "Harvesting Hope: The Story of Cesar Chavez."

ELL ENGLISH LANGUAGE LEARNERS

Preteach

Spanish Cognates

Write and discuss these Spanish cognates for Spanish-speaking students.

colorful	•	*colorido*
movement	•	*movimiento*
treatment	•	*tratamiento*

Day 1

① TEACH THE PRINCIPLE

- Administer the **Pretest**. Use the Day 5 sentences.

- Write *colorful* and *endless* on the board. Guide students to identify the suffix in each word. *(-ful, -less)* Repeat with the suffixes *-ness* and *-ment* using the chart below.

-ful	**-ful** as in color**ful**
-less	**-less** as in end**less**
-ness	**-ness** as in ill**ness**
-ment	**-ment** as in pave**ment**

② PRACTICE/APPLY

Guide students to identify words with the suffixes *-ful*, *-less*, *-ness*, and *-ment* in the remaining Spelling Words.

Practice Book p. 220

Day 2

① TEACH WORD SORT

- Set up four rows as shown. Model adding a Spelling Word to each row.

- Have students copy the chart. Guide students to write each Spelling Word where it belongs.

-ful	wasteful
-less	useless
-ness	neatness
-ment	statement

② PRACTICE/APPLY

Have students add words from "Harvesting Hope: The Story of Cesar Chavez."

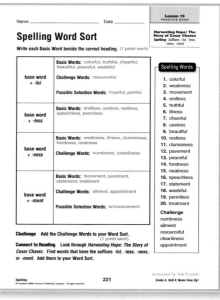

Practice Book p. 221

Day 3

① TEACH SYNONYMS

- **WRITE** *cheerful* and *happy*.

- **ASK** *How are these two words related? same meaning* Point out that words with the same meaning are called *synonyms*.

- **WRITE** *fondness*.

- With students, list and discuss words that have almost the same meaning. *sample answers: liking, love, affection, regard*

② PRACTICE/APPLY

- **WRITE** the following words in a column: *truthful, illness, beautiful, restless, peaceful, penniless.*

- Direct students to copy the words in their notebooks.

- Have students look up each word in a thesaurus or in an electronic resource to find a synonym, and ask them to write it next to that spelling word. *sample answers: truthful/honest, illness/disease, beautiful/lovely, restless/fidgety, peaceful/calm, penniless/poor*

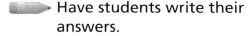 Have students write their answers.

Day 4

① CONNECT TO WRITING

- Read and discuss the prompt below.

> **Write a Personal Narrative**
> Write a story about how someone once inspired you to do something. Use words from this week's Vocabulary.

② PRACTICE/APPLY

- Remind students to proofread their writing.

- Guide students as they plan and write their narratives.

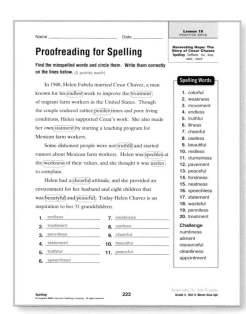

Practice Book p. 222

Day 5

ASSESS SPELLING

- Say each boldfaced word, read the sentence, and then repeat the word.

- Have students write the boldfaced word.

Basic

1. The girl wore a **colorful** hat.
2. I have a **weakness** for candy.
3. The class is reading about the civil rights **movement**.
4. The drive seemed **endless**.
5. That is not a **truthful** answer.
6. The long **illness** left me weak.
7. Play us a **cheerful** song.
8. Skis are **useless** in a desert.
9. The flowers are **beautiful**.
10. The baby is **restless** today.
11. My fall was due to my own **clumsiness**.
12. The **pavement** is cracking.
13. It was **peaceful** last night.
14. He has a **fondness** for dogs.
15. **Neatness** is not one of my virtues.
16. The vote left me **speechless**.
17. The mayor made a **statement**.
18. Using all that paper is **wasteful**.
19. The beggar was **penniless**.
20. What is the best **treatment** for the flu?

Grammar ✓ Transitions

SHARE OBJECTIVES

- Identify transition words.
- Use transition words in writing and speaking.

ELL ENGLISH LANGUAGE LEARNERS

Scaffold

Beginning Use the following sentences to demonstrate how to use transitions.

First, the player jumps to tip the ball.

Then, I run down the court.

Intermediate Use the sentences above to demonstrate how to use other transition words.

_____, the player jumps to tip the ball. *As a result*

_____, I run down the court. *Finally*

Advanced Have students use transition words to describe the order in which they get dressed every morning. Provide them with sentence frames, such as the following:

_____, I brush my teeth. *To start with*

I wash my face _____. *last*

Advanced High Have student pairs take turns orally describing their mornings using transition words or phrases.

See ELL Lesson 19, pp. E32–E41, for scaffolded support.

JOURNEYS DIGITAL **Powered by**
DESTINATIONReading®
Grammar Activities: Lesson 19

DAILY PROOFREADING PRACTICE

The soccer ball went into the ~~gole~~ *goal*.

❶ TEACH TRANSITION WORDS

- Display **Projectable 19.6**. Explain that **transition words** and phrases show when one idea ends and another begins. Point out that some transition words tell about time or order.

Projectable
19.6

- Model identifying the transition word in the example sentence: *The team cheered after I scored.*

Think Aloud *To identify the transition word I ask this Thinking Question: What word or words tell about time order? after*

❷ PRACTICE/APPLY

- Work with students to identify the transition words on **Projectable 19.6**.

- Write the following sentences on the board. Have students identify the transition word in each sentence.

First, the referee blew his whistle. *First*

The captains then ran onto the field. *then*

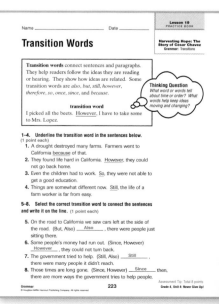

Practice Book p. 223

Day 2 TEACH

DAILY PROOFREADING PRACTICE
the next game is on friday. *The; Friday*

① EXTEND TRANSITION WORDS

Projectable **19.7**

- Display **Projectable 19.7**. Explain that some transition words tell about time order. Point out that words such as *first, next, then*, and *finally* tell the reader when things happen in a story.

- Model identifying the transition word in this sentence: *Finally, the defense stopped them from scoring.*

Think Aloud *I see a transition word in this sentence. I know that* Finally *is a word that tells about time order. So the transition word is* Finally.

② PRACTICE/APPLY

- Complete the paragraph on **Projectable 19.7** with students.

- Have students complete the following sentence frames using a transition word.

  _____, the referee tosses the coin.

  The team catches the ball _____ the kickoff.

  Sample answers:
  First, after

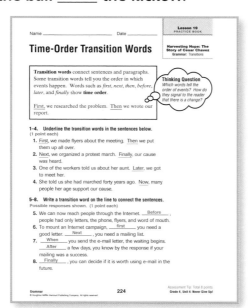

Practice Book p. 224

Day 3 TEACH

DAILY PROOFREADING PRACTICE
First, the quarterbak gives the play? *quarterback; (.)*

① TEACH TRANSITION WORDS

Projectable **19.8**

- Display **Projectable 19.8**. Explain that some transitions are phrases made of several words. Tell them that the phrases *as a result, to summarize*, and *in conclusion* are transitional phrases that show when an idea is finished.

- Model identifying the transitional phrase in the example sentence: *To sum up, the other team won because we couldn't stop them from scoring.*

Think Aloud *I see the phrase* To sum up *in the sentence, followed by a statement that sounds like the end of story. So the transitional phrase is* To sum up.

② PRACTICE/APPLY

- Complete the activity on **Projectable 19.8** with students.

- Have students use the following transition words and transitional phrases orally in sentences.

  as a result   first   after   next   then

  in addition

  in conclusion

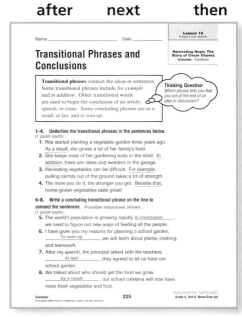

Practice Book p. 225

Day 4 REVIEW

CONNECT TO WRITING

As a result the team one the game. *As a result; won*

① REVIEW TRANSITION WORDS

Have students turn to **Student Book p. 494.** Read aloud the paragraph to review how to use **transition words**. Discuss the example paragraph. Then have students complete the Turn and Talk activity with a partner.

② SPIRAL REVIEW

Verbs in the Past Review with students that a verb in the past shows action that has already happened. Remind students that most past tense verbs end in *–ed,* but irregular verbs have different endings or different spellings.

• Write the following sentences on the board. Have students identify the past tense verb in each sentence.

The ball went into the basketball net. *went*

The guard dribbled the ball down the court.
dribbled

The player with the brown hair blocked the shot. *blocked*

In the stands, the fans cheered.
cheered

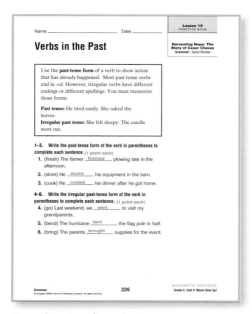

Practice Book p. 226

Day 5 REVISING AND PROOFREADING

DAILY PROOFREADING PRACTICE

finally the time ran out, and the game was over. Finally,

① CONNECT TO WRITING

• Explain that transition words help make the order of events clear to the reader.

② PRACTICE/APPLY

• Display the following sentence. Guide students to identify the transition words or phrases.

Later, we had a long practice. *Later*

As a result, we won our next game. *As a result*

• Write these sentence frames on the board. Have students orally give a transition to complete each one.

_____, my coach told us which play to run.
Sample answer: First

The goalie stopped the ball. _____, the player kicked it. *Sample answer: Then*

I _____ got a drink of water during the time out.
Sample answer: finally

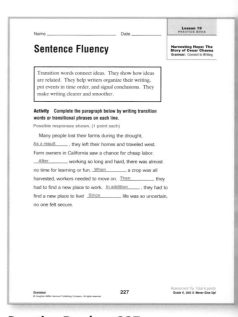

Practice Book p. 227

Grammar

What Are Transition Words? **Transition words** connect sentences and help readers make sense of what they read. Some transition words, such as *first, next, then, later,* and *finally,* can indicate time order. Others, such as *so, as a result,* and *to sum up,* can begin the conclusion of an article, speech, or essay.

Academic Language

transition words

Transition Words

Pilar, Arturo, and I stood beside the reporter in the fields. The camera operator pointed the camera at us. First the reporter asked Pilar about working conditions. Next, she asked Arturo about the shacks we live in. Finally, she asked me about our school. We answered her questions politely and honestly. As a result, the interviews were shown on the nightly news.

time-order transition words

transition words that indicate a conclusion

Turn and Talk **With a partner, identify the transition words in the sentences below. Tell which ones indicate time order and which one indicates a conclusion.**

1. First the workers met in a hall.
2. They next began their march to the north.
3. During that time, they gained many supporters.
4. After that, their leader met with the growers.
5. The end result was recognition for the new union.

494

Sentence Fluency When you write, use transition words to make the order of events clear to the reader. If you include a conclusion at the end of a piece of writing, use a transition word to indicate this.

Unclear	Clear

I began eating the sandwich. I took it out of the bag.	I began eating the sandwich after I took it out of the bag.

Connect Grammar to Writing

As you revise your personal narrative next week, check to see that you have used transition words to indicate the order of the events. Also indicate to the reader when the narrative is coming to a conclusion.

495

Turn and Talk

1. *First; time order*
2. *next; time order*
3. *During that time; time order*
4. *After that; time order*
5. *end; conclusion*

CONNECT GRAMMAR TO WRITING

- Have students turn to **Student Book p. 495** and read the page with them.

- Discuss with students how the sentences in the example are made clearer by using transition words.

- Tell students to use transition words as they revise their personal narratives.

- Review the Common Errors at the right with students.

COMMON ERRORS

Error: I started reading my book. I checked it out of the library.

Correct: I started reading my book **after** I checked it out of the library.

Error: As soon as I scored the point my teammates congratulated me.

Correct: As soon as I scored the **point,** my teammates congratulated me.

Write to Narrate ✔ Plan a Personal Narrative

- Study and evaluate personal narratives.
- Use the writing process to plan a personal narrative.
- Organize ideas to write a first draft.

Academic Language

personal narrative a story that tells something that happened in the writer's life

organize to put together in order

events things that happen in a story

topic the subject or theme of a composition

ELL ENGLISH LANGUAGE LEARNERS

Scaffold

Beginning Write the words *First, Next, Then,* and *Last.* Guide students to act out an experience by using the time-order words to help them organize the events.

Intermediate Have students say their ideas using the prompts *First, Next, Then,* and *Last.*

Advanced Have students use a flow chart to organize ideas in the order in which they happened.

Advanced High As students prewrite their personal narratives, have them review their ideas and number which parts should come first, second, third, and so on.

*See ELL Lesson 19, pp. E32–E41,
for scaffolded support.*

JOURNEYS DIGITAL | **Powered by**
DESTINATIONReading®
WriteSmart CD-ROM

Day 1 ANALYZE THE MODEL

① INTRODUCE THE MODEL

- Tell students that they will be planning a personal narrative in this lesson.

- Display **Projectable 19.9** and read the Writing Model aloud. Discuss the following points:

> **What Is a Personal Narrative?**
>
> - It describes **events** that took place, about a particular **topic**, in a person's life.
>
> - It uses interesting details in the **events.**
>
> - A **well-organized** narrative tells the events in the order in which they happened to make the narrative easy to read and understand.

- Use **Projectable 19.9** to point out that the personal narrative has main ideas that are supported by details and by the thoughts and feelings of the author.

② PRACTICE/APPLY

- With students, label the main idea, the supporting details, and the writer's thoughts and feelings in the second paragraph on **Projectable 19.9.**

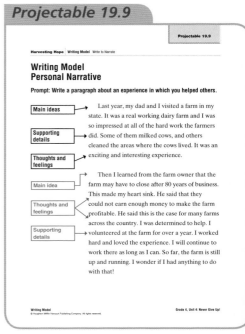

Projectable 19.9

Projectable 19.9

Harvesting Hope | Writing Model Write to Narrate

**Writing Model
Personal Narrative**

Prompt: Write a paragraph about an experience in which you helped others.

Main ideas → Last year, my dad and I visited a farm in my state. It was a real working dairy farm and I was so impressed at all of the hard work the farmers

Supporting details → did. Some of them milked cows, and others cleaned the areas where the cows lived. It was an

Thoughts and feelings → exciting and interesting experience.

Main idea → Then I learned from the farm owner that the farm may have to close after 80 years of business. This made my heart sink. He said that they

Thoughts and feelings → could not earn enough money to make the farm profitable. He said this is the case for many farms across the country. I was determined to help. I

Supporting details → volunteered at the farm for over a year. I worked hard and loved the experience. I will continue to work there as long as I can. So far, the farm is still up and running. I wonder if I had anything to do with that!

Writing Model
© Houghton Mifflin Harcourt Publishing Company. All rights reserved.

Grade 4, Unit 4: Never Give Up!

LESSON	FORM	TRAIT
16	Descriptive Paragraph	Ideas
17	Friendly Letter	Voice
18	Narrative Composition	Word Choice
19	**Prewrite: Personal Narrative**	**Organization**
20	Draft, Revise, Edit, Publish: Personal Narrative	Ideas

Language Arts

Writing

Day 2 TEACH THE FOCUS TRAIT

1 ☑ INTRODUCE THE FOCUS TRAIT: ORGANIZATION

- Tell students that writers organize their narratives in ways that help readers understand what they are reading.

- Explain that writers include clear details and thoughts to support each main idea.

Connect to "Harvesting Hope"	
Instead of this...	**...the author wrote this.**
People gave them places to stay. This helped them.	"Shelter was no longer a problem. Supporters began welcoming them each night with feasts." (p. 487)

- Point out that the author's words express details that convey how much the supporters cared about helping others.

2 PRACTICE/APPLY

- Tell students that knowing the problems of the marchers helps the reader to understand the response from the people. The author says that marchers had no place to sleep. With that information, the reader can now understand why people gave them shelter.

- Suggest a topic such as a school fundraising event, and work with students to brainstorm related ideas.

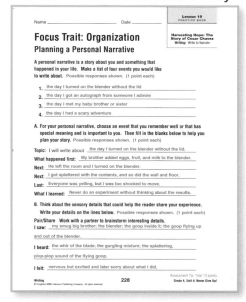

Practice Book p. 228

Day 3 PREWRITE

1 TEACH EXPLORING A TOPIC

- Explain that one way to explore ideas for a personal narrative is to use a chart to organize details.

- Tell students that you will list events from an experience, and then add details that support each event in the personal narrative.

Think Aloud *First, I'll think of who was involved in the event. I'll list that information next to the question "Who?" Then I will write details about where the event happened next to "Where?" I'll list details about the event itself next to "What?"*

Who?	my classmates, my teacher, me
Where?	the school cafeteria
What?	tables, money box, muffins

2 PRACTICE/APPLY

- Work with students to add more details to the brainstorming list. Save the list for use on Day 4.

- Write the following prompt on the board.

Write a personal narrative about your involvement in an event to help others.

- Have students begin planning their own personal narratives by brainstorming ideas.

Day 4 PREWRITE

1 TEACH PLANNING A PERSONAL NARRATIVE

- Point out that the details of how a writer feels about events make a narrative more interesting.

- Remind students of the following events from "Harvesting Hope":
  - how Chavez felt about working in the fields
  - what going to school was like for Chavez

- Ask: *Do these feelings add to the details of the story? How? These details help to give a better understanding of Chavez's experiences. I feel more and understand more about what is happening.*

- Explain that as they plan their writing, students should focus on how they felt about the events they are narrating in order to provide more detail.

2 PRACTICE/APPLY

- Review the ideas that students developed on Day 3. Display **Projectable 19.10**.

- Work with students to fill in the chart on the projectable to show what happened over the course of the narrative.

- Have students use their ideas to complete their own event charts. Remind them that feelings add to the details of each event.

Projectable 19.10

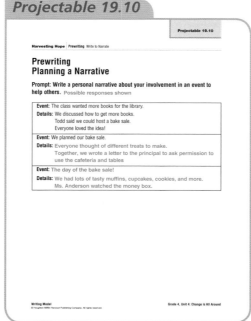

Projectable 19.10

Harvesting Hope | Prewriting Write to Narrate

**Prewriting
Planning a Narrative**

Prompt: Write a personal narrative about your involvement in an event to help others. Possible responses shown

Event: The class wanted more books for the library.
Details: We discussed how to get more books.
Todd said we could host a bake sale.
Everyone loved the idea!

Event: We planned our bake sale.
Details: Everyone thought of different treats to make.
Together, we wrote a letter to the principal to ask permission to use the cafeteria and tables

Event: The day of the bake sale!
Details: We had lots of tasty muffins, cupcakes, cookies, and more.
Ms. Anderson watched the money box.

Writing Model
© Houghton Mifflin Harcourt Publishing Company. All rights reserved.   Grade 4, Unit 4: Change is All Around

Day 5 PREWRITE

1 TEACH PLANNING A PERSONAL NARRATIVE

- Tell students they will read how one student writer organized his ideas for a personal narrative.

- Read the top of **Student Book p. 496** and the ideas written by the student writer, Steve.

- Then read Steve's events chart on **p. 497**.

- Ask: *How did Steve organize his events and details? First, he put the events in time order. Then, he added his feelings in details.*

2 PRACTICE/APPLY

- Discuss the *Reading as a Writer* questions on **Student Book p. 497**.

- Ask students to check their event charts to be sure they have included events in the order that they happened and added details that tell about each event. Tell them to add feelings and new details to support their ideas.

Reading-Writing Workshop: Prewrite

Write to Narrate

✔ **Organization** Good writers organize their ideas before they draft. You can organize ideas for a **personal narrative** by using an events chart. In your chart, write the main events in order. Below each main event, write important or interesting details about it. Use the Writing Process Checklist below as you revise your writing.

Steve decided to write about a class adventure. First he jotted down some notes. Then he organized them in a chart.

Writing Process Checklist

▶ **Prewrite**
- ✔ Did I think about my purpose for writing?
- ✔ Did I choose a topic that I will enjoy writing about?
- ✔ Did I explore my topic to remember the events and details?
- ✔ Did I organize the events in the order in which they happened?

Draft

Revise

Edit

Publish and Share

496

Exploring a Topic

Topic: my class went on the Walk to End Hunger

discuss project with class
- my idea—Walk to End Hunger
- help people
- 20-mile walk
- vote—my idea won!!!

day of Walk
- bus ride
- big crowd
- balloons, food
- walked 5 hours
- TIRED!
- band
- felt really proud

collect pledges
- got people to donate money
- total—$425

Events Chart

Event:	My class discussed ideas for a community project.
Details:	Some kids gave ideas. Mine was to go on the Walk for Hunger to help people, walk 20 miles, and get free snacks. We voted and my idea won.
Event:	We collected pledges from people.
Details:	Friends and relatives pledge to donate money. We raised $425.
Event:	Class rode bus to the Walk on May 6.
Details:	At the starting place—big crowd, balloons, free water, granola bars, caps.
Event:	We walked for 5 hours.
Details:	Easy at first, hard later—tired, sore feet.
Event:	We finished the Walk.
Details:	A band was playing. I just wanted to go home. The next day I felt really proud.

In my chart, I put the events and details in an order that makes sense. I added some new details too.

Reading as a Writer

What kind of order did Steve use to arrange his events? Which parts of your events chart can you organize more clearly?

497

Writing Traits Scoring Rubric

	Focus/Ideas	✔ Organization	Voice	✔ Word Choice	✔ Sentence Fluency	Conventions
4	Adheres to the topic, is interesting, has a sense of completeness. Ideas are well developed.	Ideas and details are clearly presented and well organized.	Connects with reader in a unique, personal way.	Includes vivid verbs, strong adjectives, specific nouns.	Includes a variety of complete sentences that flow smoothly, naturally.	Shows a strong command of grammar, spelling, capitalization, punctuation.
3	Mostly adheres to the topic, is somewhat interesting, has a sense of completeness. Ideas are adequately developed.	Ideas and details are mostly clear and generally organized.	Generally connects with reader in a way that is personal and sometimes unique.	Includes some vivid verbs, strong adjectives, specific nouns.	Includes some variety of mostly complete sentences. Some parts flow smoothly, naturally.	Shows a good command of grammar, spelling, capitalization, punctuation.
2	Does not always adhere to the topic, has some sense of completeness. Ideas are superficially developed.	Ideas and details are not always clear or organized. There is some wordiness or repetition.	Connects somewhat with reader. Sounds somewhat personal, but not unique.	Includes mostly simple nouns and verbs, and may have a few adjectives.	Includes mostly simple sentences, some of which are incomplete.	Some errors in grammar, spelling, capitalization, punctuation.
1	Does not adhere to the topic, has no sense of completeness. Ideas are vague.	Ideas and details are not organized. Wordiness or repetition hinders meaning.	Does not connect with reader. Does not sound personal or unique.	Includes only simple nouns and verbs, some inaccurate. Writing is not descriptive.	Sentences do not vary. Incomplete sentences hinder meaning.	Frequent errors in grammar, spelling, capitalization, punctuation.

See also ***Writing Rubric Blackline Master*** and Teacher's Edition pp. R18–R21.

Progress Monitoring

Assess

- **Weekly Tests**
- **Periodic Assessments**
- **Fluency Tests**

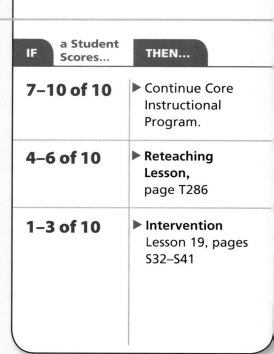

✓ Vocabulary
Target Vocabulary
Strategies: Use a Dictionary

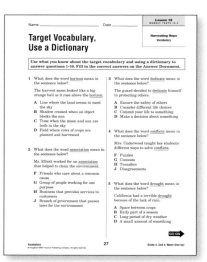

Weekly Tests 19.2–19.3

✓ Comprehension
Persuasion

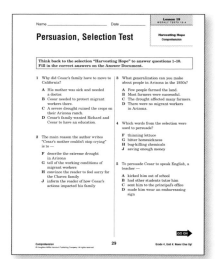

Weekly Tests 19.4–19.5

Respond to Assessment

IF	a Student Scores...	THEN...
7–10 of 10		▶ Continue Core Instructional Program.
4–6 of 10		▶ Reteaching Lesson, page T286
1–3 of 10		▶ Intervention Lesson 19, pages S32–S41

IF	a Student Scores...	THEN...
7–10 of 10		▶ Continue Core Instructional Program.
4–6 of 10		▶ Reteaching Lesson, page T286
1–3 of 10		▶ Intervention Lesson 19, pages S32–S41

Powered by DESTINATIONReading®

- **Weekly Tests**
- **Online Assessment System**

☑ Decoding
More Common Suffixes

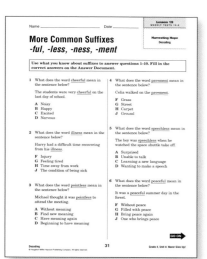

Weekly Tests 19.6–19.7

IF a Student Scores...	THEN...
7–10 of 10	▶ Continue Core Instructional Program.
4–6 of 10	▶ Reteaching Lesson, page T287
1–3 of 10	▶ Intervention Lesson 19, pages S32–S41

☑ Language Arts
Grammar: Transitions

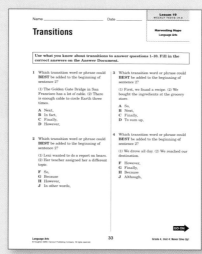

Weekly Tests 19.8–19.9

Writing Traits Rubrics
See TE pp. R18–R21.

IF a Student Scores...	THEN...
7–10 of 10	▶ Continue Core Instructional Program.
4–6 of 10	▶ Reteaching Lesson, page T287
1–3 of 10	▶ Intervention Lesson 19, pages S32–S41

☑ Fluency

Fluency Plan
Assess one group per week.
Use the suggested plan below.

	Struggling Readers	Weeks 1, 3, 5
▲	On Level	Week 2
■	Advanced	Week 4

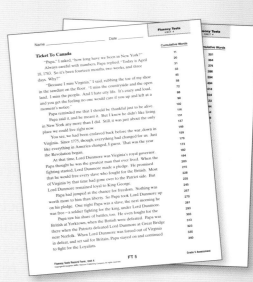

Fluency Record Forms

Fluency Scoring Rubrics
See *Grab and Go™ Resources Assessment* for help measuring progress.

✓ Progress Monitoring

Small Group

RUNNING RECORDS

To assess individual progress, occasionally use small group time to take a reading record for each student. Use the results to plan instruction.

 ● **Struggling Readers**

 ▲ **On Level**

 ■ **Advanced**

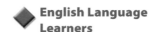 ◆ **English Language Learners**

For running records, see
Grab-and-Go™ Resources: Lesson 19, pp. 13–16.

Behaviors and Understandings to Notice

- Self-corrects errors that detract from meaning.
- Self-corrects intonation when it does not reflect the meaning.
- Rereads to solve words and resumes normal rate of reading.
- Demonstrates phrased and fluent oral reading.
- Reads dialogue with expression.

- Demonstrates awareness of punctuation.
- Automatically solves most words in the text to read fluently.
- Demonstrates appropriate stress on words, pausing and phrasing, intonation, and use of punctuation.
- Reads orally at an appropriate rate.

Weekly
Small Group Instruction

Day 1

Vocabulary Reader
* *Tough Times,* T276–T277

Vocabulary Reader

Day 2

Differentiate Comprehension
* Target Skill: Persuasion, T278–T279
* Target Strategy: Infer/Predict, T278–T279

Day 3

Leveled Readers
* ● *Songs for the People,* T280
* ▲ *The People's President,* T281
* ■ *The Story of Dorothea Lange,* T282
* ◆ *A President for the People,* T283

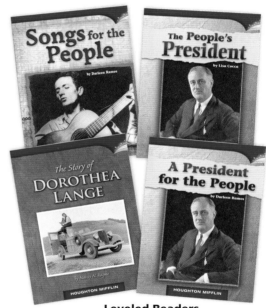

Day 4

Differentiate Vocabulary Strategies
* Use a Dictionary, T284–T285

Leveled Readers

Day 5

Options for Reteaching
* Vocabulary Strategies: Use a Dictionary, T286
* Comprehension Skill: Persuasion, T286
* Language Arts: Transitions/Write to Narrate, T287
* Decoding: More Common Suffixes, T287

Ready-Made Work Stations

Independent Practice
* Comprehension and Fluency, T226
* Word Study, T226
* Think and Write, T227
* Digital Center, T227

Comprehension and Fluency

Word Study

Think and Write

Digital Center

		Day 1	**Day 2**	**Day 3**
Teacher-Led	**Struggling Readers**	**Vocabulary Reader** *Tough Times*, Differentiated Instruction, p. T276	**Differentiate Comprehension:** Persuasion; Infer/Predict, p. T278	**Leveled Reader** *Songs for the People*, p. T280
	On Level	**Vocabulary Reader** *Tough Times*, Differentiated Instruction, p. T276	**Differentiate Comprehension:** Persuasion; Infer/Predict, p. T278	**Leveled Reader** *The People's President*, p. T281
	Advanced	**Vocabulary Reader** *Tough Times*, Differentiated Instruction, p. T277	**Differentiate Comprehension:** Persuasion; Infer/Predict, p. T279	**Leveled Reader** *The Story of Dorothea Lange*, p. T282
	English Language Learners	**Vocabulary Reader** *Tough Times*, Differentiated Instruction, p. T277	**Differentiate Comprehension:** Persuasion; Infer/Predict, p. T279	**Leveled Reader** *A President for the People*, p. T283

		Day 1	**Day 2**	**Day 3**
What are my other students doing?	**Struggling Readers**	• **Reread** *Tough Times*	• **Vocabulary in Context Cards** 181–190 *Talk It Over* Activities • **Complete** Leveled Practice SR19.1	• **Listen** to Audio of "Harvesting Hope"; Retell and discuss • **Complete** Leveled Reader SR19.2
	On Level	• **Reread** *Tough Times*	• **Reread** "Harvesting Hope" with a partner • **Complete** Practice Book p. 217	• **Reread** for Fluency: *The People's President* • **Complete** Practice Book p. 218
	Advanced	• **Vocabulary in Context Cards** 181–190 *Talk It Over* Activities	• **Reread and Retell** "Harvesting Hope" • **Complete** Leveled Practice A19.1	• **Reread** for Fluency: *The Story of Dorthea Lange* • **Complete** Leveled Practice A19.2
	English Language Learners	• **Reread** *Tough Times*	• **Listen** to Audio of "Harvesting Hope"; Retell and discuss • **Complete** Leveled Practice ELL19.1	• **Vocabulary in Context Cards** 181–190 *Talk It Over* Activities • **Complete** Leveled Practice ELL19.2

Ready-Made Work Stations

Assign these activities across the week to reinforce and extend learning.

Comprehension and Fluency
Read for Fluency

Word Study
Dissect the Definition

Day 4

Differentiate Vocabulary Strategies:
Use a Dictionary, p. T284

Differentiate Vocabulary Strategies:
Use a Dictionary, p. T284

Differentiate Vocabulary Strategies:
Use a Dictionary, p. T285

Differentiate Vocabulary Strategies:
Use a Dictionary, p. T285

Day 5

Options for Reteaching,
pp. T286–T287

Options for Reteaching,
pp. T286–T287

Options for Reteaching,
pp. T286–T287

Options for Reteaching,
pp. T286–T287

• **Partners: Reread**
Songs for the People
• **Complete** Leveled
Practice SR19.3

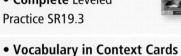

• **Vocabulary in Context Cards**
181–190
Talk It Over Activities
• **Complete** Practice Book p. 219

• **Reread** for Fluency: "Harvesting
Hope"
• **Complete** Leveled Practice A19.3

• **Partners: Reread** for
Fluency: *A President for the
People* • **Complete** Leveled
Practice ELL19.3

• **Reread** for Fluency: "Harvesting
Hope"
• **Complete** Work Station activities
• **Independent Reading**

• **Complete** Work Station activities
• **Independent Reading**

• **Complete** Work Station activities
• **Independent Reading**

• **Reread** *Tough Times* or "Harvesting
Hope"
• **Complete** Work Station Activities

Think and Write
Write a Poem

JOURNEYS DIGITAL Powered by DESTINATION Reading

Digital Center

Weekly To-Do List

This Weekly To-Do List helps students
see their own progress and move on
to additional activities independently.

Name _____ Date _____
Lesson 19
WEEKLY TO-DO LIST

Weekly To-Do List

Put an X in each box when you finish the activity.

Must Do
☐ Practice pages
_____
☐ Comprehension and
Fluency Work Station
☐ Word Study
Work Station
☐ Think and Write
Work Station
☐ Daily Independent Reading
☐ Other _____
_____

May Do
☐ Reading Log
☐ Vocabulary in Context Cards
☐ Practice Spelling Words
☐ Work on Writing Assignment
☐ Other _____
_____

Daily Independent Reading

☐ Monday	
☐ Tuesday	
☐ Wednesday	
☐ Thursday	
☐ Friday	

Weekly To-Do List
© Houghton Mifflin Harcourt Publishing Company. All rights reserved.
Grade 4, Unit 4: Never Give Up!

Reading Log

Name _____
Reading Log

Reading Log
Title _____ Author _____

Independent Reading Record
Date/Amount of Time _____ Pages _____
Date/Amount of Time _____ Pages _____
Date/Amount of Time _____ Pages _____
Date/Amount of Time _____ Pages _____
Date/Amount of Time _____ Pages _____

Summary
This book is about _____
_____

Questions for Discussion
What was your favorite part of the book? _____

What did you enjoy about the author's writing? _____

Was there something that you did not understand? If so, discuss. _____
_____

Would you recommend this book to a friend? Why or why not? _____

Reading Log
© Houghton Mifflin Harcourt Publishing Company.

Grab-and-Go!

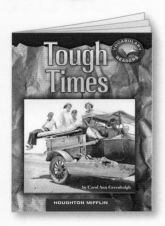

Summary

When the Great Depression began, government programs such as unemployment and food stamps did not exist. This made it hard for people to survive. Today, such programs do exist.

✓ TARGET VOCABULARY

association	overcome
brilliant	publicity
capitol	violence
dedicate	conflicts
drought	horizon

Vocabulary Reader
Tough Times

Struggling Readers

- Explain to students that the Great Depression was a long period in the 1930s when the world's economy, or financial affairs, slowed and many people lost their jobs. In response, the government created programs to help these people.

- Guide students to preview the Vocabulary Reader. Read aloud the headings. Ask students to describe the images, using Target Vocabulary words when possible.

- Have students alternate reading aloud pages of the Vocabulary Reader. Guide them to use context clues to determine the meanings of unfamiliar words. As necessary, use the Vocabulary in Context Cards to review the meanings of Vocabulary words.

- Assign the **Responding Page** and **Blackline Master 19.1**. Have partners work together to complete the pages.

On Level

- Explain to students that World War II helped end the Great Depression because it created jobs. Businesses expanded to produce supplies needed for the war. They built new factories and hired many workers. Guide students to preview the Vocabulary Reader.

- Remind students that context clues can help them determine the meaning of an unknown word. Tell students to use context clues to confirm their understanding of Target Vocabulary and to learn the meanings of new words.

- Have students alternate reading aloud pages of the Vocabulary Reader. Tell them to use context clues to determine the meanings of unknown words.

- Assign the **Responding Page** and **Blackline Master 19.1**. Have students discuss their responses with a partner.

Advanced

- Have students preview the Vocabulary Reader and make predictions about what they will read, using information from the preview and their prior knowledge.

- Remind students to use context clues to help them determine the meanings of unknown words.

- Tell students to read the selection with a partner. Ask them to stop and discuss the meanings of unknown words as necessary.

- Assign the **Responding Page** and **Blackline Master 19.1**. For the Write About It activity, remind students to use facts and details to support their ideas. Ask them why farmers affected by the Dust Bowl would have been happy to see rain clouds on the horizon.

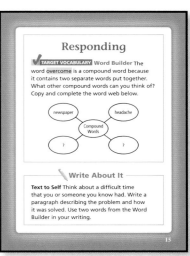

Tough Times, p. 15

Blackline Master 19.1

(ELL) English Language Learners

Group English Language Learners according to language proficiency.

Beginning

Display Vocabulary in Context Cards for *association, drought, conflicts,* and *horizon.* Read each card aloud, and have students look at the photograph on each card. Ask them how the photograph helps them learn the definition.

Advanced

Have students use the Vocabulary words in oral sentences that tell about what they learned in *Tough Times.*

Intermediate

Have partners work together to read the Vocabulary in Context Cards for Lesson 19. Have each pair choose a word that they still have difficulty understanding. Have them look the word up in a dictionary or in the glossary.

Advanced High

Have students tell about *Tough Times.* Have them give a short synopsis of the story. In the synopsis, encourage them to use at least five Vocabulary words.

Differentiate Comprehension

☑ Persuasion; Infer/Predict

Struggling Readers

I DO IT

- Remind students that the goal of persuasive text is to influence readers to think or act in a certain way.

- Explain that sometimes authors do not state a goal directly. Students may need to use text details to infer how the author wants them to think.

- Read pp. 480–481 and model identifying persuasion.

  Think Aloud *There's no water, no money, and Cesar's mother is crying. These details persuade me that the family is in a desperate situation.*

WE DO IT

- Have students read the first paragraph on p. 483.

- Help students identify the author's goal. *What is the author trying to persuade us to think? The working conditions of the farmworkers were unfair. They had no clean water, rest periods, or bathrooms, and if they complained, they were fired, beaten, or even killed.*

- Ask a volunteer to identify one text detail that supports the author's goal.

- Write the goal and reason in an Idea-Support Map on the board.

YOU DO IT

- Have students complete the Idea-Support Map with two more reasons from the text that support the author's goal.

- Have students write a paragraph explaining whether the author persuaded them to agree with her and why or why not.

- Have them read their paragraphs to the class.

On Level

I DO IT

- Read aloud p. 483 of "Harvesting Hope."

- Explain that authors of persuasive text may try to persuade the reader to identify with a character. Readers may have to infer the character's feelings, motives, and actions.

- Model inferring the author's goal of understanding the feelings and beliefs of characters with an Idea-Support Map.

  Think Aloud *Cesar is disturbed that migrant workers are not treated like human beings. That detail helps me understand Cesar's feelings.*

WE DO IT

- Have students read the first two paragraphs of p. 485.

- Help students identify the author's goal and text details that suggest what the author wants them to think or feel about Cesar's *La Causa* movement. Write students' answers in a Idea-Support Map on the board.

- Discuss how the author uses Cesar's feelings and beliefs to help support her goal.

YOU DO IT

- Have students read the rest of "Harvesting Hope" independently.

- Have pairs complete an Idea-Support Map with details about Cesar's feelings and beliefs and how the author wants the reader to feel about Cesar.

- Ask students to share their Idea-Support Maps with the class and explain how they support the goal they identified.

Advanced

I DO IT

- Read aloud p. 486 of "Harvesting Hope."

- Explain that when writers are trying to persuade their readers, the reasons they present may become stronger from the start of the text to the end.

> **Think Aloud** *The author wants us to see how determined Cesar and the marchers are. The first obstacle that the marchers face is the line of police in Delano, who try to stop them, but the marchers finally convince the police to let them continue.*

WE DO IT

- Have students read p. 487 independently.

- Have a volunteer infer the author's goal in the passage about the Delano march. *The author wants us to believe that Cesar and his marchers were determined to get their message across peacefully. What text details does she present to show the marchers are succeeding? They attract more marchers over time; people give them food, drink, and shelter; five thousand people meet the marchers.*

YOU DO IT

- Have students write a paragraph describing which reasons in "Harvesting Hope" were the strongest and which were not as strong. What inferences did they make?

- Ask students to share their thoughts with the class.

- Invite students to model how they used the Infer/Predict Strategy to write their paragraphs.

ELL English Language Learners

Group English Language Learners according to language proficiency.

Draw an Idea-Support Map on the board. Then choose one of the following activities for additional support, as appropriate.

Beginning

Read p. 484 to students. Guide them to fill in the Idea-Support Map. Ask: *What is Cesar's goal? fight for change What were two reasons for this? He didn't like working like a slave. He wanted life to be like it was in Arizona.*

Intermediate

Remind students that sometimes an author's reasons are not directly stated. Think about Cesar Chavez and what his reasons were for trying to get change. Have students give five reasons why Cesar wanted change.

Advanced

Have students pick a page from the story. Guide them to fill in the chart on the board. Next, have students explain Cesar's goal and give two reasons for his goal.

Advanced High

Have students reread "Harvesting Hope." Have them copy the chart on the board into their notebooks and fill in the chart with Cesar's goal. Have students add boxes and fill in at least five reasons Cesar Chavez was passionate about his goal.

Targets for Lesson 19

✔ TARGET SKILL
Persuasion

✔ TARGET STRATEGY
Infer/Predict

✔ TARGET VOCABULARY

association	overcome
brilliant	publicity
capitol	violence
dedicate	conflicts
drought	horizon

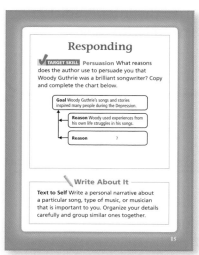

Songs for the People, p. 15

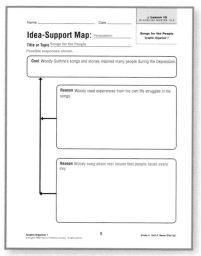

Blackline Master 19.3

Leveled Readers

Struggling Readers

 Songs for the People

GENRE: BIOGRAPHY

Summary Woody Guthrie wrote songs about the struggles that people faced, particularly during the Great Depression. Guthrie is best known for writing the song "This Land Is Your Land."

Introducing the Text

• Explain that a severe drought in the 1930s created devastating conditions for farmers across the Great Plains. The area was called the "Dust Bowl."

• Remind students that using an Idea-Support Map can help them identify an author's goal. The author's goal may be clearly stated or readers may have to infer the goal, based on supporting reasons.

Supporting the Reading

• As you listen to students read, pause to discuss these questions.

PERSUASION p. 8 *What is the author trying to persuade the reader of on this page? that Guthrie was a man of the people who wanted to help people through music*

INFER/PREDICT p. 14 *Why do many people today still love Guthrie's music? because struggling for a better life is an issue that people can still relate to*

Discussing and Revisiting the Text

CRITICAL THINKING After discussing *Songs for the People*, have students read the instructions on **Responding** p. 15. Use these points to revisit the text.

• Have partners identify a reason to support the author's goal and list it on **Blackline Master 19.3**. Then have partners discuss whether the author's goal is stated or implied based on the author's reasons.

• Distribute **Blackline Master 19.7** to develop student's critical thinking skills.

FLUENCY: STRESS Have partners echo-read p. 4 and focus on stress.

On Level

▲ *The People's President*

GENRE: BIOGRAPHY

Summary Franklin Delano Roosevelt is known for leading the country through the Great Depression and World War II. Roosevelt is remembered for working to improve life for all Americans.

Introducing the Text

- Explain that FDR was President before term limits were established. Today, a president can only serve a maximum of two terms, or eight years.

- Remind students that authors may use facts, opinions, and details to persuade the reader of the author's goal.

Supporting the Reading

- As you listen to students read, pause to discuss these questions.

PERSUASION p. 14 *How does the author persuade the reader that the country would not be the same without Roosevelt?* The author persuades the reader with details from FDR's life.

INFER/PREDICT p. 2 *What can you infer about how Americans felt about FDR? Explain.* Since he was elected to four terms, the people supported him and thought he was a great president.

Discussing and Revisiting the Text

- **CRITICAL THINKING** After discussing *The People's President*, have students read the instructions on **Responding** p.15. Use these points to revisit the text.

- Have partners identify reasons that support the author's goal. Direct them to p. 8 of *The People's President,* and tell students to list the appropriate information on **Blackline Master 19.4**.

- Have students list a second supporting reason on their own.

- Distribute **Blackline Master 19.8** to develop students' critical thinking skills.

FLUENCY: STRESS Have students read the text using appropriate stress.

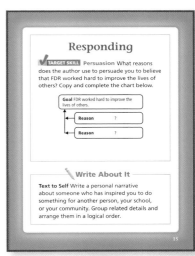

The People's President, p. 15

Blackline Master 19.4

Targets for Lesson 19

✔ TARGET SKILL

Persuasion

✔ TARGET STRATEGY

Infer/Predict

✔ TARGET VOCABULARY

association	overcome
brilliant	publicity
capitol	violence
dedicate	conflicts
drought	horizon

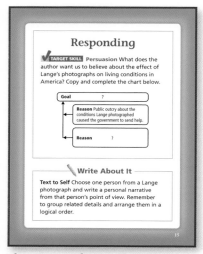

The Story of Dorothea Lange,
p. 15

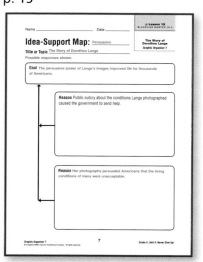

Blackline Master 19.5

Leveled Readers

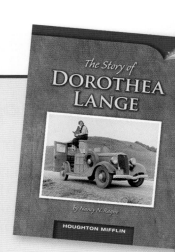

Advanced

 The Story of Dorothea Lange

GENRE: BIOGRAPHY

Summary Dorothea Lange was a well-known photographer who documented the plight of migrant farm workers during the Depression. Through her photography, she helped many people.

Introducing the Text

• Explain that by 1933 the stock market crash and the drought across the Great Plains created an economic crisis known as the Great Depression.

• Remind students that authors often have goals, or ways they want the reader to think or act after reading. Evaluating the reasons for an author's goal helps readers decide if they are persuaded by the author.

Supporting the Reading

• As you listen to students read, pause to discuss these questions.

PERSUASION pp. 2–3 *What is the author trying to persuade the reader to believe in these two pages?* That Lange was dedicated to capturing the truth.

INFER/PREDICT p. 4 *What can you infer about the way Lange's experiences as a child affected her later work?* Surviving polio gave her sympathy for others.

Discussing and Revisiting the Text

CRITICAL THINKING After discussing *The Story of Dorothea Lange*, have students read the instructions on **Responding** p. 15. Use these points to revisit the text.

• Have partners identify the author's goal on p. 3. and list the goal on **Blackline Master 19.5**. Then have students identify one or more supporting reasons for the author's goal on p. 3 and discuss whether they were persuaded by the author's goal or not.

• Distribute **Blackline Master 19.9** to develop student's critical thinking skills.

FLUENCY: STRESS Have students practice reading with appropriate stress.

JOURNEYS DIGITAL Powered by DESTINATIONReading®
Leveled Readers Online

 English Language Learners

◆ *A President for the People*

GENRE: BIOGRAPHY

Summary Franklin Delano Roosevelt led the country through the Great Depression and World War II. He is remembered for working to improve life for all Americans.

Introducing the Text

- Explain that FDR was President before there was a limit on how long a person could hold the office of President. Today, a President can only serve a maximum of two terms, or eight years.

- Remind students that authors sometimes want to persuade their readers. An author may use facts, opinions, and details to support his or her goal.

Supporting the Reading

- As you listen to students read, pause to discuss these questions.

PERSUASION p. 6 *How does the author persuade the reader that Roosevelt was determined?* with details such as "a wheelchair did not stop FDR from working"

INFER/PREDICT p. 13 *What can you infer about why people elected Roosevelt for a fourth term?* The people of the United States believed in Roosevelt's leadership.

Discussing and Revisiting the Text

CRITICAL THINKING After discussing *A President for the People*, have students read instructions on **Responding** p. 15. Use these points to revisit the text.

- Point out the goal stated on the chart and tell students to identify two supporting reasons. Have partners identify the first supporting reason on p. 8 and list it on **Blackline Master 19.6**. Help students find one more supporting reason and list it on the Idea-Support Map.

- Distribute **Blackline Master 19.10** to develop students' critical thinking skills.

FLUENCY: STRESS Have students practice read their favorite parts of the text with appropriate stress on important words.

A President for the People, p. 15

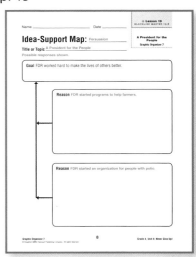

Blackline Master 19.6

Differentiate Vocabulary Strategies ✔ Use a Dictionary

Struggling Readers

I DO IT

- Display **Vocabulary in Context Card 190**: *brilliant*

- Remind students that using a dictionary entry can be helpful to find the pronunciation, part of speech, and meaning of a word.

- Look up the word *brilliant* in a dictionary. Say: Brilliant *starts with a* b. *I will look in the* B *section of the dictionary. The words are listed alphabetically.*

WE DO IT

- Read aloud the context sentence on the front of **Vocabulary in Context Card 190**.

- Guide students to use a dictionary to verify the pronunciation, part of speech, and meaning of *brilliant*. Read aloud the sample dictionary entry below:

> *brilliant* (**bril**-yuhnt) *adj.* **1.** shining very brightly **2.** very smart **3.** splendid or terrific

- Have students read aloud the context sentence on the front of the card.

YOU DO IT

- Have students restate the context sentence using the Vocabulary word *brilliant*.

- Have them write a sentence using the word *brilliant* and the meaning "shining brightly."

The brilliant diamond ring sparkled on her finger.

On Level

I DO IT

- Tell students that a dictionary's pronunciation key can help them pronounce an unfamiliar word.

- Model using a dictionary to find the meaning, pronunciation, and part of speech of the word *fracture*.

  Think Aloud *To find the word* fracture, *I look under* F *in the dictionary. I see that* fracture *is a noun that means "the act of breaking something." I also find how to correctly pronounce* fracture.

WE DO IT

- Remind students that they should use a dictionary to confirm the meanings of unfamiliar words or words with more than one meaning.

- Say: *The workmen had to fracture the rocks to help break them apart.*

- Guide students to use a dictionary to look up the correct meaning for *fracture* in the sentence.

YOU DO IT

- Have students look up and use a dictionary to locate the meanings and parts of speech of the following words: *venture, retrieve,* and *reliable.*

- Tell students to use each word in a sentence.

Advanced

I DO IT

- Remind students that they can use a dictionary to find the meanings of unfamiliar words. Explain that many words have more than one meaning.

- On the board, write *interest*. Tell students that the word *interest* has more than one meaning.

WE DO IT

- Guide students to use a dictionary to look up the meaning of the word *interest*.

- Read aloud the first definition of interest and tell students its part of speech. *Interest is a noun. It means "a desire to know or learn something."*

- Work with students to look up another meaning of the word and use it in a sentence.

YOU DO IT

- Have partners use a dictionary to look up the meaning of *express*.

- Tell students to write a sentence for each meaning of the word.

- Have partners share their sentences.

ELL English Language Learners

Group English Language Learners according to language proficiency.
Write *drought* and *crane* on the board. Have students repeat after you as you pronounce each word.

Beginning

Display **Vocabulary in Context Card 183**, and say *drought*. Have students repeat the word after you. Have them read the sentence on the card. Then read aloud the dictionary definition and part of speech for *drought*.

Intermediate

Have students look up *crane* in a dictionary and paraphrase two meanings for the word.

Advanced

Display all of the **Vocabulary in Context Cards** from Lesson 19. Have students choose a card and look up the Vocabulary word in the dictionary. Have them use two of the Vocabulary words in oral sentences.

Advanced High

Write the Target Vocabulary words on index cards. Have partners look up the words in a dictionary. Have them use an alternate meaning of each word in an oral sentence.

☑ Options for Reteaching

Vocabulary Strategies

☑ Use a Dictionary

I DO IT

- Explain that a dictionary provides many kinds of information about words.
- Point out that the dictionary provides pronunciation.
- Remind students that the dictionary can also show parts of speech, word endings, and how a word is divided into syllables.

WE DO IT

- Display **Projectable 19.5**.
- Model how to use a dictionary to find information about the word *blur*.

  Think Aloud *The word* blur *looks like a short vowel word, but it's difficult to pronounce that way. The dictionary tells me to use an* er *sound rather than an* uh *sound. It looks as if* blur *can be used as a noun or a verb. If I add an* r *and the ending -y, it can become an adjective:* blurry.

- Have a volunteer look up the dictionary entry for *blur* and recite any additional information available.

YOU DO IT

- Have partners work together to identify pronunciation, parts of speech, word endings, and syllabification for *suspicious, strike, harvest, belief,* and *rights*.
- Have them use the same dictionary entry for each aspect of the word.
- Provide corrective feedback if students need additional support.

Comprehension Skill

☑ Persuasion

I DO IT

- Remind students that persuasive messages try to convince a reader to think or act in a certain way. Persuasive messages support a goal and give facts and examples to show why the goal is important.
- Point out that readers who can evaluate persuasive messages can make up their own minds about the issues. Remind students to pay attention to word choices to better understand the writer's reasoning.

WE DO IT

- Have students read aloud the third paragraph on **Student Book p. 481** and evaluate the author's message regarding the Chavez family's first home in California.
- Model how to evaluate the persuasive message.

  Think Aloud *The family's living space was battered and old. Details include missing doors, garbage on a dirt floor, shared toilets, filth, overcrowding, noise, and fighting. These details support the message that the conditions were terrible.*

- Help volunteers identify other ideas about the Chavez family that they get from reading the passage.

YOU DO IT

- Distribute **Graphic Organizer 7**.
- Have students read paragraph 1 on **Student Book p. 483** and identify the author's message regarding the owner's treatment of migrant workers. *There was no clean drinking water, rest periods, or bathrooms. People who complained were fired, beaten or even killed. This supports the idea that workers' dignity was taken from them and they were powerless to change their lives.*
- Have students work as partners to complete the graphic organizer.
- Review the completed graphic organizers.

Language Arts

 # Transitions/Personal Narrative

I DO IT

- Remind students that a transition shows a change in ideas from one sentence to another.
- Transitions can show ideas that combine, contrast, and add to other ideas. List the following transitions on the board: *and, but, also*. Model using the transitions in sentences.

Think Aloud *To combine two thoughts, I can say: I went to the store, and I bought an apple. The transition* and *combines go to the store* and *buy an apple.*
Continue this activity with *but* and *also*.

WE DO IT

- Work together to write a sentence with a transition.
- Guide students to identify the transition in the sentence. Have them tell you if the transition combines, contrasts, or adds to two thoughts.
- Remind students that when writing narratives, using sentences with transitions can help vary their writing and make if more interesting.

YOU DO IT

- Have pairs of students write three sentences using transitions, identifying if the transitions they use combine, contrast, or add to their thoughts.

Decoding

 # More Common Suffixes: *-ful, -less, -ness, -ment*

I DO IT

- Remind students that words often break between words within a compound word and before suffixes.
- Model how to decode *homesickness* step by step.

Think Aloud *This word contains familiar base words and the suffix -ness. To pronounce this word, break between the base words* home *and* sick *and before* -ness. / home / sick / ness /

WE DO IT

- Write *careless, useless, ailment, colorful,* and *kindness* on the board.
- Guide students to break apart each word into syllables and then read the word.

Word	Base Word	Suffix
useless	use	less
ailment	ail	ment
colorful	color	ful
kindness	kind	ness

YOU DO IT

- Have partners work together to decode the remaining Spelling Words.
- Have students read the words and note the suffixes and base words that form the spelling words.
- Use the **Corrective Feedback** on **p. T255** if students need additional help.

Teacher Notes

Preteaching for Success!

Comprehension:

Main Idea and Details

Remind students of the importance of understanding the main idea as they read.

- Tell students that a main idea is what a piece of writing is mainly about. The details are ideas that support the main idea.
- Explain to students that they can find the main idea of a paragraph or of an entire story or selection.
- Have students choose a book and think about its main idea and details. Tell them to use a word web like the one on Student Book p. 502 to record this information.

Challenge Yourself!

A Letter to Sacagawea

After reading the selection "Sacagawea," have students write letters to her.

- Have students imagine that they can write letters to Sacagawea to explain how the country's landscape has changed since her days with the Lewis and Clark Expedition.
- Ask them to compare and contrast the country during these two times and explain why it changed so much.
- Ask students to share their letters with partners and discuss them.

Short Response

W.4.2b Develop the topic with facts, definitions, concrete details, quotations, or other information and examples related to the topic.

Write a paragraph to explain why someone might be able to use the selection for a school report. Give examples from the text.

Scoring Guidelines	
Excellent	Student has written a paragraph to tell why the selection might be used in a school report and has given relevant examples from the text.
Good	Student has written a paragraph to tell why the selection might be used in a school report but has not given relevant examples from the text.
Fair	Student has written a paragraph but has not addressed the writing prompt.
Unsatisfactory	Student has not written a paragraph.

Writing Minilesson

Skill: Write to Narrate—Story

Teach: Remind students that when they write to narrate, it can be in a long or short form.

Thinking Beyond the Text

Writing Prompt: Write a story about a time you took a long, difficult journey.

1. Have students decide on the main ideas and details of their stories before they begin.
2. Remind students to use abbreviations correctly when they are writing titles, addresses, months, days, or measurements.
3. When they are finished, encourage students to revise their stories to delete uninteresting or unimportant ideas.

Group Share: Have students share their stories in small groups.

Cross-Curricular Activity: Social Studies

Native Americans in Your State

Name two Native American tribes that inhabited your state. Ask students to break into two groups. Have each group research one of the tribes and write a short presentation about their customs and traditions. Lead a class discussion about the similarities and differences between these two Native American groups.

Reading Standards for Literature K–5

Key Ideas and Details

RL.4.1 Refer to details and examples in a text when explaining what the text says explicitly and when drawing inferences from the text.*

RL.4.2 Determine a theme of a story, drama, or poem from details in the text; summarize the text.*

RL.4.3 Describe in depth a character, setting, or event in a story or drama, drawing on specific details in the text (e.g., a character's thoughts, words, or actions).*

Craft and Structure

RL.4.4 Determine the meaning of words and phrases as they are used in a text, including those that allude to significant characters found in mythology (e.g., *Herculean*).*

RL.4.5 Explain major differences between poems, drama, and prose, and refer to the structural elements of poems (e.g., verse, rhythm, meter) and drama (e.g., casts of characters, settings, descriptions, dialogue, stage directions) when writing or speaking about a text.

Integration of Knowledge and Ideas

RL.4.9 Compare and contrast the treatment of similar themes and topics (e.g., opposition of good and evil) and patterns of events (e.g., the quest) in stories, myths, and traditional literature from different cultures.*

Reading Standards for Informational Text K–5

Key Ideas and Details

RI.4.1 Refer to details and examples in a text when explaining what the text says explicitly and when drawing inferences from the text.

RI.4.2 Determine the main idea of a text and explain how it is supported by key details; summarize the text.

RI.4.3 Explain events, procedures, ideas, or concepts in a historical, scientific, or technical text, including what happened and why, based on specific information in the text.

Craft and Structure

RI.4.4 Determine the meaning of general academic and domain-specific words or phrases in a text relevant to a *grade 4 topic or subject area*.

RI.4.5 Describe the overall structure (e.g., chronology, comparison, cause/effect, problem/solution) of events, ideas, concepts, or information in a text or part of a text.

Range of Reading and Level of Text Complexity

RI.4.10 By the end of year, read and comprehend informational texts, including history/social studies, science, and technical texts, in the grades 4–5 text complexity band proficiently, with scaffolding as needed at the high end of the range.

Reading Standards: Foundational Skills K–5

Phonics and Word Recognition

RF.4.3a Use combined knowledge of all letter-sound correspondences, syllabication patterns, and morphology (e.g. roots and affixes) to read accurately unfamiliar multisyllabic words in context and out of context.

Fluency

RF.4.4a Read grade-level text with purpose and understanding.

Writing Standards K–5

Text Types and Purposes

W.4.3a Orient the reader by establishing a situation and introducing a narrator and/or characters; organize an event sequence that unfolds naturally.

W.4.3b Use dialogue and description to develop experiences and events or show the responses of characters to situations.

W.4.3d Use concrete words and phrases and sensory details to convey experiences and events precisely.

W.4.3e Provide a conclusion that follows from the narrated experiences or events.

Production and Distribution of Writing

W.4.4 Produce clear and coherent writing in which the development and organization are appropriate to task, purpose, and audience.

W.4.5 With guidance and support from peers and adults, develop and strengthen writing as needed by planning, revising, and editing.

W.4.6 With some guidance and support from adults, use technology, including the Internet, to produce and publish writing as well as to interact and collaborate with others; demonstrate sufficient command of keyboarding skills to type a minimum of one page in a single sitting.*

Research to Build and Present Knowledge

W.4.7 Conduct short research projects that build knowledge through investigation of different aspects of a topic.

W.4.9a Apply *grade 4 Reading standards* to literature (e.g., "Describe in depth a character, setting, or event in a story or drama, drawing on specific details in the text [e.g., a character's thoughts, words, or actions].").*

W.4.9b Apply *grade 4 Reading standards* to informational texts (e.g., "Explain how an author uses reasons and evidence to support particular points in a text:").

Speaking & Listening Standards K–5

Comprehension and Collaboration

SL.4.1b Follow agreed-upon rules for discussions and carry out assigned roles.

SL.4.1d Review the key ideas expressed and explain their own ideas and understanding in light of the discussion.

Language Standards K–5

Conventions of Standard English

L.4.1d Order adjectives within sentences according to conventional patterns (e.g., *a small red bag* rather than *a red small bag*).*

Vocabulary Acquisition and Use

L.4.4a Use context (e.g., definitions, examples, or restatements in text) as a clue to the meaning of a word or phrase.*

L.4.4c Consult reference materials (e.g., dictionaries, glossaries, thesauruses), both print and digital, to find the pronunciation and determine or clarify the precise meaning of key words and phrases.*

L.4.5b Recognize and explain the meaning of common idioms. adages, and proverbs.*

* Extending the Common Core State Standards

SUGGESTIONS FOR BALANCED LITERACY

Use *Journeys* materials to support a Readers' Workshop approach.
See the Lesson 20 resources on pages 28, 78–79.

Lesson 20

Focus Wall

Main Selection
Sacagawea

Connect to Poetry
Native American Nature Poetry

Big Idea
There is more than one secret to success.

? Essential Question
What makes a team successful?

Comprehension

✔ **TARGET SKILL**
Main Idea and Details
✔ **TARGET STRATEGY**
Visualize

Spelling

Words with VCCV Pattern

million	canyon
collect	traffic
lumber	fortune
pepper	danger
plastic	soccer
borrow	engine
support	picture
thirty	survive
perfect	seldom
attend	effort

Fluency

Phrasing:
Punctuation

Grammar

Abbreviations

Writing

Write to Narrate
Focus Trait: Ideas

Decoding

VCCV Pattern and Word Parts

Vocabulary Strategies

Compound Words

V TARGET VOCABULARY

territory	supplies
accompany	route
proposed	corps
interpreter	clumsy
duty	landmark

Key Skills This Week

Target Skill:
Main Ideas and Details

Target Strategy:
Visualize

Vocabulary Strategies:
Compound Words

Fluency:
Phrasing: Punctuation

Decoding:
VCCV Pattern and Word Parts

Research Skill:
Taking Notes/Sorting Evidence/Citing Online Sources

Grammar:
Abbreviations

Spelling:
Words with VCCV Pattern

Writing:
Draft, Revise, Edit, Publish: Personal Narrative

Assess/Monitor

✓ **Vocabulary,**
p. T346

✓ **Comprehension,**
p. T346

✓ **Decoding,**
p. T347

✓ **Language Arts,**
p. T347

✓ **Fluency,**
p. T347

Whole Group

READING

Paired Selections

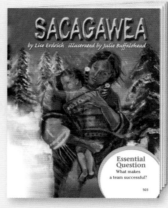

"Sacagawea"
Biography
Student Book, pp. 502–516

 Accelerated Reader
Practice Quizzes for the Selection

"Native American Nature Poetry"
Poetry
Student Book, pp. 518–520

Vocabulary

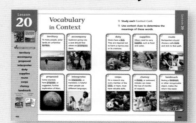

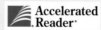

Student Book, pp. 498–499

Background and Comprehension

Student Book, pp. 500–501

LANGUAGE ARTS

Grammar
Student Book, pp. 522–523

Writing
Student Book, pp. 524–525

Small Group

See pages T354–T355 for Suggested Small Group Plan.

TEACHER-LED

Leveled Readers

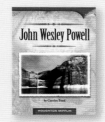
Struggling Readers

On Level

Advanced

English Language Learners

Vocabulary Reader

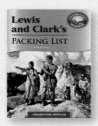

WHAT MY OTHER STUDENTS ARE DOING

Ready-Made Work Stations

Word Study

Think and Write

Comprehension and Fluency

Digital Center

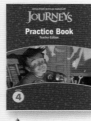

On Level

Struggling Readers

Advanced

English Language Learners

Lesson 20 Blackline Masters

- Target Vocabulary, 20.1
- Selection Summary 20.2
- Graphic Organizer 20.3–20.6 ●▲■◆
- Critical Thinking 20.7–20.10 ●▲■◆
- Running Records 20.11–20.14 ●▲■◆
- Readng Power 20.15
- Weekly Tests 20.1–20.9

Graphic Organizer Transparency 15

Additional Resources

- Genre: Biography, Autogiography, p. 8
- Reading Log, p. 12
- Vocabulary Log, p. 13
- Listening Log, p.14
- Proofreading Checklist, p.15
- Proofreading Marks, p.16
- Writing Conference Form, p. 17
- Writing Rubric, p.18
- Instructional Routines, pp.19–26
- Graphic Organizer 15: Web, p. 41

JOURNEYS DIGITAL *Powered by DESTINATION Reading*

For Students

- Student eBook
- Comprehension Expedition CD-ROM
- Leveled Readers Online
- WriteSmart CD-ROM

For Teachers

- Online TE and Focus Wall
- Online Assessment System
- Teacher One-Stop
- Destination Reading Instruction

Intervention

STRATEGIC INTERVENTION: TIER II

Use these materials to provide additional targeted instruction for students who need Tier II strategic intervention.

Supports the Student Book selections

Interactive Work-text for Skills Support

Write-In Reader:
Conquering the Mighty Colorado

- Engaging selection connects to main topic.
- Reinforces this week's target vocabulary and comprehension skill and strategy.
- Opportunities for student interaction on each page.

Assessment

Progress monitoring every two weeks.

For this week's Strategic Intervention lessons, see Teacher's Edition pages S42–S51.

INTENSIVE INTERVENTION: TIER III

- The materials in the Literacy Tool Kit help you provide a different approach for students who need Tier III intensive intervention.
- Interactive lessons provide focused instruction in key reading skills, targeted at students' specific needs.
- Lesson cards are convenient for small-group or individual instruction.
- Blackline masters provide additional practice.
- A leveled book accompanies each lesson to give students opportunities for additional reading and skill application.
- Assessments for each lesson help you evaluate the effectiveness of the intervention.

Lessons provide support for

- Phonics and Word Study Skills
- Vocabulary
- Comprehension Skills and Literary Genres
- Fluency

ELL English Language Learners

SCAFFOLDED SUPPORT

Use these materials to ensure the students acquire social and academic language proficiency.

JOURNEYS DIGITAL — Powered by DESTINATIONReading®
• Leveled Readers Online
• Picture Card Bank Online

Language Support Card

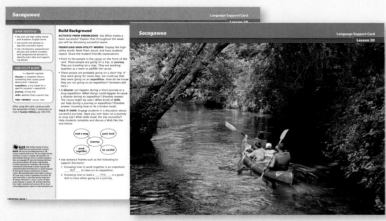

• Builds background for the main topic and promotes oral language.
• Develops high-utility vocabulary and academic language.

Leveled Reader

• Sheltered text connects to the main selection's topic, vocabulary, skill, and strategy.

Scaffolded Support

ELL ENGLISH LANGUAGE LEARNERS

Scaffold

Beginning Use the *Vocabulary in Context Cards* to ask students simple questions and describe in familiar terms the photograph on each card. Have students say each word as you hold up the card.

Intermediate Use gestures, visuals, or simplified language to explain the words *route*, *pack*, and *journey*. Have students use each word in a sentence.

Advanced Have students complete sentence frames to confirm understanding of the important ideas in the selection such as *It is important to have enough __ when taking a long trip, or__*.

Advanced High Have students work in groups to discuss why a trip to an unfamiliar place might be scary or dangerous. Have students use as many Vocabulary words as possible in their discussion.

See ELL Lesson 20, p. E42–E51, for scaffolded support.

• Notes throughout the Teacher's Edition scaffold instruction to each language proficiency level.

Vocabulary in Context Cards 191–200

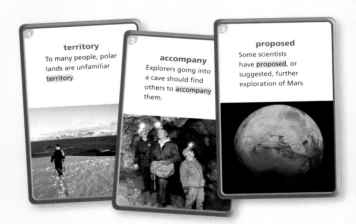

• Provide visual support and additional practice for Target Vocabulary words.

For this week's English Language Learners lessons, see Teacher's Edition, pages E42–E51.

Weekly Plan

	Day 1	Day 2
Oral Language Listening Comprehension	**Teacher Read Aloud** "Race Against Death," T300–T301 ☑ Target Vocabulary, T301	**Turn and Talk**, T307
Vocabulary Comprehension Skills and Strategies **Reading**	☑ **Comprehension** Preview the Target Skill, T301 ☑ **Introduce Vocabulary** Vocabulary in Context, T302–T303 **Develop Background** ☑ Target Vocabulary, T304–T305	**Introduce Comprehension** ☑ Main Idea and Details, T306–T307 Visualize, T306–T307 **Read "Sacagawea,"** T308–T322 Focus on Genre, T308 Stop and Think, T313, T315, T317
Cross-Curricular Connections Fluency Decoding	☑ **Fluency** Model Phrasing: Punctuation, T300	☑ **Fluency** Teach Phrasing: Punctuation, T330
Spelling Grammar Writing	☑ **Spelling** Words with VCCV Pattern: Pretest, T336 ☑ **Grammar** Daily Proofreading Practice, T338 Teach Abbreviations for People and Places, T338 ☑ **Write to Narrate: Write a Personal Narrative** Draft, T342	☑ **Spelling** Words with VCCV Pattern: Word Sort, T336 ☑ **Grammar** Daily Proofreading Practice, T339 Teach Mailing Abbreviations, T339 ☑ **Write to Narrate: Write a Personal Narrative** Draft, T343
Writing Prompt	*Describe ways you can communicate with someone other than by speaking.*	*Write about a time when teamwork was important to the success of a project.*

Whole Group

Whole Group Language Arts

COMMON CORE

Correlations

Teacher Read Aloud RF.4.4a
Introduce Vocabulary RI.4.4, L.4.6
Develop Background RI.4.4, L.4.6
Fluency RF.4.4a
Spelling L.4.2d
Write to Narrate W.4.3a, W.4.3b, W.4.4, W.4.5

Turn and Talk RI.4.1, RI.4.2
Introduce Comprehension RI.4.1, RI.4.2, RI.4.3
Read RI.4.1, RI.4.2, RI.4.3, RI.4.4, RI.4.5, RI.4.10, RF.4.4a
Fluency RF.4.4a
Spelling L.4.2d
Write to Narrate W.4.3a, W.4.3b, W.4.4, W.4.5

Suggestions for Small Groups (See pp. T354–T355.)
Suggestions for Intervention (See pp. S42–S51.)
Suggestions for English Language Learners (See pp. E42–E51.)

JOURNEYS DIGITAL Powered by DESTINATIONReading
Teacher One-Stop: Lesson Planning

Day 3

Turn and Talk, T323
Oral Language, T323

Read "Sacagawea," T308–T322
Develop Comprehension, T310, T312, T314, T316, T318, T320, T322
☑ **Target Vocabulary**
"Sacagawea," T310, T312, T314, T316, T318
Your Turn, T323
Deepen Comprehension
☑ Main Idea and Details, T328–T329

Cross-Curricular Connection
Social Studies, T311
☑ **Fluency**
Practice Phrasing: Punctuation, T321
Decoding
☑ VCCV Pattern and Word Parts, T331

☑ **Spelling**
Words with VCCV Pattern: Word Families, T337
☑ **Grammar**
Daily Proofreading Practice, T339
Teach Abbreviations for Time and Measurements, T339
☑ **Write to Narrate: Write a Personal Narrative**
Draft, T343

Write a journal entry describing why Sacagawea was so important to the team.

Turn and Talk SL.4.1a
Oral Language SL.4.1a
Read RI.4.1, RI.4.2, RI.4.3, RI.4.4, RI.4.5, RI.4.10, RF.4.4a
Deepen Comprehension RI.4.2
Cross-Curricular Connection RI.4.10
Fluency RF.4.4a
Decoding RF.4.3a
Spelling L.4.2d
Write to Narrate W.4.3a, W.4.3b, W.4.4, W.4.5

Day 4

Text to World, T327

Read "Native American Nature Poetry," T324–T326
Connect to Poetry, T324
Target Vocabulary Review, T325
Weekly Internet Challenge, T326
Making Connections, T327
☑ **Vocabulary Strategies**
Compound Words, T332–T333

☑ **Fluency**
Practice Phrasing: Punctuation, T325

☑ **Spelling**
Words with VCCV Pattern: Connect to Writing, T337
☑ **Grammar: Abbreviations**
Daily Proofreading Practice, T340
Review Abbreviations, T340
☑ **Write to Narrate: Write a Personal Narrative**
Revise, T344

Write a short poem that imitates a sound heard only at night.

Text to World W.4.7, W.4.8, W.4.10
Read RL.4.5, RF.4.4a, W.4.8
Making Connections W.4.7, W.4.8, W.4.10
Vocabulary Strategies RF.4.3a
Fluency RF.4.4a
Spelling L.4.2d
Write to Narrate W.4.3a, W.4.3b, W.4.3d, W.4.4, W.4.5

Day 5

Listening and Speaking, T335

Connect and Extend, T334–T335
Read to Connect, T334
Independent Reading, T334
Extend Through Research, T335

☑ **Fluency**
Progress Monitoring, T347

☑ **Spelling**
Words with VCCV Pattern: Assess, T337
☑ **Grammar**
Daily Proofreading Practice, T340
Connect Grammar to Writing, T340–T341
☑ **Write to Narrate: Write a Personal Narrative**
Revise, Edit, and Publish, T344

Compare and contrast Sacagawea and Charlotte Parkhurst.

Listening and Speaking SL.4.1a, SL.4.1b, SL.4.1c, SL.4.1d
Connect and Extend W.4.8, SL.4.1a, SL.4.1b, SL.4.1c, SL.4.1d
Fluency RF.4.4a
Spelling L.4.2d
Write to Narrate W.4.3a, W.4.3b, W.4.3d, W.4.4, W.4.5

Your Skills for the Week

☑ **Vocabulary**
Target Vocabulary Strategies: Compound Words

☑ **Comprehension**
Main Idea and Details
Visualize

☑ **Decoding**
VCCV Pattern and Word Parts

☑ **Fluency**
Phrasing: Punctuation

☑ **Language Arts**
Spelling
Grammar
Writing

Extending the Common Core State Standards

Read RL.4.1, RL.4.2, RL.4.10
Comprehension RL.4.9, W.4.9a
Comprehension RL.4.9, W.4.9a
Vocabulary RL.4.4, L.4.4c
Vocabulary L.4.5b
Grammar L.4.1d
Writing W.4.3e, W.4.4, W.4.5, W.4.10

Weekly Leveled Readers

Differentiated Support for This Week's Targets

✓ **TARGET SKILL**

Main Ideas and Details

✓ **TARGET STRATEGY**

Visualize

✓ **TARGET VOCABULARY**

territory	supplies
accompany	route
proposed	corps
interpreter	clumsy
duty	landmark

Additional Tools

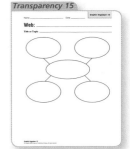

Vocabulary in Context Cards

Comprehension Tool:
Graphic Organizer
Transparency 15

❓ Essential Question

What makes a team successful?

Vocabulary Reader

Level Q

Build Target Vocabulary

• Introduce the Target Vocabulary in context and build comprehension using the Target Strategy.

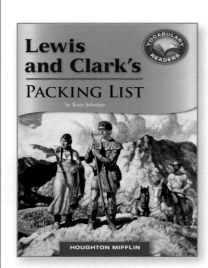

Vocabulary Reader

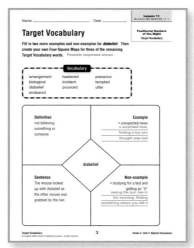

Blackline Master 20.1

Intervention

Scaffolded Support

• Provide extra support in applying the Target Vocabulary, Target Skill, and Target Strategy in context.

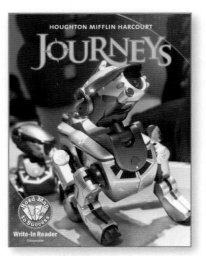

Write-In Reader

For Vocabulary Reader Lesson Plans, see Small Group pages T356–T357.

Leveled Readers

Struggling Readers

 Level O

Objective: Use main ideas and details and the visualize strategy to read *John Wesley Powell*

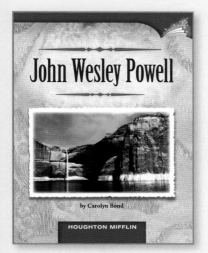

Blackline Master 20.3

On Level

Level R

Objective: Use main ideas and details and the visualize strategy to read *Writer from the Prairie*

Blackline Master 20.4

Advanced

Level U

Objective: Use main ideas and details and the visualize strategy to read *Chief Washakie*

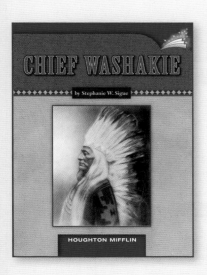

Blackline Master 20.5

English Language Learners

Level R

Objective: Use main ideas and details and the visualize strategy to read *Laura Ingalls Wilder*

Blackline Master 20.6

 For Leveled Reader Lesson Plans, see Small Group pages T360–T363.

Ready-Made Work Stations

Manage Independent Activities

Use the Ready-Made Work Stations to establish a consistent routine for students working independently. Each station contains three activities. Students who experience success with the *Get Started!* activity move on to the *Reach Higher!* and *Challenge Yourself!* activities, as time permits.

Comprehension and Fluency

Materials
- **Student Book**
- Reading Log
- **Audiotext CD**
- CD player/headphones
- stopwatch
- pencil or pen

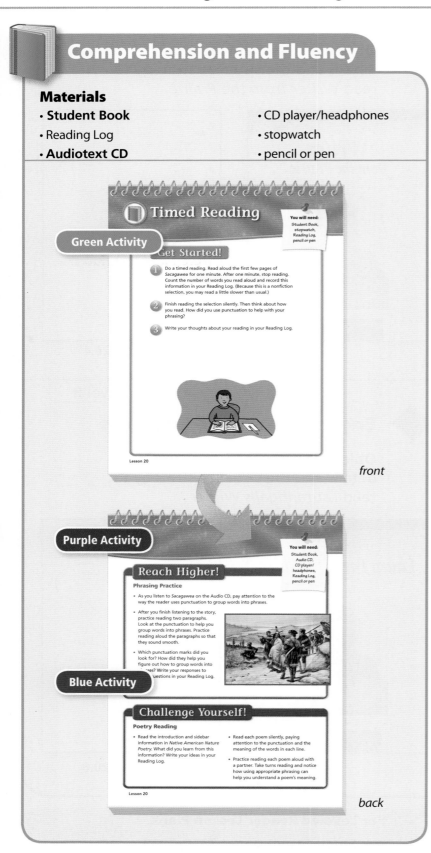

Word Study

Materials
- paper
- pencil or pen

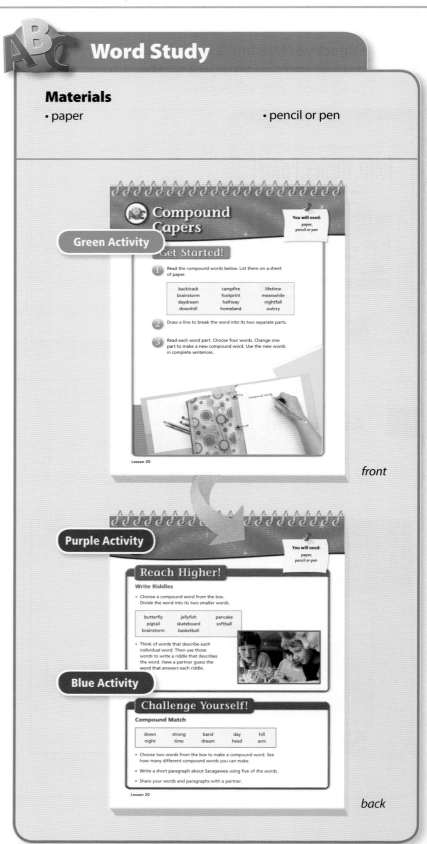

Think and Write

Materials
- computer with Internet access
- maps
- paper
- pencil or pen

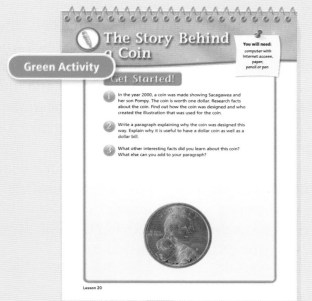

The Story Behind a Coin

Green Activity

You will need: computer with Internet access, paper, pencil or pen

Get Started!

1. In the year 2000, a coin was made showing Sacagawea and her son Pompy. The coin is worth one dollar. Research facts about the coin. Find out how the coin was designed and who created the illustration that was used for the coin.

2. Write a paragraph explaining why the coin was designed this way. Explain why it is useful to have a dollar coin as well as a dollar bill.

3. What other interesting facts did you learn about this coin? What else can you add to your paragraph?

Lesson 20

front

Purple Activity

You will need: maps, computer with Internet access, paper, pencil or pen

Reach Higher!

Write Directions

- Think of a park, zoo, museum, or other interesting place that you have visited. Find and study a map of the attraction. Then write directions to help someone get from the front gate to a particular place within the attraction. Choose a place you especially liked, or one you think other visitors might like to see.

- Share your directions with another student. If possible, have your partner try to find his or her way, using the map from which you wrote the directions.

Blue Activity

Challenge Yourself!

Computer Exploration

- Do a search on the Internet for a state or national park in your own state. Choose a place you would like to explore.

- Take notes about the place that you chose, including its location within the park. Give information about the kinds of plants and animals you might find there, trails that you can hike or walk, and special projects/classes or exhibits within your area.

- Write a description of the place you explored. You may include photographs you found on the Internet. Share your information with the class.

Lesson 20

back

Journeys DIGITAL — Powered by **DESTINATION**Reading®

Independent Activities

Have students complete these activities at a computer center or a center with an audio CD player.

LAUNCH > ## Comprehension and Grammar Activities
- Practice and apply this week's skills.

LAUNCH > ## Student eBook
- Read and listen to this week's selections and skill lessons.

LAUNCH > ## WriteSmart CD-ROM
- Review student versions of this week's writing model.

LAUNCH > ## Audiotext CD
- Listen to books or selections on CD.

Single Log In

Teacher Read Aloud

SHARE OBJECTIVES

- Listen to fluent reading.
- Listen for main idea and supporting details.
- Listen to learn the Target Vocabulary words.

Model Fluency

Phrasing: Punctuation Explain that when good readers read aloud, they group words into phrases and pause naturally at punctuation marks.

- Display **Projectable 20.1.** As you read each sentence, model how to pause at the end of each phrase and at the end of sentences.

- Point out that commas and end punctuation help show where students should pause when reading aloud.

- Reread the sentences together with students, grouping the words together in phrases and pausing at the end of each phrase.

Race Against Death

In 1925, the only doctor in the small city of Nome, Alaska, sent a desperate telegram through the U.S. Army Signal **Corps**: *"An epidemic of diphtheria is almost inevitable here…. I am in urgent need of one million units of diphtheria antitoxin…."* No one needed an **interpreter** to understand the danger. Diphtheria was a deadly, fast-spreading disease. Several children had already died, and the clock was ticking. If the doctor didn't get the antitoxin, or medicine, thousands of people in Nome and in surrounding villages would die.

1 **2** But it was January and Nome was ice-bound. A blizzard was brewing, and the only pilot who could safely fly in dangerous weather was away on a trip. Only one form of transportation was left: the dog sled. In 1925, mushers, the drivers of dog sleds, and their sled dogs were the ones who brought mail and **supplies** to Nome and other remote parts of Alaska. Most of them were Native Athabascans and Inuits, and they were the best in the **territory**. But the nearest medicine was almost 700 miles away, and it would take a musher 25 days to get it to Nome.

Then, someone **proposed** an idea: What about a relay? If each musher took a different leg of the journey and handed off the medicine to the next musher, could they make it? Believing it was their **duty** to try, a team of 20 mushers quickly organized a race against death.

Projectable 20.1

The race began in the town of Nenana where the first musher took the medicine and sped along the frozen Tanana River to the Yukon. Every village along the way offered its best team and driver. When the doctor in Nome reported more cases of diphtheria, a reporter who lived there said, "All hope is in the dogs and their heroic drivers."

With no one but their dogs to **accompany** them, each musher drove on. The **route** took them over mountains, through forests, and across the shifting ice of Norton Sound. When the blizzard hit, finding a **landmark** in the thick, swirling snow was almost impossible. One driver's team got tangled up with a reindeer. Another's hands were so **clumsy** with frostbite he could barely pass the medicine to the next driver. Several dogs died. But the mushers pushed on. And at 5:30 in the morning on February 2, the last musher and his dogs arrived in the waiting city of Nome. **3**

Together, the dedicated teams covered the distance in less than 6 days, delivering life-saving medicine to an ice-bound city, and winning the race against death.

Listening Comprehension

Preview the Target Skill

Read aloud the passage, using appropriate phrasing determined by punctuation. Then ask the following questions.

1 Main Ideas and Details

What is the main idea of the first paragraph, or what is it mostly about? The people of Nome, Alaska, were afraid a diphtheria epidemic would strike unless they received antitoxin before the disease spread.

2 Main Ideas and Details

List two details from the first paragraph that support the main idea. Sample answers: An urgent message went out through the Army Signal Corps; several children had already died; thousands of people were in danger.

3 Visualize

What words and phrases from the story help you understand the mushers' character traits? "Nome is ice-bound," "depth of winter," "heroic," and "blizzard is brewing" suggest the mushers were strong, brave, and determined people.

✓ Target Vocabulary

- Reread "Race Against Death" aloud.
- As you read, pause briefly to explain each highlighted vocabulary word.
- Discuss the meaning of each word as it is used in the Read Aloud.

corps a group

interpreter a person who translates different languages

supplies important things people need

territory land area

proposed suggested

duty job, responsibility

accompany go with

route path or way

landmark important place

clumsy awkward

☑ Introduce Vocabulary

SHARE OBJECTIVE

- Understand and use the Target Vocabulary words.

Teach

Display and discuss the **Vocabulary in Context Cards,** using the routine below. Direct students to **Student Book pp. 498–499.** See also **Instructional Routine 9.**

1 **Read and pronounce the word.** Read the word once alone, then together with students.

2 **Explain the word.** Read aloud the explanation under *What Does It Mean?*

3 **Discuss vocabulary in context.** Together, read aloud the sentence on the front of the card. Help students explain and use the word in new sentences.

4 **Engage with the word.** Ask and discuss the *Think About It* question with students.

Apply

Give partners or small groups one or two **Vocabulary in Context Cards.**

- Help students start the *Talk It Over* activity on the back of the card.
- Have students complete activities for all the cards during the week.

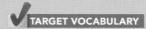

☑ TARGET VOCABULARY

territory
accompany
proposed
interpreter
duty
supplies
route
corps
clumsy
landmark

Vocabulary Reader   Context Cards

498

1 territory
To many people, polar lands are unfamiliar territory.

2 accompany
Explorers going into a cave should find others to accompany them.

3 proposed
Some scientists have proposed, or suggested, further exploration of Mars.

4 interpreter
An interpreter, or translator, is helpful when people use different languages.

ELL **ENGLISH LANGUAGE LEARNERS**

Scaffold

Beginning Use actions to demonstrate *accompany, interpreter,* and *clumsy.* Then call on volunteers to perform the action as you say each word aloud.

Advanced Have partners ask and answer questions about each Vocabulary word. For example, *Why is it your duty to help a friend in need?*

Intermediate Have students complete sentence frames for each Vocabulary word. For example, *If you are going on a hike, you should be sure to take _____, such as food and water, with you.* (supplies)

Advanced High Ask students questions to confirm their understanding. For example, *Why is it beneficial to plan your route before going on a car trip?*

See ELL Lesson 20, pp. E42–E51, for scaffolded support.

- Study each Context Card.
- Use context clues to determine the meanings of these words.

5 duty
Divers have a duty. They are required not to harm a marine area or its creatures.

6 supplies
Hikers need to carry supplies, such as food and water.

7 route
Backpackers should choose a safe route and stick to that path.

8 corps
On a research trip, every member of the corps, or team, must have valuable skills.

9 clumsy
A clumsy, or awkward, mistake can mean the loss of months of research.

10 landmark
Noting a landmark, or other recognizable object, makes the return trip easier.

499

Monitor Vocabulary

Are students able to understand and use Target Vocabulary words?

IF...	THEN...
students have difficulty understanding and using most of the Target Vocabulary words,	▶ use **Vocabulary in Context Cards** and differentiate the **Vocabulary Reader,** *Lewis and Clark's Packing List,* for Struggling Readers, p. T356. *See also Intervention Lesson 20, pp. S42–S51.*
students can understand and use most of the Target Vocabulary words,	▶ use **Vocabulary in Context Cards** and differentiate the **Vocabulary Reader,** *Lewis and Clark's Packing List,* for On Level Readers, p. T356.
students can understand and use all of the Target Vocabulary words,	▶ differentiate the **Vocabulary Reader,** *Lewis and Clark's Packing List,* for Advanced Readers, p. T357.

SMALL GROUP Options

Vocabulary Reader, pp. T356–T357
Group English Language Learners according to language proficiency.

VOCABULARY IN CONTEXT CARDS 191–200

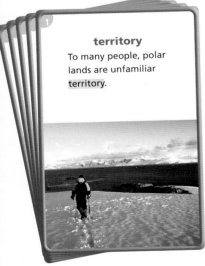

territory
To many people, polar lands are unfamiliar territory.

territory

What Does It Mean?
An area of land is a **territory**.
Spanish cognate: territorio

Think About It.
Would you like to explore **territory** that has never been explored? Why or why not?

Talk It Over.
Read each sentence to yourself. Then read aloud to a partner the sentences in which the word **territory** makes sense. Do you and your partner agree on the answers?

The _____ is on that shelf.
The state we live in was once Mexican _____
Did you _____ your homework yesterday?
My dog thinks our backyard is his _____.
Lewis and Clark explored the Northwest _____

front   back

Develop Background

 ENGLISH LANGUAGE LEARNERS

Scaffold

Beginning Use the *Vocabulary in Context Cards* to ask students simple questions and describe in familiar terms the photograph on each card. Have students say each word as you hold up the card.

Intermediate Use gestures, visuals, or simplified language to explain the words *route, pack,* and *journey*. Have students use each word in a sentence.

Advanced Have students complete sentence frames to confirm understanding of the important ideas in the selection such as, *It is important to have enough __ when taking a long trip, or __.*

Advanced High Have students work in groups to discuss why a trip to an unfamiliar place might be scary or dangerous. Have students use as many Vocabulary words as possible in their discussion.

See ELL Lesson 20, pp. E42–E51, for scaffolded support.

☑ Target Vocabulary

1 Teach/Model

- Use the map of Lewis and Clark's route on **Student Book p. 500** to explain that "Sacagawea" is about a woman who chose to **accompany** explorers on an exciting journey.
- Use **Vocabulary in Context Cards** to review the student-friendly explanations of each Target Vocabulary word.
- Have students silently read **Student Book p. 500**. Then read the passage aloud.

2 Guided Practice

Ask students the first item below and discuss their responses. Continue in this way until students have answered a question about each Target Vocabulary word.

1. If your friends **proposed** to buy some candy, would you do it? Why or why not?
2. What might you need to do to join a medical **corps**?
3. As a student, is it your **duty** to do your schoolwork? Explain.
4. Step by step, explain the **route** you take to school.
5. Describe the **territory** in your community or town.
6. Tell about a time when you were invited to **accompany** someone to a fun place.
7. If you were going on a trip to a forest in the northern United States, what **supplies** would you need?
8. When might someone need to use an **interpreter**? Explain.
9. Describe a time when you were **clumsy**. What happened?
10. Describe a **landmark** that you have seen either in person or in a book.

Background

✔ **TARGET VOCABULARY** **Exploring the West** In 1803 President Thomas Jefferson did something amazing. He doubled the size of the United States! France sold him a huge section of land west of the Mississippi River in a deal known as the Louisiana Purchase.

   Then Jefferson proposed that Captains Meriwether Lewis and William Clark lead an expedition called the Corps of Discovery. Their duty was to look for a route through this new territory by boat and to meet the Native Americans who lived there. Lewis and Clark knew the journey would be difficult. They found men to accompany them and gathered supplies. Soon they would need an interpreter to help them talk with the Native Americans and avoid clumsy communication errors.

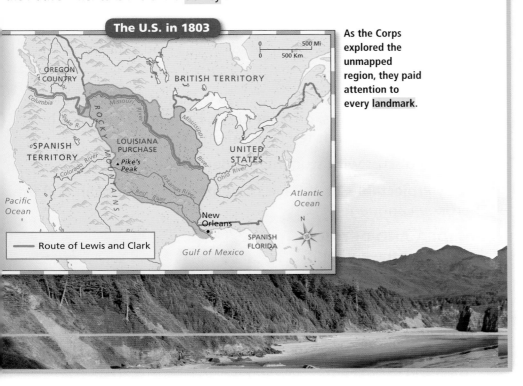

The U.S. in 1803

OREGON COUNTRY
BRITISH TERRITORY
SPANISH TERRITORY
LOUISIANA PURCHASE
Pike's Peak
UNITED STATES
Pacific Ocean
Atlantic Ocean
New Orleans
SPANISH FLORIDA
Gulf of Mexico
ROCKY MOUNTAINS
Columbia R.
Snake R.
Missouri River
Mississippi
Ohio River
Colorado River
Red River
Arkansas River
0 500 Mi
0 500 Km
N

—— Route of Lewis and Clark

As the Corps explored the unmapped region, they paid attention to every landmark.

3 | Apply

• Have partners take turns reading a paragraph on **Student Book p. 500** to one another.

• Tell partners to pause at and explain each highlighted vocabulary word as they read.

• Have each partner use one vocabulary word in a new sentence.

Introduce Comprehension

SHARE OBJECTIVES

- Identify main ideas and supporting details in informational text.
- Use details from the text to visualize

SKILL TRACE

Main Ideas and Details

Introduce	**T306–T307**, T328–T329
Differentiate	T358–T359
Reteach	T366
Review	Lesson 27
Test	Weekly Tests, Lesson 20

ELL ENGLISH LANGUAGE LEARNERS

Scaffold

Beginning Display the following sentences and read them aloud: *Ana is a good student. She scored well on the Science test.* Point out that the first sentence is the main idea and the second sentence is a detail that supports it.

Intermediate Say: *The class is writing a report about Lewis and Clark. They went to the library to find books on the topic.* Have students identify the main idea and the supporting detail.

Advanced Have students build on the Intermediate activity. Have partners add supporting details to the main idea.

Advanced High Have partners revisit a page in a nonfiction text they have already read. Have them identify the main idea and supporting details on the page.

See ELL Lesson 20, pp. E42–E51, for scaffolded support.

✔ Main Ideas and Details; Visualize

1 Teach/Model

AL *Academic Language*

main idea an important idea about the topic

supporting detail fact or example that tells more about a main idea

visualize create a mental picture of something read or heard

- Explain that writers usually organize information around the most important points, or **main ideas**. Each main idea will have **supporting details** that tell more about it.
- Read and discuss with students **Student Book p. 501.**
- Display **Projectable 20.2.** Have students read "Sequoyah and the Cherokee Language."

MAIN IDEA AND DETAILS
Point out that the author is telling an important idea about Sequoyah. The author provides details that support, or prove, the main idea.

- Explain that you will use the web to record the main idea and supporting details.

> **Think Aloud** *The title helps tell me what the passage is about. It then tells me that Sequoyah wanted to invent a way to write his language. I think that's the main idea. I'll write it in the web. Next, I will look for and add details that tell more about the main idea.*

VISUALIZE Explain that good readers **visualize** or create a picture in their mind of what is happening in a text as they read.

> **Think Aloud** *I can picture what would happen if you tried to have a symbol for each word in a language—that would be thousands of symbols. A symbol for each sound would be much easier.*

Projectable 20.2

Projectable 20.2

Sacagawea | Introduce Comprehension | Main Ideas and Details; Visualize

Main Ideas and Details; Visualize

Sequoyah and the Cherokee Language

When Sequoyah grew up in a Cherokee village he saw that the Cherokee did not have an alphabet. Sequoyah wanted to find a way to write the Cherokee spoken language.

Sequoyah tried to develop a writing system with a symbol for each Cherokee word. He found this was too hard. There would be thousands of symbols. While listening to the birds, Sequoyah realized many words have the same sounds. He decided to invent an alphabet for the Cherokee language, with a symbol for each sound in the Cherokee language. Sequoyah's finished alphabet had 86 symbols.

With the new written language the Cherokees wrote down their stories, and even wrote their own Constitution.

Main Ideas and Details Use a Web to record the main idea and details.

Detail: When Sequoyah grew up, there was no Cherokee alphabet.

Detail: Sequoyah found that a written symbol for each word did not work.

Main Idea: Sequoyah developed a written Cherokee language.

Detail: Sequoyah used a symbol for each sound.

Detail: The Cherokees wrote stories and a Constitution.

Visualize Use text details to make pictures in your mind.

Introduce Comprehension
© Houghton Mifflin Harcourt Publishing Company. All rights reserved.
Grade 4, Unit 4: Never Give Up!

Comprehension

✔ **TARGET SKILL** **Main Ideas and Details**

As you read "Sacagawea," figure out the most important ideas the author presents. Look for details that give facts or examples supporting those main ideas. Use a graphic organizer like this one to help you see the relationship between the main idea and supporting details and then summarize the most important ideas.

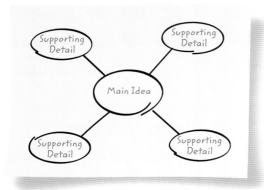

✔ **TARGET STRATEGY** **Visualize**

You can visualize various stages of Sacagawea's journey to help you identify the most important main ideas and supporting details of each stage. Descriptive details will help you create mental pictures that make the main ideas clearer.

JOURNEYS DIGITAL Powered by **DESTINATION**Reading®
Comprehension Activities: Lesson 20

501

2 Guided Practice

Guide students to copy and complete their own Webs for "Sequoyah and the Cherokee Language." Then review their Webs as a class.

3 Apply

Turn and Talk Have partners use their Webs to discuss how the supporting details can help them visualize the main idea.

Ask students to locate main ideas and supporting details in another text they have read recently. Have them record the main ideas and details in a Web and share with a partner.

Monitor Comprehension

Are students able to identify main ideas and supporting details?

IF...	THEN...
students have difficulty identifying main ideas and supporting details,	▶ **Differentiate Comprehension** for Struggling Readers, p. T358. *See also Intervention Lesson 20, pp. S42–S51.*
students can identify main ideas and supporting details,	▶ **Differentiate Comprehension** for On-Level Readers, p. T358.
students can accurately identify main ideas and supporting details,	▶ **Differentiate Comprehension** for Advanced Readers, p. T359.

Differentiate Comprehension: pp. T358–T359. *Group English Language Learners according to language proficiency. See also ELL Lesson 20, pp. E42–E51, for scaffolded support.*

Practice Book p. 229
See Grab-and-Go™ Resources for additional leveled practice.

Introduce the
Main Selection

 **TARGET SKILL**

MAIN IDEAS AND DETAILS Explain that as they read, students will use **Graphic Organizer 15: Web** to record and summarize:

- main ideas about Sacagawea's life

- facts, examples, and other details that support those main ideas

 **TARGET STRATEGY**

VISUALIZE Students will use **Graphic Organizer 15** to form mental images from text details about characters, settings, and events to better understand the author's meaning.

GENRE: Biography

- Read the genre information on **Student Book p. 502** with students.

- Share and discuss the **Genre Blackline Master: Biography, Autobiography.**

- Preview the selection and model identifying the characteristics of the genre.

Think Aloud *The title of this selection is a woman's name. The introduction mentions dates, places, and real people. Most of the illustrations show a woman. These are clues that this selection is a biography.*

- As you preview, ask students to identify other features of biography.

Main Selection

SACAGAWEA

✔ **TARGET VOCABULARY**

territory	supplies
accompany	route
proposed	corps
interpreter	clumsy
duty	landmark

✔ **TARGET SKILL**

Main Ideas and Details
Summarize a topic's key ideas and supporting details.

✔ **TARGET STRATEGY**

Visualize Use text details to form pictures in your mind of what you are reading.

GENRE

Biography tells about events in a person's life, written by another person.

Set a Purpose Before reading, set a purpose based on the genre and what you want to find out.

MEET THE AUTHOR
Lise Erdrich

Lise Erdrich is part Native American and a member of the Turtle Mountain band of Plains-Ojibway. She was inspired to become a writer by her grandfather, who was always writing or telling stories. Her sister Louise is also a writer of books for children and adults.

MEET THE ILLUSTRATOR
Julie Buffalohead

Part Ponca Indian, Julie Buffalohead researched traditional Native American art while in college. She often depicts Native American legends and traditions in her painting. She sometimes uses her painting as a way to explore important topics, such as prejudices some people may have about Native Americans.

502

Reading the Selection

	Pre-reading	Reading
Supported	**SELECTION SUMMARY** Use **Blackline Master 20.2** to help students identify main ideas. **AUDIOTEXT CD** Have students listen to the selection as they follow along in their books.	**AUTHOR'S PURPOSE** After reading the selection, discuss with students the author's purpose in explaining Sacagawea's role in the success of the expedition.
Independent	**PREVIEW** Have students look at the title and illustrations and discuss predictions and clues. Some students may read the story independently first.	**VISUALIZE** Pause after pp. 507, 511, and 513. Have students reread the page silently. Then have them tell in their own words how they visualize each scene.

SACAGAWEA

by Lise Erdrich   illustrated by Julie Buffalohead

Essential Question

What makes a team successful?

503

Blackline Master 20.2

? Essential Question

• Read aloud the **Essential Question** on **Student Book p. 503.** *What makes a team successful?*

• Tell students to think about this question as they read "Sacagawea."

Set Purpose

• Explain that good readers set a purpose for reading based on their preview of the selection and what they know about the genre, as well as what they want to learn by reading.

• Model setting a reading purpose.

Think Aloud *I have seen Sacagawea's face on the one-dollar coin, so she must be important to American history. I understand from looking at the illustrations and skimming the text that she and her husband traveled with the Lewis and Clark Corps of Discovery expedition. Since her name appears in the title, I will read to find out about her role in this journey and why she is important.*

• Have students share and record in their journals their reading purposes.

JOURNEYS DIGITAL **Powered by** DESTINATION**Reading**
Student eBook: Read and Listen

Develop Comprehension

Pause at the stopping points to ask students the following questions.

1 Infer Cause and Effect
Why do you think the members of the expedition were greeted with great excitement? The people of the villages had heard the party included a gigantic dog and a man with black skin. They may never have seen either before.

2 Draw Conclusions
How had the Corps of Discovery been traveling so far? by boat What does their need of horses tell you about the country ahead of them? There probably were no rivers they could use to travel. They would have to go by land.

3 ✔ **TARGET VOCABULARY**
If you were a leader of the Corps, why would you want an **interpreter**? *Expedition members did not speak the Shoshone language. I would want someone along who could ask the Shoshone for horses.*

4 Infer Character's Feelings
The introduction mentions an important event from Sacagawea's childhood. What happened to her? she was kidnapped How do you think she might feel about joining the Corps's journey west? She may have hope of seeing her family again.

It is the early 1800s. Teenaged Sacagawea (sak uh juh WEE uh) is a Shoshone (shoh SHOH nee) Indian living in the Knife River villages, in what is now North Dakota. When she was a child, Hidatsa (hee DAHT sah) Indians kidnapped her from her home in the Rocky Mountains. Since then, she has lived with them on the Great Plains, far from her family. Sacagawea has learned many things from the Hidatsa, including how to grow food. She is now married to a French Canadian fur trapper named Toussaint Charbonneau (too SAN shahr bohn OH).

Meanwhile, Captains Meriwether Lewis and William Clark have been preparing for the Corps (kohr) of Discovery. They and their team, which includes a large, black Newfoundland dog, are about to start a long journey of exploration, all the way to the Pacific Ocean.

On May 14, 1804, a crew of more than forty men set off against the Missouri River current in a keelboat and two large canoes called pirogues (pih ROHGZ). The Corps of Discovery was under way.

The expedition arrived at the Knife River villages at the end of October. They were greeted with great excitement. Sacagawea heard tales of a gigantic black dog that traveled with the explorers. She heard that a fierce and awesome "white man" with black skin was among the crew. This was York, the slave of Captain Clark.

The explorers built a fort and called it Fort Mandan. Then they settled in to spend the winter at the Knife River villages. Lewis and Clark soon learned they would need horses to cross the Rocky Mountains. The people of the villages told them they could get the horses from the Shoshone when the expedition reached the mountain passes.

504

ELL ENGLISH LANGUAGE LEARNERS

Scaffold

Beginning Guide students through the selection's illustrations and point out the characters by name. Have students repeat the names.	**Advanced** Have students summarize what they learned from the introduction and pp. 504–505.
Intermediate Write sentence frames such as the following for students to complete: *The Corps of Discovery was on an ___ to ____ the new land. ____ and her husband joined the ___.*	**Advanced High** Have students write three or four sentences to give a short summary of what they learned from the introduction and pp. 504–505.

See ELL Lesson 20, pp. E42–E51, for scaffolded support.

The wily Charbonneau proposed that they hire him as a guide and interpreter. He did not speak Shoshone, but Sacagawea did. He told her they would be joining the Corps of Discovery in the spring. This was exciting news, but Sacagawea's mind was on other matters. She was soon to become a mother.

3

4

505

CROSS-CURRICULAR CONNECTION

Social Studies

Have students turn to the map of the Lewis and Clark route and the Louisiana Purchase on **Student Book p. 500.** Point out the map key and explain that the Louisiana Purchase is shown in green and the route of the expedition is shown in red. Have students use their fingers to trace the route of the Lewis and Clark Corps of Discovery on the maps.

In what direction did the expedition travel? north and west *What mountain range did they have to cross to reach the Pacific Ocean?* the Rocky Mountains

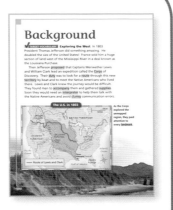

Develop Comprehension

5 **Draw Conclusions**

What conclusion can you draw about Sacagawea's importance to the expedition? She was very important to the expedition because of the many skills she had.

6 **Idioms**

What does "lost his wits" mean in the last paragraph of p. 506? He panicked and couldn't think what to do.

7 ✔ TARGET VOCABULARY

Describe a time when you needed **supplies** *to be successful.* Sample answers: I needed to bring food, a tent, and other supplies when I went camping; I needed a pencil, paper, and paints to complete an art project.

8 **Main Idea and Details**

The text says Sacagawea helped the expedition any way she could. What did she do? She gathered berries and dug for roots. She rescued the supplies when they fell overboard. She was the one who knew Shoshone language and could act as an interpreter.

In February, the time came for Sacagawea to have her baby. It was a long, difficult birth. Captain Lewis wanted to help her. He gave a crew member two rattlesnake rattles to crush and mix with water. Just a few minutes after drinking the mixture, Sacagawea gave birth to a baby boy. He was named Jean-Baptiste (zhawn bap TEEST) Charbonneau, but Captain Clark called him Pompy. Before long, the boy was known to everyone as Pomp.

On April 7, 1805, the Corps of Discovery started west, struggling upstream on the mighty, muddy Missouri in two pirogues and six smaller canoes. Pomp was not yet two months old. As Sacagawea walked along the riverbank, she carried Pomp on her back, in a cradleboard or wrapped up snug in her shawl.

Every member of the Corps of Discovery was hired for a special skill—hunter, blacksmith, woodsman, sailor. As an interpreter, Charbonneau was paid much more than the other crew members. But his skills as a sailor, guide, and outdoorsman were very poor. The only thing he did well was cook buffalo sausage.

Sacagawea did what she could to help the expedition, even though she was paid nothing. As she walked along the shore with Captain Clark, Sacagawea looked for plants to keep the crew healthy. She gathered berries or dug for wild artichoke roots with her digging stick. Her Shoshone childhood had prepared her well for this journey.

5 The Corps had been traveling less than two months when near disaster struck. Charbonneau was steering a boat through choppy waters when a sudden high wind tipped it sideways. He lost his wits and dropped the rudder while the boat filled with water. The expedition's valuables were spilling overboard! Charbonneau was ordered to right the boat or be shot. **6**

506

ELL **ENGLISH LANGUAGE LEARNERS**

Scaffold

Beginning For each question, accept one-word responses, expanding student responses into complete sentences. For example, if the answer for question 1 is "berries," expand the answer by saying, *Yes, Sacagawea found berries for food.* Have students repeat the expanded response.

Advanced Have students respond to the questions in complete sentences. Provide corrective feedback as needed.

Intermediate Provide part of a response for each question and have students complete it. Then have students repeat the complete response to confirm their understanding.

Advanced High Have students tell how they know the answer to each question based on details from the story.

See ELL Lesson 20, p. E42–E51 for scaffolded support.

Sacagawea stayed calm and rescued the captains' important things—journals, gunpowder, medicines, scientific instruments—every bundle she could reach. Without these supplies, the expedition could not have continued. **7**

A few days later, they came to a beautiful river. The grateful captains named it after Sacagawea. **8**

☑ **STOP AND THINK**
Main Ideas and Details Identify and summarize the main idea and supporting details in the last paragraph on page 506.

507

STOP AND THINK

☑ **TARGET SKILL**
Main Ideas and Details

- Remind students that recognizing details in a passage will help them understand the main idea.

- Have students complete the **Stop and Think** activity on p. 507.

- Display **Projectable 20.3a.**

- Model how to fill in the Web with the main idea and details from the last paragraph on p. 506.

- Guide students as they fill in their Webs. Then have volunteers use their Web to restate, in their own words, the main idea and details of the paragraph.

- If students have difficulty identifying the main idea and details, see **Comprehension Intervention** at left for extra support.

COMPREHENSION INTERVENTION

☑ **TARGET SKILL** Main Ideas and Details

SKILL SUPPORT Remind students that supporting details can help clarify a main idea. Discuss the main idea of the passage to this point:

- *Sacagawea, Charbonneau, and their infant had joined the Corps of Discovery as they headed up the Missouri to Shoshone territory.*

- *Sacagawea has proved very valuable to the expedition in many ways.*

Read aloud the last paragraph on p. 506. Tell students that the main idea of the paragraph is that the expedition had a near disaster. Have students name a detail from the paragraph that supports this idea. A high wind tipped the boat sideways. Explain that the other details in the paragraph support the main idea that this was a dangerous situation. Have students continue to add the details to their graphic organizers.

Projectable 20.3a

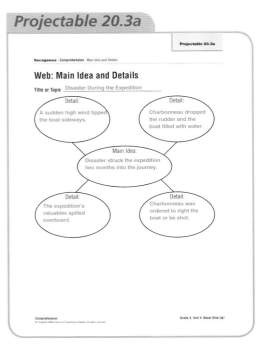

Main Selection (SB p. 507) • **T313**

Develop Comprehension

(9) Determine Cause and Effect

What caused the corps to decide to build wagons after entering mountain country? There was a waterfall and there was no way to get around it by boat.

(10) ✔ **TARGET VOCABULARY**

*Why might a **landmark** be important to people exploring an area unknown to them? Sample answer: The landmarks they had heard of, such as a waterfall or a river valley, would help them find their way.*

(11) Make Inferences

What can you infer from the fact that Sacagawea recognized several landmarks? Sample answer: She has been here before. This was probably the country where she had been born and where her people lived.

By June, the corps was entering mountain country. Soon they could hear the distant roaring sound of the Great Falls of the Missouri. Captain Lewis thought the waterfall was the grandest sight he had ever seen. But there was no way to get past it by boat. It would take the corps nearly a month to get around the Great Falls and the four waterfalls they found just beyond it.

(9) The crew built creaky, clumsy wagons to carry their boats and supplies. Battered by hail, rain, and wind, the men dragged the wagons over sharp rocks and prickly pear cactus that punctured their moccasins.

One day, a freak cloudburst caused a flash flood. Rocks, mud, and water came crashing down the canyon. Sacagawea held on to her son as tight as she could while Clark pushed and pulled them both to safety. Pomp's cradleboard, clothes, and bedding were swept away by the rushing water, but all three were unharmed.

By the middle of July, the corps was once again paddling up the Missouri. They reached a valley where three rivers came together, a place Sacagawea knew well. If she was upset to see it again, she did not show it. The captains learned how Sacagawea had been captured and her people killed.

(10) Sacagawea recognized a landmark that her people called the Beaver Head Mountain. She knew they must be nearing the summer camp of the Shoshone.

(11)

> **STOP AND THINK**
> **Author's Craft** In the first paragraph on this page is the word *roaring*. *Roar* is an example of **onomatopoeia**. That is, the sound and meaning of the word are similar. Find another example of onomatopoeia in the second paragraph on this page.

508

ELL ENGLISH LANGUAGE LEARNERS

Scaffold

Beginning Explain to students that sometimes two or more words are used together to have a specific meaning, though they are not one word. Point out the words *mountain country*, *prickly pear cactus*, and *flash flood* on p. 508. Read the sentences together and help students understand the meaning of the words.

Advanced Explain that some verbs are more than one word. Have students find the following on pp. 508–509: *get past, get around, held on, swept away.* Have students read the sentences containing the phrases. Help clarify the meaning of each phrase.

Intermediate Provide sentence frames such as the following for students to practice conjoined words: *Clark saved Sacagawea from the _____. The _____ had sharp needles.*

Advanced High Have students use the following phrasal verbs in oral sentences: *get past, get around, held on, swept away*, and *came together.*

See ELL Lesson 20, pp. E42–E51, for scaffolded support.

Nearly two weeks later, Sacagawea walked along the river, scanning the familiar territory. She spotted some men on horseback far ahead of them. Suddenly, Captain Clark saw Sacagawea dance up and down with happiness, sucking her fingers. He knew this sign meant that these were her people, the Shoshone.

An excited crowd greeted the explorers at the Shoshone camp. Although years had passed since Sacagawea had been captured, a Shoshone woman recognized her. She rushed up to Sacagawea and threw her arms around her.

509

STOP AND THINK
Author's Craft: Onomatopoeia

- Onomatopoeia is a literary device in which an author uses a word that sounds like a sound or noise made by a creature or object.

- Writers use onomatopoeia to help their readers form clear mental images of objects or events. A "roaring waterfall" suggests the sound a powerful waterfall makes.

- Model answering the Stop and Think question.

Think Aloud *On p. 508, the crew built* **creaky** *wagons to carry their supplies. Since we know the wagons were built quickly and were clumsy, they probably made squeaky sounds as they moved.* **Creaky** *and squeaky both describe sounds.* **Creaky** *must be an example of onomatopoeia.*

Develop Comprehension

12 ✔ TARGET VOCABULARY

How is a land **route** *different from a water* **route**? *Sample answer: A land route can often be chosen by the traveler, but a water route, such as a river, follows a natural course.*

13 **Main Idea and Details**

What details tell us that the journey over the Rocky Mountains was very difficult? Sample answers: The mountain paths were dangerous. The explorers' feet froze. They didn't have enough food.

14 **Draw Conclusions**

Why does the author point out that Sacagawea was allowed to vote? The author probably wants to stress Sacagawea's importance to the party and the high regard that everyone had for her. Women were not usually treated as equals at the time.

Lewis and Clark had discovered that their need for Shoshone horses was even greater than they thought. There was far more mountain country between the Missouri River and a water route to the Pacific than they expected. A grand council was called to discuss the matter. Sacagawea was to be one of the translators.

12

Interpreting for the men at the chief's council was a serious responsibility. Sacagawea wanted to do her best. But when she looked at the face of the Shoshone chief, she burst into tears. He was her brother, Cameahwait (kah mah WAY uht)! Sacagawea jumped up, threw her blanket over her brother, and wept.

Cameahwait was moved, too. But the council had to continue. Though tears kept flooding back, Sacagawea kept to her duty until the council ended.

510

Sacagawea spent the last days of August with her people. The time passed too quickly. Before long, the expedition had to mount Shoshone horses and continue across the mountains, leaving their boats behind.

The next part of their journey almost killed them. The mountain paths were narrow and dangerous, especially once it started to snow. Their feet froze, they didn't have enough to eat, and the mountains seemed without end. **(13)**

Finally, the expedition emerged on the Pacific side of the Rockies. There Nez Perce (nehz purs) Indians helped them make new boats and agreed to keep the horses in case they returned that way in the spring.

With great relief, the crew dropped their boats into the Clearwater River and let the current carry the expedition toward the ocean.

At the beginning of November, the explorers noticed a sound that could only be the crashing of waves. They had finally reached the Pacific Ocean!

The crew voted on where to make winter camp. Sacagawea was allowed to vote, too. She wanted to stay where she could find plenty of wapato roots for winter food. They set up camp not far from the ocean, in case a ship came to take them back home. But by now, people back east were sure the whole corps was long dead. No ship came for them. **(14)**

A cold rain soaked the crew as they cut logs and built Fort Clatsop. The hunters went to find game, while Sacagawea dug for wapato roots in the soggy ground.

> **STOP AND THINK**
> **Visualize** As Sacagawea reunites with the Shoshone on pages 509–510, which phrases help you visualize what happens?

511

STOP AND THINK

✔ **TARGET STRATEGY**
Visualize

Display and discuss the **Projectable S4.** Point out that forming pictures in your mind of the characters, settings, and events helps you understand what you read. Guide students to use text details to visualize of the events on pp. 509–510.

- *Which ideas on pages 509 and 510 help you form mental images of Sacagawea's first meeting with the Shoshone people?* Sacagawea dancing up and down; an excited crowd; a woman throwing her arms around Sacagawea; Sacagawea throwing her blanket over her brother and bursting into tears

- *How do these images help you picture the main idea of these pages?* They show that how Sacagawea was joyful upon returning to the people that she had not seen for many years.

- If students have difficulty visualizing, see **Comprehension Intervention** below for extra support.

COMPREHENSION INTERVENTION

✔ **TARGET STRATEGY** Visualize

STRATEGY SUPPORT Remind students that visualizing means using the author's words to form mental pictures. Model visualizing what has happened pp. 509–510: *When they were close to the village, Sacagawea recognized Shoshone riders. The text said she was jumping up and down with excitement. Then when she was asked to translate for the council, she realized the chief was her own brother. I can see her bursting into tears when she saw him. She ran up and threw her blanket over him.*

Read aloud the last paragraph on p. 511. Ask students what words or phrases in this paragraph help them to form mental pictures. cold rain, soaked, cut logs, soggy ground Have students use these mental images to describe what building Fort Clatsop was like for the Corps of Discovery. It was a time filled with hard work. They had to work in the rain and the cold. The ground was probably muddy.

Develop Comprehension

15 **Infer Character Motives**
Why might Sacagawea have given a gift to Captain Clark? Sample answers: She values and respects his leadership; she is grateful that he saved her and her son from the flood.

16 ✔ **TARGET VOCABULARY**
Why was it so important to Sacagawea that she **accompany** *Captain Clark on this journey? Sample answer: She wanted to accompany him because she did not want to travel so far without having the chance to see the ocean.*

17 **Predict Characters' Actions**
Based on text details and your reading so far, how might Sacagawea have been helpful to Captain Clark at the Pacific shore? Sample answers: She may have helped to arrange buying the blubber; she may have carried back some of the whale blubber.

15 Christmas Day was rainy and dreary, but the corps was determined to celebrate. The men fired a salute with their guns and sang. Sacagawea gave Captain Clark a fine gift of two dozen white weasel tails.

In early January, Clark heard from some Indians that a whale had washed up onshore. He decided to go to the ocean to get blubber for the crew to eat. They were tired of their diet of lean spoiled meat and fish.

512

ELL **ENGLISH LANGUAGE LEARNERS**

Scaffold

Beginning Using drawings and gestures, explain that some words describe, or tell more about nouns. For example, *large* whale, *little* boy, *rainy* day. Help students also to recognize the adjectives in sentences such as "Christmas Day was *rainy* and *dreary*."

Advanced Explain that some phrases, called *idioms*, have a specific meaning that is different than the meanings of the separate words. Guide students to find an example of an idiom on p. 512. fired a salute Clarify the meaning if necessary.

Intermediate Point out the phrase *two dozen white weasel tails*. Work with students to understand how the meaning is built by using several adjectives with a single noun: *weasel tails, white weasel tails, two dozen white-weasel tails.*

Advanced High Point out that writers often compare one thing to another to help readers "see" what they are describing. Have partners find an example of a simile on p. 513 and explain its meaning.

See ELL Lesson 20, pp. E42–E51, for scaffolded support.

Sacagawea gathered up her courage and insisted that she be allowed to accompany Clark. She hadn't traveled so far to leave without ever seeing the ocean! And she wanted to see that monstrous creature. The captains agreed to let her go. **16**

At last, Sacagawea saw the Pacific Ocean. She stood and stared at the great waters stretching endlessly in front of her. On the beach was the great skeleton of the whale. It was an amazing sight, nearly as long as twenty men lying end to end. The whale had been picked clean, but Clark was able to buy some blubber from the Indians to feed his men. **17**

513

✓ **TARGET STRATEGY**

Visualize

Model the Strategy

Remind students that creating mental images while reading helps readers gain a richer understanding and appreciation of what the author is describing.

- Discuss with students what it might be like to see the ocean for the first time. Have them share what someone might see, hear, smell, and feel.

- Have students use **Graphic Organizer 15** to show the main idea and supporting details on p. 513.

- Have students use the details on their Webs to visualize the scene. Ask: *What did Sacagawea see and hear? What might she have felt?*

- Have partners identify words and phrases on p. 513 that best help them visualize the scene on the beach. *Sample answers: the enormous creature, the great water stretching endlessly, the sound of waves lapping on the beach, and the sight of the whale's great skeleton, the smell of salty air*

Projectable 20.3b

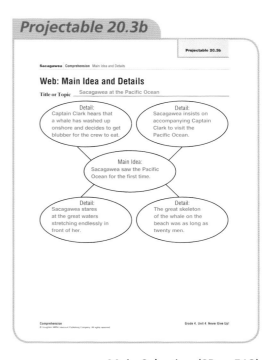

Develop Comprehension

18 Use Graphic Features

Look at the illustrations on pp. 514–515. Why do you think the author included these pieces of art to illustrate this part of the story? To show a reproduction of an actual page from Lewis' journal, including one of his drawings from the trip, and his actual carving on the rock. It makes us feel a little more connected to the experience.

19 Draw Conclusions

Why might the Corps of Discovery have divided into two groups at this point in their mission? Sample answer: They probably wanted to explore the Marias River, but didn't want to send the entire expedition to do it.

20 Using Context

The text says Sacagawea gazed at the earth lodges of the villages. What is a lodge? Sample answer: a kind of shelter

18 The crew stayed busy all winter, hunting, sewing moccasins, and making repairs on their equipment. Clark made maps, while Lewis worked on his report to President Jefferson.

Sacagawea watched over Pomp as he began to walk. Captain Clark called him "my little dancing boy." He had become very attached to Sacagawea and her son. When the time came, it would be hard for them to part.

Spring arrived, and it was time to go back the way they had come. In late March, the Corps of Discovery headed up the Columbia River to retrieve their horses from the Nez Perce.

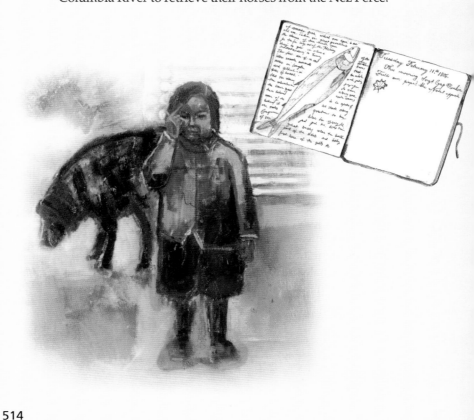

514

At a place called Travelers' Rest, the expedition divided into two groups. Sacagawea would help guide Clark's group south to the Yellowstone River. Lewis's group would head northeast to explore the Marias River. **19**

At the end of July, Clark's group came across an enormous rock tower on the banks of the Yellowstone. Clark named it Pompy's Tower in honor of his beloved little friend. In the side of the rock, he carved:

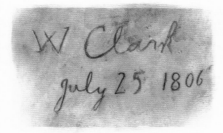

The two groups met up on August 12. Two days later, Sacagawea gazed once again upon the round earth lodges of the Knife River villages. She had been gone a year and four months. **20**

Lewis and Clark prepared to return to St. Louis. Before they left, Captain Clark came to talk to Sacagawea and Charbonneau. He offered to take Pomp back to St. Louis with him. He would see that the boy had a good education and would raise him as his own son.

515

Practice Fluency

Phrasing: Punctuation Read aloud the first paragraph on **Student Book p. 514** as students follow along.

- *After which words did you hear me pause?* winter, hunting, moccasins, equipment, maps, and Jefferson

- *What punctuation marks in the paragraph signal places to pause during reading?* commas and periods

- Tell students that in long sentences with no punctuation, good readers naturally group words into phrases and pause after each one.

- Have students echo-read the paragraph, taking care to pause after each comma and period.

The Fluency lesson on **Teacher Edition p. T330** provides further opportunities for modeling and practice in phrasing using punctuation.

? Essential Question

Discuss with students what made the Corps of Discovery successful. Ask: *How did the various members of the team contribute to the team's success?*

Develop Comprehension

㉑ Cause and Effect

Why didn't Sacagawea let Captain Clark take Pomp with him to St. Louis? He was not even two years old, she knew he still needed her, and she was not ready to give him up.

㉒ Understanding Characters

What do you think Sacagawea was thinking and feeling as she watched the Corps of Discovery set off?
Sample answer: She may have felt proud of her adventures and the way she contributed to the expedition's success. She probably also felt glad to be home. She may have felt a little sad at seeing her friends leave.

Sacagawea knew that Captain Clark would take good care of her child. But he was not even two years old. She couldn't let him go yet. Sacagawea and Charbonneau promised they would bring Pomp to visit Clark in a year or so.

On August 17, 1806, Sacagawea watched as the Corps of Discovery set off again down the Missouri River. Her journey of exploration was over, but the Corps of Discovery still had hundreds of miles to go.

516

Your Turn

Join the Corps

Write an Explanation Imagine that you had been invited to go on Lewis and Clark's expedition. What qualities or skills would you have brought to the team? What would you have enjoyed most about the trip? What would you have found most difficult? Write a paragraph explaining your ideas.

PERSONAL RESPONSE

Action!

Act Out a Scene Work in a small group. Imagine that you are actors starring in a movie about the Corps of Discovery. Choose a scene from the selection and decide who will play the roles in that scene. Include a narrator, if necessary. Collect some props that will help bring your scene to life. Practice the scene and perform it for the class.

SMALL GROUP

Team Players

 With a partner, discuss what made the Corps of Discovery team successful. What challenges did they face? How did they work together to meet these challenges? How important was Sacagawea as a member of this team? Use details from the selection to support your thoughts.

MAIN IDEAS AND DETAILS

517

Retelling Rubric

4	Excellent	Students provide a thorough retelling supported by several relevant examples from the text.
3	Good	Students provide an adequate retelling supported by relevant examples from the text.
2	Fair	Students provide an incomplete retelling supported by few to no examples from the text.
1	Unsatisfactory	Students provide an off-topic, retelling summary with no support from the text.

Your Turn

Have students complete the activities on page 517.

Join the Corps Have students write a list of qualities and skills that the expedition members needed to be successful. Then have students circle the qualities and skills that apply to them. Have students skim the text to find highlights and challenges that the Corps members faced. PERSONAL RESPONSE

Action! Have students scan the selection and choose a scene that has enough roles for the whole group. Remind them that the *narrator* is the person who helps tell the story to move the scene along. Help students come up with a list of props, encouraging them to draw or make props that they cannot find. SMALL GROUP

Team Players Have students make a quick list of the Corps of Discovery team members. Ask: *How did each team member contribute to the challenges the Corps faced? What skills did Sacagawea have that the rest of the Corps did not have?* MAIN IDEAS AND DETAILS

Oral Language Have small groups talk about Sacagawea's adventures. Students should use examples from the text to help them briefly retell the main events of Sacagawea's journey. Use the Retelling Rubric at the left to evaluate students' responses.

Connect to Poetry

PREVIEW THE POETRY

- Tell students that poetry uses the sounds and rhythms of words to create images and express feelings.

DISCUSS FREE VERSE

- Tell students that some poetry has rhyming words and an identifiable rhythm pattern, or meter.

- Tell students that **free verse** does not have rhyme, but sometimes has rhythm.

- Point out that the appeal of free verse poetry comes from its flow and rhythm.

- Define key terms. Tell students that free verse poetry can also use sensory language to create vivid mental pictures.

Connect to

Poetry

Native American
NATURE POETRY

✓ TARGET VOCABULARY

territory	supplies
accompany	route
proposed	corps
interpreter	clumsy
duty	landmark

GENRE

Poetry uses the sound and rhythm of words to suggest images and express feelings.

TEXT FOCUS

Free verse is poetry without a regular rhyme or regular rhythm. As you read "The Wind," note how the poem does not have rhyme or rhythm like other poems you have read. How do the line breaks help create the poem's feeling of wind movement?

Native American NATURE POETRY

Nature and a person's relationship to nature are two important themes in Native American poetry. A poem might include details that describe a common territory, such as a forest with wind rustling through the trees. It might personify an object, giving human characteristics to it. Then again, a poem might tell what is important in life.

518

ELL **ENGLISH LANGUAGE LEARNERS**

Scaffold

Beginning Read the poems aloud to students. Use the illustrations and gestures to help students understand the subject of each poem.

Advanced Have students echo-read the poems with you. Then have them tell in their own words what they think the poem is saying.

Intermediate Have students complete similes about the moon, the wind, or the day. For example, *The moon shines like a _____.*

Advanced High Have partners write their own simple free verse poem about something in nature.

See ELL Lesson 20, pp. E42–E51, for scaffolded support.

Here am I
Behold me **1**
It said as it rose,
I am the moon **2**
Behold me.
Teton Sioux

THE WIND

At night,
The wind keeps us awake,
Rustling through the trees.
We don't know how we'll get to sleep,
Until we do--
Dropping off as suddenly
As the wind dying down.
Crow

PRESERVING ORAL TRADITIONS

For centuries Native Americans passed their poems, songs, and stories orally from one generation to the next. People who did not speak Native American languages needed an interpreter to help them understand and write down these stories.

By the late 1800s, people could use cylinder recorders to record and play sounds. Compared to today's small electronic recorders, cylinder recorders were clumsy to use. Yet they preserved sounds exactly. In 1890 this recorder became important to scientist Jesse Fewkes, who was asked to accompany a corps of researchers to the southwestern United States. The cylinder recorder was among Fewkes's supplies. He used it to record and preserve Native American oral stories.

A cylinder recorder

519

Practice Fluency

Phrasing: Punctuation Have students listen as you read aloud the second poem on **Student Book p. 519.**

- Remind students that good readers pay attention to punctuation such as commas and periods. Explain that the line breaks in free verse often help them know where to pause.

- Have students practice reading the poems with a partner. Remind them to pay attention to the punctuation.

JOURNEYS DIGITAL **Powered by** DESTINATIONReading
Teacher One-Stop: Lesson Planning

TARGET VOCABULARY REVIEW

✔ **TARGET VOCABULARY** **Vocabulary in Context Cards—Word Clues**

Have students work in pairs to play a game with the cards. Have students turn all cards face up, and then take turns turning one over without their partner seeing the word. The first partner uses the word in a sentence, but leaves out the word. The second partner must supply the Vocabulary word to complete the sentence.

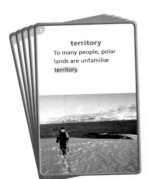

Develop Comprehension

1 **Identify Point of View**
Who is speaking in the poem at the top of p. 519? the moon

2 **Figurative Language**
Which words in this poem might make a reader think of a full, round moon? behold, rose, moon

3 **Main Idea and Details**
What do you think the poet of "I Think Over Again My Small Adventures" is saying? The most important thing is to be alive.

Interpret a Poem

- Tell students that people may have different interpretations of what a poem means, and that it may mean different things to different people.

- Explain that readers may enjoy a poem simply because of the sensory language. Point out examples of sensory language, such as *rustling through the trees* and *the light that fills the world*.

WRITE A POEM

- Have students work independently to write poems about something they think is beautiful using language that appeals to the senses. Have students share their poems with the class.

You, whose day it is,
Make it beautiful.
Get out your rainbow colors,
So it will be beautiful.

Nootka

I THINK OVER AGAIN MY SMALL ADVENTURES

I think over again my small adventures,
My fears,
Those small ones that seemed so big,
For all the vital things
I had to get and to reach;
And yet there is only one great thing,
The only thing,
To live to see the great day that dawns
And the light that fills the world.

3

*Anonymous
(North American Indian;
nineteenth century)*

Write a Poem About Beauty

The poem "You, whose day it is" suggests that it is one's duty to make the day beautiful. How would you make your day beautiful? Would you help someone you care about? Would you take a special route to visit a favorite landmark? Would you make a picture or admire a sunset? Have friends proposed ideas to you in the past? Write a poem that tells what you would do.

520

Weekly Internet Challenge

Synthesize Information

- Review Internet Strategy, Step 5: Synthesize

- Remind students they should use more than one website.

- Explain that they may find different information about the topic by using different websites.

- Point out to students that they should take notes, and then combine the information from the different sites.

INTERNET STRATEGY

1. **Plan a Search** by identifying what you are looking for and how to find it.

2. **Search and Predict** which sites will be worth exploring.

3. **Navigate** a site to see how to get around it and what it contains.

4. **Analyze and Evaluate** the quality and reliability of the information.

5. **Synthesize** the information from multiple sites.

Making Connections

 Text to Self

Write a Journal Entry We know details of the Corps of Discovery expedition because Lewis and Clark kept journals. Recall an interesting trip you have taken. Write a journal entry about it. Explain why the trip was important to you.

 Text to Text

Write a Poem Think about one of the natural sights that Sacagawea saw during her journey. Then write a poem about that sight. Include sensory details that help readers picture the scene. You may draw on the poems in "Native American Nature Poetry" for ideas.

 Text to World

Research Native Americans Choose a Native American group that lived in your state in the past. Find at least three interesting facts about this group, and list them on a poster, along with drawings or photographs that help explain your facts.

The Cherokee Nation in Georgia
-The Cherokee migrated from the area around the Great Lakes to the Southeast. Cherokees lived in log houses in Georgia.

521

"Native American Nature Poetry" Challenge

- Have students search the Internet to learn more about the Nootka. Decide if more keywords are needed to get a good number of results.

- Guide students to look at more than one website.

- Have students open the sites they find and take notes on what they learn about the Nootka.

- Tell students to synthesize the information from the websites to write a paragraph about the Nootka.

Making Connections

 Text to Self

Have students write a list of places they visited, jotting down sensory words to help them describe what they saw.

 Text to Text

To guide students' writing, have them name the five senses, and then make a list of sensory words or phrases that describe their subject.

 Text to World

Have students use the Internet or their Social Studies text to research Native American groups of your state. Suggest they show on a map where in the state these groups of people lived. Have students ask and answer questions about the posters, explaining and clarifying the text and illustrations presented.

Deepen Comprehension

SKILL TRACE

Main Idea and Details

Introduce	T306–T307, **T328–T329**
Differentiate	T358–T359
Reteach	T366
Review	Lesson 27
Test	Weekly Tests, Lesson 20

ELL ENGLISH LANGUAGE LEARNERS

Scaffold

Beginning Remind students that a main idea is the most important idea in a section of text. The details support the main idea.

Intermediate Go through the selection, stating main ideas as sentence frames and having students fill in key words.

Advanced Have students summarize the main ideas in the selection in their own words. Then have them give one detail to support each main idea.

Advanced High Have students write a short summary of the selection, telling the main ideas and details that support them.

See ELL Lesson 20, pp. E42–E51, for scaffolded support.

✔ Infer Main Ideas and Details

1 Teach/Model

AL *Academic Language*

main idea, **infer**, **supporting detail**

- Explain to students that an author usually presents several **main ideas** about a topic. **Supporting details** explain, prove, or give examples of the main ideas.

- Point out that authors do not always state the main ideas in the text. Readers must think carefully about the supporting details to **infer** the main idea.

- Tell students that paying attention to the main ideas and supporting details in a passage can help them find and remember important information about the topic.

- Display **Projectable 20.4.** and discuss **Deepen Comprehension Question 1.**

- Remind students that a Web can help them organize main ideas and details. Model finding details to infer the main idea to complete the Web.

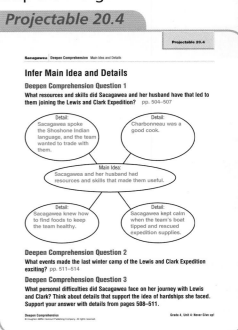

Projectable 20.4

> Think Aloud *The Corps of Discovery needed a guide and an interpreter. They had to get horses from the Shoshone. They needed to find food along the way. Charbonneau was a good cook. His wife, Sacagawea, spoke Shoshone. She also knew how to find food. Even though the author does not directly state it, I can infer from these details that Sacagawea and her husband were important to the expedition because they had useful skills and knowledge.*

2 Guided Practice

- Reread with students pp. 511–514 of "Sacagawea." Discuss **Deepen Comprehension Question 2** on **Projectable 20.4.** Have students draw a web and identify details that support the main idea: *The crew stayed busy all winter making camp and repairing equipment.* Use these prompts to guide students:

- *What did the crew do in camp? They built a fort, celebrated Christmas, and worked on repairs. Lewis kept a journal and Clark made maps.*

- *What did Captain Clark learn that interested him? A whale had washed up on the shore. He wanted to get blubber for the crew to eat.*

- *What did Sacagawea want to do? She wanted to go with them so she could see the ocean.*

- Guide students to complete a web for **Deepen Comprehension Question 2.** *Sample details: the crew built a fort (p. 511); the crew celebrated Christmas (p. 512); they visited the ocean and saw a whale; Clark bought blubber from Indians (p. 513)*

GUIDED DISCUSSION Ask students to identify and summarize main ideas and details from other parts of the selection. For example, ask students the following: *Why didn't a ship come for the expedition crew? People back east thought the crew was long dead.*

3 Apply

 Have students reread pp. 508–511 of "Sacagawea." Then have partners discuss and complete **Deepen Comprehension Question 3** on **Projectable 20.4.** Have students share their responses, retelling the events in sequence. Remind them that their summaries should maintain the meaning of the text.

✏️ **WRITE ABOUT READING** Have students write their responses to **Deepen Comprehension Question 3.** Ask volunteers to share their responses.

Monitor Comprehension

Are students able to infer main ideas and details in a selection?

IF...	THEN...
students have difficulty inferring main ideas and details,	▶ use the Leveled Reader for **Struggling Readers,** *John Wesley Powell,* p. T360.
students can infer one or more main idea, and supporting details,	▶ use the Leveled Reader for **On-Level Readers,** *Writer from the Prairie,* p. T361.
students can accurately infer main ideas and supporting details,	▶ use the Leveled Reader for **Advanced Readers,** *Chief Washakie,* p. T362.

Leveled Readers: pp. T360–T363
Use the Leveled Reader for **English Language Learners,** *Laura Ingalls Wilder,* p. T363.

Practice Book p. 230
See Grab-and-Go™ Resources for additional leveled practice.

Fluency

✔ Phrasing: Punctuation

1 Teach/Model

- Tell students that good readers pay attention to punctuation and natural grouping of words into phrases.

- Have students turn to "Sacagawea," **Student Book p. 506.** Help students find the last sentence in the first paragraph ("Before long, the boy…").

- Read the sentence rapidly in one breath. Then reread it in a more expressive voice, modeling how to pause after a comma. Discuss how you grouped words into meaningful phrases and paused slightly when you saw a comma.

2 Guided Practice

- Together, read aloud the last two paragraphs on **Student Book p. 506.**

- Work with students to read the passage using punctuation and other natural pauses to guide phrasing.

- See also **Instructional Routine Card 6: Echo Reading** for additional practice.

3 Apply

- Tell students that with practice, they can improve their phrasing and learn to read with fluency.

- Have partners take turns reading paragraphs in the selection aloud with natural phrasing, paying attention to punctuation. Listen in to monitor fluency. Allow each student to read a paragraph three or four times.

Decoding

 ## VCCV Pattern and Word Parts

SHARE OBJECTIVES
- Recognize words with the VCCV pattern.
- Use the VCCV pattern to decode longer words.

1 Teach/Model

ANALYZE WORDS WITH VCCV PATTERN Explain to students that when dividing a VCCV word that has an affix, they should first find the affix and separate it from the base word. Then they can divide the remaining syllables using what they know about VCCV words.

- Model how to divide *misfortune* into syllables. Write the word on the board and read it aloud with students. First, locate the prefix, *mis-*, and underline it. Then divide the word *fortune* between the consonants: for | tune.

- Remind students that an affix can be either a prefix or a suffix. Common prefixes include *non-, re-, un-, pre-,* and *dis-*. Common suffixes include *-ment, -tion, -age, -ant,* and *-less.*

2 Practice/Apply

DECODE WORDS WITH VCCV PATTERN AND WORD PARTS Write on the board the following words. Guide students to identify the affix and then break the words into parts. Model how to decode the first word step by step.

affection
af | fec | tion

collection
col | lec | tion

ar | range | ment
ar | range | ment

discontinue
dis | con | tin | ue

presuppose
pre | sup | pose

effortless
ef | fort | less

- Have partners work to decode the other words. Call on students to read the words and note common letter patterns and word parts, such as *-ment* in *arrangement* and *un-* in *unexpected.* Use **Projectable S1** as needed to guide instruction with the decoding strategy.

- Use **Corrective Feedback** if students need additional help.

Corrective Feedback

If students have trouble dividing words with the VCCV pattern that contain affixes, use the model below.

Correct the error. *Arrangement* is divided before the suffix and between the consonants *rr. ar | range | ment*

Model the correct way to decode the word. *This word has a VCCV pattern. However, it also has a suffix, -ment. You have to divide the word between the two consonants and before the suffix to decode the word.*

Guide students to decode the word again. *What is the first syllable?* (ar) *What is the second syllable?* (range) *What is the third syllable?* (ment)

Check students' understanding. *What is the word?* (arrangement)

Reinforce Have students repeat the process with the word *wilderness.*

Vocabulary Strategies

✓ Compound Words

1 Teach/Model

AL *Academic Language*

compound word a word made up of two shorter words

- Explain that a **compound word** is formed from two shorter words.

- Point out that a compound word can be written as a single word, as two words, or as two words connected by a hyphen.

- Tell students that to determine the meaning of a compound word, they should break the word into its two recognizable base words. If students understand the meaning of the base words individually, tell them to use context clues to determine the meaning of the compound word. Students can use a dictionary to confirm the meaning of the word.

- Point out that not all compound words can be understood by looking at the individual words, such as the word *butterfly*.

- Write the following sentence on the board: "A mountain is one kind of landmark." Say the sentence aloud with students. Repeat the word *landmark* with students.

- Display **Projectable S8**. Model using Steps 1 and 2 of the strategy to understand the meaning of *landmark*.

Think Aloud *In this sentence I see two short words that I know,* land *and* mark. Land *is part of the earth, and a* mark *is a spot or something noticeable. From the context of the sentence I learn that a mountain is a landmark. Using what I know about the base words* land *and* mark, *and the context of the sentence, a landmark must be a large or important feature on land.*

- **Ask:** *Does this meaning fit with the context of the sentence? Is a mountain one kind of large or important feature on land? (Yes, a mountain is a large land mass. This makes sense.)*

2 Guided Practice

- Display the top of **Projectable 20.5** and read aloud "Traveling the Lewis and Clark Historic Trail."

- Display the web at the bottom of **Projectable 20.5**.

- Have students identify the compound words from the passage. Circle or highlight the words and use them to complete the Web.

Projectable 20.5

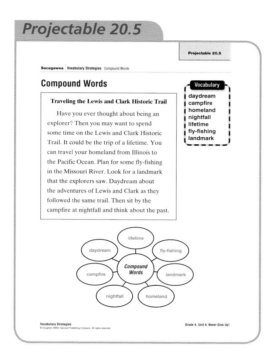

3 Apply

- For each compound word on the Projectable, have students apply steps 1 and 2 of the Vocabulary Strategy on **Projectable 20.5**.

- Have students look in a dictionary to locate the definition of any words that are still unfamiliar.

Monitor Vocabulary Strategies

Are students able to identify and use compound words?

IF...	THEN...
students have difficulty identifying and using compound words,	▶ **Differentiate Vocabulary Strategies** for Struggling Readers, p. T364. *See also Intervention Lesson 20, pp. S42–S51.*
students can identify and use some compound words,	▶ **Differentiate Vocabulary Strategies** for On-Level Readers, p. T364.
students can identify and use compound words,	▶ **Differentiate Vocabulary Strategies** for Advanced Readers, p. T365.

 Differentiate Vocabulary Strategies: pp. T364–T365
Group English Language Learners according to language proficiency.

Practice Book p. 231
See Grab-and-Go™ Resources for additional leveled practice.

Vocabulary Strategies • **T333**

Connect and Extend

- Make connections across texts.
- Read independently for a sustained period of time.
- Learn to categorize and sort information.
- Listen to interpret poetry.

"Sacagawea" "Native American Nature Poetry"

Vocabulary Reader

Struggling Readers *On-Level Readers*

Advanced Readers *English Language Learners*

Read to Connect

SHARE AND COMPARE TEXTS Have students compare and contrast this week's reading selections. Use the following prompts to guide the discussion.

- How is the idea of working well with others similar in this week's readings?

- Using evidence from this week's selections, explain how the different settings affected the people and their lives.

CONNECT TEXT TO WORLD Use this prompt to help deepen student thinking and discussion. Accept students' opinions, but encourage them to support their ideas with text details and other information from their reading.

- What comparisons can you draw about past explorations and explorations today, such as space exploration?

Independent Reading

BOOK TALK Have student pairs discuss their independent reading for the week. Tell them to refer to their Reading Log or journal and paraphrase what the reading was about. To focus students' discussions further, tell them to talk about one or more of the following:

- what the characters accomplished in their lives

- how the times in which they lived affected what they accomplished

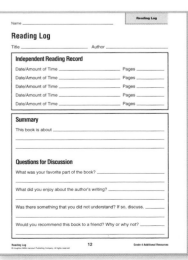

Reading Log

Extend Through Research

TAKING NOTES/SORTING EVIDENCE/CITING ONLINE SOURCES Remind students that they should take notes from at least three sources of information when they are writing a research report. They can then read through their notes to sort information and evidence into categories, eliminate unnecessary details, and narrow an answer to their research question. Tell students that they should double-check that their notes are written in their own words. If they have used direct quotes from their sources, remind them to properly credit their quotes and cite all sources.

- Ask partners to identify a research topic that interests them. Have them use at least three sources to research their topic. Tell them to take notes on what they find.

- Have partners review their notes. Tell them to discuss which note might give unnecessary or misleading details about the research topic, and why. Have students sort their notes into categories. Finally, have students trade notes to confirm that correct citations have been given for each source.

Listening and Speaking

INTERPRET POETRY Read aloud a poem to students and discuss with them what message they think the author is trying to convey. Have them consider the following questions:

- What is the tone of the poem?
- Why might the poet have written the poem?
- What words or images help make the author's point?

Have groups choose a favorite poem and discuss its meaning. Then have groups read aloud their poem to the class, and share their interpretations.

Have students use the Listening Log to record their personal interpretation of the poem and how well the poet made his or her purpose and point clear. Tell them to write down the specific words and images they enjoyed or thought worked best.

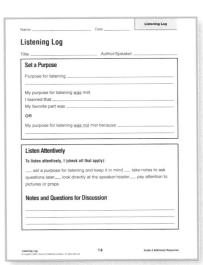

Listening Log

Spelling Words with VCCV Pattern

• Spell words with the VCCV pattern.

Spelling Words
Basic

million	thirty	soccer
collect	perfect	engine
lumber	attend	picture
pepper	⭐ canyon	survive
plastic	traffic	seldom
borrow	fortune	effort
support	⭐ danger	

Review ⭐ until, invite, happen, forget, letter

Challenge
occur, venture, challenge, rascal, splendid

⭐ Forms of these words appear in "Sacagawea."

ELL ENGLISH LANGUAGE LEARNERS

Preteach

Spanish Cognates

Write and discuss these Spanish cognates for Spanish-speaking students.

plastic	•	*plastico*
perfect	•	*perfecto*
canyon	•	*cañón*

Day 1

① TEACH THE PRINCIPLE

• Administer the **Pretest**. Use the Day 5 sentences.

• Write *support* and *traffic* on the board. Guide students to identify the VCCV pattern in each. *(u-p-p-o, a-f-f-i)* Point out that the two middle consonants are the same letter. Repeat with words in which the two consonants are different using the chart below.

VCCV (consonants the same)	s**upp**ort tr**aff**ic
VCCV (consonants different)	pl**ast**ic s**eld**om

② PRACTICE/APPLY

Guide students to identify the VCCV pattern in the remaining Spelling Words.

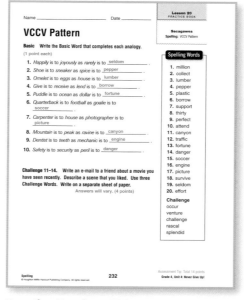

Practice Book p. 232

Day 2

① TEACH WORD SORT

• Set up two rows as shown. Model adding a Spelling Word to each row.

• Have students copy the chart. Guide students to write each Spelling Word where it belongs.

VCCV [consonants the same]	attend
VCCV [consonants different]	danger

② PRACTICE/APPLY

Have students add words from "Sacagawea."

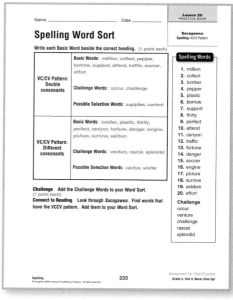

Practice Book p. 233

Day 3

❶ TEACH WORD FAMILIES

- **WRITE** *perfect*. Define it: "without faults or errors."

- **WRITE** *perfection*. Define it: "highest excellence."

- **ASK** *What is the connection between these words? Both contain p-e-r-f-e-c-t; something of the highest excellence does not have faults or errors.*

- With students, list and discuss more words related to *perfect*. sample answers: *perfectly, perfectionist, imperfect, perfectionism*

❷ PRACTICE/APPLY

- **WRITE** *collect*. Define it: "gather together."

- **WRITE** *collectible, collection, collective*. Have students look these words up in a dictionary or in an electronic resource.

- **ASK** *What is the connection among* collect, collectible, collection, *and* collective?

➤ Have students write their answers.

Day 4

❶ CONNECT TO WRITING

- Read and discuss the prompt below.

> ✏ **WRITE TO NARRATE**
> Write a personal narrative about how you worked with a team to achieve a goal. Use what you've learned from your readings this week.

❷ PRACTICE/APPLY

- Guide students as they plan and write their personal narratives.

- Remind students to proofread their writing.

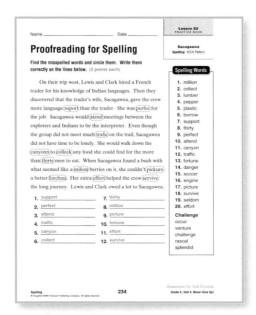

Practice Book p. 234

Day 5

ASSESS SPELLING

- Say each boldfaced word, read the sentence, and then repeat the word.

- Have students write the boldfaced word.

Basic

1. A **million** people came to the parade.
2. I will **collect** the reports.
3. He bought **lumber** to build a shed.
4. I like **pepper** on my eggs.
5. The radio has a **plastic** case.
6. May I **borrow** five dollars?
7. Columns **support** the roof.
8. This month has **thirty** days.
9. The girl made a **perfect** dive.
10. I plan to **attend** the party.
11. A **canyon** is a deep valley.
12. Our car is in heavy **traffic**.
13. His family **fortune** was gone.
14. There is **danger** in skating on thin ice.
15. My sister likes to play **soccer**.
16. The **engine** makes the car move.
17. I took a **picture** of a lion.
18. Plants need water to **survive**.
19. Maria is **seldom** ill.
20. Climbing a mountain takes great **effort**.

Grammar ✓ Abbreviations

SHARE OBJECTIVES

• Identify abbreviations.
• Use correct abbreviations in writing.

ELL **ENGLISH LANGUAGE LEARNERS**

Scaffold

Beginning

Use the following names to demonstrate abbreviations.

Doctor Maria Sanchez *Dr.*
Mister Kirk Chapman *Mr.*

Intermediate

Use the following address to demonstrate how to use abbreviations.

Doctor Maria Sanchez *Dr.*

The Sanchez Company *Co.*

109 Nelson Avenue *Ave.*

Chicago, Illinois *IL*

Advanced

Have students use abbreviations to write dates and names. Use the following as examples.

Sunday, January 10, 1999 *Sun., Jan.*

Mister Liam McDonald *Mr.*

Advanced High

Have student pairs take turns orally giving dates and writing the abbreviations for the dates.

See ELL Lesson 20, pp. E42–E51, for scaffolded support.

JOURNEYS DIGITAL **Powered by DESTINATIONReading®**
Grammar Activities: Lesson 20

Day 1 TEACH

DAILY PROOFREADING PRACTICE

As soon as I finished my book I went to the library for a knew one. *book,; new*

Projectable
20.6

1 **TEACH ABBREVIATIONS FOR PEOPLE AND PLACES**

• Display **Projectable 20.6**. Explain that an **abbreviation** is a short form of a word. Point out that most abbreviations begin with a capital letter and end with a period.

• Model identifying the abbreviations in the example: *Dr. Lewis Clark, 16 River Rd., Buckner, MO 64016*

Think Aloud *To identify the abbreviation I ask this Thinking Question:* **What parts of the address are shortened forms of words?** *Dr., Rd. and MO are all abbreviations in this address. The abbreviation Dr. is short for Doctor, Rd. is short for Road and MO is short for Missouri.*

2 **PRACTICE/APPLY**

• Complete items 1–8 on **Projectable 20.6** with students.

• Write the following groups of words on the board. Ask students to identify where abbreviations can be used.

2819 Cherrywood Lane Mister Jesse Madrid, Junior

Lane–Ln., Mister–Mr., Junior–Jr.

Practice Book p. 235

Day 2 TEACH

DAILY PROOFREADING PRACTICE
My doctors name is dr James. *doctor's; Dr.*

Projectable 20.7

① EXTEND MAILING ABBREVIATIONS

• Display **Projectable 20.7**. Point out that abbreviations are short forms of whole words. Explain how they are used in addresses to write street names and state names. Tell students that *floor, suite,* and *apartment* can be abbreviated.

• Model abbreviating the following sample address:
14 State Street
Apartment 304
Austin, Texas 78730

Think Aloud *To identify the abbreviation I ask these Thinking Questions:* **What parts of an address can I make shorter?** *Street, Apartment, Texas* **How can I shorten the whole word?** *St., Apt., TX*

Point out that both letters in the abbreviation of state names are capital letters, and no period is used.

② PRACTICE/APPLY

• Complete items 1–9 on **Projectable 20.7** with students.

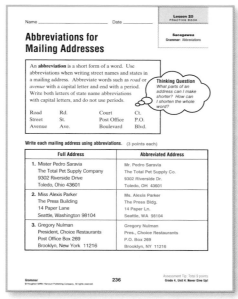

Practice Book p. 236

Day 3 TEACH

DAILY PROOFREADING PRACTICE
My mother lives in Santa Fe Nm. *Santa Fe, NM.*

Projectable 20.8

① TEACH ABBREVIATIONS FOR TIME AND MEASUREMENTS

• Display **Projectable 20.8**. Explain that abbreviations for days and months begin with a capital letter and end with a period. Point out that many abbreviations for measurements begin with a lower case letter.

• Model abbreviating the following example:
Tuesday, January 18, 1805
8 inches of snow in 2 hours

Think Aloud *To identify the abbreviation I ask these Thinking Questions:* **What parts can I make shorter?** *time: Tuesday, January; measurements: inches, hours* **How can I shorten the whole word?** *Tues., Jan., in., hr.*

② PRACTICE/APPLY

• Complete items 1–10 on **Projectable 20.8** with students.

• Have students write the days of the week and months of the year in a column. Then, have students write the abbreviation of each day and month in a second column.

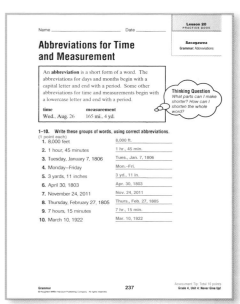

Practice Book p. 237

Abbreviations • **T339**

Day 4 REVIEW

DAILY PROOFREADING PRACTICE
my birthday is on jan 12. *My; Jan.*

❶ REVIEW ABBREVIATIONS

• Have students turn to **Student Book p. 522**. Read aloud the paragraph to review how to correctly use **abbreviations**. Discuss the examples in the chart. Then have students complete the Try This! activity.

❷ SPIRAL REVIEW

Irregular Verbs Review with students that an irregular verb is a verb that does not end with -*ed* to show past tense. Point out that students must memorize the spellings of irregular verbs.

• Ask students to say sentences with irregular verbs and write them on the board. Have the class point out the irregular verbs and tell their present-tense forms.

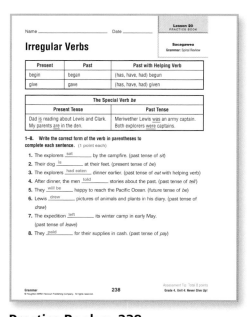

Practice Book p. 238

Day 5 CONNECT TO WRITING

DAILY PROOFREADING PRACTICE
I have an appointment with Dr Thompson on feb. 9. *Dr.; Feb.*

❶ CONNECT TO WRITING

• Explain that good writers use abbreviations when writing *titles, addresses, days, months,* and *measurements* in special kinds of writing.

❷ PRACTICE/APPLY

• Display the following name and address. Guide students to identify which words should be abbreviated and how to abbreviate them.

> **Captain Joan Ming** *Captain–Capt.*
>
> **1802 Castle Court** *Court–Ct.*
>
> **Arlington, Virginia 22201** *Virginia–VA*

• Write the following words on the board. Have students write the abbreviations for each word.

> **Road** *Rd.*   **March** *Mar.*
>
> **miles** *mi.*   **Wednesday** *Wed.*
>
> **inches** *in.*   **Boulevard** *Blvd.*

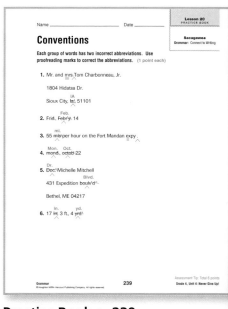

Practice Book p. 239

Grammar

What Is an Abbreviation? How Are Abbreviations Written? Some words have a shortened form called an **abbreviation**. An abbreviation stands for a whole word. Most abbreviations begin with a capital letter and end with a period. Use them only in special kinds of writing, such as addresses and lists.

Academic Language

abbreviation

Some Common Abbreviations			
Titles	Mr. → Mister Jr. → Junior	Capt. → Captain Dr. → Doctor	Mrs. → married woman Ms. → any woman
Addresses	Rd. → Road St. → Street	Ave. → Avenue Blvd. → Boulevard	Ct. → Court P.O. → Post Office
Months	Feb. → February	Aug. → August	Oct. → October
Days	Mon. → Monday	Wed. → Wednesday	Thurs. → Thursday
Measurements	in. → inch/inches	ft. → foot/feet	mi. → mile/miles

Try This! **Proofread the items below. On another sheet of paper, rewrite each group of words, using the correct abbreviations.**

❶ Andrew Perkins
438 Groat Avenue
Grapevine, TEX 76051

❷ 5280 feet = 1 mile

❸ Thursday, Feb'y 8, 2010

❹ Doctor Linda Cheung
4195 Buffalo Street
Chadron, Nebraska 69337

522

Conventions Good writers use abbreviations only in special kinds of writing, such as addresses and lists. When you use abbreviations, make sure you write them correctly.

Incorrect Abbreviations	Correct Abbreviations
Doct. James Sekiguchi The Bradley Comp 127 Saratoga Boul. Montgomery, Ala. 36104 Weds, Sep. 18 4 ft, 7 in	Dr. James Sekiguchi The Bradley Co. 127 Saratoga Blvd. Montgomery, AL 36104 Wed., Sept. 18 4 ft., 7 in.

Connect Grammar to Writing

As you edit your personal narrative, correct any errors in capitalization or punctuation that you discover. If you used any abbreviations, make sure you used proper capitalization and punctuation.

523

Try This!

- *Mr. Andrew Perkins*
  438 Groat Ave.
  Grapevine, TX 76051
- *5,280 ft = 1 mi.*
- *Thurs., Feb. 8, 2010*
- *Dr. Linda Cheung*
  4195 Buffalo St.
  Chadron, NE 69370

CONNECT GRAMMAR TO WRITING

- Have students turn to **Student Book p. 523** and read the page with them.
- Discuss with students the special kinds of writing where abbreviations are appropriate, such as addresses and lists.
- Tell students to use abbreviations with correct capitalization and punctuation as they revise their personal narratives.
- Review the Common Errors at the right with students.

COMMON ERRORS

Error: Jacksonville, Fl.

Correct: Jacksonville, FL

Error: 5 ft, 8 in

Correct: 5 ft., 8 in.

Error: PO Box 234

Correct: P.O. Box 234

Error: Cap. Bryant

Correct: Capt. Bryant

Write to Narrate ✔ Write a Personal Narrative

SHARE OBJECTIVES

- Write a personal narrative.
- Draft, revise, proofread, and edit a personal narrative.
- Publish final drafts.

Academic Language

personal narrative a narrative that tells about a true event in the writer's life

elaboration details that help clarify events in a narrative

 ENGLISH LANGUAGE LEARNERS

Scaffold

Beginning Write the following sentences on the board: *The camping trip was fun. The camping trip was fun because we all had fun together.* Point out that the second sentence added details to help the reader understand the writer's feelings.

Intermediate Work with students to make a list of the details that appear in a familiar story. Ask them to identify the details that are the most interesting and note who is speaking and what is being said.

Advanced Guide students to change verbs to show details. Tell them that instead of saying *Jason said*, they can use a more descriptive phrase such as, *Jason shouted*.

Advanced High Have partners take turns telling their story to each other before writing their drafts.

*See ELL Lesson 20, pp. E42–E51,
for scaffolded support.*

JOURNEYS DIGITAL | **Powered by** DESTINATIONReading·
WriteSmart CD-ROM

Day 1 DRAFT

❶ TEACH DRAFTING

- Tell students that they will be writing drafts of the personal narratives that they planned in Lesson 19. Discuss the following:

  > What Is a Personal Narrative?
  >
  > - It is a story about something that happened to the writer.
  > - It includes interesting details.
  > - It begins with a detail that catches the reader's attention.
  > - It shows the personal feelings of the writer.

- Explain that a good **personal narrative** begins in a way that draws readers in, making them want to find out what happens next.

- Read aloud the first paragraph on **Student Book p. 504.** Discuss how the author introduces the narrative. Ask: *What is the setting of the story? the Missouri River in 1804 What is happening at the beginning? A crew of 40 men set out on canoes. What line makes the reader want to continue reading? "The Corps of Discovery was under way."*

❷ PRACTICE/APPLY

- Have students use their completed charts from Lesson 19 to begin drafting their personal narratives.

- Remind students that their opening should include something that makes the reader want to continue reading.

LESSON	FORM	TRAIT
16	Descriptive Paragraph	Ideas
17	Friendly Letter	Voice
18	Narrative Composition	Word Choice
19	Prewrite: Personal Narrative	Organization
20	**Draft, Revise, Edit, Publish: Personal Narrative**	**Ideas**

Day 2 DRAFT

① INTRODUCE THE FOCUS TRAIT: IDEAS

- Remind students that personal narratives are organized by including important events and details in the order in which they happened.

- Explain that writers can use dates, months, or even other events to mark time in a narrative. Use this example to discuss how the author organized events in *Sacagawea*.

Connect to "Sacagawea"	
Instead of this...	**...the author wrote this.**
Then the corps headed up the Missouri.	"By the middle of July, the corps was once again paddling up the Missouri." (p. 508)

② PRACTICE/APPLY

- Read aloud on **Student Book p. 506.** Have students identify what details the writer used to indicate the passage of time. *The writer used the birth of Sacagawea's baby, dates, and the changing age of the baby to show when important events happened.*

- Have students continue drafting their personal narratives. Remind them to use important details that explain the order of events.

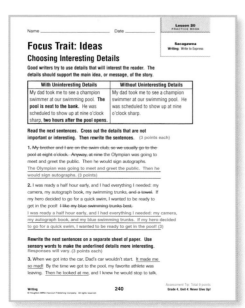

Practice Book p. 240

Day 3 DRAFT

① TEACH ELABORATION

- Explain that good writers use details and feelings to help clarify the events in their narratives. This is called **elaboration**.

- Read aloud the last paragraph on **Student Book p. 506.** Have students identify the details in this event. Discuss this sentence *"Charbonneau was ordered to right the boat or be shot." This tells about the feelings of the crew. It reveals that the crew was very upset at his mistake.*

- Point out that good details help to make events easier to understand.

② PRACTICE/APPLY

- Work with students to find places in their narratives where they can elaborate by adding more details or feelings.

- Read this sentence from **Student Book p. 508:** *"Captain Lewis thought the waterfall was the grandest sight he had ever seen."* Discuss how his feelings give more information about the waterfall for the reader.

- Have students review their completed story maps to identify places where they can add details.

- Have students complete the first drafts of their personal narratives.

Day 4 REVISE

1 TEACH/MODEL

- Remind students that their personal narratives should be organized in time order.

- Review these points:

- The beginning should grab readers' attention to make them want to continue reading.

- The narrative should show the writer's feelings.

- Explain that a good personal narrative includes details that clarify the events and keep the reader interested.

2 PRACTICE/APPLY

- Tell students to revise their drafts to include details that will keep their readers interested in the narrative.

- Remind them to make sure they have used elaboration to clarify events in their narratives for readers.

Day 5 EDIT AND PUBLISH

1 INTRODUCE THE STUDENT MODEL

- Read aloud the top of **Student Book p. 524**. Discuss the revisions made by the student writer. Ask: *What did the writer change? Why did he make these changes? The writer deleted when the teacher called on him and which project came in second. Those were not interesting details.*

2 PRACTICE/APPLY

- Display **Projectable 20.9**. Work with students to proofread the rest of the draft, including suggestions from students. Point out where details have been added to clarify events.

- Have students turn to **Student Book p. 525**. Have students read Steve's Final Copy and discuss the *Reading as a Writer* questions.

- **Proofreading** For proofreading support, have students use the **Proofreading Checklist Blackline Master**.

- **Publish** Tell students to create a final copy of their personal narratives. Provide the following publishing options:

1. **Dramatic Reading** Writers can give dramatic readings of their narratives.

2. **Booklet** Students can illustrate their stories and publish them in booklets.

3. **Classroom Literary Journal** Students can collect their narratives in a classroom literary journal.

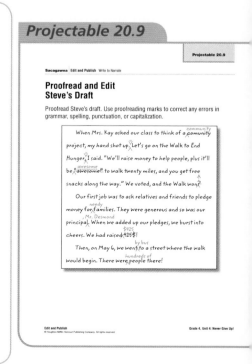

Projectable 20.9

Reading-Writing Workshop: Revise

Write to Narrate

☑ **Ideas** In "Sacagawea," the author does not tell every detail about the explorers' journey. Instead, she includes only the most interesting and important parts. When you revise your **personal narrative**, look at each detail. Is it important to your story? Is it interesting? Use the Writing Process Checklist below as you revise your writing.

Steve drafted his story about a class adventure. When he revised it, he took out some uninteresting details and made other changes too.

Writing Process Checklist

Prewrite

Draft

▶ Revise

☑ Did I begin with an attention-grabber?

☑ Did I include only interesting parts and tell them in order?

☑ Did I use vivid details and dialogue?

☑ Do my feelings come through?

☑ Are my sentences smooth and varied?

☑ Does my ending show how the events worked out?

Edit

Publish and Share

524

Revised Draft

When Mrs. Kay asked our class to think of a community project, my hand shot up. ~~Mrs. Kay called on me fifth.~~ "Let's go on the Walk to End Hunger," I said. "We'll raise money to help people, plus it'll be <u>awesome</u> to walk twenty miles. And you get free snacks along the way." We voted, and the Walk won! ~~A park clean-up came in second.~~

Final Copy

Our Walk to End Hunger
by Steve Jones

When Mrs. Kay asked our class to think of a community project, my hand shot up. "Let's go on the Walk to End Hunger," I said. "We'll raise money to help people, plus it'll be <u>awesome</u> to walk twenty miles, and you get free snacks along the way." We voted, and the Walk won!

Our first job was to ask relatives and friends to pledge money for needy families. They were generous and so was our principal, Mr. Desmond. When we added up our pledges, we burst into cheers. We had raised $425!

Then, on May 6, we went by bus to a street where the Walk would begin. Hundreds of people were there. We saw balloons, banners, and tables with juice and granola bars.

> I took out some unimportant details. I also made sure to use correct punctuation.

Reading as a Writer

How did Steve keep his story interesting? What parts of your story could you make more interesting?

525

Writing Traits Scoring Rubric

	Focus/Ideas	☑ Organization	Voice	☑ Word Choice	☑ Sentence Fluency	Conventions
4	Adheres to the topic, is interesting, has a sense of completeness. Ideas are well developed.	Ideas and details are clearly presented and well organized.	Connects with reader in a unique, personal way.	Includes vivid verbs, strong adjectives, specific nouns.	Includes a variety of complete sentences that flow smoothly, naturally.	Shows a strong command of grammar, spelling, capitalization, punctuation.
3	Mostly adheres to the topic, is somewhat interesting, has a sense of completeness. Ideas are adequately developed.	Ideas and details are mostly clear and generally organized.	Generally connects with reader in a way that is personal and sometimes unique.	Includes some vivid verbs, strong adjectives, specific nouns.	Includes some variety of mostly complete sentences. Some parts flow smoothly, naturally.	Shows a good command of grammar, spelling, capitalization, punctuation.
2	Does not always adhere to the topic, has some sense of completeness. Ideas are superficially developed.	Ideas and details are not always clear or organized. There is some wordiness or repetition.	Connects somewhat with reader. Sounds somewhat personal, but not unique.	Includes mostly simple nouns and verbs, and may have a few adjectives.	Includes mostly simple sentences, some of which are incomplete.	Some errors in grammar, spelling, capitalization, punctuation.
1	Does not adhere to the topic, has no sense of completeness. Ideas are vague.	Ideas and details are not organized. Wordiness or repetition hinders meaning.	Does not connect with reader. Does not sound personal or unique.	Includes only simple nouns and verbs, some inaccurate. Writing is not descriptive.	Sentences do not vary. Incomplete sentences hinder meaning.	Frequent errors in grammar, spelling, capitalization, punctuation.

See also ***Writing Rubric Blackline Master*** and Teacher's Edition pp. R18–R21.

Progress Monitoring

Assess

- **Weekly Tests**
- **Periodic Assessments**
- **Fluency Tests**

✓ Vocabulary
Target Vocabulary
Strategies: Compound Words

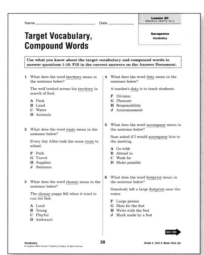

Weekly Tests 20.2–20.3

✓ Comprehension
Main Ideas and Details

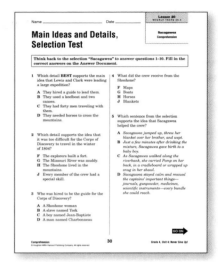

Weekly Tests 20.4–20.5

Respond to Assessment

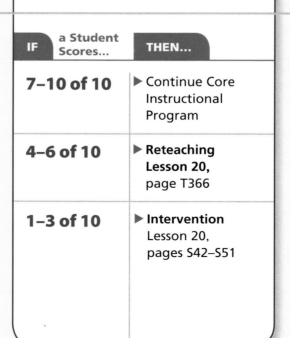

IF a Student Scores...	THEN...
7–10 of 10	▶ Continue Core Instructional Program
4–6 of 10	▶ **Reteaching Lesson 20,** page T366
1–3 of 10	▶ **Intervention** Lesson 20, pages S42–S51

IF a Student Scores...	THEN...
7–10 of 10	▶ Continue Core Instructional Program
4–6 of 10	▶ **Reteaching Lesson 20,** page T366
1–3 of 10	▶ **Intervention** Lesson 20, pages S42–S51

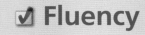 **Powered by** DESTINATIONReading®

- **Weekly Tests**
- **Online Assessment System**

☑ Decoding
VCCV Pattern and Word Parts

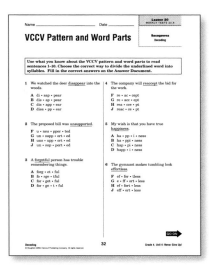

Weekly Tests 20.6–20.7

IF	a Student Scores...	THEN...
7–10 of 10		▶ Continue Core Instructional Program
4–6 of 10		▶ Reteaching Lesson 20, page T367
1–3 of 10		▶ Intervention Lesson 20, pages S42–S51

☑ Language Arts
Grammar: Abbreviations

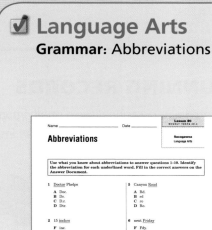

Weekly Tests 20.8–20.9

Writing Traits Rubrics
See TE pp. R18–R21.

IF	a Student Scores...	THEN...
7–10 of 10		▶ Continue Core Instructional Program
4–6 of 10		▶ Reteaching Lesson 20, page T367
1–3 of 10		▶ Intervention Lesson 20, pages S42–S51

☑ Fluency

Fluency Plan
Assess one group per week.
Use the suggested plan below.

	Struggling Readers	Weeks 1, 3, 5
▲	On Level	Week 2
■	Advanced	Week 4

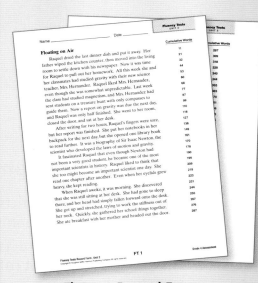

Fluency Record Forms

Fluency Scoring Rubrics
See *Grab-and-Go™ Resources Assessment* for help in measuring progress.

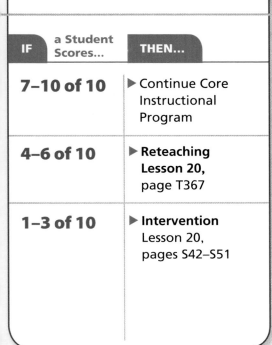

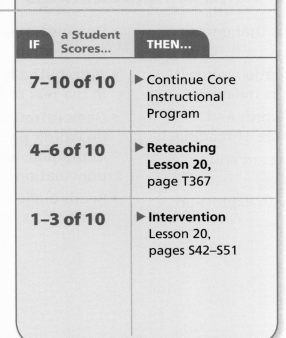

Progress Monitoring

Small Group

RUNNING RECORDS

To assess individual progress, occasionally use small group time to take a reading record for each student. Use the results to plan instruction.

 **Struggling Readers**

 On Level

 Advanced

 **English Language Learners**

For running records, see
Grab-and-Go™ Resources: Lesson 20, pp. 13–16.

Behaviors and Understandings to Notice

- Self-corrects errors that detract from meaning.
- Self-corrects intonation when it does not reflect the meaning.
- Rereads to solve words and resumes normal rate of reading.
- Demonstrates phrased and fluent oral reading.
- Reads dialogue with expression.

- Demonstrates awareness of punctuation.
- Automatically solves most words in the text to read fluently.
- Demonstrates appropriate stress on words, pausing and phrasing, intonation, and use of punctuation.
- Reads orally at an appropriate rate.

Discuss Reading Strategies

Remind students that using strategies that help them become successful readers is useful for reading passages on a test. Tell students that they should try using different strategies during practice tests and think about the strategies that best help them understand what they read. Display and discuss the following strategies:

• Read the title and preview the text.

• Look at the photographs and illustrations. Read the captions.

• Read the questions after the passage to help you focus as you read.

• Make notes in your test booklet or underline things that seem to be important.

• Ask yourself questions as you read: *Can I picture what the author is describing? What can I do to form clearer pictures?*

Also remind students of the Target Strategies they have learned. Tell them to practice using the strategies with test passages as well.

• **Question**	• **Monitor/Clarify**
• **Infer/Predict**	• **Summarize**
• **Analyze/Evaluate**	• **Visualize**

SKILL TRACE

Test Power Focus

Unit 1	Read Fiction
Unit 2	Read Nonfiction
Unit 3	Read Fiction
Unit 4	**Compare Texts**
Unit 5	Compare Texts

1 Teach/Model

Tell students that a test may ask them to read two selections back-to-back and then answer questions about how the pieces of writing are alike and different.

- Tell students that paired reading selections on a test will have something in common. They may have similar main ideas, subjects, themes, plots, characters, or organization.

- Have students turn to **Student Book pp. 526–527.** Call on a volunteer to read aloud the direction line on **Student Book p. 526**.

Read the next two selections. Think about how they are alike and different.

A Lesson Learned the Hard Way

Ryan and Ahmed sat on their bicycles at the start of the cyclocross course. Ahmed had been competing in cyclocross for three years, but this was Ryan's first race. He wished he could remember everything Ahmed had taught him.

Ryan reviewed the last six months in his mind. From the moment Ahmed had first asked whether he would like to try the sport, Ryan had been excited. Ahmed helped Ryan find safety gear. He also explained the importance of practicing and set up a schedule for the two friends to practice together.

Practicing was hard. Ryan soon grew bored with working on the same skills over and over. He was ready to race! Ryan ended up skipping many of the practices. When Ryan did go to practices, he spent more time doing tricks with his bike than he did listening to Ahmed's tips.

"Now the real fun begins," Ryan thought as he sat at the starting line.

"You need to get serious," Ahmed warned. "Cyclocross can be dangerous."

Bang! The starting gun went off. The boys exploded off the starting line. Ryan saw the first obstacle ahead. It was a series of small hurdles.

"Here I go!" Ryan yelled when he reached the hurdles. He jumped off his bike and landed hard on his foot. Next, he had to get his bike onto his shoulder. Ryan could not recall what Ahmed had said about shouldering the bike. He tried to pick it up by the wheels but dropped it. Finally, he got his bike off the ground. As he ran, he tried to balance the bike on his shoulder. The bike was heavy, and his ankle hurt. Before he knew it, he fell face-down into the mud.

"Are you okay?" Ryan heard his friend ask. Ahmed reached down to help Ryan. Ryan was grateful that Ahmed cared more about him than about the race. He grabbed Ahmed's hand and stood.

"Ouch!" Ryan shouted. It hurt to put weight on his ankle. "You were right, Ahmed. Cyclocross is about more than strength and speed. Can we spend a few more months training together? I want to finish my next cyclocross race!"

526

ELL ENGLISH LANGUAGE LEARNERS

Scaffold

Beginning Show a photo of a bicycle and point out the illustration of the safety gear to prompt students to say or repeat descriptive words about cyclocross.

Advanced Have students use these terms in oral sentences: *practice, racing, athlete,* and *shoulder.*

Intermediate Ask yes/no questions and encourage students to add a statement after their *yes* or *no* response. Examples: *Would everyone like cyclocross? Is cyclocross easy to learn?*

Advanced High Have partners use details in both selections to discuss cyclocross.

Is Cyclocross for You?

by Rick Spears, Staff Writer

Cyclocross is cross-country bicycle racing. Cyclocross racers spend only part of a race on their bikes because only part of the two-mile course is smooth. Other parts of the course present challenges such as sandpits, mud puddles, and piles of wood. When racers reach these obstacles, they have two choices. They can ride over them, or they can pick up their bikes and run.

You must be a strong athlete with good skills to compete in this sport. Here are some basics you should learn and practice before you enter a cyclocross race.

Dismounting

To be a top racer, you must dismount without slowing down at all. To do this, swing your right leg over the bike seat. At the same time, move the bike away from your body. This makes room for your right foot to hit the ground next to your left foot. As your right foot nears the ground, remove your left foot from the pedal. Put both feet on the ground and start running!

Carrying Your Bike

As soon as you are running, you have to decide what to do with your bike. You may shoulder it or lift it.

Sometimes you will need to run fast and jump over a series of obstacles. In these cases, you will probably want to shoulder your bike. As your feet hit the ground during a dismount, reach down and grab the bottom of your bike's downtube. Lift up gently and toss the bicycle frame onto your right shoulder. Hold on to the handlebar to keep the bike from bouncing while you run.

Sometimes you will want to lift your bike to get through obstacles. Lifting is like shouldering, except that you grab the bike's toptube instead of its downtube. Then you lift the bike high enough to get over the obstacles. After you have cleared the obstacles, gently set the bike on the ground.

Remounting

After you have successfully dismounted and carried your bike across an obstacle, you will need to remount. As soon as your bike is on the ground, push off with your left leg, swing your right leg over the bike seat, and slide into riding position. Remounting can be the hardest skill of cyclocross.

Imagine this: You are coming to a single, low obstacle. You want to clear it without taking time to dismount. You can do this with a bunny hop. To do a bunny hop, raise your whole body. This causes the bike to hop like a rabbit right over the obstacle.

Cyclocross is a great way to stay active and have fun. However, it can be dangerous. Make sure that you are well prepared and have the safety gear you need. Then, you will be ready and set. You'll just need to go!

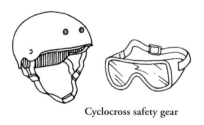

Cyclocross safety gear

527

2 Practice/Apply

- Call on volunteers to read the two selections aloud as students follow along. You may want to pause after the first selection to have students summarize what happens before and during the race. Pause periodically during the reading of the magazine article to discuss similarities students have noticed between the selections.

- Then distribute **Blackline Master 20.15**. Work with students to answer the questions, using the passages in the **Student Book**.

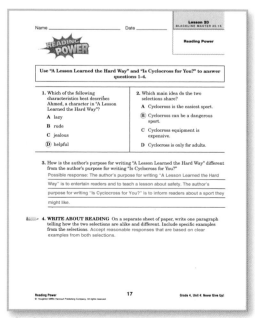

Blackline Master 20.15

Unit 4 Wrap-Up

The Big Idea

- Read the activity with students, and discuss how the characters in the Unit 4 selections achieve success in different ways.

- To help students come up with ideas for accomplishments, tell them to think about different areas of their lives, such as schoolwork, sports, music, community service, the arts, and home life.

- Show students an example of a recipe card. Point out text features such as the recipe title, the list of ingredients and quantities, and the list of cooking steps.

Listening and Speaking

- Choose one character from Unit 4 or a previous unit. Model choosing what award he or she should get and give several reasons explaining why he or she deserves that award.

- Discuss aspects of an effective speech, such as knowing your audience, starting with an exciting introduction, organizing your ideas, and speaking loudly and clearly.

- Give students time to practice their speeches with a partner. Have listeners provide one compliment and one suggestion for improvement.

Unit 4 Wrap-Up

The Big 💡 Idea

Recipe for Success Make a recipe card for achieving success. What is one accomplishment that would make you feel successful? List the qualities you need to achieve success. Then list the steps you would take to achieve it. Share your recipe with your class.

> **My Recipe for Success**
>
> Quantities Needed:
> • :
> Steps:
> 1.
> 2.
> 3.
> 4.

Listening and Speaking

Present an Award
The characters in Unit 4 are successful in different ways. Brainstorm an award to give to one of them. Prepare a short speech to present the award. Your speech should answer these questions: *What is the award? Who is receiving it? Why does the character deserve the award?* Practice your speech. Then deliver it to the class.

528

Small Group Instruction

Day 1

Vocabulary Reader
- *Lewis and Clark's Packing List,* T356–T357

Vocabulary Reader

Day 2

Differentiate Comprehension
- Target Skill: Main Ideas and Details, T358–T359
- Target Strategy: Visualize, T358–T359

Day 3

Leveled Readers
- ● *John Wesley Powell,* T360
- ▲ *Writer from the Prairie,* T361
- ■ *Chief Washakie,* T362
- ◆ *Laura Ingalls Wilder,* T363

Day 4

Differentiate Vocabulary Strategies
- Compound Words, T364–T365

Day 5

Options for Reteaching
- Vocabulary Strategies: Compound Words, T366
- Comprehension Skill: Main Ideas and Details, T366
- Language Arts: Abbreviations/Write to Narrate, T367
- Decoding: VCCV Pattern and Word Parts, T367

Leveled Readers

Ready-Made Work Stations

Independent Practice
- Comprehension and Fluency, T298
- Word Study, T298
- Think and Write, T299
- Digital Center, T299

Comprehension and Fluency

Word Study

Think and Write

Digital Center

		Day 1	Day 2	Day 3	
Teacher-Led	**Struggling Readers**	**Vocabulary Reader** *Lewis and Clark's Packing List*, Differentiated Instruction, p. T356	**Differentiate Comprehension**: Main Ideas and Details; Visualize, p. T358	**Leveled Reader** *John Wesley Powell*, p. T360	
	On Level	**Vocabulary Reader** *Lewis and Clark's Packing List*, Differentiated Instruction, p. T356	**Differentiate Comprehension**: Main Ideas and Details; Visualize, p. T358	**Leveled Reader** *Writer from the Prairie*, p. T361	
	Advanced	**Vocabulary Reader** *Lewis and Clark's Packing List*, Differentiated Instruction, p. T357	**Differentiate Comprehension**: Main Ideas and Details; Visualize, p. T359	**Leveled Reader** *Chief Washakie*, p. T362	
	English Language Learners	**Vocabulary Reader** *Lewis and Clark's Packing List*, Differentiated Instruction, p. T357	**Differentiate Comprehension**: Main Ideas and Details; Visualize, p. T359	**Leveled Reader** *Laura Ingalls Wilder*, p. T363	

		Day 1	Day 2	Day 3
What are my other students doing?	**Struggling Readers**	• **Reread** *Lewis and Clark's Packing List*	• **Vocabulary in Context Cards** 191–200 *Talk It Over* Activities • **Complete** Leveled Practice SR20.1	• **Listen** to Audiotext CD of "Sacagawea"; Retell and discuss • **Complete** Leveled Reader SR20.2
	On Level	• **Reread** *Lewis and Clark's Packing List*	• **Reread** "Sacagawea" with a partner • **Complete** Practice Book p. 229	• **Reread** for Fluency: *Writer from the Prairie* • **Complete** Practice Book p. 230
	Advanced	• **Vocabulary in Context Cards** 191–200 *Talk It Over* Activities	• **Reread and Retell** "Sacagawea" • **Complete** Leveled Practice A20.1	• **Reread** for Fluency: *Chief Washakie* • **Complete** Leveled Practice A20.2
	English Language Learners	• **Reread** *Lewis and Clark's Packing List*	• **Listen** to Audiotext CD of "Sacagawea"; Retell and discuss • **Complete** Leveled Practice ELL20.1	• **Vocabulary in Context Cards** 191–200 *Talk It Over* Activities • **Complete** Leveled Practice ELL20.2

Ready-Made Work Stations
Assign these activities across the week to reinforce and extend learning.

Comprehension and Fluency
Timed Reading

Word Study
Compound Capers

Day 4

Differentiate Vocabulary Strategies:
Compound Words, p. T364

Differentiate Vocabulary Strategies:
Compound Words, p. T364

Differentiate Vocabulary Strategies:
Compound Words, p. T365

Differentiate Vocabulary Strategies:
Compound Words, p. T365

Day 5

Options for Reteaching,
pp. T366–T367

Options for Reteaching,
pp. T366–T367

Options for Reteaching,
pp. T366–T367

Options for Reteaching,
pp. T366–T367

• **Partners: Reread** *John Wesley Powell*
• **Complete** Leveled Practice SR20.3

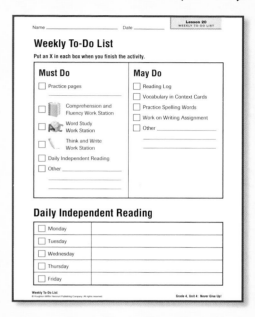

• **Vocabulary in Context Cards**
191–200 *Talk It Over* Activities
• **Complete** Practice Book p. 231

• **Reread** for Fluency: "Sacagawea"
• **Complete** Leveled Practice A20.3

• **Partners: Reread** for Fluency: *Laura Ingalls Wilder*
• **Complete** Leveled Practice ELL20.3

• **Reread** for Fluency: "Sacagawea"
• **Complete** Work Station activities
• **Independent Reading**

• **Complete** Work Station activities
• **Independent Reading**

• **Complete** Work Station activities
• **Independent Reading**

• **Reread** *Lewis and Clark's Packing List* or "Sacagawea"
• **Complete** Work Station activities

 **Think and Write**
The Story Behind a Coin

 JOURNEYS DIGITAL Powered by DESTINATIONReading **Digital Center**

Weekly To-Do List

This Weekly To-Do List helps students see their own progress and move on to additional activities independently.

Reading Log

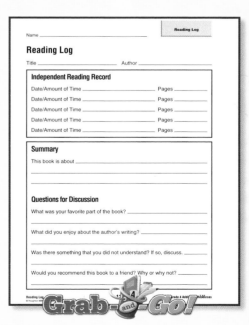

Vocabulary Reader
Lewis and Clark's Packing List

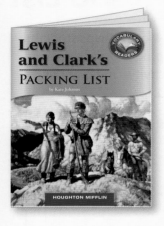

Summary

Lewis and Clark crossed America seeking a water route. To prepare for the long journey, they had a packing list including clothing, food, cooking supplies, bedding, shelter, and medicine.

✓ **TARGET VOCABULARY**

territory	duty
corps	accompany
interpreter	proposed
landmark	supplies
route	clumsy

Struggling Readers

- Explain to students that Lewis and Clark packed supplies for their journey because there was no store or depot in the wilderness for them to restock. It was essential that they plan carefully for what they might need.

- Guide students to preview the Vocabulary Reader. Read aloud the headings. Ask students to describe the images, using Target Vocabulary words when possible.

- Have students alternate reading pages of the Vocabulary Reader aloud. Guide them to use context clues to determine the meanings of unfamiliar words. As necessary, use the Vocabulary in Context Cards to review the meanings of Vocabulary words.

- Assign the **Responding Page** and **Blackline Master 20.1.** Have partners work together to complete the pages.

On Level

- Explain to students that Lewis and Clark carried along gifts for the American Indians in the hopes that they might exchange them for information about plants, animals, and travel routes. Guide students to preview the Vocabulary Reader.

- Remind students that context clues can help them determine the meaning of an unfamiliar word. Tell students to use context clues to confirm their understanding of Target Vocabulary words and to learn the meanings of new words.

- Have students alternate reading pages of the Vocabulary Reader aloud. Tell them to use context clues to determine the meanings of unfamiliar words.

- Assign the **Responding Page** and **Blackline Master 20.1.** Have students discuss their responses with a partner.

JOURNEYS
DIGITAL

Powered by
DESTINATIONReading®
Leveled Readers Online

Day 1

Advanced

- Have students preview the Vocabulary Reader and make predictions about what they will read, using information from the preview and their prior knowledge.

- Remind students to use context clues to help them determine the meanings of unfamiliar words.

- Tell students to read the Vocabulary Reader with a partner. Ask them to stop and discuss the meanings of unfamiliar words as necessary.

- Assign the **Responding Page** and **Blackline Master 20.1.** For the Write About It activity, remind students to use facts and details to support their ideas. Ask them why the corps brought books and journals to keep records.

Lewis and Clark's Packing List, p. 15

⒠ English Language Learners

Group English Language Learners according to language proficiency.

Beginning

Display Context Card 194: *interpreter.* Read the card aloud. Have students tell why a person might need an interpreter. Ask if they or someone they know has ever used an interpreter and for what reason.

Advanced

Have students reread *Lewis and Clark's Packing List.* Check students' understanding of the Target Vocabulary words words by having partners use the words in oral sentences.

Intermediate

Have partners reread *Lewis and Clark's Packing List.* Have students find a sentence in the story with a Target Vocabulary word. Have them write the sentence in their notebooks, circling the words around it that help them understand the meaning of the word.

Advanced High

Have students reread *Lewis and Clark's Packing List.* Have partners use the Target Vocabulary words in an oral summary of the book.

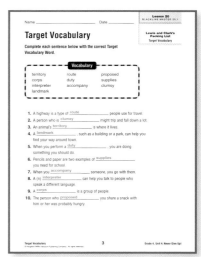

Blackline Master 20.1

Differentiate Comprehension

☑ Main Ideas and Details; Visualize

Struggling Readers

I DO IT

- Remind students that main ideas are important ideas about the topic. Supporting details are facts that tell about the main idea.

- Tell them that *visualizing* characters and events can help them understand the main idea and supporting details. Tell students to picture the text details in their heads as they read.

- Read the first two paragraphs on p. 504 of "Sacagawea" and model using the visualize strategy to help picture the main idea and details.

WE DO IT

- Have students read the first three paragraphs on p. 508.

- Help students identify the main idea. *The trip was dangerous and difficult.*

- Discuss supporting details. *sounds of the waterfall; creaky wagons; rain, hail, and wind; the cloudburst; rushing water*

- Ask: *What is this passage about? The journey from the Great Falls and Captain Clark's rescue of Pomp.*

- Write responses in a Web on the board.

YOU DO IT

- Have students copy and complete the Web with other supporting details.

- Have volunteers share their responses and explain how they used the visualize strategy to help them recall the supporting details.

On Level

I DO IT

- Read aloud p. 509 of "Sacagawea."

- Explain that visualizing the details helps students understand the main idea.

- Model visualizing Sacagawea's excitement about returning to the Shoshone camp.

> **Think Aloud** *I can picture Sacagawea seeing the men on horses and jumping up and down because she is excited. The woman is hugging her. She is sucking her fingers. She is happy.*

WE DO IT

- Have students read p. 511. Guide students to complete the following.

- *Name details that the author provides about the challenges the expedition faces in the mountain. narrow, dangerous paths; snow; not enough to eat; frozen feet; mountains that seemed without end*

- Write students' responses in a Web on the board.

- Ask a volunteer to identify the main idea of the selection.

YOU DO IT

- Have partners complete a Web with the main idea and supporting details about the expedition's journey from the beginning of the story to the end.

- Ask students to share their answers. Have them explain how they used visualized text events to help understand the main idea and recall the details.

Advanced

I DO IT

- Read aloud the last three paragraphs of pp. 506–507 of "Sacagawea."

- Explain that students may need to infer a main idea from the supporting details if it is not stated directly.

- Model identifying the main idea and supporting details using a Web.

Supporting Detail: She found plants to keep the crew healthy.
Main Idea: She was more useful than her husband on the expedition, even though she was not paid.

WE DO IT

- Have students read pp. 509–510 independently.

- Say: *The author shows us another side of Sacagawea. What are some of the things we learn? she is very happy when she sees the Shoshone people; she cries when she sees her brother; she tries to control her tears and keeps to her duty during the council meeting*

- Ask a volunteer to suggest a main idea for this selection based on the details discussed.

YOU DO IT

- Have students read the rest of "Sacagawea" and write a paragraph describing the main idea and supporting details about Sacagawea's role in the expedition.

- Tell students to describe how they visualized the supporting details to confirm their understanding of the text events.

- Have volunteers share their paragraphs with the class.

ELL English Language Learners

Group English Language Learners according to language proficiency.
Draw a Web on the board. Choose one of the following activities for additional support, as appropriate.

Beggining

Show students a simple map. Tell them a map is a picture that helps people find their way. Draw a Web on the board and tell students that a Web will help them find out about a story.

Intermediate

Write *Pomp* in the middle circle of the Web. Help students find details about Pomp to put in the surrounding circles. Pantomine some of the details after you have written the word or words in each circle.

Advanced

Have students copy the Web on the board into their notebooks and fill it in with the main idea and details from "Sacagewea". Have them share their Webs with the class.

Advanced High

Have students use their Webs and other details in the book to make a simple time line of Pomp's life with the expedition. They can decorate the timeline with drawings.

SMALL GROUP Options

Targets for Lesson 20

TARGET SKILL

Main Ideas and Details

TARGET STRATEGY

Visualize

TARGET VOCABULARY

territory	duty
corps	accompany
interpreter	proposed
landmark	supplies
route	clumsy

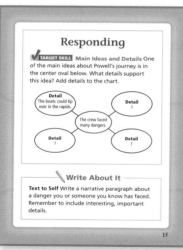

John Wesley Powell, p. 15

Blackline Master 20.3

Leveled Readers

Struggling Readers

 John Wesley Powell

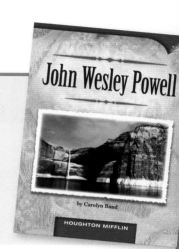

GENRE: BIOGRAPHY

SUMMARY In 1869, John Wesley Powell led a team by boat through the Grand Canyon. The group survived thanks to Powell's leadership.

Introducing the Text

- Explain that the Grand Canyon is located in Arizona.

- Remind students that using a Web can help them understand how the main idea and details are connected in the selection.

Supporting the Reading

- As you listen to students read, pause to discuss these questions.

MAIN IDEAS AND DETAILS p. 3 *What details support the main idea that Powell was always adventurous?* *He spent a lot of time exploring as a teenager.*

VISUALIZE p. 5 *What details help you visualize the Flaming Gorge canyon?* *brilliant colors, rock walls, power of the river, carved rock, deep canyon*

Discussing and Revisiting the Text

CRITICAL THINKING After discussing *John Wesley Powell*, have students read the instructions on **Responding** p. 15. Use these points as they revisit the text.

- Have partners identify the main idea and details from *John Wesley Powell* and list them in the ovals on **Blackline Master 20.3**.

- Distribute **Blackline Master 20.7** to further develop students' critical thinking skills.

FLUENCY: PHRASING: PUNCTUATION Model using punctuation as a guide to correct phrasing. Then have partners echo-read p. 7 and focus on using punctuation to read with proper phrasing.

JOURNEYS DIGITAL
Powered by DESTINATIONReading®
Leveled Readers Online

On Level

▲ Writer from the Prairie

GENRE: BIOGRAPHY

Summary Laura Ingalls Wilder turned her journals into a series of successful novels. The books tell what it was like to grow up on the Great Plains during the mid-1800s.

Introducing the Text

• Explain that life could be very hard for homesteaders like the Ingalls family. Weather, illness, and difficulty farming made life on the plains challenging.

• Remind students that the main idea is what the selection is about, and details support the main idea.

Supporting the Reading

• As you listen to students read, pause to discuss these questions.

MAIN IDEAS AND DETAILS p. 4 *What details give more information about the way Laura's father farmed? He used a plow. He cut through the thick sod.*

VISUALIZE p. 10 *Use your imagination to visualize Laura's house, now a landmark in South Dakota. Describe what you visualize. Answers will vary.*

Discussing and Revisiting the Text

CRITICAL THINKING After discussing *Writer from the Prairie*, have students read the instructions on **Responding** p. 15. Use these points as they revisit the text.

• Have partners identify the main idea and details from *Writer from the Prairie* in **Blackline Master 20.4** and write them in the ovals.

• Distribute **Blackline Master 20.8** to further develop students' critical thinking skills.

FLUENCY: PHRASING: PUNCTUATION Have students practice reading their favorite parts of *Writer from the Prairie* with correct phrasing. Remind them to pause and stop according to the punctuation.

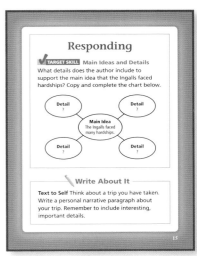

Writer from the Prairie, p. 15

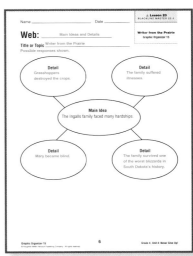

Blackline Master 20.4

Targets for Lesson 20

TARGET SKILL

Main Ideas and Details

TARGET STRATEGY

Visualize

TARGET VOCABULARY

territory	duty
corps	accompany
interpreter	proposed
landmark	supplies
route	clumsy

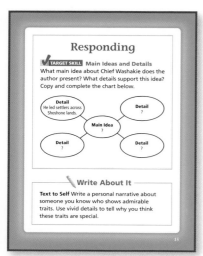

Chief Washakie, p. 15

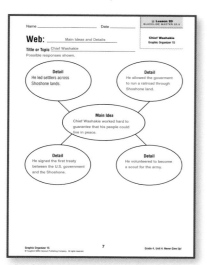

Blackline Master 20.5

Leveled Readers

Advanced

■ Chief Washakie

GENRE: BIOGRAPHY

Summary Chief Washakie led the Shoshone from around 1840 until 1900. This peaceful Native American leader negotiated with the U.S. government.

Introducing the Text

• Explain that Chief Washakie led the Shoshone during a time of great change when large numbers of pioneers settled in the West.

• Remind students that biographers use descriptive details to create a vivid portrait of a person.

Supporting the Reading

• As you listen to students read, pause to discuss these questions.

MAIN IDEAS AND DETAILS pp. 4–5 *How was Chief Washakie different than other Native American leaders? He guided the pioneers who traveled though Wyoming. He chose to make deals with the U.S. government. He chose peace over war.*

VISUALIZE p. 9 *What details help you visualize what the frontier was like before the settlers arrive? The frontier had mountains, deserts, rivers, and grasslands.*

Discussing and Revisiting the Text

CRITICAL THINKING After discussing *Chief Washakie*, have students read the instructions on **Responding** p. 15. Use these points as they revisit the text.

• Have partners identify the main idea and details from *Chief Washakie* and list them in the ovals on **Blackline Master 20.5**.

• Distribute **Blackline Master 20.9** to further develop students' critical thinking skills.

FLUENCY: PHRASING: PUNCTUATION Have students read their favorite parts of *Chief Washakie* with correct phrasing.

JOURNEYS DIGITAL **Powered by** DESTINATIONReading®
Leveled Readers Online

 ELL English Language Learners

◆ **Laura Ingalls Wilder**

GENRE: BIOGRAPHY

Summary Laura Ingalls Wilder and her family lived on the Great Plains during the mid-1800s. She turned her journals about growing up on the prairie into a series of successful novels.

Introducing the Text

- Explain that homesteaders were people who staked a claim to the land and raised crops and animals to provide for themselves. Homesteaders like Laura's family faced many challenges.

- Remind students that the main idea supports the topic of the selection. Supporting details give additional information about the main idea.

Supporting the Reading

- As you listen to students read, pause to discuss these questions.

MAIN IDEAS AND DETAILS p. 2 *What is the main idea on this page? Laura Ingalls Wilder was a beloved writer who wrote about her childhood.*

VISUALIZE p. 8 *What details help you to visualize a sod house? blocks of dirt, under the ground and above the ground, dirt walls with white paint*

Discussing and Revisiting the Text

CRITICAL THINKING After discussing *Laura Ingalls Wilder* have students read the instructions on **Responding** p. 15. Use these points as they revisit the text.

- Have partners identify the main idea and details in *Laura Ingalls Wilder* and list them in the ovals on **Blackline Master 20.6**.

- Distribute **Blackline Master 20.10** to further develop students' critical thinking skills.

FLUENCY: PHRASING: PUNCTUATION Have students practice reading their favorite parts of *Laura Ingalls Wilder* with correct phrasing and expression. Remind students that punctuation marks will help them determine when to pause and stop.

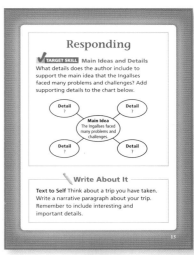

Laura Ingalls Wilder, p. 15

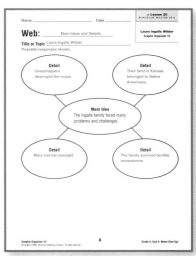

Blackline Master 20.6

Differentiate Vocabulary Strategies ☑ Compound Words

Struggling Readers

I DO IT

- Display **Vocabulary in Context Card 200**: *landmark*.

- Explain that compound words are formed from two or more shorter words. They may be written as one word, include a space, or include a hyphen.

- Remind students that looking at the text around a word can help them understand the word's meaning.

WE DO IT

- Read aloud the context sentence on the front of the card.

- Look at the two words that make up *landmark*: *land* and *mark*. *Land* means "an area of ground," and *mark* means "an object that shows position."

- Discuss the meaning of *landmark* and have students read aloud the **Vocabulary in Context Card**.

YOU DO IT

- Have students write short sentences for the word *landmark*, using examples of landmarks they have seen or read about.

- Tell students to draw a picture of a famous or local landmark.

On Level

I DO IT

- Remind students that a compound word is formed by combining two or more shorter words.

- A compound word can be one word, include a space, or contain a hyphen.

- Explain that not all words can form compound words. On the board, write *duty*. Ask students to make the word into a compound word.
  Possible answers heavy-duty

WE DO IT

- On the board, list student suggestions for compound words.

- Go through the list together, and see which words, if any, need a space or a hyphen. Examples include *dead end, fly-fishing, schoolhouse*.

YOU DO IT

- Have students select words from the list on the board and write sentences to demonstrate their understanding.

- Have students exchange sentences with a partner. Partners should use a dictionary to confirm that the words were used correctly.

Advanced

I DO IT

- Write the word *life* on the board. Then write the following sets of compound words:

  lifetime, lifelong, life cycle, lifeguard, life-size

- Tell students that many compound words can often be formed from one simple word.

WE DO IT

- As a class, list more compound words that contain the word *life*.

- Then work with students to list compound words with the word *day*. *Possible answers: daybreak, day-to-day, daylight, Sunday*

YOU DO IT

- Have partners create a compound Web for either the word *down* or the word *back*.

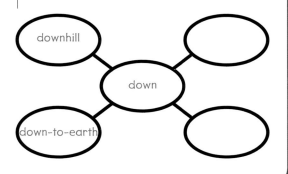

ELL English Language Learners

Group English Language Learners according to language proficiency.

Write the words *bedroom, keyboard, weekend,* and *hometown* on the board. Have students repeat after you as you pronounce each word.

Beginning

Say and point to *bedroom*. Have student repeat after you. Point out the words *bed* and *room* and explain the meaning of each word. Have students then say the meaning of *bedroom*.

Intermediate

Point out the words that make up each compound word. Have students tell what each base word means. Then discuss the meanings of each compound word.

Advanced

Have students point out the words that make up each compound word. Guide them to use the meanings of the words to determine the meaning of each compound word.

Advanced High

Have partners determine the meaning of each compound word using the meaning of the smaller word. Have them use each compound word in an oral sentence.

☑ Options for Reteaching

Vocabulary Strategy

☑ Compound Words

I DO IT

- Remind students that compound words are words made up of two shorter words.
- Point out that compound words are sometimes separated by a space, as in *cell division,* or connected by a hyphen, as in *baby-sit.*

WE DO IT

- Display **Projectable 20.5.**
- Help students identify the compound words and note whether any of the words have spaces or hyphens between them.
- Model how to determine the meaning of *daydream.*

 Think Aloud *The word* daydream *has two words in it:* day *and* dream. *A daydream might be a dream that happens during the day. Based on the passage, which tells the reader to daydream. I think it must be a kind of dreaming, or imagining, someone does when they are awake.*

- Have a volunteer look up *daydream* in a dictionary and read the definitions aloud.

YOU DO IT

- Have partners work together to identify the definitions of *campfire, homeland, nightfall, lifetime, fly-fishing,* and *landmark.*
- Have them use dictionaries to help define the words.
- Provide corrective feedback if students need additional support.

Comprehension Skill

☑ Main Ideas and Details

I DO IT

- Remind students that a main idea is the most important fact or idea in a selection. The details are additional ideas or information that support the main idea.
- Point out that a reader can infer the main idea by visualizing and by thinking carefully about what idea each of the supporting details helps explain.

WE DO IT

- Have students read the first two paragraphs on **Student Book p. 506** aloud and identify the main idea and supporting details.
- Model how to infer the main idea from the selection.

 Think Aloud *The author tells us Sacagawea had a difficult birth. Captain Lewis gave Sacagawea a rattlesnake mixture to drink, and she gave birth to a baby boy. While the explorers traveled in canoes, Sacagawea continued to help the team and walked along the riverbank carrying Pomp in a cradleboard. Though unstated, the main idea seems to be that while Sacagawea became a mother on the journey west, it did not slow the expedition down. Instead, Sacagawea continued to be an important team member.*

- Help volunteers identify the details that show Sacagawea's continued value to the crew.

YOU DO IT

- Distribute **Graphic Organizer 15.**
- Have students identify the main idea of the second paragraph on **Student Book p. 508.** *Travel was slow, difficult, and uncomfortable.*
- Have partners complete the graphic organizer with details that support the main idea.
- Review the completed graphic organizers.

Language Arts

 # Abbreviations/Write to Narrate

I DO IT

- Remind students that an abbreviation stands for a whole word. Most abbreviations begin with a capital letter and end with a period.
- List the following abbreviations on the board: *Feb., Aug., Oct.* Model using each.

Think Aloud *To abbreviate February, I will use the first three letters of the word followed by a period. The abbreviation is* Feb. *This works for August and October, too.*

WE DO IT

- Work together to write abbreviations that may be used in special kinds of writing such as addresses and lists.
- Guide students to identify the abbreviations in the following sentences that you write on the board. *My birthday is Oct. 22. I live on Tyndall Ave.* Have students identify the abbreviations and tell you the whole word. Discuss when the abbreviations may be used.
- Have partners work together to write a birthday date using abbreviations. If the month doesn't have an abbreviation, have them write another date.

YOU DO IT

- Have pairs of students write addresses and today's date using abbreviations.
- Have partners exchange their papers with another pair, asking them to check for correct punctuation.

Decoding

 # VCCV Pattern and Word Parts

I DO IT

- Review **Routine Card1.**
- Remind students that a closed syllable is a word part that ends with a consonant and has a short vowel sound.
- Point out that words with a VCCV pattern may be divided before or after an affix.
- Model how to decode the word *unsupportive* step by step.
un/sup/port/ive

WE DO IT

- Write *collection, dangerous,* and *effortless* on the board.
- Help students decode each word.

Word	Base Word	Affix
collection	col/lect	tion
dangerous	dan/ger	ous
effortless	ef/fort	less

YOU DO IT

- Have partners work together to decode *misfortune* and identify the base word, prefix, or suffix. Have students read the word and note the letter pattern.
- Tell partners to find and decode additional examples in the **Student Book.**
- Use the **Corrective Feedback** on page T331 if students need additional help.

Teacher Notes

Never Give Up!

 STRATEGIC INTERVENTION

SHARE OBJECTIVES

- Identify adjectives and the nouns they describe.
- Discuss transportation in the 1880s and today.
- Read to build meaning for Target Vocabulary words.

MATERIALS

Write-In Reader pages 152–153

ACADEMIC LANGUAGE

adjective   noun

pronoun

Warm Up

Oral Grammar

Adjectives

- Point out the photograph of the wagons on page 152 in students' **Write-In Reader**.

- Ask, *What word could you use to describe the wagons?* (old) *What other words can you use?* (covered, white, wooden) Ask students to think of a word that tells how many wagons they see. (two)

- Ask, *What are these describing words called?* (adjectives) *What do adjectives describe?* (nouns or pronouns)

Talk About It

Help focus students' attention on living in the 1800s. Ask, *If you had been born 150 years ago, how would you have traveled from place to place—by car or train? by bicycle or horse?*

Discuss the question, emphasizing these points:

- Not by car; they hadn't been invented yet.

- Probably not by train; they were new and many people might never have seen one.

- Not by bicycle; they were not made in America until 1878.

- Maybe by horse, but students would need to own one, and they were expensive.

- For sure by foot! In fact, students probably would have walked a lot more than most of us do today!

Target Vocabulary

Write-In Reader pages 152–153

- Read and discuss each paragraph. Then discuss the meaning of each Target Vocabulary word. Suggest that students underline words or phrases that provide clues to meaning. Also point out the following:

  Contrast the meaning of *defended* in this instance with the more familiar meaning of "protected someone or something."

  Satisfied can mean "happy with something," such as *I'm satisfied with the work you are doing in reading this year.* But *satisfied* can also mean "believe to be true."

- Point out and read the caption. Ask, *What extra information does the caption give us?* (the name of the animal pictured)

- Ask students to choose an answer they would like to read aloud.

Possible responses:

1. stood up for

2. Responses will vary.

3. My school should have the reputation for being a great place to learn.

4. contented

5. Responses will vary.

Quick Check Target Vocabulary

Ask each student to use one of the Target Vocabulary words in a sentence.

✓ **TARGET VOCABULARY**

If a person protected something from physical or verbal attack, he or she **defended** it.

If you **relied** on someone, you depended on him or her to do something for you.

The general public's opinions of a person form his or her **reputation**.

A person who feels **satisfied** is happy with things that have happened or the work he or she has done.

A **situation** is what is happening at a specific time or place.

EXTRA PRACTICE

Build Fluency Have students read **Write-In Reader** pages 152–153 with a partner or a family member.

SHARE OBJECTIVES

- Read words with vowel pair syllables.
- Understand the skill of compare and contrast.
- Read to apply skills and strategies.

MATERIALS

Write-In Reader pages 154–157

ACADEMIC LANGUAGE

| compare | contrast |
| monitor | clarify |

Warm Up

Multisyllable Words

Focus: Vowel Pair Syllables

Write these words on the board or on a pad. Note that the words in each column have the same vowel pair.

1	trail	please	coach	shout
2	gain	reach	road	proud
3	paid	clean	coat	found

Row 1: Circle the vowel pairs in these words. Say the sound for each vowel pair. Remind students that each vowel pair stands for one sound. Model reading each word.

Row 2: Ask a student volunteer to circle the vowel pairs in each word. Choral read the words with students.

Row 3: Listen to each student read the words. Make corrections as needed. Record your findings.

RETEACH

Compare and Contrast

- Hold up two articles of clothing such as a hat and a scarf. Ask, *How are these alike? How are they different?*

- Review the skill of comparing and contrasting with students. Say, *When you told me how the scarf and hat were alike, you* compared *the articles of clothing. When you told me how the scarf and hat were different, you* contrasted *them.*

- Remind students that authors often make comparisons in their writing. Ask, *What are some of the things that authors compare and contrast?* (characters and settings) Explain that keeping track of how such things as characters and settings are alike and different helps readers to keep track of important information in a story or informational article.

- Discuss signal words. Remind students that authors often use words to signal that they are making a comparison. Ask, *What do the words* like *or* also *signal?* (that two or more things are being compared) *What do the words* however *or* but *signal?* (that two or more things are being contrasted).

Quick Check Comprehension

Have students compare and contrast two story characters.

READ

"The Fastest Rider in the West"

Write-In Reader pages 154–157

- Preview the selection with students using the **Think Aloud** to predict the setting (both time and place). Guide students to use headings and photos to make predictions. Record their ideas.

> **Think Aloud** *I see a map that looks old. I think this story takes place a long time ago. What other clues help you predict the setting?*

- Together, review the steps to the Monitor/Clarify Strategy, **Write-In Reader** page 304. As needed, guide students in applying the strategy as they read.

READ

Ask students to read to confirm their predictions. Have students take turns reading the selection with partners. Discuss, confirm, and revise student predictions based upon story details.

REREAD

Call on individuals to read aloud while others follow along. Point out words that have a vowel pair pattern, such as *pleased, trail*, and *speed*. Stop to discuss each question. Allow time for students to write their responses before proceeding. Sample answers are provided.

Page 154: Based on the title, what event do you think Nathan Mott wrote about? (the fastest horseback ride in the West)

Help unpack meaning, if needed, by asking, *What is the title of the article?* ("The Fastest Rider in the West") *What does the photo show?* (It shows a person riding a galloping horse.)

Unpack Meaning: For questions on pages 155–157, you may want to use the notes in the right-hand column.

Page 155: Who is a faster rider, Nathan Mott or Francis Aubry? Explain. (Francis Aubry is a faster rider. He is ahead of Mott.)

Turn and Talk **Page 156:** What is Francis Aubry's reputation? (He has a reputation as a person who loves to set speed records.) Have partners discuss this question and then share with the group.

Page 157: Why do you think Aubry didn't carve his name into Pawnee Rock? (He was trying to beat his speed record.)

UNPACK MEANING

Use prompts such as these if students have difficulty with a **Stop•Think•Write** question:

Page 155 *Underline the words in the text that help you respond to the question.* (Now Aubry is ahead of me.)

Page 156 *What is the meaning of the word* reputation? (people's opinion of someone) *Where would the answer to the question most likely appear in the text?* (near the word *reputation*)

Page 157 *It takes time to carve rock. What is Aubry trying to do?* (He is trying to break a speed record.)

EXTRA PRACTICE

Build Fluency Have students read **Write-In Reader** pages 154–157 with a partner or a family member.

SHARE OBJECTIVES

- Identify articles and the nouns they describe.
- Read aloud fluently to improve rate.
- Read to apply skills and strategies.

MATERIALS

Write-In Reader pages 158–160

ACADEMIC LANGUAGE

definite article

indefinite article

rate

Warm Up

Oral Grammar

Articles

- Direct students to look at the photo on page 158. Say, *If I had a choice, I'd like to ride the horse with the white foot.* Have students point to your preferred horse. (the one on the left)

- Ask, *If I said I'd like to ride a horse, which horse would I be talking about?* (They wouldn't be able to answer because you said *a* horse. You weren't definite.)

- Explain that when we use the definite article *the*, we are referring to a particular person, place, or thing. When we use an indefinite article, *a* or *an*, we aren't naming a particular person, place, or thing.

- Provide additional examples, if needed, using classroom objects. (I prefer **the** illustration with the...; I like to eat **a** sandwich for lunch.)

RETEACH

Fluency: Rate

Write-In Reader page 158

Explain that you are going to read from page 158 in two different ways, and you want students to evaluate your reading.

- First, read very slowly, pausing between words. Then read quickly, running words together.

- Ask, *What did you think of my first reading? Explain. Was my second reading better? Explain.* Be sure students recognize how hard it is to understand meaning when someone reads too quickly or too slowly.

- Now read the page at an appropriate rate. Ask, *Why is it easier to understand what the story is about now?* Have students practice reading aloud sentences from the page, concentrating on reading at a rate that would enable listeners to better understand what the story is about.

READ

"The Fastest Rider in the West"

Write-In Reader pages 158–160

Review the first part of the story with students. Ask, *What have we learned about Aubry so far?* Then preview today's reading. Have students look for clues to help them predict how this story will end.

READ

Ask students to read to confirm their predictions. Have students take turns reading the selection with partners. Discuss, confirm, and revise predictions based upon story details. Ask if there was anything about the way the story ended that surprised them.

REREAD

Call on individuals to read aloud while others follow along. Stop to discuss each question. Allow time for students to write their responses before proceeding. Sample answers are provided.

Page 158: Why do you think the reporter <u>defended</u> Aubry? (He admires Aubry.)

Help unpack meaning, if needed, by asking, *What does* defended *mean?* (stood up for) *Was the answer to this question written anywhere?* (no) *Which details served as clues?* (The reporter has been trying to catch up with Aubry for days.)

Unpack Meaning: For questions on pages 159–160, you may want to use the notes in the right-hand column.

Page 159: Who has more time to talk, Nathan Mott or Francis Aubry? Explain. (Nathan has more time to talk. Aubry is in a hurry because he is on his way to meet with some traders.)

Turn and Talk **Page 160:** Is it faster to travel by wagon train or by horse? Explain. (It is faster to travel by horse. The data on the chart supports my answer.) Have partners discuss this question and then share with the group.

Quick Check **Retelling**

Have students retell the end of the story. Support the retelling by asking, *Why was it so hard for the reporter to catch up to Aubry? What happened when he finally did catch up with him?*

UNPACK MEANING

Use prompts such as these if students have difficulty with a **Stop•Think•Write** question:

Page 159 *Where is Aubry going?* (to meet with some traders) *If he were going to meet with someone, would he have time to talk?* (probably not) *What does the story say about how Nathan Mott felt about talking to Aubry?* (that Mott could have talked all day)

Page 160 *Look at the chart. How fast does a wagon train travel?* (2 miles an hour) *How fast does a horse travel?* (20 miles an hour) *Which travels faster?* (the horse)

EXTRA PRACTICE

Build Fluency Have students read **Write-In Reader** pages 158–160 with a partner or a family member.

SHARE OBJECTIVES

- Read words with vowel pair syllables.
- Identify adjectives and articles and the nouns they describe.
- Answer questions using evidence from the text.

MATERIALS

Write-In Reader pages 154–161

ACADEMIC LANGUAGE

adjective

Warm Up

Multisyllable Words

Focus: Vowel Pair Syllables

Write these words on the board or on a pad. Space the letters so you can draw a line before the ending. Remind students that we can divide a longer word in front of a suffix to make it easier to read.

1	gain / ing	sound / ed
2	waiting	scouted
3	training	pounded

Row 1: Circle the vowel pairs in these words. Say the sound for each vowel pair. Remind students that each vowel pair stands for one sound. Model the reading of each word.

Row 2: Ask a student to circle the vowel pairs in each word and then say the sound. Choral read the words with students.

Row 3: Listen to each student read the words. Make corrections as needed. Record your findings.

RETEACH

Adjectives

- Review that adjectives are words that tell about nouns. They may tell what kind or how many. Read the first four sentences on page 159 aloud.

- Ask, *What adjective tells about Aubry? What kind of man is he?* (strong) *What other adjectives could you use to describe him, using evidence in the text?* (short, small, energetic)

Turn and Talk Have students reread the remaining sentences on this page and list other adjectives to describe Aubry. Tell them to find evidence to support their answers.

Possible answers: busy, restless (evidence: He didn't have time to talk for long.); determined, positive, hopeful (evidence: He wants to ride the trail in just six days.)

Quick Check Grammar

Have students write a sentence with two or three adjectives.

Look Back and Respond

Write-In Reader pages 154–161

Help students complete the Look Back and Respond page. Model how to use the hint in question 1 to find evidence that can be used to support answers.

• Explain that evidence is proof, clues, or information.

• Remind students that they can circle or underline the specific words in the selection that they used as evidence for their answers.

1. How are Nathan Mott and Francis Aubry different? (Aubry is faster than Mott. Aubry doesn't travel like other people; he can travel on little sleep and skip meals. Aubry is not a big man.)

Help unpack meaning, if needed, by saying, *Underline the clues on page 156 that helped you answer the question.* (I am not as fast as he is.) *Now underline the clues on pages 158 and 159.* (Page 158: Aubry doesn't travel like other people. They say he can get along on two hour's sleep. They say he can go without meals. Page 159: He isn't a big man at all.)

Turn and Talk Have students work independently on questions 2, 3, and 4. When students have completed the page, have partners discuss their responses and then share them with the group. Sample responses are provided.

Unpack Meaning: For questions 2–4, you may want to use the notes in the right-hand column to guide the discussion about student responses.

2. What is one way that Mott's trip and Aubry's trip are the same? (They are both traveling by horse.)

3. How would you describe Aubry? (Aubry won't let anything stop him. He is strong and full of energy. He is never satisfied and keeps trying to do better.)

4. Is the ride in the story faster or slower than the six-day ride Aubry hopes to take after the summer? (The ride was slower. He left on May 20th and reached Santa Fe on June 3. That is 15 days.)

UNPACK MEANING

Use prompts such as these if students have difficulty with a question:

2. *What clue on page 156 did you use to figure out one way that Mott's and Aubry's trips are alike?* (That's how I'm traveling, too.)

3. *What part of your answer to question 1 can help you answer this question?* (Question 1 was about Aubry's actions and reputation. I can use that to begin my description.) *What other information on page 159 can you add to your answer?* (I can add his physical description and how the reporter observed him acting.)

4. *Look at the heading on page 155. When did Aubry leave?* (May 20) *Look at the heading on page 159. When did he reach Santa Fe?* (June 3) *How many days is that?* (15)

EXTRA PRACTICE

Build Fluency Have students retell "The Fastest Rider in the West" to a partner or a family member.

SHARE OBJECTIVES

- Read words with vowel pair syllables in context.
- Demonstrate understanding of Target Vocabulary words.
- Preview Sequence of Events and the Summarize Strategy.

MATERIALS

Context Cards: *churning, defended, deserve, escorted, relied, reputation, satisfied, situation, swelled, worthy*

Write-In Reader pages 154–160 **Leveled Reader:** *Elizabeth's Stormy Ride*

ACADEMIC LANGUAGE

sequence   summarize

 TARGET VOCABULARY

Something that is **churning** is stirred up and moving with great force.

If you **deserve** something, you have a right to it or have earned it.

To have **escorted** someone is to have gone with that person as a guide or protector.

If something **swelled**, it grew larger than usual.

When something is **worthy**, it has value.

Multisyllable Words
Cumulative Review

- Write these sentences on the board or on a pad.

  1. The coach was loaded to the top.
  2. Each horse waited as the scout looked around.
  3. "Let's go!" he shouted at last. "Get out of here!"
  4. The horses' feet pounded the ground!

- Have student volunteers circle the vowel pairs in each sentence. Check their work. Then assign students to work with a partner to practice reading the sentences. Remind them to use the end punctuation to help them read with expression. Then listen to each student read one sentence. Make corrections as needed. Record your findings.

REVIEW

Target Vocabulary
Context Cards

- Display the **Context Cards** for *churning, deserve, escorted, swelled,* and *worthy*. Review the meanings of these words. Then have students use the words in oral sentences about traveling in the 1800s.

- Add the **Context Cards** for *defended, relied, reputation, satisfied,* and *situation*. Give one card to each student. Have each student make up a riddle for his or her word. Have the rest of the group guess the answer.

▬▬▶ **WRITE ABOUT IT**

- Ask students to write about a scary situation that a traveler on the Santa Fe Trail might face in the 1800s. Have them tell about what happened, using the word *situation* in their descriptions.

Sequence of Events
Summarize

Write-In Reader pages 154–160

- Introduce skill and strategy. Say, *In the next lesson, we are going to focus on the order of events in a story. We'll also work on ways to summarize events.*

- Explain, *Many writers organize their stories by sequence. Sequence is the order in which events happen. Sometimes, they use sequence words, such as* first, next, then, *and* finally.

- Ask, *What clues did the writer of this week's story use to make the sequence clear?* (Starting on page 155, dates are given throughout the story.)

- List on the board with students the sequence of events in the selection.

  1. Mott leaves Independence, Missouri, trying to catch Aubry.

  2. Mott makes several stops along the Santa Fe Trail, always behind Aubry.

  3. Mott catches up to Aubry in Santa Fe.

- Turn to and review the Summarize Strategy found on page 302 in the **Write-In Reader**. Tell students that when they summarize, they should briefly tell the important parts of the story in their own words. Have them use the Sequence of Events to summarize the selection.

APPLY READING SKILLS

Introduce *Elizabeth's Stormy Ride*. Choral read the first few pages with students. Depending on their abilities, have students continue reading with partners or as a group.

Quick Check **Fluency**

Listen to individual students as they read the **Write-In Reader** selection. Make specific notes about words that presented difficulty to them.

● **Leveled Reader**

SUMMARIZE STRATEGY

When you **summarize**, you briefly explain the most important ideas in a text in your own words. Organize a summary in a way that makes sense, and do not change the meaning of the text. A summary can be as short as one or two sentences.

In narrative texts, explain

- who the main character is and where the story takes place.

- the problem that the main character faces.

- the most important events.

- how the problem is resolved.

In informational texts, explain

- the main idea.

- the most important details that support the main idea.

EXTRA PRACTICE

Independent Reading Have students read from a book of their choice and describe what they read in their reading logs.

SHARE OBJECTIVES

- Use adverbs correctly.
- Discuss monkeys and their abilities.
- Read to build meaning for Target Vocabulary words.

MATERIALS

Write-In Reader pages 162–163

ACADEMIC LANGUAGE

adverb

Oral Grammar

Adverbs

- Remind students that adverbs are words that can help us understand *how* something is happening. Add that adverbs tell readers something about a verb.

- Tell students that you are going to say a *bare* (very simple) sentence, and you want them to help you bring it to life by telling *how* something is happening.

- Say the sentence. Prompt students by asking *how.*

Examples	
1. The monkey climbed the tree. **Prompt:** *How did it climb? Give me some words to show how.*	The monkey slowly (rapidly, gracefully) climbed the tree.
2. Jerrell wrote her own story. **Prompt:** *How did she write?*	Jerrell confidently (quickly, happily, sadly) wrote her own story.
3. The parents walked into the school. **Prompt:** *How did they walk?*	The parents expectantly (happily, joyfully, nervously) walked into the school.

Talk About It

Help focus students' attention on monkeys. Ask, *What do you know about monkeys?*

Discuss the question, emphasizing these points:

- Live: Where can you see monkeys? In the wild; at zoos; in the circus; with families

- Eat: What do they like to eat? Bananas; grapes; oranges

- Play: What can they do? Tricks; mimic people; make us laugh

- Work: How can monkeys help people? They are trained to help people with disabilities.

Target Vocabulary

Write-In Reader pages 162–163

- Read and discuss the passage. Then discuss the meaning of each Target Vocabulary word. Suggest that students underline words or phrases that provide clues to meaning. Also point out the following:

   Foster can mean "having to do with the care of someone else's animal or child," such as *The baby lived in a foster home until he was adopted by a family.* But *foster* can also mean "to encourage" as in *to foster good reading habits in students.*

   The word *performs* can be used in different ways. A person *performs* different tasks at work. An animal *performs* tricks. A singer *performs* in a show. A computer *performs* calculations.

- Have students complete items 1–3. Explain that they should use a vocabulary word only once in this section. Then have them answer the questions. Ask students to choose an answer they would like to read aloud.

Responses:

   1. reward

   2. foster

   3. performs

   4. Possible response: on line for the bus

   5. Possible response: remind that person of all the things she has been successful at in the past

Quick Check **Target Vocabulary**

Ask each student to use one of the Target Vocabulary words in a sentence.

✔ **TARGET VOCABULARY**

When a person has a strong belief in his or her abilities, that person has **confidence**.

A **foster** caretaker takes care of someone else's animal or child.

If you do something **patiently**, you do it calmly and without complaining.

When a person **performs** a task, he or she does that task.

To **reward** someone is to give that person something in return for doing something.

EXTRA PRACTICE

Build Fluency Have students read **Write-In Reader** pages 162–163 with a partner or a family member.

SHARE OBJECTIVES

- Read words with vowel pair syllables.
- Determine sequence of events.
- Read to apply skills and strategies.

MATERIALS

Write-In Reader pages 164–167

ACADEMIC LANGUAGE

sequence   event   summarize

Multisyllable Words

Focus: Vowel Pair Syllables

Write these words on the board or on a pad.

1	canteen	fifteen	elbow
2	contain	dugout	fellow
3	sixteen	coffee	monkey

Row 1: Help students divide words into syllables using the vowel and consonant letter patterns. Remind students that vowel pairs keep their sound in a syllable.

c a n / t e e n	f i f / t e e n	e l / bow
VC C V	VC C V	VC CV

Circle the vowel pairs. Then read each word.

Row 2: Have volunteers identify the VCCV letter patterns, then divide the words between consonants. Have them circle the vowel pairs and read the word. Then choral read the words.

Row 3: Listen to each student read the words. Make corrections as needed. Record your findings.

RETEACH

Sequence of Events

- Remind students that a sequence of events is a group of events that are usually listed or written out in the order in which they take place. Explain that identifying a sequence of events helps readers keep track of a story plot and recognize how different story events are related.

- Discuss farming, specifically how to grow vegetables. Ask, *What do you do first? Next? Then what? And then?* Use a chart to organize students' ideas.

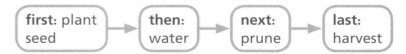

first: plant seed → then: water → next: prune → last: harvest

- Review the labels. Explain that authors use such words to signal a sequence of events.

Quick Check Comprehension

Have students write a short paragraph that describes a sequence of events. Tell them to include signal words in their writing.

READ

"Monkey Business"

Write-In Reader pages 164–167

- Preview the selection with students using the **Think Aloud** to help set a purpose for reading. Guide students to use headings and photos to help them set a purpose. Record their ideas.

Think Aloud   *The photos show monkeys learning different things. I wonder why they are learning these things. I will read to find out.*

- Together, review the steps to the Summarize Strategy, **Write-In Reader** page 304. As needed, guide students in applying the strategy as they read.

READ

Ask students to read to find out why monkeys are learning how to perform these tasks. Have students take turns reading the selection with partners. Discuss how reading the selection helped them find out more about monkeys. Ask students what details they read that surprised them.

REREAD

Call on individuals to read aloud while others follow along. Point out words with vowel pair syllables such as *follow* and *teeth*. Stop to discuss each question. Allow time for students to write their responses before proceeding. Sample answers are provided.

Page 164: In what situation would you not be able to pick something up? (Possible response: If I were injured.)

Help unpack meaning, if needed, by asking, *What might make it difficult for a person to move?* (They could be sick in bed; they could be paralyzed or disabled in another way.)

Unpack Meaning: For questions on pages 165–167, you may want to use the notes in the right column.

Page 165: A monkey performs many jobs. Which would be most helpful to you? (Possible response: Help me tidy my room.)

Page 166: What changes after the baby monkey gets teeth? (It stops drinking from a bottle and begins to eat monkey food.)

Turn and Talk   Page 167: Why is working patiently important when teaching something new? (Possible response: If you are impatient when teaching something, your pupil will probably get nervous and take longer to learn.)

UNPACK MEANING

Use prompts such as these if students have difficulty with a **Stop•Think•Write** question:

Page 165 *What does* performs *mean?* (that someone does a task) *What kinds of jobs do monkeys learn to perform?* (pick up things, open doors, turn lights on and off, feed a person)

Page 166 *What does the word* after *signal?* (that this question relates to a sequence of events) *What should you look for in the story to help you respond?* (other signal words such as *first, later, next,* and *so* that signal the order in which events took place)

Page 167 *What does* patiently *mean?* (calmly do something) *What does it feel like to be around someone who is patient?* (calm) *What does it feel like to be around someone who is not patient?* (unsettling) *Which person do you think would make a better teacher?* (someone who is patient) *Why?* (A patient person is better able to deal with a pupil's mistakes.)

EXTRA PRACTICE

Build Fluency Have students read **Write-In Reader** pages 164–167 with a partner or a family member.

Warm Up

Oral Grammar

Adverbs

- Remind students that an adverb is a word that describes a verb. Adverbs can help tell us *where, when,* and *how* an event is taking place.

- Tell students that you want them to help you bring a plain or simple sentence to life by telling *where* or *when* the action is occurring.

- Say the sentence. Prompt students by asking *when* or *where.*

Examples	
1. *The parents walked into the school.* **Prompt:** *When did they walk into the school?*	Soon the parents walked into the school.
2. *Jerrell wrote her own story.* **Prompt:** *When or where did she write?*	Jerrell wrote her own story here. First, Jerrell wrote her own story.
3. *The monkey climbed the tree.* **Prompt:** *When did it climb? Where did it climb?*	Later, the monkey climbed down the tree.

RETEACH

Fluency: Intonation

Write-In Reader page 164

Explain that you are going to read from page 164 in two different ways, and you want students to evaluate your reading.

- First, read the paragraph in a monotone voice. Then reread in a more expressive manner, adjusting your intonation, or pitch, to help communicate information such as a question or emphasize such words as *Who* and *Sometimes.*

- Ask, *What did you think of my first reading? Explain. Was my second reading better? Explain.* Be sure students recognize how important it is to change their pitch, or intonation, as they read to help communicate important information to the listener. Then have students practice reading aloud page 165, focusing on intonation.

READ

"Monkey Business"

Write-In Reader pages 168–170

Review the first part of the story with students. Ask, *What have we learned about the kinds of things that monkeys are trained to do?* Then preview today's reading. Have students predict what else they might learn about how monkeys help people.

READ

Ask students to read to confirm their predictions. Have students take turns reading the selection with partners. Discuss the additional information that students learned. Have them cite selection details that helped them. Ask, *What did you find most surprising about monkeys?*

REREAD

Call on individuals to read aloud while others follow along. Stop to discuss each question. Allow time for students to write their responses before proceeding. Sample answers are provided.

Page 168: What does the monkey have to do before it is rewarded? (The monkey must accomplish a specific task.)

Help unpack meaning, if needed, by asking, *What does* reward *mean? (to give someone something for doing a good job) When might a monkey be rewarded?* (when it completes a task) *What task is described on page 168? (A dot of red light shines on something. The monkey must get the thing and bring it back.)*

Unpack Meaning: For questions on pages 169–70, you may want to use the notes in the right-hand column.

Turn and Talk **Page 169:** Does the person or the monkey get the most out of this relationship? Why? (Possible response: Both the monkey and the person get something special.) Have partners discuss this question and then share with the group.

Page 170: Why can't a dog perform the tasks a monkey can? (Dogs don't have thumbs.)

Quick Check | Retelling

Have students retell the end of the story. Support the retelling by asking, *How are monkeys trained? How do a monkey and a person benefit from each other?*

UNPACK MEANING

Use prompts such as these if students have difficulty with a **Stop•Think•Write** question:

Page 169 *What does the monkey do for the person?* (helps make life easier) *What does the person do for the monkey?* (feeds and cares for it)

Page 170 *What do monkeys have that most animals do not?* (thumbs) *What does a thumb enable a monkey to do?* (complete different tasks such as open a bottle, comb someone's hair, or dial 911)

EXTRA PRACTICE

Build Fluency Have students read **Write-In Reader** pages 168–169 with a partner or a family member.

SHARE OBJECTIVES

- Read words with vowel pair syllables
- Identify adverbs and the verbs they modify.
- Answer questions using evidence from the text.

MATERIALS

Write-In Reader pages 162–171

ACADEMIC LANGUAGE

adverb   verb   modify

Multisyllable Words

Focus: Vowel Pair Syllables

Write these words on the board or on a pad.

1	follow	indeed	discount
2	pillow	Sunday	obtain
3	mislead	display	yellow

Row 1: Ask, *How are these words alike?* (They have a VCCV letter pattern. The first syllable is closed. The second is a vowel pair syllable.) Model reading each word. Note that the letters *sh* stand for one consonant sound.

Row 2: Have volunteers underline the VCCV pattern to divide the words, and circle the vowel pair syllable. Then choral read the words.

Row 3: Listen to each student read the words. Make corrections as needed. Record your findings.

RETEACH

Adverbs

Write-In Reader page 162–170

- Review that adverbs are words that can help us understand how something is happening. Adverbs tell more about verbs. Read the third paragraph on page 162 as students follow along.

- Ask, *What adverbs are in this paragraph?* (patiently, soon) *What verbs do they tell more about?* (wait, learn)

Turn and Talk Have students skim through the selection *Monkey Business* for other examples of adverbs. Remind them that not all adverbs end with -*ly*.

Possible answers: patiently, p. 162; easily, p. 165; At first, p. 166; fast, p. 167; hard, p. 167

Quick Check Grammar

Have students write a sentence for each of the following adverbs: *slowly* and *yesterday.*

Look Back and Respond

Write-In Reader pages 164–171

Help students complete the Look Back and Respond page. Model how to use the hint in question 1 to find evidence that can be used to support answers.

- Explain that evidence is proof, clues, or information.

- Remind students that they can circle or underline the specific words in the selection that they used as evidence for their answers.

1. Why do some people need monkeys? (Some people can't move their arms or legs. Monkeys can help these people do things that they can't do by themselves.)

Help unpack meaning, if needed, by asking, *What details about people who need the help of monkeys can you find on page 165?* (Some people who can't move their arms and legs need the help of monkeys.) *Underline ways that monkeys can help them.* (They can pick up things, open doors, turn lights on and off, and even feed a person.)

Turn and Talk Have students work independently on questions 2, 3, and 4. When students have completed the page, have partners discuss their responses and then share them with the group. Sample responses are provided. Accept reasonable responses.

Unpack Meaning: For questions 2–4, you may want to use the notes in the right-hand column to guide the discussion about student responses.

2. Where does a monkey live before it goes to school? (The monkey lives in the home of a human foster family.)

3. What happens to a monkey after it has lived with its foster family for four years? (The monkey goes to school where it learns to follow orders.)

4. What other jobs do you think a monkey might do to help people? (fold clothes; throw things away)

UNPACK MEANING

Use prompts such as these if students have difficulty with a question:

2. *What information can you find on page 166 about where a monkey lives after it is two months old? Circle the information.* (When a monkey is two months old, it moves into a home with a human foster family.)

3. *What do you know about the kinds of tasks the monkeys perform?* (They help people who can't help themselves.) *HINT: Look on page 167 to find out where monkeys learn these skills.*

4. *What body part enables monkeys to do jobs like dialing the phone, putting a CD into a recorder, or putting a straw into a drink? HINT: Look on page 170 to help you.* (They have thumbs.) *What other jobs would thumbs enable them to do?* (water plants, fold clothes)

EXTRA PRACTICE

Retell Have students retell "Monkey Business" to a partner..

Day 5

SHARE OBJECTIVES

- Read words with vowel pair syllables in context.
- Demonstrate understanding of Target Vocabulary words.
- Preview Understanding Characters and the Question Strategy.

MATERIALS

Context Cards: *ceremony, confesses, confidence, disobey, foster, graduate, patiently, performs, reward, symbol*

Write-In Reader pages 34–40

Leveled Reader *Animal Doctors*

ACADEMIC LANGUAGE

character	traits
behavior	question

 TARGET VOCABULARY

A **ceremony** is an event that celebrates something special.

When a person **confesses**, he or she admits to having done something wrong.

To **disobey** is to not follow orders.

To **graduate** from school is to complete it.

A **symbol** is something that stands for something else.

Multisyllable Words

Cumulative Review

- Write these sentences on the board or on a pad.

    1. A guide dog will follow orders in the classroom.

    2. I explain why I don't approach guide dogs.

    3. On Sunday, the dog will display a new behavior.

- Have students circle all of the words with vowel pair syllables. Then assign students to work with a partner to practice reading the sentences. Listen to each student read one sentence. Record your findings.

REVIEW

Target Vocabulary

Context Cards

- Display the **Context Cards** for *ceremony, confesses, disobey, graduate,* and *symbol.* Review the meanings of these words. Then have students use the words in oral sentences about the monkeys, their training, and what they do to help people.

- Add the **Context Cards** for *confidence, foster, patiently, performs,* and *reward.* Give one card to each student. Then say a sentence that describes the meaning of a vocabulary word. The student holding that card should raise his or her hand and give you the card. Continue until you have all of the cards.

▶ WRITE ABOUT IT

- Ask students to describe a time when they had to teach someone how to do something. Tell students to use the word *patiently* in their description.

Understanding Characters Question

Write-In Reader pages 34–40

- Introduce skill and strategy. Say, *In the next lesson, we are going to focus on understanding why a character in a story behaves in a certain way and what that behavior, or trait, tells about the character. We'll also work on the Question Strategy.*

- Explain,*"The Fastest Rider in the West" is based on a real person, Francis Aubry. The author tells about his actions to give the reader an idea of the kind of person Aubry was. On page 35 we learn that Aubry wants to ride alone to break the speed record for the trail. What does this tell us about the kind of person Aubry is?* (He is daring and wants to do something that no one else has ever done.)

- Have students turn to page 38. Ask, *What trait does Aubry show by going without food or much sleep in order to move quickly?* (The fact that he will do almost anything to be the fastest rider in the West shows his determination. It also shows that once he decides to do something, there is practically nothing that will stop him.)

- Turn to and review the Question Strategy found on page 306 in the **Write-In Reader**. Tell students that by questioning as they read, they can check how well they understand the important ideas in a story. For example, have students describe questions they had about Francis Aubrey as they read "The Fastest Rider in the West" and the answers they found to these questions.

APPLY READING SKILLS

Introduce *Animal Doctors*. Choral read the first few pages with students. Depending on their abilities, have students continue reading with partners or as a group.

Quick Check Fluency

Listen to individual students as they read the **Write-In Reader** selection. Make specific notes about words that presented difficulty to them.

Leveled Reader

EXTRA PRACTICE

Independent Reading Have students read from a book of their choice and describe what they read in their reading logs.

Warm Up

Oral Grammar

Prepositions

- Tell students that prepositions are mostly little words that we use for many different purposes. Some prepositions help us tell *when* something happened.

- Write a few prepositions on the board or on a pad.

Prepositions That Tell W*hen*		
about	at	before
after	on	around
between	near	during
past	in	since

- Look at the clock, and give students a few examples of time-related prepositions. Begin by asking a few questions. Then have students suggest examples.

  *Is it **past** 10:00 yet? What can we do **before** lunch? Is it **near** lunchtime yet? **About** what time will we eat today?*

Talk About It

Help focus students' attention on preparing for a sports-team tryout. Ask, *How do athletes prepare for team tryouts?*

Discuss the question, emphasizing these points:

- They practice.
- They watch other players to learn from them.
- They get enough rest.
- They exercise.
- They think positively.

Target Vocabulary

Write-In Reader pages 172–173

- Read and discuss each paragraph. Then discuss the meaning of each Target Vocabulary word. Suggest that students underline words or phrases that provide clues to meaning. Also point out the following:

    Contrast the meaning of *deliberately* in this instance, "when someone does something on purpose," with another meaning for the word, "done with careful consideration," as in *He made his decision* deliberately, *by carefully comparing all of his choices.*

    As used in the story, *lure* means "to tempt a person into doing something." A *lure* is also "a small object, often bright in color, that is attached to a fishing line to attract fish."

- Allow time for students to write their responses. Then ask students to choose an answer they would like to read aloud.

Possible responses:

  1. by placing a bowl of food on the ground next to it

  2. wanting another person's things so much that you begin to dislike that person

  3. disappeared

  4. basketball, tennis, running

  5. I do my homework every night.

Quick Check Target Vocabulary

Ask each student to use one of the Target Vocabulary words in a sentence.

> ✔ **TARGET VOCABULARY**
>
> When someone does something on purpose, he or she does it **deliberately**.
>
> If something is done **especially**, it is done in a special or specific way.
>
> A person who wants something that another person has feels **jealous**.
>
> To **lure** someone is to tempt him or her to do something.
>
> If something **vanished**, it disappeared or was missing.

> **EXTRA PRACTICE**
>
> **Build Fluency** Have students read **Write-In Reader** pages 172–173 with a partner or a family member.

SHARE OBJECTIVES

- Read words with vowel pair syllables.
- Understand a character's motivations and behaviors.
- Read to apply skills and strategies.

MATERIALS

Write-In Reader pages 174–177

ACADEMIC LANGUAGE

prefix	character
motive	question

Warm Up

Multisyllable Words

Focus: Vowel Pair Syllables

Write these words on the board or on a pad.

1	unload	recook	subway
2	untrue	retrains	disown
3	unpaid	preheat	unclean

Row 1: Say, *These words all begin with a prefix. Identify the prefix in each word.* Point out that some of these prefixes are closed syllables (Columns 1 and 3) and some are open syllables (Column 2). Demonstrate how to divide each word after the prefix.

un / load   re / cook   sub / way

Ask, *How are the second syllables in these words alike?* (They are vowel pair syllables.) Model reading the words.

Row 2: Have volunteers underline the prefixes and circle the vowel pair syllables. Then choral read the words.

Row 3: Listen to each student read the words. Make corrections as needed. Record your findings.

RETEACH

Understanding Characters

- Look for a set of keys in your pocket. Then hold up the keys and ask, *What was I looking for? Why do I need these keys?*

- Explain that you had a **motive**, or reason, for your action. Draw a chart to show how the events are related.

Action	**Motive**
I looked for my keys.	I need to unlock my car and get my briefcase.

- Explain that characters also have motives that explain their actions. A reader can better understand the plot when he or she understands a character's motives.

- Display a familar book. Have students name a character and describe a motive for his or her actions.

Quick Check | Comprehension

Have students tell about a time when they had specific motives or reasons for their actions.

READ

"Right on Track"

Write-In Reader pages 174–177

- Preview the selection with students using the **Think Aloud** to predict what this story will be about. Guide students to use the title and pictures to make predictions. Record their ideas.

Think Aloud *The pictures show runners. I think this story must have something to do with racing. What other clues help you predict what the story will be about?*

- Together, review the steps to the Question Strategy, **Write-In Reader** page 305. As needed, guide students in applying the strategy as they read.

READ

Ask students to read to confirm their predictions. Have students take turns reading the selection with partners. Discuss, confirm, and revise student predictions based upon story details.

REREAD

Call on individuals to read aloud while others follow along. Stop to discuss each question. Allow time for students to write their responses before proceeding. Sample answers are provided.

Page 174: Why did Rachel run after Anya? (The two girls walk to school together, and Anya was ahead of Rachel.)

Help unpack meaning, if needed, by asking, *Why did Rachel call to Anya?* (to get her to wait up) *What did Rachel and Anya do next?* (They walked to school together.)

Unpack Meaning: For questions on pages 175–177, you may want to use the notes in the right-hand column.

Page 175: Why might people be jealous of someone like Anya? (because she was good at sports)

Page 176: Was Anya being mean when she laughed? Why, or why not? (No. Anya was trying to encourage her friend, and she laughed at Rachel to let Rachel know that she had a good chance at making the cross-country team.)

Turn and Talk **Page 177:** How can you tell that Anya really cares about her friend? (She tells Rachel that it isn't speed but being able to keep on running that counts in this kind of race. By reassuring Rachel, Anya shows that she is a good friend.) Have partners discuss this question and then share with the group.

UNPACK MEANING

Use prompts such as these if students have difficulty with a **Stop•Think•Write** question:

Page 175 *What does* jealous *mean?* (wanting something that another person has) *What is Anya able to do that some people might be jealous of?* (She's good at sports.)

Page 176 *Why did Anya laugh at Rachel?* (because Rachel didn't realize that she ran a long way almost every day) *How did Anya help Rachel by reminding her that she often ran a long way?* (It gave Rachel confidence to think that she could run a cross-country race.)

Page 177 *Underline what Anya whispers to Rachel. How does what Anya says make Rachel's fears vanish?* (Anya reminds Rachel that the race is not about speed, but about the kind of running that Rachel is good at.)

EXTRA PRACTICE

Build Fluency Have students read **Write-In Reader** pages 174–177 with a partner or a family member.

Day 3

SHARE OBJECTIVES

- Understand prepositions.
- Read aloud fluently to improve accuracy and self-correction.
- Read to apply skills and strategies.

MATERIALS

Write-In Reader pages 178–180

ACADEMIC LANGUAGE

preposition   accuracy   self-correction

Oral Grammar

Prepositions

- Tell students that prepositions are mostly little words that we use for many different purposes. Prepositions can be difficult to explain, but some prepositions tell how one object is positioned or located compared to another object. These prepositions help us explain *where* something is.

- Gather a few objects: a box, a book, or a ball. Place the objects in a variety of locations and say, *The book is* behind *the desk,* by *the desk,* under *the desk,* inside *the box…*

- Then name a preposition and have students place objects in places that demonstrate where they are the appropriate location.

Prepositions That Tell *Where*		
beside	behind	below
across	by	outside
on	off	under
over	above	between
underneath	near	inside

RETEACH

Fluency: Accuracy and Self-Correction

Write-In Reader page 174

- Have students follow along as you read aloud the last paragraph on page 174. Say *cross-county* for *cross-country*. Then pause and say *cross-country* to model self-correction.

- Say, *I knew I misread something. I had never heard of a cross-county race before. So, I looked at the sentence again and realized that I had misread* country.

- Explain, *It's important to read with accuracy. Think about what you are saying. Ask yourself, "Does this make sense?" If the answer is "no" look back at the text. You may have misread a word or a phrase.*

- Have students take turns reading aloud sentences from the story. Encourage them to read with accuracy, self-correcting when they make mistakes.

READ

"Right on Track"

Write-In Reader pages 178–180

Review the first part of the story with students. Ask, *What have we learned so far?* Then preview today's reading. Have students look for clues to help them predict how this story will end.

READ

Ask students to read to confirm their predictions. Have students take turns reading the selection with partners. Discuss, confirm, and revise predictions based upon story details. Ask if there was anything about the way the story ended that surprised them.

REREAD

Call on individuals to read aloud while others follow along. Stop to discuss each question. Allow time for students to write their responses before proceeding. Sample answers are provided.

Page 178: What does the author mean by saying that Anya didn't slow down underlined(deliberately)? (She didn't slow down on purpose; she slowed down because she got tired.)

Help unpack meaning, if needed, by asking, *What does deliberately mean?* (on purpose) *Why did Anya slow down?* (She got tired.) *Did Anya get tired on purpose?* (no)

Unpack Meaning: For questions on pages 179–180, you may want to use the notes in the right-hand column.

Turn and Talk **Page 179:** Do you think Rachel expected to beat Damon? (Responses will vary, but students should recognize that all through the story Rachel kept on saying that she couldn't run fast enough to win the race.) Have partners discuss this question and then share with the group.

Page 180: Do you think the other team members will like having Rachel on the team? Why? (Yes. Damon gives Rachel a high-five, then says that the whole team owes Rachel's aunt a big thank you.)

Quick Check **Retelling**

Have students retell the end of the story. Support the retelling by asking, *What happened once the race began? Did Rachel make the team? Why?*

UNPACK MEANING

Use prompts such as these if students have difficulty with a **Stop•Think•Write** question:

Page 179 *Why did Rachel win the race?* (She had a lot of energy left and used it to overtake Damon.) *Why might Rachel have known that she could run and run and still have one more burst of energy?* (Anya convinced Rachel that her runs back and forth to her aunt's house showed that she had that ability.)

Page 180 *What does Damon give to Rachel after the race is over?* (a high-five) *What does a high-five mean?* (good job)

EXTRA PRACTICE

Build Fluency Have students read **Write-In Reader** pages 178–180 with a partner or a family member.

SHARE OBJECTIVES

- Read words with prefixes that have vowel pair syllables.
- Identify prepositions and prepositional phrases.
- Answer questions using evidence from the text.

MATERIALS

Write-In Reader pages 174–181

ACADEMIC LANGUAGE

preposition   prepositional phrase

Warm Up

Multisyllable Words

Focus: Vowel Pair Syllables

Write these words on the board or on a pad.

1	misread	displease	reteach
2	refreeze	unchain	upstream
3	mistreat	recount	preclean

Row 1: Say, *These words all have a prefix. I'm going to read the prefix, then blend it with the rest of the word.* Then ask, *How are the second syllables in these words alike?* (They are vowel pair syllables.)

Row 2: Have volunteers underline the prefix and circle the vowel pair syllable. Then choral read the words with students.

Row 3: Listen to each student read the words. Make corrections as needed. Record your findings.

RETEACH

Prepositions

- Review that a preposition is a little word that can tell such things as when something is happening, how it is happening, and where something is located. Ask, *What are some prepositions you know?* (Possible answers: *at, in, by, near, above, beyond*) Have students use the prepositions in sentences.

- Write one of the students' sentences on the board. Circle the preposition. Then underline the prepositional phrase. Explain that a prepositional phrase includes both a preposition and a noun, or the "object of the preposition."

Turn and Talk Have students find examples of prepositional phrases in the selection. Have them identify the preposition and the object of the preposition in the example sentences they find.

Quick Check Grammar

Write the following prepositions on the board: *during, before, since,* and *past.* Have students use the words in oral sentences. Remind them that each prepositional phrase includes both a preposition and an object.

Look Back and Respond

Write-In Reader pages 174–181

Help students complete the Look Back and Respond page. Model how to use the hint in question 1 to find evidence that can be used to support answers.

• Explain that evidence is proof, clues, or information.

• Remind students that they can circle or underline the specific words in the selection that they used as evidence for their answers.

1. Which character is good at many sports? (Anya)

Help unpack meaning, if needed, by asking, *Which character were some people jealous of?* (Anya) *Why?* (She is good at many sports.)

Turn and Talk Have students work independently on questions 2, 3, and 4. When students have completed the page, have partners discuss their responses and then share them with the group. Sample responses are provided. Accept reasonable responses.

Unpack Meaning: For questions 2–4, you may want to use the notes in the right-hand column to guide the discussion about student responses.

2. Why did Anya think Rachel would be a good cross-country runner? (Anya knew that the distance that Rachel ran to visit her aunt was about as long as a cross-country race.)

3. Why was it important for Rachel to believe in herself? (As soon as Anya convinced Rachel that she could do it, Rachel began to believe in herself. When that happened, her fear vanished and she was no longer nervous.)

4. What makes Anya a good friend? (Responses will vary, but students should recognize that Anya is constantly encouraging her friend by bringing up evidence that Rachel "can do it!")

UNPACK MEANING

Use prompts such as these if students have difficulty with a question:

2. *What evidence can you find on page 176 to help you write your answer?* (Anya knows that the distance that Rachel runs to her aunt's every day is about as long as a cross-country race.)

3. *Lots of times nerves make a person lose confidence in themselves. What happened when Rachel's fears vanished?* (She stopped being nervous and felt confident.)

4. *How does Anya respond when Rachel says that she is not good at sports?* (Anya challenges her friend's opinion.) *What does Anya's behavior say about her feelings toward Rachel?* (that she cares for Rachel and wants her to be a success)

EXTRA PRACTICE

Retell Have students retell "Right on Track" to a partner or a family member.

SHARE OBJECTIVES

- Read words with vowel pairs syllables in context.
- Demonstrate understanding of Target Vocabulary words.
- Preview Persuasion and the Infer/Predict strategy.

MATERIALS

Context Cards: *crisp, deliberately, especially, gigantic, haze, jealous, lapped, lure, miniature, vanished,*

Write-In Reader pages 164–170

Leveled Reader: *Tammy's Goal*

ACADEMIC LANGUAGE

persuade   infer   predict

✓ TARGET VOCABULARY

Crisp means sharp and clear.

Haze is foggy or smoky air.

Something that is **gigantic** is huge or enormous.

If something **lapped** against you, it splashed or brushed lightly against you.

Something that is much smaller than the usual size is **miniature**.

Multisyllable Words
Cumulative Review

- Write these sentences on the board or on a pad.

    1. Let's recount the yellow cakes for the Moon Festival.

    2. The girls display their Fellow Friends ribbons.

    3. Friends esteem and never mistreat each other.

- Have student volunteers circle the vowel pairs. Check their work. Assign students to work with a partner to practice reading the sentences. Then listen to each student read one sentence. Record your findings.

REVIEW

Target Vocabulary
Context Cards

- Display the **Context Cards** for *crisp, gigantic, haze, lapped,* and *miniature*. Review the meanings of these words. Then have students use the words in oral sentences about preparing for and running a cross-country race.

- Add the **Context Cards** for *deliberately, especially, jealous, lure,* and *vanished*. Give one card to each student. Have students make up riddles for their words. Have the rest of the group guess the answer.

✏️ WRITE ABOUT IT

- Ask students to write about a book they have read or a movie or TV program that they have seen in which one character is jealous of another. Have students describe why this character was jealous. Tell students to use the word *jealous* in their descriptions.

PRETEACH

Persuasion
Infer/Predict

Write-In Reader pages 164–170

- Introduce skill and strategy. Say, *In the next lesson, we are going to focus on ways that authors try to persuade, or convince, readers to agree with their ideas or point of view. We'll also work on ways to infer and then predict events in a story.*

- Explain, *Remember, authors have different purposes for writing. One purpose is to persuade readers to think or feel in a certain way. We read a story called "Monkey Business" a while ago. In this story, the author's goal, or purpose, was to try to persuade us that monkeys can be helpful to people who cannot help themselves.*

- Ask, *What examples did the author give to persuade the reader that monkeys were good companions and helpers to people who are not able to do certain things for themselves?*

- List on the board with students some examples, such as those below:

  1. Monkeys can use their hands to pick up things, to open doors, and to turn lights off and on for people who can't do these things.

  2. Monkeys can bring things to people who can't walk.

  3. Monkeys can comb someone's hair, put a straw in a drink, and even dial 911 on the telephone if there's an emergency.

- Turn to and review the Infer/Predict Strategy found on page 304 in the **Write-In Reader**. Have students review "Monkey Business." Ask, *What inferences or predictions can you make based on what you read?* Have them identify their inferences and predictions as well as the clues they used to make them.

APPLY READING SKILLS

- Introduce *Tammy's Goal.* Choral read the first few pages with students. Depending on their abilities, have students continue reading with partners or as a group.

Quick Check Fluency

● Leveled Reader

Listen to individual students as they read the **Write-In Reader** selection. Make specific notes about words that presented difficulty to them.

INFER/PREDICT STRATEGY

When you make an **inference**, you use clues in the text and what you already know to figure out what the author does not tell you.

Look for clues like these to help you make an inference:

- what characters say
- characters' actions
- plot events
- description of the setting
- main ideas and details
- characteristics of the genre
- your prior knowledge and experiences

A **prediction** is a type of inference. When you make a prediction, you use clues to guess what will happen.

EXTRA PRACTICE

Independent Reading Have students read from a book of their choice and describe what they read in their reading logs.

SHARE OBJECTIVES

- Identify and use transition words.
- Discuss slavery in America.
- Read to build meaning for Target Vocabulary words.

MATERIALS

Write-In Reader pages 182–183

ACADEMIC LANGUAGE

transition word

Warm Up

Oral Grammar

Transition Words

- Write these words on the board or on a pad. Point to and chorus read each word with students.

after	before	while	when	now
first	next	then	finally	later

- Explain to students that these are good transition words to use when you are telling a story about an event that occurred. Ask, *Why do you think these are good words for telling a story?* (These words help the speaker or writer make it clear in which order events occur.)

- Play a game of "grapevine." Start the story yourself, using one of the words in a phrase or sentence. For example, you might say, *One night after dinner, I heard a noise downstairs.* (Then turn over the next story event to a volunteer.) Make sure that each student uses at least one of the transition words in her or his part of the story.

- Summarize the use of transition words by explaining that these words give clues about which action occurs before another one takes place.

Talk About It

Help focus students' attention on the traits of a good leader. Ask, *What are some of the character traits that make someone a hero?*

Discuss the question, emphasizing these points:

- Heroes are selfless. They are willing to put the needs of others before themselves.

- Heroes inspire. They set an example for others to follow.

- Heroes are enthusiastic. They feel strongly about their beliefs and their interest in helping and inspiring others.

- Heroes are brave and daring. They take chances that many other people are afraid to take.

Target Vocabulary

Write-In Reader pages 182–183

- Read and discuss each paragraph. Then discuss the meaning of each Target Vocabulary word. Suggest that students underline words or phrases that provide clues to meaning. Also point out the following:

  The word *publicity* is related to the word *public*, which can help you remember the meaning of *publicity*, "information given out to get the public's attention."

- Allow time for students to write their responses. Then ask students to choose an answer they would like to read aloud.

Responses:

1. disagreements

2. Possible response: Violence is the use of physical force to cause harm. When someone inflicts violence on someone else he or she can cause injury or even death to that person.

3. Possible response: They give a lot of time and energy to something.

4. Possible response: so that you can accomplish things, even if they are frightening or overwhelming

5. Possible response: give speeches, write newspaper articles

Quick Check Target Vocabulary

Ask each student to use one of the Target Vocabulary words in a sentence.

✔ **TARGET VOCABULARY**

When people have **conflicts**, they have problems or disagreements with each other.

To **dedicate** something is to devote it to a special purpose.

To **overcome** a difficulty is to solve it or conquer it.

Publicity is information given out to get the public's attention.

Violence is the use of physical force to cause harm.

EXTRA PRACTICE

Build Fluency Have students read **Write-In Reader** pages 182–183 with a partner or a family member.

SHARE OBJECTIVES

- Read words with vowel pair syllables.
- Recognize persuasive text.
- Read to apply skills and strategies.

MATERIALS

Write-In Reader pages 184–187

ACADEMIC LANGUAGE

persuasion   infer   predict

Warm Up

Multisyllable Words

Focus: Vowel Pair Syllables

Write these words on the board or on a pad.

1	player	peaceful	speechless
2	cleaner	needy	joyless
3	eater	gloomy	meaty

Row 1: Say, *These words have endings.* Explain that we can divide before an ending to make words easier to read.

play / er   peace / ful   speech / less

Circle the vowel pair syllable. Model reading each word.

Row 2: Have volunteers identify the ending, divide before it, and circle the vowel pair syllable. Then choral read the words.

Row 3: Listen to each student read the words. Make corrections as needed. Record your findings.

RETEACH

Persuasion

- Show the class an advertisement from a newspaper or magazine. The ad should contain persuasive language designed to convince the consumer to buy a product. Ask, *What does the writer say to persuade or convince you to want to buy the product?*

- Review that authors sometimes write to **persuade**, or convince readers to think and act in a certain way, or to buy or do something.

- Ask students to brainstorm different types of persuasive writing. List their ideas on the board. (Possible answers include editorials, advertisements, letters to the editor, political flyers.)

- Point out that authors often use emotional language in persuasive writing. An author who is writing persuasive material usually wants the reader to agree with him or her.

Quick Check Comprehension

Ask students to describe something they read recently where the author's purpose was to persuade.

READ

"Harriet Tubman: American Hero"

Write-In Reader pages 184–187

• Preview the selection with students using the **Think Aloud** to predict what the story will be about.

> **Think Aloud** *The title tells me the story is about Harriet Tubman. What other clues help you predict what you will learn?*

• Together, review the steps to the Infer/Predict Strategy, **Write-In Reader** page 304. Guide students in applying the strategy.

READ

Ask students to read to confirm their predictions. Have students take turns reading the selection with partners. Discuss, confirm, and revise student predictions based upon selection details.

REREAD

Call on individuals to read aloud while others follow along. Point out multisyllable words with vowel pairs such as *owner* and *freedom*. Stop to discuss each question. Sample answers are provided.

Page 184: How does the author want you to feel about the boss? How do you know? (The author wants us to really dislike the boss. She describes him as cruel and gives an example of how he was cruel.)

Help unpack meaning, if needed, by asking, *What adjective does the author use to describe the boss?* (cruel) *What did the boss do to Harriet?* (threw a heavy weight at her head)

Unpack Meaning: For questions on pages 185–187, you may want to use the notes in the right-hand column.

Turn and Talk **Page 185:** What made Harriet Tubman want to escape slavery? (She was being sold to a new owner and would have to leave her family.) Have partners discuss this question and then share with the group.

Page 186: Why do you think that Harriet wanted to <u>dedicate</u> herself to helping enslaved people escape? (She knew how difficult their lives were. She wanted to free her family.)

Page 187: What are two challenges that Harriet and her passengers had to <u>overcome</u>? (crossing swamps, forests, and mountains without getting caught; traveling back roads at night)

UNPACK MEANING

Use prompts such as these if students have difficulty with a **Stop•Think•Write** question:

Page 185 *Something happened right before Harriet decided to escape. What was that event?* (She was being sold to a new owner.) *What did this mean for Harriet?* (She would have to leave her family.) *How do you think this made her feel?* (sad and scared)

Page 186 *What does* dedicate *mean in this paragraph?* (give a lot of time and energy to) *Why does Harriet want to give time and energy to helping slaves?* (because she was a slave, too)

Page 187 *What does* overcome *mean?* (solve) *What are some problems people had to face when escaping from slavery?* (crossing swamps, forests, and mountains without getting caught; traveling back roads at night)

EXTRA PRACTICE

Build Fluency Have students read **Write-In Reader** pages 184–187 with a partner or a family member.

Day 3

SHARE OBJECTIVES

- Identify and use transition words and phrases.
- Read aloud fluently to improve stress.
- Read to apply skills and strategies.

MATERIALS

Write-In Reader pages 188–190

ACADEMIC LANGUAGE

conjunction   stress

Warm Up

Oral Grammar

Transition Words and Phrases

- Write these words and phrases on the board or on a pad. Point to and read each word with students.

as	as if	as long as	unless
because	so that	whenever	where

- Explain to students that these words can help them connect sentences together. Provide an example, such as, *I am happy as long as I get enough sleep.*

- Tell students that these words are conjunctions. They join sentence parts and make meaning clear.

- Have student partners write sentences containing three of these conjunctions. Provide more examples if necessary.

  *I am **as** hungry **as** a bear.*

  *He acts **as if** he knows everything.*

  *I will leave now **unless** you want me to stay.*

  *He acts like that **because** he is worried.*

  *I know **where** you are going.*

RETEACH

Fluency: Stress

Write-In Reader page 188

Explain that you are going to read from page 188 in two different ways, and you want students to evaluate your reading.

- First, read the first five sentences on the page in a natural way. Emphasize words that help to communicate the danger and drama of escaping slavery such as *scared, tired, hungry, cold, conflicts, begged, one rule, there was no going back.* Then read the sentences in a flat way. Avoid adding stress to any of the words as you read.

- Ask, *What did you think of my first reading? Explain. Was my second reading better or worse? Explain.* Be sure students recognize that when a reader puts emphasis, or stress, on a word or phrase, a listener will pay special attention to the words.

- Have students take turns reading aloud one of the remaining sentences from the page, concentrating on stress as they read.

READ

"Harriet Tubman: American Hero"

Write-In Reader pages 188–190

Review the first part of the story with students. Ask, *What have we learned about Harriet Tubman so far?* Then preview today's reading. Have students look for clues to help them predict how this story will end.

READ

Ask students to read to confirm their predictions. Have students take turns reading the selection with partners. Discuss, confirm, and revise predictions based upon story details. Ask if there was anything about the way the story ended that surprised them.

REREAD

Call on individuals to read aloud while others follow along. Stop to discuss each question. Point out multisyllable words with vowel pairs and endings such as *leader*. Allow time for students to write their responses before proceeding. Sample answers are provided.

Page 188: Why do you think that Harriet never lost a passenger? (She was a skilled and capable conductor.)

Help unpack meaning, if needed, by asking, *What did Harriet do?* (help people escape slavery) *She never lost a passenger. What does that say about Harriet's ability as a conductor?* (She was a very good conductor.)

Unpack Meaning: For questions on pages 189–190, you may want to use the notes in the right-hand column.

Page 189: In what two ways did Harriet help the North during the Civil War? (She served as a nurse and she spied for the North.)

Turn and Talk **Page 190:** What words tell how the author feels about Harriet Tubman? (brave, great American hero) Have partners discuss this question and then share with the group.

Quick Check | **Retelling**

Have students retell the end of the story. Support the retelling by asking, *What was Harriet's rule for the slaves she was helping escape? How did Harriet help during the Civil War? How is Harriet Tubman remembered?*

UNPACK MEANING

Use prompts such as these if students have difficulty with a **Stop•Think•Write** question:

Page 189 *What facts do you see about Harriet during the Civil War?* (She made special tea for soldiers to help cure them. She spied for the North.)

Page 190 *What adjective does the author use to describe Harriet in the second paragraph?* (brave) *What does the author call Harriet in the last sentence?* (a great American Hero)

EXTRA PRACTICE

Build Fluency Have students read **Write-In Reader** pages 188–190 with a partner or a family member.

SHARE OBJECTIVES

- Read words with vowel pair syllables.
- Recognize and use transition words.
- Answer questions using evidence from the text.

MATERIALS

Write-In Reader pages 184–191

ACADEMIC LANGUAGE

transition word

Warm Up

Multisyllable Words

Focus: Vowel Pair Syllables

Write these words on the board or on a pad.

1	smoothest	weakness	payment
2	deepest	neatness	ailment
3	meanest	greatness	treatment

Row 1: Say, *These words all have an ending. I'm going to divide these words before the ending.* Then ask, *How are the first syllables in these words alike?* (They are vowel pair syllables.) Model reading the words, blending the first syllable with the ending.

Row 2: Have volunteers underline the ending and circle the vowel pair syllable. Then choral read the words.

Row 3: Listen to each student read the words. Make corrections as needed. Record your findings.

RETEACH

Transition Words

- Review that transition words and phrases connect one idea to the next, one sentence to the next, or one paragraph to the next. Transitions help readers connect the author's thoughts and ideas. Some transitions show time order, such as *first*, *then*, *next*, *before*, and *after*. Writers also use transitions to conclude, such as *in conclusion*, *as a result*, and *in summary*.

- Have students turn to page 190 and read the first two sentences aloud. Ask, *What transition words connect events in the order that they happened?* (After, In 1908)

Turn and Talk Have students reread the remaining sentences on this page and list other transition words to describe the order of events in Harriet Tubman's later life.

Possible answers: Over time, In 1913, In 1944, In 1995

Quick Check **Grammar**

Have students write a paragraph describing an event, such as a birthday party, and have them include at least two transition words or phrases.

Look Back and Respond

Write-In Reader pages 184–191

Help students complete the Look Back and Respond page. Model how to use the hint in question 1 to find evidence that can be used to support answers.

- Explain that evidence is proof, clues, or information.

- Remind students that they can circle or underline the specific words in the selection that they used as evidence for their answers.

1. What opinion does the author want readers to have about Harriet Tubman? Why do you think that? (**brave**, evidence: author tells how Harriet stepped between the boss and a slave and got hurt as a result; **selfless**, evidence: Harriet dedicated her life to helping other slaves escape to freedom despite putting herself in danger; **strong leader**, evidence: she did not let the slaves she was helping give up)

Help unpack meaning, if needed, by asking, *What does* opinion *mean?* (what someone thinks or believes) *How does the author show readers what Harriet Tubman was like?* (She tells readers what Harriet did and said, and we can see how others respected and followed her instructions.)

Turn and Talk Have students work independently on questions 2 and 3. When students have completed the page, have partners discuss their responses and then share them with the group. Sample responses are provided. Accept reasonable responses.

Unpack Meaning: For questions 2 and 3, you may want to use the notes in the right-hand column to guide the discussion about student responses.

2. When escaping slaves became scared, how did Harriet persuade them not to turn back? (She told them if they go back, slave hunters might find the rest of them. She said they would be free or die.)

3. What words would you use to describe Harriet? Explain. (brave, selfless, a hero; she risked her life to help others escape slavery)

Day 5

SHARE OBJECTIVES

- Read words with vowel pair syllables.
- Demonstrate understanding of Target Vocabulary words.
- Preview Main Ideas and Details and the Visualize Strategy.

MATERIALS

Context Cards: *association, brilliant, capitol, conflicts, dedicate, drought, horizon, overcome, publicity, violence*

Write-In Reader pages 184–190

Leveled Reader: *Songs for the People*

ACADEMIC LANGUAGE

main Idea   detail   visualize

✓ TARGET VOCABULARY

An **association** is a group of people officially organized for a certain purpose.

Something that is **brilliant** is very bright.

A **capitol** is a building in which government meets to create laws.

During a **drought**, there is little or no rain.

The place where the earth and sky meet is the **horizon**.

Multisyllable Words

Cumulative Review

- Write these sentences on the board or on a pad.

  1. Workers did not receive fair payment or treatment.

  2. Some men were displeased with their fellow workers.

  3. Bosses did indeed mistreat some workers.

- Have student volunteers circle vowel pair syllables in these multisyllable words. Assign students to work with a partner to practice reading the sentences. Then listen to each student read one sentence. Make corrections as needed. Record your findings.

REVIEW

Target Vocabulary

Context Cards

- Display the **Context Cards** for *association, brilliant, capitol, drought,* and *horizon*. Review the meanings of these words. Then give one card to each student. Have them make up a riddle for their word. Have the rest of the group guess the answer.

- Add the **Context Cards** for *conflicts, dedicate, overcome, publicity,* and *violence*. Then have students use the words in oral sentences about what it means to be a strong leader.

✏ WRITE ABOUT IT

- Have students write a diary entry from the point of view of a person being helped to freedom by Harriet Tubman. Have them use the word *overcome* in their descriptions.

Main Ideas and Details
Visualize

Write-In Reader pages 184–190

- Introduce skill and strategy. Say, *In the next lesson, we are going to focus on identifying main ideas and details. We'll also work on ways to visualize events.*

- Explain, *Main ideas are the most important ideas in a selection. An author provides details, such as facts and examples, to explain more about a main idea and to make it clearer.*

- Say, *One main idea in this week's story is that Harriet was a good conductor. What details support this main idea?*

- List on the board with students the details to support this main idea.

  1. Harriet made nineteen trips and overcame many challenges to lead enslaved people to freedom.

  2. Harriet did not stop even when slave hunters were willing to pay $40,000 to anyone who found her.

  3. She never lost a passenger.

- Turn to and review the Visualize Strategy, found on page 305 in the **Write-In Reader**. Tell students that when they visualize, they use details in a selection and what they already know to create pictures in their minds. Have them use the main ideas and details to visualize events in the selection.

APPLY READING SKILLS

Introduce *Songs for the People*. Choral read the first few pages with students. Depending on their abilities, have students continue reading with partners or as a group.

Quick Check Fluency

Leveled Reader

Listen to individual students as they read the **Write-In Reader** selection. Make specific notes about words that presented difficulty to them.

VISUALIZE STRATEGY

When you **visualize**, you use details in a text to help you create mental pictures. Use the author's words plus your own knowledge and experiences. Visualizing can help you understand and remember what you are reading.

In narrative texts, visualize

- how characters look and act.
- settings and plot events.
- how one event leads to the next event.

In informational texts, visualize

- what an object, a real person, or place looks like.
- how something works or how it is built.
- steps to complete a task.
- how one event leads to another event.
- how things are alike and different.

Be ready to change your mental pictures as you read new details.

EXTRA PRACTICE

Independent Reading Have students read from a book of their choice and describe what they read in their reading logs.

SHARE OBJECTIVES

- Use abbreviations correctly.
- Discuss the early exploration and settlement of America's West.
- Read to build meaning for Target Vocabulary words.

MATERIALS

Write-In Reader pages 192–193

ACADEMIC LANGUAGE
abbreviation

Oral Grammar

Abbreviations

- Write the abbreviations below on the board or on a pad. Have students practice reading them.

Months		Days		Directions and Locations
Jan.	Feb.	Mon.	Tues.	E (East)
Aug.	Sept.	Wed.	Thurs.	W (West)
Oct.	Nov.	Fri.	Sat.	N (North)
Dec.		Sun.		S (South)
				Ave. (Avenue)
				St. (Street)
				Rd. (Road)

- Have students write and read dates:
  - their birthdays
  - holidays
  - special events

- Have students write and read addresses:
  - their own
  - their school's
  - their relatives'
  - their friends'

Talk About It

Help focus students' attention on river travel in the 1800s. Ask, *What challenges might people face traveling down a major river in small wooden boats?*

Discuss the question, emphasizing these points:

- The water on a river can sometimes get rough. Small boats can easily capsize in rapids.
- Waterfalls can halt a boat trip on a river. Even worse, a boat could go over the falls.
- Traveling on a river in a small boat loaded with supplies can be dangerous.
- Boats can spring leaks or get damaged on sharp rocks.

Target Vocabulary

Write-In Reader pages 192–193

• Read and discuss each paragraph. Suggest that students underline words or phrases that provide clues to the missing words. Then discuss the meaning of each Target Vocabulary word to figure out how to complete the cloze sentence. Also point out the following:

Route and *root* are homophones—they sound alike, but have different meanings and spellings. A *route* is "a road or path between two places." A *root* is "the part of the plant that grows underground, securing the plant and collecting water and nutrients from the soil."

In this instance, *accompany* means "to go somewhere with someone." The word is also used in music ("to play or sing a part to support a larger part") as in *The singer always has a piano player to accompany him.*

A *duty* is "a person's job or responsibility." A *duty* can also be "a tax paid on goods, especially those imported or exported," as in *Souvenirs sold at the airport are duty-free.*

• Allow time for students to write their responses. Then ask students to choose an answer they would like to read aloud.

Responses:

1. supplies

2. accompany

3. territory

4. route

5. duty

Quick Check | Target Vocabulary

Ask each student to use one of the Target Vocabulary words in a sentence.

✔ **TARGET VOCABULARY**

To go somewhere with someone is to **accompany** him or her.

A person's **duty** is his or her job or responsibility.

A **route** is a road or path between two places.

Supplies are the important items that people need.

An area of land is a **territory**.

EXTRA PRACTICE

Build Fluency Have students read **Write-In Reader** pages 192–193 with a partner or a family member.

SHARE OBJECTIVES

- Read words with vowel pair syllables.
- Identify main ideas and details.
- Read to apply skills and strategies.

MATERIALS

Write-In Reader pages 194–196

ACADEMIC LANGUAGE

main idea   detail   visualize

Warm Up

Multisyllable Words

Cumulative Review

- Write these sentences on the board or on a pad.

  1. Sacagawea took them upstream past the teepees.

  2. He tried not to be fearful or show weakness.

  3 The tribe displays a peaceful nature.

- Have student volunteers circle multisyllable words with vowel pair syllables. Assign students to work with a partner to practice reading the sentences. Then listen to each student read one sentence. Record your findings.

RETEACH

Main Ideas and Details

- Display a nonfiction book with chapters (such as a book about animals). Read the title and point out the topic of the book. Then read a chapter title. Ask, *What is the main idea of this chapter?*

- Remind students that a **topic** tells what a book or selection is about. The **main idea** is an important idea about the topic. **Details** tell more about the main idea.

- Read a paragraph from the chapter. Use an Idea-Support Map to show the main idea and details in the paragraph.

- Ask students to use the map to summarize the paragraph. Point out that identifying the main idea and details can help a reader understand, summarize, and remember.

Quick Check Comprehension

Ask students to find and read a paragraph in a classroom nonfiction book or magazine. Have them identify the main idea and at least two supporting details.

READ

"Conquering the Mighty Colorado"

Write-In Reader pages 194–196

- Preview the selection with students using the **Think Aloud** to predict the setting (both time and place). Guide students to use headings and pictures to make predictions. Record their ideas.

Think Aloud   *The title tells me where the story takes place. I think it takes place on the Colorado River. What clues can you find to figure out when the story takes place?*

- Together, review the steps to the Visualize Strategy, **Write-In Reader** page 305. As needed, guide students in applying the strategy as they read.

READ

Ask students to read to confirm their predictions. Have students take turns reading the selection with partners. Discuss, confirm, and revise student predictions based upon text details.

REREAD

Call on individuals to read aloud while others follow along. Stop to discuss each question. Point out examples of multisyllable words with vowel pairs, such as *easy* and *afraid*. Allow time for students to write their responses before proceeding. Sample answers are provided.

Page 194: Where did Powell and his team plan to go? (down the Colorado River)

Help unpack meaning, if needed, by asking, *What is the title of the story?* ("Conquering the Mighty Colorado") *What does the illustration show?* (a man and several boats)

Unpack Meaning: For questions on pages 195–196, you may want to use the notes in the right-hand column.

Turn and Talk   **Page 195:** Why was it important for Powell to pick strong, brave men to <u>accompany</u> him? (The Colorado was fast-moving and dangerous; no one had ever traveled down it; it would not be easy.) Have partners discuss this question and then share with the group.

Page 196: What kind of <u>supplies</u> might the men have brought? (food, guns, water)

UNPACK MEANING

Use prompts such as these if students have difficulty with a **Stop•Think•Write** question:

Page 195 *How does the author describe the Colorado River on page 194?* (fast-moving, dangerous) *What kind of person is willing to travel down a fast-moving, dangerous river?* (a strong, brave one)

Page 196 *What does* supplies *mean in this paragraph?* (items the men needed on the trip) *Where were the men going?* (down the Colorado) *What kinds of supplies would a person need to stay alive in this wilderness region?* (food, water, weapons)

EXTRA PRACTICE

Build Fluency Have students read **Write-In Reader** pages 194–196 with a partner or a family member.

Day 3

SHARE OBJECTIVES

- Identify abbreviations.
- Read aloud fluently to improve phrasing.
- Read to apply skills and strategies.

MATERIALS

Write-In Reader pages 197–200

ACADEMIC LANGUAGE

abbreviation   phrasing

Oral Grammar

Abbreviations

- Discuss with students why we use abbreviations in our writing. Then ask, *What abbreviations have you used in math?* You may want to prompt with the unabbreviated word. Say, *What unit of measurement would I use to describe the length of my desk?* (feet, yards) *How would I abbreviate that unit of measurement?*

Common Examples	
Length customary	foot (ft), inch (in.), yard (yd), mile (mi)
Length metric	centimeter (cm), kilometer (km), meter (m)

- Point out to students that abbreviations for customary measurements in math often include a period, but metric measurement abbreviations do not. Also, point out that these (and most) math abbreviations are not capitalized. Exceptions include F (for Fahrenheit) and C (for Celsius).

RETEACH

Fluency: Phrasing

Write-In Reader page 199

Read a paragraph from page 199 in two different ways, and have students evaluate your reading.

- First, read the text rapidly, almost in one breath. Do not chunk text into phrases or pause for punctuation. Then reread the paragraph in a more expressive voice. Model how to group words into phrases and how to pause naturally after each phrase and punctuation mark.

- Then ask, *Which reading was better? Why?* Be sure students recognize that "chunking" groups of words into meaningful phrases and pausing slightly between the phrases and at punctuation marks can help listeners understand a story.

- Have student pairs or small groups practice reading aloud a paragraph of their choice from pages 194–197. Encourage them to concentrate on phrasing and on pausing appropriately for punctuation.

READ

"Conquering the Mighty Colorado"

Write-In Reader pages 197–200

Review the first part of the story with students. Ask, *What have we learned so far about John Wesley Powell and his journey on the Colorado River?* Then preview today's reading. Have students look for clues to help them predict how this story will end.

READ

Ask students to read to confirm their predictions. Have students take turns reading the selection with partners. Discuss, confirm, and revise predictions based upon story details.

REREAD

Call on individuals to read aloud while others follow along. Stop to discuss each question. Point out words with vowel pair syllables, including *feeding*, *supplies*, and *journey*. Allow time for students to write their responses before proceeding.

Page 197: Tell one way the land changed as the men moved along the river. (Possible answers: steep mountainsides, open grassland)

Help unpack meaning, if needed, by asking, *What did Powell notice as the men sailed down the river?* (sheep on steep sides of mountains; elk feeding in open grassland)

Unpack Meaning: For questions on pages 198–200, you may want to use the notes in the right-hand column.

Page 198: Why did one of the men leave the team? (The trip was too dangerous.)

Page 199: Why didn't the men ride in the boats all the way down the river? (The water was too rough.)

Turn and Talk **Page 200:** How did Powell's trip help other Americans? (They learned about lands in the West and then moved there to build along the Colorado River.) Have partners discuss this question and then share with the group.

Quick Check Retelling

Have students retell the end of the story. Support the retelling by asking, *What happened at the waterfall? What was the Colorado River like? What effect did the trip have on Americans?*

UNPACK MEANING

Use prompts such as these if students have difficulty with a **Stop•Think•Write** question:

Page 198 *What happened right before the man decided to leave?* (His boat went over a waterfall and smashed into the rocks.) *How do you think the men felt?* (scared)

Page 199 *What did the men do when the water was too rough?* (They walked on the shore.)

Page 200 *What did Americans do when they learned about the West from Powell?* (Families moved to the West to build homes along the Colorado River.)

EXTRA PRACTICE

Build Fluency Have students read **Write-In Reader** pages 197–200 with a partner or a family member.

SHARE OBJECTIVES

- Read words with vowel pair syllables.
- Identify abbreviations.
- Answer questions using evidence from the selection.

MATERIALS

Write-In Reader pages 194–201

ACADEMIC LANGUAGE

abbreviation

Warm Up

Multisyllable Words

Cumulative Review

- Write these sentences on the board or on a pad.
  1. Did they complain about being mistreated?
  2. He finds a treatment for her ailment.
  3. They are fellow travelers from her viewpoint.
- Have student volunteers circle multisyllable words with vowel pair syllables. Assign students to work with a partner to practice reading the sentences. Then listen to each student read one sentence. Record your findings.

RETEACH

Abbreviations

- Review that abbreviations are a shortened form of a word, such as *Dr.* for *Doctor*, *Rd.* for *Road*, or *Tues.* for *Tuesday*. Discuss why writers use abbreviations. For example, it takes less time to write an abbreviation than a full word, name, or title in an address or list.
- Remind students that many abbreviations begin with a capital letter and are followed by a period. State names are exceptions; both letters are capital letters, and no periods are used.
- Write abbreviations for places on the board or a pad. Have students identify the words they represent.

  Places: Ave. TX

  Time: hr. Tues.

  Measurements: mi. in.

- Have students write the date, the address of your school or another community building, and your name. Tell them to use at least one abbreviation in each response.

Turn and Talk Have students make a list of abbreviations they use in their daily lives, from teachers' names to addresses to measurements to days and months.

Quick Check Grammar

Write several types of abbreviations on the board or a pad. Have students identify words represented by the abbreviations.

Look Back and Respond

Write-In Reader pages 194–201

Help students complete the Look Back and Respond page. Model how to use the hint in question 1 to find evidence that can be used to support answers.

- Explain that evidence is proof, clues, or information.

- Remind students that they can circle or underline the specific words in the selection that they used as evidence for their answers.

1. Why did Powell explore the Colorado? (His love of science led him to explore the river.)

Help unpack meaning, if needed, by asking, *What clues can you find on page 195 to help you answer the question?* (His love of science led him to explore the Colorado.)

Turn and Talk Have students work independently on questions 2, 3, and 4. When students have completed the page, have partners discuss their responses and then share them with the group. Sample responses are provided. Accept reasonable responses.

Unpack Meaning: For questions 2–4, you may want to use the notes in the right-hand column to guide the discussion about student responses.

2. Why had no one ever gone down the Colorado before? (It was dangerous.)

3. Was Powell's team brave? Explain. (Yes. They were doing something no one had done before, and they knew it was dangerous.)

4. Do you think the men who left early regretted their decisions? Explain. (Responses will vary, but may include: Yes they regretted leaving early because the team completed the expedition sucessfully.)

UNPACK MEANING

Use prompts such as these if students have difficulty with a question:

2. *The author directly states the reason why no one had ever gone down the Colorado River before. What is the reason?* (It was too dangerous.)

3. *What part of your answer to question 2 can help you answer this question?* (My answer to question 2 was that no one had gone down the Colorado because it was dangerous. Knowing it was dangerous helps me know that Powell's team had to be brave.)

4. *What happened to the men who did not leave early?* (They completed their journey and helped Americans learn about land in the West.) *How do you think the men felt at the end?* (proud, happy)

EXTRA PRACTICE

Retell Have students retell "Conquering the Mighty Colorado" to a partner or a family member.

Day 5

SHARE OBJECTIVES

- Read sentences with vowel pair syllables.
- Demonstrate understanding of Target Vocabulary words.
- Preview Theme and the Summarize Strategy.

MATERIALS

Context Cards: *accompany, clumsy, corps, duty, interpreter, landmark, proposed, route, supplies, territory,*

Write-In Reader pages 194–200

Leveled Reader: *John Wesley Powell*

ACADEMIC LANGUAGE

theme   summarize

 TARGET VOCABULARY

Something that is **clumsy** is awkward or done without skill.

A **corps** is a group that works together.

An **interpreter** translates words from one language to another.

A **landmark** is a familiar or easily seen object that identifies a place.

If something is **proposed**, it is suggested.

Multisyllable Words
Cumulative Review

- Write these sentences on the board or on a pad.
    1. She fills her canteen and reheats the meat.
    2. This is one of the deepest and smoothest rivers.
    3. We will follow the path upstream.

- Have student volunteers circle multisyllable words with vowel pair syllables. Assign students to work with a partner to practice reading the sentences. Then listen to each student read one sentence. Record your findings.

REVIEW

Target Vocabulary
Context Cards

- Display the **Context Cards** for *clumsy, corps, interpreter, landmark*, and *proposed*. Review the meanings of these words. Then have students use the words in oral sentences about taking a journey down the Colorado River.

- Add the **Context Cards** for *accompany, duty, route, supplies*, and *territory*. Give one card to each student. Have students think of a synonym for their words. Have them take turns sharing their synonyms. Ask the rest of the group to identify the correct vocabulary word for each synonym.

WRITE ABOUT IT

- Ask students to write about a dangerous situation that an explorer going down the Colorado River might have faced back in the late 1800s. Have them tell about what happened, using the word *route* in their descriptions.

PRETEACH

PRETEACH

Theme
Summarize

Write-In Reader pages 194–200

- Introduce skill and strategy. Say, *In the next lesson, we are going to focus on theme in a story. We'll also work on ways to summarize events.*

- Explain, *Most stories have a theme. A theme is a message about life. The theme of a story is different from the subject. The subject is the topic. An author does not state the theme directly, but communicates it in different ways, including what happens in a story, how the characters behave and feel, and what the characters think.*

- Ask, *What do you think is the theme of this week's story?*

- List on the board with students what themes they think are in the story, along with evidence of each theme.

    1. Bravery is rewarded. (The men who finished the expedition made a difference in the lives of Americans who decided to build their lives around the Colorado River.)

    2. Quit while you're ahead. (Some men quit because the journey was dangerous.)

    3. Listen to, and respect, nature. (When the men saw how rough the water was, they decided to walk on the shore.)

- Turn to and review the Summarize Strategy found on page 302 in the **Write-In Reader**. Tell students that when they summarize, they should briefly tell the important parts of the story in their own words. Have students think about the story themes to help them summarize the selection.

APPLY READING SKILLS

- Introduce *John Wesley Powell*. Choral read the first few pages with students. Depending on their abilities, have students continue reading with partners or as a group.

Quick Check Fluency

Listen to individual students as they read the **Write-In Reader** selection. Make specific notes about words that presented difficulty to them.

John Wesley Powell

● **Leveled Reader**

SUMMARIZE STRATEGY

When you **summarize**, you briefly explain the most important ideas in a text in your own words. Organize a summary in a way that makes sense, and do not change the meaning of the text. A summary can be as short as one or two sentences.

In narrative texts, explain

- who the main character is and where the story takes place.

- the problem that the main character faces.

- the most important events.

- how the problem is resolved.

In informational texts, explain

- the main idea.

- the most important details that support the main idea.

EXTRA PRACTICE

Independent Reading Have students read from a book of their choice and describe what they read in their reading logs.

Teacher Notes

Unit 4 Never Give Up!

Lesson 16 "Riding Freedom"

Build Background: How can someone overcome great difficulties?

Comprehension: Compare and Contrast; Monitor/Clarify

Target Vocabulary: churning, defended, deserve, escorted, relied, reputation, satisfied, situation, swelled, worthy

High-Utility Words: accident, collapsed, convince, disguise, train

Lesson 17 "The Right Dog for the Job: Ira's Path from Service Dog to Guide Dog"

Build Background: How does training lead to success?

Comprehension: Sequence of Events; Summarize

Target Vocabulary: ceremony, confesses, confidence, disobey, foster, graduate, patiently, performs, reward, symbol

High-Utility Words: blind, difficulty, disabilities, special, training

Lesson 18 "Moon Runner"

Build Background: How do athletes achieve their goals?

Comprehension: Understanding Characters; Question

Target Vocabulary: crisp, deliberately, especially, gigantic, haze, jealous, lapped, lure, miniature, vanished

High-Utility Words: apologize, celebrate, compete, fault, trouble

Lesson 19 "Harvesting Hope: The Story of Cesar Chavez"

Build Background: What makes a good leader?

Comprehension: Persuasion; Infer/Predict

Target Vocabulary: association, brilliant, capitol, conflicts, dedicate, drought, horizon, overcome, publicity, violence

High-Utility Words: choice, justice, miserable, rebel, struggle

Lesson 20 "Sacagawea"

Build Background: What makes a team successful?

Comprehension: Main Idea and Details; Visualize

Target Vocabulary: accompany, clumsy, corps, duty, interpreter, landmark, proposed, route, supplies, territory

High-Utility Words: disaster, expedition, journey, skills

SHARE OBJECTIVES

- Participate in discussion about driving a stagecoach in the 1800s
- Say, read, and use Target Vocabulary and high-utility words
- Practice comparing and contrasting and complete a Venn Diagram

MATERIALS

Language Support Card 16
Context Cards
Chant ELL16.1 (A Worthy Stagecoach Driver)
Student Book (pp. 406–416)
Main Selection Summary ELL16.2
Graphic Organizer Transparency 14

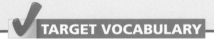

✔ TARGET VOCABULARY

• = Spanish cognate

churning	
defended	• defendieron
deserve	
escorted	• escoltar
relied	
reputation	• reputación
satisfied	• satisfechos
situation	• situación
swelled	
worthy	

ACADEMIC LANGUAGE

• = Spanish cognate

compare	• comparar
contrast	• contrastar

Listening, Speaking, and Viewing

USE LANGUAGE SUPPORT CARD
Present **Language Support Card 16**. Use the activities on the back of the card to introduce concepts and vocabulary from "Riding Freedom" and to practice **Academic English**.

Develop Target Vocabulary

USE CONTEXT CARDS Show the **Context Cards** for *situation* and *reputation*. Present the cards using Steps 1–3 of the Introduce Vocabulary routine on **Teacher's Edition** p. T14.

- Help students use *situation* and *reputation* to discuss how someone can overcome great difficulties.

- Encourage students to use high-utility words in their responses.

USE ORAL LANGUAGE CHANT Distribute **Chant ELL16.1**. Read the title aloud, and have students repeat. Have students look at the title, images, and other information on the page. Then have them predict what they think the chant will be about.

BLM ELL16.1

- As you read the chant aloud, display the **Context Cards** for *worthy, reputation, deserve,* and *defended*. After you read the chant, have students use each word in an original sentence.

- Lead students in a discussion about what it would take to drive a stagecoach in the 1800s. Compare the requirements to driving a car today. List student responses.

- Allow students to include language from **Chant ELL16.1**. Encourage them to use high-utility words.

▬▬▶ **WRITE-PAIR-SHARE** Display sentence frames such as the following, and have partners use them to write complete sentences.

1. Stagecoach drivers _____relied_____ on their skills in order to drive safely.

2. If you have a good _____reputation_____, you are viewed well by other people.

Scaffold Comprehension

PREVIEW "RIDING FREEDOM" Explain that, before reading, students will skim "Riding Freedom" in order to predict what the selection is about. Help students scan illustrations, highlighted words, and other text features on **Student Book** pp. 406–416. Have them predict one thing they may learn by reading the text.

USE MAIN SELECTION SUMMARY Distribute **Summary ELL16.2**. Read the summary aloud, and then have partners take turns naming the meaning of each vocabulary word.

BLM
ELL16.2

RETEACH
Compare and Contrast

TEACH/MODEL Read aloud the first paragraph in **Summary ELL16.2**. Write *compare* and *contrast*. Say the words aloud, and have students repeat.

- Remind students that to compare things is to tell how they are alike, and to contrast things is to tell how they are different.

GUIDED PRACTICE Have students read the first paragraph in **Summary ELL16.2**. Write *Alike* and *Different*.

- Display **Graphic Organizer Transparency 14**. Explain that a Venn Diagram can help students identify how things are alike and how they are different.

- Draw a blank Venn Diagram. Label the left circle *The 1800s* and the right circle *Today*. Label the overlapping area of the circles *Both*.

- Have students read the first paragraph in order to identify how things in the 1800s are similar to or different from today.

- Display a completed Venn Diagram as a reference throughout the week.

CHECK PROGRESS

Do students…
- correctly pronounce and use vocabulary words in discussion?
- compare and contrast details?

REVIEW TOGETHER

- Have partners use **Context Cards** to review the Target Vocabulary words and their meanings. Have them complete the activities on the backs of the cards.
- Have partners write *alike* and *different* on index cards and use them as they take turns retelling how the activities they like to do are alike and different.

Graphic Organizer 14

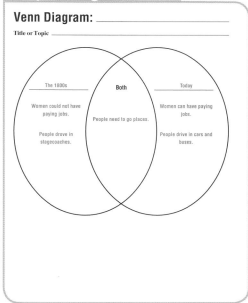

Venn Diagram: _____

Title or Topic

The 1800s — Women could not have paying jobs. People drove in stagecoaches.

Both — People need to go places.

Today — Women can have paying jobs. People drive in cars and buses.

✏️ Scaffolded Practice and Application

Beginning	**Intermediate**	**Advanced**	**Advanced High**
Help students label their Venn Diagrams. Provide language to help them act out and describe details that show how things today are similar to and different from the 1800s.	Have partners discuss their Venn Diagrams and write additional words or phrases that show how things today are similar to and different from the 1800s.	Have partners label their Venn Diagrams and write complete sentences in the columns to describe how things today are similar to and different from the 1800s.	Have partners use their completed diagrams to write a paragraph comparing and contrasting how things today are similar to and different from the 1800s.

- Use Target Vocabulary words to discuss "Riding Freedom"
- Listen to and recite a chant about driving a stagecoach in the 1800s
- Identify sound and spelling changes in words
- Monitor events to clarify information

MATERIALS

Student Book (pp. 406–416)
Student Book Audiotext CD
Chant ELL16.1 (A Worthy Stagecoach Driver)
Context Cards
Main Selection Summary ELL16.2
Language Support Card 16

ACADEMIC LANGUAGE

• = Spanish cognate

historical fiction	• *ficción histórica*
monitor	
clarify	• *clarificar*

Scaffold Comprehension

DISCUSS "RIDING FREEDOM" Use the following picture-text prompts to discuss "Riding Freedom." Remind students that "Riding Freedom" is **historical fiction**. Historical fiction is a story whose characters and events are set in real periods in history.

PAGE 407: Have students read the title aloud. *What does the word freedom mean to you?* Discuss student responses.

PAGE 412: Have students find and point to the word *worthy*. Charlotte checks to make sure the bridge is worthy of carrying the stage coach. She wants to make sure it will be safe. How do Charlotte's actions prove that she is a *worthy* stagecoach driver? (She is careful and thoughtful. This helps her drive the stagecoach through a storm.)

PAGE 416: *Describe the expressions on the passengers' faces. Do they seem amazed by what Charlotte did? What type of reputation do you think she will have after this ride?* (Yes; She will have a good reputation after this ride.)

AUDIOTEXT CD Make the **Audiotext CD** for "Riding Freedom" available. Have students follow in the **Student Book** as they listen.

Practice Target Vocabulary

USE ORAL LANGUAGE CHANT Distribute **Chant ELL16.1**. Have a student read the title aloud.

BLM
ELL16.1

- Read the chant aloud, or have a proficient reader model reading aloud.

- Have students identify Target Vocabulary and high-utility words in the chant and read the words aloud with you.

- Have them restate each Target Vocabulary word and share the meaning of each word in their own words. Then have them complete the activity on the page.

PRACTICE FLUENCY: EXPRESSION Read aloud or choral read **Chant ELL16.1** with a few students. Have students who are not reading follow along on their pages as they listen. Have them listen as you model appropriate expression. Have partners echo you and take turns repeating each stanza with appropriate expression.

PRETEACH
Sound/Spelling Changes

INTRODUCE Write *public*. Explain that *public* means "having to do with people" or "known to people." Then write and pronounce *publicity*. Explain that *publicity* can mean "attracting the attention of people" or "making something known to the public."

• *How is the word* publicity *the same as* public*? How are the two words different?* Point out that *publicity* is formed by adding *-ity* to the end of *public*. The spelling change causes the /k/ sound in *public* to become the /s/ sound in *publicity*.

PRACTICE Have students use **Context Cards**, the chant, the summary, or *Riding Freedom* to look for and name words that change their sounds and how they are spelled. *(relied, situation, satisfied)*

RETEACH
Monitor/Clarify

TEACH/MODEL Remind students that they should **monitor**, or pay attention to, what they read. If they don't understand something in a text, they should **clarify**, or clear up, their understanding of it. Use a Think Aloud to model monitoring and clarifying information from "Riding Freedom."

Think Aloud *On page 411, it says that the rain "came down in washtubs." I read that the rain "came flying in every direction." This tells me that the phrase means it was raining very hard.*

GUIDED PRACTICE As a class, reread sections of "Riding Freedom," and monitor and clarify students' understanding of the story. Remind students that they can use this strategy to help them compare and contrast story details.

• Review **Teach Academic English** on **Language Support Card 16**. Remind students to use the causative verb *made* and phrases with *because of* when they monitor and clarify events from the story.

CHECK PROGRESS
Do students…
• demonstrate fluency as they read the chant with appropriate expression?
• identify words with sound and spelling changes?
• correctly monitor and clarify details from "Riding Freedom"?

REVIEW TOGETHER
• Have partners take turns reading **Chant ELL16.1** aloud. Encourage them to recite the chant together with appropriate expression.
• Have partners work together to identify sound and spelling changes in words from the selection.
• Have students reread "Riding Freedom" and use a Venn Diagram to help them monitor and clarify details that compare and contrast.

✏️ Scaffolded Practice and Application

Beginning	Intermediate	Advanced	Advanced High
Have partners compare and contrast one detail from the story. Help them use the monitor and clarify strategy to make the comparison.	Have partners identify information from the story that they may not understand. Then have them use the strategy to clarify the information.	Have partners clarify details from the story. Have them read the original details and their clarifications to the class.	Have students choose three or four details from the story. Have them write sentences that clarify the details. Have students read their sentences to the class.

Scaffold Comprehension

REVIEW "RIDING FREEDOM" Use a Think Aloud and the following prompts to lead students on a guided review of "Riding Freedom." Remind students that reviewing and retelling what they read will help them compare and contrast story details.

Think Aloud **PAGE 408:** *In the first paragraph of the story, we read that Charlotte is learning to drive a stagecoach all over again after losing sight in one eye. I wonder if she will be able to drive as well as before.*

PAGE 409: Ask students to look for the word *relied*. Have a student read the sentence aloud. *When you rely on something, you depend on it. What did Charlotte have to rely on to drive the coach?* (her good eye)

PAGE 411: Point to James. *How would you describe the look on his face?* Point to Charlotte. *How would you describe the look on Charlotte's face? Why does Charlotte look excited while James looks scared?* (She knows she can drive the stagecoach, even in the rain.)

PAGE 412: *Find the words* worthy *and* satisfied *on this page.* Have a student read the paragraph aloud. *Why did Charlotte check to see if the bridge was worthy?* (to see if she was satisfied with it)

CHECK COMPREHENSION If students need additional support with the main selection, direct them to **Summary ELL16.2**. Read the summary aloud, and have them listen and follow along on their pages.

BLM
ELL16.2

Have students take turns reading sections of the summary aloud. Have them answer the following comprehension questions:

1. Why did Charlotte disguise herself as a man?

2. How did Charlotte learn to drive again?

3. Why did the passengers praise Charlotte?

Have students work in pairs to circle high-utility words and highlight Target Vocabulary words found in **Summary ELL16.2**. Then have students use each word in an original sentence.

AUDIOTEXT CD Make the **Audiotext CD** for "Riding Freedom" available. Have students follow in the **Student Book** as they listen.

PRETEACH
Context Clues

INTRODUCE *Sometimes when you read, you will see words that you don't know.* **Context clues** *are nearby words that can help you figure out the meaning of words you don't know.*

- Write *The bridge collapsed and dropped into the churning river.* Circle *collapsed.* *Look at this sentence.* Collapsed *means "fell down." If you didn't know the meaning of this word, you should look for context clues to help you. What context clue in this sentence can help you figure out what* collapsed *means?* (The bridge dropped after collapsing.)

THINK-PAIR-SHARE Write the following sentences. Have students read the sentences together and use context clues to orally figure out the meanings of the underlined words.

1. The teacher <u>escorted</u> her students as she led them to the classroom. (accompanied)

2. The passengers were <u>satisfied</u> and happy with their journey. (pleased)

RETEACH
Compare and Contrast

TEACH/MODEL Explain that when you **infer**, you use what you know, plus story details, to figure out more about events or characters in a story or selection.

GUIDED PRACTICE Guide students to make an **inference** from "Riding Freedom" that **compares** and **contrasts**. *Is James as good a stagecoach driver as Charlotte? How do you know?* (Yes. He says he will take the reins if Charlotte can't handle it, so he must be a good driver.)

CHECK PROGRESS

Do students…
- use Target Vocabulary words appropriately to discuss "Riding Freedom"?
- correctly answer questions about the summary?
- use context clues to identify the meanings of unknown words?
- infer story details that compare and contrast?

REVIEW TOGETHER

- Provide additional practice with **Context Cards.**
- Have partners take turns reading aloud **Summary ELL16.2.**
- Have partners discuss unknown words or phrases from "Riding Freedom." Guide them to use context clues to figure out the meanings of the unknown words or phrases.
- As a class, review inferences the students made that compare and contrast. Have students use keywords such as *alike* and *different* to discuss their inferences.

Scaffolded Practice and Application

Beginning Have students draw and label a Venn Diagram. Then have them use simple words and phrases to infer details that compare and contrast James and Charlotte.	**Intermediate** Have partners make inferences about James and Charlotte. Then have them draw and fill in a Venn Diagram with their details.	**Advanced** Have partners draw and label a Venn Diagram. Then have them write complete sentences that describe an inference comparing and contrasting James and Charlotte.	**Advanced High** Have partners draw a Venn Diagram and write complete sentences that infer a comparison of James and Charlotte. Have them use their completed diagrams to write a paragraph.

Day 4

- Use Target Vocabulary words to discuss "Spindletop"
- Practice identifying and using adjectives

MATERIALS

Student Book (pp. 412, 418–420, 422)
Leveled Reader
Context Cards

ACADEMIC LANGUAGE

• = Spanish cognate

informational text	• texto informativo
adjective	• adjetivo

Scaffold Content-Area Reading

DISCUSS "SPINDLETOP" Use the following picture-text prompts to lead students on a review of "Spindletop." Tell them that "Spindletop" is **informational text**. Remind them that informational text gives factual information about a topic.

PAGE 418: *What was Spindletop?* (a salt dome) *Where was Spindletop located?* (near Beaumont, Texas)

- *How is a salt dome formed?* (by rising underground mineral salts)

PAGE 419: *How would you describe the early efforts to drill oil at Spindletop?* (unsuccessful)

- *How was the Lucas Geyser more successful than other oil fields in Texas?* (It produced 100,000 barrels of oil per day.)

PAGE 420: *How did Spindletop affect the town of Beaumont?* (Beaumont became one of the first oil-fueled boomtowns.)

Leveled Reader

READ *A DANGEROUS TRIP* To read more about life in the 1800s, direct students to the **Leveled Reader**. Have partners or small groups take turns rereading the selection aloud to one another.

BUDDY READING Pair more proficient readers with slightly less proficient readers. Have students take turns reading to each other. Display these tips that more proficient readers can use when their less proficient buddies read to them.

◆ **English Language Learners**

1. Help with pronunciation when you know words that your buddy doesn't know.

2. Help your buddy sound out difficult words. If necessary, model reading the word aloud.

3. Ask questions to help your buddy understand the story:

   - What is happening in this picture?

   - Where are the people in the story?

   - What is the problem in the story?

RETEACH
Adjectives

TEACH/MODEL Write *adjective*. Explain that adjectives such as *strong* are words that describe nouns. *Some adjectives tell what kind. Some adjectives tell how many.*

- Have students turn to **Student Book** p. 422. Remind students that they can combine sentences by using *and* to join adjectives that follow a form of the verb *be*.

- Have students use adjectives to describe Charlotte from "Riding Freedom." List the adjectives. Then use *and* to combine the adjectives into one sentence, such as *Charlotte is strong and brave.*

GUIDED PRACTICE Point to the picture of the horses on **Student Book** p. 412. Have a student count the horses. *How do you think the six horses feel during the storm?* Write *The six horses are scared and nervous.*

- Remind students that *six* tells how many horses there are in the picture. *Scared and* nervous *are also adjectives that describe the horses.* Have a student underline the adjectives in the sentence.

> **Extend Language**
> **Synonyms for *strong***
> robust, stout, solid, durable, resilient, tough
> **Synonyms for *brave***
> courageous, valiant, heroic, bold, daring, fearless, plucky
> **Synonyms for *scared***
> frightened, afraid, terrified, fearful, petrified, worried, anxious, timid

---

CHECK PROGRESS

Do students…
- use Target Vocabulary words appropriately to talk about "Spindletop" and *A Dangerous Trip*?
- identify and use adjectives in sentences?

REVIEW TOGETHER

- Provide additional practice with **Context Cards**.
- Have partners read sections of "Spindletop" and *A Dangerous Trip* to each other.
- List several adjectives. Have students write sentences using at least two adjectives and *and* in a sentence.

✏️ **Scaffolded Practice and Application**

Beginning Write *The stagecoach is strong and fast.* Read the sentence aloud. Then have partners write the sentence and work together to underline the adjectives.	**Intermediate** Write *Several horses were tired* and *Every passenger was frightened.* Tell students to copy the sentences. Then have them underline the adjectives.	**Advanced** Write *The passengers were _____ and _____.* Have students copy the sentence and complete it with adjectives. Then have students read their sentence to the class.	**Advanced High** Have students write their own sentences using adjectives, then exchange with a partner. Have them underline the adjectives in their partner's sentences.

Compare Texts

MAKE COMPARISONS Use the model below to help students complete a chart comparing life in the 1800s. Have students refer to their **Leveled Reader** and **Student Book** pp. 406–416 and 418–420.

Title	"Riding Freedom"	"Spindletop"	*A Dangerous Trip*
Characters	Charlotte, James, passengers	Patillo Higgins, Captain Anthony F. Lucas	the Ambrose family
Difficult Situations	Charlotte is blind in one eye; drives a stagecoach in a big storm	drilling for oil in Texas was difficult; hard to get people to provide money for drilling	hard life in Missouri, river floods
How They Overcame Situations	Charlotte relearns how to drive; she saves the passengers	convinces people to invest; strikes oil	family moves to Oregon; manages to cross over the river

- Have students orally form sentences based on the information in the chart. Provide sentence frames such as the following:

1. ___James___ and ___Charlotte___ are characters in "Riding Freedom."

2. ___The Ambrose family___ overcame a difficult situation by moving to a new place.

3. One difficult situation in ___"Riding Freedom"___ was Charlotte's blindness.

DISCUSS COMPARISONS To help students compare and contrast life in the 1800s, ask questions such as *What difficult situations did people in the 1800s have to overcome? How were the situations alike? How were they different?* Provide sentence frames such as:

4. Life in the 1800s was ___difficult___.

5. People in the 1800s had to ___move from place to place___.

6. In both "Riding Freedom" and *A Dangerous Trip,* the characters had to ___cross over a river___.

Write to Narrate

TEACH/MODEL Review the features of a **descriptive paragraph**. *In a paragraph that describes, you need a **main idea**. A sentence that states your main idea is a **topic sentence**. **Details** can support your main idea. In descriptive writing, the details should show, not just tell, what something is like.*

- Read and discuss the Writing Traits Checklist on **Student Book** p. 424 and the Writing Model on **Student Book** pp. 424–425. Point out examples of similes that paint vivid pictures.

GUIDED PRACTICE Explain that the class will work together to write a descriptive paragraph.

- Write *Life in the 1800s was difficult.* Have the group read the statement aloud chorally. Explain that this sentence will be the main idea. *The paragraph will have details about life in the 1800s that will support this main idea.* Remind students that in descriptive writing, the writer shows, not just tells, what something is like.

> **Extend Language**
> **Synonyms for *difficult***
> hard, tough, demanding, arduous, tiring, strenuous, grueling, challenging

- Have individuals suggest descriptive sentences to include in the paragraph. Tell them to refer to the sentence frames they used to discuss the chart and the ones they used to compare the selections. Remind students to include adjectives and similes in the sentences.

- Write students' suggestions in the paragraph. Then, as a group, review the paragraph and make suggestions for combining any sentences so they aren't choppy.

- Have a student read the completed paragraph aloud to the class.

CHECK PROGRESS

Do students…
- participate in discussion about life in the 1800s?
- correctly identify similarities and differences between life in the 1800s?
- use adjectives and similes in their writing?

REVIEW TOGETHER

- Have students work in pairs or small groups to read and review the rows and columns of the life in the 1800s comparison chart.
- Have partners help each other check for and include vocabulary words in their writing.
- Have students review the **Writing Rubric** on p. 18 of the **Grab-and-Go™ Resources**.

✏️ Scaffolded Practice and Application

| **Beginning** Provide the sentence frame *The _____ waters of the river were rough.* Write *churning* and *swift.* Have students use each word in the sentence and read the sentences chorally. | **Intermediate** Have students write completions for the following sentence frame: *Life in the 1800s was difficult because _____.* | **Advanced** Have partners add descriptive words to these sentences: *The stagecoach traveled across the bridge; The passengers were scared.* | **Advanced High** Have students use the comparison chart to write a descriptive paragraph about how life is different today than it was in the 1800s. |

✔ TARGET VOCABULARY

	• = Spanish cognate
ceremony	• ceremonia
confesses	• confesar
confidence	• confianza
disobey	
foster	
graduate	• graduar
patiently	• pacientemente
performs	
reward	
symbol	• símbolo

ACADEMIC LANGUAGE

	• = Spanish cognate
sequence	• secuencia
events	• eventos

Listening, Speaking, and Viewing

USE LANGUAGE SUPPORT CARD
Present **Language Support Card 17**. Use the activities on the back of the card to introduce concepts and vocabulary from "The Right Dog for the Job" and to practice **Academic English**.

Develop Target Vocabulary

USE CONTEXT CARDS Show the **Context Cards** for *performs* and *reward*. Present the cards using Steps 1–3 of the Introduce Vocabulary routine on **Teacher's Edition** p. T86.

- Help students use *performs* and *reward* to discuss how training leads to success.

- Encourage students to use high-utility words in their responses.

USE DIALOGUE Distribute **Dialogue ELL17.1**. Read the title aloud, and have students repeat. Have students look at the title, images, and other information on the page. Then have them predict what they think the dialogue will be about.

BLM
ELL17.1

- As you read the dialogue aloud, display the **Context Cards** for *performs, reward, confidence,* and *patiently*. After you read the dialogue, have partners take turns reading each character's lines aloud.

- Brainstorm tasks or professions that require training. List student ideas.

- Have students describe the training needed for each task or profession, such as school or hands-on experience.

- Allow students to include language from **Dialogue ELL17.1**. Encourage them to use high-utility words. Have groups choose one task or profession and make an illustration about the training needed to succeed. Have students label their illustrations with words, phrases, or complete sentences.

▰▰▰▶ **WRITE-PAIR-SHARE** Display sentence frames such as the following, and have partners use them to write complete sentences.

1. A ___reward___ can make people and animals work harder during training.

2. It's important to have ___confidence___ that you can do a job well.

Scaffold Comprehension

PREVIEW "THE RIGHT DOG FOR THE JOB" Explain that students will skim "The Right Dog for the Job" in order to predict what the selection is about. Help students scan the illustrations, captions, and other text features on **Student Book** pp. 430–440. Have them predict one thing they may learn by reading the text.

USE MAIN SELECTION SUMMARY Distribute **Summary ELL17.2**. Read the summary aloud, and then have students reread the summary independently.

BLM ELL17.2

RETEACH

Sequence of Events

TEACH/MODEL Read aloud the third paragraph in **Summary ELL17.2**. Write *sequence* and *events*. Say the words aloud, and have students repeat.

• Explain that a sequence is an order. *A sequence of events tells the order in which things happen.* Point out that adverbs and adverb phrases of time often signal sequences.

GUIDED PRACTICE Have students read the third paragraph in **Summary ELL17.2** and circle the words *later* and *finally*.

• Display **Graphic Organizer Transparency 4**. Explain that a Flow Chart can help students determine the order in which events happened.

• Label the cells of the Flow Chart *First*, *Next*, and *Finally*.

• Write the following events from the summary: *Ira attends service-dog training; Ira learns to wait at lights; Ira graduates from training. Which event came first? Next? Finally?* Have students read the sentences aloud and complete the Flow Chart.

• Display a completed Flow Chart as a reference throughout the week.

CHECK PROGRESS

Do students…
• correctly pronounce and use vocabulary words in discussion?
• identify a sequence of events?

REVIEW TOGETHER

• Have partners use **Context Cards** to review the Target Vocabulary words and their meanings. Have them complete the activities on the backs of the cards.
• Have students make sentences with verbs in a series to describe a sequence of events.

Graphic Organizer

Flow Chart: _____

Title or Topic _____

First, Ira attends service-dog training.

Next, Ira learns to wait at lights.

Finally, Ira graduates from training.

Scaffolded Practice and Application

Beginning Have students write *first, next,* and *finally* in the correct sequence in the Flow Chart. Provide language as needed to help them act out and describe a sequence of events from the summary.

Intermediate Have partners discuss a sequence of events from the summary. Then have them write words or phrases to describe each event in the Flow Chart.

Advanced Have partners discuss a sequence of events from the summary. Then have them use sentences to describe each event in the Flow Chart.

Advanced High Have students write sentences in the Flow Chart about a sequence of events from the summary. Then have them use the Flow Chart to write a paragraph about the events.

SHARE OBJECTIVES

- Use Target Vocabulary words to discuss "The Right Dog for the Job"
- Listen to and recite a dialogue about service dogs
- Identify words that change the -y to -i when adding -es
- Summarize information from "The Right Dog for the Job"

MATERIALS

Student Book (pp. 430–440)
Audiotext CD
Dialogue ELL17.1 (A Special Dog)
Context Cards
Main Selection Summary ELL17.2
Language Support Card 17

ACADEMIC LANGUAGE

• = Spanish cognate

narrative nonfiction	• *narrativa de no ficción*
vowel	• *vocal*
summary	• *resumen*
summarize	• *resumir*

Scaffold Comprehension

DISCUSS "THE RIGHT DOG FOR THE JOB" Use the following picture-text prompts to discuss "The Right Dog for the Job." Remind students that "The Right Dog for the Job" is **narrative nonfiction**. It gives factual information by telling a true story.

PAGE 431: Have students read the title aloud. *What job is the title probably referring to?* (service dog, guide dog)

PAGE 433: Point to the picture, and read the caption. *Why do service dogs perform tasks like picking up keys?* (The people they are helping have difficulty doing such tasks.)

PAGE 434: Point to the plastic lid. *How did Kathleen train Ira to recognize the wheelchair access button?* (She gave him a reward for scratching on the lid with his foot.) *How do rewards help us learn?* (They give us confidence that we are doing well.)

PAGE 436: Point to the picture, and read the caption. *How did the children in Kathleen's classroom help teach Ira?* (They trained him to come when called.)

AUDIOTEXT CD Make the **Audiotext CD** for "The Right Dog for the Job" available. Have students follow in the **Student Book** as they listen.

Practice Target Vocabulary

USE ORAL LANGUAGE DIALOGUE Distribute **Dialogue ELL17.1**. Have a student read the title aloud.

BLM
ELL17.1

- Read the dialogue aloud, or have proficient readers model reading aloud.

- Have students identify Target Vocabulary and high-utility words in the dialogue and read the words aloud with you.

- Have them restate each Target Vocabulary word and tell in their own words what it means. Then have them complete the activity on the page.

PRACTICE FLUENCY: RATE Read or have a fluent reader read **Dialogue ELL17.1** aloud, varying the rate of reading according to the difficulty of the words. Have students echo the reader, using the same rate he or she used.

More Sound/Spelling Changes

INTRODUCE Remind students that spelling changes sometimes cause changes in how a word sounds. Write *puppy* and *fly*. *What vowel sound does each of these words end in?* (long e and long i) Have students underline the *y* in each word.

- Write *puppies* and *flies*. Circle *-ies* in each word. *When you need to add -es to a word that ends in -y, you must change the -y to -i before adding -es. What is the ending sound in* puppies *and* flies? (/z/)

PRACTICE Have students use **Context Cards**, the dialogue, the summary, or "The Right Dog for the Job" to look for and name words that change the *-y* to *-i* when adding *-es*. (*difficulty, abilities, disabilities, family, try, company, university, library*)

Summarize

TEACH/MODEL Write *summary* and *summarize,* and explain the terms. Remind students that a summary tells the most important information in a story. Use a Think Aloud to model summarizing "The Right Dog for the Job."

Think Aloud *On page 435 it says that dogs practice getting on and off buses and staying calm. The puppy raisers take the dogs all over town and teach them how to do tasks and wait quietly.*

GUIDED PRACTICE As a class, retell the important details from other pages of "The Right Dog for the Job." Help students identify only details that are important to include in a summary.

- Review **Teach Academic English** on **Language Support Card 17**. Remind students to use sequencing, adverb phrases of time, and verbs in a series when summarizing.

CHECK PROGRESS

Do students…

- demonstrate fluency as they recite the dialogue at different rates?
- correctly identify words that change the *-y* to *-i* when adding *-es*?
- correctly summarize "The Right Dog for the Job"?

REVIEW TOGETHER

- Have partners take turns reading **Dialogue ELL17.1** aloud. Encourage them to recite the dialogue together, using different rates to compensate for the difficulty of the language.
- Have partners work together to identify words that change the *-y* to *-i* when adding *-es*.
- Have partners take turns summarizing each paragraph of "The Right Dog for the Job" in one or two sentences.

Scaffolded Practice and Application

Beginning	Intermediate	Advanced	Advanced High
Beginning Ask questions to help students identify important details in the selection. Have them answer in one or two words.	**Intermediate** Have students identify important details from the selection. Help them use the details to create sentences summarizing the selection.	**Advanced** Have partners brainstorm details and events from the selection. Have them put the events in sequence and use them to summarize the selection.	**Advanced High** Have partners list details and events from the selection. Have them sequence the events and orally summarize the selection.

SHARE OBJECTIVES

- Use Target Vocabulary words to discuss "The Right Dog for the Job"
- Read and discuss a summary of "The Right Dog for the Job"
- Identify suffixes *-ion*, *-ation*, and *-ition*
- Infer sequence of events

MATERIALS

Student Book (pp. 430–440)
Main Selection Summary ELL17.2
Audiotext CD
Dictionaries
Language Support Card 17
Context Cards

ACADEMIC LANGUAGE

• = *Spanish cognate*

suffix	• *sufijo*
infer	• *inferir*
inference	• *inferencia*

Scaffold Comprehension

REVIEW "THE RIGHT DOG FOR THE JOB" Use a Think Aloud and the following prompts to lead students on a guided review of "The Right Dog for the Job." Remind students that reviewing and retelling what they read can help them better understand the sequence of events and summarize important information.

Think Aloud **PAGE 432:** *On this page, I see the puppies playing at the farm. I see the word* foster. *Someone who fosters a puppy gives the puppy a place to live and takes care of it.*

PAGE 436: Point to the picture. *Where is Ira?* (in a classroom) Have a student read the second paragraph aloud. *How does being in a classroom full of students help with Ira's training?* (He learns to be around noise and people.)

PAGE 438: Point out the picture of the dog leading the person. *Why do service dogs need to have confidence?* (to be able to deal with different situations; to know when to disobey their owner to keep him or her safe)

PAGE 440: *This is Ira at a graduation ceremony. What is a graduation ceremony?* (a special celebration of finishing school) Have students describe what is happening in the picture.

CHECK COMPREHENSION If students need additional support with the main selection, direct them to **Summary ELL17.2**. Read the summary aloud, and have them listen and follow along on their pages.

BLM
ELL17.2

Have students take turns reading sections of the summary aloud. Have them answer the following comprehension questions:

1. How are service dogs helpful?

2. Why do service dogs live in foster homes first?

3. Why does Ira go to live with Don?

Have students work in pairs to circle high-utility words and highlight Target Vocabulary words found in **Summary ELL17.2**. Have them take turns reading each sentence with a vocabulary word and then using the word in an original sentence.

AUDIOTEXT CD Make the **Audiotext CD** for "The Right Dog for the Job" available. Have students follow in the **Student Book** as they listen.

Do students…
- use Target Vocabulary words appropriately to discuss "The Right Dog for the Job"?
- correctly answer questions about the summary?
- identify suffixes -*ion, -ation,* and -*ition*?
- infer a sequence of events?

PRETEACH

Suffixes -*ion*, -*ation*, -*ition*

INTRODUCE Write *suffix*. *A suffix is a word part that is added to the end of a base word or root word. It changes the meaning of the word.* Explain that a suffix has meaning, but it is not a word by itself.

- Write *confess, declare,* and *add*. *These words are verbs. We can add suffixes to change each one to a noun.* Add -*ion, -ation,* and -*ition* to each word, noting that the -e must be dropped before adding the suffix.

THINK-PAIR-SHARE Write *direction, conversation,* and *competition*. Have partners identify the suffix of each word. Then have them use dictionaries to find each word's meaning. Discuss the meanings as a class. Have students use the words to orally complete the following sentences:

1. What ____direction____ is your home from the school?

2. It is hard for Lex to have ____conversation____ with new people.

3. Anna won the athletic ____competition____ because she is so strong.

REVIEW TOGETHER

- Provide additional practice with **Context Cards**.
- Have partners take turns reading aloud **Summary ELL17.2**.
- Write -*ion, -ation,* and -*ition* words, and have partners copy them and break them into word roots and other word parts.
- Write or say a single sequence of events, but omit one step or event. Have students infer what information is missing from the sequence.

RETEACH

Sequence of Events

TEACH/MODEL Write and pronounce *infer* and *inference*. Explain that *infer* is a verb. *When you infer, you use clues to guess about events that aren't in the story.* Inference *is the noun form of* infer.

GUIDED PRACTICE Write *The dog waited patiently. He ran quickly to the front of the room*. Have students read the sentences aloud. *Can you infer what event is missing from this sequence?* (Possible answers: He heard his name; He was called by his owner.)

- Review **Teach Academic English** on **Language Support Card 17**. Remind students that adverb phrases of time can help them infer the order in which events occurred.

✏️ Scaffolded Practice and Application

Beginning Have students copy events from a sequence in a jumbled order. Help them order the events in the correct sequence, using adverb phrases of time as clues.	**Intermediate** Have partners write a familiar sequence of events on strips of paper using adverb phrases of time. Have them exchange sentence strips and correctly order each sequence.	**Advanced** Have partners write a familiar sequence of events in the correct order, leaving out one event. Then have partners exchange sequences and infer each missing event.	**Advanced High** Have partners write a familiar sequence of events on strips of paper, leaving out one event. Have partners exchange sentence strips, order each sequence, and infer the missing event.

SHARE OBJECTIVES

- Use Target Vocabulary words to discuss "The Sticky Coyote"
- Identify and use adverbs that tell how, where, and when

MATERIALS

Student Book (pp. 433, 436, 438, 442–444)
Leveled Reader
Context Cards

ACADEMIC LANGUAGE

• = *Spanish cognate*

trickster tale
adverb   • *adverbio*

Scaffold Content-Area Reading

DISCUSS "THE STICKY COYOTE" Use the following picture-text prompts to lead students on a review of "The Sticky Coyote." Remind them that "The Sticky Coyote" is a **trickster tale**. Remind them that in a trickster tale, a character plays tricks on other characters and is sometimes tricked in return.

PAGE 442: Point to the child holding the shoes. *Who is this character?* (Shoemaker)

- *Why does Coyote offer to help Shoemaker?* (He wants to perform a good deed so the villagers will like him.)

PAGE 443: *What symbol is on the jar?* (a bee) *Find the word* symbol *on this page.* Have a student read the sentence. *What is a symbol?* (something that stands for something else) *What does Coyote think the bee stands for?* (honey)

- Point to Coyote. *How does Coyote wait for the beekeeper?* (patiently) *How does someone act when they are waiting patiently?* (They are quiet and calm.)

PAGE 444: Point to the leaves on Coyote. *What is Coyote covered in? Why?* (leaves; He rolled on the ground when he was sticky with honey.) *Why do the villagers run away from him?* (They think he's a monster.)

- *What does Coyote confess?* (that he tricked Beekeeper and ate the honey) *How do the villagers react?* (They laugh.) Point out the laughing girl in the picture.

Leveled Reader

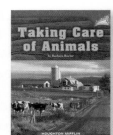

READ *TAKING CARE OF ANIMALS* To read more about animals, direct students to the **Leveled Reader.** Have partners or small groups take turns rereading the selection aloud to one another.

BUDDY READING Pair more proficient readers with struggling or less proficient readers. Have the more proficient reader read aloud for 10–15 minutes, while the less proficient reader follows along in the text. Have the more proficient reader ask questions to help his or her buddy understand the story:

◆ **English Language Learners**

- What is happening in this picture?

- Who are the people in the story?

- What happened in the part of the story I just read to you?

RETEACH
Adverbs

TEACH/MODEL Write *adverb*. Explain that an adverb can modify or change the meaning of a verb. *Some adverbs tell how an action happened, while others tell when and where the action happened.*

• Point to the picture of Ira on **Student Book** p. 433 of "The Right Dog for the Job." Have a student describe the picture. *What is Ira doing?* Write *Ira is learning quickly. Ira practices outside the home.*

• Point to *quickly,* and explain that it is an adverb that tells how Ira learns. Point to *outside,* and explain that this adverb tells where Ira practices.

GUIDED PRACTICE Write sentences with adverbs that tell information from "The Right Dog for the Job." For example, point to the picture on **Student Book** p. 438, and write *Ira will be a guide dog soon.*

• Have students underline the verb and circle the adverb. *Does* soon *tell us how, where, or when?* Point out that adverbs that tell when sometimes come at the end of a sentence instead of after the verb.

Transfer Skills
Adverb Placement

In Cantonese, adverbs usually come before, rather than after, verbs. Speakers of Cantonese may carry over this practice into English, using phrases such as *slowly talk.* Provide additional practice placing adverbs after verbs, for example, *You should eat slowly.*

• Continue this procedure using additional examples from **Student Book** p. 436: *Ira lies quietly on the rug. Ira stays close to the person he is helping. Sandy must train Ira correctly.*

CHECK PROGRESS

Do students…
• use Target Vocabulary words appropriately to talk about "The Sticky Coyote" and *Taking Care of Animals*?
• identify and use adverbs that tell how, where, and when?

REVIEW TOGETHER

• Provide additional practice with **Context Cards**.
• Have partners read sections of "The Sticky Coyote" and *Taking Care of Animals* to each other.
• Review the function and placement of adverbs as a group.

Scaffolded Practice and Application

Beginning Have students write *He sits quietly* and *She stays inside.* Then have partners circle the adverb that tells how and underline the adverb that tells where.

Intermediate Have students write *The service dogs learned quickly and easily* and *Ira waited inside.* Then have them read the sentences aloud, circle the adverbs that tell how, and underline the adverbs that tell where.

Advanced Have partners write two or three sentences using adverbs and read them aloud. Then have students explain to each other whether the adverbs tell how, where, or when.

Advanced High Have students write a paragraph using adverbs that tell how, where, and when. Then have partners exchange papers and identify each adverb, explaining how it modifies or changes the meaning of the verb.

SHARE OBJECTIVES

- Discuss and compare how animals and humans help each other
- Make a chart to compare and contrast how animals and humans help each other
- Use vocabulary words to write about how animals and humans help each other

MATERIALS

Student Book (pp. 430–440, 442–444, 448–449)
Leveled Reader
Chart Paper
Grab-and-Go™ Resources (p. 18)

ACADEMIC LANGUAGE

• = *Spanish cognate*

friendly letter
narrate   • *narrar*
informal

Compare Texts

MAKE COMPARISONS Use the model below to help students complete a chart comparing how animals and humans help each other. Have students refer to their **Leveled Reader** and **Student Book** pp. 430–440 and 442–444.

Title	"The Right Dog for the Job"	"The Sticky Coyote"	*Taking Care of Animals*
Who/What is helping?	service dogs and guide dogs	Coyote	veterinarian
What help is given?	retrieves objects; leads people; opens doors; protects owner from danger	makes people laugh; protects the village	helps with birth; gives check-ups; cures hoof and leg problems; cures stomach problems
What is the reward for helping?	praise; loving relationship with owner	Coyote can stay in the village; he is happy and the people like him	eases animal pain; helps farmers who love their animals

- Have students orally form sentences based on the information in the chart. Provide sentence frames such as the following:

1. One job that a service dog performs is ___retrieving objects___ .

2. When Coyote helps people, one reward is ___staying in the village___ .

3. One way a veterinarian can help animals is by ___easing their pain___ .

DISCUSS COMPARISONS To help students compare and contrast how animals and humans help each other, ask questions such as *How are the tasks the animals and people perform similar? How are they different? What rewards do animals and people receive for helping?* Provide sentence frames such as:

4. Both ___Coyote___ and ___dogs___ perform tasks to help people.

5. A service dog helps by ___leading people___, but Coyote helps by ___making people laugh___ .

6. Both Coyote and ___service dogs___ protect people from danger.

7. One reward for a veterinarian is ___easing pain___, but a reward for a service dog is ___praise___ .

RETEACH
Write to Narrate

TEACH/MODEL Review the features of a **friendly letter**. *When you write to **narrate**, you tell a story. You can tell your story in a friendly letter—a letter you write to someone you know well.* Explain that friendly letters have a greeting at the beginning, a closing at the end, and use **informal** language in the body.

- Read and discuss the Writing Traits Checklist on **Student Book** p. 448 and the Writing Model on **Student Book** pp. 448–449. Point out examples of voice.

GUIDED PRACTICE Explain that the class will work together to write a friendly letter.

- Write *We learned about how a dog becomes a service dog*. Have the group read the statement aloud chorally. Explain that the class will write their letter about this topic.

- *What goes at the top of a letter?* Write the date on chart paper to begin the letter. Have the class choose a person to write to, and suggest a greeting.

- Have individuals suggest sentences that tell how Ira became a service dog. Remind students to use adverbs in their writing to describe how, when, or where. Write their suggestions in the letter.

> **Extend Language**
> **Topic-Related Terms**
> mobility cane, seeing-eye dog, visually impaired, legally blind, independence, hearing/mobility impairment

- Explain that in a friendly letter, you can also tell feelings or opinions about the topic. Have students add their personal thoughts about what they learned, as appropriate.

- Write a closing for the letter, and then read it aloud chorally. Have students suggest changes to reflect their voice.

CHECK PROGRESS

Do students…
- participate in discussion about how animals and humans help each other?
- correctly identify similarities and differences between how animals and humans help each other?
- use voice in their writing?

REVIEW TOGETHER

- Have students work in pairs or small groups to read and review the rows and columns of the comparison chart.
- Have partners help each other check for and include vocabulary words in their writing.
- Have students review the **Writing Rubric** on p. 18 of the **Grab-and-Go™ Resources**.

✏️ **Scaffolded Practice and Application**

| **Beginning** Show students a short friendly letter with the date and closing missing. Have students tell you what is missing and then read the complete letter chorally. | **Intermediate** Have partners write two or three sentences about "The Right Dog for the Job" to include in a friendly letter. Then have them write one sentence that tells their personal thoughts on the topic. | **Advanced** Have partners write a friendly letter about "The Right Dog for the Job." Have them include adverbs that tell how, where, and when. | **Advanced High** Have students write a friendly letter about "The Right Dog for the Job." Have them include adverbs that tell how, where, and when, as well as details that tell their personal thoughts on the topic. |

Day 1

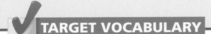

SHARE OBJECTIVES

- Participate in discussion about doing one's best
- Say, read, and use Target Vocabulary and high-utility words
- Practice understanding characters and complete a Column Chart

MATERIALS

Language Support Card 18
Context Cards
Dialogue ELL18.1 (Fast Friends)
Student Book (pp. 454–464)
Main Selection Summary ELL18.2
Graphic Organizer Transparency 1

✔ TARGET VOCABULARY

• = Spanish cognate

crisp	
deliberately	• deliberadamente
especially	• especialmente
gigantic	• gigantesco
haze	
jealous	
lapped	
lure	
miniature	• miniatura
vanished	

ACADEMIC LANGUAGE

character
trait

Listening, Speaking, and Viewing

USE LANGUAGE SUPPORT CARD
Present **Language Support Card 18**.
Use the activities on the back of the card to introduce concepts and vocabulary from "Moon Runner" and to practice **Academic English**.

Develop Target Vocabulary

USE CONTEXT CARDS Show the **Context Cards** for *deliberately* and *lure*. Present the cards using Steps 1–3 of the Introduce Vocabulary routine on **Teacher's Edition** p. T158.

- Help students use *deliberately* and *lure* to discuss how athletes achieve their goals.

- Encourage students to use high-utility words in their responses.

USE ORAL LANGUAGE DIALOGUE Distribute **Dialogue ELL18.1**. Read the title aloud, and have students repeat. Have students look at the title, images, and other information on the page. Then have them predict what they think the dialogue will be about.

BLM
ELL18.1

- As you read the dialogue aloud, display the **Context Cards** for *deliberately, especially,* and *lure*. After you read the dialogue, have partners read it together.

- Have students share activities they do very well.

- Have them brainstorm the qualities they needed to do those activities. Have them explain why they enjoy doing the activities.

- Allow students to include language from **Dialogue ELL18.1**. Encourage them to use high-utility words. List the qualities discussed.

WRITE-PAIR-SHARE Display sentence frames such as the following, and have partners use them to write complete sentences.

1. Students who do well ___deliberately___ try their best.

2. One quality ___especially___ needed to win is determination.

Scaffold Comprehension

PREVIEW "MOON RUNNER" Explain that students will skim "Moon Runner" in order to predict what the selection is about. Help students scan the title, illustrations, and other text features on **Student Book** pp. 454–464. Have them predict one thing they may learn by reading the text.

USE MAIN SELECTION SUMMARY Distribute **Summary ELL18.2**. Read the summary aloud, and then have students chorally reread with you.

BLM
ELL18.2

RETEACH

Understanding Characters

TEACH/MODEL Read aloud the first paragraph in **Summary ELL18.2**. Point out the names *Ruth* and *Mina*. Explain that Ruth and Mina are **characters**. *Characters are the people you read about in stories.*

- Explain that character **traits** can be the thoughts, actions, and words of a character. *You can learn a lot about characters by understanding their traits.*

GUIDED PRACTICE Have students read the first paragraph in **Summary ELL18.2** and circle *Mina*.

- Display **Graphic Organizer Transparency 1**. Explain that a Column Chart can help students understand characters. Label the columns *Thoughts, Actions,* and *Words.*

- Write *Mina is worried about her friendship with Ruth. Is this a thought, an action, or a word?* Write the sentence in the *Thoughts* column. *What does this thought tell you about Mina?* Write the trait below the Column Chart.

- Continue to discuss how Mina's words and actions inform readers about her traits.

- Display a completed Column Chart as a reference throughout the week.

Graphic Organizer

Column Chart: _____

Title or Topic Mina

Thoughts	Actions	Words
Mina is worried about her friendship with Ruth.	Mina deliberately loses the race.	

✏️ **Scaffolded Practice and Application**

Beginning Write three sentences about Mina. Help students decide if each sentence contains Mina's thoughts, actions, or words.	**Intermediate** Have students read another paragraph from the summary. Help them write words describing Mina's character traits. Have them put the information in the Column Chart.	**Advanced** Have partners use phrases with *tells + that* to write sentences that describe Mina's traits, for example, *Mina's determination tells you that she is special.*	**Advanced High** Have students use the completed Column Chart to write a paragraph describing Mina's character traits.

SHARE OBJECTIVES

- Use Target Vocabulary words to discuss "Moon Runner"
- Listen to and recite a dialogue about doing one's best
- Identify prefixes
- Question details from "Moon Runner"

MATERIALS

Student Book (pp. 454–464)
Audiotext CD
Dialogue ELL18.1 (Fast Friends)
Context Cards
Language Support Card 18

ACADEMIC LANGUAGE

• = Spanish cognate

realistic fiction	• *ficción realista*
prefix	• *prefijo*
question	

Scaffold Comprehension

DISCUSS "MOON RUNNER" Use the following picture-text prompts to discuss "Moon Runner." Remind students that "Moon Runner" is **realistic fiction**. It is a present-day story that could happen in real life.

PAGE 455: Have students read the title aloud. *What do you think* Moon Runner *means?* (Possible answer: someone who runs at night)

PAGES 462-463: *How do runners practice?* (They practice by racing with other runners.) Point to the picture of Mina and Ruth. Explain that Mina and Ruth are racing to see who is the fastest. *Athletes must always try their hardest, especially when they compete against other athletes.*

PAGE 464: Point to *gigantic* and *miniature*. Gigantic *means "very large," and* miniature *means "very small." What does Mina take that is gigantic?* (She takes a gigantic leap, or step.) *What do the girls lay down by that is miniature?* (They lay down by miniature white flowers.)

AUDIOTEXT CD Make the **Audiotext CD** for "Moon Runner" available. Have students follow in the **Student Book** as they listen.

Practice Target Vocabulary

USE ORAL LANGUAGE DIALOGUE Distribute **Dialogue ELL18.1**. Have a student read the title aloud.

BLM
ELL18.1

- Read the dialogue aloud, or have proficient readers model reading aloud.

- Have students identify Target Vocabulary and high-utility words in the dialogue and read the words aloud with you.

- Have them restate each Target Vocabulary word and paraphrase the sentence it is used in. Then have them complete the activity on the page.

PRACTICE FLUENCY: INTONATION Have two fluent readers read **Dialogue ELL18.1** aloud, varying intonation at the phrase or sentence level. Have students follow along on their pages as they listen. Then guide them to echo the reader, reminding them to focus on their own intonation.

PRETEACH

Recognizing Prefixes

INTRODUCE *Prefixes are word parts added to the beginning of a word. A prefix changes the meaning of the word.*

- Write *redo, unpaid,* and *dislike.* Circle *re-, un-,* and *dis-. These are prefixes.*

- Explain what each prefix means. *The prefix* re- *means "again," and the prefixes* un- *and* dis- *both mean "not."* Have students discuss what *redo, unpaid,* and *dislike* mean.

PRACTICE Write *remake, unread,* and *disbelieve.* Have students write the words on slips of paper and the meaning of each on separate slips. Have partners match the words and their meanings.

RETEACH

Question

TEACH/MODEL Remind students that when you ask **questions,** you want to find out more information about a story. Remind students to use question words such as *why, what,* and *when* when applying the Question strategy. Use a Think Aloud to model asking questions about "Moon Runner."

> Think Aloud *Mina deliberately lost a race. Why did she think she should lose? What did she do then? I would ask this question while reading "Moon Runner."*

GUIDED PRACTICE As a class, generate additional questions about "Moon Runner." Write the questions, and have partners answer them.

- Review **Teach Academic English** on **Language Support Card 18**.

- Remind students to use *tell* + *that* clauses and irregular past-tense verbs when they ask and answer questions about what happened in a story or selection.

CHECK PROGRESS

Do students…
- demonstrate fluency as they recite the dialogue with proper intonation?
- recognize prefixes?
- ask questions about "Moon Runner"?

REVIEW TOGETHER

- Have partners take turns reading **Dialogue ELL18.1** aloud. Encourage them to recite the dialogue together, focusing on intonation.
- List words with prefixes and without prefixes. Have partners identify the prefixes and discuss how they change the meaning of the word.
- Have students reread "Moon Runner" and write questions that will help them understand the characters better.

✏ Scaffolded Practice and Application

Beginning Write *What is the character thinking or feeling?* Then help students identify sentences in "Moon Runner" that answer the question.	**Intermediate** Have students write *What is the character thinking or feeling?* Then have partners work together to identify sentences in "Moon Runner" that answer the question.	**Advanced** Have partners brainstorm questions about a character in "Moon Runner." Have them find and write the sentences that answer their questions.	**Advanced High** Have students write questions about characters and events from "Moon Runner." Then have them write sentences to answer their questions.

- Use Target Vocabulary words to discuss "Moon Runner"
- Read and discuss a summary of "Moon Runner"
- Identify homophones, homonyms, and homographs
- Use clues to infer understanding of characters

MATERIALS

Student Book (pp. 454–464)

Main Selection Summary ELL18.2

Audiotext CD

Language Support Card 18

Dictionaries

Context Cards

ACADEMIC LANGUAGE

• = Spanish cognate

homophone	• *homófono*
homonym	• *homónimo*
homograph	• *homógrafo*
infer	• *inferir*
inference	• *inferencia*
character trait	

Scaffold Comprehension

REVIEW "MOON RUNNER" Use a Think Aloud and the following prompts to lead students on a guided review of "Moon Runner." Remind students that reviewing and retelling what they read will help them remember vocabulary words.

Think Aloud **PAGES 456–457:** *Mina and Ruth are talking about their friendship. I see the word* jealous *on page 456. Mina thinks Ruth is jealous. I think Ruth may be jealous because Mina is a faster runner.*

PAGE 459: Tell students to find the word *lure*. Have a student read the sentence aloud. *Why is Ruth trying to lure the bird?* (She wants to bring it closer.)

PAGE 462: *Look at the picture of Mina and Ruth racing. Describe what you see.* Have students point to the word *vanished*. *What does* vanished *mean?* (*Vanished* means "went away" or "disappeared.") Invite a student to read the paragraph with *vanished*. *What vanished in this paragraph?* (Mina vanished.)

PAGE 463: *Look at the word* lapped. *Here, the meaning of* lapped *is "wrapped somebody in something." How can a breeze lap at you?* (It can surround you.)

CHECK COMPREHENSION If students need additional support with the main selection, direct them to **Summary ELL18.2**. Read the summary aloud, and have them listen and follow along on their pages.

BLM ELL18.2

Have students take turns reading sections of the summary aloud. Have them answer the following comprehension questions:

1. Why did Mina deliberately lose the race?

2. What was Mina doing when she smelled the haze of flowers?

3. When did Mina see the crisp crescent moon?

Have students work in pairs to circle high-utility words and highlight Target Vocabulary words found in **Summary ELL18.2**. Have students take turns reading each sentence with a vocabulary word and use it in an original sentence.

AUDIOTEXT CD Make the **Audiotext CD** for "Moon Runner" available. Have students follow in the **Student Book** as they listen.

Homophones, Homonyms, Homographs

INTRODUCE Write *homophone, homonym,* and *homograph*. Pronounce the words, and have students repeat.

- *Homographs are words that are spelled the same but have different meanings. Homonyms are spelled or pronounced the same, but have different meanings. Homophones sound the same, but have different spellings and meanings.*

THINK-PAIR-SHARE Write and pronounce the two forms of *bass*. Direct students to use dictionaries to find the meanings of the word. Discuss the meanings as a class, and elicit that the words are homographs. Have students use the words to orally complete the following sentences:

1. You can hear the ___bass___ over the other instruments.

2. A ___bass___ is a type of fish.

Understanding Characters

TEACH/MODEL *You can use clues to **infer character traits**, or characteristics of a character. Then you can make an **inference** about that character.*

GUIDED PRACTICE Write *Ruth didn't want to tell Mina how she felt. She knew that Mina would want to race her again. What inference can we make about how Ruth felt?* (Possible answers: Ruth felt jealous of Mina; Ruth was scared to race Mina.)

- Review **Teach Academic English** on **Language Support Card 18**. Remind students that complex sentences with *tell + that* and irregular past-tense verbs can be used to make an inference about a character.

CHECK PROGRESS

Do students…
- use Target Vocabulary words appropriately to discuss "Moon Runner"?
- correctly answer questions about the summary?
- correctly identify homophones, homonyms, and homographs?
- correctly make an inference about characters?

REVIEW TOGETHER

- Provide additional practice with **Context Cards**.
- Have partners take turns reading aloud **Summary ELL18.2**.
- Write examples of homophones, homonyms, and homographs. Have partners identify and discuss the differences in each word pair.
- Write or say a sentence showing a character's actions from "Moon Runner." Have partners make an inference about the character.

✏️ Scaffolded Practice and Application

Beginning	Intermediate	Advanced	Advanced High
Beginning Write *Mina wonders if the birds ever get jealous or scared.* Help students make an inference about Mina's character.	**Intermediate** Write *Mina wonders if the birds ever get jealous or scared.* Have students write a sentence that makes an inference about Mina's character.	**Advanced** Have partners find a sentence from "Moon Runner" that will help them make an inference about a character. Have them write a sentence explaining the inference they made.	**Advanced High** Have students find three sentences to support an inference they made about a character from "Moon Runner." Have them write a sentence explaining the inference.

Day 4

SHARE OBJECTIVES

- Use Target Vocabulary words to discuss "A Day for the Moon"
- Identify prepositions and prepositional phrases

MATERIALS

Student Book (pp. 462–463, 466–468)
Leveled Reader
Context Cards

ACADEMIC LANGUAGE

• = *Spanish cognate*

informational text	• *texto informativo*
preposition	• *preposición*
prepositional phrase	• *frase preposicional*

Scaffold Content-Area Reading

DISCUSS "A DAY FOR THE MOON" Use the following picture-text prompts to lead students on a review of "A Day for the Moon." Remind them that "A Day for the Moon" is **informational text**. Remind them that informational text gives facts and examples about a topic.

PAGE 466: Point to the chart. *What does the chart show?* (It shows the dates China celebrates the Moon Festival.) *What date will the Moon Festival be on in 2010?* (It will be on September 22.)

PAGE 467: *What did Chang E do with the potion given to her husband?* (She drank it all.) *When the haze clears around a full moon, what can you see?* (You can see Chang E.)

- *What do people use as miniature moons?* (They use candles.)

- Point to the picture of the family. *What is an especially popular symbol of the holiday?* (Moon cakes are an especially popular symbol of the holiday.) *Describe a moon cake.* (A moon cake has a crisp outside and a sweet filling inside.)

PAGE 468: *Where does this banner lure people?* (It lures them to the Moon Festival.)

Leveled Reader

READ *BASEBALL FRIENDS* To read more about achieving goals, direct students to the **Leveled Reader**. Have partners or small groups take turns rereading the selection aloud to one another.

English Language Learners

READING WITH STICKY NOTES

1. Have individuals read the story and put sticky notes on pages they have difficulty with or would like to discuss.

2. Have them talk about the sections they marked, either with a partner or in groups.

Prepositions and Prepositional Phrases

TEACH/MODEL Write *preposition* and *prepositional phrase*. Pronounce the words, and have students repeat. *Prepositions show the connection between parts of a sentence. A prepositional phrase begins with a preposition and ends with a noun or pronoun.*

- Work with students to create a list titled *Prepositions*. Include words such as *for, on, around, down, beside, at,* and *with*. Discuss with students how to use these words to create prepositional phrases such as *with the athletes*.

GUIDED PRACTICE Point to the picture of the girls running on **Student Book** pp. 462–463. Have a student describe the picture. *Where do runners practice for a race?* Write *Runners practice for a race on a track*.

- Remind students that *for* and *on* are prepositions. Elicit that *for a race* and *on the track* are prepositional phrases.

Transfer Skills
Omission of Prepositions

Cantonese does not have an equivalent of English prepositions, so students may not be familiar with them. Provide extra practice with prepositions. For example, *Where do athletes end a race? They end a race at the finish line.*

- Have a student circle the prepositions. Then have another student underline the prepositional phrases.

CHECK PROGRESS

Do students…
- use Target Vocabulary words appropriately to talk about "A Day for the Moon" and *Baseball Friends*?
- correctly identify prepositions and prepositional phrases?

REVIEW TOGETHER

- Provide additional practice with **Context Cards**.
- Have partners read sections of "A Day for the Moon" and *Baseball Friends* to each other.
- Write sentences with prepositional phrases. Have students circle the preposition and underline the prepositional phrase.

Scaffolded Practice and Application

Beginning	Intermediate	Advanced	Advanced High
Write *A runner races around the track*. Have students read the sentence chorally with you. Then have students circle the preposition and underline the prepositional phrase.	Write two sentences with prepositional phrases. Have students read the sentences aloud. Then have them circle the prepositions and underline the prepositional phrases.	Have partners write their own sentence using a prepositional phrase. Have them circle the preposition and underline the prepositional phrase.	Have students write their own sentences using prepositional phrases. Then have students exchange with a partner. Have them circle the prepositions and underline the prepositional phrases.

SHARE OBJECTIVES

• Discuss and compare achieving goals
• Make a chart to compare and contrast achieving goals
• Use vocabulary words to write about achieving goals

MATERIALS

Student Book (pp. 454–464, 466–468, 472–473)
Leveled Reader
Grab-and-Go™ Resources (p. 18)

ACADEMIC LANGUAGE

• = *Spanish cognate*

narrative composition
synonym   • *sinónimo*

Compare Texts

MAKE COMPARISONS Use the model below to help students complete a chart comparing achieving goals. Have students refer to their **Leveled Reader** and **Student Book** pp. 454–464 and 466–468.

Selection Title	"Moon Runner"	"A Day for the Moon"	*Baseball Friends*
Genre	realistic fiction	informational text	realistic fiction
Goal	keep friendship, be great athletes	have people enjoy celebrating the Moon Festival	make new friends
What Characters Do to Achieve Their Goals	talk about problems, try their best when they compete	organize activities, use banner to let people know to come	spend time with new students

• Have students orally form sentences based on the information in the chart. Provide sentence frames such as the following:

1. __Realistic fiction__ is the genre of *Baseball Friends*.

2. Characters in "Moon Runner" achieve their goals by __talking about their problems and trying their best when they compete__.

3. The goal of "A Day for the Moon" is to __celebrate the Moon Festival__.

DISCUSS COMPARISONS To help students compare and contrast achieving goals, ask questions such as *How are some of the goals we've read about this week the same? How are they different?* Provide sentence frames such as:

4. In all three stories, the goals are similar because __they involve people being together__.

5. The goals in "Moon Runner" are __to maintain friendship and be great athletes__, but the goal in "A Day for the Moon" is __to have people enjoy the Moon Festival__.

6. The characters in __"Moon Runner"__ try to achieve their goals by talking about their problems, but in *Baseball Friends* they __spend time with new students__.

Write to Narrate

TEACH/MODEL Review the features of a **narrative composition**. Review words about writing a narrative composition. *When you write a narrative composition, you tell something that happened. Many times, a narrative will tell the order in which events happened. One way to keep a narrative interesting is to use* **synonyms**, *words that have the same meaning.*

- Read and discuss the Writing Traits Checklist on **Student Book** p. 472.

- Read and discuss the Writing Model on **Student Book** pp. 472–473. Point out examples of word choice.

GUIDED PRACTICE Explain that the class will work together to write a narrative composition.

- Write *We competed in a field day today*. Have the group read the statement aloud chorally. *This will be the first sentence of the narrative.*

- *The rest of the narrative will include the events of the field day in the order that they happened.* **Have students suggest statements to include in the composition. Write their suggestions.**

> ### Extend Language
> **Athletic Homophones**
> course/coarse, peddle/petal/pedal, road/rode/rowed, root/route

- Then have students suggest words that describe how they felt during the events of the field day. Write their responses.

- Have students read the completed narrative composition chorally. Discuss the composition, and have students suggest changes to the order of the sentences.

> ### CHECK PROGRESS
> Do students…
> - participate in discussion about achieving goals?
> - correctly identify similarities and differences between achieving goals?
> - use order of events and synonyms in their writing?

> ### REVIEW TOGETHER
> - Have students work in pairs or small groups to read and review the rows and columns of the achieving goals comparison chart.
> - Have partners help each other check for and include vocabulary words in their writing.
> - Have students review the **Writing Rubric** on p. 18 of the **Grab-and-Go™ Resources**.

▭▷ Scaffolded Practice and Application

Beginning Provide the sentence frames *I practiced _____ today. I have to practice each day so I can _____.* Have students complete the sentence frames and read the sentences aloud.	**Intermediate** Have students write completions for the sentence *At our school, athletes train hard because _____.* (Possible answer: They want to compete well.)	**Advanced** Have students write sentences to narrate something that happened at school last week. Have them check their sentences for sequence and descriptive words.	**Advanced High** Have students write a paragraph that narrates an event. Have students put the events in order and include descriptive words. Invite students to read their paragraph to the class.

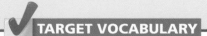

TARGET VOCABULARY

	• = *Spanish cognate*
association	• *asociación*
brilliant	• *brillantes*
capitol	• *capitolio*
conflicts	• *conflictos*
dedicate	• *dedicar*
drought	
horizon	• *horizonte*
overcome	
publicity	• *publicidad*
violence	• *violencia*

ACADEMIC LANGUAGE

	• = *Spa nish cognate*
persuasion	• *persuasión*
author's goal	• *objetivo del autor*

Listening, Speaking, and Viewing

USE LANGUAGE SUPPORT CARD
Present **Language Support Card 19**. Use the activities on the back of the card to introduce concepts and vocabulary from "Harvesting Hope: The Story of Cesar Chavez" and to practice **Academic English**.

Develop Target Vocabulary

USE CONTEXT CARDS Show the **Context Cards** for *overcome* and *conflicts*. Present the cards using Steps 1–3 of the Introduce Vocabulary routine on **Teacher's Edition** p. T230.

- Help students use *overcome* and *conflicts* to discuss what makes a good leader.

USE ORAL LANGUAGE CHANT Distribute **Chant ELL19.1**. Read the title aloud, and have students repeat. Have students look at the title, images, and other information on the page. Then have them predict what they think the chant will be about.

BLM
ELL19.1

- As you read the chant aloud, display the **Context Cards** for *overcome, conflicts, drought,* and *publicity*. After you read the chant, have students read it chorally with you, practicing rhythm and emphasizing rhyme.

- Have students turn their papers over. Read most of the first line of the chant, omitting the final two or three words. Have students finish the line from memory.

- Continue the process with each line of the chant. Write keywords and rhymes as necessary. Next, have students illustrate a scene from the chant.

- Have students label their illustrations with words, phrases, or sentences that describe what they have drawn. Allow students to include language from **Chant ELL19.1**.

WRITE-PAIR-SHARE Display sentence frames such as the following, and have partners use them to write complete sentences.

1. Cesar Chavez migrated because of a __drought__.

2. The landowners got bad __publicity__ because they used violence.

Scaffold Comprehension

PREVIEW "HARVESTING HOPE: THE STORY OF CESAR CHAVEZ"
Explain that, before reading, students will skim "Harvesting Hope: The Story of Cesar Chavez" in order to predict what the selection is about. Help students scan illustrations, pronunciation guides, and other text features on **Student Book** pp. 478–488. Have them predict one thing they may learn by reading the text.

USE MAIN SELECTION SUMMARY Distribute **Summary ELL19.2.** Read the summary aloud, and then have partners rere to each other.

BLM
ELL19.2

RETEACH

Persuasion

TEACH/MODEL Read aloud the first paragraph in **Summary ELL19.2.** Write *persuasion* and *author's goal.* Explain that sometimes an author's goal is to persuade people to agree with what he or she believes.

• *When we persuade, we try to convince someone to agree with our ideas. In this story, the author wants to persuade us that Cesar Chavez was a great man who overcame great obstacles.*

GUIDED PRACTICE Have students read the first paragraph in **Summary ELL19.2** and look for words that describe the living conditions and situation of Chavez and his family in California.

• Display **Graphic Organizer Transparency 7**. Explain that an Idea-Support Map can help students analyze the reasons an author gives when trying to persuade the reader. Label the bottom three cells, *Reason 1, Reason 2,* and *Reason 3.*

• *What does the author say life was like in California for the Chavez family?* Write responses in the top cell. Have students find reasons to support the author's idea and read them aloud. Help students complete the Idea-Support Map.

• Display a completed Idea-Support Map as a reference.

Graphic Organizer

Idea-Support Map: _____
Title or Topic _____

Life was miserable in California for Cesar and the Chavez family.

Reason 1
little money

Reason 2
tiny, dirty shacks

Reason 3
landowners treated workers badly

✏️ Scaffolded Practice and Application

Beginning Have students think of a product they like. Help them complete graphic organizers with the name of the product and one or two reasons telling why they like it.

Intermediate Have students complete graphic organizers about a product they like. Have them write three phrases or short sentences as reasons to describe why they like the product.

Advanced Have students complete graphic organizers about a product they like. Have them write complex sentences with *because* and *that* clauses to explain reasons why they like the product.

Advanced High Have students complete graphic organizers about a product they like. Have them use the organizers to write a persuasive paragraph explaining their reasons for liking the product.

Scaffold Comprehension

DISCUSS "HARVESTING HOPE: THE STORY OF CESAR CHAVEZ"
Use the following picture-text prompts to discuss "Harvesting Hope: The Story of Cesar Chavez." Remind students that "Harvesting Hope: The Story of Cesar Chavez" is a **biography**. It tells about events in a person's life, written by another person.

PAGE 479: Have students read the title aloud. *Have you heard of Cesar Chavez? What do you know about him?* Explain that Cesar Chavez was a farm worker and a great leader. Have students tell what the word *harvesting* means. *How do you think Cesar Chavez harvested hope?*

PAGE 480: *Why did Cesar and his family have to leave their farm?* (There was a drought.) Discuss how a drought can ruin fields. *If there is not enough rain, plants won't grow. If the plants don't grow, the landowners and the workers won't make any money.*

PAGE 484: *Describe what you see in this illustration.* (Cesar is talking to people about rebelling against the landowners.)

PAGE 486: *What did Cesar plan in order to gain publicity for the farm workers' struggle?* (a march from the grapevines to the state capitol)

AUDIOTEXT CD Make the **Audiotext CD** for "Harvesting Hope: The Story of Cesar Chavez" available. Have students follow in the **Student Book** as they listen.

Practice Target Vocabulary

USE ORAL LANGUAGE CHANT Distribute **Chant ELL19.1**. Have a student read the title aloud.

BLM
ELL19.1

- Read the chant aloud, or have a proficient reader model reading aloud.

- Have students identify Target Vocabulary and high-utility words in the chant and read the words aloud with you.

- Have them restate each Target Vocabulary word and use it in an original sentence. Then have them complete the activity on the page.

PRACTICE FLUENCY: ACCURACY AND SELF-CORRECTION Read or have a fluent reader read **Chant ELL19.1** aloud, practicing accuracy and self-correcting at the phrase or sentence level. Have students follow along as they listen. Then have them echo the reader, focusing on their own accuracy and self-correction.

Suffixes: *-ful, -less, -ness, -ment*

INTRODUCE Write *suffix*. Remind students that suffixes are word parts that are added to the end of words.

- Write *peaceful, fearless, fairness,* and *treatment.* Say each word aloud, and have students repeat. Circle the suffixes.

- Explain that *-ful* means "full of" or "having," *-ness* means "being," and *-less* means "without." *Words with the suffix -ment are nouns, or things.* Discuss the meanings of each root word and of the words with suffixes.

PRACTICE Have students use **Context Cards,** the chant, the summary, or "Harvesting Hope: The Story of Cesar Chavez" to look for and name words that have the suffixes *-ful, -less, -ness,* and *-ment.* (*homesickness, powerless, hopeful, announcement*)

Infer/Predict

TEACH/MODEL Write *infer* and *predict,* and remind students that to infer is to guess about information that isn't stated directly. Explain that to predict is to guess what will happen in the future. Use a Think Aloud to model inferring and predicting while reading "Harvesting Hope: The Story of Cesar Chavez."

> Think Aloud   *I can infer that the author thinks the workers were treated unfairly. I predict that Chavez will do something to change this.*

GUIDED PRACTICE As a class, reread sections of "Harvesting Hope: The Story of Cesar Chavez," and make **inferences** and **predictions** about the events and characters' feelings.

- Review **Teach Academic English** on **Language Support Card 19**.

- Remind students that reading explanations can help them infer the author's goal and predict events.

Do students…

- demonstrate fluency as they recite the chant with accuracy and self-correction?
- identify and use the suffixes *-ful, -less, -ness,* and *-ment*?
- make inferences and predictions about "Harvesting Hope: The Story of Cesar Chavez"?

- Have partners take turns reading **Chant ELL19.1** aloud. Encourage them to recite the chant together, focusing on accuracy and self-correction.
- Have partners work together to identify words from the weekly selections with the suffixes *-ful, -less, -ness,* and *-ment.*
- Have partners reread "Harvesting Hope: The Story of Cesar Chavez" and discuss inferences and predictions that they can make.

✏️ **Scaffolded Practice and Application**

Beginning Ask students questions to make inferences or to predict what will happen in the selection. Have them answer in one or two words.	**Intermediate** Have students work in groups to make predictions about the selection. Have them write their best two or three ideas and share them with the class.	**Advanced** Have partners make inferences and predictions about the selection using *because* and *that.* Have them write their best ideas and share with the class.	**Advanced High** Have students make inferences and predictions about the selection using *because* and *that.* Have them write a persuasive paragraph telling their ideas.

Scaffold Comprehension

REVIEW "HARVESTING HOPE: THE STORY OF CESAR CHAVEZ" Use a Think Aloud and the following prompts to lead students on a guided review of "Harvesting Hope: The Story of Cesar Chavez." Remind students that reviewing and retelling what they read can help them understand it better and make predictions.

Think Aloud **PAGES 480–481:** *The children look so sad because they are leaving their home. The* drought *was so terrible that they had no choice.*

PAGE 482: Have a student read the last paragraph aloud. *Find the word* conflicts *in this paragraph. What is a conflict?* (a disagreement) *Who is having a conflict in the picture?* (a landowner and two workers) *What were some of the conflicts that Chavez faced?* (He couldn't go into stores or restaurants; he couldn't speak Spanish in school.)

PAGE 485: *Find the words* violence *and* overcome *on this page.* **Have a student read the paragraph aloud.** *What did Chavez feel was a better weapon than violence?* (truth) *How did he overcome his problems?* (He became a leader for migrant workers, and together they changed their working and living conditions.)

CHECK COMPREHENSION If students need additional support with the main selection, direct them to **Summary ELL19.2.** Read the summary aloud, and have them listen and follow along on their pages.

BLM ELL19.2

Have students take turns reading sections of the summary aloud. Have them answer the following comprehension questions:

1. How did the drought affect Cesar's family?

2. What did Cesar dedicate himself to doing?

3. Why did the landowners finally agree to better working conditions?

Have students work in pairs to circle high-utility words and highlight Target Vocabulary words found in **Summary ELL19.2.** Have them take turns reading each sentence containing a vocabulary word and restating the meaning of the sentence in their own words.

AUDIOTEXT CD Make the **Audiotext CD** for "Harvesting Hope: The Story of Cesar Chavez" available. Have students follow in the Student Book as they listen.

PRETEACH

Use a Dictionary

INTRODUCE Write *dictionary* and *entry*. *Each word listed in a dictionary is called an entry. Entries are listed in alphabetical order. An entry has different parts that give different information.*

• Write *horizon,* and have students look it up in a dictionary. Explain the features of the entry, including the pronunciation guide, part of speech, and definition.

THINK-PAIR-SHARE Write *brilliant, capitol,* and *violence*. Have partners use dictionaries to help them pronounce and define each word. Discuss the meanings as a class, pointing out that some words have multiple meanings. Have students use *brilliant, capitol,* and *violence* to orally complete the following sentences:

1. Our state ___capitol___ building is in the city of _____.

2. The room was filled with ___brilliant___ light.

3. Some movies have too much ___violence___ in them.

RETEACH

Persuasion

TEACH/MODEL Write and pronounce *persuade* and *evaluate*. *Authors use reasons to persuade readers, or explain why they should think a certain way. When you analyze a text, you should remember the author's reasons when you evaluate, or judge the text.*

GUIDED PRACTICE Show students persuasive advertisements from magazines. Have students discuss each ad, evaluating the reasons or other methods it uses to persuade the reader. Write their opinions in sentences using *because* and *that*.

• Review **Teach Academic English** on **Language Support Card 19**.

• Remind students that clauses with *because* often signal reasons and can be helpful in evaluating persuasive writing.

CHECK PROGRESS

Do students…
• use Target Vocabulary words appropriately to discuss "Harvesting Hope: The Story of Cesar Chavez"?
• correctly answer questions about the summary?
• use dictionaries to determine meaning?
• evaluate persuasive messages effectively?

REVIEW TOGETHER

• Provide additional practice with **Context Cards**.
• Have partners take turns reading aloud **Summary ELL19.2**.
• Have partners use a dictionary to look up unfamiliar words from this week's selections.
• As a class, choose events from the main selection, and evaluate what message the author is trying to persuade the audience to believe.

> **Scaffolded Practice and Application**

| **Beginning** Help students look at magazine ads and circle words or pictures that are persuasive. Ask guiding questions, having students answer with one or two words. | **Intermediate** Have partners identify persuasive information in magazine ads. Have them write two or three simple sentences restating the information. | **Advanced** Have partners write sentences that evaluate persuasive information in magazine ads. Have them use *because* and *that* to tell the reasons the ad is persuasive. | **Advanced High** Have students write a paragraph that evaluates persuasive information in a magazine ad. Have them use *because* and *that* to tell the reasons the ad is persuasive. |

Day 4

SHARE OBJECTIVES

- Use Target Vocabulary words to discuss "The Edible Schoolyard"
- Identify and use transitions

MATERIALS

Student Book (pp. 482, 483, 490–492)
Leveled Reader Context Cards

ACADEMIC LANGUAGE

• = *Spanish cognate*

informational text	• *texto informativo*
transition	• *transición*
time order	

Scaffold Content-Area Reading

DISCUSS "THE EDIBLE SCHOOLYARD" Use the following picture-text prompts to lead students on a review of "The Edible Schoolyard." Remind them that "The Edible Schoolyard" is **informational text**. Remind them that informational text gives facts and examples about its topic.

PAGE 491: Point to the girls. *What are the students in this picture doing?* (They are working in a garden.) *Do they seem to be working well together?* (yes)

- *Find the word* drought *on this page.* Have a student read the sentence aloud. *What would the plants in the picture look like during a drought, if they weren't watered?* (They would be dry, brown, or dead.)

- *Find the word* conflicts *on this page.* Have a student read the sentence aloud. *What conflicts might these students have when working together? How can they resolve these problems?* (Answers will vary.)

PAGE 492: *Look at the chart. What does the chart show?* (foods that are healthy and how much you should eat of them) Have students read the first sentence. *Why is the Edible Schoolyard gaining so much publicity?* (It promotes healthy eating.)

Leveled Reader

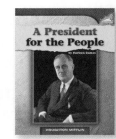

READ *A PRESIDENT FOR THE PEOPLE* To read more about leadership and helping others, direct students to the **Leveled Reader**. Have partners or small groups take turns rereading the selection aloud to one another.

◆ **English Language Learners**

READING WITH A KWL CHART Make a table with three columns. Label the columns *K*, *W,* and *L*. Explain that *K* is for "what I know," *W* is for "what I want to learn," and *L* is for "what I learned." Explain that you will fill out the first two columns as a class before you read, and complete the chart after reading.

1. Complete the *K* and *W* columns of the chart as a class.

2. Have students read the selection you have chosen. Students can read and fill in the *L* column in pairs or groups, or complete the chart as a class after reading.

Transitions

TEACH/MODEL Explain that **transitions** are words or phrases that connect sentences and help readers understand an author's meaning. *Transitions such as* next *and* finally *show* **time order,** *and transition words such as* so *and* to sum up *indicate results or conclusions.*

- Read aloud the second paragraph on **Student Book** p. 482. *Which words seem like a transition? Why?* Write *As the years blurred together. This tells us that time is passing, and it connects Chavez's childhood with his adulthood.*

- Read aloud the second paragraph on **Student Book** p. 483. Have students identify the transition word *so. How does the word* so *connect ideas in this part of the story?* Help students understand that it shows why Chavez was afraid and that he felt the same as other migrant workers.

GUIDED PRACTICE Explain that time-order transitions help the reader follow events over the course of time.

- Have students name words that can be used for time-order transitions, such as *then, after, when,* and *later.*

- Help students identify two or three time-order transitions from the week's reading selections.

- *Some transitions tell us that the author is drawing conclusions or finishing an idea.* Give examples of words such as *thus, as a result, because of this,* and *in conclusion.*

> **Transfer Skills**
> *If* **versus** *When*
> Speakers of Tagalog may confuse *if* and *when* since the language has one word that covers both. Provide additional practice with *if* and *when,* for example, *If it rains, we will stay inside. When the sun rises, we will wake up.*

- Help students identify two or three transitions that show results or conclusions in the week's reading selections.

CHECK PROGRESS

Do students…
- use Target Vocabulary words appropriately to talk about "The Edible Schoolyard" and *A President for the People*?
- identify and use transitions?

REVIEW TOGETHER

- Provide additional practice with **Context Cards.**
- Have partners read sections of "The Edible Schoolyard" and *A President for the People* to each other.
- Write transition words. Then have partners use the words in oral sentences.

Scaffolded Practice and Application

| **Beginning** Help students identify transition words from the week's selections. Have them copy sentences and circle the transition words or phrases in each one. | **Intermediate** Have partners make notes about the week's selections. Have them choose two events and write a sentence linking them with a transition word or phrase. | **Advanced** Have partners make notes about events or ideas from the week's selections. Have them choose several events and write sentences linking them with transition words or phrases. | **Advanced High** Have students write a paragraph linking several events and ideas from the week's selections, using transition words or phrases to show how the information is connected. |

SHARE OBJECTIVES

- Discuss and compare leaders
- Make a chart to compare and contrast leaders
- Use vocabulary words to write about leaders

MATERIALS

Student Book (pp. 478–488, 496–497)
Leveled Reader

ACADEMIC LANGUAGE

• = *Spanish cognate*

personal narrative • *narrativa personal*

prewrite

Compare Texts

MAKE COMPARISONS Use the model below to help students complete a chart comparing types of leadership. Have students refer to their **Leveled Reader** and **Student Book** pp. 478–488.

Leader	Cesar Chavez	Franklin D. Roosevelt
Childhood and Education	poor family, moved from school to school, graduated eighth grade	wealthy family, home-schooled, university graduate
Personal Challenges Faced	poor living and working conditions as a migrant worker	got polio as an adult and spent the rest of his life in a wheelchair
Leadership Years	1960s–1990s	1910–1945, from state senate to presidency
How He Showed Leadership	as a labor leader; began the National Farm Workers Association, led strikes and marches, negotiated with grape company for better pay and working conditions	as a political leader; helped people keep homes and farms, created jobs, built camps for migrants, raised money for polio

- Have students orally form sentences based on the information in the chart. Provide sentence frames such as the following:

1. ___Cesar Chavez___ was able to overcome poor living and working conditions.

2. ___FDR___ was educated at home but graduated from a university.

3. Cesar Chavez was a dedicated leader from the ___1960s–1990s___.

DISCUSS COMPARISONS To help students compare and contrast leaders, ask questions such as *How was each man a leader? How did they help others? How were their lives different? What leadership qualities did both men probably have?* Provide sentence frames such as:

4. ___Cesar Chavez___ graduated from eighth grade, but ___FDR___ graduated from a university.

5. ___Cesar Chavez___ struggled with poverty, while ___FDR___ faced the challenge of polio.

6. Both men wanted to help ___migrant workers___.

RETEACH
Write to Narrate

TEACH/MODEL Review the features of a **personal narrative**.

When you write a personal narrative, you write about something that happened to you. It is important to organize your ideas first by prewriting. Prewriting is all the things you do to get ready to write.

- Read and discuss the Writing Process Checklist on **Student Book** p. 496.

- Read and discuss the events chart on **Student Book** p. 497. Point out examples of organization.

GUIDED PRACTICE Explain that the class will work together to prewrite a personal narrative by first organizing their ideas.

- Tell the class that they will write a personal narrative about a field trip or activity that the class did together recently. Write the topic of the personal narrative.

- *Before we write, we will prewrite. Let's start by listing our ideas.* Have students brainstorm events that happened. Write their ideas.

- *What should we do next?* (organize the ideas) Have students number the events in order. Have them link supporting details and reasons by drawing arrows to the events they support.

- Review the completed graphic organizer as a class. Have students suggest changes to the order of the details.

CHECK PROGRESS

Do students…
- participate in discussion about leaders?
- correctly identify similarities and differences between leaders?
- organize ideas in their writing?

REVIEW TOGETHER

- Have students work in pairs or small groups to read and review the rows and columns of the leader comparison chart.
- Have partners help each other check for and include vocabulary words in their writing.

Scaffolded Practice and Application

Beginning	Intermediate	Advanced	Advanced High
Have students write about events that happened using one or two words. Have students number the events if possible.	Have students list events that happened using phrases or sentences. Have them number the events in the order in which they happened.	Have students write sentences about events that happened to them, including supporting details. Have them use time-order transition words to show the order in which the events happened.	Have students write sentences about events that happened to them, using time-order transitions. Have them write additional sentences with transitions that tell results or conclusions.

✓ TARGET VOCABULARY

• = *Spanish cognate*

accompany	• *acompañar*
clumsy	
corps	• *cuerpo*
duty	
interpreter	• *intérprete*
landmark	
proposed	• *propuesto*
route	• *ruta*
supplies	
territory	• *territorio*

ACADEMIC LANGUAGE

• = *Spanish cognate*

topic	
main idea	• *idea principal*
supporting detail	

Listening, Speaking, and Viewing

USE LANGUAGE SUPPORT CARD
Present **Language Support Card 20**. Use the activities on the back of the card to introduce concepts and vocabulary from "Sacagawea" and to practice **Academic English**.

Develop Target Vocabulary

USE CONTEXT CARDS Show the **Context Cards** for *duty* and *accompany*. Present the cards using Steps 1–3 of the Introduce Vocabulary routine on **Teacher's Edition** p. T302.

- Help students use *duty* and *accompany* to discuss what makes a successful team.

- Encourage students to use high-utility words in their responses.

USE ORAL LANGUAGE CHANT Distribute **Chant ELL20.1**. Read the title aloud, and have students repeat. Have students look at the title, images, and other information on the page. Then have them predict what they think the chant will be about.

BLM
ELL20.1

- As you read the chant aloud, display the **Context Cards** for *landmark, route, accompany,* and *territory*. After you read the chant, have partners read it chorally.

- Draw or post a picture of Sacagawea. Explain that Sacagawea was a member of an expedition, or team of explorers.

- Have students brainstorm skills Sacagawea might have had that would help an expedition.

- Allow students to include language from **Chant ELL20.1**. Encourage them to use high-utility words. List responses around the picture of Sacagawea.

WRITE-PAIR-SHARE Display sentence frames such as the following, and have partners use them to write complete sentences.

1. Sacagawea went to accompany ___Lewis and Clark___.

2. One duty she had in the corps was to be an ___interpreter___.

Scaffold Comprehension

PREVIEW "SACAGAWEA" Explain that, before reading, students will skim "Sacagawea" in order to predict what the selection is about. Help students scan illustrations, highlighted words, and other text features on **Student Book** pp. 502–516. Have them predict one thing they may learn by reading the text.

USE MAIN SELECTION SUMMARY Distribute **Summary ELL20.2**. Read the summary aloud, and then have students read it independently.

BLM
ELL20.2

RETEACH
Main Idea and Details

TEACH/MODEL Read aloud the last paragraph in **Summary ELL20.2**. Write *topic, main idea,* and *supporting detail*. Review the meaning of each term.

* *A topic is what a selection is mostly about. The main idea is the most important idea in a paragraph or selection. Supporting details tell more information about the main idea.*

GUIDED PRACTICE Have students read the last paragraph in **Summary ELL20.2** and underline the first sentence. *This is the topic sentence or main idea of the paragraph.*

* Display **Graphic Organizer Transparency 15**. Explain that a Web can help students organize the main idea and supporting details. Write *main idea* at the top of the center oval and *supporting detail* at the top of each outside oval. Write *Sacagawea used her skills to help the explorers* in the center oval.

* Help students find details to support the main idea.

* Write *found food, interpreted for the men, saved supplies,* and *acted as a guide*. Read the phrases aloud, and have students repeat. Have students fill in the details in the Web.

* Display a completed Web as a reference throughout the week.

Do students…
* correctly pronounce and use vocabulary words in discussion?
* correctly identify main idea and details?

REVIEW TOGETHER

* Have partners use **Context Cards** to review the Target Vocabulary words and their meanings. Have them complete the activities on the backs of the cards.
* Have partners write sentences about the main ideas from the summary using introductory prepositional phrases.

Graphic Organizer

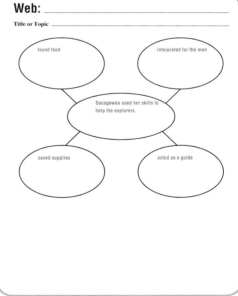

Web: _____
Title or Topic _____

found food
interpreted for the men
Sacagawea used her skills to help the explorers.
saved supplies
acted as a guide

✏️ **Scaffolded Practice and Application**

Beginning Help students pronounce *main idea* and *supporting detail*. Have them copy the words and then copy a main idea and supporting detail from the Web.

Intermediate Have partners discuss a main idea from the summary. Have them use supporting details to describe the main idea.

Advanced Have students use the main idea from the Web to write complete sentences that describe supporting details from the summary.

Advanced High Have students use the completed Web to write the main idea and supporting details in paragraph form. Have partners read their paragraphs aloud.

Scaffold Comprehension

DISCUSS "SACAGAWEA" Use the following picture-text prompts to discuss "Sacagawea." Remind students that "Sacagawea" is a **biography**. It tells about the events in a person's life, written by another person.

PAGE 503: Have students read the title aloud. *Who is Sacagawea?* Have students look at the picture and describe what they see.

PAGE 507: *What is Sacagawea doing? Why is it important?* (She is getting supplies. Without these supplies, the expedition would not have been able to continue.)

PAGES 512–513: *Sacagawea wanted to* accompany *Clark to see the ocean. What does* accompany *mean?* (to go with someone else) *Look at the picture. What did she see?* (She saw a whale.)

AUDIOTEXT CD Make the **Audiotext CD** for *Sacagawea* available. Have students follow in the **Student Book** as they listen.

Practice Target Vocabulary

USE ORAL LANGUAGE CHANT Distribute **Chant ELL20.1**. Have a student read the title aloud.

BLM
ELL20.1

- Read the chant aloud, or have a proficient reader model reading aloud.

- Have students identify Target Vocabulary and high-utility words in the chant and read the words aloud with you.

- Have them restate each Target Vocabulary word and give an example of the word. Then have them complete the activity on the page.

PRACTICE FLUENCY: STRESS Read or have a fluent reader read aloud **Chant ELL20.1**, having students follow along on their pages as they listen. Then guide them to repeat after the reader chorally, focusing on emphasizing certain words as they read.

VCCV Pattern and Word Parts

INTRODUCE Write *syllables* and *disaster*. Say the words aloud, and have students repeat.

- *Syllables are word parts.* Disaster *has three syllables, dis/as/ter.* Have students clap out the syllables with you as you say them.

- Write *V* or *C* over each letter, then draw a vertical line between the two letters labeled *C*. *The VCCV pattern can help you figure out how to pronounce a word.* Point out that each syllable has only one vowel sound.

PRACTICE Have students use **Context Cards**, the chant, the summary, or *Sacagawea* to look for and name words that have the VCCV pattern. *(accompany, clumsy, interpreter, territory)*

RETEACH

Visualize

TEACH/MODEL Write *visualize,* and explain the term. Remind students that when you visualize something you hear or read, you create a picture in your mind. Use a Think Aloud to model visualizing details from "Sacagawea."

> Think Aloud *Charbonneau was steering the boat in choppy waters. The boat turned over. I can picture the boat turning over in the choppy waters. I can use descriptive words in the selection to help me visualize this part of "Sacagawea."*

GUIDED PRACTICE As a class, identify and list two or three descriptive details from "Sacagawea." Have students close their eyes to visualize the events from the story as you read the details aloud.

CHECK PROGRESS

Do students…

- demonstrate fluency as they recite the chant with proper stress?
- identify syllables and the VCCV pattern in word parts?
- visualize details from "Sacagawea"?

REVIEW TOGETHER

- Have partners take turns reading **Chant ELL20.1** aloud. Encourage them to recite the chant together, emphasizing certain words as they read.
- Have partners work together to clap out syllables and identify vowels and consonants.
- Have partners visualize different sections of "Sacagawea."

✏️ Scaffolded Practice and Application

Beginning Have students copy the details from "Sacagawea." Tell them to circle the keywords and phrases they think are descriptive and help them visualize events from the story.	**Intermediate** Have groups identify and write two or three descriptive details from "Sacagawea." Have them use the listed details or other details they found.	**Advanced** Have partners find and list descriptive details from "Sacagawea." Have them use these details to write a two- or three-sentence description of the story.	**Advanced High** Have partners find descriptive details from "Sacagawea" and write a full paragraph description of the story using these details.

Scaffold Comprehension

REVIEW "SACAGAWEA" Use a Think Aloud and the following prompts to lead students on a guided review of "Sacagawea." Remind students that reviewing and retelling what they read will help them understand and remember the story.

> **Think Aloud** **PAGE 504:** *I see the word* corps *on page 504. A* corps *is a group of people that work together. The Corps of Discovery went on a journey to the Pacific Ocean.*

PAGE 506: Have students read the third paragraph aloud. *Why were the men on the team hired?* (They were hired for their special skills.) *Why was Charbonneau paid more than the others?* (He was an *interpreter*.) *What is an interpreter?* (someone who translates what people are saying) *Why did Lewis and Clark need an interpreter?* (They didn't speak the Native American language.)

PAGE 508: Point to the word *landmark*. Have students read the sentence aloud. *What is a landmark?* (A landmark is an object that identifies a location.) *What was the landmark that Sacagawea saw?* (a mountain)

PAGE 509: *Describe what you see in the picture. Why was Sacagawea so happy to be back in her territory?* (She hadn't seen her people in a long time.)

CHECK COMPREHENSION If students need additional support with the main selection, direct them to **Summary ELL20.2**. Read the summary aloud, and have them listen and follow along on their pages.

BLM
ELL20.2

Have students take turns reading sections of the summary aloud. Have them answer the following comprehension questions:

1. Lewis and Clark were looking for a route to where?

2. Who saved the captain's supplies?

3. What landmark did Sacagawea see?

Have students work in pairs to circle high-utility words and highlight Target Vocabulary words found in **Summary ELL20.2**. Have partners chorally read each sentence containing a vocabulary word and paraphrase the meaning of the sentence.

AUDIOTEXT CD Make the **Audiotext CD** for "Sacagawea" available. Have students follow in the **Student Book** as they listen.

Compound Words

INTRODUCE Write *compound words*. *Compound words are words made up of two shorter words.*

* Write *landmark*. Say the word aloud, and have students repeat. *What two shorter words do you see?* Have a student write *land* and *mark* under *landmark*. *Landmark is a compound word.*

THINK-PAIR-SHARE Write *footprints* and *arrowhead*. Have partners look at the two words to determine the meaning of the compound word. Discuss the meanings as a class. Have students use compound words to orally complete the following sentences:

1. The Corps of Discovery made ___footprints___ in the snow.

2. They found an ___arrowhead___ left by Indians.

Main Idea and Details

TEACH/MODEL Write and pronounce *infer*. Have students repeat. Explain that sometimes readers may not know the **main idea** of a selection. *If you don't know everything about a selection, you sometimes have to use **details** to infer the main idea.*

GUIDED PRACTICE Write *Sacagawea made Captain Clark take her to the ocean. She had never seen the ocean.* Have students infer the main idea from these supporting details. (Possible answer: Sacagawea wanted to see the ocean.)

* Review **Teach Academic English** on **Language Support Card 20**.

* Remind students that introductory prepositional phrases and ordinal numbers with prepositional phrases can be used when inferring main ideas and supporting details.

Scaffolded Practice and Application

Beginning Write a main idea and two supporting details. Help students identify and circle the main idea and underline the supporting details.	**Intermediate** Write a main idea and two supporting details. Have partners identify and circle the main idea and underline the supporting details.	**Advanced** Write three supporting details from the story, and have students infer the main idea. Have them write the main idea in a complete sentence.	**Advanced High** Have students find supporting details from the story and infer the main idea. Have them write the main idea and supporting details in a paragraph.

CHECK PROGRESS

Do students…

* use Target Vocabulary words appropriately to discuss "Sacagawea"?
* correctly answer questions about the summary?
* correctly identify and use compound words?
* correctly infer main idea and details?

REVIEW TOGETHER

* Provide additional practice with **Context Cards**.
* Have partners take turns reading aloud **Summary ELL20.2**.
* Write compound words, and have students find the two words that make up each compound word.
* Write or say details from the story. Have students infer the main idea.

Day 4

SHARE OBJECTIVES

- Use Target Vocabulary words to discuss "Native American Nature Poetry"
- Identify abbreviations

MATERIALS

Student Book (pp. 505, 518–520)
Leveled Reader
Context Cards

ACADEMIC LANGUAGE

• = Spanish cognate

poetry	• *poesia*
abbreviation	• *abreviatura*

Scaffold Content-Area Reading

DISCUSS "NATIVE AMERICAN NATURE POETRY" Use the following picture-text prompts to lead students on a review of "Native American Nature Poetry." Remind them that "Native American Nature Poetry" is **poetry**. Remind them that poetry uses the sound and rhythm of words to suggest images and feelings.

PAGE 518: *Describe what you see in the picture.* Have a student find the word *territory* and read the sentence aloud. *What is a territory?* (A territory is an area of land.) *What type of territory do we see in the picture?* (a territory with forests, mountains, and a river)

PAGE 519: Remind students that an interpreter is someone who translates a language. Have students read the first paragraph aloud. *How is it that we have Native American poems like the one we just read?* (An interpreter had to write them down.)

PAGE 520: Have a student read the poem "You, whose day it is." *According to the poem, what is our duty?* (Our duty is to make the day beautiful.)

- Read the poem "I Think Over Again My Small Adventures" aloud. *What do you think the poet is saying in this poem?* (We make small things seem bigger than they are.) Explain that an important part of the Native American culture was to appreciate nature and what it gave to them, such as food, light, water, and beauty.

Leveled Reader

READ *LAURA INGALLS WILDER* To read more about successful teams, direct students to the **Leveled Reader**. Have partners or small groups take turns rereading the selection aloud to one another.

◆ **English Language Learners**

READING WITH A KWL CHART Have readers make a Column Chart and label the columns *K, W,* and *L*. Explain that *K* stands for "What I Know," *W* for "What I Want to Learn," and *L* for "What I Learned." Explain that the readers should fill out the first two columns before reading, and complete the chart after reading.

1. Have readers complete the *K* and *W* columns.

2. Have them read the selection. Have them read and fill in the *L* column after reading.

Abbreviations

TEACH/MODEL Point to the picture of Sacagawea, Captain Lewis, and Charbonneau on **Student Book** p. 505. Have a student describe the picture. *Where did Lewis and Clark begin their expedition?*

• Write *Captain Lewis and Captain Clark began their expedition in North Dakota.*

• Point to *Captain* and *North Dakota,* and remind students that some words can be written in shorter ways. Remind students that abbreviations are the shorter forms of these words.

GUIDED PRACTICE Explain that abbreviations are shorter ways to write words.

• Circle *Captain* both times it appears in the sentence, and write *Capt.* above each. Tell students that *Capt.* is the abbreviation for *Captain.*

• Circle *North Dakota,* and write *ND* above it. Explain that *ND* is the abbreviation for *North Dakota.* Elicit other abbreviations from students. *What is the abbreviation for our state?*

• Work with students to create a list of common abbreviations.

CHECK PROGRESS

Do students…

• use Target Vocabulary words appropriately to talk about "Native American Nature Poetry" and *Laura Ingalls Wilder?*
• correctly identify and use abbreviations?

REVIEW TOGETHER

• Provide additional practice with **Context Cards**.
• Have partners read sections of "Native American Nature Poetry" and *Laura Ingalls Wilder* to each other.
• Make a list of words on one side and their abbreviations in random order on the other side. Have students match words with the correct abbreviations.

✏️ **Scaffolded Practice and Application**

Beginning Say *Mister* and *Mrs.* Help students write the abbreviations *Mr.* and *Mrs.*	**Intermediate** Have students write sentences from the story that include dates or titles. Help them write the appropriate abbreviations.	**Advanced** Read aloud three sentences from the story with dates or titles. Have students write the appropriate abbreviations.	**Advanced High** Have students write three original sentences containing words that can be abbreviated. Then have partners trade sentences, circle the words, and write the abbreviated version of the word.

Compare Texts

MAKE COMPARISONS Use the model below to help students complete a chart comparing successful teams. Have students refer to their **Leveled Reader** and **Student Book** pp. 502–516 and 518–520.

Team	Lewis and Clark	Jesse Fewkes's Team	Laura Ingalls Wilder and Her Daughter
How They Were Successful	explored the Western United States	interpreted Native American stories	wrote stories about life in the West
Skills That Helped Them Be Successful	hunt, read maps, sail, interpret	interpret, know how to use cylinder	write stories
Supplies	journals (pencil and paper), gunpowder, medicines, scientific instruments	cylinder recorder	pencil, paper

- Have students orally form sentences based on the information in the chart. Provide sentence frames such as the following:

1. <u>Jesse Fewkes's team</u> was successful because they interpreted Native American stories.

2. One skill that helped Laura Ingalls Wilder to be successful was <u>Possible answer: writing well</u>.

3. Lewis and Clark were successful because they <u>explored the United States</u>.

4. The <u>cylinder recorder</u> was one of the supplies used by Jesse Fewkes's team.

DISCUSS COMPARISONS To help students compare and contrast successful teams, ask questions such as *How are the teams' skills and supplies similar? How are they different?* Provide sentence frames such as:

5. Both Lewis and Clark and Laura Ingalls Wilder used <u>pencil and paper</u> as supplies.

6. Jesse Fewkes's team was successful in <u>interpreting stories</u>, but Lewis and Clark were successful in <u>exploring</u>.

7. Skills that helped Lewis and Clark were <u>hunting, reading maps, sailing, and interpreting</u>, but the skills that helped Jesse Fewkes's team were <u>interpreting and using the cylinder recorder</u>.

Write to Express

TEACH/MODEL Review the features of a **personal narrative**. Review words about writing a personal narrative. *When you write a personal narrative, you write about something that happened to you.* Tell students that today they will draft the personal narrative that they began last week.

- Read and discuss the Writing Process Checklist on **Student Book** p. 524.

- Read and discuss the Writing Model on **Student Book** pp. 524–525. Point out examples of interesting **details**.

GUIDED PRACTICE Explain that the class will work together to write a personal narrative.

- Have students use the events chart that they completed for their personal narrative last week. Remind students that the topic of their narrative is a field trip or activity they did with others.

- *What ideas can we use from the events chart to write our personal narrative?* List the ideas as students say them. Explain that a narrative should include interesting details of the event.

Extend Language
Words About the Outdoors
cloudy, forest, hot, insects, plants, rainy, sunny, windy

- *What details can we add to the sentences to make them more interesting?* Make any necessary corrections.

- Read the completed narrative aloud chorally. Discuss the narrative, and have students suggest places they could add details to make it more interesting.

CHECK PROGRESS

Do students…
- participate in discussion about successful teams?
- correctly identify similarities and differences between successful teams?
- use interesting details in their writing?

REVIEW TOGETHER

- Have students work in pairs or small groups to read and review the rows and columns of the successful teams comparison chart.
- Have partners help each other check for and include vocabulary words in their writing.
- Have students review the **Writing Rubric** on p. 18 of the **Grab-and-Go™ Resources**.

Scaffolded Practice and Application

Beginning Provide the sentence frame *A field trip is enjoyable because ____.* Guide students to suggest interesting details to complete it.

Intermediate Have students write *A field trip is enjoyable because ____.* Have students add details to make the sentence interesting.

Advanced Have students write sentences about what makes field trips enjoyable. Have partners exchange sentences and add descriptive details.

Advanced High Have students write a paragraph about what makes field trips enjoyable. Have them exchange paragraphs with a partner and add descriptive details.

Teacher Notes

Resources

Unit 4

Contents

✔ Brainstorm

1 TEACH/MODEL

Ask students to name situations when people must develop new, creative ideas, such as an advertiser thinking up a slogan, or an inventor working on an invention.

Explain that students have just brainstormed ideas. When people brainstorm, they try to come up with as many ideas as they can think of, with few or no restrictions. Discuss the background of brainstorming:

- No idea is too silly or strange.
- Every idea is a good suggestion.
- The goal of brainstorming is to think creatively, without judging or being judged.

Point out the advantages and challenges of brainstorming in a group:

- The group benefits from many people's experience and creativity.
- One person's idea may spark an idea in someone else.
- All ideas should be considered without criticism. Acceptance is essential to the process.
- Everyone must stay focused on the task or goal.

2 PRACTICE/APPLY

- Ask small groups to brainstorm ideas for a poster illustrating the Unit Big Idea: *There is more than one secret to success.* Note that the poster can be any form, with or without words.
- Have each group list their ideas on a large sheet of paper. Allow time for sharing.

✔ Solve Problems

1 TEACH/MODEL

Remind students that, like story characters, they too must figure out ways to solve their problems. Point out that knowing a process for problem solving will help them find solutions more easily.

- Introduce the problem-solving process:

  1. Define the problem. State it clearly in your own words. Figure out possible causes of the problem and potential effects.

  2. Consider possible solutions. Make a list of your ideas.

  3. Examine possible solutions. Analyze and evaluate all the information you have. Consider the pros and cons of each possible solution.

  4. Decide on the best solution. Offer convincing evidence as to why it is the best solution.

  5. Carry out the solution.

- Discuss the following problem and demonstrate how to work through each step. Have students contribute their ideas and help decide on the best solution.

Problem: *What should you do if your aunt's wedding is the same day as your best friend's birthday party? Which event should you attend?*

2 PRACTICE/APPLY

- Display a list of problems faced by characters in the Unit selections. Discuss the ways the characters could have solved those problems.

- Ask small groups to use the problem-solving process to identify the best solutions.

- Allow time to share and discuss solutions.

SHARE OBJECTIVES
- Use a process to solve a problem.
- Share and discuss solutions.

Make a Hypothesis

1 TEACH/MODEL

Explain that a hypothesis is a statement that describes an inference made from observing available evidence. Scientists make hypotheses to explain what they observe in the world around them. Good readers make hypotheses about story elements and selection concepts using details presented by an author.

Discuss how to make and test a hypothesis:

1. Ask a question. As you read, think of questions about the characters, setting, or plot. Choose one question to investigate.

2. Make a hypothesis. Think of what you already know about the question. Form an idea and write it down. That is your hypothesis.

3. Find evidence. Test your hypothesis by looking for evidence as you read.

4. Adjust the hypothesis. As you read, you may find new evidence that requires you to change your hypothesis.

5. Draw a conclusion. Does the evidence support your hypothesis, or should you revise it? Write your conclusion.

2 PRACTICE/APPLY

• Have partners write a hypothesis about a character from their reading. Have them find evidence to test the hypothesis and then write a conclusion. Have volunteers share their hypothesis and evidence with the class.

Support a Proposition

SHARE OBJECTIVES

• Make and support a proposition.
• Express supported opinions/communicate effectively.

1 TEACH/MODEL

Explain that a proposition is a statement of opinion that tries to persuade others by providing reasons for the statement. It often proposes a solution to a problem.

• Remind students that persuasion tries to influence others to think or act in certain ways. It is most effective when ideas or opinions are supported by well thought-out reasons, which are supported by facts and evidence.

• Point out that a writer or speaker should expect questions and be able to answer the audience's concerns and arguments.

• Help students develop a proposition or strong opinion statement, such as *All children should play a sport.*

• Demonstrate how to justify the proposition, or prove its importance. Name a reason people should agree with the opinion and state facts or evidence to support it. For example, *Sports provide good exercise.*

• Have students suggest other reasons and supporting evidence or "proof."

2 PRACTICE/APPLY

• Have partners make a proposal for how to solve a problem, such as how to keep the school playground or a local park clean. Have them write an opinion statement and identify reasons and evidence that people should support their opinion and proposal.

Follow Multi-Step Directions

1 TEACH/MODEL

Explain that following directions is a step-by-step way of learning how to do something. Review the process:

- Read the directions carefully, from beginning to end. Become familiar with special terms or techniques needed.

- Gather any necessary materials.

- Follow the steps in order, finishing each one. Pay attention to numbers or any order words such as *first*, *next*, or *finally*.

- If a step is unclear, reread the directions again.

- Study any diagrams or illustrations to understand how they relate to the steps.

- If possible, ask questions.

2 PRACTICE/APPLY

- Have students reread the directions in "Pizza Pizzazz" and "Making Wet Chalk Drawings," on **Student Book p. 83** and **p. 216**.

- Have students compare and contrast the two sets of directions. Have them determine which set of directions was easier to follow, and why.

- Have partners create a set of directions for a simple, familiar activity such as changing a light bulb or making a bed.

Collect Information from Surveys

1 TEACH/MODEL

Remind students that a survey is a way of collecting information by asking people questions. Review the steps in conducting a survey:

- Start with a good question, such as *What makes the best pet, a dog or a cat?* Decide what you want to know and figure out how to best ask about it. Be specific. The answer to your question should be short, such as a number, name, or just yes or no.

- Ask a good sample of the people you want to study, such as classmates or family members. It is usually not necessary to ask everyone in an area to get an idea of what people think or do. You just need to ask a representative group. Be sure you pick a fair and random one.

- Collect and record the data. Be fair and complete, because every answer counts.

- Organize the answers, and report what you found. You can use charts, tables, diagrams, or graphs to show your results.

2 PRACTICE/APPLY

- Have small groups conduct a survey.

- Have groups decide on a survey question such as *Who is your favorite book character?* or *What type of award would you give for your favorite book character?*

- Have group members collect information and present the results to the class using a simple graph.

Prepare Oral Reports

SHARE OBJECTIVE

• Organize thoughts before speaking.

MATERIALS

• note cards

1 TEACH/MODEL

Explain that before students give an oral presentation, they must plan for what they are going to say. Discuss how students can prepare to give a speech. Provide these tips:

• Choose a topic to speak about.

• Write notes telling important ideas about the topic on note cards.

• Organize the note cards in an order that makes sense.

• Practice speaking aloud, using the note cards to help organize talking points.

2 PRACTICE/APPLY

Have students prepare a speech on the importance of good nutrition.

• Tell students to write notes on cards about healthy foods.

• Ask students to arrange the cards in a logical order.

• Have students practice their speech aloud.

Make Oral Presentations

SHARE OBJECTIVE

• Make an oral presentation about how to conserve energy at home.

MATERIALS

• notes on index cards

1 TEACH/MODEL

Remind students that before anyone gives a talk, he or she must prepare what to say. Once the notes are written and the speech has been practiced, the speaker is ready to present it. Discuss what students should remember when giving a speech:

• Stay focused on the chosen topic.

• Present the information in an order that makes sense.

• Speak loudly and clearly.

• Make good eye contact with the audience.

• Speak with appropriate expression.

2 PRACTICE/APPLY

Have students prepare a speech on conserving energy at home.

• Have students write and organize notes on index cards.

• Have students present their speech.

• Remind students to speak loudly, clearly, and with expression. Encourage students to look at the audience as they speak.

Use Text Structure to Outline

1 TEACH/MODEL

Remind students that authors use structural patterns to organize information and ideas so that readers understand what is meant. The patterns can also be used when outlining. Organizing information in the same pattern helps retell or summarize it briefly but clearly.

Review sections of an outline. Then explain how to outline by using structural patterns such as these:

• Cause and effect: List each primary cause and effect as a main topic. List secondary causes and effects as subtopics. Add details for clarification.

• Compare and contrast: List likenesses as one main topic and differences as another. List subtopics and details in order of importance.

• Order of importance: List the most important facts and ideas as main topics and less important facts as subtopics.

• Proposition and support: Provide a proposition or opinion statement. List reasons supporting it as main topics; list facts, evidence, or proof, as subtopics.

• Demonstrate how to outline using the cause and effect text structure in *Riding Freedom* on **Student Book pp. 412–414**.

2 PRACTICE/APPLY

• Have small groups identify selections that feature different types of text structures.

• Ask students to outline one selection using the text structure to organize their thoughts.

Analyze Incorrect Inferences

1 TEACH/MODEL

Explain that when an author doesn't state something directly, a reader may make a conclusion, or inference, using text clues or personal experience. An inference may be based on incorrect thinking, rather than facts. Identify these types:

• An overgeneralization is a broad statement not based on facts or evidence: *All video games are expensive.*

• Faulty cause and effect wrongly connects two events: *It was sunny, and she was happy.* One event does not necessarily cause the other.

• Unreliable evidence is a reason not supported by accurate or reliable proof: *He won't understand because I heard he doesn't speak English.*

• False comparison is based on poor reasoning skills: *This phone looks just like that phone, so it should cost the same.*

2 PRACTICE/APPLY

• Have students discuss times when they have made an overgeneralization or wrongly connected two events.

• Have partners search magazine and newspaper articles to find examples of incorrect inferences.

Review Internet Strategy: Steps 1 and 2

SHARE OBJECTIVE

• Synthesize information from websites and other sources.

MATERIALS

• notes on a topic from several websites

1 TEACH/MODEL

Review Steps 1–2 of the Internet Strategy. Refer to the Internet Strategies on **pp. T34** and **T106**.

• Explain that a successful Internet search requires planning. The key to success is to decide what students want to know and how best to find it.

• To go to a specific website, students must type in its address, or URL. Identify a possible site to explore. Note that an extension such as *.gov* or *.org* is a possible source of reliable information.

• To use a search engine, students must first devise questions about a topic.

• Next, students must use their questions to identify keywords that focus on specific areas of the topic.

• Type in keywords such as dogs + service + Texas, and display the list of sites identified by the search engine.

Remind students that their choice of keywords will narrow their search to create more useful lists, or "hits."

• Discuss the list of sites. Have students predict which ones will give information about the topic and which will not be useful.

• Point out details from an entry, such as the description or quote, site URL, and links.

2 PRACTICE/APPLY

• Have partners type topics and focused keywords into a search engine and analyze the results. Then have partners list the URLs of two promising websites and one that is not helpful.

Word Lists

Reaching Out

Lesson 1

TARGET VOCABULARY		Spelling Words			Academic Language
comfort	consisted	blade	drain	raft	plot
mention	positive	gray	maybe	jail	conflict
mood	advanced	past	break	crayon	resolution
properly	peculiar	afraid	sale	fact	infer
intends	talent	magic	hang	stale	complete sentences
		delay	stain	steak	simple subject
		amaze	glass		simple predicate

Lesson 2

TARGET VOCABULARY		Spelling Words			Academic Language
injustice	dream	west	steam	greed	author's purpose
numerous	encounters	steep	beast	shelf	infer
segregation	preferred	member	believe	least	author's viewpoint
nourishing	recall	gleam	speck	eager	complete subject
captured	example	fresh	kept	reason	complete predicate
		freedom	cheap	chief	compound subject
		speed	pretend		compound predicate

Lesson 3

TARGET VOCABULARY		Spelling Words			Academic Language
welcomed	negative	skill	chill	district	cause
sensitive	honor	crime	delight	inch	effect
observes	included	grind	build	sigh	infer
unspoiled	glances	tonight	ditch	fright	statement
prepared	encouragement	brick	decide	remind	question
		flight	witness	split	command
		live	wind		exclamation

Lesson 4

TARGET VOCABULARY		Spelling Words			Academic Language
assist	misjudged	block	odd	solve	theme
burglaries	suspect	shown	locate	known	analyze
innocent	favor	oatmeal	slope	remote	evaluate
scheme	speculated	wrote	throat	stock	simple sentence
regretfully	prior	fellow	host	boast	compound sentence
		scold	online	globe	conjunction
		coast	shock		subject-verb agreement

Lesson 5

TARGET VOCABULARY		Spelling Words			Academic Language
yearning	shortage	wait	heal	feat	character traits
memorable	tidal	weight	peak	vain	relationships
betrayed	outcast	heard	peek	vane	infer
condition	foaming	herd	sent	vein	traits
seafaring	horrified	days	cent	miner	singular noun
		daze	scent	minor	plural noun
		heel	feet		common noun
					proper noun

Unit 2

Do You Know What I Mean?

	TARGET VOCABULARY		☑ Spelling Words			Academic Language
Lesson 6	rescue	refused	bunch	refuse	rude	compare
	hideous	invisible	fruit	truth	trust	contrast
	exploding	hired	argue	young	dew	suffix
	battle	immense	crumb	clue	stuck	affix
	wealthy	warrior	crew	trunk	rescue	baseword
			tune	amuse	brush	action verb
			juice	suit		linking verb
						helping verb
Lesson 7	entertaining	critics	bloom	proof	booth	fact
	promote	target	cookbook	prove	raccoon	verify
	focus	thrilling	tool	group	hook	opinion
	advertise	angles	shampoo	brook	groom	root
	jolts	generated	put	foolish	roof	present tense
			wool	bush	soup	past tense
			stool	crooked		future tense
Lesson 8	glorious	ruined	aloud	tower	drown	motivation
	studio	yanked	bald	stalk	pause	relationship
	concerned	streak	hawk	couple	fault	visualize
	model	schedule	south	howl	cause	analyze
	smeared	feast	faucet	false	amount	traits
			proud	dawn	cloudier	conjunction
			claw	allow		compound sentence
						complex sentence
						correlative conjunction
Lesson 9	fault	local	spark	earring	hairy	conclusions
	borrow	apologize	prepare	scarce	compare	generalizations
	reference	proof	cheer	weird	alarm	antonyms
	fainted	slimy	tear	sharp	harsh	analogy
	genuine	insisted	scarf	rear	upstairs	comma
			scare	spare	square	series
			repair	gear		
Lesson 10	debut	towered	learn	cure	world	author's purpose
	stubborn	triumph	dirty	board	search	implied
	permission	discouraged	worn	course	worse	pronoun
	hauling	toured	sore	worth	thirteen	antecedent
	mournful	border	thirst	early	sport	reflexive pronoun
			burn	return	current	
			record	pure		

Word Lists • **R9**

Word Lists

Natural Encounters

	TARGET VOCABULARY		☑ Spelling Words			Academic Language
Lesson 11	presence	arrangement	somebody	all right	driveway	fact
	disbelief	pounced	fireplace	goodbye	alarm clock	opinion
	tempted	utter	nearby	forehead	baby-sit	distinguish
	biological	hastened	toothbrush	classmate	airport	suffix
	endeared	incident	homesick	flashlight	forever	baseword
			make-believe	haircut	mailbox	affix
			anything	twenty-two		
Lesson 12	trembles	crushing	rising	snapping	hitting	sequence of events
	wreckage	rubble	traced	bragging	spotted	visualize
	slab	debris	stripped	handled	raced	synonyms
	possessions	timbers	slammed	dripped	dimmed	possessive noun
	tenement	constructed	dancing	begged	spinning	apostrophe
			striped	dared	escaped	problem
			winning	skipped		solution
						composition
Lesson 13	display	vision	wiped	seeking	hiking	cause
	alert	huddle	covered	visiting	checking	effect
	weariness	graceful	mapped	mixed	fainted	infer
	fractured	stranded	pleasing	shipped	landed	root
	standards	concluded	slipped	phoning	becoming	regular verb
			putting	offered	wandering	helping verb
			traveled	smelling		past participle
						persuasive letter
						voice
Lesson 14	social	transport	turkey	starry	daily	text features
	exchanges	chamber	lonely	melody	alley	boldface print
	excess	scarce	colony	movie	fifty	graphic features
	reinforce	obstacles	steady	duty	empty	participle
	storage	transfers	hungry	drowsy	injury	present participle
			valley	chimney	prairie	past participle
			hockey	plenty		support
						persuasive essay
						goal
Lesson 15	organisms	habitats	tiniest	families	breezier	main idea
	directly	variety	hobbies	spied	prettiest	supporting details
	affect	species	copied	happiest	noisier	infer
	traces	banned	countries	ladies	healthier	facts and examples
	vast	radiation	pitied	friendlier	butterflies	persuade
			easier	studied	funniest	multiple-meaning words
			laziest	busier		context

Unit 4

Never Give Up!

	TARGET VOCABULARY		☑ Spelling Words			Academic Language
Lesson 16	escorted swelled relied reputation worthy	churning situation deserve defended satisfied	risky track topic blank question pocket monkey	junk equal ache public attack struck earthquake	picnic banker electric blanket mistake stomach	compare contrast context similarity adjective adjective of purpose vivid detail topic sentence
Lesson 17	reward graduate symbol foster disobey	confidence patiently confesses ceremony performs	glance judge damage package twice stage carriage	since practice marriage baggage office message bridge	chance notice ridge manage palace bandage	chronological order infer sequence of events adverb adverb of frequency adverb of intensity greeting closing
Lesson 18	gigantic miniature especially lapped vanished	jealous haze lure deliberately crisp	unused refresh dislike replace unpaid redo disorder	unplanned distrust rewind untrue unload recall displease	uneven rebuild restart uncover untidy discolor	character traits homonyms homophones narrative synonym
Lesson 19	overcome association capitol drought dedicate	publicity violence conflicts horizon brilliant	colorful weakness movement endless truthful illness cheerful	useless beautiful restless clumsiness pavement peaceful fondness	neatness speechless statement wasteful penniless treatment	author's goal persuade evaluate dictionary entry pronunciation pronunciation key personal narrative organize topic
Lesson 20	territory accompany proposed interpreter duty	supplies route corps clumsy landmark	million collect lumber pepper plastic borrow support	thirty perfect attend canyon traffic fortune danger	soccer engine picture survive seldom effort	topic main idea supporting detail compound word abbreviation revise dialogue

Word Lists • R11

Word Lists

Change Is All Around

	TARGET VOCABULARY		✓ Spelling Words			Academic Language
Lesson 21	appreciate	nocturnal	event	unite	punish	theme
	blaring	feats	humor	frozen	defend	summarize
	combination	effort	rapid	figure	relay	multiple-meaning words
	promptly	suggest	music	siren	habit	summary
	introduce	racket	relief	polite	student	important details
			planet	hotel	moment	
			detail	protest		
Lesson 22	politics	legislature	dentist	hollow	dinner	cause
	intelligent	amendment	final	divide	minus	effect
	disorderly	candidates	finish	famous	minute	negative
	approve	informed	narrow	recent	value	transitions
	polls	denied	shelter	silver	reward	etymology
			ahead	capture	broken	
			corner	cabin		
Lesson 23	resources	civilized	poster	bucket	degree	text features
	dense	continent	secret	ticket	gather	graphic features
	evaporate	opportunities	whether	declare	achieve	visuals
	shallow	customs	author	chicken	rather	caption
	moisture	independent	rocket	clothing	bracket	prefix
			bushel	apron	machine	procedural composition
			agree	whiskers		supporting facts
						process transitions
Lesson 24	bond	inseparable	hundred	sandwich	sample	compare
	suffered	charged	supply	instead	although	contrast
	intruder	chief	single	complete	turtle	analyze
	companion	exhausted	middle	monster	athlete	evaluate
	enclosure	affection	explain	settle	orchard	suffix
			surprise	address	kingdom	outline
			pilgrim	farther		research
						source
Lesson 25	progress	insert	idea	piano	period	author's purpose
	calculated	waste	lion	January	February	infer
	dispute	inspector	usual	quiet	cereal	question
	centuries	mechanical	radio	poet	video	author's purpose
	superior	average	liar	science	meteor	apostrophe
			poem	diary	rodeo	contraction
			India	violin		research report
						introductory paragraph

Unit 6 — Paths to Discovery

	TARGET VOCABULARY		✓ Spelling Words			Academic Language
Lesson 26	peculiar intends captured nourishing glances	observes assist favor condition memorable	enter banner sugar shower motor collar labor	finger mirror beggar favor bother fever doctor	temper actor polar sweater traitor whenever	story elements setting character(s) plot conflict resolution root stanza rhythm rhyme
Lesson 27	shortage betrayed species continent scarce	focus included alert introduce opportunities	title towel battle pedal metal simple eagle	special total trouble nickel gentle barrel model	tangle ankle marvel juggle squirrel riddle	topic main idea supporting detail analogy journal entry
Lesson 28	apologize genuine triumph arrangement biological	display concluded obstacles affect vast	library another hospital example deliver history however	several vacation important victory imagine camera potato	remember together memory favorite continue president	fact opinion prefix distinguish public service announcement analyze
Lesson 29	defended satisfied confidence symbol vanished	deliberately brilliant publicity territory proposed	half comb mortgage honor fasten kneel wreath	calm answer handsome wrinkle listen fetch yolk	climb honest knuckle plumber limb folktale	infer predict trait behavior word origin genre multi-genre collage
Lesson 30	appreciate effort denied informed shallow	resources average suffered inspector progress	meant routine style flood month pleasant guess	women either against disguise sweat magazine guard	receive wonder league type ceiling money	conclusion generalization summarize suffix contraction homophone

Using Rubrics

A **rubric** *is a tool a teacher can use to score a student's work.*

A **rubric** *lists the criteria for evaluating the work, and it describes different levels of success in meeting those criteria.*

Rubrics *are useful assessment tools for teachers, but they can be just as useful for students. In fact, rubrics can be powerful teaching tools.*

RUBRIC

Rubrics for Retelling and Summarizing

- There is a separate rubric for narrative and for nonfiction. Before students begin their retellings or summaries, ask them which rubric should be used. Then point out the criteria and discuss each one.

- Have students focus on the criteria for excellence listed on the rubric so that they have specific goals to aim for.

RUBRIC

Rubric for Presentations

- Before students make a presentation, discuss the criteria listed on the rubric. Have students focus on the criteria for excellence listed on the rubric so that they can aim for specific goals.

- Discuss the criteria for listening with students who will be in the audience. Point out the criteria for excellence listed on the rubric so that they can target specific goals.

RUBRIC

Rubrics for Writing

- When you introduce students to a new kind of writing through a writing model, discuss the criteria listed on the rubric, and ask students to decide how well the model meets each criterion.

- Before students attempt a new kind of writing, have them focus on the criteria for excellence listed on the rubric so that they have specific goals to aim for.

- During both the drafting and revising stages, remind students to check their writing against the rubric to keep their focus and to determine if there are any aspects of their writing they can improve.

- Students can use the rubrics to score their own writing. They can keep the marked rubric in their portfolios with the corresponding piece of writing. The marked rubrics will help students see their progress through the school year. In conferences with students and family members, you can refer to the rubrics to point out both strengths and weaknesses in students' writing.

- See *Grab-and-Go™ Resources* for weekly writing rubrics.

Scoring RUBRIC for Retelling Narratives

Score of 4

The student:

- names and describes the main and supporting characters and tells how they change or learn.
- tells about the setting.
- retells the plot in detail.
- describes the problems and resolutions in the story.
- uses phrases, language, vocabulary, sentence structure, or literary devices from the story.
- accurately describes the theme or meaning of the story.
- provides extensions of the story, such as making connections to other texts, and relating relevant experiences, and/or making generalizations.
- requires little or no prompting.

Score of 3

The student:

- names and describes the main characters.
- tells about the setting.
- retells most of the plot accurately.
- describes some of the problems and resolutions in the story.
- uses some phrases, language, vocabulary, or literary devices from the story.
- relates some aspects of the theme or meaning of the story.
- provides some extensions of the story, such as making connections to other texts or relating relevant experiences.
- may require some prompting.

Score of 2

The student:

- tells some details about the story elements, including characters, setting, and plot, with some omissions or errors.
- uses little language and vocabulary from the story.
- shows minimal understanding of the theme or meaning of the story.
- provides minimal extensions of the story.
- requires some prompting to retell the story.

Score of 1

The student:

- tells few, if any, details about the story elements, with errors.
- has little or no awareness of the theme of the story.
- provides no extensions of the story.
- is unable to retell the story without prompting.

Scoring RUBRIC for Summarizing Nonfiction

Score of 4

The student:

- provides a summarizing statement.
- relates the main idea and important supporting details.
- creates a focused, coherent, logical, and organized structure; stays on topic; and relates important points to the text.
- understands relationships in the text such as cause-and-effect, chronological order, or classifying, grouping, comparing, or contrasting information.
- discriminates between reality and fantasy, fact and fiction.
- uses phrases, language, vocabulary, or sentence structure from the text.
- clearly tells the conclusion or point of the text with details.
- identifies the author's purpose for recreating the text.
- provides extensions of the text, such as making connections to other texts, relating relevant experiences, and/or making generalizations.
- requires little or no prompting.

Score of 3

The student:

- tells the topic of the text.
- relates the main idea and relevant details.
- creates a coherent structure and stays on topic.
- mostly understands relationships in the text, such as cause-and-effect, chronological order, or classifying, grouping, or comparing information.
- discriminates between reality and fantasy.
- uses some phrases, language, or vocabulary from the text.
- tells the conclusion or point of the text.
- identifies the author's purpose.
- provides some extensions of the story, such as making connections to other texts or relating relevant experiences.
- may require some prompting.

Score of 2

The student:

- minimally relates the topic of the text.
- shows minimal understanding of the main idea, and omits many important details.
- provides some structure; might stray from topic.
- understands few, if any, relationships in the text, such as chronological order, classifying, or grouping.
- uses little or no language and vocabulary from the text.
- does not fully understand the conclusion or point of the text.
- shows some awareness of the author's purpose.
- provides few, if any, extensions of the text.
- requires some prompting.

Score of 1

The student:

- shows little or no understanding of the topic of the text.
- shows little or no understanding of the main idea, and omits important details.
- provides a poorly organized or unclear structure.
- does not understand relationships in the text.
- does not understand the conclusion of the text.
- provides no extensions of the text.
- is unable to summarize the text without prompting.

Scoring RUBRIC for Presentations

	HANDWRITING	WORD PROCESSING	MARKERS	VISUALS	SPEAKING
Score of 4	The slant of the letters is the same throughout the whole paper. The letters are clearly formed and the spacing between words is equal, which makes the text very easy to read.	Fonts and sizes are used very well, which helps the reader enjoy reading the text.	The title, subheads, page numbers, and bullets are used very well. They make it easy for the reader to find information in the text. These markers clearly show organized information.	The writer uses visuals such as illustrations, charts, graphs, maps, and tables very well. The text and visuals clearly relate to each other.	The speaker uses very effective pace, volume, intonation, and expression.
Score of 3	The slant of the letters is usually the same. The letters are clearly formed most of the time. The spacing between words is usually equal.	Fonts and sizes are used fairly well, but could be improved upon.	The title, subheads, page numbers, and bullets are used fairly well. They usually help the reader find information.	The writer uses visuals fairly well.	The speaker uses effective pace, volume, intonation, and expression.
Score of 2	The handwriting is readable. There are some differences in letter shape and form, slant, and spacing that make some words easier to read than others.	Fonts and sizes are used well in some places, but make the paper look cluttered in others.	The writer uses some markers such as a title, page numbers, or bullets. However, the use of markers could be improved upon to help the reader get more meaning from the text.	The writer uses visuals with the text, but the reader may not understand how they are related.	The speaker uses somewhat effective pace, volume, intonation, and expression.
Score of 1	The letters are not formed correctly. The slant spacing is not the same throughout the paper, or there is no regular space between words. The paper is very difficult to read.	The writer has used too many different fonts and sizes. It is very distracting to the reader.	There are no markers such as title, page numbers, bullets, or subheads.	The visuals do not make sense with the text.	The speaker's techniques are unclear or distracting to the listener.

Scoring Rubrics

Scoring RUBRIC for Narrative Writing

	FOCUS/IDEAS	ORGANIZATION	VOICE	WORD CHOICE	SENTENCE FLUENCY	CONVENTIONS
Score of 4	The narrative fits the purpose for writing and the intended audience very well. The ideas are very interesting.	A beginning introduces characters, setting, and problem. A middle tells events in order. An ending gives the solution.	Characters and events are presented in rich detail, in a very clear and authentic way.	There are many exact, vivid, and sensory words and some dialogue.	All of the sentences are smooth and varied.	There are no grammar, spelling, capitalization, or punctuation errors.
Score of 3	The narrative fits the purpose for writing and the intended audience well. The ideas are interesting.	A beginning introduces characters and problem. Events in the middle are not always in order. An ending gives the solution.	Characters and events are presented in some detail, in a mostly clear and authentic way.	There are some exact, vivid, and sensory words and some dialogue.	Most of the sentences are smooth and varied.	There are a few grammar, spelling, capitalization, or punctuation errors.
Score of 2	The purpose for writing and the intended audience are not very clear. The ideas are not very interesting.	A beginning introduces characters, middle, or ending. There is a problem, but not a good solution. Events are not in order.	There is no clear beginning, middle, or ending. There is a problem, but not a good solution. Events are not in order.	Characters and events are presented with few details and not enough authenticity.	There are few descriptive words and no dialogue.	Few of the sentences are smooth, and there is little sentence variety.	There are some grammar, spelling, capitalization, and punctuation errors.
Score of 1	The purpose for writing and the intended audience are not clear. The ideas are uninteresting.	The purpose for writing and the intended audience are not clear. The ideas are uninteresting.	There is no beginning, middle, or ending. There is no problem. Events are hard to follow.	Characters and events are presented with little detail and authenticity.	There are no descriptive words and no dialogue.	None of the sentences are smooth, and there is no sentence variety.	There are many grammar, spelling, capitalization, and punctuation errors.

Scoring RUBRIC for Expository Writing

	FOCUS/IDEAS	ORGANIZATION	VOICE	WORD CHOICE	SENTENCE FLUENCY	CONVENTIONS
Score of 4	Writing adheres to a clearly stated topic. All of the main ideas are supported by facts.	Facts and examples are always presented in a clear and logical order.	The writing shows a strong and confident connection to the topic.	All of the facts are clear and exact, and all words readers might not know are defined.	There is excellent sentence variety, and all the verb tenses are the same.	There are no grammar, spelling, capitalization, or punctuation errors.
Score of 3	Writing mostly adheres to the topic. Most of the main ideas are supported by facts.	Facts and examples are mostly presented in a clear and logical order.	The writing mostly shows a confident connection to the topic.	Most of the facts are clear and exact, and many words readers might not know are defined.	There is adequate sentence variety, and most of the verb tenses are the same.	There are a few grammar, spelling, capitalization, or punctuation errors.
Score of 2	Writing does not always adhere to the topic. Some of the main ideas are supported by facts.	Facts and examples are sometimes presented in a clear and logical order.	The writing sometimes shows a confident connection to the topic.	Some of the facts are clear and exact, and some words readers might not know are defined.	There is some sentence variety, and some of the verb tenses are the same.	There are some grammar, spelling, capitalization, and punctuation errors.
Score of 1	Writing does not adhere to the topic. There are few main ideas and supporting facts.	Facts and examples are rarely presented in a clear and logical order.	The writing shows a weak connection to the topic.	Few of the facts are clear and exact, and none of the words readers might not know are defined.	There is little sentence variety, and the verb tenses are confusing and often different.	There are many grammar, spelling, capitalization, and punctuation errors.

Scoring Rubrics

Scoring RUBRIC for Persuasive Writing

	FOCUS/IDEAS	ORGANIZATION	VOICE	WORD CHOICE	SENTENCE FLUENCY	CONVENTIONS
Score of 4	The position is very clear and well supported by three or more good reasons. There is a strong call to action.	There are plenty of facts and details arranged in a logical order.	Feelings about the topic are very clear and strongly expressed.	There are many exact words and phrases.	There is excellent variety in sentence types and lengths.	There are no grammar, spelling, capitalization, or punctuation errors.
Score of 3	The position is clear and supported by two good reasons. There is a call to action.	There are adequate facts and details, mostly arranged in a logical order.	Feelings about the topic are mostly clear and adequately expressed.	There are some exact words and phrases.	There is adequate variety in sentence types and lengths.	There are a few grammar, spelling, capitalization, or punctuation errors.
Score of 2	The position is not clearly stated and is inadequately supported. There is a vague call to action.	There are few facts and details and no logical order.	Feelings about the topic are somewhat clear and weakly expressed.	There are a few exact words and phrases.	There is some variety in sentence types and lengths.	There are some grammar, spelling, capitalization, and punctuation errors.
Score of 1	The position is unclear, and there are no supporting reasons. There is no call to action.	There are no facts or details.	Feelings about the topic are not clear, and there is no personal expression.	There are no exact words and phrases.	There is little variety in sentence types and lengths.	There are many grammar, spelling, capitalization, and punctuation errors.

Scoring RUBRIC for Multipurpose Writing

	FOCUS/IDEAS	ORGANIZATION	VOICE	WORD CHOICE	SENTENCE FLUENCY	CONVENTIONS
Score of 4	Adheres to the topic, is interesting, has a sense of completeness. Ideas are well developed.	Ideas and details are clearly presented and well organized.	Connects with reader in a unique, personal way.	Includes vivid verbs, strong adjectives, specific nouns.	Includes a variety of complete sentences that flow smoothly, naturally.	Shows a strong command of grammar, spelling, capitalization, punctuation.
Score of 3	Mostly adheres to the topic, is somewhat interesting, has a sense of completeness. Ideas are adequately developed.	Ideas and details are mostly clear and generally organized.	Generally connects with reader in a way that is personal and sometimes unique.	Includes some vivid verbs, strong adjectives, specific nouns.	Includes some variety of mostly complete sentences. Some parts flow smoothly, naturally.	Shows a good command of grammar, spelling, capitalization, punctuation.
Score of 2	Does not always adhere to the topic, has some sense of completeness. Ideas are superficially developed.	Ideas and details are not always clear or organized. There is some wordiness or repetition.	Connects somewhat with reader. Sounds somewhat personal, but not unique.	Includes mostly simple nouns and verbs, and may have a few adjectives.	Includes mostly simple sentences, some of which are incomplete.	Some errors in grammar, spelling, capitalization, punctuation.
Score of 1	Does not adhere to the topic, has no sense of completeness. Ideas are vague.	Ideas and details are not organized. Wordiness or repetition hinders meaning.	Does not connect with reader. Does not sound personal or unique.	Includes only simple nouns and verbs, some inaccurate. Writing is not descriptive.	Sentences do not vary. Incomplete sentences hinder meaning.	Frequent errors in grammar, spelling, capitalization, punctuation.

Handwriting

Individual students have various levels of handwriting skills, but they all have the desire to communicate effectively. To write correctly, they must be familiar with concepts of

- size (tall, short)
- open and closed
- capital and lowercase letters
- manuscript vs. cursive letters
- letter and word spacing
- punctuation

To assess students' handwriting skills, review samples of their written work. Note whether they use correct letter formation and appropriate size and spacing. Note whether students follow the conventions of print such as correct capitalization and punctuation. Encourage students to edit and proofread their work and to use editing marks. When writing messages, notes, and letters, or when publishing their writing, students should leave adequate margins and indent new paragraphs to help make their work more readable for their audience.

Stroke and Letter Formation

Most manuscript letters are formed with a continuous stroke, so students do not often pick up their pencils when writing a single letter. When students begin to use cursive handwriting, they will have to lift their pencils from the paper less frequently and will be able to write more fluently. Models for manuscript and D'Nealian handwriting are provided on pages R24–R27.

Position for Writing

Establishing the correct posture, pen or pencil grip, and paper position for writing will help prevent handwriting problems.

Posture   Students should sit with both feet on the floor and with hips to the back of the chair. They can lean forward slightly but should not slouch. The writing surface should be smooth and flat and at a height that allows the upper arms to be perpendicular to the surface and the elbows to be under the shoulders.

Writing Instrument   An adult-sized number-two lead pencil is a satisfactory writing tool for most students. As students become proficient in the use of cursive handwriting, have them use pens for writing final drafts. Use your judgment in determining what type of instrument is most suitable.

Paper Position and Pencil Grip   The paper is slanted along the line of the student's writing arm, and the student uses his or her nonwriting hand to hold the paper in place. The student holds the pencil or pen slightly above the paint line—about one inch from the lead tip.

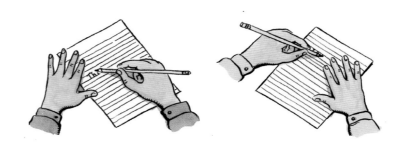

Developing Handwriting

The best instruction builds on what students already know and can do. Given the wide range in students' handwriting abilities, a variety of approaches may be needed.

Writing for Different Purposes　For students who need more practice keeping their handwriting legible, one of the most important understandings is that legible writing is important for clear communication. Provide as many opportunities for classroom writing as possible. For example, students can

- **make a class directory listing the names of their classmates;**
- **draw and label graphic organizers, pictures, and maps;**
- **contribute entries weekly to their vocabulary journals;**
- **write and post messages about class assignments or group activities; and**
- **record observations during activities.**

Meaningful Print Experiences　Students should participate in meaningful print experiences. They can

- **write signs, labels for centers, and other messages;**
- **label graphic organizers and drawings;**
- **contribute in group writing activities; and**
- **write independently in notebooks.**

You may also want to have students practice handwriting skills in their first language.

Writing Fluently　To ensure continued rapid advancement of students who come to fourth grade writing fluently, provide

- **a wide range of writing assignments, and**
- **opportunities for independent writig on self-selected and assigned topics.**

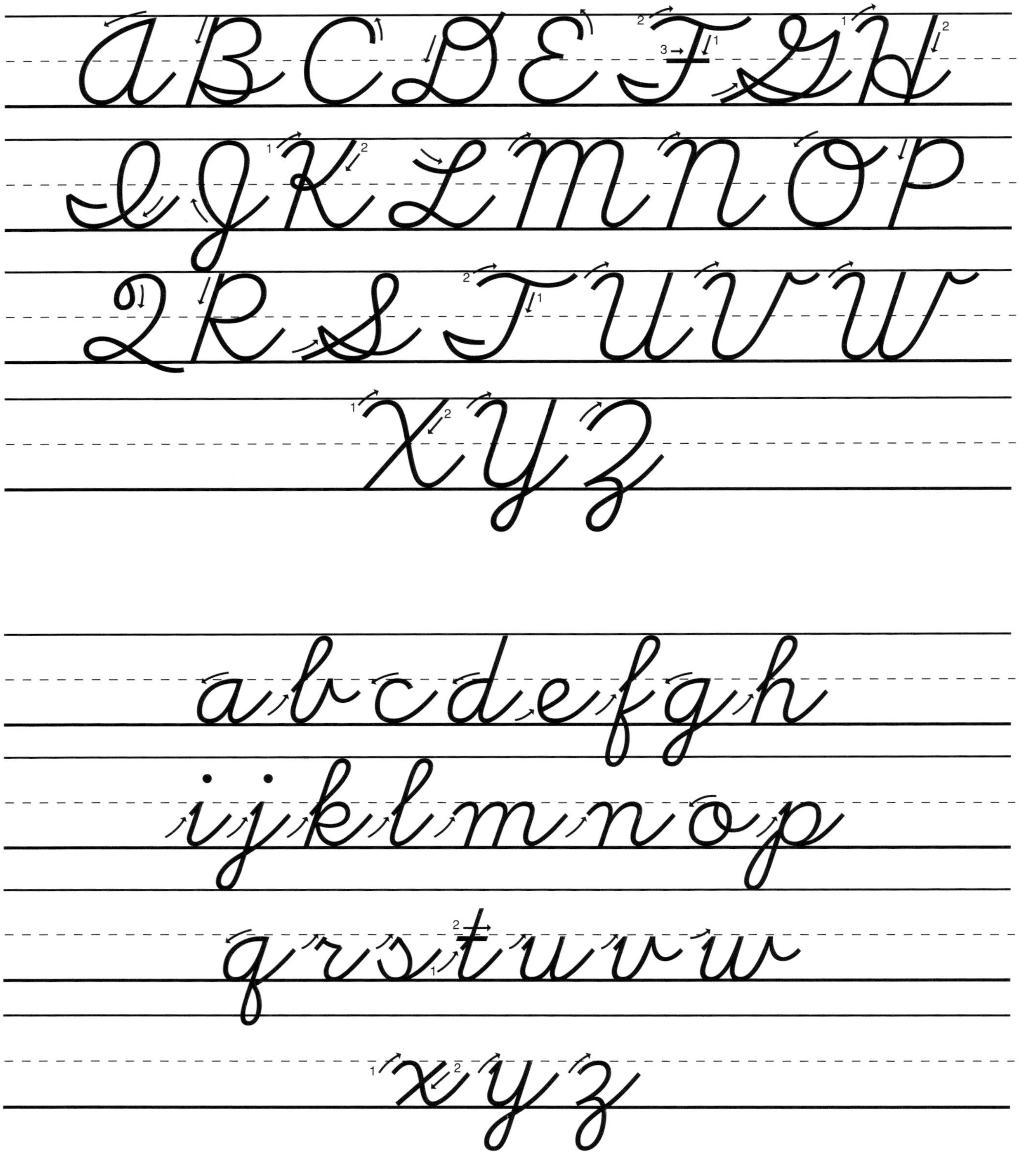

A B C D E F G H
I J K L M N O P
Q R S T U V W
X Y Z

a b c d e f g h
i j k l m n o p
q r s t u v w
x y z

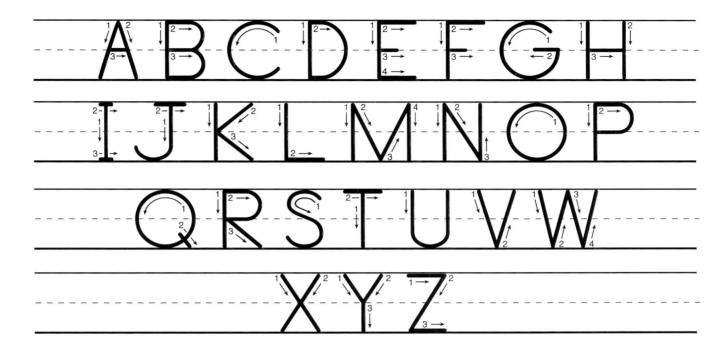

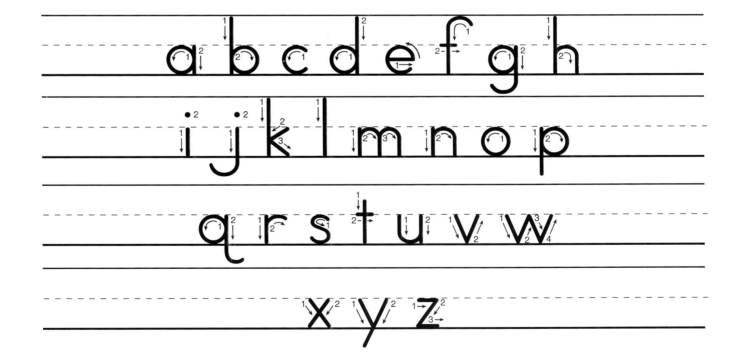

$$A\ B\ C\ D\ E\ F\ G\ H$$

$$I\ J\ K\ L\ M\ N\ O\ P$$

$$Q\ R\ S\ T\ U\ V\ W$$

$$X\ Y\ Z$$

$$a\ b\ c\ d\ e\ f\ g\ h$$

$$i\ j\ k\ l\ m\ n\ o\ p$$

$$q\ r\ s\ t\ u\ v\ w$$

$$x\ y\ z$$

ABCDEFGH
IJKLMNOP
QRSTUVW
XYZ

abcdefgh
ijklmnop
qrstuvw
xyz

Glossary

This glossary contains meanings and pronunciations for some of the words in this book. The Full Pronunciation Key shows how to pronounce each consonant and vowel in a special spelling. At the bottom of the glossary pages is a shortened form of the full key.

Full Pronunciation Key

Consonant Sounds

b	**bib, cabbage**	kw	**choir, quick**	t	**tight, stopped**
ch	**church, stitch**	l	**lid, needle, tall**	th	**bath, thin**
d	**deed, mailed, puddle**	m	**am, man, dumb**	th	**bathe, this**
f	**fast, fife, off, phrase, rough**	n	**no, sudden**	v	**cave, valve, vine**
		ng	**thing, ink**	w	**with, wolf**
g	**gag, get, finger**	p	**pop, happy**	y	**yes, yolk, onion**
h	**hat, who**	r	**roar, rhyme**	z	**rose, size, xylophone, zebra**
hw	**which, where**	s	**miss, sauce, scene, see**	zh	**garage, pleasure, vision**
j	**judge, gem**	sh	**dish, ship, sugar, tissue**		
k	**cat, kick, school**				

Vowel Sounds

ă	**pat, laugh**	ŏ	**horrible, pot**	ŭ	**cut, flood, rough, some**
ā	**ape, aid, pay**	ō	**go, row, toe, though**	û	**circle, fur, heard, term, turn, urge, word**
â	**air, care, wear**	ô	**all, caught, for, paw**		
ä	**father, koala, yard**	oi	**boy, noise, oil**	yōō	**cure**
ĕ	**pet, pleasure, any**	ou	**cow, out**	yōō	**abuse, use**
ē	**be, bee, easy, piano**	ŏŏ	**full, book, wolf**	ə	**ago, silent, pencil, lemon, circus**
ĭ	**if, pit, busy**	ōō	**boot, rude, fruit, flew**		
ī	**ride, by, pie, high**				
î	**dear, deer, fierce, mere**				

Stress Marks

Primary Stress ´: bi·ol·o·gy [bī **ŏl´** ə jē]
Secondary Stress ˈ: bi·o·log·i·cal [bī´ ə **lŏj´** ĭ kəl]

Pronunciation key and definitions copyright © 2007 by Houghton Mifflin Harcourt Publishing Company. Reproduced by permission from *The American Heritage Children's Dictionary* and *The American Heritage Student Dictionary*.

G1

A

ac·com·pa·ny (ə **kŭm´** pə nē) *v.* To go along with: *I was told to accompany them to the concert.*

ad·vanced (ăd **vănst´**) *adj.* Highly developed or complex; beyond in progress: *The advanced high school student was able to take college courses.*

ad·ver·tise (**ăd´** vər tīz´) *v.* To announce to the public: *Posters sometimes advertise movies.*

af·fect (ə **fĕkt´**) *v.* To cause a change in something or someone: *Problems in the rain forest affect the animals living in it.*

af·fec·tion (ə **fĕk´** shən) *n.* A feeling of fondness or love for a person, animal, or thing: *My affection for my dog grew after he brought me the morning paper.*

a·lert (ə **lûrt´**) *adj.* Watching out for danger; attentive: *A good driver must always be alert.*

amendment
The base word of *amendment* is the verb *amend*. It comes from the Latin word *emendare*, which means "to correct." The word *mend*, which means "to fix or repair," comes from the same Latin word root. When you *make amends*, you try to correct or mend a wrong you did to someone.

a·mend·ment (ə **mĕnd´** mənt) *n.* A change made to improve, correct, or add something: *An amendment to the United States Constitution limits the President to two full terms in office.*

an·gle (**ăng´** gəl) *n.* A way of looking at something: *There are many different angles from which we could film this movie.*

a·pol·o·gize (ə **pŏl´** ə jīz´) *v.* To make an apology; say one is sorry: *Did you apologize to your mother for burning the pancakes?*

ap·pre·ci·ate (ə **prē´** shē āt´) *v.* To be thankful for: *Will the child appreciate my help?*

ap·prove (ə **prōōv´**) *v.* To consent to officially: *The Senate is expected to approve the treaty.*

ar·range·ment (ə **rānj´** mənt) *n.* **1.** The act or an example of arranging; order in which things are arranged: *I studied the alphabetical arrangement of the books on the shelf.* **2.** Preparations for an undertaking; plan: *Pigeons find that living among people is a fine plan, or arrangement.*

as·sist (ə **sist´**) *v.* To give help; aid: *Did you assist him in moving the box?*

as·so·ci·a·tion (ə sō sē ā´ shən) *n.* A group of people organized for a common purpose: *The students formed an association to help stop global warming.*

av·er·age (**ăv´** ər ij) *adj.* Typical or ordinary: *The average kid loves to play.*

B

ban (băn) *v.* To forbid by making illegal: *Fishing can be banned in certain areas to protect fish.*

bat·tle (**băt´** l) *n.* A fight between two armed forces, usually in war: *The two ants were in a battle over a breadcrumb.*

be·tray (bĭ **trā´**) *v.* To be unfaithful to: *When he heard the lie, Tom knew his friend had betrayed him.*

bi·o·log·i·cal (bī´ ə **lŏj´** ĭ kəl) *adj.* Of, relating to, or affecting living things: *She had a biological need to sleep.*

blar·ing (**blâr´** ing) *adj.* Loud, harsh: *The concert began with a fanfare of blaring trumpets.*

bond (bŏnd) *n.* A force that unites; a tie: *I feel a close bond with my sister.*

bor·der (**bôr´** dər) *n.* The line where an area, such as a country, ends and another area begins: *The Americans had to cross the Mexican border on their way to South America.*

bor·row (**bôr´** ō) *v.* To get from someone else with the understanding that what is gotten will be returned or replaced: *I want to borrow that toy.*

bril·liant (**brĭl´** yənt) *adj.* Very vivid in color: *The sky was a brilliant blue.*

bur·gla·ry (**bûr´** glə rē) *n.* The crime of breaking into a building with the intention of stealing: *The unlocked door led to many burglaries.*

C

cal·cu·late (**kăl´** kyə lāt´) *v.* To find by using addition, subtraction, multiplication, or division: *I calculated the amount of fabric I would need to make the bedspread.*

can·di·date (**kăn´** dĭ dāt´) *n.* A person who seeks or is put forward by others for an office or honor: *The candidates walked in the morning parade, shaking people's hands and asking for their votes.*

capitol

cap·i·tol (**kăp´** ĭ tl) *n.* The building in which a state legislature meets: *The governor went to the capitol to sign a bill that the legislature created.*

cap·ture (**kăp´** chər) *v.* **1.** To seize and hold, as by force or skill: *The play captured my imagination.* **2.** To get hold of, as by force or craft: *The enemy captured the general.*

cen·tu·ry (**sĕn´** chə rē) *n.* A period of 100 years: *The United States Constitution was written more than two centuries ago.*

cer·e·mo·ny (**sĕr´** ə mō´ nē) *n.* A formal act or series of acts performed in honor of an event or special occasion: *Our school had a graduation ceremony today.*

ă rat / ā pay / â care / ä father / ĕ pet / ē be / ĭ pit / ī pie / î fierce / ŏ pot / ō go / ô paw, for / oi oil / ŏŏ book

G2

conclude
One meaning of *conclude* is "to bring to an end; close; finish." *Conclude* comes from the Latin: the prefix *com-* plus *claudere*, "to close." When you decide something or form an opinion, you *conclude* or reach a *conclusion*, bringing your thoughts to a close. The word *include* comes from the same Latin root. When you include people, you "enclose" them.

cham·ber (chām´ bər) *n.* An enclosed space in a machine or in an animal's living space; compartment: *The yellow jackets' nest was in a chamber in the soil next to the house.*

charge (chärj) *v.* To rush or rush at with force; attack: *The soldiers charged the fort.*

chief (chēf) *adj.* Most important: *The chief problem is to decide what to do first.*

churn·ing (chûrn´ ing) *adj.* Moving forcefully: *The churning winds picked up dirt.*

civ·i·lized (sĭv´ ə līzd´) *adj.* Having an advanced culture and society: *The civilized city had strict rules.*

clas·si·fy (klăs´ ə fī) *v.* To put together into groups or classes; sort: *The books were classified by reading level.*

continent

clum·sy (klŭm´ zē) *adj.* Done or made without skill: *The clumsy shelter fell apart.*

com·bi·na·tion (kŏm´ bə nā´ shən) *n.* The condition of being combined; union: *Salt and pepper make a good combination.*

com·fort (kŭm´ fərt) *v.* To soothe when sad or frightened: *She tried to comfort the lost child.*

com·pan·ion (kəm păn´ yən) *n.* A friend or associate: *My dog Sam was my favorite companion.*

con·cerned (kən sûrnd´) *adj.* Worried or anxious: *The concerned citizens went to the town meeting.*

con·clude (kən klōōd´) *v.* To think about something and then reach a decision or form an opinion: *I have concluded that the best way to make a friend is to be one.*

con·di·tion (kən dĭsh´ an) *n.* General health and fitness: *Athletes train before a competition so they are in good condition.*

con·fess (kən fĕs´) *v.* 1. To admit that one has done something bad, wrong, or illegal: *This woman confesses to eating the apple.* 2. To own or admit as true: *This girl confesses, or admits, that daily care of a dog is hard work.*

con·fi·dence (kŏn´ fĭ dans) *n.* Trust or faith in someone else or in something: *The coach had a brief moment of confidence in his team before they started losing again.*

con·flict (kŏn´ flĭkt´) *n.* A clash or struggle, as of ideas, feelings, or interests: *The differences between the rich and the poor cause many conflicts about taxes.*

con·sist (kən sĭst´) *v.* To be made up: *The biology class today consisted of a pop quiz and a lecture on always doing your homework.*

con·struct (kən strŭkt´) *v.* To make by fitting parts together; build: *We constructed a bookcase.*

con·ti·nent (kŏn´ tə nant) *n.* One of the main land masses of the earth: *North America and South America are two continents.*

corps (kôr) *n.* A group of people acting or working together: *We belong to a drum and bugle corps.*

crisp (krĭsp) *adj.* Brief and clear: *It was a crisp picture in which I could see every hair on my dog's head.*

crit·ic (krĭt´ ĭk) *n.* A person whose work is judging the value of books, plays, or other artistic efforts: *There were many critics at the premier of the movie.*

crush (krŭsh) *v.* To press, squeeze, or bear down on with enough force to break or injure: *The tree fell, crushing the car.*

cus·tom (kŭs´ təm) *n.* Something that the members of a group usually do: *Shaking hands when meeting someone is one of many customs our society has.*

D

de·bris (də brē´) *n.* The scattered remains of something broken or destroyed: *The man used a bulldozer to clear away the debris after the storm.*

debris

de·but (dā byōō´) *n.* A first public appearance, as of a performer: *The juggler had his debut on television that night.*

ded·i·cate (dĕd´ ĭ kāt´) *v.* To set apart for a special purpose; devote: *The scientists will dedicate themselves to research after graduating from college.*

de·fend (dĭ fĕnd´) *v.* 1. To protect from attack, harm, danger, or challenge: *They defended themselves from the wolves with spears.* 2. To support or maintain, as by argument; justify: *The child defended taking the cookie, saying he was hungry.*

de·lib·er·ate·ly (dĭ lĭb´ ər ĭt lē) *adv.* Done or said on purpose; intentional: *She told a lie deliberately to fool him.*

dense (dĕns) *adj.* Having the parts packed together closely: *I could not move in the dense crowd.*

de·ny (dĭ nī´) *v.* To refuse to give; withhold: *He denied the rabbit the carrot.*

de·serve (dĭ zûrv´) *v.* To be worthy of or have a right to; merit: *You deserve the reward.*

di·rect·ly (dĭ rĕkt´ lē) *adv.* In a direct line or way; straight: *My teacher is directly responsible for my interest in science.*

ă rat / ā pay / â care / ä father / ĕ pet / ē be / ĭ pit / ī pie / î fierce / ŏ pot / ō go / ô paw, for / oi oil / ōō book

ōō boot / ou out / ŭ cut / û fur / hw which / th thin / th this / zh vision / ə ago, silent, pencil, lemon, circus

---

dis-
The prefix *dis-* has several senses, but its basic meaning is "not, not any." Thus *disbelieve* means "to refuse to believe" and *discomfort* means "a lack of comfort." *Dis-* comes ultimately from the Latin adverb *dis*, meaning "apart, asunder." *Dis-* is an important prefix that occurs very often in English in words such as *discredit*, *disrepair*, *disrespect*, and *disobey*.

dis·be·lief (dĭs´ bĭ lēf´) *n.* The refusal or unwillingness to believe: *The audience was in disbelief after the magician pulled the rabbit from the hat.*

dis·cour·aged (dĭs kûr´ ĭjd) *adj.* Less hopeful or enthusiastic: *After getting a nail in the foot, the discouraged child stopped running barefoot.*

dis·o·bey (dĭs´ ə bā´) *v.* To refuse or fail to obey: *Why did you disobey a direct order to eat your spinach?*

dis·or·der·ly (dĭs ôr´ dər lē) *adj.* Not behaving according to rules or customs; unruly: *The classroom became disorderly after the substitute teacher did not tell the students the rules.*

dis·play (dĭ splā´) *n.* A public showing; exhibition: *A display of moon rocks is in the museum.*

dis·pute (dĭs pyōōt´) *v.* To argue about; debate: *In the debate, did the students dispute the question of a dress code?*

dream (drēm) *n.* Something hoped for; aspiration: *I have a dream of world peace.*

drought (drout) *n.* A period of little or no rain: *The farmers' crops could not grow because of the drought.*

du·ty (dōō´ tē) *n.* The obligation to do what is right: *The president had a duty to serve his country.*

E

ef·fort (ĕf´ ərt) *n.* The use of physical or mental energy to do something: *Doing it this way will save time and effort.*

en·clo·sure (ĕn klō´ zhər) *n.* An enclosed area: *I kept my pets in an enclosure made of wood.*

en·coun·ter (ĕn koun´ tər) *n.* 1. An often unexpected meeting with a person or thing: *I had many encounters with animals as a kid.* 2. A hostile confrontation: *The two armies had several encounters on the battlefield.*

en·cour·age·ment (ĕn kûr´ ij mant) *n.* The act of encouraging: *He gave his son encouragement to do the right thing.*

en·deared (ĕn dîr´) *v.* To make beloved or very sympathetic: *The child endeared himself to everyone who met him because of his charming personality.*

en·ter·tain·ing (ĕn´ tər tān´ ing) *adj.* Holding the attention in an agreeable way: *The movie was entertaining.*

es·cort (ĕs´ kôrt´) *v.* To go with as an escort: *Police escorted the senator during the parade.*

es·pe·cial·ly (ĕ spĕsh´ ə lē) *adv.* In a special way; specifically: *These coats are designed especially for tall people.*

e·vap·o·rate (ĭ văp´ ə rāt´) *v.* To change into a vapor or gas: *The water will evaporate quickly under the hot sun.*

ex·am·ple (ĭg zăm´ pal) *n.* Someone or something that should be copied; model: *Their courage was an example to all of us.*

ex·cess (ĕk´ sĕs´) *adj.* More than is needed or usual: *I brushed the excess salt off my pretzel.*

ex·change (ĭks chānj´) *n.* A giving of one thing for another: *I did not feel that the several exchanges I had with that man were fair.*

ex·haust·ed (ĭg zôst´ad) *adj.* Worn out completely; tired: *I was exhausted from the long swim.*

ex·plode (ĭk splōd´) *v.* To burst or cause to burst with a loud noise; blow up: *The fireworks were exploding over the hotel.*

ex·traor·di·nar·y (ĭk strôr´ dn ĕr´ ē) *adj.* Very unusual; remarkable: *Landing on the moon was an extraordinary event.*

F

faint (fānt) *v.* To lose consciousness for a short time: *She fainted after he took off his mask.*

fault (fôlt) *n.* Responsibility for a mistake or an offense: *Failing the test was my own fault because I did not study.*

fa·vor (fā´ vər) *n.* A kind or helpful act: *She granted him a favor.*

feast (fēst) *n.* A fancy meal; banquet: *We prepared a feast for the wedding.*

explode
Explode comes from a Latin word meaning "drive out or off by clapping." It was originally used in theatres to mean "to drive an actor off the stage by making noise."

feat (fēt) *n.* An act or accomplishment that shows skill, strength, or bravery: *The gymnasts performed remarkable feats.*

foam·ing (fō´ ming) *adj.* Full of bubbles that form in a liquid such as soap; frothing: *Foaming bubbles from the puppy shampoo spilled outside the tub.*

feast

fo·cus (fō´ kas) *v.* To concentrate or center; fix: *I could not focus on the test.*

fos·ter (fō´ stər) *adj.* Receiving, sharing, or giving care like that of a parent, although not related by blood or adoption: *There are three foster children in our home.*

frac·tured (frăk´ chərd) *adj.* Broken: *The fractured television had to be thrown away.*

G

gen·er·ate (jĕn´ ə rāt´) *v.* To bring about or produce: *Water and steam generated electricity.*

gen·u·ine (jĕn´ yōō ĭn) *adj.* Sincere; honest: *They showed genuine interest in my work.*

gi·gan·tic (jī găn´ tĭk) *adj.* Being like a giant in size, strength, or power: *Some of the dinosaurs were gigantic creatures.*

ă rat / ā pay / â care / ä father / ĕ pet / ē be / ĭ pit / ī pie / î fierce / ŏ pot / ō go / ô paw, for / oi oil / ōō book

ōō boot / ou out / ŭ cut / û fur / hw which / th thin / th this / zh vision / ə ago, silent, pencil, lemon, circus

glance (glăns) *v.* To take a quick look: *She glances outside to make sure it isn't snowing yet.*

glo·ri·ous (glôr´ē əs) *adj.* Having great beauty; magnificent: *We saw a glorious sunset.*

grace·ful (grās´ fəl) *adj.* Showing grace, as in movement: *The deer is a graceful animal.*

grad·u·ate (grăj´ŏŏ āt´) *v.* To finish a course of study and receive a diploma: *My cousin will graduate from high school next Saturday.*

graduate

graduate
Graduate comes from the Latin word root *gradus*, meaning "step." The word *grade*, meaning a slope that changes a little at a time, also comes from the same word root. *Gradual*, which means "occurring in small steps over time," is another related word.

H

hab·i·tat (hăb´ i tăt´) *n.* The place where a plant or animal naturally lives: *When ecosystems change, animals often have to leave their habitats.*

has·ten (hā´ sən) *v.* To move or act swiftly; hurry: *I hastened home to tell my family the news.*

haul (hôl) *v.* To move from one place to another, as with a truck: *I was hauling the bed from my house to hers when I heard the news.*

haze (hāz) *n.* Fine dust, smoke, or water vapor floating in the air: *The haze along the beach did not allow the lifeguard to see who was swimming.*

hid·e·ous (hid´ ē əs) *adj.* Very ugly or disgusting: *The man looked hideous after he put on the Halloween mask.*

hire (hīr) *v.* To use the work or services of; employ: *He was hired to mow the grass, but instead he fell asleep.*

hon·or (ŏn´ ər) *n.* Special respect or high regard: *We display the flag to show honor to the United States.*

ho·ri·zon (hə rī´ zən) *n.* The line along which the earth and the sky appear to meet: *The sun dropped beneath the horizon and the day grew into the night.*

hor·ri·fy (hôr´ rə fī´) *v.* To surprise unpleasantly: *The farmer was horrified to find his cows in the neighbor's field.*

hud·dle (hŭd´ l) *v.* To crowd close or put close together: *We huddled around the campfire to keep warm.*

I

im·mense (ĭ mĕns´) *adj.* Of great size, extent, or degree: *Antarctica is covered by an immense sheet of ice.*

in·ci·dent (ĭn´ sĭ dənt) *n.* An event that causes trouble: *The newspaper reported the fire incident.*

in·clude (ĭn klŏŏd´) *v.* To put into a group, set, or total: *She was included in the kids' package even though she was too old.*

in·de·pend·ent (ĭn´ dĭ pĕn´ dənt) *adj.* Not dependent: *My brother is not independent of mom and dad. He receives a monthly check to help pay his rent.*

in·formed (ĭn fôrmd´) *adj.* Having or prepared with information or knowledge: *The informed driver knew the correct directions to the city.*

in·jus·tice (ĭn jŭs´ tĭs) *n.* Unfair treatment of a person or thing: *They protested the injustice of not having a snow day.*

in·no·cent (ĭn´ ə sənt) *adj.* Not guilty of a crime or fault: *The jury found them innocent.*

in·sep·a·ra·ble (ĭn sĕp´ ər ə bəl) *adj.* Impossible to separate or part: *The two best friends were inseparable.*

in·sert (ĭn sûrt´) *v.* To put, set, or fit into: *Insert the key in the lock.*

in·sist (ĭn sĭst´) *v.* To demand: *I insisted on going to the beach.*

in·spec·tor (ĭn spĕk´ tər) *n.* A person who makes inspections: *The inspector found mold in the walls.*

in·tel·li·gent (ĭn tĕl´ ə jənt) *adj.* Having or showing the ability to learn, think, understand, and know: *The intelligent man read the whole book in five minutes.*

in·tend (ĭn tĕnd´) *v.* To have in mind as an aim or goal; plan: *He intends to bake his friend a cake for her birthday.*

in·ter·pret·er (ĭn tûr´ prĭ tər) *n.* A person who translates orally from one language to another: *An interpreter was needed to find out what the foreign president was saying.*

in·tro·duce (ĭn´ trə dŏŏs´) *v.* To bring or put in something new or different: *Will you introduce the cat to the dog?*

in·trud·er (ĭn trŏŏd´ ər) *n.* A person who intrudes, especially into a building, with criminal intent: *I called the police after the intruder refused to leave my house.*

in·vis·i·ble (ĭn vĭz´ ə bəl) *adj.* Not capable of being seen; not visible: *Air is invisible.*

J

jeal·ous (jĕl´ əs) *adj.* Having a bad feeling toward another person who is a competitor; envious: *Were you jealous of the winner?*

jolt (jōlt) *n.* A feeling or something that causes a feeling of sudden shock or surprise: *The audience felt a jolt every time the car turned a corner in the movie.*

invisible
The word *invisible* comes from the Latin prefix *in-* ("not") and the Latin word root *vis*, meaning "sight." *Visual*, "relating to the sense of sight"; *visible*, "able to be seen"; *envision*, "to picture in the mind"; and *television*, "a device that receives and reproduces visual images" all contain the word root *vis.*

ă rat / ā pay / â care / ä father / ĕ pet / ē be / ĭ pit / ī pie / î fierce / ŏ pot / ō go / ô paw, for / oi oil / ŏŏ book

G8

L

land·mark (lănd´ märk´) *n.* A familiar or easily seen object or building that marks or identifies a place: *The Golden Gate Bridge is a landmark of San Francisco.*

lap (lăp) *v.* To wash or splash with a light, slapping sound: *The waves lapped at his feet as he stared across the ocean.*

leg·is·la·ture (lĕj´ ĭs lā´ chər) *n.* A body of people with the power to make and change laws: *The legislature made a law that forced people to throw away their trash.*

lo·cal (lō´ kəl) *adj.* Of a certain limited area or place: *The town has its own local government.*

lure (lŏŏr) *v.* To attract by offering something tempting: *He can lure the mouse out of the hole with cheese.*

miniature

M

me·chan·i·cal (mə kăn´ ĭ kəl) *adj.* Of or relating to machines or tools: *It takes mechanical skill to repair a clock.*

mem·o·ra·ble (mĕm´ ər ə bəl) *adj.* Worthy of being remembered: *Our class trip to the circus was a memorable event.*

men·tion (mĕn´ shən) *v.* To speak of or write about briefly: *I mentioned my idea during class.*

min·i·a·ture (mĭn´ ē ə chər) *adj.* Much smaller than the usual size: *We have a miniature train.*

mis·judge (mĭs jŭj´) *v.* To judge wrongly: *I misjudged the distance to the boat and fell into the ocean.*

mod·el (mŏd´ l) *adj.* Serving as a model: *Since we have to move, we looked at a number of model homes.*

mois·ture (mois´ chər) *n.* Liquid, as water, that is present in the air or in the ground or that forms tiny drops on a surface: *I wiped away the moisture on the window so I could see outside.*

mood (mŏŏd) *n.* A person's state of mind: *Playing with my friends puts me in a happy mood.*

mourn·ful (môrn´ fəl) *adj.* Feeling, showing, or causing grief; sad: *The mournful owner buried his dog in the back of the yard.*

N

na·ture (nā´ chər) *n.* The basic character or quality of a person or thing: *She has a friendly nature.*

neg·a·tive (nĕg´ ə tĭv) *adj.* Lacking in positive qualities such as enthusiasm and hope: *Your negative attitude is not helping you to make friends.*

noc·tur·nal (nŏk tûr´ nəl) *adj.* Active at night: *Owls are nocturnal birds.*

nour·ish·ing (nûr´ ĭsh ĭng) *adj.* Helping to promote life, growth, or strength: *The vitamins were parts of a nourishing diet.*

nu·mer·ous (nŏŏ´ mər əs) *adj.* Including or made up of a large number: *They have numerous problems.*

O

ob·serve (əb zûrv´) *v.* To say; remark: *"This hot dog is tasty," the man observes.*

ob·sta·cle (ŏb´ stə kəl) *n.* Something that blocks or stands in the way: *Fallen rocks and other obstacles made it impossible to use the road.*

op·por·tu·ni·ty (ŏp´ ər tŏŏ´ ni tē) *or* (ŏp´ ər tyŏŏ´ ni tē) *n.* A good chance, as to advance oneself: *That summer job offers many opportunities.*

or·gan·ism (ôr´ gə nĭz´ əm) *n.* An individual form of life, such as a plant or animal: *On the field trip, we looked at sea organisms under the microscope.*

out·cast (out´ kăst´) *n.* A person blocked from participation in a group or society: *Stormy felt like an outcast because he had outgrown Cape Cod.*

o·ver·come (ō´ vər kŭm´) *v.* To get the better of; conquer: *I had to overcome my fear of heights to climb the mountain.*

P

pa·tient·ly (pā´ shənt lē) *adv.* Putting up with trouble, hardship, annoyance, or delay without complaining: *He waited patiently for his food to arrive.*

pe·cu·liar (pĭ kyŏŏl´ yər) *adj.* Not usual; strange or odd: *I smell a peculiar odor.*

per·form (pər fôrm´) *v.* To carry out; do: *She performs very well onstage after a lot of practice.*

per·mis·sion (pər mĭsh´ ən) *n.* Consent granted by someone in authority: *Our parents gave us permission to go to the movies.*

pol·i·tics (pŏl´ ĭ tĭks´) *n.* The science, art, or work of government: *My father felt politics got in the way of people doing their regular jobs.*

poll (pōl) *n.* Often **polls.** The place where votes are cast: *I went to the polls to vote for the President of the United States.*

pos·i·tive (pŏz´ ĭ tĭv) *adj.* Having no doubts; sure: *I'm positive that we've met before.*

pos·ses·sion (pə zĕsh´ ən) *n.* Something that is owned; belonging: *They fled the burning building, leaving their possessions behind.*

pounce (pouns) *v.* To seize swiftly or as if by swooping: *The kitten pounced on the ball.*

ă rat / ā pay / â care / ä father / ĕ pet / ē be / ĭ pit / ī pie / î fierce / ŏ pot / ō go / ô paw, for / oi oil / ŏŏ book

G10

pre·fer (pri **fûr´**) *v.* To like better: *I preferred dancing to jogging.*

pre·pare (pri **pâr´**) *v.* To put together the ingredients of: *I prepare my lunch each morning.*

pres·ence (**prĕz´** əns) *n.* The fact or condition of being present: *Your presence is not required.*

pri·or (**prī´** ər) *adj.* Coming before in time or order; earlier: *Tell me about your prior grades.*

prog·ress (**prŏg´** rĕs) *n.* Steady improvement: *After I passed the test, I realized I was making very good progress.*

pro·mote (prə **mōt´**) *v.* To try to sell or make popular, as by advertising; publicize: *Television ads promote many products.*

prompt·ly (**prŏmpt´** lē) *adv.* Done or given without delay: *I promptly sent my message.*

proof (prōof) *n.* Evidence of truth or accuracy: *We have no proof that the money was stolen.*

prop·er·ly (**prŏp´** ər lē) *adv.* In a proper manner: *Jim did not hold his fork properly.*

pro·pose (prə **pōz´**) *v.* To put forward for consideration; suggest: *I proposed a trip to Florida. We went to Ohio instead.*

pub·lic·i·ty (pŭ **blĭs´** ĭ tē) *n.* Information that is given out to let the public know about something or to get its approval: *There was no publicity for the new movie, so few people watched it.*

R

rack·et (**răk´** ĭt) *n.* A loud, unpleasant noise: *The several parrots outside my window made a racket this morning.*

ra·di·a·tion (rā´ dē **ā´** shən) *n.* Energy that travels through space as rays or waves: *Sunscreen helps protect people from the sun's radiation.*

re·call (ri **kôl´**) *v.* To bring back to mind; remember: *I can't recall their phone number.*

ref·er·ence (**rĕf´** ər əns) *adj.* A book, such as an encyclopedia or dictionary, that gives special information arranged according to a plan or system: *This book has a reference glossary.*

re·fuse (ri **fyōoz´**) *v.* To decline to do or give: *The cat refused to go out in the snow.*

re·gret·ful·ly (ri **grĕt´** fə lē) *adv.* Full of regret: *Looking down regretfully, she cancelled the party.*

re·in·force (rē´ ĭn **fôrs´**) *v.* To make stronger with more material, help, or support: *The construction crew will reinforce this building with a single beam.*

re·ly (ri **lī´**) *v.* To be dependent for support, help, or supply: *I relied on my brother to give me money for dinner.*

rep·u·ta·tion (rĕp´ yə **tā´** shən) *n.* The general worth or quality of someone or something as judged by others or by the general public: *The senator has a very good reputation.*

res·cue (**rĕs´** kyōo) *v.* To save from danger or harm: *Lifeguards learn how to rescue swimmers.*

re·source (**rē´** sôrs´) *or* (ri **sôrs´**) *n.* Something that is a source of wealth to a country: *Our forests and trees are great natural resources.*

re·ward (ri **wôrd´**) *v.* To give a reward for or to: *The son rewarded his mother with breakfast in bed.*

route (rōot) *n.* A road or lane of travel between two places: *The hikers climbed the mountain, using a well-known route.*

rub·ble (**rŭb´** əl) *n.* Broken or crumbled material, as brick, that is left when a building falls down: *The building exploded and left rubble everywhere.*

ru·in (**rōo´** ĭn) *v.* To damage beyond repair; wreck: *She ruined the clay castle by stepping on it.*

S

sat·is·fy (**săt´** ĭs fī´) *v.* To fulfill or gratify: *The steak satisfied my hunger.*

scarce (skârs) *adj.* Not enough to meet a demand: *Food is scarce in many countries.*

sched·ule (**skĕj´** ōol) *n.* A program of events, appointments, or classes: *We have a full schedule of activities after school.*

scheme (skēm) *n.* A plan or plot for doing something: *He created a scheme to break out of prison.*

sea·far·ing (**sē´** fâr´ ing) *adj.* Earning one's living at sea: *The seafaring life of a fisherman is dangerous.*

seg·re·ga·tion (sĕg´ ri **gā´** shən) *n.* The act of segregating or the condition of being segregated: *Laws on segregation once kept African Americans and white Americans separate.*

sen·si·tive (**sĕn´** si tiv) *adj.* Easily affected, influenced, or hurt: *Don't be so sensitive to criticism.*

shal·low (**shăl´** ō) *adj.* Measuring little from bottom to top or from back to front; not deep: *The fish swam in the shallow end of the river.*

short·age (**shôr´** tij) *n.* An amount of something that is not enough: *We donate items to a food pantry when there is a food shortage.*

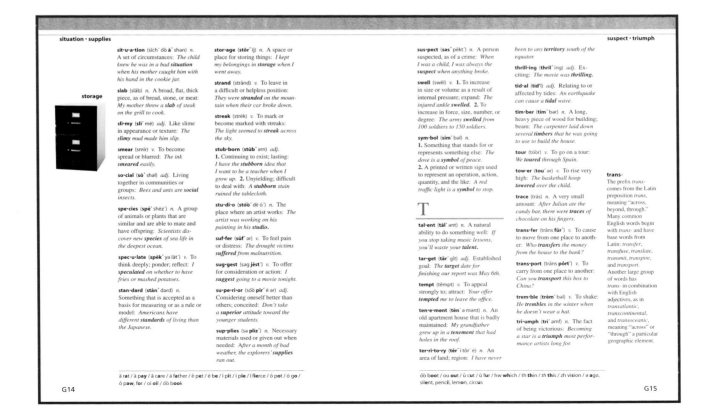

reference

à rat / ā pay / â care / ä father / ĕ pet / ē be / ĭ pit / ī pie / î fierce / ŏ pot / ō go / ô paw, for / oi oil / ōo book

ōo boot / ou out / ŭ cut / û fur / hw which / th thin / th this / zh vision / ə ago, silent, pencil, lemon, circus

G12

G13

---

sit·u·a·tion (sĭch´ ōo **ā´** shən) *n.* A set of circumstances: *The child knew he was in a bad situation when his mother caught him with his hand in the cookie jar.*

slab (slăb) *n.* A broad, flat, thick piece, as of bread, stone, or meat: *My mother threw a slab of steak on the grill to cook.*

sli·my (**slī´** mē) *adj.* Like slime in appearance or texture: *The slimy mud made him slip.*

smear (smîr) *v.* To become spread or blurred: *The ink smeared easily.*

so·cial (**sō´** shəl) *adj.* Living together in communities or groups: *Bees and ants are social insects.*

spe·cies (**spē´** shēz´) *n.* A group of animals or plants that are similar and are able to mate and have offspring: *Scientists discover new species of sea life in the deepest ocean.*

spec·u·late (**spĕk´** yə lāt´) *v.* To think deeply; ponder; reflect: *I speculated on whether to have fries or mashed potatoes.*

stan·dard (**stăn´** dərd) *n.* Something that is accepted as a basis for measuring or as a rule or model: *Americans have different standards of living than the Japanese.*

stor·age (**stôr´** ij) *n.* A space or place for storing things: *I kept my belongings in storage when I went away.*

strand (strănd) *v.* To leave in a difficult or helpless position: *They were stranded on the mountain when their car broke down.*

streak (strēk) *v.* To mark or become marked with streaks: *The light seemed to streak across the sky.*

stub·born (**stŭb´** ərn) *adj.* **1.** Continuing to exist; lasting: *I have the stubborn idea that I want to be a teacher when I grow up.* **2.** Unyielding; difficult to deal with: *A stubborn stain ruined the tablecloth.*

stu·di·o (**stōo´** dē ō´) *n.* The place where an artist works: *The artist was working on his painting in his studio.*

suf·fer (**sŭf´** ər) *v.* To feel pain or distress: *The drought victims suffered from malnutrition.*

sug·gest (səg **jĕst´**) *v.* To offer for consideration or action: *I suggest going to a movie tonight.*

su·pe·ri·or (sōo **pîr´** ē ər) *adj.* Considering oneself better than others; conceited: *Don't take a superior attitude toward the younger students.*

sup·plies (sə **plīz´**) *n.* Necessary materials used or given out when needed: *After a month of bad weather, the explorers' supplies ran out.*

sus·pect (**sŭs´** pĕkt´) *n.* A person suspected, as of a crime: *When I was a child, I was always the suspect when anything broke.*

swell (swĕl) *v.* **1.** To increase in size or volume as a result of internal pressure; expand: *The injured ankle swelled.* **2.** To increase in force, size, number, or degree: *The army swelled from 100 soldiers to 150 soldiers.*

sym·bol (**sĭm´** bəl) *n.* **1.** Something that stands for or represents something else: *The dove is a symbol of peace.* **2.** A printed or written sign used to represent an operation, action, quantity, and the like: *A red traffic light is a symbol to stop.*

T

tal·ent (**tăl´** ənt) *n.* A natural ability to do something well: *If you stop taking music lessons, you'll waste your talent.*

tar·get (**tär´** gĭt) *adj.* Established goal: *The target date for finishing our report was May 6th.*

tempt (tĕmpt) *v.* To appeal strongly to; attract: *Your offer tempted me to leave the office.*

ten·e·ment (**tĕn´** ə mənt) *n.* An old apartment house that is badly maintained: *My grandfather grew up in a tenement that had holes in the roof.*

ter·ri·to·ry (**tĕr´** i tôr´ ē) *n.* An area of land; region: *I have never been to any territory south of the equator.*

thrill·ing (**thrĭl´** ing) *adj.* Exciting: *The movie was thrilling.*

tid·al (**tīd´** l) *adj.* Relating to or affected by tides: *An earthquake can cause a tidal wave.*

tim·ber (**tĭm´** bər) *n.* A long, heavy piece of wood for building; beam: *The carpenter laid down several timbers that he was going to use to build the house.*

tour (tōor) *v.* To go on a tour: *We toured through Spain.*

tow·er (**tou´** ər) *v.* To rise very high: *The basketball hoop towered over the child.*

trace (trās) *n.* A very small amount: *After Julian ate the candy bar, there were traces of chocolate on his fingers.*

trans·fer (trăns **fûr´**) *v.* To cause to move from one place to another: *Who transfers the money from the house to the bank?*

trans·port (trăns **pôrt´**) *v.* To carry from one place to another: *Can you transport this box to China?*

trem·ble (**trĕm´** bəl) *v.* To shake: *He trembles in the winter when he doesn't wear a hat.*

tri·umph (**trī´** əmf) *n.* The fact of being victorious: *Becoming a star is a triumph most performance artists long for.*

trans- The prefix *trans-* comes from the Latin preposition *trans*, meaning "across, beyond, through." Many common English words begin with *trans-* and have base words from Latin: *transfer, transfuse, translate, transmit, transpire,* and *transport.* Another large group of words has *trans-* in combination with English adjectives, as in *transatlantic, transcontinental,* and *transoceanic,* meaning "across" or "through" a particular geographic element.

storage

à rat / ā pay / â care / ä father / ĕ pet / ē be / ĭ pit / ī pie / î fierce / ŏ pot / ō go / ô paw, for / oi oil / ōo book

ōo boot / ou out / ŭ cut / û fur / hw which / th thin / th this / zh vision / ə ago, silent, pencil, lemon, circus

G14

G15

Unit 4 Acknowledgements

U

un•spoiled (un spoyld) *adj.* To be not lessened or diminished by flaws or imperfections: *The snow was **unspoiled** until Jimmy made a snow angel.*

ut•ter (ŭt´ ər) *v.* To express out loud: *Did she **utter** a sigh of relief after the test?*

V

van•ish (văn´ ĭsh) *v.* To disappear or become invisible: *My smile **vanished** when I heard the bad news.*

va•ri•e•ty (və rī´ ĭ tē) *n.* A number of different things within the same group or category: *The market sells a **variety** of bread.*

vast (văst) *adj.* Very great in area; huge: *The Amazon River flows through a **vast** rain forest.*

vi•o•lence (vī´ ə ləns) *n.* The use of physical force to cause damage or injury: *The **violence** of war caused many to die.*

vi•sion (vĭzh´ ən) *n.* A mental picture produced by the imagination: *I had a **vision** of a pink elephant bouncing on a trampoline.*

W

war•ri•or (wôr´ ē ər) *n.* A person who is involved or experienced in war or fighting: *The **warrior** went to battle without armor.*

waste (wāst) *n.* The act of wasting or the condition of being wasted: *If you aren't going to read the newspaper, you should recycle it. It would be such a **waste** if you do not.*

wealth•y (wĕl´ thē) *adj.* Having wealth; rich: *She came from a **wealthy** family.*

wea•ri•ness (wîr´ ē nĕs) *n.* Temporary loss of strength and energy resulting from hard physical or mental work: *Chasing the dog for hours caused great **weariness.***

wel•comed (wĕl´ kəmd) *adj.* Greeted, received, or accepted with pleasure: *She was a **welcomed** visitor.*

wor•thy (wûr´ thē) *adj.* Having merit or value: *We contribute to **worthy** causes.*

wreck•age (rĕk´ ĭj) *n.* The remains of something that has been wrecked: *The **wreckage** of the car was hauled away.*

Y

yank (yăngk) *v.* To pull with a sudden, sharp movement: *We **yanked** the heavy door open.*

yearn•ing (yûr´ nĭng) *n.* A deep longing or strong desire: *Grandfather felt a **yearning** to visit his childhood home in the mountains.*

ă **rat** / ā **pay** / â **care** / ä **father** / ĕ **pet** / ē **be** / ĭ **pit** / ī **pie** / î **fierce** / ŏ **pot** / ō **go** / ô **paw, for** / oi **oil** / ŏŏ **book**

Acknowledgments

Main Literature Selections

"Ancestors of Tomorrow/Futuros ancestros" from *Iguanas in the Snow and Other Winter Poems/Iguanas en la nieve y otras poemas de invierno* by Francisco X. Alarcón. Copyright © 2001 by Francisco X. Alarcón. Reprinted by permission of the publisher, Children's Book Press, San Francisco, CA, www.childrensbookpress.org.

Antarctic Journal: Four Months at the Bottom of the World written and illustrated by Jennifer Owings Dewey. Copyright © 2001 by Jennifer Owings Dewey. Reprinted by permission of Houghton Mifflin Harcourt Publishing Company and Kirchoff/Wohlberg, Inc.

Because of Winn-Dixie by Kate DiCamillo. Copyright © 2000 by Kate DiCamillo. Reprinted by permission of the publisher Candlewick Press Inc., and Listening Library, a division of Random House, Inc.

"Over 5,000 attend Chinatown Center's 1-Year Anniversary & Moon Festival Celebration." Copyright © 2007 by Tan International Group, Ltd. Reprinted by permission of Red Velvet Events, Inc. on behalf of Tan International Group, Ltd.

Coming Distractions: Questioning Movies by Frank E. Baker. Copyright © 2007 by Capstone Press. All rights reserved. Reprinted by permission of Capstone Press.

Dear Mr. Winston by Ken Roberts. Copyright © 2001 by Ken Roberts. Reprinted by permission of Groundwood Books Limited, Toronto.

"Dreams" from *The Collected Poems of Langston Hughes* by Langston Hughes, edited by Arnold Rampersad with David Roessel, Associate Editor, copyright © 1994 by The Estate of Langston Hughes. Reprinted by permission of Alfred A. Knopf, a division of Random House, Inc., and Harold Ober Associates, Inc.

"The Dream Keeper" from *The Collected Poems of Langston Hughes* by Langston Hughes, edited by Arnold Rampersad with David Roessel, Associate Editor, copyright © 1994 by The Estate of Langston Hughes. Reprinted by permission of Alfred A. Knopf, a division of Random House, Inc., and Harold Ober Associates, Inc.

The Earth Dragon Awakes: The San Francisco Earthquake of 1906 by Laurence Yep. Copyright © 2006 by Laurence Yep. All rights reserved. Reprinted by permission of HarperCollins Publishers and Curtis Brown, Ltd.

Ecology for Kids by Federico Arana. Originally published as *Ecologia para los ninos*. Text copyright © 1994 by Federico Arana. Text © 1994 by Editorial Joaquin Mortiz, S.A. DE C.V. Reprinted by permission of Editorial Planeta Mexicana, S.A. DE C.V.

The Ever-Living Tree: The Life and Times of a Coast Redwood by Linda Vieira, illustrations by Christopher Canyon. Copyright © 1994 by Linda Vieira. Illustrations copyright © 1994 by Christopher Canyon. All rights reserved. Reprinted by permission of Walker & Company.

"First Recorded 6,000-Year-Old Tree in America" from *A Burst of Firsts* by J. Patrick Lewis. Published by Dial Books for Young Readers. Copyright © 2001 by J. Patrick Lewis. Reprinted by permission of Curtis Brown, Ltd.

The Fun They Had by Isaac Asimov. Copyright © 1957 by Isaac Asimov from Isaac Asimov: The Complete Stories of Vol. 1 by Isaac Asimov. Reprinted by permission of Doubleday, a division of Random House, Inc.

"Giant Sequoias/Secoyas gigantes" from *Iguanas in the Snow and Other Winter Poems/Iguanas en la nieve y otras poemas de invierno* by Francisco X. Alarcón. Copyright © 2001 by Francisco X. Alarcón. Reprinted by permission of Children's Book Press, San Francisco, CA, www.childrensbookpress.org.

Harvesting Hope: The Story of Cesar Chavez by Kathleen Krull, illustrated by Yuyi Morales. Text copyright © 2003 by Kathleen Krull. Illustrations copyright © 2003 by Yuyi Morales. Reprinted by permission of Houghton Mifflin Harcourt Publishing Company and Writer's House, LLC, acting as agent for the author.

How Tía Lola Came to (Visit) Stay by Julia Alvarez. Copyright © 2001 by Julia Alvarez. Published by Dell Yearling and in hardcover by Alfred A. Knopf Children's Books, a division of Random House, New York. Reprinted by permission of the Susan Bergholz Literary Services, New York, NY and Lamy, NM. All rights reserved.

I Could Do That! Esther Morris Gets Women to Vote by Linda Arms White, illustrated by Nancy Carpenter. Text copyright © 2005 by Linda Arms White. Illustrations copyright © 2005 by Nancy Carpenter. Reprinted by permission of Farrar, Straus & Giroux LLC.

José! Born to Dance By Susanna Reich, illustrated by Raúl Colón. Text copyright © 2005 by Susanna Reich. Illustrations copyright © 2005 by Raúl Colón. All rights reserved. Reprinted by permission of Simon & Schuster Books for Young Readers, an Imprint of Simon & Schuster Inc., and Adams Literary.

The Life and Times of the Ant written and illustrated by Charles Micucci. Copyright © 2003 by Charles Micucci. All rights reserved. Reprinted by permission of Houghton Mifflin Harcourt Publishing Company.

"Lightning Bolt" *from Flicker Flash* by Joan Bransfield Graham. Copyright © 1999 by Joan Bransfield Graham. Reprinted by permission of Houghton Mifflin Harcourt Publishing Company.

Excerpt from "Lines Written for Gene Kelly to Dance To" from *Wind Song* by Carl Sandburg. Copyright © 1960 Carl Sandburg and renewed 1998 by Margaret Sandburg, Janet Sandburg, and Helga Sandburg Crile. Reprinted by permission of Houghton Mifflin Harcourt Publishing Company.

Me and Uncle Romie: A Story Inspired by the Life and Art of Romare Bearden by Claire Hartfield, illustrated by Jerome Lagarrigue. Text copyright © 2002 by Claire Hartfield. Illustrations copyright © 2002 by Jerome Lagarrigue. Reprinted by permission of Dial Books for Young Readers, a Division of Penguin Young Readers Group, A Member of Penguin Group (USA) Inc., 345 Hudson Street, New York, NY 10014. All rights reserved.

Moon Runner by Carolyn Marsden. Copyright © 2005 by Carolyn Marsden. Reprinted by permission of the publisher Candlewick Press Inc.

My Brother Martin: A Sister Remembers Growing Up with the Rev. Dr. Martin Luther King Jr. by Christine King Farris, illustrated by Chris Soentpiet. Text copyright © 2003 by Christine King Farris. Illustrations copyright © 2003 by Chris Soentpiet. Reprinted by the permission of The Permissions Company and Simon & Schuster Books for Young Readers, an imprint of Simon & Schuster Children's Publishing Division.

Once Upon a Cool Motorcycle Dude by Kevin O'Malley, illustrated by Kevin O'Malley, Carol Heyer, and Scott Goto. Text copyright © 2005 by Kevin O'Malley. Illustrations copyright © Kevin O'Malley, Carol Heyer, and Scott Goto. All rights reserved. Reprinted by permission of Walker & Company.

Owen and Mzee by Isabella Hatkoff, Craig Hatkoff, and Dr. Paula Kahumbu, photographs by Peter Greste. Copyright © 2006 by Turtle Pond Publications, LLC and Lafarge Eco Systems, Ltd. Photographs copyright © 2006, 2005 by Peter Greste. All rights reserved. Reprinted by permission of Scholastic Press, an imprint of Scholastic Inc., and Turtle Pond Publications, LLC.

"Race Day" excerpted from *Ice Marathon 2006*, by Evgeniy Gorkov. Text and photographs © 2006 by Evgeniy Gorkov. http://run.gorkov.org/antarctica2006.html. Reprinted by permission of the author.

Riding Freedom by Pam Muñoz Ryan. Text copyright © 1998 by Pam Muñoz Ryan. Reprinted by permission of Scholastic Press, a division of Scholastic Inc.

The Right Dog for the Job: Ira's Path from Service Dog to Guide Dog by Dorothy Hinshaw Patent, photographs by William Muñoz. Copyright © 2004 by Dorothy Hinshaw Patent. Photographs copyright © 2004 by William Muñoz. All rights reserved. Reprinted by permission of Walker & Company.

Sacagawea by Lise Erdrich, illustrated by Julie Buffalohead. Text copyright © 2003 by Lise Erdrich. Illustrations copyright © 2003 by Julie Buffalohead All rights reserved. Reprinted by permission of Carolrhoda Books, a division of Lerner Publishing Group, Inc.

"The Screech Owl Who Liked Television" from *The Tarantula in My Purse and 172 Other Wild Pets* by Jean Craighead George. Copyright © 1996 by Jean Craighead George. Reprinted by permission of HarperCollins Publishers and Curtis Brown, Ltd.

"The Song of the Night" by Leslie D. Perkins from *Song and Dance*, published by Simon & Schuster.

"Stormalong" from *American Tall Tales*, by Mary Pope Osbourne. Text copyright © 1991 by Mary Pope Osbourne. Reprinted by permission of Alfred A. Knopf, a division of Random House, Inc.

"Three/Quarters Time" from *Those Who Rode the Night Winds* by Nikki Giovanni. Copyright © 1983 by Nikki Giovanni. Reprinted by permission of HarperCollins Publishers.

"To You" from *The Collected Poems of Langston Hughes* by Langston Hughes, edited by Arnold Rampersad with David Roessel, Associated Editor, copyright © 1994 by The Estate of Langston Hughes. Reprinted by permission of Alfred A. Knopf, a division of Random House, Inc., and Harold Ober Associates, Inc.

"Weather" from *Always Wondering* by Aileen Fisher. Copyright © 1991 by Aileen Fisher. Reprinted by permission of the Boulder Public Library Foundation, Inc., c/o Marian Reiner, Literary Agent.

"Weatherbee's Diner" from *Flamingos on the Roof* by Calef Brown. Copyright © 2006 by Calef Brown. Reprinted by permission of Houghton Mifflin Harcourt Publishing Company and Dunham Literary as agent of the author.

The World According to Humphrey by Betty G. Birney. Copyright © 2004 by Betty G. Birney. Reprinted by permission of G. P. Putnam's Sons, A Division of Penguin Young Readers Group, A Member of Penguin Group (USA) Inc., and Faber & Faber, Ltd.

Credits

Photo Credits

TOC Norbert Wu/Getty Images; **TOC** Three Lions/Getty Images; **TOC** Alan and Sandy Carey/Photo Researchers Inc.; **TOC** Travis Rowan/Alamy; **TOC** Creatas Images/Jupiter Images; **TOC** Courtesy of the Pebbles Project, www.pebblesproject.org; **TOC** Yellow Dog Productions/Getty Images; **TOC** © CORBIS; **TOC** © Bettmann/CORBIS; **TOC** ©SHOUT/Alamy; **TOC** Diane Ferlatte; **TOC** © Robbie Jack/Corbis; **TOC** © Royalty-Free/CORBIS; **TOC** GoodShoot/SuperStock; **TOC** © Mapi/age fotostock; **TOC** Richard Donovan/www.IceMarathon.com; **TOC** © Buddy Mays/Corbis; **TOC** © Bettmann/CORBIS; **2** (bl) Yellow Dog Productions/Getty Images; **8** b © Buddy Mays/Corbis; **9** c ©Jeff Greenberg/ The Image Works; **9** c © Oote Boe Photography / Alamy; **17** c © Charles Bowma/age fotostock; **18** tl Yellow Dog Productions/Getty Images; **18** cl Juan Silva/Getty Images; **18** cr Butch Martin/Alamy; **18** bl Image Source Black/Getty Images; **18** br Creatas Images/Jupiter Images; **19** tl Blend Images/Alamy; **19** tc © Myrleen Ferguson Cate/PhotoEdit; **19** tr © Brian Pieters/Masterfile; **19** bl © Hill Street Studios/AgeFotostock; **19** bc Terry Vine/Getty Images; **19** br © Terry Vine/age fotostock; **20-21** © Andersen Ross/Blend Images/Corbis; **22** © Kate DiCamillo; **23** "BECAUSE OF WINN-DIXIE"©2005 Twentieth Century Fox. All rights reserved.; **24** "BECAUSE OF WINN- DIXIE"©2005 Twentieth Century Fox. All rights reserved.; **25** "BECAUSE OF WINN- DIXIE"©2005 Twentieth Century Fox. All rights reserved.; **27** "BECAUSE OF WINN- DIXIE"©2005 Twentieth Century Fox. All rights reserved.; **29** "BECAUSE OF WINN- DIXIE"©2005 Twentieth Century Fox. All rights reserved.; **31** "BECAUSE OF WINN- DIXIE"©2005 Twentieth Century Fox. All rights reserved.; **32** "BECAUSE OF WINN- DIXIE"©2005 Twentieth Century Fox. All rights reserved.; **33** (br) PhotoDisc / Getty Images; **34** br Purestock/Getty Images; **34** tl Yellow Dog Productions/Getty Images; **35** Yellow Dog Productions/Getty Images; **36** © Houghton Mifflin Company/School Division; **37** c © Frank Siteman / PhotoEdit; **37** b Getty Images/Stockdisc Premium; **37** tr Yellow Dog Productions/Getty Images; **39** © Pat Doyle/Corbis; **41** Masterfile (Royalty-Free Div.); **42** cl © Steve Schapiro/Corbis; **42** cr © S»bastien D»sarmaux/Godong/Corbis; **42** bl Danny Lyon/Magnum Photos; **42** br JUPITERIMAGES/ Brand X / Alamy; **42** tl © CORBIS; **42** bkgd tl © Bettmann/CORBIS; **43** tl © Patrick Durand/CORBIS SYGMA; **43** tc © Kevin Dodge/Corbis; **43** tr © Robert Maass/CORBIS; **43** bl © Steve Schapiro/Corbis; **43** bc © Andrea Thrussell / Alamy; **43** br © Dennis MacDonald / PhotoEdit; **44** bl ASSOCIATED PRESS; **44** bkgd © Steve Schapiro/Corbis; **46** t Getty Images; **46** b Michael Tamborinno/Mercury Pictures; **60** b © CORBIS; **60** tl © CORBIS; **60** bkgd tl © Bettmann/CORBIS; **60-61** bkgd © Bettmann/CORBIS; **62** © Blend Images/Alamy; **63** c © Flip Schulke/CORBIS; **63** tr © CORBIS; **63** bkgd tr © Bettmann/CORBIS; **67** Masterfile (Royalty-Free Div.); **68** cl © Myrleen Ferguson Cate / PhotoEdit; **68** cr Todd Warnock/Getty Images; **68** bl Masterfile (Royalty-Free Div.); **68** br © Roy Ooms / Masterfile; **68** tl © Mapi/age fotostock; **69** tl Asia Images Group/Getty Images; **69** tc Gary Houlder/Getty Images; **69** tr © Masterfile (Royalty-Free Div.); **69** bl © Kayte M. Deioma/PhotoEdit; **69** bc © Big Cheese Photo LLC / Alamy; **69** br Masterfile (Royalty-Free Div.); **70** c ©Ellen B. Senisi/The Image Works; **70-71** bkgd Ryan McVay; **72** Courtesy Davkd Diaz; **81** (tl) Comstock/Whimsical Pop-Ins; **82** bkgd © Mapi/age fotostock; **82** tl © Mapi/age fotostock; **84** br © David Young-Wolff/PhotoEdit; **84-85** bkgd Michael Goldman/Getty Images; **85** b Robert Glusic; **85** tr © Mapi/AgeFotostock; **87** Masterfile (Royalty-Free Div.); **89** Masterfile (Royalty-Free Div.); **90** cl © Yael Kadish/AgeFotostock; **90** cr © Photodisc / SuperStock; **90** bl © Michael Newman / PhotoEdit; **90** br © Simon Marcus/CORBIS; **90** tl ©SHOUT/Alamy; **91** tl © JG Photography / Alamy; **91** tc © Corbis; **91** tr © Will & Deni McIntyre/Corbis; **91** bl © Michael Newman / PhotoEdit; **91** bc © SW Productions/Brand X/Corbis; **91** br MIXA/Getty Images; **92** © Pinto/zefa/Corbis; **94** Michael Greenlar/Mercury Pictures; **105** (tr) Brand X Pictures; **112** tl © SHOUT/Alamy; **112-113** © SHOUT/Alamy; **113** tr Jean Louis Aubert/Getty Images; **114-115** © Jean-Bernard Vernier/CORBIS SYGMA; **115** tr © SHOUT/Alamy; **117** Stockdisc; **119** © RubberBall/SuperStock; **120** tl © age fotostock / SuperStock; **120** tr AP Photo/Tsunemi Kubodera of the National Science Museum of Japan, HO; **120** bl Alexis Rosenfeld/Photo Researchers, Inc.; **120** br © Darryl Leniuk/Masterfile; **121** tl © Catherine Karnow/CORBIS; **121** tc © Denis Scott/Corbis; **121** tr Georgette Douwma/ Photo Researchers, Inc.; **121** bl Jonathan Blair/CORBIS; **121** bc © Galen Rowell/CORBIS; **121** br © Stephen Frink/CORBIS; **122** Andre Seale/Alamy; **124** Courtesy Steve Swinburne; **133** (tr) Comstock/Whimsical Pop-Ins; **133** (br) Corel Stock Photo Library - royalty free; **137** c © Kevin Schafer/Alamy; **137** b © R. Ian Lloyd/Masterfile; **139** Masterfile (Royalty-Free Div.); **141** © RubberBall/SuperStock; **143** b © Houghton Mifflin Company/School Division/Angela Coppola; **144** Nicolas Russell/Getty Images; **144** tc © Jeff Greenberg/age fotostock; **145** c © Jeff Greenberg/PhotoEdit; **146** cl © Lisa Berkshire/Illustration Works/Corbis; **146** cr Carol Kohen/Getty Images; **146** bl © Garry Black/Masterfile; **146** br Scala/Art Resource, NY; **146** tl Diane Ferlatte; **147** tl © Christie's Images/CORBIS; **147** tc Radius Images / Alamy; **147** tr © Sean Justice/Corbis; **147** bl Fine Art Photographic Library, London / Art Resource, NY; **147** bc © Paul Hardy/Corbis; **147** br © Photos 12/Alamy; **148-149** © Kevin Jordan/Corbis; **150** tl Courtesy Kevin O'Malley; **150** c Courtesy Carol Heyer; **150** cr Courtesy Scott Goto; **163** (tr) Getty Images/PhotoDisc; **164** tc Courtesy of Diane Ferlatte; **164** tl Diane Ferlatte; **165** Courtesy of Diane Ferlatte; **166** Courtesy of Diane Ferlatte; **167** c Masterfile (Royalty-Free Div.); **167** tr Diane Ferlatte; **171** Masterfile (Royalty-Free Div.); **172** cl © Michael Ochs Archives/Corbis; **172** cr © John Springer Collection/CORBIS; **172** bl Joe Sohm/drr.net; **172** br Hulton Archive/Getty Images; **172** tl Three Lions/Getty Images; **173** tl Peter Beavis/Getty Images; **173** tc © Rob Wilkinson / Alamy; **173** tr Eric O'connell/Getty Images; **173** bl © moodboard/Corbis; **173** bc © Photodisc / Alamy; **173** br © Purestock/AgeFotostock; **174-175** bkgd © Randy Faris/Corbis; **174** c © Creatas/SuperStock; **176** Courtesy Frank W. Baker; **187** (tl) Getty Images Royalty Free; **187** (tr) Artville / Getty Images; **187** (br) Corel Stock Photo Library - royalty free; **188-189** b Three Lions/Getty Images; **188** tl Three Lions/Getty Images; **189** cr SOTHEBY'S/AFP/Getty Images; **189** tr SOTHEBY'S/AFP/Getty Images; **190** tr © TWPhoto/Corbis; **191** tr Three Lions/Getty Images; **193** D. Hurst/Alamy; **195** © Image Source Pink / SuperStock; **196** tl © Rafael Macia/AgeFotostock; **196** tr DAJ/Getty Images; **196** bl Masterfile (Royalty-Free Div.); **196** br Kim Heacox/Getty Images; **197** tl © neal and molly jansen / Alamy; **197** tc Shalom Ormsby/Getty Images; **197** tr © The Photolibrary Wales / Alamy; **197** bl © Farinaz Taghavi/Corbis; **197** bc © Photodisc/AgeFotostock; **197** br © Michael Mahovlich / Masterfile; **198-199** bkgd © Bettmann/CORBIS; **198** cl Art Resource, NY; **198** cr AP Photo/F. Ruesch; **200** Courtesy Jerome Lagarrigue; **213** (br) Getty Images/PhotoDisc; **217** c Mark Leibowitz/Masterfile; **221** Sean Justice/Getty Images; **222** cl © Myrleen Ferguson Cate / PhotoEdit; **222** cr © David Young-Wolff / PhotoEdit; **222** bl © Bill Aron / PhotoEdit; **222** br © Reg Charity/CORBIS; **222** tl Alan and Sandy Carey/Photo Researchers Inc; **223** tl © Big Cheese Photo/AgeFotostock; **223** tc © Layne Kennedy/Corbis; **223** tr © Tony Freeman / PhotoEdit; **223** bl © JUPITERIMAGES/ Comstock Premium / Alamy; **223** bc © George Disario/CORBIS; **223** br © Bryan Allen/CORBIS; **224-225** bkgd © Brownstock Inc./Alamy; **224** bl © Houghton Mifflin Company/School Division/Ray Boudreau; **224** br © 1997 PhotoDisc, Inc. All rights reserved. Images provided by © 1997 C Squared Studios; **226** t Courtesy House of Anansi Press and Groundwood Books; **226** b Courtesy Andy Hammond; **237** (tr) Ingram; **237** (br) Corbis; **238-239** bkgd Craig Brewer/Getty Images; **238** tl Alan and Sandy Carey/Photo Researchers Inc.; **239** tr Suzanne L. Collins/Photo Researchers Inc.; **239** br Alan and Sandy Carey/Photo Researchers Inc.; **240-241** bkgd © Atlantide

Phototravel/Corbis; **240** tr blickwinkel/Alamy; **240** inset © Photospin; **241** tr Alan and Sandy Carey/Photo Researchers Inc.; **245** Steven Puetzer/Getty Images; **246** cl © UpperCut Images / Alamy; **246** cr ©David Grossman / The Image Works; **246** bl © images-of-france / Alamy; **246** br © Lebrecht Music and Arts Photo Library / Alamy; **246** tl © Robbie Jack/Corbis; **247** tl © Robbie Jack/Corbis; **247** tc © Joseph Sohm/Visions of America/Corbis; **247** tr Alamy; **247** bl © Yukmin/AgeFotostock; **247** bc © image100 / Alamy; **247** br © Anthony Cooper; Ecoscene/ CORBIS; **248-249** © Julie Lemberger/Corbis; **250** t Courtesy Susanna Reich; **250** c Courtesy Morgan Gaynin; **261** (tr) Rubberball / Getty Images; **262-263** bkgd © Robbie Jack/Corbis; **262** tl © Robbie Jack/Corbis; **263** br Time & Life Pictures/Getty Images; **264-265** bkgd © Corbis Premium RF/Alamy; **265** c Time & Life Pictures/ Getty Images; **265** tr © Robbie Jack/Corbis; **267** © Blend Images/SuperStock; **269** Steven Puetzer/Getty Images; **271** b © Houghton Mifflin Company/School Division; **272** Digital Vision/Getty Images; **272** tc Richard Hutchings/ Photo Edit; **273** c William Ervin/Science Photo Library; **274** tl Susan Watts/New York Daily News; **274** tr Michael Eudenbach/Getty Images; **274** bl © Nahum Budin / Alamy; **274** br Alamy; **274** bkgd tl © Hans Weisenhoffer; **275** tl GERRY ELLIS/Minden Pictures; **275** tc Renee Morris / Alamy; **275** tr M.Varesvuo /Peter Arnold Inc.; **275** bl © Getty; **275** bc © James L. Amos/CORBIS; **275** br © Comstock; **276-277** © Charles Campbell/Alamy; **278** t Courtesy Harper Collins; **278** b Courtesy Tim Bowers; **291** (tr) Comstock; **291** (tl) PhotoDisc - royalty free; **295** b © Big Cheese Photo LLC/Alamy; **299** Amos Morgan/ Getty Images; **300** cl © Jim Cornfield/CORBIS; **300** cr Robert Yager/Getty Images; **300** bl © Lloyd Cluff/ CORBIS; **300** br © SuperStock, Inc. / SuperStock; **300** bkgd tl © Royalty-Free/CORBIS; **300** tl GoodShoot/ SuperStock; **301** tl © Photodisc / Alamy; **301** tc © CORBIS; **301** tr © Mark Richards / PhotoEdit; **301** bl © Lloyd Cluff/CORBIS; **301** bc Chuck Franklin / Alamy; **301** br © Lloyd Sutton/Masterfile; **302** bl © Bettmann/ CORBIS; **302-303** b © David Sailors/CORBIS; **304** t Courtesy Harper Collins; **304** b Courtesy of Yuan Lee; **315** (tl) Corbis; **316** bkgd tl © CORBIS; **316** tl GoodShoot/ SuperStock; **316-317** bkgd © CORBIS; **318-319** bkgd Robert Glusic; **317** r © GoodShoot/ SuperStock; **319** cr © Bettmann/CORBIS; **319** br Zephyr/Photo Researchers, Inc.; **319** bkgd tr © Royalty-Free/CORBIS; **319** bkgd tr GoodShot/Superstock; **323** Masterfile (Royalty-Free Div.); **324** cl © Digital Vision; **324** cr ROBYN STEWART/ Minden Pictures; **324** bl © Rolf Nussbaumer / Alamy; **324** br © Steve Allen Travel Photography / Alamy; **324** tl Mike King/www.icemarathon.com; **325** tl © Steven J. Kazlowski / Alamy; **325** tc © image100/Corbis; **325** tr © Terrance Klassen / Alamy; **325** bl © Emilio Ereza / Alamy; **325** bc KONRAD WOTHE /Minden Pictures; **325** br © Momatiuk - Eastcott/Corbis; **326-327** b © Jorge Fernandez/Alamy; **326** cr © Eye Ubiquitous/Alamy; **328** Courtesy Harper Collins; **339** (tr) Getty Images/ PhotoDisc; **339** (br) Corbis; **339** (tl) JupiterImages/ Brand X/Alamy; **340-341** c Mike King/www.icemarathon.com; **340-343** border © 1997 PhotoDisc, Inc. All rights reserved. Images provided by © 1997 Don Farrall, LightWorks Studio; **340** tl Mike King/www.icemarathon.com; **342** bkgd © Ann Hawthorne/CORBIS; **342** br Courtesy of Antarctic Mike/www.AntarcticMike.com; **343** c Mike King/www. icemarathon.com; **343** tr Mike King/www.icemarathon. com; **345** David Tipling/Getty Images; **347** © Digital Vision / Alamy; **348** tl Getty Images/Terje Rakke; **348** tr © Redmond Durrell / Alamy; **348** bl © Michael Busselle/ CORBIS; **348** br Martin Harvey / Alamy; **349** tl Tony Herbert / Alamy; **349** tc Nick Servian / Alamy; **349** tr Corwin,Jim/Jupiter Images; **349** bl ©GERALD HINDE/ ABPL / Animals Animals; **349** bc Pat Bennett / Alamy; **349** br © Paul Conklin/ PhotoEdit; **350-351** © Antonio L€pez RomΣn/age fotostock; **352** Peggy Micucci; **369** c Gary Vestal/Jupiter Images; **373** © Photodisc / SuperStock; **374** tl © John Sevigny/epa/Corbis; **374** tr © CNP/Corbis; **374** bl Mira / Alamy; **374** br © Brownie Harris/CORBIS; **375** tl © Michael Newman / PhotoEdit; **375** tc © Peter Kneffel/ dpa/Corbis; **375** tr Ashley Cooper / Alamy; **375** bl © PhotoDisc; **375** bc Jeff Greenberg / Alamy; **375** br © Eric Nguyen/Corbis; **376-377** bkgd © 1997 PhotoDisc, Inc. All rights reserved. Images provided by © 1997 Don Farrall, LightWorks Studio; **376** c Houghton Mifflin Company/ School Division; **378** John Lei; **389** (tl) Brand X Pictures; **389** (br) Robert Yin/Corbis; **395** © Image Source Pink/ SuperStock; **397** © Photodisc / SuperStock; **398-399** b © Houghton Mifflin Company/School Division; **400** tc © moodboard/Corbis; **401** c Sean Rowland/Covered Images/ ASP via Getty Images; **402** tl © Bettmann/CORBIS; **402** tr © Dave G. Houser/Corbis; **402** bl © CORBIS; **402** br © North Wind Picture Archives / Alamy; **402** tl © Bettmann/ CORBIS; **403** tl © Robert Estall/CORBIS; **403** tc © Digital Vision; **403** tr © J.C. Leacock/Alamy; **403** bl © North Wind Picture Archives / Alamy; **403** bc dk / Alamy; **403** br North Wind Picture Archives / Alamy; **404** E.J. Baumeister Jr./Alamy; **406** t Courtesy Pam Munoz Ryan; **406** b Courtesy of Marc Scott; **418-421** bkgd Digital Stock; **418** tc Iconsinternational.Com/Alamy; **418** bl © Bettmann/CORBIS; **418** tl © Bettmann/CORBIS; **419** The Granger Collection, New York; **420** Photodisc/ SuperStock; **421** c North Wind Picture Archives/Alamy; **421** b UPITTERIMAGES/ Creatas/Alamy; **421** tr © Bettmann/CORBIS; **425** © Bananastock/age fotostock; **426** tl Margaret Miller / Photo Researchers, Inc.; **426** tr © Charles Gupton/CORBIS; **426** bl © Tim Davis/CORBIS; **426** br ©Sean Cayton/The Image Works; **427** tl © Ashley Cooper/Corbis; **427** tc Daniel Dempster Photography/ Alamy; **427** tr © Juniors Bildarchiv/Alamy; **427** bl © Blend Images/Alamy; **427** bc © tbkmedia.de / Alamy; **427** br © Fred Lord / Alamy; **428** t altrendo images/Getty Images; **428** c © Frank Siteman/PhotoEdit; **428** b © ARCO/De Meester/age fotostock; **430** Courtesy Dorothy Hinshaw Patent; **441** Getty Images/PhotoDisc; **447** Minden Pictures/Getty Images; **449** Masterfile (Royalty-Free Div.); **450** cl © Tom Stewart/zefa/Corbis; **450** cr © COMSTOCK Images/age fotostock; **450** bl © Blend Images/Alamy; **450** br © Radius Images/Alamy; **450** tl Travis Rowan/Alamy; **450** bkgd tl Creatas Images/Jupiter Images; **451** tl © Patrik Giardino/CORBIS; **451** tc © PhotoStockFile / Alamy; **451** tr © Michael Prince/Corbis; **451** bl © Ted Grant/Masterfile; **451** bc © Aflo Foto Agency/Alamy; **451** br © SW Productions/Brand X/ Corbis; **452** c Richard Hutchings/Photo Edit; **452-453** b Sascha Pflaeging /Getty Images; **454** t Courtesy Carolyn

Marsden; **454** b Courtesy Cornelius Van Wright; **465** Image100 / Corbis; **466-467** b Travis Rowan/Alamy; **466-467** tc Creatas Images/Jupiter Images; **466** tl Travis Rowan/Alamy; **466** bkgd tl Creatas Images/Jupiter Imagescom; **468-469** bkgd Johnny Greig Travel Photography/Alamy; **467** c ImagineChina; **468** br Gary Conner/Photo Edit; **468** c Creatas Images/Jupiter Images; **469** c © Digital Vision/Alamy; **469** b ©Beaconstox/Alamy; **469** tr Travis Rowan/Alamy; **473** Houghton Mifflin Company/School Division/Ray Boudreau; **474** cl © Bettmann/CORBIS; **474** cr ©Bob Daemmrich / The Image Works; **474** bl © Bruce Burkhardt/CORBIS; **474** br © Arthur Rothstein/CORBIS; **474** tr ©Jeff Greenberg/ The Image Works; **474** bkgd tl Oote Boe Photography/ Alamy; **475** tl © Hulton-Deutsch Collection/CORBIS; **475** tc © Horacio Villalobos/Corbis; **475** tr ©Marilyn Humphries/ The Image Works; **475** bl © Richard Hutchings / PhotoEdit; **475** bc © Gary Crabbe/ Alamy; **475** br Masterfile (Royalty-Free Div.); **476-477** bkgd © Gary Crabbe/Alamy; **476** c AP Photo/Sakuma; **478** t Ken Krull; **478** b Courtesy Yuyi Morales; **490-491** bkgd Oote Boe Photography /Alamy; **492-493** bkgd Yoshio Sawargai/ Getty Images; **490** cl © Iconotec; **490** bc C Squared Studios; **490** tl ©Jeff Greenberg/ The Image Works; **490** bkgd tl Oote Boe Photography /Alamy; **491** br Jeff Greenberg/The Image Works; **491** tc C Squared Studios; **492** c D. Hurst / Alamy; **492** tc C Squared Studios; **493** c ©C.W. McKeen/Syracuse Newspapers0/The Image Works; **493** tr ©Jeff Greenberg/The Image Works; **493** bkgd tr Oote Boe Photography/Alamy; **497** © RubberBall/ SuperStock; **498** cl © Paul A. Souders/CORBIS; **498** cr AP Photo/Great Falls Tribune, Robin Loznak; **498** bl © PhotoDisc; **498** br Dennis MacDonald / Alamy; **498** tl © Buddy Mays/Corbis; **499** tl MARK SPENCER/ AUSCAPE/Minden Pictures; **499** tr © Jeremy Woodhouse/age fotostock; **499** bl KATHERINE FENG/ GLOBIO/Minden Pictures; **499** bc © PhotoDisc; **499** br Peter Barritt/Alamy; **500-501** b © Purestock/Alamy; **502** © Bettina Strauss; **518** tl © Buddy Mays/Corbis; **518-519** bkgd © Buddy Mays/Corbis; **519** br The Print Collector/ Alamy; **520-521** bkgd Digital Vision; **521** c © Connie Ricca/Corbis; **521** tr © Buddy Mays/Corbis; **523** Jupiter Images; **525** © RubberBall / SuperStock; **526-527** b © Houghton Mifflin Company/School Division/Angela Coppola; **528** © CORBIS/AegFotostock; **528** tc; **529** c Mitchell Funk/Getty Images; **529** bkgd © 1997 PhotoDisc, Inc. All rights reserved. Images provided by © 1997 Don Farrall, LightWorks Studio; **530** tl Aura/Getty Images; **530** tr © DENNIS HALLINAN / Getty Images.; **530** bl © Stanley Fellerman/Corbis; **530** Peter Dazeley/Getty Images; **530** bkgd bl Rick Lew/Getty Images; **531** tl © Don Mason/Corbis; **531** tc © Robert Pickett/CORBIS; **531** tr Gary Gerovac / Masterfile; **531** bl Juniors Bildarchiv / Alamy; **531** bc Steve Lyne/Getty Image; **531** br Martin Harvey/Getty Images; **532-533** b © Photospin; **532** br ©Digital Vision Ltd./SuperStock; **532** bc © Burke/Triolo Productions/Brand X/Corbis; **534** t Courtesy Penguin Group; **534** b Courtesy Teri Farrell Gittins; **547** PhotoDisc, Inc.; **547** Comstock; **553** © Kreber/Corbis; **555** © Image Source Pink/SuperStock; **556** tl Digital Vision/Getty Images; **556** tr © Michael Newman / PhotoEdit; **556** br © image100/Corbis; **556** bl © Najlah Feanny/Corbis; **557** tl © Mike Blake/Reuters/Corbis; **557** tc Terry Farmer/Jupiter Images; **557** tr © Bettmann/ CORBIS; **557** bl ©John Berry / Syracuse Newspapers / The Image Works; **557** bc ©WireImageStock/Masterfile; **557** br © Beathan/Corbis; **558** © Bettmann/CORBIS; **560** Courtesy Linda Arms White; **574** bl Michael Ventura/ Alamy; **574** bc © Bettmann/CORBIS; **574** br © Bettmann/ CORBIS; **575** c © Jeff Greenberg/age fotostock; **577** © North Wind/North Wind Picture Archives; **579** © Rubberball Productions; **580** cl © Wolfgang Kaehler / Alamy; **580** cr Brent Waltermire / Alamy; **580** bl © Craig Tuttle/CORBIS; **580** br John Henshall / Alamy; **580** tl James Randklev/Getty Images; **581** tl Papilio / Alamy; **581** tc © CORBIS; **581** tr Cartesia/PhotoDisc Imaging; **581** bl © Bob Rowan; Progressive Image/CORBIS; **581** bc © Jack Fields/CORBIS; **581** br Leland Bobbe/Getty Images; **582-583** bkgd b © Getty; **582** bl Adam Jones/Photo Researchers, Inc.; **582** br Adam Jones/Photo Researchers, Inc.; **582** bc Adam Jones/Photo Researchers, Inc.; **584** t Courtesy Linda Vieira; **584** b Courtesy Christopher Canyon; **599** Adam DeMelo/Alamy; **599** Corbis; **599** Comstock; **600-01** bkgd James Randklev/Getty Images; **600** br Image Farm Inc./Alamy; **600** tl James Randklev/ Getty Images; **601** tr ©1995 PhotoDisc, Inc. All rights reserved. Images ©1995 PhotoLink; **601** br Andre Jenny/ Alamy; **601** bkgd © Digital Stock; **601** cl Image Farm Inc./ Alamy; **602-603** bkgd © Digital Stock; **602** cr ©1995 PhotoDisc, Inc. All rights reserved. Images ©1995 PhotoLink; **602** tl Image Farm Inc./Alamy; **603** tr James Randklev/Getty Images; **603** cr © Galen Rowell/CORBIS; **603** tr James Randklev/Getty Images; **605** Ambient Images Inc./Alamy; **607** © RubberBall/SuperStock; **608** cl © Royalty-Free/Corbis; **608** cr Juniors Bildarchiv / Alamy; **608** bl Mike Parry/Getty Images; **608** br Jose Luis Pelaez Inc/Getty Images; **608** tl Norbert Wu/Getty Images; **609** tl © Kelly Redinger/age fotostock; **609** tc © Thierry Prat/ Sygma/Corbis; **609** tr Tim Platt/Getty Images; **609** bl ©SHAEN ADEY/ABPL / Animals Animals; **609** bc © GoGo Images/age fotostock; **609** br Jupiter Images; **610-611** REUTERS/Pawan Kumar; **612** tl Courtesy Scholastic; **612** tc Courtesy Scholastic; **612** tr Courtesy Scholastic; **624** tl Norbert Wu/Getty Images; **624-625** Norbert Wu/Getty Images; **627** tr Norbert Wu/Getty Images; **629** Frans Lanting/Minden Pictures; **631** © Photodisc/SuperStock; **632** tl © Richard Cummins/ CORBIS; **632** tc © Bonnie Kamin / PhotoEdit; **632** bl © moodboard/Corbis; **632** br © LL / Roger-Viollet / The Image Works; **632** tl Courtesy of the Pebbles Project, www. pebblesproject.org; **633** tl Brand X Pictures; **633** tc Elvele Images / Alamy; **633** tr © Don Mason/Corbis; **633** bl Jeremy Trew, Trewimage / Alamy; **633** bc © Liba Taylor/ CORBIS; **633** br George Doyle/Getty Images; **634** b © Carol & Mike Werner/SuperStock; **636** t Getty Images; **636** b Courtesy Alan Flinn; **646** bc AP Photo/Karen Vibert-Kennedy; **646** tl Courtesy of the Pebbles Project, www.pebblesproject.org; **647** Courtesy of the Pebbles Project, www.pebblesproject.org/; **648** b © Najlah Feanny/ Corbis; **649** tr Courtesy of the Pebbles Project, www. pebblesproject.org; **653** © Photodisc/SuperStock; **656** b © Myrleen Ferguson Cate / PhotoEdit; **656** tc © Werner Dieterich/age fotostock; **665** ©Digital Stock; **666** © Cartesia/PhotoDisc Imaging; **667** © Digital Stock; **669** ©

Artville; **670** © Ryan McVay; **671** ©1995 PhotoDisc, Inc. All rights reserved. Images ©1995 CMCD, Inc.; **672** ©Stockbyte; **675** © Artville; **676** ©1995 PhotoDisc, Inc. All rights reserved. Images provided by © 1995 CMCD;

Illustration

Cover Brandon Dorman. **5** (bl) © Scott Goto; **7** (tml) Ann Boyajian; **8** (ml, b) Peter Grosshauser, (b) Tim Bower; **9** (ml) Gerardo Suzan, (bl) Linda Bronson; **10** (bl) Lisa Perrett; **12** (ml) Jackie Stafford-Snider, (bl) Renee Graef, (bc) Alan Flinn. **17** Sally Vitsky; **38–39** Rob McClurken; **63** (mr) Kristine Walsh; **63** (tr) Lesley Withrow; **64** Rob McClurken; **72–81** David Diaz **83** Lesley Withrow; **85** Lesley Withrow; **86** Rob McClurken; **115** LesleyWithrow; **116** Rob McClurken. **116** Rob McClurken; **122** Ortelius Design Inc; **134–137** © Scott Goto; **138** Rob McClurken **143** Sally Vitsky; **144** Tim Johnson **148** Argosy **168–169** Rob McClurken **191** Ken Bowser; **192** Rob McClurken **214–217** Ann Boyajian **218–219** Rob McClurken **226–237** Andy Hammond **241** Tim Johnson **242–243** Rob McClurken **265** Lesley Withrow **266** Rob McClurken **270** Sally Vitsky. **272** Sally Vitsky; **278–291** Tim Bowers **292–295** Peter Grosshauser **296–297** Rob McClurken; **304–315** Yuan Lee. **316–317** Patrick Gnan; **318–319** Patrick Gann; **320–321** Rob McClurken; **326** Susan Carlson. **341** Ortelius Design Inc; **343** Daniel Delvalle; **344–345** Rob McClurken; **366–368** Gerardo Suzan; **370** Rob McClurken; **390–391** Linda Bronson. **392** Sally Vitsky; **394–395** Rob McClurken; **398** Sally Vitsky; **400** Sally Vitsky; **404** Peter Bull; **406–417** Marc Scott; **422** Steve Mack; **442–444** Lisa Perrett; **445**. Kristine Walsh; **446-447** Rob McClurken. **454–465** Cornelius Van Wright; **470–471** Rob McClurken; **494–495** Rob McClurken; **500** Susan Carlson; **521** Kristine Walsh; **522** Rob McClurken. **526** Sally Vitsky; **528** Tim Johnson; **534–546** Teri Farrell-Gittins; **548–550** Jackie Stafford-Snider; **551** Tim Johnson; **552** Rob McClurken. **553** Rob McClurken; **572–575** Renee Graef. **576–577** Rob McClurken; **604** Rob McClurken; **610** Ortelius Design Inc; **624** Rob McClurken. **624** Robert Schuster; **628** Rob McClurken; **636–645** Alan Flinn. **650-651** Rob McClurken. **654-655** Sally Vitsky.

All other photos: Houghton Mifflin Harcourt Photo Libraries and Photographers.

Research Bibliography

Adams, M.J. (2000). *Beginning to Read: Thinking and Learning About Print*. Cambridge: MIT Press.

Armbruster, B., Anderson, T.H., & Ostertag, J. (1987). Does text structure/summarization instruction facilitate learning from expository text? *Reading Research Quarterly*, 22 (3), 331–346.

Armbruster, B., Lehr, F., & Osborn, J. (2001). *Put Reading First: The Research Building Blocks for Teaching Children to Read* (pp. 21-31). Washington, D.C.: National Institute for Literacy.

Askew, B.J. & Fountas, I.C. (1998). Building an early reading process: Active from the start! *The Reading Teacher,* 52 (2), 126–134.

Baker, S.K., Chard, D.J., Ketterlin-Geller, L.R., Apichatabutra, C., & Doabler, C. (in press). The basis of evidence for Self-Regulated Strategy Development for students with or at risk for learning disabilities. *Exceptional Children.*

Ball, E., & Blachman, B. (1991). Does phoneme awareness training in kindergarten make a difference in early word recognition and developmental spelling? *Reading Research Quarterly*, 26 (1), 49–66.

Baumann, J.F. & Bergeron, B.S. (1993). Story map instruction using children's literature: Effects on first graders' comprehension of central narrative elements. *Journal of Reading Behavior*, 25 (4), 407–437.

Baumann, J.F. & Kame'enui, E.J. (Eds.). (2004). *Vocabulary Instruction: Research to Practice.* New York: Guilford Press.

Baumann, J.F., Seifert-Kessell, N., & Jones, L.A. (1992). Effect of think-aloud instruction on elementary students' comprehension monitoring abilities. *Journal of Reading Behavior*, 24 (2), 143–172.

Bear, D.R. & Templeton, S. (1998). Explorations in developmental spelling: Foundations for learning and teaching phonics, spelling, and vocabulary. *The Reading Teacher,* 52 (3), 222–242.

Beck, I.L. (2006). *Making Sense of Phonics: The Hows and Whys*. New York: Guilford Press.

Beck, I.L. & McKeown, M. (2006). *Improving Comprehension with Questioning the Author: A Fresh and Expanded View of a Powerful Approach (Theory and Practice)*. New York, NY: Scholastic.

Beck, I.L., McKeown, M., Hamilton, R., & Kucan, L. (1998). Getting at the meaning. *American Educator*, Summer, 66–71.

Beck, I.L., McKeown, M., Hamilton, R., & Kucan, L. (1997). *Questioning the Author: An Approach for Enhancing Student Engagement with Text*. Newark, DE: International Reading Association.

Beck, I.L., & McKeown, M.G., (2001). Text talk: Capturing the benefits of read-aloud experiences for young children. *The Reading Teacher*, 55 (1), 10–20.

Beck, I.L., McKeown, M.G. & Kucan, L. (2002). *Bringing Words to Life: Robust Vocabulary Instruction*. New York: Guilford Press.

Beck, I.L., Perfetti, C.A., & McKeown, M.G. (1982). Effects of long-term vocabulary instruction on lexical access and reading comprehension. *Journal of Educational Psychology*, 74 (4), 506–521.

Bereiter, C. & Bird, M. (1985). Use of thinking aloud in identification and teaching of reading comprehension strategies. *Cognition and Instruction*, 2, 131–156.

Biemiller, A. (2005). Size and sequence in vocabulary development: Implications for choosing words for primary grade vocabulary. In E.H. Hiebert & M.L. Kamil (Eds.), *Teaching and Learning Vocabulary* (pp. 223–242). Mahwah, NJ: Lawrence Erlbaum.

Biemiller, A. (2001) Teaching vocabulary: Early, direct, and sequential. *American Educator*. Spring.

Biemiller, A. (2001). Vocabulary development and instruction: A prerequisite for school learning. In D. Dickinson & S. Neuman (Eds.), *Handbook of Early Literacy Research,* (Vol. 2), New York: Guilford Press.

Biemiller, A. & Slonim, N. (2001). Estimating root word vocabulary growth in normative and advantaged populations: Evidence for a common sequence of vocabulary acquisition. *Journal of Educational Psychology,* 93 (3), 498–520.

Blachman, B. (2000). Phonological awareness. In M. Kamil, P. Mosenthal, P.D. Pearson, & R. Barr (Eds.), *Handbook of Reading Research,* (Vol. 3). Mahwah, NJ: Lawrence Erlbaum.

Blachman, B., Ball, E.W., Black, R.S., & Tangel, D.M. (1994). Kindergarten teachers develop phoneme awareness in low-income, inner-city classrooms: Does it make a difference? *Reading and Writing: An Interdisciplinary Journal* 6 (1), 1–18.

Brown, I.S. & Felton, R.H. (1990). Effects of instruction on beginning reading skills in children at risk for reading disability. *Reading and Writing: An Interdisciplinary Journal*, 2 (3), 223–241.

Carlo, M. (2004). Closing the gap: Addressing the vocabulary needs of English-language learners in bilingual and mainstream classrooms. *Reading Research Quarterly,* 39 (2), 188–215.

Chall, J. (1996). *Learning to Read: The Great Debate (revised, with a new foreword)*. New York: McGraw-Hill.

Chard, D.J., Ketterlin-Geller, L.R., Baker, S.K., Doabler, C., & Apichatabutra, C. (in press). Repeated reading interventions for students with learning disabilities: Status of the evidence. *Exceptional Children.*

Chard, D.J., Stoolmiller, M., Harn, B., Vaughn, S., Wanzek, J., Linan-Thompson, S., & Kame'enui, E.J. (2008). Predicting reading success in a multi-level school-wide reading model: A retrospective analysis. *Journal of Learning Disabilities,* 41 (2), 174–188.

Charity, A.H., Scarborough, H.E., & Griffin, D.M. (2004). Familiarity with school English in African American children and its relation to early reading achievement. *Child Development*, 75 (5), 1340–1356.

Chiappe, P. & Siegel, L.S. (2006). A longitudinal study of reading development of Canadian children from diverse linguistic backgrounds. *Elementary School Journal,* 107 (2), 135–152.

Coyne, M.D., Kame'enui, E.J., & Simmons, D.C. (2004). Improving beginning reading instruction and intervention for students with LD: Reconciling "all" with "each." *Journal of Learning Disabilities*, 37 (3), 231–239.

Coyne, M.D., Kame'enui, E.J., Simmons, D.C., & Harn, B.A. (2004). Beginning reading intervention as inoculation or insulin: First-grade reading performance of strong responders to kindergarten intervention. *Journal of Learning Disabilities*, 37 (2), 90–104.

Coyne, M.D., Zipoli Jr., R.P., Chard, D.J., Faggella-Luby, M., Ruby, M., Santoro, L.E., & Baker, S. (2009). Direct instruction of comprehension: Instructional examples from intervention research on listening and reading comprehension. *Reading & Writing Quarterly*, 25 (2), 221–245.

Coyne, M.D., Zipoli Jr., R.P., & Ruby, M. (2006). Beginning reading instruction for students at risk for reading disabilities: What, how, and when. *Intervention in School and Clinic*, 41 (3), 161–168.

Craig, H.K. & Washington, J.A. (2006). *Malik Goes to School: Examining the Language Skills of African American Students From Preschool-5th Grade.* Mahwah, NJ: Lawrence Erlbaum Associates.

Craig, H.K. & Washington, J.A. (2001). Recent research on the language and literacy skills of African American students in early years . In D. Dickinson & S. Neuman (Eds.), *Handbook of Early Literacy Research,* (Vol. 2), New York: Guilford Press.

Dixon, R.C., Isaacson, S., & Stein, M. (2002). Effective strategies for teaching writing. In E.J. Kame'enui, D.W. Carnine, R.C. Dixon, D.C. Simmons, & M.D. Coyne (Eds.), *Effective Teaching Strategies That Accommodate Diverse Learners* (2nd ed., pp. 93–119). Upper Saddle River, NJ: Merrill Prentice Hall.

Dowhower, S.L. (1987). Effects of repeated reading on second-grade transitional readers' fluency and comprehension. *Reading Research Quarterly*, 22 (4), 389–406.

Duke, N.K. (2000). 3.6 minutes a day: The scarcity of informational text in first grade. *Reading Research Quarterly*, 35 (2), 202–224.

Duke, N.K. & Pearson, P.D. (2002). Effective practices for developing reading comprehension. In A.E. Farstrup & S.J. Samuels (Eds.), *What Research Has to Say About Reading Instruction* (3rd ed., pp. 205–242). Newark, DE: International Reading Association.

Durán, E., Shefelbine, J., Carnine, L., Maldonado-Colón, E., & Gunn, B. (2003). *Systematic Instruction in Reading for Spanish-Speaking Students.* Springfield, IL: Charles C. Thomas.

Edwards Santoro, L., Chard, D.J., Howard, L., & Baker, S.K. (2008). Making the VERY most of classroom read alouds: How to promote comprehension and vocabulary in K-2 classrooms. *The Reading Teacher,* 61 (5), 396–408.

Ehri, L.C. (1998). Grapheme-phoneme knowledge is essential for learning to read words in English. In J. Metsala & L. Ehri (Eds.), *Word Recognition in Beginning Literacy* (pp. 3–40). Hillsdale, NJ: Lawrence Erlbaum Associates.

Ehri, L. & Nunes, S.R. (2002). The role of phonemic awareness in learning to read. In A.E. Farstrup & S.J. Samuels (Eds.), *What Research Has to Say About Reading Instruction* (3rd ed., pp. 110–139). Newark, DE: International Reading Association.

Ehri, L. & Wilce, L. (1987). Does learning to spell help beginners learn to read words? *Reading Research Quarterly*, 22 (1), 48–65.

Farr, R. (1990). Reading. *Educational Leadership,* 47 (5), 82–83.

Farr, R., Lewis, M., Faszholz, J., Pinsky, E., Towle, S., Lipschutz, J. & Faulds, B.P. (1990). Writing in response to reading. *Educational Leadership*, 47 (6), 66–69.

Fletcher, J.M. & Lyon, G.R. (1998) Reading: A research-based approach. In Evers, W.M. (Ed.), *What's Gone Wrong in America's Classroom?* Palo Alto, CA: Hoover Institution Press, Stanford University.

Foorman, B. (Ed.). (2003). *Preventing and Remediating Reading Difficulties*. Baltimore, MD: York Press.

Foorman, B.R., Francis, D.J., Fletcher, J., Schatschneider, C., & Mehta, P. (1998). The role of instruction in learning to read: Preventing reading failure in at-risk children. *Journal of Educational Psychology*, 90 (1), 37–55.

Francis D.J., Rivera, M., Lesaux, N., Kieffer, M., & Rivera, H. (2006). Practical Guidelines for the Education of English Language Learners: Research-based recommendations for instruction and academic interventions (Book 1). Texas Institute for Measurement, Evaluation, and Statistics. University of Houston for the Center on Instruction.

Francis D.J., Rivera, M., Lesaux, N., Kieffer, M., & Rivera, H. (2006). Practical Guidelines for the Education of English Language Learners: Research-based recommendations for serving adolescent newcomers (Book 2). Texas Institute for Measurement, Evaluation, and Statistics. University of Houston for the Center on Instruction.

Fuchs, L., Fuchs, D., & Hosp, M. (2001). Oral reading fluency as an indicator of reading competence: A theoretical, empirical, and historical analysis. *Scientific Studies of Reading*, 5 (3), 239–256.

Fukkink, R.G. & de Glopper, K. (1998). Effects of instruction in deriving word meaning from context: A meta-analysis. *Review of Educational Research*, 68 (4), 450–469.

Gambrell, L.B., Morrow, L.M., & Pennington, C. (2002). Early childhood and elementary literature-based instruction: Current perspectives... *Reading Online,* 5 (6), 26–39.

Gersten, R. (2005). Behind the scenes of an intervention research study. *Learning Disabilities Research & Practice,* 20 (4), 200–212.

Gersten, R. & Baker, S. (2000). What we know about effective instructional practices for English learners. *Exceptional Children*, 66 (4), 454–470.

Gersten, R., Baker, S.K., Haager, D., & Graves, A.W. (2005). Exploring the role of teacher quality in predicting reading outcomes for first-grade English learners: An observational study. *Remedial and Special Education,* 26 (4), 197–206.

Gersten, R. & Geva, E. (2003). Teaching reading to early language learners. *Educational Leadership,* 60 (7), 44–49.

Gersten, R. & Jiménez, R. (2002). Modulating instruction for English-language learners. In E.J. Kame'enui, D.W. Carnine, R.C. Dixon, D.C. Simmons, & M.D. Coyne (Eds.), *Effective Teaching Strategies That Accommodate Diverse Learners*. Upper Saddle River, NJ: Merrill Prentice Hall.

Gipe, J.P. & Arnold, R.D. (1979). Teaching vocabulary through familiar associations and contexts. *Journal of Reading Behavior*, 11 (3), 281–285.

Griffith, P.L., Klesius, J.P., & Kromrey, J.D. (1992). The effect of phonemic awareness on the literacy development of first grade children in a traditional or a whole language classroom. *Journal of Research in Childhood Education*, 6 (2), 85–92.

Guthrie, J. & Wigfield, A. (2000). Engagement and motivation in reading. In M. Kamil, P. Mosenthal, P. Pearson, & R. Barr, (Eds.), *Handbook of Reading Research, Vol. III*, 403–422.

Guthrie, J.T., Wigfield, A., Barbosa, P., Perencevich, K.C., Taboada, A., Davis, M.H., et al. (2004). Increasing reading comprehension and engagement through concept-oriented reading instruction. *Journal of Educational Psychology*, 96 (3), 403–423.

Hall, S.L. & Moats, L.C. (1999). *Straight Talk About Reading*. Chicago, IL: Contemporary Books.

Harm, M.W., McCandliss, B.D. & Seidenberg, M.S. (2003). Modeling the successes and failures of interventions for disabled readers. *Scientific Studies of Reading*, 7 (2), 155–182.

Harn, B.A., Stoolmiller, M., & Chard, D. (2008). Identifying the dimensions of alphabetic principle on the reading development of first graders: The role of automaticity and unitization. *Journal of Learning disabilities,* 41 (2), 143–157.

Hasbrouck, J. & Tindal, G.A. (2006). Oral reading fluency norms: A valuable assessment tool for reading teachers. *The Reading Teacher*, 59 (7), 636–644.

Research Bibliography

Hiebert, E.H. & Kamil, M.L. (Eds.). (2005). *Teaching and Learning Vocabulary: Bringing Research to Practice*. Mahwah, NJ: Lawrence Erlbaum Associates.

Hudson, R., (2006). Using Repeated Reading and Readers Theater to Increase Fluency. Reading First National Conference. Website: http://www3.ksde.org/sfp/rdgfirst/natl_rdgfirst_conf_2006/hudson_using_repeated_reading_to_increase_fluency.pdf.

Hudson, R., Lane, H., & Pullen, P. (2005). Reading fluency assessment and instruction: What, why, and how? *The Reading Teacher*, 58 (8), 702–714.

Juel, C. (1988). Learning to read and write: A longitudinal study of fifty-four children from first through fourth grades. *Journal of Educational Psychology*, 80 (4), 437–447.

Juel, C., & Minden-Cupp, C. (2000). Learning to read words: Linguistic units and instructional strategies. *Reading Research Quarterly*, 35 (4), 458–492.

Kamil, M.L., Mosenthal, P.B., Pearson, P.D., & Barr, R. (2000). *Handbook of Reading Research*. Vol. III. Mahwah, NJ: Lawrence Erlbaum Associates.

Lehr, F. & Osborn, J. (2005). A Focus on Comprehension. Pacific Resources for Education and Learning (PREL) Monograph. U.S. Department of Education. Website: www.prel.org/programs/rel/rel.asp.

Lehr, F., Osborn, J., & Hiebert, E.H. (2004). A Focus on Vocabulary. Pacific Resources for Education and Learning (PREL) Monograph. U.S. Department of Education. Website: www.prel.org/programs/rel/rel.asp.

Lesaux, N.K. & Siegel, L.S. (2003). The development of reading in children who speak English as a second language. *Developmental Psychology*, 39 (6), 1005–1019.

Lipson, M.Y., Mosenthal, J.H., Mekkelsen, J., & Russ, B. (2004). Building knowledge and fashioning success one school at a time. *The Reading Teacher*, 57 (6), 534–542.

Lipson, M.Y. & Wixson, K.K. (2008). New IRA commission will address RTI issues. *Reading Today*, 26 (1), 1, 5.

Lonigan, C.J., Burgess, S.R., & Anthony, J.L. (2000). Development of emergent literacy and early reading skills in preschool children: Evidence from a latent-variable longitudinal study. *Developmental Psychology*, 36 (5), 596–613.

Lundberg, I., Frost, J., & Petersen O. (1988). Effects of an extensive program for stimulating phonological awareness in preschool children. *Reading Research Quarterly*, 23 (3), 263–284.

McCardle, P. & Chhabra, V. (Eds.). (2004). *The Voice of Evidence in Reading Research*. Baltimore: Brooks.

McIntosh, A.S., Graves, A., & Gersten, R. (2007). The effects of response to intervention on literacy development in multiple-language settings. *Learning Disability Quarterly*, 30 (3), 197–212.

McIntosh, K., Chard, D.J., Boland, J.B., & Horner, R.H. (2006). Demonstration of combined efforts in school-wide academic and behavioral systems and incidence of reading and behavior challenges in early elementary grades. *Journal of Positive Behavior Interventions*, 8 (3), 146–154.

McIntosh, K., Horner, R.H., Chard, D.J., Boland, J.B., Good, R.H. (2006). The use of reading and behavior screening measures to predict non-response to school-wide positive behavior support: A longitudinal analysis. *School Psychology Review*, 35 (2), 275–291.

McIntosh, K., Horner, R.H., Chard, D.J., Dickey, C.R., & Braun, D.H. (2008). Reading skills and function of problem behavior in typical school settings. *The Journal of Special Education*, 42 (3), 131–147.

McKenna, M.C. & Stahl, S.A. (2003). *Assessment for Reading Instruction*, New York: Guilford Press.

McKeown, M.G. & Beck, I.L. (2001). Encouraging young children's language interactions with stories. In D. Dickinson & S. Neuman (Eds.), *Handbook of Early Literacy Research* (Vol. 2). New York: Guilford Press.

McKeown, M.G., Beck, I.L., Omanson, R.C., & Pople, M.T. (1985). Some effects of the nature and frequency of vocabulary instruction on the knowledge and use of words. *Reading Research Quarterly*, 20 (5), 522–535.

Merino, B. & Scarcella, R. (2005). Teaching science to English learners. *University of California Linguistic Minority Research Institute Newsletter*, 14 (4).

Moats, L. (2004). Efficacy of a structured, systematic language curriculum for adolescent poor readers. *Reading & Writing Quarterly*, 20 (2), 145–159.

Moats, L. (2001). When older students can't read. *Educational Leadership*, 58 (6), 36–46.

Moats, L.C. (2000). *Speech to Print: Language Essentials for Teachers*. Baltimore, MD: Paul H. Brooks Publishing Co., Inc.

Moats, L.C. (1998). Teaching decoding. *American Educator*, 22 (1 & 2), 42–49, 95–96.

Moats, L.C. (1999). *Teaching Reading Is Rocket Science*. Washington, DC: American Federation of Teachers.

Morrow, L.M. (2004). Developmentally appropriate practice in early literacy instruction. *The Reading Teacher*, 58 (1), 88–89.

Morrow, L.M., Kuhn, M.R., & Schwanenflugel, P.J. (2006/2007). The family fluency program. *The Reading Teacher*, 60 (4), 322–333.

Morrow, L.M. & Tracey, D.H. (1997). Strategies used for phonics instruction in early childhood classrooms. *The Reading Teacher*, 50 (8), 644–651.

Morrow, L.M., Tracey, D.H., Woo, D.G., & Pressley, M. (1999). Characteristics of exemplary first-grade literacy instruction. *The Reading Teacher*, 52 (5), 462–476.

Mosenthal, J.H., Lipson, M.Y., Torncello, S., Russ, B., & Mekkelsen, J. (2004). Contexts and practices of six schools successful in obtaining reading achievement. *Elementary School Journal*, 104 (5), 343–367. ABSTRACT ONLY.

Nagy, W.E. & Scott, J.A. (2000). Vocabulary processes. In M.L. Kamil, P.B. Mosenthal, P.D. Pearson, & R. Barr (Eds.), *Handbook of Reading Research*, (Vol. 3, 269–284). Mahwah, NJ: Erlbaum.

National Center to Improve Tools of Educators. Website: NCITE: http://idea.uoregon.edu/~ ncite/.

National Commission on Writing. (2004). *Writing: A Ticket to Work…or a Ticket Out*. New York: The College Board.

National Reading Panel (2000). Teaching children to read: An evidence-based assessment of the scientific research literature on reading and its implications for reading instruction. NIH Publication No. 00–4754. Washington, DC: National Institute of Child Health and Human Development.

Neuman, S.B., & Dickinson, D.K., (Eds.). (2002). *Handbook of Early Literacy Research*. New York: Guilford Press.

O'Connor, R., Jenkins, J.R., & Slocum, T.A. (1995). Transfer among phonological tasks in kindergarten: Essential instructional content. *Journal of Educational Psychology*, 87 (2), 202–217.

O'Shea, L.J., Sindelar, P.T., & O'Shea, D.J. (1985). The effects of repeated readings and attentional cues on reading fluency and comprehension. *Journal of Reading Behavior*, 17 (2), 129–142.

Orkwis, R. & McLane, K. (1998, Fall). *A Curriculum Every Student Can Use: Design Principles for Student Access*. ERIC/OSEP Special Project, ERIC Clearinghouse on Disabilities and Gifted Education, Council for Exceptional Children.

Osborn, J. & Lehr, F. (2003). *A Focus on Fluency: Research-Based Practices in Early Reading Series*. Honolulu, HI: Pacific Resources for Education and Learning.

Paris, S.G., Cross, D.R., & Lipson, M.Y. (1984). Informed strategies for learning: A program to improve children's reading awareness and comprehension. *Journal of Educational Psychology*, 76 (6), 1239–1252.

The Partnership for Reading. (2003). *Put Reading First: The Research Building Blocks for Teaching Children to Read*. (2nd ed.). MD: National Institute for Literacy.

Payne, B.D., & Manning, B.H. (1992). Basal reader instruction: Effects of comprehension monitoring training on reading comprehension, strategy use and attitude. *Reading Research and Instruction*, 32 (1), 29–38.

Phillips, B.M. & Torgesen, J.K. (2001). Phonemic awareness and reading: Beyond growth of initial reading accuracy. In D. Dickinson & S. Neuman (Eds.), *Handbook of Early Literacy Research* (Vol. 2). New York: Guilford Press.

Pikulski, J.J., (1998). Business we should finish. *Reading Today*, 15 (5), 30.

Pikulski, J.J., & Chard, D.J. (2005). Fluency: Bridge between decoding and reading comprehension. *The Reading Teacher,* 58 (6), 510–519.

Pressley, M. (1998). *Reading Instruction That Works: The Case for Balanced Teaching*. New York: The Guilford Press.

Rasinski, T. (2003). *The Fluent Reader: Oral Reading Strategies for Building Word Recognition, Fluency and Comprehension*. New York: Scholastic.

Rasinski, T.V., Padak, N., Linek, W., & Sturtevant, E. (1994). Effects of fluency development on urban second-grade readers. *Journal of Educational Research*, 87 (3), 158–165.

Rayner, K., Foorman, B.R., Perfetti, C.A., Pesetsky, D., & Seidenberg, M.S. (2001). How psychological science informs the teaching of reading. *Psychological Science in the Public Interest*, 2 (2), 31–74.

Rayner, K., Foorman, B.R., Perfetti, C.A., Pesetsky, D., & Seidenberg, M.S. (2002) How should reading be taught? *Scientific American*, pp. 85–91.

Report from the National Reading Panel. (2000). *Teaching Children to Read: An Evidence-Based Assessment of the Scientific Research Literature on Reading and its Implications for Reading Instruction*. Bethesda, MD: National Institute of Child Health and Human Development. Website: http://www.nationalreadingpanel.org/Publications/summary.htm.

Rinehart, S.D., Stahl, S.A., & Erickson, L.G. (1986). Some effects of summarization training on reading and studying. *Reading Research Quarterly*, 21 (4), 422–438.

Robbins, C. & Ehri, L.C. (1994). Reading storybooks to kindergartners helps them learn new vocabulary words. *Journal of Educational Psychology*, 86 (1), 54–64.

Rosenshine, B., & Meister, C. (1994). Reciprocal teaching: A review of research. *Review of Educational Research*, 64 (4), 479–530.

Rosenshine, B., Meister, C., & Chapman, S. (1996). Teaching students to generate questions: A review of the intervention studies. *Review of Educational Research*, 66 (2), 181–221.

Samuels, S., Schermer, N., & Reinking, D. (1992). Reading fluency: Techniques for making decoding automatic. In S.J. Samuels, J. Samuels, & A.E. Farstrup (Eds.), *What Research Has to Say About Reading Instruction* (pp. 124–143). Newark, DE: International Reading Association.

Samuels, S.J. & Farstrup, A.E. (2006). *What Research Has to Say About Fluency Instruction*. Newark, DE: International Reading Association.

Scarcella, R. (2003) Academic English: A conceptual framework. *The University of California Linguistic Minority Research Institute, Technical Report* 2003-1.

Scarcella, R. English learners and writing: Responding to linguistic diversity. On-line pdf. http://wps.ablongman.com/wps/media/objects/133/136243/english.pdf.

Scarcella, R. (1990). *Teaching Language Minority Students in the Multicultural Classroom*. Englewood Cliffs, NJ: Prentice Hall Regents.

Scharer, P.L., Pinnell, G.S., Lyons, C., & Fountas, I. (2005). Becoming an engaged reader. *Educational Leadership,* 63 (2), 24–29.

Schleppegrell, M. (2004). *Teaching Academic Writing to English Learners,* 13 (2). Grant Report: University of California Linguistic Minority Research Institute.

Sénéchal, M. (1997). The differential effect of storybook reading on preschoolers' acquisition of expressive and receptive vocabulary. *Journal of Child Language*, 24 (1), 123–138.

Shanahan, T. (2005). FAQs about Fluency. http://www.springfield.k12.il.us/resources/languagearts/readingwriting/readfluency.html.

Shany, M.T. & Biemiller, A. (1995). Assisted reading practice: Effects on performance for poor readers in grades 3 and 4. *Reading Research Quarterly*, 30 (3), 382–395.

Shaywitz, S. (2003). *Overcoming Dyslexia*. New York: Alfred A Knopf.

Simmons, D.C., Kame'enui, E.J, Coyne, M.D. & Chard, D.J. (2002). Effective strategies for teaching beginning reading. In E.J. Kame'enui, D.W. Carnine, R.C. Dixon, D.C. Simmons, & M.D. Coyne (Eds.), *Effective Teaching Strategies That Accommodate Diverse Learners*. Upper Saddle River, NJ: Merrill Prentice Hall.

Sindelar, P.T., Monda, L.E., & O'Shea, L.J. (1990). Effects of repeated readings on instructional- and mastery-level readers. *Journal of Educational Research*, 83 (4), 220–226.

Snow, C., Burns, M., & Griffin, P. (Eds.). (1998). *Preventing Reading Difficulties in Young Children*. Washington, D.C.: National Academy Press.

Stahl, S.A. & Fairbanks, M.M. (1986). The effects of vocabulary instruction: A model-based meta-analysis. *Review of Educational Research*, 56 (1), 72–110.

Stanovich, K.E. (1986). Matthew effects in reading: Some consequences of individual differences in acquisition of literacy. *Reading Research Quarterly*, 21 (4), 360–407.

Research Bibliography

Stanovich, K.E. & Stanovich, P.J. (2003). Using research and reason in education: How teachers can use scientifically based research to make curricular & instructional decisions. Jessup, MD: National Institute for Literacy. Retrieved January, 26, 2006, from http://www.nifl.gov/partnershipforreading/publications/pdf/Stanovich_Color.pdf.

Strickland, D.S. (2002). The importance of effective early intervention. In A.E. Farstrup & S.J. Samuels (Eds.), *What Research Has to Say About Reading Instruction* (3rd ed., pp. 69–86). Newark, DE: International Reading Association.

Strickland, D.S. & Morrow, L.M. (2000). *Beginning Reading and Writing*. Newark, DE: International Reading Association.

Strickland, D.S., Snow, C., Griffin, P., Burns, S.M. & McNamara, P. (2002). *Preparing Our Teachers: Opportunities for Better Reading Instruction*. Washington, D.C.: Joseph Henry Press.

Tabors, P.O. & Snow, C.E. (2002). Young bilingual children and early literacy development. In S. Neuman & D.K. Dickinson (Eds.), *Handbook of Early Literacy Research* (pp. 159–178). New York: Guilford Press.

Templeton, S. (1986). Synthesis of research on the learning and teaching of spelling. *Educational Leadership,* 43 (6), 73–78.

Templeton, S., Cain, C.T., & Miller, J.O. (1981). Reconceptualizing readability: The relationship between surface and underlying structure analyses in predicting the difficulty of basal reader stories. *Journal of Educational Research,* 74 (6), 382–387.

Torgesen, J., Morgan, S., & Davis, C. (1992). Effects of two types of phonological awareness training on word learning in kindergarten children. *Journal of Educational Psychology*, 84 (3), 364–370.

Torgesen, J., Wagner, R., Rashotte, C., Rose, E., Lindamood, P., Conway, T., & Garvan, C. (1999). Preventing reading failure in young children with phonological processing disabilities: Group and individual responses to instruction. *Journal of Educational Psychology*, 91 (4), 579–593.

Torgesen, J.K. & Hudson, R. (2006). Reading fluency: Critical issues for struggling readers. In S.J. Samuels & A. Farstrup (Eds.), *What Research Has to Say About Fluency Instruction*. Newark, DE: International Reading Association.

Torgesen, J.K., & Mathes, P. (2000). *A Basic Guide to Understanding, Assessing, and Teaching Phonological Awareness*. Austin, TX: PRO-ED.

Torgesen, J.K., Rashotte, C.A., & Alexander, A. (2001). Principles of fluency instruction in reading: Relationships with established empirical outcomes. In M. Wolf (Ed.), *Dyslexia, Fluency, and the Brain*. Parkton, MD: York Press.

Valencia, S.W., Au, K.H., Scheu, J.A., & Kawakami, A.J. (1990). Assessment of students' ownership of literacy. *The Reading Teacher,* 44 (2), 154–156.

Valencia, S.W. & Buly, M.R. (2004). Behind test scores: What struggling readers *really* need. *The Reading Teacher,* 57 (6), 520–531.

Valencia, S.W. & Sulzby, E. (1991). Assessment of emergent literacy: Storybook reading. *The Reading Teacher,* 44 (7), 498–500.

Vaughn, S. & Linan-Thompson, S. (2004). *Research-Based Methods of Reading Instruction: Grades K–3*. Alexandria, VA: ASCD.

Vaughn, S., Linan-Thompson, S., Pollard-Durodola, S.D., Mathes, P.G. & Hagan, E.C. (2001). Effective interventions for English language learners (Spanish-English) at risk for reading difficulties. In D. Dickinson & S. Neuman (Eds.), *Handbook of Early Literacy Research* (Vol. 2, pp. 185–197). New York: Guilford Press.

Vaughn, S., Moody, S.W., & Shuman, J.S. (1998). Broken promises: Reading instruction in the resource room. *Exceptional Children*, 64 (2), 211–225.

Vellutino, F.R., & Scanlon, D.M. (1987). Phonological coding, phonological awareness, and reading ability: Evidence from a longitudinal and experimental study. *Merrill-Palmer Quarterly*, 33 (3), 321–363.

Vogt, M. (2004/2005). Fitful nights. *Reading Today*, 22 (3), 6.

Vogt, M. & Nagano, P. (2003). Turn it on with light bulb reading!: Sound-switching strategies for struggling readers. *The Reading Teacher*, 57 (3), 214–221.

Washington, J.A. (2001). Early literacy skills in African-American children: Research considerations. *Learning Disabilities Research and Practice,* 16 (4), 213–221.

White, T.G., Graves, M.F., & Slater, W.H. (1990). Growth of reading vocabulary in diverse elementary schools: Decoding and word meaning. *Journal of Educational Psychology*, 82 (2), 281–290.

Wixson, K.K. (1986). Vocabulary instruction and children's comprehension of basal stories. *Reading Research Quarterly*, 21 (3), 317–329.

Index

Magazine Article. *See* Genre.

Main Idea. *See* Comprehension, Target Skills.

Main Selections. *See* Student Book, Literature Selections.

Making Connections. *See* Student Book, Making Connections.

Mass Media. *See* Research; Technology Resources.

Meeting Individual Needs. *See* Differentiated Instruction.

Media Literacy. *See* Connect and Extend.

Model Fluency. *See* Fluency, Modeling.

Modeled Writing. *See* Writing, Modeled Writing.

Modeling. *See* Think Aloud.

Monitor/Clarify. *See* Comprehension, Target Strategies.

Monitor Comprehension. *See* Comprehension, Target Strategies.

Multiple-Meaning Words. *See* Vocabulary, Strategies.

Mystery. *See* Genre.

Myth. *See* Genre.

Narrative Nonfiction. *See* Genre.

Narrative Writing. *See* Writing, Forms.

Negatives. *See* Grammar.

Nonfiction. *See* Genre; Writing.

Notes. *See* Writing, Process, Prewrite.

Nouns. *See* Grammar.

Ongoing Assessment. *See* Assessment.

Online Teacher Book and Planning Resources. *See* Technology Resources.

Oral Language. *See* Listening and Speaking; Your Turn.

Oral Language Conventions. *See* Grammar; Listening and Speaking.

Organization. *See* Writing, Traits.

Paragraphs. *See* Writing, Forms.

Parent Involvement. *See* Grab-and-Go™.

Participles. *See* Grammar.

Periodic Progress-Monitoring. *See* Assessment.

Periods. *See* Grammar, Punctuation.

Personal Narratives. *See* Writing, Forms.

Persuasion. *See* Genre.

Phonics. *See* Decoding.

Photo Cards. *See* Student Book, Vocabulary in Context.

Photo Essay. *See* Genre.

Phrasing. *See* Fluency.

Planning. *See* Focus Wall; Suggested Small Group Planner; Suggested Weekly Plan; Unit Planning and Pacing; Week at a Glance; Technology Resources.

Plays. *See* Genre; Writing, Form.

Plot. *See* Comprehension, Target Skills.

Plural Nouns. *See* Grammar, Nouns.

Poetry. *See* Genre; Writing, Form.

Poetry Place. *See* Magazine, Poetry Place.

Possessive Pronouns. *See* Grammar.

Predictions, Make. *See* Comprehension, Target Skills.

Prefixes. *See* Vocabulary, Strategies.

Prepositions. *See* Grammar.

Prepositional Phrases. *See* Grammar.

Prewriting. *See* Writing, Process, Brainstorming; Generating Ideas.

Prior Knowledge. *See* Develop Background; Differentiated Instruction, English Language Learners.

Progress Monitoring. *See* Assessment.

Pronouns. *See* Grammar.

Proofreading. *See* Grammar; Writing.

Proper Mechanics. *See* Grammar.

Proper Nouns,. *See* Grammar.

Prosody. *See* Fluency.

Publishing. *See* Writing, Process.

Punctuation. *See* Fluency, Phrasing; Grammar.

Purposes for Reading. *See* Set Purpose.

Purposes for Writing. *See* Writing, Process, Prewrite.

Questions. *See* Comprehension; Essential Questions; Grammar; Research; Writing.

Quotation Marks. *See* Grammar, Punctuation.

Rate. *See* Fluency.

***R*-Controlled Vowels.** *See* Decoding.

Read Aloud. *See* Fluency; Teacher Read Aloud.

Readers' Theater. *See* Genre.

Reading

T199, T273, T345; **4-4:** T53, T125, T197, T269, T345; **4-5:** T55, T127, T203, T274, T345; **4-6:** T43, T87, T131, T177, T223

Your Turn, **4-1:** T31, T105, T175, T247, T323; **4-2:** T33, T105, T179, T251, T323; **4-3:** T33, T105, T177, T251, T323; **4-4:** T31, T103, T175, T247, T323; **4-5:** T33, T105, T181, T253, T323

Study Skills, 4-1: R2–R7; **4-2:** R2–R7; **4-3:** R2–R7; **4-4:** R2–R7; **4-5:** R2–R7; **4-6:** R2–R5;

Suffixes. *See* Vocabulary, Strategies.

Suggested Small Group Plan, 4-1: T58–T59, T132–T133, T202–T203, T274–T275, T354–T355; **4-2:** T60–T61, T132–T133, T206–T207, T278–T279, T354–T355; **4-3:** T60–T61, T132–T133, T204–T205, T278–T279, T354–T355; **4-4:** T58–T59, T130–T131, T202–T203, T274–T275, T354–T355; **4-5:** T60–T61, T132–T133, T208–T209, T280–T281, T354–T355; **4-6:** T6–T7, T52–T53, T96–T97, T140–T141, T186–T187

Suggested Weekly Plan, 4-1: T6–T7, T78–T79, T152–T153, T222–T223, T294–T295; **4-2:** T6–T7, T80–T81, T152–T153, T226–T227, T298–T299; **4-3:** T6–T7, T80–T81, T152–T153, T224–T225, T298–T299; **4-4:** T6–T7, T78–T79, T150–T151, T222–T223, T294–T295; **4-5:** T6–T7, T80–T81, T152–T153, T228–T229, T300–T301; **4-6:** T4–T5, T50–T51, 94–T95, T138–T139, T184–T185

Summarize. *See* Comprehension, Target Strategies; Writing.

Summary, 4-1: T64–T67, T138–T141, T208–T211, T280–T283, T360–T363; **4-2:** T66–T69, T138–T141, T212–T215, T284–T287, T360–T363; **4-3:** T66–T69, T138–T141, T210–T213, T284–T287, T360–T363; **4-4:** T64–T67, T136–T139, T208–T211, T280–T283, T360–T363; **4-5:** T66–T69, T138–T141, T214–T217, T286–T289, T360–T363

Summative Assessment. *See* Assessment.

Syllable Patterns. *See* Decoding.

Synonyms. *See* Vocabulary, Strategies.

Tall Tales. *See* Genre.

Target Skills. *See* Comprehension.

Target Strategies. *See* Comprehension.

Teacher Read Aloud, 4-1: T12–T13, T84–T85, T158–T159, T228–T229, T300–T301; **4-2:** T12–T13, T86–T87, T158–T159, T232–T233, T304–T305; **4-3:** T12–T13, T86–T87, T158–T159, T230–T231, T304–T305; **4-4:** T12–T13, T84–T85, T156–T157, T228–T229, T300–T301; **4-5:** T12–

T13, T86–T87, T158–T159, T234–T235, T306–T307; **4-6:** T8–T9, T54–T55, T98–T99, T142–T143, T188–T189

Technology Resources

Audiotext CD, **4-1:** T3, T75, T149, T219, T291; **4-2:** T3, T77, T149, T223, T295; **4-4:** T3, T75, T147, T219, T291; **4-5:** T3, T77, T149, T225, T297; **4-6:** T3, T49, T03, T137, T183

Grammar Songs CD, **4-1:** T190, T262, T338; **4-2:** T266, T338; **4-3:** T120, T338; **4-4:** T46, T190, **4-5:** T48, T196, T268, T338; **4-6:** T38, T126, T172

Journeys Digital, **4-1:** T3, T75, T149, T219, T291; **4-2:** T3, T79, T151, T223, T295; **4-3:** T3, T77, T149, T221, T295; **4-4:** T3, T75, T147, T219, T291; **4-5:** T3, T77, T149, T225, T297; **4-6:** T3, T49, T93, T137, T183

Online TE & Planning Resources **4-1:** T6–T7, T57, T78–T79, T131, T152–T153, T201, T222–T223, T273, T294–T295, T353; **4-2:** T6–T7, T59, T80–T81, T131, T152–T153, T205, T226–T227, T277, T298–T299, T353; **4-3:** T6–T7, T59, T80–T81, T131, T152–T153, T203, T224–T225, T277, T298–T299, T353; **4-4:** T6–T7, T57, T78–T79, T129, T150–T151, T201, T222–T223, T273, T294–T295, T353; **4-5:** T6–T7, T59, T80–T81, T131, T152–T153, T207, T228–T229, T279, T300–T301, T353; **4-6:** T4–T5, T50–T51, 94–T95, T138–T139, T184–T185

Student eBook, **4-1:** T3, T75, T149, T219, T291; **4-2:** T3, T77, T149, T223, T295; **4-3:** T3, T77, T149, T221, T295; **4-4:** T3, T75, T147, T219, T291; **4-5:** T3, T77, T149, T225, T297; **4-6:** T3, T49, T93, T137, T183

Tenses. *See* Grammar.

Text and Graphic Features. *See* Comprehension, Target Skills.

Text to Self/Text/World. *See* Making Connections; Read to Connect.

Theme. *See* Comprehension, Target Skills

Think Aloud, 4-1: T18, T90, T164, T234, T306; **4-2:** T18, T92, T164, T238, T310; **4-3:** T18, T92, T164, T236, T310; **4-4:** T18, T90, T162, T234, T306; **4-5:** T18, T92, T164, T240, T312

Think Critically. *See* Student Book, Your Turn.

Tier II. *See* Intervention, Strategic.

Tier III. *See* Intervention, Intensive.

Trade Books

Informational Text

Sea Turtles: Ocean Nomads, **4-6:** T339

Realistic Fiction

Justin and the Best Biscuits in the World, **4-6:** T227

Phineas L. MacGuire…Gets Slimed!, **4-6:** T283

Traditional Tales. *See* Genre.

Traits of Good Writing. *See* Writing, Traits.

Transitions. *See* Grammar.

Trickster Tales. *See* Genre.

Unit Wrap-Up, 4-1: T352; **4-2:** T352; **4-3:** T352; **4-4:** T352; **4-5:** T352

Usage. *See* Grammar.

Variant Vowels. *See* Decoding.

Verbs. *See* Grammar.

Visualize. *See* Comprehension, Target Strategies.

Vocabulary

Academic Language, **4-1:** T18, T36, T90, T110, T164, T180, T234, T252, T306, T328; **4-2:** T18, T38, T92, T110, T164, T184, T238, T256, T310, T328; **4-3:** T18, T38, T92, T110, T164, T182, T236, T256, T310, T328; **4-4:** T18, T36, T90, T108, T162, T180, T234, T252, T306, T328; **4-5:** T18, T38, T92, T110, T164, T186, T240, T258, T312, T328; **4-6:** T12, T58, T102, T146, T192

Lists, **4-1:** T13, T85, T159, 229, T301; **4-2:** T13, T87, T159, T233, T305; **4-3:** T13, T87, T159, T231, T305; **4-4:** T13, T85, T157, T229, T301; **4-5:** T13, T87, T159, T235, T307

Reader, **4-1:** T60–T61, T134–T135, T204–T205, T276–T277, T356–T357; **4-2:** T62–T63, T134–T135, T208–T209, T280–T281, T356–T357; **4-3:** T62–T63, T134–T135, T206–T207, T280–T281, T356–T357; **4-4:** T60–T61, T132–T133, T204–T205, T276–T277, T356–T357; **4-5:** T62–T63, T134–T135, T210–T211, T282–T283, T356–T357

Strategies

Analogies, **4-2:** T332–T333, T366; **4-6:** T76–T77

Antonyms, **4-2:** T260–T261, T290

Compound Words, **4-4:** T332–T333, T366

Figurative Language, **4-2:** T188–T189, T218

Greek and Latin Word Parts, **4-2:** T114–T115, T144; **4-3:** T186–T187, T216; **4-5:** T332–T333, T366; **4-6:** T32–T33

Homographs, **4-4:** T184–T185, T214

Homonyms, **4-4:** T184–T185, T214

Homophones, **4-4:** T184–T185, T214

Multiple-Meaning Words, **4-3:** T332–T333, T366; **4-5:** T42–T43, T72

Acknowledgments

All photos from the HMH Photo Library or shot by Houghton Mifflin Harcourt Photographers.

Teacher Notes

Teacher Notes

Teacher Notes

Teacher Notes

Teacher Notes

Teacher Notes

Teacher Notes

Teacher Notes

Teacher Notes